£1-50P

The Pope John Sunday Missal

The Pope John Sunday Missal

A Treasury of Catholic Spirituality

Edited by
Mgr. MICHAEL BUCKLEY

Designed and illustrated by
MICHAEL GREEN

REDEMPTORIST PUBLICATIONS

Redemptorist Publications
Alphonsus House
Chawton
Alton, Hants. GU34 3HQ.

Compilation, design, artwork and editorial matter
© Copyright 1984 Redemptorist Publications.

First Published in 1978 by Kevin Mayhew Ltd.

This revised edition published in 1984 by
Redemptorist Publications.

Concordat cum originali	John P. Dewis
Nihil obstat	Michael Munnelly, B.D.
Imprimatur	✠ Basil Hume
Westminster, July 25 1978	

Standard
ISBN 0 85231 068 4
Superior
ISBN 0 85231 069 2
De-Luxe
ISBN 0 85231 075 7

The editor and publisher gratefully acknowledge permission to use the following copyright material in this missal:
   Excerpts from the English translation of the Roman Missal © 1973, International Committee on English in the Liturgy, Inc. All rights reserved.
   Psalm texts are from *The Psalms: A New Translation* © Copyright The Grail (England) 1973, published by William Collins Sons & Co. Ltd.
   Material from the *Jerusalem Bible,* published and © Copyright 1966, 1967 and 1968 by Darton, Longman and Todd Ltd., and Doubleday & Co., Inc., is used by permission of the publishers.

Printed and bound in Britain by Knight and Forster, Water Lane, Leeds LS11 9UB.

Table of Contents

Foreword by Cardinal Hume — vii
Editor's Introduction — ix
Table of Movable Feasts — xii

THE CHRISTIAN LIFE

The Christian Life — 1
The Sacraments — 9-38
  Baptism, 16
  Confirmation, 21
  Communion, 22
  Reconciliation, 25
  Anointing of the Sick, 28
  Marriage, 32
  Holy Orders, 34
Liturgy and Renewal — 39
Liturgical Symbols — 45
The Liturgical Year — 55

THE ORDER OF MASS

Introduction — 518
Prayers before Mass — 530
The Order of Mass — 538
Prefaces — 558
Solemn Blessings — 598
Prayers after Mass — 602

THE SUNDAY MASSES

The Season of Advent — 61-114
  Year A, 65
  Year B, 82
  Year C, 99
The Season of Christmas — 115-173
  Midnight Mass, 119
  Dawn Mass, 123
  Mass During the Day, 126
  The Holy Family, 131
  Mary, Mother of God, 145
  Second Sunday of Christmas, 149
  The Epiphany, 154
  The Baptism of the Lord, 159

The Season of Lent   175-260
   Ash Wednesday, 183
   Year A, 189
   Year B, 216
   Year C, 238

Holy Week   261-328
   Passion (Palm) Sunday, 262
   Holy Thursday, 295
   Good Friday, 307

The Season of Easter   329-467
   Holy Saturday (Easter Vigil), 332
   Easter Sunday, 371
   Sundays of Easter
     Year A, 376
     Year B, 407
     Year C, 438
   Pentecost Sunday, 469
   The Most Holy Trinity
     Year A, 477
     Year B, 481
     Year C, 485
   Corpus Christi
     Year A, 489
     Year B, 494
     Year C, 499
   The Sacred Heart
     Year A, 503
     Year B, 508
     Year C, 513
   Sundays in Ordinary Time
     Year A, 609
     Year B, 737
     Year C, 867

SOLEMNITIES AND FEASTS

February 2	The Presentation of the Lord	1009
March 1	St David	1015
March 17	St Patrick	1019
March 19	St Joseph	1024
March 25	The Annunciation of the Lord	1029

April 23	St George	1033
June 24	Birth of St John the Baptist	1036
June 29	Ss Peter and Paul	1041
August 6	The Transfiguration of the Lord	1046
August 15	The Assumption of the BVM	1051
September 14	The Triumph of the Cross	1056
October 25	The Forty Martyrs	1060
November 1	All Saints	1063
November 2	All Souls	1068
November 30	St Andrew	1075
December 8	The Immaculate Conception of the BVM	1078
Anniversary of the Dedication of a Church		1083

PRAYER AND DEVOTION

Personal Prayer	1091
Prayer Groups	1096
Praying the Bible	1099
General Prayers	1101
The Jesus Prayer	1125
Litanies	1127
The Rosary	1136
The Stations of the Cross	1145-1171
Traditional Form, 1148	
Modern Form, 1156	
Prayers Before the Blessed Sacrament	1174
Eucharistic Exposition and Benediction	1182
Latin Texts for the Mass	1189

*The shorter forms of the Sunday Readings are indicated by an indentation and a vertical line.

Foreword

WHEN we gather each Sunday at Mass we proclaim to each other and to the world the saving power of Christ's death and resurrection. The 'Pope John Sunday Missal' is designed to help us to do this more fully by making the christian faith come alive for us as individuals within the worshipping community.

The missal maintains a sensitive balance between those aspects of belief and practice with which we have been long familiar and the fresh insights which came from Vatican II. It should allay the fears of those who are suspicious of change and also remind young people of the heritage of tradition which has brought the christian message down through the ages. By thus renewing the hallowed, and hallowing the new, the 'Pope John Sunday Missal' should become, in addition, a vehicle of reconciliation.

Its lucid Introduction, outlining the history of salvation, provides a source of meditation on God's love for us that can be tapped again and again. The explanations of liturgical renewal, the liturgical year, the use of symbols and the order of Mass, should help both young and old to grow in the love and service of God, and to be renewed once more as each annual season comes round. Prayer is at the heart of our union with God, and the missal also contains other aids to prayer — both prayer alone and with others.

It is my hope that all users of the 'Pope John Sunday Missal' will come to a deeper understanding of their christian life as active members of a baptismal and eucharistic people who proclaim Christ's kingdom 'until he comes again'.

✠ Basil Hume
Archbishop of Westminster

Editor's Introduction

THIS missal is dedicated to the memory of Pope John XXIII. He called all the bishops of the Roman Catholic Church together in the famous Second Vatican Council. His aim was twofold: firstly to renew the Church spiritually so that she would be a clear sign of Christ's presence to everyone; secondly to make the Gospel come alive for christians who are called to live in a rapidly changing world. It was, therefore, at one and the same time, a council of renewal and relevance. This missal follows through the twofold thinking of the Council. It has as its aim the spiritual renewal of all the faithful who gather together every Sunday to praise the Lord in the Eucharist so that renewed and refreshed they may bring God's saving word to those who walk in darkness. We are called to be the light of the world *(lumen gentium)* and we can only do this if we make our light shine before men. "You are the light of the world. A city built on a hill-top cannot be hidden. No one lights a lamp to put it under a tub; they put it on the lampstand where it shines for everyone in the house." Matthew 5:14-15. Revelance does not mean compromise with the world. We are not to water down the christian message but we need to live and preach it in such a way that people can understand it in a language suited to our age and so be attracted by its beauty.

We are to take an active part in the liturgy. The Church will only come alive when the liturgy is dynamic and meaningful. Vatican II declared that the liturgy was 'the summit towards which the activity of the Church is directed; at the same time it is the fountain from which all her power flows'. Recent changes in the liturgy were specifically designed to make us more aware that we are all members of a community in which everyone has a role to play. The Church is the people of God and we all share in Christ's priesthood offering prayers and adoration to God our Father. Each Sunday has its own theme on which we should meditate so that we can be together at the eucharist as one in mind and heart with Christ and with each other. There are special sections in the missal which give us a fuller understanding of liturgy and renewal as well as a deeper insight into the meaning of liturgical symbols. The section on the Order of Mass is essential to a fuller realisation of what we are doing at the eucharist. These sections are directed not only to the mind but also to the heart so that as whole persons we can live out their meaning in our daily lives. We are the Paschal Candle, the Risen Christ, to everyone we meet.

The theology of the sacraments is very clearly expressed in the new rites. Here indeed the Church has opened to us the rich treasury of her household, "every scribe who becomes a disciple of the kingdom of heaven is like a householder who brings out from his storeroom things both new and old." Matthew 13:52. There has been a massive interest in recent years in the nature and function of the Church and this is reflected in the emphasis which she places on the community aspect of the sacraments. We are baptized for each other in Christ. No one is a christian for himself alone since we are all parts of the same body which is Christ.

We come in Christ to the Father through prayer and the sacraments. We are above all a prayer-filled people who are moved by the Spirit to call God 'Father'. This is our heritage and our mission. The sections on the christian life and prayer, both personal and in groups, should give a deeper meaning to all we say and do in the Lord. There is a combination of old and new prayers and devotions so that this missal may become a reconciling and healing factor in a changing Church and world. Vatican II adds to the riches of the Church and future generations will grasp more fully its spirit and meaning. This missal is a treasury of spirituality of the Church down the ages even though 'we are only the earthenware jars that hold this treasure, to make it clear that such an overwhelming power comes from God and not from us.' 2 Corinthians 4:7.

Many people are apprehensive about the passing of the catechism from our schools. They do not seem to realise that the Church has her own programme of catechetical instruction set into the framework of the liturgy. The centrality of the Gospels in our spiritual lives is highlighted by the new lectionary which feeds us on 'the more representative portions of the holy scripture read to the people over a set cycle of years'. We are a Gospel-orientated people who are fed daily on the Word of God. Scripture and tradition, our two main sources of inspiration, are wedded beautifully in the Sunday Missal.

The editing of this missal was undertaken in a spirit of openness and gratitude to the Spirit who draws us ever closer to the Father. If it helps others to thank God for his generosity to his people then the work involved will be more than amply repaid. However the results depend ultimately on the Spirit. I make my prayer that of St. Paul: 'This, then, is what I pray, kneeling before the Father, from whom every family, whether spiritual or natural, takes its name: Out of his infinite glory, may he give you the power through his Spirit for your hidden self to grow strong, so that Christ may live in your hearts through faith, and then, planted in love and built on love, you will with all the saints have strength to grasp the breadth and the length, the height and the depth, until, knowing the love of Christ, which is beyond all knowledge, you are filled with the utter fulness of God. Glory be to him whose power, working in us, can do infinitely more than we can ask or imagine; glory be to him from generation to generation in the Church and in Christ Jesus for ever and ever. Amen.' Ephesians 3:14-21.

In the preparation of the Pope John Sunday Missal I am deeply indebted to many people whose guidance and criticism made my task much easier than it might otherwise have been. Cardinal Basil Hume graciously wrote a Foreword. Father Anthony Boylan's comments on the structure of the missal were invaluable, and he was especially helpful in the lay-out of the Ordinary of the Mass. Father John Fitzsimons generously furnished me with the background of the scheme for the lectionary readings for the three year cycle. Sister Patricia and our beloved community of Carmelite Sisters at Wood Hall Centre encouraged me to edit the missal and their prayers were a spur to my endeavours. Their reading of the proofs was but a small part of all they have contributed to what this missal has become. Michael Green's beautiful artistic work speaks for itself. Kevin Mayhew, in his own inimitable way, not only instigated the missal but played a key role in the planning of its actual format. Finally, Marjory Fenton worked tirelessly and joyfully at the mammoth task of typing the manuscript.

In the peace of my home set in lovely woods on the outskirts of the unlikely city of Leeds this missal was born. In its preparation I discovered a deeper appreciation and understanding of what our faith means in our daily lives.

Michael J. Buckley
Feast of Pentecost 1978

Table of Movable Feasts

Year	Sunday Cycle	Ash Wednesday	Easter	Ascension	Pentecost
1984	A	Mar. 7	Apr. 22	May 31	June 10
1985	B	Feb. 20	Apr. 7	May 16	May 26
1986	C	Feb. 12	Mar. 30	May 8	May 18
1987	A	Mar. 4	Apr. 19	May 28	June 7
1988	B	Feb. 17	Apr. 3	May 12	May 22
1989	C	Feb. 8	Mar. 26	May 4	May 14
1990	A	Feb. 28	Apr. 15	May 24	June 3
1991	B	Feb. 13	Mar. 31	May 9	May 19
1992	C	Mar. 4	Apr. 19	May 28	June 7
1993	A	Feb. 24	Apr. 11	May 20	May 30
1994	B	Feb. 16	Apr. 3	May 12	May 22
1995	C	Mar. 1	Apr. 16	May 25	June 4
1996	A	Feb. 21	Apr. 7	May 16	May 26
1997	B	Feb. 12	Mar. 30	May 8	May 18
1998	C	Feb. 25	Apr. 12	May 21	May 31
1999	A	Feb. 17	Apr. 4	May 13	May 23

Corpus Christi	Ordinary Weeks of the Year				First Sunday of Advent	Year
	Before Lent		After Pentecost			
	Until	Week	From	Week		
June 21	Mar. 6	9	June 11	10	Dec. 2	1984
June 6	Feb. 19	6	May 27	8	Dec. 1	1985
May 29	Feb. 11	5	May 19	7	Nov. 30	1986
June 18	Mar. 3	8	June 8	10	Nov. 29	1987
June 2	Feb. 16	6	May 23	8	Nov. 27	1988
May 25	Feb. 7	5	May 15	6	Dec. 3	1989
June 14	Feb. 27	8	June 4	9	Dec. 2	1990
May 30	Feb. 12	5	May 20	7	Dec. 1	1991
June 18	Mar. 3	8	June 8	10	Nov. 29	1992
June 10	Feb. 23	7	May 31	9	Nov. 28	1993
June 2	Feb. 15	6	May 23	8	Nov. 27	1994
June 15	Feb. 28	8	June 5	9	Dec. 3	1995
June 6	Feb. 20	7	May 27	8	Dec. 1	1996
May 29	Feb. 11	5	May 19	7	Nov. 30	1997
June 11	Feb. 24	7	June 1	9	Nov. 29	1998
June 3	Feb. 16	6	May 24	8	Nov. 28	1999

The Christian Life

The Christian Life

GOD calls us to fullness of life in Jesus Christ. 'God loved the world so much that he gave his only Son so that everyone who believes in him may not be lost but may have eternal life.' John 3:16. It is the unique vocation of christians that through the powerful intercession of Jesus Christ we have as our final destiny the capacity to share the very life of God himself. God sent his only Son on earth in human form — 'the word was made flesh, he lived among us'. John 1:14. — and if we accept Christ in faith as our Redeemer then we will live with God for eternity, knowing and loving him as Christ does. 'To all who did accept him [Christ] he gave power to become children of God' John 1:12.

By this divine plan we are united to God. Before time began it was God's purpose for the whole world to respond perfectly to the love of his Son who would be Lord of the Universe. Christ 'is the image of the unseen God and the first-born of all creation, for in him were created all things in heaven and on earth' Colossians 1:15. Christ was intended by God to be the crowning point of his creation. He sums up the ideal of the divine invitation to holiness and the perfect human response. The christian life is a communion of love joining us with God and with each other. Christ is at the centre of the love-exchange which will be complete and perfect in heaven.

Through Christ, God personally intervenes in the history of the human race. Christ is God's invitation to the eternal banquet not written on a decorative card but in human flesh and blood. 'When the appointed time came, God sent his Son, born of a woman, born a subject of the Law, to redeem the subjects of the Law and to enable us to be adopted as sons. The proof that you are sons is that God has sent the Spirit of his Son into our hearts; the Spirit that cries, Abba, Father, and it is this that makes you a son, you are not a slave any more; and if God has made you a son, then he has made you heir.' Galatians 4:4-7. We were to share the lot of the Son and to come to the Father through him. As sons of God we would be given the power of the Spirit so that we could in pure love call God our Father [Abba].

God, however, created people free but they abused their freedom. Thus a foreign element, sin, invaded our world. Sin disturbed the balance of loving obedience between us and God,

THE CHRISTIAN LIFE

set brother against brother in the human family and finally disorientated us in ourselves so that we were wounded people whose wholeness was shattered into fragments. Sin distracted us from the two poles which direct our lives — love of God and love of neighbour. Humanity could only be described as a fallen race. We were like a ship without a compass; like sheep we had all gone astray.

The Incarnation means that Christ took to himself this sin-laden human race. Though himself personally sinless, he had to live as man his divine Sonship in a certain mysterious estrangement from his loving Father. This all came about because of the damage sin had done to the world. However God's love in Christ overcomes our sinfulness. 'God loved us with so much love that he was generous with his mercy: when we were dead through our sins, he brought us to life with Christ — it is through grace that you have been saved — and raised us up with him and gave us a place with him in heaven, in Christ Jesus. This was to show for all ages to come, through his goodness towards us in Christ Jesus, how infinitely rich he is in grace. Because it is by grace that you have been saved, through faith; not by anything of your own, but by a gift from God; not by anything that you have done, so that nobody can claim the credit. We are God's work of art, created in Christ Jesus to live the good life as from the beginning he has meant us to live it.' Ephesians 2:4-10.

Christ's life on earth was lived in perfect, loving obedience to his Father's will. 'My food is to do the will of the one who sent me.' John 4:34. His perfect sonship is manifested in perfect obedience even to the death on a cross. The life and death of the Son of God who had become a slave for our sake reveal God as a saving God who gave us his only begotten Son as our brother. It also reveals the Son who, because he loved us, freely handed over to his Father his human life in testimony of his love of the human race. The perfect gift from God to us becomes our perfect gift to Him.

The testimony to the Father by the Son given in conditions of this sin-filled world draws from the Father his testimony to his Son. The humiliated servant is enthroned in glory and power as the Lord of Glory. The resurrection, ascension, setting of Christ at his right hand, and the sending of the Holy Spirit are the Father's response to our human race now reconciled to him through the new covenant established in Christ. A new age is

THE CHRISTIAN LIFE

inaugurated. We are now living in the last [eschatological] stage when God our Father will bring the whole of creation under the rule of his Son so that 'of his kingdom there shall be no end.' Christ has passed beyond sin, death and corruption to the conditions of a heavenly existence. There he awaits those who believe in him and from whence he will come once again at the 'Final Consummation' of all things. We who have been faithful in life will enter with him into the glory which he promised his followers. 'Father, I want those you have given me to be with me where I am, so that they may always see the glory you have given me because you loved me before the foundation of the world.' John 17:24.

We often have a tendency to look on the death, resurrection and exaltation [ascension] of Christ as if they were dramatic events of a past age which has little to do with the world of our time. It is *true* that the exaltation of Christ meant the end of his visible, physical presence on earth but it did not mean that he left us orphans. The popular picture of Christ disappearing into the clouds of heaven represents only part of the story of salvation.

The other part is this. Christ is the *beginning* of a new, restored humanity. Through his death and resurrection he returns to the Father as the *exalted* man who has become one with God. He has risen from the death to bestow life on those who lay in the tomb. 'Through him, with him and in him' we are reconciled to God and so give perfect praise to God 'through Christ our Lord.'

The second Vatican Council not only stressed the humanity of Christ but also emphasised the need to renew our resurrection piety. This does not mean that we sentimentalize our Gospel understanding of Christ and so reduce him to the status of a man who was only a teacher or our moral example. He is much more than that. The new emphasis on his humanity is on his *exalted* humanity for it is in his exalted humanity that we are redeemed. Christ is not just the man for others. He is God's son for everyone.

There is a danger too that resurrection piety may overlook the passion of Christ. We needed the passion and cross in order to be saved. The cross will always be hailed as our only hope. *[ave crux spes unica]* But today we are renewing and rediscovering the spirituality of the early Church which taught that suffering and death in our own lives have a meaning precisely because we are

THE CHRISTIAN LIFE

saturated with the power of the resurrection. *We are a joy-filled people.* Suffering and death are tragic but they are not the ultimate tragedies because in the Spirit of the risen Christ we will overcome them. Without the resurrection the passion and death of Christ are the ultimate absurdity. 'Now if Christ raised from the dead is what has been preached, how can some of you be saying that there is no resurrection of the dead? If there is no resurrection of the dead, Christ himself cannot have been raised, and if Christ has not been raised then our preaching is useless and your believing it is useless; indeed, we are shown up as witnesses who have committed perjury before God, because we swore in evidence before God that he had raised Christ to life. For if the dead are not raised, Christ has not been raised, and if Christ has not been raised, you are still in your sins. And what is more serious, all who have died in Christ have perished. If our hope in Christ has been for this life, we are the most unfortunate of all people.' 1 Corinthians 15:12-19.

The resurrection piety called for by the Second Vatican Council required that as christians we balance the awesomeness and majesty of Christ with the fact that he is tender and close to us. Popular piety of the past few centuries highlighted the historically completed passion of Christ and his awe-inspiring divinity. We were left perhaps with a distance between Christ and ourselves. We over-emphasised the fact that we were sinners and so tended to obscure the great truth that we were also children of God, members of Christ's body and heirs to his kingdom. The Church encourages us to *rejoice* and give thanks as well as make prayers of petition. Our lives are to be lived in love. Our actions must not be done out of fear but rather in gratitude to a loving Father who has redeemed us through his Son. 'Everyone moved by the Spirit is a son of God. The spirit you received is not the spirit of slaves bringing fear into your lives again; it is the spirit of sons, and it makes us cry out, 'Abba Father!' The Spirit himself and our spirit bear united witness that we are children of God. And if we are children we are heirs as well: heirs of God and coheirs with Christ, sharing his sufferings so as to share his glory.' Romans 8:14-17.

The conviction of Christ's ultimate triumph takes pride of place in our lives as christians. Since the resurrection no sorrow is final. Even on occasions of deepest mourning we remember that God is still our loving Father to whom 'we do well always and

THE CHRISTIAN LIFE

everywhere to give thanks'. The Church constantly invites us to rejoice and be glad in the light of the resurrection. The Church, for example, while conscious of her own shortcomings still calls herself the bride of Christ because she is aware of what she is through the loving power of God. God our Father has also endowed us as individuals with sublime dignity as christians yet we often fall short of what we are called to be. This is the paradox of the christian life. 'This seems to be the rule, that every single time I want to do good it is something evil that comes to hand. In my inmost self I dearly love God's Law, but I can see that my body follows a different law that battles against the law which my reason dictates. This is what makes me a prisoner of that law of sin which lives inside my body. What a wretched man I am! Who will rescue me from this body doomed to death? Thanks be to God through Jesus Christ our Lord! In short, it is I who with my reason serve the Law of God, and no less I who serve in my unspiritual self the law of sin.' Romans 7:21-25.

We cannot overlook the fact that the cross is very much part of our lives. There is a place for penance in our christian lives and we are the poorer when we dismiss it as old-fashioned and irrelevant. The triumph of Christ is not yet fully achieved in us. We still have to face sin, suffering and death. We require prayers and acts of penance, and we need the annual observance of Advent and Lent to remind us that we are still in the process of becoming full persons in Christ. 'For we must hope to be saved since we are not saved yet — it is something we must wait for with patience.' Romans 8:24-25. Christ is not just a part of history [Christ *has* died] or a hope to look forward to [Christ *will* come again] but the most important influence in our daily lives [Christ *is* risen].

Because Christ is man as well as God, his exaltation is ours as well. The ascension means that the risen Christ is with God. If he is with God then so are we because we are one with him as his spiritual brothers and sisters. The Gospel account of Pentecost follows swiftly after the Ascension showing the link between them both. 'It is for your own good that I am going because unless I go, the Advocate will not come to you; but if I do go, I will send him to you.' John 16:7. The risen, ascended Lord communicates his Spirit to us so that like the apostles we too are 'filled with the Holy Spirit.' Through baptism we receive the Spirit of Christ and the presence of the Spirit is our infallible

THE CHRISTIAN LIFE

guarantee of the enduring presence of Christ among us. We *now*, today, in every situation in which we find ourselves, walk with Christ in our midst. 'Know that I am with you always; yes, to the end of time.' Matthew 28:20

The Sacraments

The Sacraments

THE Church is the body of Christ. It is the communion of the faithful in the life of its risen Lord. Conscious of its 'oneness' with Christ, the Church continues his saving ministry. As Christ laid his hands on the sick, or in blessing, so does the Church. As Christ gave thanks and shared with his disciples the bread and wine which were his body and blood so do we. The Church in its sacramental life is the visible focus of God's presence and activity in the world. She is the 'sign lifted up among the nations' for all to see.

Our religion is sacramental. Through the sacraments the Church expresses in the most effective possible way God's loving care for us as individuals and as a community [church]. Sacraments are not to be thought of as impersonal things which stand between us and God. The relationship between God and us is, on the contrary, very personal. God has chosen to communicate with us in a human way precisely because we are human. We communicate with each other, for example, through words and gestures. The rites we call sacraments are the extension of this pattern of personal relationship between God and us into our own situation of time and place. God after all has chosen to meet us in this world and not in some other. The sacraments therefore are points of personal contact here and now between a loving Father and his children in Christ.

From the most primitive times to the first great civilizations in Mesopotamia there is ample proof that the divine is to be found in those things which make up the fabric of human life and relationships. The exaggerations and superstitions of much of this kind of religion should not blind us to the beauty and simplicity of our human insight into nature. The Church harnesses all the signs and symbols of nature and uses them with thrilling effect in her celebration of the sacraments. We live in time and we carry our history with us. God's plan is not to destroy human life or history but to gather them to himself in love. From this perspective we cannot afford to ignore the primitive element in man which appeals especially to his senses, since we are composed of body as well as soul.

As christians we are especially indebted to the Jews for the main lines of our patterns of worship and sacraments. The sacrament of baptism has its roots in the practice of ritual bathing in Jewish synagogues and homes. There is a very profound and striking similarity between the Jewish passover meal and our celebration of the eucharist. The christian liturgy of the word has its counterpart in the daily synagogue service. Our attitude to sin and the need of penance is Jewish in origin. Both christian vespers and the blessing of the paschal candle have their roots in the Jewish domestic lighting of lamps and evening prayer. Jerusalem and its temple passed over into our tradition to provide us with a powerful symbolism which gives life and colour to our language and ceremonial. The pattern of relationship established between God and us through both nature and the covenant with Israel should not be discarded as though they were artificial props or means to a succeeding stage. Our understanding of the sacraments and their visible expression is an ongoing process. Christ in his Church is the fulfilment of history and of God's dealing with his people.

Our liturgical celebration of the sacraments is impoverished when we gloss over or ignore altogether those elements which are regarded as out of date or 'primitive'. We have manifested an unhealthy dislike in Western Europe for any gestures which involve bodily contact such as the sign of peace. The result has been that we suffered from a sterile form of celebration of the sacraments in which words tended to so dominate as to become the only form of communication. The new approach of the Church to the sacraments gives us great cause for hope in the way it combines relevance to our age with our great traditions of the past.

The growing emphasis on the central role of the resurrection of Christ as highlighted time and again in the Second Vatican Council has had a profound effect on our understanding of the nature and function of the Church. As christians we live now 'in the risen Lord'. It is the sense of being 'in Christ' which prompted us to a deepening of our perception of the meaning and significance of the sacraments. We *celebrate* all the sacraments in the risen Lord because above everything else the ultimate triumph of Christ has pride of place in our lives. We celebrate the sacrament of reconciliation as his triumph over sin just as truly as we celebrate the eucharist. In Christ there is no death and through him we triumph. Our concern in the Church is always and everywhere to express hope through resurrection.

THE SACRAMENTS

'If our hope in Christ has been for this life only, we are the most unfortunate people of all. But Christ has, in fact, been raised from the dead, the first fruits of all who have fallen asleep. Death came through one man and in the same way the resurrection of the dead has come through one man. Just as all men die in Adam so all men will be brought to life in Christ'. 1 Corinthians 15.19-22.

Before we can celebrate the death and resurrection of Christ we must be 'made ready' or initiated. The *sacraments of initiation* are baptism, confirmation and eucharist. For adults these sacraments are preceded ideally by several years preparation known as the catechumenate. The whole process of initiation marks the beginning of a person's life in that community of faith which we call the Church. It also marks the beginning of the christian's life of worship in the Church so that christian initiation is an entry by stages into a worshipping body whose core is union with the risen Lord in the eucharist.

Baptism is the sacrament of new life that comes to us through our death in Christ so as to be born again. It is a sacrament of resurrection in so far as it is a passage through water which signifies life from death to life and is the promise of our own resurrection in Christ. Confirmation is inseparably linked to baptism and is its proper completion, thus completing our entry into the Church. The risen Lord whose life we share through baptism sends his spirit upon us and we are called to be witnesses to the kingdom of God. Participation in the eucharist is itself the expression of our baptism for in it the unity between Christ and his Church is made visible as he gives himself to us as food and drink.

We are surrounded on all sides by sin. Even though we have been redeemed we are still conscious that we live in a sin-filled world. We need God's protection lest we fall and we have recourse to his mercy when having fallen we wish like the prodigal son to return to our father's home. The mercy of God, uniquely revealed in the life, death and resurrection of Jesus Christ remains forever in his Church. It is in Christ that we are reconciled to God through the mystical body of the Church. In the sacrament of reconciliation we receive the merciful forgiveness of God our Father.

We are children not only of the world to come in its perfection in God but also of this world. Called to live in God's presence in communion and friendship with him we remain on earth as the living link between him and his creation. Marriage in a special way reflects God's presence in the world which husband and wife are together to bring before him in prayer and praise. Christ and his Church are united in love and this is the abiding sign of the relationship between husband and wife.

Christ the high priest while sharing his priesthood with all believers nevertheless calls certain of his followers to a unique sharing in his ministerial service. The sacrament of holy orders is that means by which the Church continues Christ's ministry in a special way. By their ministry priests perfect the spiritual lives of the faithful by uniting them to the eucharistic sacrifice of Christ. The sacrifice is offered sacramentally in an unbloody manner through the hands of the priests who, by their example, are to recall the mystery of the death and resurrection of the Lord.

Finally we must all suffer death as the consequence of sin. The Church surrounds christian death and burial with hope. The new funeral rites use many symbols of baptism. Death is in a real sense the completion of baptism for through suffering and death we join Christ in glory. Through baptism we already live the new life of grace and physical death releases us from the bonds of our earthly existence so that we may live fully in Christ. The highlighting by the Second Vatican Council of the resurrection gave us further insights into the meaning of baptism.

One of the deepest concerns of liturgical renewal is to communicate to us all the need to become aware of what it means to live the life of a christian. In the weekly celebration of Sunday the liturgy of the Word makes us aware of who we are: 'You have been taught that when we were baptized in Christ Jesus we were baptized in his death, in other words, when we were baptized we went into the tomb with him and joined him in death, so that as Christ was raised from the dead by the Father's glory, we too might live a new life'. Romans 6:3-4. In a sense we are always beginners, always finding something new and glorious in what it means to become a christian. Our baptism is not merely something past but a call from God in Christ every day to live a life which is continually renewed in his Spirit. The light of the resurrection which drew us from the dark of the empty tomb of self opens to us a whole new horizon of life and glory: 'We believe that having died with Christ we shall return to life with him: Christ, as we know, having been raised from the dead will

THE SACRAMENTS

never die again. Death has no power over him any more. When he died, he died, once for all, to sin, so his life now is life with God; and in that way, you too must consider yourselves to be dead to sin but alive for God in Christ Jesus'. Romans 6:8-11.

Baptism

BAPTISM is an Easter sacrament through which we die to sin and enter into the life of the risen Lord, 'you too must consider yourselves to be dead to sin but alive for God in Christ Jesus.' Romans 6:11. Through baptism we enter into Christ's own dying and rising. The seasons of Lent and Easter highlight the concern of the Church for all its members to enter more deeply into an awareness of the meaning of our own baptism. Sunday, the day of the resurrection, when we gather together as a community to celebrate the eucharist, stands as a continual reminder both of the new life to which we are called as well as a sign to the Church of its own life in Christ.

As baptism brings life to the whole Church so also it is the concern of the whole Church. The entry of new members of Christ into our community is a cause for rejoicing by all since God draws us to himself not just as individuals but as a people whom he has made his own. Baptism is not a private affair and its celebration is encouraged at the Sunday eucharist as a witness to all of us who are already baptised that we must constantly undergo rebirth and change. Christ's dying and rising is made visible as new members themselves turn to him as the source of new life to which they are called and freely respond. Nowadays the fact that baptism and confirmation take place within the Mass indicate that the eucharist is the fulfilment and expression of our new life in Christ.

Baptism is the first of the three sacraments of initiation; baptism, confirmation and eucharist. Through these we come to full participation in the life of the Church. Confirmation is the

BAPTISM

completion of baptism since the risen Lord who makes us one with him in baptism, sends his life-giving Spirit upon us and in the eucharist we share the sacrament of unity with Christ and his body, the Church. The eucharist in which Christ gives himself to us as food and drink is the visible expression of unity between Christ and his Church to which we belong through baptism.

Baptism leads to the eucharist which in turn nourishes our baptismal life. Baptism signs and seals us as members of God's royal priesthood, whose privilege it is to proclaim his kingdom through prayer and lives of loving service. We live out our baptismal commitment in our daily lives as we move ever closer to its fulfilment in the resurrection. We are Gospel people whose lives make peace 'Be at peace among yourselves. And this is what we ask you to do, brothers: warn the idlers, give courage to those who are apprehensive, care for the weak and be patient with everyone. Make sure that people do not try to take revenge; you must all think of what is best for each other and for the community. Be happy at all times; pray constantly; and for all things give thanks to God, because this is what God expects you to do in Christ Jesus.' 1 Thessalonians 5:14-18.

As well as restoring the profound unity which exists between the three sacraments of initiation, baptism, confirmation and eucharist, the reform of the liturgy links them with the liturgical year. The new rites urge that their preparation be completed during Lent so that at the Easter Vigil the new members of Christ's Church may be baptised, confirmed and receive the eucharist. Easter begins the new life of the resurrection until he comes in glory. In its new members the Church itself is renewed and revitalised.

Initiation of Adults

The *Instruction for the Rite of Christian Initiation of Adults* calls for the restoration of adult baptism as a central event in the life of the Church. 'The initiation of catechumens takes place in the midst of the community of the faithful. Together with the catechumens, the faithful reflect upon the value of the paschal mystery, renew their own conversion, and by their example lead the catechumens to obey the Holy Spirit more generously'. (n.4.)

We all need today to grasp more fully the idea of the catechumenate which was a common feature of life among the early christians. The new rites and prayers for the catechumens, a word with which we are not as familiar as we should be, are only the expression of something much deeper which affects the life of the whole christian community. They presuppose that we as a loving, caring community are getting to know the new christians and guiding them by our example and fellowship on the path to baptism. We are called to *renew* our own commitment and understanding of what it means to be a christian. It is in this communal preparation of catechumens that the Church hopes for a renewal of her liturgy and life.

The process of initiation takes many forms in different dioceses and cultures but certain common principles are to be found which help us to understand the pastoral care of the Church in the preparation of catechumens. People who have a general desire for faith for a long time may eventually appreciate the need to share that faith with others. They are then *enrolled* in the catechumenate, a Church structure. The purpose of this is to help them to think and act with others according to the demands of Christ's gospel. *The catechumen is already a member of the Church* but yet not fully one of the faithful through baptism. It is difficult for us to understand this in our present fixed way of thinking but explanations of the catechumenate from the pulpit will help us grow in our appreciation of what the catechumenate means to the individual as well as to the community of the Church.

Christian initiation is an entry-by-stages into the Church whose centre is communion with the risen Lord in the eucharist. The eucharist is the centre to which one is led through the whole conversion process prior to baptism and from which one emerges through the continuing process of becoming more Christ-like after baptism in order to become the 'outreach' of the Church's mission of love and service. We are not baptised for ourselves alone but for the sake of the Church and the world. The reception of already baptized christians into full communion with the Catholic Church and the baptism of children are all to take their meaning from the full rites of adult initiation which it will be the privilege of the present day Church to absorb and understand. One of the deepest concerns of liturgical renewal is to communicate to all the faithful the full sense of their baptism with its christian commitment. Renewal of baptismal awareness means liturgical renewal in the very best sense of the term.

BAPTISM

The rite itself of becoming catechumens while basically simple generally begins with the celebrant greeting the candidates and their sponsors. When the candidates one by one signify their intention to become members of the Church the celebrant welcomes them in the name of the community and signs them on the forehead and senses reminding them that they are to follow Christ. The candidates are then invited formally to hear the liturgy of the word and the whole congregation pray for them. Special celebrations of the liturgy of the word are to be held for catechumens

to guide them in the christian way of life
to explain the symbols and actions of the liturgy
to instruct them on methods of prayer
to lead them gradually into eucharistic worship.

In addition special prayers are said that the catechumenate may grow in faith, hope and love through the power of the Holy Spirit. The laying-on of hands is another sign of God's special love for them and of the Church's concern for their spiritual growth.

At the beginning of Lent they are formally enrolled as catechumens and signify their intention of receiving the sacraments of baptism, confirmation and eucharist. On the third, fourth and fifth Sundays of Lent special reading at Mass emphasise the meaning of baptism while at the same time there are prayers for the candidates together with exorcisms. These exorcisms do not mean that the catechumens are possessed by demons but are prayers that they may be released from the powers of sin and darkness. During these weeks there may also be 'presentations' at which the candidates learn the profession of faith and the Lord's Prayer. Since the Easter Vigil is the most appropriate time for the sacraments of initiation, Holy Saturday is kept as a day of fasting and prayer for those who are to be baptised. They may also be anointed with oil as a final strengthening before baptism.

The Baptism of Children

Every baptism is a sign to the Church of its own life in Christ. Whenever possible the baptism should take place in the presence of the Sunday congregation at the eucharist. Since the new rite emphasises the responsibilities of parents to prepare their children for the christian life the parents themselves should also be prepared to take on their task before God and the community. The celebrant in the name of the community claims the child for Christ our Saviour by the sign of the cross. After special readings from the lectionary the water is blessed except during the Easter season when a prayer of thanksgiving is said instead. There are special booklets readily available, and in use in most parishes, which explain in detail the various rites used in the baptism of children.

Reception of Baptized Christians into Full Communion with the Catholic Church

The new rite for the reception of baptized people into the Catholic Church acknowledges that those who have been baptized are christians and most of them have already begun to live true christian lives as members of churches separated from Catholicism. The emphasis in the new rite is on 'full communion' which means not only participation in the eucharist but also that the elements of truth and sanctification in other christian churches have brought them to the point of seeking full admission into the Catholic community. The reception of such christians must never be construed as being against ecumenism since their decision has been taken under the guidance of the Holy Spirit. The main part of the rite consists in the profession of faith in the presence of the assembly.

Confirmation

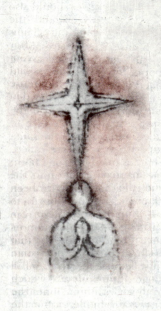

WE are called like Christ to be witnesses to God's kingdom. This 'calling' is made in baptism through which we share the life of the risen Lord. The sacrament of confirmation is the completion of baptism with which it is linked in the tradition of the Church. The spirit of the risen Lord is sent upon the confirmed and candidates for confirmation are anointed with the oil of chrism as a reminder that they have a special place in the mission of God's anointed Son. In Jewish tradition, as well as christian, sweet fragrance is often associated with worship or sacrifice acceptable to God. Through the fragrance of oil of chrism in confirmation we offer our lives to the service of God as a sacrifice which is pleasing to Him.

The candidates accompanied by one of their sponsors or parents are presented for confirmation by the priest or another person. Wherever possible each candidate is called by name and comes individually to the sanctuary. The candidates then renew their baptismal promises.

The bishop or other minister extends his hands over all who are to be confirmed and prays for the coming of the Holy Spirit. After he has laid his hands on each of the candidates the bishop then anoints them with chrism. The sponsors also place their hands on the candidates' shoulders, a sign that the Holy Spirit is shared by the whole Church, priests and people. The congregation prays for those who have been confirmed, for the parents, the Church and the world.

Holy Communion

THE EUCHARISTIC COMMUNITY OF PRAISE AND SACRIFICE

AS christians we are above all else a eucharistic community. We are a people called together in Christ and it is in him that we find our true unity: 'There is one body, one Spirit, just as you were all called into one and the same hope when you were called. There is one Lord, one faith, one baptism and one God who is Father of all, through all and within all'. Ephesians 4:4-6. In this unity we are fulfilling God's plan for us since it is his purpose to unite everyone under one head, Jesus Christ. We do not come together like other human societies just because we have similar interests. Christ is the beginning of a new humanity and we are called to follow him by growing into unity with him. "I am the vine, you are the branches. Whoever remains in me, with me in him, bears fruit in plenty; for cut off from me you can do nothing'. John 5:5. It is the community which unites to God each one of its members and through them calls towards God those who are not yet members. The community is for sanctification and mission. The Church is a perfect community and as such is the visible embodiment of the most profound unity possible between Christ and us. Christ at the Last Supper prayed for this unity. 'May they all be one, Father, may they be one in us, as you are in me and I am in you, so that the world may believe it was you who sent me'. John 17:21.

The Church is nowhere more united than when its people gather together to celebrate the eucharist — 'The eucharist makes the Church'. The eucharistic assembly of the local church is the universal Church made present here and now in its most

HOLY COMMUNION

effective way. The eucharist is our banquet of praise and thanksgiving at which we commemorate all that God has done and continues to do for us, through Christ. The very word 'eucharist' means praise and thanksgiving and we celebrate our unity in the risen Lord which draws out from us expressions of gratitude and wonder of God who has done marvels for us. We can never thank him enough and that is why we come together as a community to praise him through Christ. When we seek to approach God it is not sufficient to let our own hearts speak. Christ is present among us as our great high priest and all we offer is done in and through him. He is our high priest and 'it is the duty of every high priest to offer gifts and sacrifices'. **Hebrews 8:3.**

Through prayers of praise and thanksgiving we enter more fully into an understanding of the eucharist as a sacrifice. The eucharist is a banquet *because* it is a sacrifice. The one includes the other. The Gospel writers place the eucharist within the context of the Jewish passover meal portraying Christ's command to 'do this' as a command to keep *his* passover. The passover supper of the old covenant was a celebration of all that God had done for Israel. It was a sacred banquet of thanksgiving recalling the formation of Israel as God's people and their deliverance from Egypt. It embodied the joyful anticipation of the Messiah's coming and involved the slaying of a sacrificial lamb. Christ is our paschal lamb of the New Covenant who sacrificed himself for us so that we might celebrate as a new people all that God does for us as we anticipate the coming joy of God's kingdom.

Christ's death was sacrificial not simply because he died but above all because his death was a loving act of surrender to his Father for the salvation of mankind. In the eucharist the Church presents Christ's sacrifice to the Father in thanksgiving for all he has done for us together with the prayer that God's blessings will continue to be given to us in this world and in the one to come. The eucharist is also the sacrificial offering of the Church itself to the Father and thus involves each member of the congregation in offering himself with the Lord Jesus to our Father.

We are consecrated by the Holy Spirit in baptism and so are made a royal priesthood. We lift up our hearts in surrender and adoration to the Father. The eucharist is a mystery. It is not only

HOLY COMMUNION

the sacramental presence of Christ's sacrifice revealed by signs of bread and wine and made present by the power of the Spirit and the word. It is also that sacred action by which God gives himself to us and through which we give glory to him through our Redeemer, Jesus Christ. It is a two-way action, towards God and towards us. God gives us his Son and through His Son we give thanks to God so that God's gift becomes our response. Christ's death and resurrection make us want to praise God and also provides us with the perfect gift and sacrifice of praise and thanksgiving. Christ restores us to our proper relationship with God. 'How much more effectively the blood of Christ, who offered himself as the perfect sacrifice to God through the eternal Spirit, can purify our inner self from dead actions so that we do our service to the living God. He brings a new covenant, as the mediator, only so that the people who were called to an eternal inheritance may actually receive what was promised: his death took place to cancel the sins that infringed the earlier covenant.'
Hebrews 9:14-15.

Reconciliation

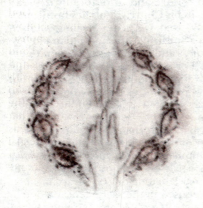

THROUGH baptism we share in the life of the risen Lord but the inward struggle still remains. 'I cannot understand my own behaviour, I fail to carry out the things I want to do, and I find myself doing the very things I hate. In fact, this seems to be the rule, that every single time I want to do good it is something evil that comes to hand. In my inmost self I dearly love God's law, but I can see that my body follows a different law that battles against the law which my reason dictates. This is what makes me a prisoner of that law of sin which lives inside my body.' Romans 7:15.21-23. We live surrounded on all sides by sin and even within ourselves there is a constant inclination to abandon God's law and love. 'The fact is, I know nothing good living in me — living, that is, in my unspiritual self — for though the will to do what is good is in me, the performance is not, with the result that instead of doing the good things I want to do, I carry out the sinful things I do not want. When I act against my will, then, it is not my true self doing it, but sin which lives in me.' Romans 7:18-20.

This disorientation within ourselves caused by sin is rectified through the saving power of Christ. He is the perfect reconciler who heals us like prodigal sons returning to our Father's home. 'It was God who reconciled us to himself through Christ and gave us the work of handing on this reconciliation. In other words, God in Christ was reconciling the world to himself, not holding men's faults against them, and he has entrusted to us the news that they are reconciled.' 2 Corinthians 5:18-19 Jesus came for the sake of sinners and those who feel lost and abandoned

RECONCILIATION

since he is the Good Shepherd who gives his life for his sheep. The Gospel is meaningless if it is denuded of God's loving forgiveness and reconciliation manifested visibly in Christ.

Christ's power to heal, to forgive and to restore us in God's love and friendship remains in his Church. This has been and is our constant belief, namely, that we are a healing Church through the power of Christ's Spirit. We are engaged in warfare with powers of sin and darkness and our baptismal commitment is under constant challenge. 'For we must be content to hope that we shall be saved — our salvation is not in sight, we should not have been hoping for it if it were — but, as I say, we must hope to be saved since we are not saved yet — it is something we must wait for with patience.' Romans 8:24-25.

The sacrament of reconciliation, formerly called penance, is now celebrated with a liturgy of the word which proclaims God's forgiveness and Christ's triumph over sin and death. We *celebrate* the sacrament with true christian joy and gratitude. However brief the readings may be a proclamation of God's word makes it evident that the ministry exercised in the sacrament is alone in obedience to a commissioning of God's Word as remembered effectively by the Church and, at the same time it is as a 'Church' here and now that we are healed and reconciled.

The liturgical dimension of the sacrament of forgiveness is clearly intended to be visible in the celebration of the new rite of reconciliation. Through the visible reconciliation of the local assembly of believing christians we receive the mercy of God's forgiveness. It is important therefore that penitential services be held regularly in parish or other local communities so that we can express the theological truth that we are reconciled to God in Jesus Christ through the mystical body of the Church. Many dioceses hold penitential services with the bishop present within the context of the eucharist, especially during the season of Lent, so that we can be seen to be a baptismal and eucharistic people.

This communal act of penitence instead of detracting from the necessity of individual confession highlights it. The community joins together in its preparation for the moment of individual confession and the fact that such a confession is made within the assembly aids the penitent to understand the communal or social nature of his sin. We sin against God and against our neighbour by what we have failed to do as much as by what we have done. The communal examination of conscience

RECONCILIATION

sensitively led by the priest is of inestimable value in building up the body of Christ in our midst. It encourages us to be more sincere in our usual Sunday celebration of the penitential rite. We are encouraged to witness to our conversion of heart through the visible testimony of seeing one another going to confess our sins to God through the necessary action of the priest.

Individual Reconciliation

Confession is to take place within the context of prayer and the reading of the scriptures. This is to some extent pastorally impossible when there are large numbers who wish to receive the sacraments hence the importance of frequent communal services of reconciliation. For the moment we can refer to the directives laid down in the new rites as expressing the ideal rather than the norm. These rites allow for a great variety of alternatives depending upon the needs and preferences of those who are celebrating the sacrament. In accord with ancient tradition by extending his hands over the penitent when he gives absolution the priest signifies Christ who welcomes the penitent in the Father's name and upon whom he invokes God's Spirit.

Communal Reconciliation

This rite generally begins with a hymn and opening prayer followed by a liturgy of the word. We examine the conformity of our lives in relation to the word of God which we have heard and then there follows a general confession of sins. Each penitent goes to the priest(s) for individual confession and after these are completed the priest leads the congregation in prayers of praise and thanksgiving and gives the final blessing.

Anointing the Sick

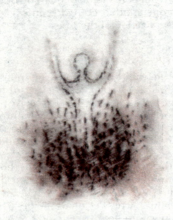

WE are surrounded on all sides by the effects of sin since everyone must suffer its penalty — death. 'Sin entered the world through one man, and through sin death, and thus death has spread through the whole human race because everyone has sinned.' Romans 5:12. Christ by his death and resurrection put an end to the power of death over us. 'If it is certain that death reigned over everyone as the consequence of one man's fall, it is even more certain that one man, Jesus Christ, will cause everyone to reign in life who receives the free gift that he does not deserve, of being made righteous. Again, as one man's fall brought condemnation on everyone, so the good act of one man brings everyone life and makes them justified. As by one man's disobedience many were made sinners, so by one man's obedience many will be made righteous. When law came, it was to multiply the opportunities of falling, but however great the number of sins committed, grace was even greater; and so, just as sin reigned wherever there was death, so grace will reign to bring eternal life thanks to the righteousness that comes through Jesus Christ our Lord.' Romans 5:17-21.

Christ came into our sin-filled world in order to overcome evil in all its forms. During the three years of his public ministry he restored health to the sick, sight to the blind, and even life to the dead. 'Then Jesus gave the messengers their answer, "Go back and tell John what you have seen and heard: the blind see again, the lame walk, lepers are cleansed, and the deaf hear, the dead are raised to life, the Good News is proclaimed to the poor and happy is the man who does not lose faith in me." ' Luke 7:22-23.

ANOINTING THE SICK

Christ's ministry to the sick is continued in his Church both through the sacrament of the anointing of the sick as well as through the charism of healing which has been manifest in every age and which has seen a rapid growth in recent years. Sickness and death remain for the christian as great evils to be feared. Christ's victory over sickness and death reveals his power to take away the sins of the world. Accordingly the Church urges us to pray for the recovery of those who are ill. Illness, if used properly, is a participation in Christ's suffering and death which will prepare us to share in his rising glory. The sick are anointed so that they will be strengthened with the power of Christ either to bear their suffering in union with his passion or to show the power of his resurrection in their restoration to health. All those who are seriously ill, handicapped or aged are encouraged to receive the anointing with confidence. This anointing is not to be confused with *viaticum* which is the sacrament of the dying. Since the Church's ministry is an extension of Christ's own healing ministry we should gather together as a community along with those who wish to be anointed so that we may witness to Christ's healing power. The rite of anointing includes suitable readings from the Bible followed by a short homily which links the readings with the anointing. In silence the priest lays his hands on the sick and then says a prayer of thanksgiving over the oil. This prayer recalls with gratitude God's saving action in history. The sick person is anointed on the forehead and hands and after prayers for his spiritual and physical well-being he receives a blessing from the priest.

Christian Death and Burial

Since the Church is essentially baptismal, in that we die to ourselves in order to rise with Christ, so we treat death not so much in sorrow as those who have no hope, but in triumph. Death is an on-going process into life which has no end. 'If there is no resurrection of the dead, Christ himself cannot have been raised, and if Christ has not been raised then our preaching is useless and your believing it is useless; indeed, we are shown up as witnesses who have committed perjury before God, because we swore in evidence before God that he had raised Christ to life. For if the dead are not raised, Christ has not been raised, and if Christ has not been raised, you are still in your sins. And what is

ANOINTING THE SICK

more serious, all who have died in Christ have perished. If our hope in Christ has been for this life only, we are the most unfortunate of all people. But Christ has in fact been raised from the dead, the first-fruits of all who have fallen asleep. Death came through one man and in the same way the resurrection of the dead has come through one man. Just as all men die in Adam, so all men will be brought to life in Christ.' **1 Corinthians 15:13-22.**

The new funeral rites emphasise our christian hope through its use of many symbols of baptism. The Easter candle of light and life in the resurrection is placed at the head of the coffin which is draped in a white pall [cloth] symbol of our baptismal robe. Nowadays white vestments are often used as a sign of triumph in the knowledge that we will rise again in Christ to the glory of the Father. Baptism does not mean that our lives can be lived without pain but we believe that when we face suffering and death with courage and acceptance of God's saving will for us then we come at last to the joy of the resurrection. Death therefore is the completion of our earthly baptism and we begin to live fully the life of the risen Lord.

Through baptism we take up our cross daily to follow him through death. By the death of one of its members the Church also lives its common baptism in so far as it undergoes loss and change. The Church in this world has become different but it is also changed for the better through the mystical body of the saints in heaven whose number has been increased through the entry of another who has been sealed by the Holy Spirit. 'Flesh and blood cannot inherit the kingdom of God: and the perishable cannot inherit what lasts for ever. I will tell you something that has been secret: that we are not all going to die, but we shall all be changed. This will be instantaneous, in the twinkling of an eye, when the last trumpet sounds. It will sound, and the dead will be raised, imperishable, and we shall be changed as well, because our present perishable nature must put on imperishability and this mortal nature must put on immortality, then the words of scripture will come true: Death is swallowed up in victory. Death, where is your victory? Death, where is your sting?' **1. Corinthians 15:50-55.**

The wake service when the body is brought to church is coming into more frequent usage. It begins with either psalm 130 or psalm 23 and is followed by appropriate readings from

ANOINTING THE SICK

scripture. After a prayerful silence or a short meditation on the resurrection the priest leads the people in prayers for the deceased and the strengthening comfort of the relatives. The service concludes with a blessing.

Marriage

THE sacrament of matrimony is called the 'family sacrament'. The family is the basic unit of the Church and society. St. Paul compares the love of Christ for his Church with the relationship between husband and wife. 'Give way to one another in obedience to Christ. Wives should regard their husbands as they regard the Lord, since as Christ is head of the Church and saves the whole body, so is a husband the head of his wife; and as the Church submits to Christ, so should wives to their husbands, in everything. Husbands should love their wives just as Christ loved the Church and sacrificed himself for her to make her holy.' Ephesians 5:21-25.

Marriage is not a legal arrangement between two people but a living sign of Christ's loving presence among us. Together husband and wife are God's image and likeness so they are no longer two but one in Christ who is constantly with them through the grace of this sacrament helping them at all times whether good or bad. They take each other in love for better or worse in a bond which no one has the power to break. They are faithful to each other as God is forever faithful to them.

The married couple themselves are the ministers of the sacrament to one another. The Church witnesses publicly to their marriage through the presence of the priest and the members of the community since matrimony is very much a sacrament of the assembly, the community. Christians come together in a local congregation to celebrate God's love for the newly-married couple and their love for one another. That is why the Church encourages the celebration of marriage within the eucharistic celebration itself. By celebrating the eucharist with the new couple the Church shows publicly that marriage is not merely for

MARRIAGE

two people but for the whole Church which celebrates this sacrament of joy. The Church prays publicly for them and gives them a nuptial blessing as an expression of Christ's love for them not only on their wedding day but also in the years ahead. The readings in the marriage rite are so varied that it is customary for couples to supply their own order of service in small booklets.

Blessing of an engagement

The months before marriage are an important time of preparation and many couples now seek the blessing of the Church and ask for the support of the parish through its prayers on their behalf. The rite of the blessing is very simple. There is a short bible reading followed by an exchange of promises together with the blessing of the engagement ring(s). It is becoming more common too for a young couple to have a bible service on the night before a wedding in conjunction with their wedding rehearsal.

Holy Orders

The Ordination of Bishops

THE role of bishop is essential to the hierarchical structure of the Church. He is appointed by special mandate from the Holy Father and his importance in the sacramental life of the Church has always been part of our belief and tradition as Catholics. The principal consecrator reminds the bishop-elect what his role is to be in the following words: 'In the person of the bishop surrounded by his priests, our Lord Jesus Christ, who is high priest for ever, is present among you. In the ministry of the bishop, Christ himself continues to proclaim the word of God and to unfold the mysteries of faith to those who believe. In the paternal functions of the bishop, Christ adds to his body and incorporates new members into it. In the bishop's wisdom and prudence Christ guides you in your earthly pilgrimage towards eternal happiness.

'Take to yourselves therefore in a thankful and happy spirit our brother whom we bishops make a colleague in our order by laying hands upon him. Respect him as a minister of Christ and a steward entrusted with the mysteries of God. He has been assigned to bear witness to the truth of the Gospel, as well as to minister the Spirit and God's power to make men just. Remember the words of Christ which he addressed to the apostles: "Whoever listens to you listens to me: whoever rejects you rejects me, and those who reject me reject the one who sent me."

'You, beloved brother, have been chosen by the Lord. Reflect

HOLY ORDERS

on the fact that you have been taken from among men and appointed to act for men in their relations with God. The title of bishop derives not from rank but from his duty, and it is the part of a bishop to serve rather than to rule. Such is the counsel of the master that the most important should behave as if he were the last, and the leader as if he were the one who serves. Proclaim the message whether it be welcome or unwelcome; correct error with the greatest patience and in a spirit of teaching. Make it your business to pray and offer sacrifice for the people committed to your care and so draw every kind of grace for them from the overflowing holiness of Christ.

'As a steward of the mysteries of Christ in the church assigned to you, be a faithful supervisor and guardian. Since you are chosen by the Father to rule over his family, be mindful always of the good shepherd who knows his sheep and is known by them and who did not hesitate to lay down his life for his sheep.

'Love with the charity of a father and a brother all those whom God places in your care, the priests and deacons who are partners with you in the ministry of Christ, the poor and the infirm as well, and also strangers and aliens. Encourage the faithful to work with you in your apostolic task and do not refuse to listen to them willingly. Never relax in your concern for those who do not belong as yet to the one fold of Christ, since they are commended to you in the Lord. Never forget that the Catholic Church is made one by the bond of charity and that you are joined to the collegiate body of bishops. You will consequently maintain a deep concern for all the churches and gladly come to the aid and support of churches in need. Give your attention therefore to the whole flock in which the Holy Spirit appoints you an overseer of the assembly of God — in the name of the Father whose image you personify in the Church — and in the name of his Son Jesus Christ whose triple role of teacher, priest and pastor you undertake — and in the name of the Holy Spirit who gives life to the Church of Christ and supports our weakness with his power.'

When the bishop-elect affirms that he is resolved to carry out his duties then all the bishops present lay hands on him as a sign of the presence of the Holy Spirit. The open book of Gospels is placed on his head as a sign that he is to live its life in word and deed. The consecrating bishops pray that the Spirit which was given to the apostles will now pour out his power on the bishop-

HOLY ORDERS

elect to the praise and glory of God the Father so that he will serve God by reconciling us to him, by offering the eucharist and by the forgiveness of sins. The head of the new bishop is anointed and he is presented with the book of the Gospels which he is to proclaim. He receives the ring, mitre and staff, signs of his office, and is reminded that he is to be a shepherd of his flock. He is invited to take the first place in the church and then receives the kiss of peace from the other bishops. Finally he goes through the church blessing the people of God whom he is now to serve as the apostles did before him.

The Ordination of Priests

The priest is very much part of the life and service of the Church. Following a special calling by the Holy Spirit he chooses to follow the priesthood of Christ by dedicating himself to a life of celibacy. He is above all else the minister of the eucharist. Every high priest has been taken out of mankind and is appointed to act for men in their relations with God, to offer gifts and sacrifices for sins; and so he can sympathise with those who are ignorant or uncertain because he too lives in the limitations of weakness. That is why he has to make sin offerings for himself as well as for the people. No one takes this honour on himself, but each one is called by God, as Aaron was.' Hebrews 5:1-4.

Those who are to be ordained are presented in the name of the people for acceptance by the bishop who reminds them that it is their duty to instruct the people and to celebrate the sacraments. 'It is your ministry which will make the spiritual sacrifices of the faithful perfect by uniting them to the eucharistic sacrifice of Christ. That sacrifice of Christ will be offered sacramentally in an unbloody way through your hands. Understand the meaning of what you do; put into practice what you celebrate. When you recall the mystery of the death and resurrection of the Lord, try to die to sin and to walk in the new life of Christ. In baptizing men you will bring them into the people of God; in the sacrament of penance you will forgive sins in the name of Christ and the Church; with holy oil you will relieve and console the sick. You will celebrate the liturgy, offer thanks and praise to God through every hour of the day, praying for the people of God and the whole world as well. As you do this, always keep in mind that you are a man chosen from among men and appointed to act for men in their relations with God. Do your part in the work of Christ the priest with the unfailing gladness of genuine charity, and look after the concerns of Christ, not your own.' (From the bishop's instruction to the candidates.)

The bishop then questions the candidates about their willingness to accept the duties and obligations of the priesthood and accepts their promise of obedience and respect to him and his successors. Priests are ordained by the laying-on of hands and prayer. The bishop first lays his hands on them and this is also done by all the priests present at the ceremony thus signifying the oneness of the priesthood in which all of them share. The bishop completes the ordination when in a solemn prayer he thanks God for his unfailing gift of ministry to the Church.

The new priests are invested with the stole and chasuble which are the eucharistic garments of their office for which they are now set aside. The bishop anoints their hands to signify that like Christ priests are anointed to bless, consecrate and sanctify. He also presents them with a chalice of wine and the paten [plate] of bread urging them to know what they are doing, to be as holy as the actions they perform and to model their lives on the mystery of the cross. The bishop exchanges the kiss of peace with each of the new priests welcoming them as co-workers with him. It is becoming more customary to ordain the candidates for the priesthood in their own parishes thus showing the link between the people and the priest.

The Ordination of Deacons

The ordination of deacons is deeply rooted in the tradition of the Church from the earliest times since when it has undergone a change from a more administrative role to the more specific one of proclaiming the Gospel. 'So the twelve called a full meeting of the disciples and addressed them, "It would not be right for us to neglect the word of God so as to give out food; you, brothers, must select from among yourselves seven men of good reputation, filled with the Spirit and with wisdom; we will hand over this duty to them, and continue to devote ourselves to

HOLY ORDERS

prayer and to the service of the word." The whole assembly approved of this proposal and elected Stephen, a man full of faith and of the Holy Spirit, together with Philip, Prochorus, Nicanor, Timon, Parmenas, and Nicolaus of Antioch, a convert to Judaism. They presented these to the apostles, who prayed and laid their hands on them.' **Acts 6:2-6.**

In the Second Vatican Council the role of deacon was restored in its own right so that now married men may also be ordained to this office in the hierarchical structure of the Church.

The candidates are presented in the name of the people to the bishop who reminds them that they are to assist the bishop and priests in the ministry of the word, at the liturgy and in the Church's work of charity. He instructs them as follows 'Let them excel in every virtue: in sincere love, in the use of authority with moderation, in concern for the sick and the poor, in purity and irreproachable conduct, and in a deeply spiritual life. Let your commandments be evident in their conduct, so that the faithful may follow their good example. Let them offer the world a witness of a clear conscience. Help them to persevere, firm and steadfast in Christ. Just as your own Son came not to be served, but to give himself in service to others, may these deacons imitate him on earth and reign with him in heaven.'

As in the case of ordination of priests they promise the bishop and his successors obedience and respect. After the laying-on of hands and the prayer of consecration they are invested with the stole and dalmatic which are their signs of office. They are then presented with the book of Gospels and urged to believe what they read, teach what they believe and to practise what they preach. The bishop exchanges the kiss of peace with each of the new deacons.

Liturgy and Renewal

Liturgy and Renewal

GOD, our Father, has appointed his Son, Jesus Christ, to be our eternal High Priest. 'In Jesus, the Son of God we have the supreme high priest who has gone through to the highest heaven.' Hebrews 4:14. The mediating action of Christ works in two directions in the love exchange between God and us. On the one hand through Christ we give glory to God and offer him a worship which is perfect and on the other we receive God's grace and so through Christ our salvation is being achieved.

Liturgy is quite simply God's life with us and our lives with him. Christ brings the two elements together namely the glory of God and the salvation of his people. The whole of the liturgy whether of praise or of grace is thus embodied in Christ who is united with his Church as a bridegroom with his bride. Christ is the head which gives life to the body of which we are the members. 'Now you together are Christ's body; but each of you is a different part'. 1 Corinthians 12.27. The Church is therefore associated with the death, resurrection and exaltation of her saviour and acts in his name. 'The sacred liturgy is the public worship which our Redeemer, as the Church's head, offers to the heavenly Father; it is the worship which the community of Christ's faithful gives to its founder and through him to the eternal Father; briefly it is the public worship of the mystical body of Jesus Christ, head and members'. *Encyclical letter of Pope Pius XII Mediator Dei et hominum.*

The liturgy is the source and summit of our christian life. The concern of the Sacred Vatican Council was to *renew* the Church's life through a reform and renewal of the Church's liturgy. Liturgical renewal is not simply a matter of moving the altar round to face the people or of changing the language. It refers to what happens in our hearts and minds so that our worship may take place in a new, richer and more meaningful way. Ceremonial was not at the heart of the liturgical movement's concern. Rather it looked to a renewal of the Church's life and spirituality through a return to the depths of our heritage in scripture and tradition. That is why the liturgy of the Word has such a prominent part in our worship today.

The reform of the liturgy through the improvement and revision of our liturgical book and rites is just a means to an end.

LITURGY AND RENEWAL

Renewal means the improvement of the quality of our worship, a much more rewarding and demanding task than simple liturgical reform. Because many people hoped that liturgical reform would of itself produce the desired results of a renewed christian community they were disappointed with all the changes in our manner of worship when these results failed to materialise. Criticism soon followed and even hostility to 'modernization' set in. This happened because liturgical reform was equated with renewal in the Church's life.

Liturgical renewal in its deepest sense involves us as christians in an ever-deepening awareness of our commitment as christians through a fuller understanding of the sacrament of baptism. Both the new rites for the baptism of children and adults make it clear that only those who have been formed in the Church's life can properly join in the celebration of the eucharist. We live out our lives as baptised people through the liturgy.

In the larger perspective of the history of the Church's worship we soon discover that her worship has always exhibited two complementary principles namely a basic uniformity in essentials together with a wealth of variety of details. The liturgy most of us identify as 'the Catholic liturgy' is in point of fact only one of the great family of Catholic liturgies, all of equal age and dignity. Over the course of history change has been the rule rather than the exception. Sometimes the change has been dramatic such as in the Church's penitential discipline in which there was a shift from a system of public penance to that of private penance still familiar to us. The new emphasis in the sacrament of reconciliation combines both the public and private expressions of penance. It is a wedding of the 'old' and the 'new'.

At the beginning of the Middle Ages when the local churches of Western Europe began to adopt the Roman rite they still retained many local customs and variations. The Roman rite is a combination of a variety of practices and styles so that liturgy may be seen as an interplay of the universal and the local. Greater emphasis is placed today on the value of a dynamic liturgy for the local church. A number of recent liturgical reforms have made it possible for the liturgical celebration to become a more evident sign of the Church's unity in diversity.

The renewed stress on the importance of the 'local church' has also meant a particular emphasis on the liturgy as the action of all the people, the community, who are positively encouraged to

LITURGY AND RENEWAL

take an active part in the Church's worship. The liturgy is not simply a gathering of like-minded individuals who 'shop around' for their kind of liturgy nor is it an impersonal crowd. It is an *interactive* congregation of priests and people who are called together by God as the body of Christ and as such represent the whole Church scattered throughout the world as well as the assembly of saints in Heaven. Those who gather together for the liturgy must be one with the whole community of the faithful. It is a unity of faith, hope and charity and not just the superficial unity of language. The importance of Latin as a common language for worship, while having its advantages, has been over-played as a sign of the Church's unity.

The liturgical assembly functions more perfectly as a sacramental sign when those who take part whether rich or poor, young or old, educated or illiterate find their unity and meaning as a congregation in what is really a living, loving community. We have to work hard at the community aspect in our local churches if liturgy is ever going to come alive. We do not encounter the risen Lord in some vague, abstract, impersonal way but as he is present in our midst in our local church. In the sacramental plan which God has established for us we find that it is the local community of faith which is the incarnation 'here and now' of God's enduring presence with us and for us. This emphasis has resulted in variation in the celebration of liturgy from one place to another, and even from one celebration to another. The local liturgy is therefore the focal point of the risen Christ in our world. Liturgy is never imposed by elite groups but grows out of the community. In this way priests and people will discover a new force which will weld them together in the bonds of community.

In its deepest sense the Church is the body of Christ, the communion of the faithful, in the life of its risen Lord. Sacramental actions are not merely things or rites interposed between man and God; they are the activity of Christ in our midst offering praise to the Father and reconciling us to one another and to God. We need to penetrate and understand more fully the new or restored symbols and revivify the old ones. It is a matter of hallowing the new and renewing the hallowed. We urgently need a true spirit of liturgical celebration which communicates the holy not as unapproachable and distant but as loved and present among us. Ecclesiastical structures need to be reassessed so that the local church is not just a community which meets in a building for an hour on Sunday but reflects Christ's loving pastoral care of the world outside. When we set our sights on these priorities liturgical renewal will not be accomplished but it will have begun.

Liturgical Symbols

Liturgical Symbols

GOD is a spirit whom we cannot see, hear or touch. He incarnates himself in the humanity of his Son who is the perfect link in communication between God and us. We too wish to communicate with God in a manner which will raise our minds and hearts above mundane matters and so we make use of symbols which convey to us the deeper meaning behind the obvious reality which we know through our senses. Bread for example is food which sustains our bodily life but it also conveys the idea of Christ who is the bread of life. We use four main types of symbols in our worship:

1. Persons
2. Places
3. Things
4. Gestures

1. PERSONS

The community of the faithful itself is the primary symbolic element of the liturgy. The Second Vatican Council encourages us, as the people of God gathered together in a eucharistic community, to take an active part according to our function in all liturgical celebrations. We do this in the eucharist by listening prayerfully and attentively to scripture readings, joining in the prayers, giving our 'amen' or assent to the actions offered in our name, bringing gifts of bread and wine to the altar, joining in the acclamations and sharing in communion. Whenever liturgical celebration tends to become private or exclusive the sign of the liturgy as an assembly of the faithful is diminished. 'Our Saviour instituted the Eucharistic Sacrifice of His Body and Blood to perpetuate the sacrifice of the Cross throughout the centuries and entrust to His Church a memorial of His death and resurrection, a sacrament of love, a sign of unity, a bond of charity . . .'

Therefore the Church earnestly desires that when Christ's faithful are present at this mystery of faith, they should not be there as strangers or silent spectators, but through a proper appreciation of the rites and prayers they should participate knowingly, devoutly and actively.

Instructed by God's word and refreshed at the table of the

LITURGICAL SYMBOLS

Lord's body, they should give thanks to God by offering the Immaculate Victim, not only through the hands of the Priest, but also with him, they should offer themselves too.

Through Christ the Mediator they should be drawn day by day into ever closer union with God and with each other, so that finally, God may be all in all'. *[Vatican II; Document on Liturgy]*.

The liturgical assembly is an ordered gathering and thus requires a variety of ministers each to play his role in and for the assembly.

The Bishop, or the celebrant who takes his place, is the head or president of the assembly. He presides over the prayers, preaches the homily, dedicates and consecrates the offerings and ministers the sacraments.

The Deacon proclaims the Gospel at Mass, sings the Easter proclamation [Exultet] and assists at the altar especially in the distribution of communion.

The reader reads all the biblical lessons except the Gospel.

The acolyte serves at the altar, carries the processional cross and candles and assists in the distribution of communion.

The choir aids the people in participating in the liturgy by leading the congregation in song especially in the Kyrie, the Gospel Alleluia, the response to the general intercessions, the eucharistic acclamations, the Lord's Prayer and the Lamb of God.

2. PLACES

The church is the building in which the christian community usually gathers together to worship and pray. It should be planned primarily to suit the requirements of the liturgy and only secondarily as a place for recollection and private devotions. We must not, however, look upon the church merely as a building since it is designed to house ourselves the living stones of the spiritual temple which Christ the cornerstone is building up day by day. For this reason the church is consecrated or at least blessed before it is used.

The baptistery is located near the entrance to the church. During the Easter season the font contains the baptismal water blessed during the paschal vigil on Easter Eve. During the other seasons the water is blessed at each baptismal liturgy. The

LITURGICAL SYMBOLS

baptistery is becoming a more prominent feature in the architectural design of newly-built churches. This is going back to the tradition of the early christians and helps us to appreciate even more the importance of baptism in our lives. The font is 'the fountain of living water' promised by Christ [John 4:14.] which springs up into eternal life in those who are baptised. It is the Jordan which we must cross in order to enter into the promised land. We are reminded of the great mystery of water every Sunday in the blessing and sprinkling of holy water and by the bowl of holy water which we find by the door of the church.

The cemetery is also a holy place and proclaims the promise of eternal life. We place the bodies of the dead in the cemetery with the same trust that we plant grains of wheat in the soil, since we believe that in due time they will spring up from death into everlasting life.

The altar like the 'Holy of Holies' in the temple of Jerusalem is the focal point of the church. It is both the place of sacrifice and the table at which we celebrate the Lord's supper. The altar is a sacred stone which at its consecration was, as it were, baptised with holy water and confirmed by being anointed with holy oil. It is a symbol of Christ himself and receives special marks of reverence such as bows and incensation in the liturgy. The altar is also the focal point of liturgies other than the eucharist, for example, the rite of baptism concludes with a procession to the altar and marriage vows, religious vows and ordinations all take place in front of the altar. The keeping of the blessed sacrament at a shrine to the side of the altar or in a small chapel of its own has caused unnecessary misunderstanding. The reason that the altar is a holy place is not because the tabernacle is usually placed on it but rather the tabernacle is put there because the altar is *in itself* the holy place. We treat the altar reverently in its own right and we are encouraged to focus our attention on the liturgical action which takes place at this place of worship.

The lectern has a special place and significance in the church for it is from there that God's saving word is proclaimed.

The Blessed Sacrament chapel with its tabernacle is the abiding presence of Christ under the sacramental species of bread and is a special place of private devotion reminding us that Christ is always with us day and night. It is the most decorated part of the church to show our respect for the Risen Lord.

LITURGICAL SYMBOLS

3. THINGS

Bread. The most important of the sacred things are those which are themselves made sacred or sacramental — bread, wine, oils and water. The eucharist is a meal. It supplies us with our daily food as we continue our journey as pilgrims back to the Father. It is to us spiritually what manna was to the Jewish people materially as they journeyed through the desert for forty years on their way to the promised land. It is the food of wayfarers *[cibus viatorum]* reminding us that we are still on our way supported and strengthened by Christ as the bread of life. 'I am the bread of life. He who comes to me will never be hungry' John 6:35.

Wine is a symbol of celebration and through it we celebrate with Christ his victory over sin, death and the world. When we present bread and wine to the Lord we do what Melchisedech did to thank God for Abraham's victory. 'The cup of salvation I will raise: I will call on the Lord's name. Ps. 115:13.

Oil has a symbolic importance which stretches back into the heart of Jewish history. Kings were anointed with oil by the prophets as a sign of consecration and strength. On Holy Thursday morning at the bishop's eucharist the holy oils are blessed. The oil of catechumens is a sign of the Church's strengthening of the weak. With the oil of chrism the Church seals with the Spirit those who bear his life in the world [confirmation], commissions those whose lives are to be a living sign of Christ's sacrificial service [ordination] and brings his ministry of healing to the sick [anointing of the sick]. Holy oils are very much part of the Church's life of service and mission.

Water is above all a symbol of the new life which comes to us through death. Just as Christ died that we might live so we must die to self in order that Christ may live in us through grace. Water, with its power for destruction, signifies death, recalling the story of the flood. Water also signifies life in so far as it causes things to grow. Without water the earth would be a barren wasteland. God's spirit moves over the waters and brings all things into existence. Through the waters of baptism we are a new creation. Water is a sign of the resurrection of the Lord, who conquers death in us, and a promise of our own resurrection in Christ. The baptismal font is a continual reminder that the whole of christian life is marked by baptism.

LITURGICAL SYMBOLS

Smoke or cloud is an ancient symbol of divinity or the sacred. The children of Israel were led by the pillar of cloud as they journeyed from Egypt. 'Yahweh went before them, by day in the form of a pillar of cloud to show them the way, and by night in the form of a pillar of fire to give them light; thus they could continue their march by day and by night.' Exodus 13:21. It was in a cloud of smoke that Moses received the Ten Commandments from God. 'Then Moses led the people out of the camp to meet God; and they stood at the bottom of the mountain. The mountain of Sinai was entirely wrapped in smoke, because Yahweh had descended on it in the form of fire. Like smoke from a furnace the smoke went up, and the whole mountain shook violently.' Exodus 19:17-18. A cloud of divine glory filled Jerusalem's temple and it was in a cloud that the Father spoke at Jesus' baptism and at his transfiguration. 'Jesus was still speaking when suddenly a bright cloud covered them with shadow, and from the cloud there came a voice which said, 'This is my Son, the Beloved; he enjoys my favour. Listen to him.' Matthew 17:5.

The smoke of incense is also used as a symbol of the Church's prayer which rises up before God as a 'sweet savour' with which he is pleased. The smoke of incense is used to envelop everything which belongs to God: the altar, the cross, the gifts for sacrifice, the living members of Christ [clergy and people] and even their mortal remains — relics of the saints and the bodies of those who have died believing in Christ.

Light. The risen Christ, whose life is given to us in baptism, is the light of the world. The Easter candle, solemnly blessed on Easter Eve, and the candles used at baptism take on unique importance as signifying the radiance of Christ dispelling the darkness of sin and death. Candles carried before processions or which flank the altar or gospel book convey the same message. A lighted candle in the hands of a christian is a symbol of faith and a sharing in the divine life of Christ. Candles are used at the renewal of baptismal vows during the Easter Vigil, at the procession on the feast of the Presentation of the Lord, at first communion, at religious profession or ordination, at the point of death and also accompany the body of the believer to the grave. From birth to death we are aglow with the light of Christ.

Vestments — their use developed historically out of ordinary street clothes worn by everyone until eventually they became the

LITURGICAL SYMBOLS

dress of the clergy alone for use in the liturgy. They represent the deeply felt human need to surround any important event with solemnity. Clothes have had a special significance ever since man's fall. It was sin which gave rise to the sense of shame of Adam and Eve who received from God the skins of animals with which they clothed themselves. The baptismal garment of white shows us that we really have 'put on' Christ himself, that is, his grace. The garment of grace is a sign of the garment of glory which with the blessed in heaven one day we will share.

Vessels. Since the recent liturgical reform, considerable freedom has been allowed with regard to the kind of material used for the chalice [cup] and paten [plate]. Formerly they were made of the most precious metals and gold since they touched the sacramental body and blood of Christ but today they are often fashioned so as to convey the meal aspect of the eucharist.

4. GESTURES

Processions are not merely activities to keep us occupied in church but vivid reminders that we are pilgrims on a journey through life on earth to our heavenly home. The people's presentation of the gifts and their procession to the altar at communion are integral parts of the liturgical action. Processions create a sense of movement and purpose for the congregation and are part of our christian tradition.

Peace greeting or pax is a very important gesture. It expresses our unity in Christ and our willingness to be reconciled with one another.

Hands upraised or outstretched in prayer are now associated with the priest but originally all christians prayed in this manner in the liturgy. The practice is returning with the resurgence of charismatic life in the church.

Sign of the cross is one of the oldest christian gestures and immerses our prayers and actions in the life of the Trinity through the saving cross of Christ.

Prayer postures are very important and vary from culture to culture. In Africa, for example, many congregations sit or kneel for the reading of the Gospel as a sign that they are its servants and wish to listen to the words of Christ, their chief. They consider standing to be a sign of confrontation and hostility.

LITURGICAL SYMBOLS

However, in our culture the following is generally accepted: *standing* indicates attentiveness and a sense of dignity, *kneeling* denotes humility and sorrow, and *bowing* is a gesture of adoration and honour.

Communion in the hand is the most ancient custom of receiving communion and has rightly been restored. The reverent gesture of stretching out our hands indicates that we come before the Lord as suppliant beggars in response to Christ's command to 'take and eat'. Any controversy in this matter is due to a lack of historical sense and ill-founded fears that doctrinal implications are involved.

The Liturgical Year

The Liturgical Year

WE are a people united in and with Christ. As a community we remember and celebrate his saving work on our behalf from his incarnation until he comes in glory. Throughout the year the Church unfolds the entire mystery of Christ so that we may always give thanks to our Father for the new life of grace in which we now live. 'Out of his infinite glory, may he give you the power through his Spirit for your hidden self to grow strong, so that Christ may live in your hearts through faith, and then, planted in love and built on love, you will with all the saints have strength to grasp the breadth and the length, the height and the depth; until, knowing the love of Christ, which is beyond all knowledge, you are filled with the utter fullness of God. Glory be to him whose power, working in us, can do infinitely more than we can ask or imagine; glory be to him from generation to generation in the Church and in Christ Jesus for ever and ever. Amen.' Ephesians 3:16-21.

LITURGICAL DAYS

The Day: Each day is made holy through the liturgical celebrations of God's people especially the holy eucharist and the office or the liturgy of the hours [chiefly, morning and evening prayer]. We not only grow old with the passage of time: we also grow more in the likeness of our Saviour. In every moment of time we are being raised in Christ to the new life of grace by means of the Church's liturgy. We are called to live out each day the life of the resurrection of the Lord. 'Since you have been brought back to true life with Christ, you must look for the things that are in heaven, where Christ is, sitting at God's right hand. Let your thoughts be on heavenly things, not on the things that are on the earth, because you have died, and now the life you have is hidden with Christ in God. But when Christ is revealed — and he is your life — you too will be revealed in all your glory with him.' Corinthians 3:1-4.

Sunday: The resurrection is at the heart and centre of our lives as christians. In the very earliest days the Church celebrated no feasts at all except the resurrection. It was the original feast day and the most important. All other feasts were celebrated in relation to it. The Church celebrated the resurrection every

THE LITURGICAL YEAR

Sunday which we call the Lord's day. The weekly observance of Sunday is the cornerstone on which the Church's liturgy is built. Sunday is the very day of Christ's resurrection when God as it were resumed his work of creation in a new and spiritual way. This is in symbolic contrast to the Jewish Sabbath when God is thought of as resting after his six days of material creation. Christ is the beginning of the new creation. We *begin* our week with our 'holy day' remembering the new creation whereas the Jews *end* their week with their 'holy day' remembering the old creation. Sunday was also commonly known as the 'eighth day', a day that was considered as going on throughout the rest of time until Christ comes again. It was a custom among the early christians to assemble before dawn on the Lord's day to celebrate the eucharist, thereby calling to mind the resurrection of their Lord, while at the same time looking forward to the dawn of their own resurrection when the risen Christ would return to them in glory.

Special Days of Celebration: These are divided into solemnities, feasts and memorials. *Solemnities* are remembrances of our Lord, the Virgin Mary, and the celebration of the days of saints who have universal significance throughout the entire Church. *Feasts* are commemorations of lesser importance and finally *memorials* complete the cycle of christian remembrance, celebration and prayer.

Days of Special Prayer and Penance: Lent is the chief period of penance and Ash Wednesday together with all the Fridays of the year, especially Good Friday, are the appointed days of penance. Through penance we change the direction of our lives towards God by hearing and following the Gospel of Jesus Christ.

THE YEAR

Easter Triduum: Easter is the centre of our annual cycle of feasts and seasons. The Easter Triduum is the peak of the liturgical year in which we recall how Christ redeemed the whole human race and gave glory to the Father by his death and resurrection. We begin the Triduum by the celebration of the Lord's Supper on Holy Thursday evening, continue with the celebration of the Lord's Passion on Good Friday afternoon, reach the high point with the evening Easter Vigil of the Lord's resurrection and close with evening prayer on Easter Sunday.

THE LITURGICAL YEAR

The solemnity of Easter is to the liturgical year what Sunday is to the week.

The Easter Season is sometimes called 'the great Sunday'. It continues for fifty days, a week of weeks, with the Ascension on the fortieth day and the sending of the Holy Spirit at Pentecost as the completion of Easter. The weekdays after the Ascension to the Saturday before Pentecost are a preparation for the coming of the Holy Spirit. The sending of the Holy Spirit begins the 'last age' and it was for this purpose that Christ died, rose again and ascended to his Father. 'It is for your own good that I am going because unless I go, the Advocate will not come to you; but if I do go, I will send him to you.' John 16:7.

The Season of Lent prepares us for Easter. Formerly it was a preparatory season of fasting and prayer varying from place to place according to different cultures until it took the form of Lent as we know it today. The positive aspects of 'renewal' are very strongly emphasised in our present understanding of Lent whose baptismal character dominates the whole season. We prepare ourselves for Easter by recalling our own baptism and committing ourselves to prayer and penance out of love of the Lord. In this way we identify ourselves with his saving passion. The Second Vatican Council gave great prominence to the preparation of catechumens, a process which was for centuries largely ignored. This takes the form of several stages of christian initiation in order to prepare them for the celebration of the paschal mystery. It is in this season that the 'scrutinies' of catechumens takes place and our growing understanding in future years of this approach to baptism will help towards liturgical renewal in the church. A fuller explanation of the catechumenate is given in the section on the 'initiation of adults'. The sixth Sunday of Lent, which marks the beginning of Holy Week, is known as Passion Sunday [Palm Sunday]. It recalls the passion of Christ beginning with his messianic entry into Jerusalem. During this week we listen to the readings of the Passion which lead us into a fuller appreciation of the Easter Triduum.

The Christmas Season which celebrates the birth of our Lord and his early manifestations is second in importance only to the annual celebration of the Easter Triduum.

THE LITURGICAL YEAR

Advent not only prepares us for Christmas and Epiphany but also for the second coming of Christ in glory at the end of time.

Ordinary Time consists of the thirty-three or thirty-four weeks of the year in which the mystery of Christ in all its fullness is celebrated. Ordinary time begins on Monday after the Sunday following January 6th until Tuesday before Ash Wednesday inclusive and begins again on the Monday after Pentecost and ends before the first evening prayer of the First Sunday of Advent.

Solemnities, feasts and memorials are interwoven into the basic pattern of our liturgical year. Mary the Mother of God is especially honoured and the martyrs and other saints are proposed as examples to us of what it means to model our lives on Christ. Like them if we suffer with Christ we shall also rise in glory with him. The liturgical year therefore constantly keeps before our minds the saving power of Christ who has called us to share the glory of God our Father. 'With God on our side who can be against us? Since God did not spare his own Son, but gave him up to benefit us all, we may be certain, after such a gift, that he will not refuse anything he can give.' Romans 8:31-32.

The Season of Advent

The Season of Advent

THE christian is *waiting* for the glory of Christ to be revealed in all its fullness. This aspect of waiting conveys the real meaning of Advent as we wait in joyful hope until he comes in glory. We live in the in-between period in the history of man's salvation. Christ has come to Bethlehem. This is the *first coming* and we who have received Him have been given the power to become sons of God. Now we wait for his *second coming* when the light of Christ in all its beauty will finally rise upon the darkness of the world. We do not know when this will happen and so in Advent we watch and wait in hope.

The Church is the bride of Christ waiting for the second coming of the Lord who is her Bridegroom. We know that this will happen in God's good time because he is faithful to his promise. He proved that fidelity when he sent his only son on earth in human flesh. The prophecies of the Old Testament once delivered to Israel have been fulfilled in Bethlehem. This is our assurance that Christ's prophecy concerning himself will also be fulfilled: 'You will see the Son of Man seated at the right hand of the Power and coming on the clouds of heaven' Matthew 26:24. Christ risen from the dead and now present among us in mystery will be revealed to everyone on the Last Day as the glorious son of our heavenly Father.

During Advent with John the Baptist we too are called to 'prepare the way of the Lord'. Matthew 3:3. We listen with special alertness to the scripture readings which remind us that the darkness of the night will soon be dispelled by the brightness of the coming of the Lord, 'the people who walked in darkness have seen a great light' Isaiah 9:1. Like the dark days of winter which will slowly give way to the brightness and promise of spring so the light of Christ will finally rise upon the darkness of our world giving a true meaning to all the hardships we endure in our daily lives. We must keep the lamp of our christian faith alive and alight so that when the bridegroom comes he will find us waiting. Matthew 25:1-13.

Advent is also a time of *expectancy*. We are filled with joy because we who have received the good news believe that when Christ comes again his presence will exceed all our dreams 'no eye has seen, no ear has heard, things beyond the mind of man, all that God has prepared for those who love him' 1 Corinthians 2:2.

THE SEASON OF ADVENT

The long night of our waiting is nearly over. We pray in hope trusting in his power to save us. It is our christian hope which makes us joyful. Advent is, therefore, a time of great joy. During Advent we prepare with Our Lady for the coming of the Lord. Our souls too will magnify him for he who is mighty has done great things for us and holy is his name.

FIRST SUNDAY OF ADVENT/A

Be prepared!
During Advent we prepare ourselves for the
birth of Christ. We make ourselves ready as the
new homes into which he will come. The long hours
of waiting are nearly over and the dawn of
our salvation is about to break. Soon we will walk
in the light of the Lord.

Entrance Antiphon

To you, my God, I lift my soul, I trust in you; let me never come to shame. Do not let my enemies laugh at me. No one who waits for you is ever put to shame.
Psalm 24:1-3

The Gloria is not said today.

Opening Prayer

Let us pray
   [that we may take Christ's coming seriously]

All-powerful God,
increase our strength of will for doing good
that Christ may find an eager welcome at his coming
and call us to his side in the kingdom of heaven,
where he lives and reigns with you and the Holy Spirit,
one God, for ever and ever.
or

Let us pray
   [in Advent time
   with longing and waiting
   for the coming of the Lord]

Father in heaven,
our hearts desire the warmth of your love

FIRST SUNDAY OF ADVENT/A

and our minds are searching for the light of your Word.

Increase our longing for Christ our Saviour
and give us the strength to grow in love,
that the dawn of his coming
may find us rejoicing in his presence
and welcoming the light of his truth.

First Reading   Isaiah 2:1-5

The Lord gathers all nations together into the eternal peace of God's kingdom.

The vision of Isiah son of Amoz, concerning Judah and Jerusalem.
In the days to come
the mountain of the Temple of the Lord
shall tower above the mountains
and be lifted higher than the hills.
All the nations will stream to it,
peoples without number will come to it; and they will say:
"Come, let us go up to the mountain of the Lord,
to the Temple of the God of Jacob
that he may teach us his ways
so that we may walk in his paths;
since the Law will go out from Zion,
and the oracle of the Lord from Jerusalem."
He will wield authority over the nations
and adjudicate between many peoples;
these will hammer their swords into ploughshares,
their spears into sickles.
Nation will not lift sword against nation,
there will be no more training for war.
O House of Jacob, come,
let us walk in the light of the Lord.

Responsorial Psalm   Psalm 121

℟ **I rejoiced when I heard them say:
"Let us go to God's house."**

1. I rejoiced when I heard them say:
   "Let us go to God's house."
   And now our feet are standing
   within your gates, O Jerusalem. ℟

FIRST SUNDAY OF ADVENT/A

2. It is there that the tribes go up,
   the tribes of the Lord.
   For Israel's law it is,
   there to praise the Lord's name.
   There were set the thrones of judgement
   of the house of David. ℟
3. For the peace of Jerusalem pray:
   "Peace be to your homes!"
   May peace reign in your walls,
   in your palaces, peace!" ℟
4. For love of my brethren and friends
   I say: "Peace upon you!"
   For love of the house of the Lord
   I will ask for your good. ℟

Second Reading   Romans 13:11-14
Our salvation is near.

You know "the time" has come: you must wake up now: our salvation is even nearer than it was when we were converted. The night is almost over, it will be daylight soon — let us give up all the things we prefer to do under cover of dark; let us arm ourselves and appear in the light. Let us live decently as people do in the daytime: no drunken orgies, no promiscuity or licentiousness, and no wrangling or jealousy. Let your armour be the Lord Jesus Christ.

Alleluia
Alleluia, alleluia! Let us see, O Lord, your mercy and give us your saving help. Alleluia! **Psalm 84:8**

Gospel   Matthew 24:37-44
Stay awake so that you may be ready.

Jesus said to his disciples: "As it was in Noah's day, so will it be when the Son of Man comes. For in those days before the Flood people were eating, drinking, taking wives, taking husbands, right up to the day Noah went into the ark, and they suspected nothing till the Flood came and swept all away. It will be like this when the Son of Man comes. Then of two men in the fields one is taken, one left; of two women at the millstone grinding, one is taken, one left. So stay awake, because you do not know the day

FIRST SUNDAY OF ADVENT/A

when your master is coming. You may be quite sure of this that if the householder had known at what time of the night the burglar would come, he would have stayed awake and would not have allowed anyone to break through the wall of his house. Therefore, you too must stand ready because the Son of Man is coming at an hour you do not expect."

Prayer over the Gifts

Father,
from all you give us
we present this bread and wine.
As we serve you now,
accept our offering
and sustain us with your promise of eternal life.

Preface of Advent I, page 558.

Communion Antiphon

The Lord will shower his gifts, and our land will yield its fruit.

Psalm 84:13

Prayer after Communion

Father,
may our communion
teach us to love heaven.
May its promise and hope
guide our way on earth.

The priest may give the Solemn Blessing for Advent on page 598.

SECOND SUNDAY OF ADVENT/A

Prepare a way for the Lord!
We prepare ourselves for the
coming of Christ through repentance.
We need to change the pattern of our lives
in order to be ready when indeed he does come.
In the next few weeks we must straighten
out our lives so that the Lord
will have no obstacle in his path.

Entrance Antiphon People of Zion, the Lord will come to save all nations, and your hearts will exult to hear his majestic voice. cf. Isaiah 30:19.30

There is no Gloria today.

Opening Prayer

Let us pray
  [that nothing may hinder us
  from receiving Christ with joy]

God of power and mercy,
open our hearts in welcome.
Remove the things that hinder us from receiving Christ with joy,
so that we may share his wisdom
and become one with him
when he comes in glory,
for he lives and reigns with you and the Holy Spirit,
one God, for ever and ever.

or

Let us pray
  [in Advent time
  for the coming Saviour to teach us wisdom]

Father in heaven,
the day draws near when the glory of your Son

SECOND SUNDAY OF ADVENT/A

will make radiant the night of the waiting world.

May the lure of greed not impede us from the joy
which moves the hearts of those who seek him.
May the darkness not blind us
to the vision of wisdom
which fills the minds of those who find him.

First Reading   Isaiah 11:1-10

He judges the wretched with integrity.

A shoot springs from the stock of Jesse,
a scion thrusts from his roots:
on him the spirit of the Lord rests,
a spirit of wisdom and insight,
a spirit of counsel and power,
a spirit of knowledge and of the fear of the Lord.
(The fear of the Lord is his breath.)
He does not judge by appearances,
he gives no verdict on hearsay,
but judges the wretched with integrity,
and with equity gives a verdict for the poor of the land.
His word is a rod that strikes the ruthless,
his sentences bring death to the wicked.
Integrity is the loincloth round his waist,
faithfulness the belt about his hips.

The wolf lives with the lamb,
the panther lies down with the kid,
calf and lion cub feed together
with a little boy to lead them.
The cow and the bear make friends,
their young lie down together.
The lion eats straw like the ox.
The infant plays over the cobra's hole;
into the viper's lair
the young child puts his hand.
They do no hurt, no harm,
on all my holy mountain,
for the country is filled with the knowledge of the Lord
as the waters swell the sea.

That day, the root of Jesse

SECOND SUNDAY OF ADVENT/A

shall stand as a signal to the peoples.
It will be sought out by the nations
and its home will be glorious.

Responsorial Psalm   Psalm 71

℟ **In his days justice shall flourish
and peace till the moon fails.**

1. O God, give your judgement to the king,
   to a king's son your justice,
   that he may judge your people in justice
   and your poor in right judgement.   ℟

2. In his days justice shall flourish
   and peace till the moon fails.
   He shall rule from sea to sea,
   from the Great River to earth's bounds.   ℟

3. For he shall save the poor when they cry
   and the needy who are helpless.
   He will have pity on the weak
   and save the lives of the poor.   ℟

4. May his name be blessed for ever
   and endure like the sun.
   Every tribe shall be blessed in him,
   all nations bless his name.   ℟

Second Reading   Romans 15:4-9

Christ is the saviour of all men.

Everything that was written long ago in the scriptures was meant to teach us something about hope from the examples scripture gives of how people who did not give up were helped by God. And may he who helps us when we refuse to give up, help you all to be tolerant with each other, following the example of Christ Jesus, so that united in mind and voice you may give glory to the God and Father of our Lord Jesus Christ.
It can only be to God's glory, then, for you to treat each other in the same friendly way as Christ treated you. The reason Christ became the servant of circumcised Jews was not only so that God could faithfully carry out the promises made to the patriarchs, it was also to get the pagans to give glory to God for his mercy, as scripture says in one place: For this I shall praise you among the pagans and sing to your name.

SECOND SUNDAY OF ADVENT/A

Alleluia Alleluia, alleluia! Prepare a way for the Lord, make his paths straight. And all mankind shall see the salvation of God. Alleluia! **Luke 3:4.6**

Gospel   Matthew 3:1-12

Repent, for the kingdom of heaven is close at hand.

In due course John the Baptist appeared; he preached in the wilderness of Judaea and this was his message: "Repent, for the kingdom of heaven is close at hand." This was the man the prophet Isaiah spoke of when he said:
A voice cries in the wilderness:
Prepare a way for the Lord,
make his paths straight.
This man John wore a garment made of camel-hair with a leather belt round his waist, and his food was locusts and wild honey. Then Jerusalem and all Judaea and the whole Jordan district made their way to him, and as they were baptised by him in the river Jordan they confessed their sins. But when he saw a number of Pharisees and Sadducees coming for baptism he said to them, "Brood of vipers, who warned you to fly from the retribution that is coming? But if you are repentant, produce the appropriate fruit, and do not presume to tell yourselves, 'We have Abraham for our father,' because, I tell you, God can raise children for Abraham from these stones. Even now the axe is laid to the roots of the trees, so that any tree which fails to produce good fruit will be cut down and thrown on the fire. I baptise you in water for repentance, but the one who follows me is more powerful than I am, and I am not fit to carry his sandals; he will baptise you with the Holy Spirit and fire. His winnowing-fan is in his hand; he will clear his threshing-floor and gather his wheat into the barn; but the chaff he will burn in a fire that will never go out."

Prayer over the Gifts
Lord,
we are nothing without you.
As you sustain us with your mercy,
receive our prayers and offerings.

Preface of Advent I, page 558.

SECOND SUNDAY OF ADVENT/A

Communion Antiphon Rise up, Jerusalem, stand on the heights, and see the joy that is coming to you from God. Baruch 5:5; 4:36

Prayer after Communion

Father,
you give us food from heaven.
By our sharing in this mystery
teach us to judge wisely the things of earth
and to love the things of heaven.

The priest may give the Solemn Blessing for Advent on page 598.

THIRD SUNDAY OF ADVENT/A

Rejoice, the Lord is coming soon!
God sends his own Son to save us. Joy and
gladness are ours and the time for sorrow
and lamenting is over. Christ is standing at the
gates and we know he is the one for whom
we have been waiting. Do not lose heart.
Take courage! Your God is coming!

Entrance Antiphon   Rejoice in the Lord always; again I say, rejoice! The Lord is near.

Philippians 4:4.5

There is no Gloria today.

Opening Prayer

Let us pray
  [that God will fill us with joy
  at the coming of Christ]

Lord God,
may we, your people,
who look forward to the birthday of Christ
experience the joy of salvation
and celebrate that feast with love and thanksgiving.

or

Let us pray
  [this Advent
  for joy and hope in the coming Lord]

Father of our Lord Jesus Christ,
ever faithful to your promises
and ever close to your Church:
the earth rejoices in hope of the Saviour's coming
and looks forward with longing

THIRD SUNDAY OF ADVENT/A

to his return at the end of time.

Prepare our hearts and remove the sadness
that hinders us from feeling the joy and hope
which his presence will bestow,
for he is Lord for ever and ever.

First Reading   Isaiah 35:1-6.10
God himself is coming to save you.

Let the wilderness and the dry-lands exult,
let the wasteland rejoice and bloom,
let it bring forth flowers like the jonquil,
let it rejoice and sing for joy.

The glory of Lebanon is bestowed on it,
the splendour of Carmel and Sharon;
they shall see the glory of the Lord,
the splendour of our God.

Strengthen all weary hands, steady all trembling knees
and say to all faint hearts,
"Courage! Do not be afraid.

"Look, your God is coming,
vengeance is coming,
the retribution of God;
he is coming to save you."

Then the eyes of the blind shall be opened,
the ears of the deaf unsealed,
then the lame shall leap like a deer
and the tongues of the dumb sing for joy;
for those the Lord has ransomed shall return.

They will come to Zion shouting for joy,
everlasting joy on their faces;
joy and gladness will go with them
and sorrow and lament be ended.

Responsorial Psalm   Psalm 145

R/ **Come, Lord, and save us.**
or R/ **Alleluia!**

1. It is the Lord who keeps faith for ever,
   who is just to those who are oppressed.
   It is he who gives bread to the hungry,
   the Lord, who sets prisoners free. R/

THIRD SUNDAY OF ADVENT/A

2. It is the Lord who gives sight to the blind,
   who raises up those who are bowed down,
   the Lord, who protects the stranger
   and upholds the widow and orphan. R/

3. It is the Lord who loves the just
   but thwarts the path of the wicked.
   The Lord will reign for ever,
   Zion's God, from age to age. R/

Second Reading   James 5:7-10

Do not lose heart, because the Lord's coming will be soon.

Be patient, brothers, until the Lord's coming. Think of a farmer: how patiently he waits for the precious fruit of the ground until it has had the autumn rains and the spring rains! You too have to be patient; do not lose heart, because the Lord's coming will be soon. Do not make complaints against one another, brothers, so as not to be brought to judgement yourselves; the Judge is already to be seen waiting at the gates. For your example, brothers, in submitting with patience, take the prophets who spoke in the name of the Lord.

Alleluia

Alleluia, alleluia! The spirit of the Lord has been given to me. He has sent me to bring good news to the poor. Alleluia! Luke 4:18.

Gospel   Matthew 11:2-11

Are you the one who is to come, or have we got to wait for someone else?

John in his prison had heard what Christ was doing and he sent his disciples to ask him, "Are you the one who is to come, or have we got to wait for someone else?" Jesus answered, "Go back and tell John what you hear and see; the blind see again, and the lame walk, lepers are cleansed, and the deaf hear, and the dead are raised to life and the Good News is proclaimed to the poor; and happy is the man who does not lose faith in me".

As the messengers were leaving, Jesus began to talk to the people about John: "What did you go out into the wilderness to see? A reed swaying in the breeze? No? Then what did you go out to see? A man wearing fine clothes? Oh no, those who wear fine clothes are to be found in palaces. Then what did you go out for? To see a prophet? Yes, I tell you, and much more than a prophet:

THIRD SUNDAY OF ADVENT/A

he is the one of whom scripture says:
Look, I am going to send my messenger before you;
he will prepare your way before you.

"I tell you solemnly, of all the children born of women, a greater than John the Baptist has never been seen; yet the least in the kingdom of heaven is greater than he is."

Prayer over the Gifts

Lord,
may the gift we offer in faith and love
be a continual sacrifice in your honour
and truly become our eucharist and our salvation.

Preface of Advent I or II, page 558.

Communion Antiphon

Say to the anxious: be strong and fear not, our God will come to save us.

cf. Isaiah 35:4

Prayer after Communion

God of mercy,
may this eucharist bring us your divine help,
free us from our sins,
and prepare us for the birthday of our Saviour,
who is Lord for ever and ever.

The priest may give the Solemn Blessing for Advent on page 598.

FOURTH SUNDAY OF ADVENT/A

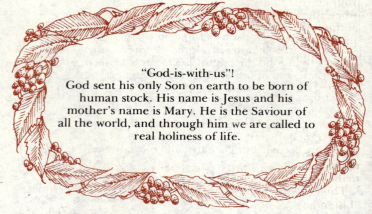

"God-is-with-us"!
God sent his only Son on earth to be born of
human stock. His name is Jesus and his
mother's name is Mary. He is the Saviour of
all the world, and through him we are called to
real holiness of life.

Entrance Antiphon   Let the clouds rain down the Just One,
and the earth bring forth a Saviour.

Isaiah 45:8

There is no Gloria today.

Opening Prayer

Let us pray
 [as Advent draws to a close,
  that Christ will truly come into our hearts]

Lord,
fill our hearts with your love,
and as you revealed to us by an angel
the coming of your Son as man,
so lead us through his suffering and death
to the glory of his resurrection,
for he lives and reigns with you and the Holy Spirit,
one God, for ever and ever.

or

Let us pray
 [as Advent draws to a close
  for the faith that opens our lives
  to the Spirit of God]

Father, all-powerful God,

FOURTH SUNDAY OF ADVENT/A

your eternal Word took flesh on our earth
when the Virgin Mary placed her life
at the service of your plan.

Lift our minds in watchful hope
to hear the voice which announces his glory
and open our minds to receive the Spirit
who prepares us for his coming.

First Reading   Isaiah 7:10-14
The maiden is with child.

The Lord spoke to Ahaz and said, "Ask the Lord your God for a sign for yourself coming either from the depths of Sheol or from the heights above." "No," Ahaz answered "I will not put the Lord to the test."

Then he said:
"Listen now, House of David:
are you not satisfied with trying the patience of men
without trying the patience of my God, too?
The Lord himself, therefore,
will give you a sign.
It is this: the maiden is with child
and will soon give birth to a son
whom she will call Immanuel,
a name which means 'God-is-with-us'."

Responsorial Psalm   Psalm 23

R/ **Let the Lord enter! He is the king of glory.**

1. The Lord's is the earth and its fullness,
   the world and all its peoples.
   It is he who set it on the seas;
   on the waters he made it firm. R/

2. Who shall climb the mountain of the Lord?
   Who shall stand in his holy place?
   The man with clean hands and pure heart,
   who desires not worthless things. R/

3. He shall receive blessings from the Lord
   and reward from the God who saves him.
   Such are the men who seek him,
   seek the face of the God of Jacob. R/

FOURTH SUNDAY OF ADVENT/A

Second Reading   Romans 1:1-7
Jesus Christ, descendant of David, Son of God.

From Paul, a servant of Christ Jesus who has been called to be an apostle, and specially chosen to preach the Good News that God promised long ago through his prophets in the scriptures.

This news is about the Son of God who, according to the human nature he took, was a descendant of David: it is about Jesus Christ our Lord who, in the order of the spirit, the spirit of holiness that was in him, was proclaimed Son of God in all his power through his resurrection from the dead. Through him we received grace and our apostolic mission to preach the obedience of faith to all pagan nations in honour of his name. You are one of these nations, and by his call belong to Jesus Christ. To you all, then, who are God's beloved in Rome, called to be saints, may God our Father and the Lord Jesus Christ send grace and peace.

Alleluia   Alleluia, alleluia! The virgin will conceive and give birth to a son and they will call him Emmanuel, a name which means "God-is-with-us". Alleluia!

Matthew 1:23

Gospel   Matthew 1:18-24
Jesus is born of Mary who was betrothed to Joseph, son of David.

This is how Jesus Christ came to be born. His mother Mary was betrothed to Joseph; but before they came to live together she was found to be with child through the Holy Spirit. Her husband Joseph, being a man of honour and wanting to spare her publicity, decided to divorce her informally. He had made up his mind to do this when the angel of the Lord appeared to him in a dream and said, "Joseph son of David, do not be afraid to take Mary home as your wife, because she has conceived what is in her by the Holy Spirit. She will give birth to a son and you must name him Jesus, because he is the one who is to save his people from their sins." Now all this took place to fulfil the words spoken by the Lord through the prophet:
The virgin will conceive and give birth to a son
and they will call him Emmanuel,
a name which means "God-is-with-us". When Joseph woke up he did what the angel of the Lord had told him to do: he took his wife to his home.

FOURTH SUNDAY OF ADVENT/A

Prayer over the Gifts

Lord,
may the power of the Spirit,
which sanctified Mary the mother of your Son,
make holy the gifts we place upon this altar.

Preface of Advent II, page 558.

Communion Antiphon

The Virgin is with child, and shall bear a son, and she will call him Emmanuel. Isaiah 7:14.

Prayer after Communion

Lord,
in this sacrament
we receive the promise of salvation;
as Christmas draws near
make us grow in faith and love
to celebrate the coming of Christ our Saviour,
who is Lord for ever and ever.

The priest may give the Solemn Blessing for Advent on page 598.

The Masses for the Christmas Season will be found on pages 119ff.

FIRST SUNDAY OF ADVENT/B

Stay Awake.
Advent is a time of waiting and watching for the second coming of the Lord Jesus.
The Holy Spirit is our constant help that we may always be on our guard and remain awake so that we are prepared for the last day.
The best preparation is a good life lived in the knowledge that God is our father and we are the work of his hands.

Entrance Antiphon To you, my God, I lift my soul, I trust in you; let me never come to shame. Do not let my enemies laugh at me. No one who waits for you is ever put to shame.

Psalm 24:1-3

The Gloria is not said today.

Opening Prayer

Let us pray
   [that we may take Christ's coming seriously]

All-powerful God,
increase our strength of will for doing good
that Christ may find an eager welcome at his coming
and call us to his side in the kingdom of heaven,
where he lives and reigns with you and the Holy Spirit,
one God, for ever and ever.

or

Let us pray
   [in Advent time
   with longing and waiting
   for the coming of the Lord]

FIRST SUNDAY OF ADVENT/B

Father in heaven,
our hearts desire the warmth of your love
and our minds are searching for the light of your Word.

Increase our longing for Christ our Saviour
and give us the strength to grow in love,
that the dawn of his coming
may find us rejoicing in his presence
and welcoming the light of his truth.

First Reading   Isaiah 63:16-17; 64:1, 3-8
Oh, that you would tear the heavens open and come down.

You, Lord, yourself are our Father,
Our Redeemer is your ancient name.
Why, Lord, leave us to stray from your ways
and harden our hearts against fearing you?
Return, for the sake of your servants,
the tribes of your inheritance.
Oh, that you would tear the heavens open and come down
— at your Presence the mountains would melt.

No ear has heard,
no eye has seen
any god but you act like this
for those who trust him.
You guide those who act with integrity
and keep your ways in mind.
You were angry when we were sinners;
we had long been rebels against you.
We were all like men unclean,
all that integrity of ours like filthy clothing.
We have all withered like leaves
and our sins blew us away like the wind.
No one invoked your name
or roused himself to catch hold of you.
For you hid your face from us
and gave us up to the power of our sins.
And yet, Lord, you are our Father;
we the clay, you the potter,
we are all the work of your hand.

FIRST SUNDAY OF ADVENT/B

Responsorial Psalm   Psalm 79

**R/ God of hosts, bring us back;
let your face shine on us and we shall be saved.**

1. O shepherd of Israel, hear us,
   shine forth from your cherubim throne.
   O Lord, rouse up your might,
   O Lord, come to our help. R/

2. God of hosts, turn again, we implore,
   look down from heaven and see.
   Visit this vine and protect it,
   the vine your right hand has planted. R/

3. May your hand be on the man you have chosen,
   the man you have given your strength.
   And we shall never forsake you again:
   give us life that we may call upon your name. R/

Second Reading   1 Corinthians 1:3-9
We are waiting for our Lord Jesus Christ to be revealed.

May God our Father and the Lord Jesus Christ send you grace and peace.

I never stop thanking God for all the graces you have received through Jesus Christ. I thank him that you have been enriched in so many ways, especially in your teachers and preachers; the witness to Christ has indeed been strong among you so that you will not be without any of the gifts of the Spirit while you are waiting for our Lord Jesus Christ to be revealed; and he will keep you steady and without blame until the last day, the day of our Lord Jesus Christ, because God by calling you has joined you to his Son, Jesus Christ; and God is faithful.

Alleluia
Alleluia, alleluia! Let us see, O Lord, your mercy and give us your saving help. Alleluia! Psalm 84:8

Gospel   Mark 13:33-37
Stay awake, because you do not know when the master of the house is coming.

Jesus said to his disciples: "Be on your guard, stay awake, because you never know when the time will come. It is like a man

FIRST SUNDAY OF ADVENT/B

travelling abroad: he has gone from home, and left his servants in charge, each with his own task; and he has told the doorkeeper to stay awake. So stay awake, because you do not know when the master of the house is coming, evening, midnight, cockcrow, dawn; if he comes unexpectedly, he must not find you asleep. And what I say to you I say to all: Stay awake!"

Prayer over the Gifts
Father,
from all you give us
we present this bread and wine.
As we serve you now,
accept our offering
and sustain us with your promise of eternal life.

Preface of Advent I, page 558.

Communion Antiphon
The Lord will shower his gifts, and our land will yield its fruit.

Psalm 84:13

Prayer after Communion
Father,
may our communion
teach us to love heaven.
May its promise and hope
guide our way on earth.

The priest may give the Solemn Blessing for Advent on page 598.

SECOND SUNDAY OF ADVENT/B

Prepare a way for the Lord!
We prepare each day of our lives for the
coming of the Lord. We have to straighten
out those things in our behaviour which
prevent us from living holy and
saintly lives. The new heavens and the
new earth where God reigns are what
is promised to us and that is why
we should always try to be joyful.

Entrance Antiphon   People of Zion, the Lord will come to save all nations, and your hearts will exult to hear his majestic voice.

cf. Isaiah 30:19.30

The Gloria is not said today.

Opening Prayer

Let us pray
  [that nothing may hinder us
  from receiving Christ with joy]

God of power and mercy,
open our hearts in welcome.
Remove the things that hinder us from receiving Christ with
  joy,
so that we may share his wisdom
and become one with him
when he comes in glory,
for he lives and reigns with you and the Holy Spirit,
one God, for ever and ever.

or

Let us pray
  [in Advent time
  for the coming Saviour to teach us wisdom]

SECOND SUNDAY OF ADVENT/B

Father in heaven,
the day draws near when the glory of your Son
will make radiant the night of the waiting world.

May the lure of greed not impede us from the joy
which moves the hearts of those who seek him.
May the darkness not blind us
to the vision of wisdom
which fills the minds of those who find him.

We ask this in the name of Jesus the Lord.

First Reading   Isaiah 40:1-5.9-11
Prepare a way for the Lord

"Console my people, console them"
says your God.
"Speak to the heart of Jerusalem
and call to her
that her time of service is ended,
that her sin is atoned for,
that she has received from the hand of the Lord
double punishment for all her crimes."

A voice cries, "Prepare in the wilderness
a way for the Lord.
Make a straight highway for our God
across the desert.
Let every valley be filled in,
every mountain and hill be laid low,
let every cliff become a plain,
and the ridges a valley;
then the glory of the Lord shall be revealed
and all mankind shall see it;
for the mouth of the Lord has spoken."

Go up on a high mountain,
joyful messenger to Zion.
Shout with a loud voice,
joyful messenger to Jerusalem.
Shout without fear,
say to the towns of Judah,
"Here is your God."

Here is the Lord coming with power,

SECOND SUNDAY OF ADVENT/B

his arm subduing all things to him.
The prize of his victory is with him,
his trophies all go before him.
He is like a shepherd feeding his flock,
gathering lambs in his arms,
holding them against his breast
and leading to their rest the mother ewes.

Responsorial Psalm   Psalm 84

℟ **Let us see, O Lord, your mercy
and give us your saving help.**

1. I will hear what the Lord God has to say,
a voice that speaks of peace,
peace for his people.
His help is near for those who fear him
and his glory will dwell in our land. ℟

2. Mercy and faithfulness have met;
justice and peace have embraced.
Faithfulness shall spring from the earth
and justice look down from heaven. ℟

3. The Lord will make us prosper
and our earth shall yield its fruit.
Justice shall march before him
and peace shall follow his steps. ℟

Second Reading   2 Peter 3:8-14

We are waiting for the new heavens and new earth.

There is one thing, my friends, that you must never forget: that with the Lord, "a day" can mean a thousand years, and a thousand years is like a day. The Lord is not being slow to carry out his promises, as anybody else might be called slow; but he is being patient with you all, wanting nobody to be lost and everybody to be brought to change his ways. The Day of the Lord will come like a thief, and then with a roar the sky will vanish, the elements will catch fire and fall apart, the earth and all that it contains will be burnt up.

Since everything is coming to an end like this, you should be living holy and saintly lives while you wait and long for the Day of God to come, when the sky will dissolve in flames and the

SECOND SUNDAY OF ADVENT/B

elements melt in the heat. What we are waiting for is what he promised: the new heavens and new earth, the place where righteousness will be at home. So then, my friends, while you are waiting, do your best to live lives without spot or stain so that he will find you at peace.

Alleluia   Alleluia, alleluia! Prepare a way for the Lord, make his paths straight. And all mankind shall see the salvation of God. Alleluia! Luke 3:4.6.

Gospel   Mark 1:1-8

Make his paths straight.

The beginning of the Good News about Jesus Christ, the Son of God. It is written in the book of the prophet Isaiah:
Look, I am going to send my messenger before you;
he will prepare your way.
A voice cries in the wilderness:
Prepare a way for the Lord,
make his paths straight,
and so it was that John the Baptist appeared in the wilderness, proclaiming a baptism of repentance for the forgiveness of sins. All Judaea and all the people of Jerusalem made their way to him, and as they were baptised by him in the river Jordan they confessed their sins. John wore a garment of camel-skin, and he lived on locusts and wild honey. In the course of his preaching he said, "Someone is following me, someone who is more powerful than I am, and I am not fit to kneel down and undo the strap of his sandals. I have baptised you with water, but he will baptise you with the Holy Spirit."

Prayer over the Gifts

Lord,
we are nothing without you.
As you sustain us with your mercy,
receive our prayers and offerings.

Preface of Advent I, page 558.

Communion Antiphon   Rise up, Jerusalem, stand on the heights, and see the joy that is coming to you from God. Baruch 5:5;4:36

SECOND SUNDAY OF ADVENT/B

Prayer after Communion

Father,
you give us food from heaven.
By our sharing in this mystery,
teach us to judge wisely the things of earth
and to love the things of heaven.

The priest may give the Solemn Blessing for Advent on page 598.

THIRD SUNDAY OF ADVENT/B

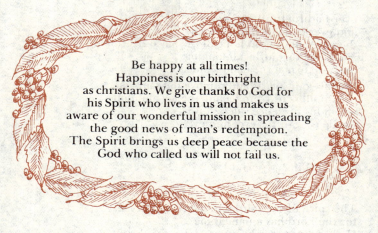

Be happy at all times!
Happiness is our birthright
as christians. We give thanks to God for
his Spirit who lives in us and makes us
aware of our wonderful mission in spreading
the good news of man's redemption.
The Spirit brings us deep peace because the
God who called us will not fail us.

Entrance Antiphon   Rejoice in the Lord always; again I say, rejoice! The Lord is near.

Philippians 4:4.5

The Gloria is not said today.

Opening Prayer

Let us pray
  [that God will fill us with joy
  at the coming of Christ]

Lord God,
may we, your people,
who look forward to the birthday of Christ
experience the joy of salvation
and celebrate that feast with love and thanksgiving.

or

Let us pray
  [this Advent
  for joy and hope in the coming Lord]

Father of our Lord Jesus Christ,

THIRD SUNDAY OF ADVENT B

ever faithful to your promises
and ever close to your Church:
the earth rejoices in hope of the Saviour's coming
and looks forward with longing
to his return at the end of time.

Prepare our hearts and remove the sadness
that hinders us from feeling the joy and hope
which his presence will bestow,
for he is Lord for ever and ever.

First Reading   Isaiah 61:1-2.10-11

I exult for joy in the Lord.

The spirit of the Lord has been given to me,
for the Lord has anointed me.
He has sent me to bring good news to the poor,
to bind up hearts that are broken;

to proclaim liberty to captives,
freedom to those in prison;
to proclaim a year of favour from the Lord.

"I exult for joy in the Lord,
my soul rejoices in my God,
for he has clothed me in the garments of salvation,
he has wrapped me in the cloak of integrity,
like a bridegroom wearing his wreath,
like a bride adorned in her jewels.

"For as the earth makes fresh things grow,
as a garden makes seeds spring up,
so will the Lord make both integrity and praise
spring up in the sight of the nations."

Responsorial Psalm   Luke 1:46-50.53-54

℟ **My soul rejoices in my God.**

1. My soul glorifies the Lord,
   my spirit rejoices in God, my Saviour.
   He looks on his servant in her nothingness;
   henceforth all ages will call me blessed. ℟

THIRD SUNDAY OF ADVENT/B

2. The Almighty works marvels for me.
   Holy his name!
   His mercy is from age to age,
   on those who fear him. ℟

3. He fills the starving with good things,
   sends the rich away empty.
   He protects Israel, his servant,
   remembering his mercy. ℟

Second Reading   1 Thessalonians 5:16-24

May you all be kept safe, spirit, soul and body, for the coming of the Lord.

Be happy at all times; pray constantly; and for all things give thanks to God, because this is what God expects you to do in Christ Jesus.

Never try to suppress the Spirit or treat the gift of prophecy with contempt; think before you do anything — hold on to what is good and avoid every form of evil.

May the God of peace make you perfect and holy; and may you all be kept safe and blameless, spirit, soul and body, for the coming of our Lord Jesus Christ. God has called you and he will not fail you.

Alleluia   Alleluia, alleluia! The spirit of the Lord has been given to me. He has sent me to bring good news to the poor. Alleluia! Luke 4:18

Gospel   John 1:6-8.19-28

There stands among you — unknown to you — the one who is coming after me.

A man came, sent by God.
His name was John.
He came as a witness,
as a witness to speak for the light,
so that everyone might believe through him.
He was not the light,
only a witness to speak for the light.

This is how John appeared as a witness. When the Jews sent priests and Levites from Jerusalem to ask him, "Who are you?" he not only declared, but he declared quite openly, "I am not the Christ." "Well then," they asked "are you Elijah?" "I am not" he

THIRD SUNDAY OF ADVENT/B

said. "Are you the Prophet?" He answered, "No." So they said to him, "Who are you? We must take back an answer to those who sent us. What have you to say about yourself?" So John said, "I am, as Isaiah prophesied:
a voice that cries in the wilderness:
Make a straight way for the Lord."
Now these men had been sent by the Pharisees, and they put this further question to him, "Why are you baptising if you are not the Christ, and not Elijah, and not the prophet?" John replied, "I baptise with water; but there stands among you — unknown to you — the one who is coming after me; and I am not fit to undo his sandal-strap." This happened at Bethany, on the far side of the Jordan, where John was baptising.

Prayer over the Gifts

Lord,
may the gift we offer in faith and love
be a continual sacrifice in your honour
and truly become our eucharist and our salvation.

Preface of Advent I or II, page 558.

Communion Antiphon

Say to the anxious: be strong and fear not, our God will come to save us.

cf. Isaiah 35:4

Prayer after Communion

God of mercy,
may this eucharist bring us your divine help,
free us from our sins,
and prepare us for the birthday of our Saviour,
who is Lord for ever and ever.

The priest may give the Solemn Blessing for Advent on page 598.

FOURTH SUNDAY OF ADVENT/B

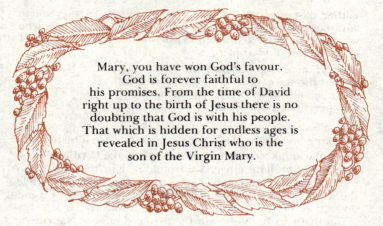

Mary, you have won God's favour.
God is forever faithful to
his promises. From the time of David
right up to the birth of Jesus there is no
doubting that God is with his people.
That which is hidden for endless ages is
revealed in Jesus Christ who is the
son of the Virgin Mary.

Entrance Antiphon   Let the clouds rain down the Just One,
and the earth bring forth a Saviour.
Isaiah 45:8

The Gloria is not said today.

Opening Prayer

Let us pray
  [as Advent draws to a close,
  that Christ will truly come into our hearts]

Lord,
fill our hearts with your love,
and as you revealed to us by an angel
the coming of your Son as man,
so lead us through his suffering and death
to the glory of his resurrection,
for he lives and reigns with you and the Holy Spirit,
one God, for ever and ever.

or

Let us pray
  [as Advent draws to a close
  for the faith that opens our lives
  to the Spirit of God]

FOURTH SUNDAY OF ADVENT/B

Father, all-powerful God,
your eternal Word took flesh on our earth
when the Virgin Mary placed her life
at the service of your plan.

Lift our minds in watchful hope
to hear the voice which announces his glory
and open our minds to receive the Spirit
who prepares us for his coming.

First Reading   2 Samuel 7:1-5. 8-12. 14.16
The kingdom of David will always stand secure before the Lord.

Once David had settled into his house and the Lord had given him rest from all the enemies surrounding him, the king said to the prophet Nathan, "Look, I am living in a house of cedar while the ark of God dwells in a tent." Nathan said to the king, "Go and do all that is in your mind, for the Lord is with you."

But that very night the word of the Lord came to Nathan:

"Go and tell my servant David, 'Thus the Lord speaks: Are you the man to build me a house to dwell in? I took you from the pasture, from following the sheep, to be leader of my people Israel; I have been with you on all your expeditions; I have cut off all your enemies before you. I will give you fame as great as the fame of the greatest on earth. I will provide a place for my people Israel; I will plant them there and they shall dwell in that place and never be disturbed again; nor shall the wicked continue to oppress them as they did, in the days when I appointed judges over my people Israel; I will give them rest from all their enemies. The Lord will make you great; the Lord will make you a House. And when our days are ended and you are laid to rest with your ancestors, I will preserve the offspring of your body after you and make his sovereignty secure. I will be a father to him and he a son to me. Your House and your sovereignty will always stand secure before me and your throne be established for ever.'"

Responsorial Psalm   Psalm 88

℟ **I will sing forever of your love, O Lord.**

1. I will sing for ever of your love, O Lord;
   through all ages my mouth will proclaim your truth.
   Of this I am sure, that your love lasts for ever,
   that your truth is firmly established as the heavens.   ℟

FOURTH SUNDAY OF ADVENT/B

2. "I have made a covenant with my chosen one;
   I have sworn to David my servant:
   I will establish your dynasty for ever
   and set up your throne through all ages." ℟

3. He will say to me: "You are my father,
   my God, the rock who saves me."
   I will keep my love for him always
   for him my covenant shall endure. ℟

Second Reading   Romans 16:25-27

The mystery, which was kept secret for endless ages, is now made clear.

Glory to him who is able to give you strength to live according to the Good News I preach, and in which I proclaim Jesus Christ, the revelation of a mystery kept secret for endless ages, but now so clear that it must be broadcast to pagans everywhere to bring them to the obedience of faith. This is only what scripture has predicted, and it is all part of the way the eternal God wants things to be. He alone is wisdom; give glory therefore to him through Jesus Christ for ever and ever. Amen.

Alleluia

Alleluia, alleluia! I am the handmaid of the Lord: let what you have said be done to me. Alleluia!

Luke 1:38

Gospel   Luke 1:26-38

Listen! You are to conceive and bear a son.

The angel Gabriel was sent by God to a town in Galilee called Nazareth, to a virgin betrothed to a man named Joseph, of the House of David; and the virgin's name was Mary. He went in and said to her, "Rejoice, so highly favoured! The Lord is with you." She was deeply disturbed by these words and asked herself what this greeting could mean, but the angel said to her, "Mary, do not be afraid: you have won God's favour. Listen! You are to conceive and bear a son, and you must name him Jesus. He will be great and will be called Son of the Most High. The Lord God will give him the throne of his ancestor David; he will rule over the House of Jacob for ever and his reign will have no end." Mary said to the angel, "But how can this come about, since I am a virgin?" "The Holy Spirit will come upon you" the angel answered "and the power of the Most High will cover you with its shadow. And so the

FOURTH SUNDAY OF ADVENT/B

child will be holy and will be called Son of God. Know this too; your kinswomen Elizabeth has, in her old age, herself conceived a son, and she whom people called barren is now in her sixth month, for nothing is impossible to God." "I am the handmaid of the Lord," said Mary "let what you have said be done to me." And the Angel left her.

Prayer over the Gifts

Lord,
may the power of the Spirit,
which sanctified Mary the mother of your Son,
make holy the gifts we place upon this altar.

Preface of Advent II, page 558.

Communion Antiphon

The Virgin is with child and shall bear a son, and she will call him Emmanuel. Isaiah 7:14

Prayer after Communion

Lord,
in this sacrament
we receive the promise of salvation;
as Christmas draws near
make us grow in faith and love
to celebrate the coming of Christ our Saviour,
who is Lord for ever and ever.

The priest may give the Solemn Blessing for Advent on page 598.

The Masses for the Christmas Season will be found on pages 119ff.

FIRST SUNDAY OF ADVENT/C

Your liberation is near at hand.
We have no reason to fear the second coming of
Christ if we allow God to teach us how to grow in
holiness. We ask him to help us to love one another
with generosity and integrity. In this way we will be
able to hold our heads high and have the strength
necessary to survive all that will happen in our
lives so that when the time comes we will stand in
confidence before Christ and his saints.

Entrance Antiphon   To you, my God, I lift my soul, I trust in you; let me never come to shame. Do not let my enemies laugh at me. No one who waits for you is ever put to shame. Psalm 24:1-3

There is no Gloria today.

Opening Prayer

Let us pray
  [that we may take Christ's coming seriously]

All-powerful God,
increase our strength of will for doing good
that Christ may find an eager welcome at his coming
and call us to his side in the kingdom of heaven,
where he lives and reigns with you and the Holy Spirit,
one God, for ever and ever.

or

Let us pray
  [in Advent time
  with longing and waiting
  for the coming of the Lord]

Father in heaven,
our hearts desire the warmth of your love
and our minds are searching for the light of your Word.

FIRST SUNDAY OF ADVENT/C

Increase our longing for Christ our Saviour
and give us the strength to grow in love,
that the dawn of his coming
may find us rejoicing in his presence
and welcoming the light of his truth.

First Reading   Jeremiah 33:14-16.

I will make a virtuous Branch grow for David.

See, the days are coming — it is the Lord who speaks — when I am going to fulfil the promise I made to the House of Israel and the House of Judah:
"In those days and at that time,
I will make a virtuous Branch grow for David,
who shall practise honesty and integrity in the land.
In those days Judah shall be saved
and Israel shall dwell in confidence.
And this is the name the city will be called:
The Lord-our-integrity."

Responsorial Psalm   Psalm 24

R/ To you, O Lord, I lift up my soul.

1. Lord, make me know your ways.
   Lord, teach me your paths.
   Make me walk in your truth, and teach me:
   for you are God my saviour. R/

2. The Lord is good and upright.
   He shows the path to those who stray,
   he guides the humble in the right path;
   he teaches his way to the poor. R/

3. His ways are faithfulness and love
   for those who keep his covenant and will.
   The Lord's friendship is for those who revere him;
   to them he reveals his covenant. R/

Second Reading   1 Thessalonians 3:12-4:2

May the Lord confirm your hearts in holiness when Christ comes.

May the Lord be generous in increasing your love and make you love one another and the whole human race as much as we love you. And may he so confirm your hearts in holiness that you may

FIRST SUNDAY OF ADVENT/C

be blameless in the sight of our God and Father when our Lord Jesus Christ comes with all his saints.

Finally, brothers, we urge you and appeal to you in the Lord Jesus to make more and more progress in the kind of life that you are meant to live: the life that God wants, as you learnt from us, and as you are already living it. You have not forgotten the instructions we gave you on the authority of the Lord Jesus.

Alleluia   Alleluia, alleluia! Let us see, O Lord, your mercy and give us your saving help. Alleluia! Psalm 84:8

Gospel   Luke 21:25-28. 34-36

Your liberation is near at hand.

Jesus said to his disciples, "There will be signs in the sun and moon and stars; on earth nations in agony, bewildered by the clamour of the ocean and its waves; men dying of fear as they await what menaces the world, for the powers of heaven will be shaken. And then they will see the Son of Man coming in a cloud with power and great glory. When these things begin to take place, stand erect, hold your heads high, because your liberation is near at hand."

"Watch yourselves, or your hearts will be coarsened with debauchery and drunkenness and the cares of life, and that day will be sprung on you suddenly, like a trap. For it will come down on every living man on the face of the earth. Stay awake, praying at all times for the strength to survive all that is going to happen, and to stand with confidence before the Son of Man."

Prayer over the Gifts

Father,
from all you give us
we present this bread and wine.
As we serve you now,
accept our offering
and sustain us with your promise of eternal life.

Preface of Advent I, page 558.

Communion Antiphon   The Lord will shower his gifts, and our land will yield its fruit.

Psalm 84:13

FIRST SUNDAY OF ADVENT/C

Prayer after Communion

Father,
may our communion
teach us to love heaven.
May its promise and hope
guide our way on earth.

The priest may give the Solemn Blessing for Advent on page 598.

SECOND SUNDAY OF ADVENT/C

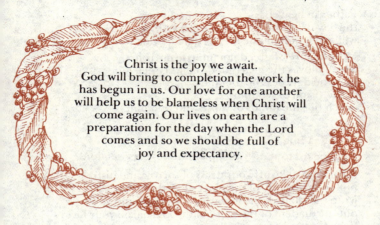

Christ is the joy we await.
God will bring to completion the work he has begun in us. Our love for one another will help us to be blameless when Christ will come again. Our lives on earth are a preparation for the day when the Lord comes and so we should be full of joy and expectancy.

Entrance Antiphon People of Zion, the Lord will come to save all nations, and your hearts will exult to hear his majestic voice. cf. Isaiah 30:19.30

There is no Gloria today.

Opening Prayer
Let us pray
   [that nothing may hinder us
   from receiving Christ with joy]

God of power and mercy,
open our hearts in welcome.
Remove the things that hinder us from receiving Christ with joy,
so that we may share his wisdom
and become one with him
when he comes in glory,
for he lives and reigns with you and the Holy Spirit,
one God, for ever and ever.

or
Let us pray
   [in Advent time
   for the coming Saviour to teach us wisdom]

SECOND SUNDAY OF ADVENT/C

Father in heaven,
the day draws near when the glory of your Son
will make radiant the night of the waiting world.

May the lure of greed not impede us from the joy
which moves the hearts of those who seek him.
May the darkness not blind us
to the vision of wisdom
which fills the minds of those who find him.

First Reading   Baruch 5:1-9.
God means to show your splendour to every nation.

Jerusalem, take off your dress of sorrow and distress,
put on the beauty of the glory of God for ever,
wrap the cloak of the integrity of God around you,
put the diadem of the glory of the Eternal on your head:
since God means to show your splendour to every nation under
   heaven,
since the name God gives you for ever will be,
"Peace through integrity, and honour through devotedness."
Arise, Jerusalem, stand on the heights
and turn your eyes to the east:
see your sons reassembled from west and east
at the command of the Holy One, jubilant that God has
   remembered them.

Though they left you on foot,
with enemies for an escort,
now God brings them back to you
like royal princes carried back in glory.

For God has decreed the flattening
of each high mountain, of the everlasting hills,
the filling of the valleys to make the ground level
so that Israel can walk in safety under the glory of God.

And the forests and every fragrant tree will provide shade
for Israel at the command of God;
for God will guide Israel in joy by the light of his glory
with his mercy and integrity for escort.

SECOND SUNDAY OF ADVENT/C

Responsorial Psalm   Psalm 125

℟ **What marvels the Lord worked for us!
Indeed we were glad.**

1. When the Lord delivered Zion from bondage,
   it seemed like a dream.
   Then was our mouth filled with laughter,
   on our lips there were songs. ℟

2. The heathens themselves said: "What marvels
   the Lord worked for them!"
   What marvels the Lord worked for us!
   Indeed we were glad. ℟

3. Deliver us, O Lord, from our bondage
   as streams in dry land.
   Those who are sowing in tears
   will sing when they reap. ℟

4. They go out, they go out, full of tears,
   carrying seed for the sowing:
   they come back, they come back, full of song,
   carrying their sheaves. ℟

Second Reading   Philippians 1:3-6. 8-11

Be pure and blameless for the day of Christ.

Every time I pray for all of you, I pray with joy, remembering how you have helped to spread the Good News from the day you first heard it right up to the present. I am quite certain that the One who began this good work in you will see that it is finished when the Day of Christ Jesus comes. God knows how much I miss you all, loving you as Christ Jesus loves you. My prayer is that your love for each other may increase more and more and never stop improving your knowledge and deepening perception so that you can always recognise what is best. This will help you to become pure and blameless, and prepare you for the Day of Christ, when you will reach the perfect goodness which Jesus Christ produces in us for the glory and praise of God.

Alleluia

Alleluia, alleluia! Prepare a way for the Lord, make his paths straight. And all mankind shall see the salvation of God. Alleluia! **Luke 3:4.6**

SECOND SUNDAY OF ADVENT/C

Gospel   Luke 3:1-6
All mankind shall see the salvation of God.

In the fifteenth year of Tiberius Caesar's reign, when Pontius Pilate was governor of Judaea, Herod tetrarch of Galilee, his brother Philip tetrarch of the lands of Ituraea and Trachonitis, Lysanias tetrarch of Abilene, during the pontificate of Annas and Caiaphas, the word of God came to John son of Zechariah, in the wilderness. He went through the whole Jordan district proclaiming a baptism of repentance for the forgiveness of sins, as it is written in the book of the sayings of the prophet Isaiah:
A voice cries in the wilderness:
Prepare a way for the Lord,
make his paths straight.
Every valley will be filled in
every mountain and hill be laid low,
winding ways will be straightened
and rough roads made smooth.
And all mankind shall see the salvation of God.

Prayer over the Gifts

Lord,
we are nothing without yout.
As you sustain us with your mercy,
receive our prayers and offerings.

Preface of Advent I, page 558.

Communion Antiphon
Rise up, Jerusalem, stand on the heights, and see the joy that is coming to you from God. Baruch 5:5; 4:36

Prayer after Communion

Father,
you give us food from heaven.
By our sharing in this mystery,
teach us to judge wisely the things of earth
and to love the things of heaven.

The priest may give the Solemn Blessing for Advent on page 598.

THIRD SUNDAY OF ADVENT/C

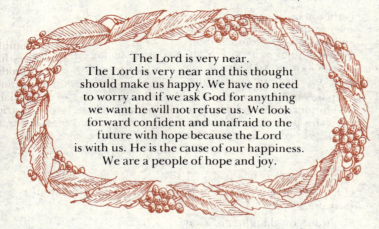

The Lord is very near.
The Lord is very near and this thought
should make us happy. We have no need
to worry and if we ask God for anything
we want he will not refuse us. We look
forward confident and unafraid to the
future with hope because the Lord
is with us. He is the cause of our happiness.
We are a people of hope and joy.

Entrance Antiphon   Rejoice in the Lord always; again I say, rejoice! The Lord is near.
Philippians 4:4.5

There is no Gloria today.

Opening Prayer

Let us pray
   [that God will fill us with joy
   at the coming of Christ]

Lord God,
may we, your people,
who look forward to the birthday of Christ
experience the joy of salvation
and celebrate that feast with love and thanksgiving.

or

Let us pray
   [this Advent
   for joy and hope in the coming Lord]

THIRD SUNDAY OF ADVENT/C

Father of our Lord Jesus Christ,
ever faithful to your promises
and ever close to your Church:
the earth rejoices in hope of the Saviour's coming
and looks forward with longing
to his return at the end of time.

Prepare our hearts and remove the sadness
that hinders us from feeling the joy and hope
which his presence will bestow,
for he is Lord for ever and ever.

First Reading   Zephaniah 3:14-18

The Lord will dance with shouts of joy for you as on a day of festival.

Shout for joy, daughter of Zion,
Israel, shout aloud!
Rejoice, exult with all your heart,
daughter of Jerusalem!
The Lord has repealed your sentence;
he has driven your enemies away.
The Lord, the king of Israel, is in your midst;
you have no more evil to fear.
When that day comes, word will come to Jerusalem:
Zion, have no fear,
do not let your hands fall limp.
The Lord your God is in your midst,
a victorious warrior.
He will exult with joy for you,
he will renew you by his love;
he will dance with shouts of joy for you
as on a day of festival.

Responsorial Psalm   Isaiah 12:2-6

R/ **Sing and shout for joy
for great in your midst is the Holy One of Israel.**

1. Truly, God is my salvation,
   I trust, I shall not fear.
   For the Lord is my strength, my song,

THIRD SUNDAY OF ADVENT/C

    he became my saviour.
With joy you will draw water
from the wells of salvation. ℟

2. Give thanks to the Lord, give praise to his name!
make his mighty deeds known to the peoples!
Declare the greatness of his name. ℟

3. Sing a psalm to the Lord
for he has done glorious deeds,
make them known to all the earth!
People of Zion, sing and shout for joy
for great in your midst is the Holy One of Israel. ℟

Second Reading   Philippians 4:4-7

The Lord is very near.

I want you to be happy, always happy in the Lord; I repeat, what I want is your happiness. Let your tolerance be evident to everyone: the Lord is very near. There is no need to worry; but if there is anything you need, pray for it, asking God for it with prayer and thanksgiving, and that peace of God, which is so much greater than we can understand, will guard your hearts and your thoughts, in Christ Jesus.

Alleluia   Alleluia, alleluia! The spirit of the Lord has been given to me. He has sent me to bring good news to the poor. Alleluia! Isaiah 61:1 (Luke 4:18).

Gospel   Luke 3:10-18

What must we do?

When all the people asked John. "What must we do." he answered, "If anyone has two tunics he must share with the man who has none, and the one with something to eat must do the same." There were tax collectors too who came for baptism, and these said to him, 'Master, what must we do?' He said to them, "Exact no more than your rate." Some soldiers asked him in their turn, "What about us? What must we do?" He said to them, "No intimidation! No extortion! Be content with your pay!"

    A feeling of expectancy had grown among the people, who were beginning to think that John might be Christ, so John declared before them all, "I baptise you with water, but someone is coming, someone who is more powerful than I am, and I am not fit

THIRD SUNDAY OF ADVENT/C

to undo the strap of his sandals; he will baptise you with the Holy Spirit and fire. His winnowing-fan is in his hand to clear his threshing-floor and to gather the wheat into his barn; but the chaff he will burn in a fire that will never go out." As well as this, there were many other things he said to exhort the people and to announce the Good News to them.

Prayer over the Gifts

Lord,
may the gift we offer in faith and love
be a continual sacrifice in your honour
and truly become our eucharist and our salvation.

Preface of Advent I or II, page 558.

Communion Antiphon

Say to the anxious: be strong and fear not, our God will come to save us.

cf. Isaiah 35:4

Prayer after Communion

God of mercy,
may this eucharist bring us your divine help,
free us from our sins,
and prepare us for the birthday of our Saviour,
who is Lord for ever and ever.

The priest may give the Solemn Blessing for Advent on page 598.

FOURTH SUNDAY OF ADVENT/C

Mary, Mother of my Lord.
Mary does the will of God perfectly.
When God speaks to her she is prompt
to obey and in her flesh God's word
becomes incarnate. Of all women she is
the most blessed because she believed that
God's promises would be fulfilled in the
humblest of his creatures. She is the
servant of everyone. She was for Elizabeth
the cause of her joy. She is the same for us.

Entrance Antiphon   Let the clouds rain down the Just One, and
the earth bring forth a Saviour.

Isaiah 45:8

There is no Gloria today.

Opening Prayer

Let us pray
  [as Advent draws to a close,
  that Christ will truly come into our hearts]

Lord,
fill our hearts with your love,
and as you revealed to us by an angel
the coming of your Son as man,
so lead us through his suffering and death
to the glory of his resurrection,
for he lives and reigns with you and the Holy Spirit,
one God, for ever and ever.

or

Let us pray
  [as Advent draws to a close
  for the faith that opens our lives
  to the Spirit of God]

FOURTH SUNDAY OF ADVENT/C

Father, all-powerful God,
your eternal Word took flesh on our earth
when the Virgin Mary placed her life
at the service of your plan.

Lift our minds in watchful hope
to hear the voice which announces his glory
and open our minds to receive the Spirit
who prepares us for his coming.

First Reading   Micah 5:1-4

Out of you will be born the one who is to rule over Israel.

The Lord says this:
You, Bethlehem Ephrathah,
the least of the clans of Judah,
out of you will be born for me
the one who is to rule over Israel;
his origin goes back to the distant past,
to the days of old.
The Lord is therefore going to abandon them
till the time when she who is to give birth gives birth.
Then the remnant of his brothers will come back
to the sons of Israel.
He will stand and feed his flock
with the power of the Lord,
with the majesty of the name of his God.
They will live secure, for from then on he will extend his power
to the ends of the land.
He himself will be peace.

Responsorial Psalm   Psalm 79

**R/ God of hosts, bring us back;
let your face shine on us and we shall be saved.**

1. O shepherd of Israel, hear us,
   shine forth from your cherubim throne.
   O Lord, rouse up your might,
   O Lord, come to our help. R/

2. God of hosts, turn again, we implore,
   look down from heaven and see.
   Visit this vine and protect it,
   the vine your right hand has planted. R/

FOURTH SUNDAY OF ADVENT/C

3. May your hand be on the man you have chosen,
   the man you have given your strength.
   And we shall never forsake you again:
   give us life that we may call upon your name. ℟

Second Reading   Hebrews 10:5-10

Here I am! I am coming to obey your will.

This is what Christ said, on coming into the world:
You who wanted no sacrifice or oblation,
prepared a body for me.
You took no pleasure in holocausts or sacrifices for sin;
then I said,
just as I was commanded in the scroll of the book,
"God, here I am! I am coming to obey your will."
Notice that he says first: You did not want what the Law lays down as the things to be offered, that is: the sacrifices, the oblations, the holocausts and the sacrifices for sin, and you took no pleasure in them; and then he says: Here I am! I am coming to obey your will. He is abolishing the first sort to replace it with the second. And this will was for us to be made holy by the offering of his body made once and for all by Jesus Christ.

Alleluia

Alleluia, alleluia! I am the handmaid of the Lord: let what you have said be done to me. Alleluia!

                                                                                                                        Luke 1:38

Gospel   Luke 1:39-44

Why should I be honoured with a visit from the mother of my Lord?

Mary set out and went as quickly as she could to a town in the hill country of Judah. She went into Zechariah's house and greeted Elizabeth. Now as soon as Elizabeth heard Mary's greeting, the child leapt in her womb and Elizabeth was filled with the Holy Spirit. She gave a loud cry and said, "Of all women you are the most blessed, and blessed is the fruit of your womb. Why should I be honoured with a visit from the mother of my Lord? For the moment your greeting reached my ears, the child in my womb **leapt for joy. Yes, blessed is she who believed that the promise made her by the Lord would be fulfilled.**"

FOURTH SUNDAY OF ADVENT/C

Prayer over the Gifts

Lord,
may the power of the Spirit,
which sanctified Mary the mother of your Son,
make holy the gifts we place upon this altar.

Preface of Advent II, page 558.

Communion Antiphon

The Virgin is with child and shall bear a son, and she will call him Emmanuel.

Isaiah 7:14

Prayer after Communion

Lord,
in this sacrament
we receive the promise of salvation;
as Christmas draws near
make us grow in faith and love
to celebrate the coming of Christ our Saviour,
who is Lord for ever and ever.

The priest may give the Solemn Blessing for Advent on page 598.

The Season of Christmas

The Season of Christmas

THE Saviour is born and the work of our redemption has already begun. He is Emmanuel — God with us — and in him we find a new life. His final coming in glory may still be far off but the whole world has been changed by the event at Bethlehem. God, through a tiny baby, enters the course of human history and the world will never be the same again.

During the Christmas season we celebrate two great feasts — Christmas and Epiphany. As in Advent, the season has a double significance — the coming of Christ in flesh and his final coming in glory. We rejoice in the Lord's coming at Bethlehem and this gives us the assurance and hope that he will come again. At Christmas we are filled with thanksgiving and awe at the magnificence of God's gift to us. This is but a foretaste of the gladness that will fill us completely when Christ our Saviour will finally be revealed as Lord of the Universe.

In the birth of Christ 'the kindness and love of God our Saviour for mankind were revealed' Titus 3:4. Christ is born in a stable and his presence is made known to a few simple shepherds. The circle of those who find him will grow until the season of Christmas comes to its full significance in the Epiphany [revealing]. This is a foretaste of the Last Day when God's glory will be fully revealed in Christ.

The date of his birth — December 25th — roughly coincides with the winter solstice when the sun begins to rise in its orbit and the long winter nights grow shorter. Pagans kept festivals to celebrate the return of light with its promise of spring when once again they would sow their crops. It was for them a time of joy and hope after the long dark days of winter. How much more joyful are we now that the life of Christ has dawned on us. In his name we sow the seeds of a good christian life until the harvest time when Christ will gather us all to take us back to our heavenly Father.

CHRISTMAS DAY: MASS AT MIDNIGHT

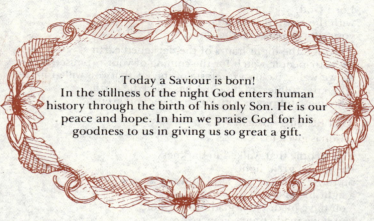

Today a Saviour is born!
In the stillness of the night God enters human history through the birth of his only Son. He is our peace and hope. In him we praise God for his goodness to us in giving us so great a gift.

Entrance Antiphon The Lord said to me: You are my Son; this day have I begotten you. **Psalm 2:7**

or

Let us all rejoice in the Lord, for our Saviour is born to the world. True peace has descended from heaven.

Opening Prayer

Let us pray
   [in the peace of Christmas midnight
   that our joy in the birth of Christ
   will last for ever]

Father,
you make this holy night radiant
with the splendour of Jesus Christ our light.
We welcome him as Lord, the true light of the world.
Bring us to eternal joy in the kingdom of heaven,
where he lives and reigns with you and the Holy Spirit,
one God, for ever and ever.

or

Let us pray
   [with joy and hope
   as we await the dawning of the Father's Word]

CHRISTMAS DAY: MASS AT MIDNIGHT/A/B/C

Lord God,
with the birth of your Son,
your glory breaks on the world.

Through the night hours of the darkened earth
we your people watch for the coming of your promised Son.
As we wait, give us a foretaste of the joy that you will grant us
when the fullness of his glory has filled the earth,
who lives and reigns with you for ever and ever.

First Reading   Isaiah 9:1-7
A son is given to us.

The people that walked in darkness
has seen a great light;
on those who live in a land of deep shadow
a light has shone.
You have made their gladness greater,
you have made their joy increase;
they rejoice in your presence
as men rejoice at harvest time,
as men are happy when they are dividing the spoils.
For the yoke that was weighing on him,
the bar across his shoulders,
the rod of his oppressor,
these you break as on the day of Midian.
For all the footgear of battle,
every cloak rolled in blood,
is burnt,
and consumed by fire.
For there is a child born for us,
a son given to us
and dominion is laid on his shoulders;
and this is the name they give him:
Wonder-Counsellor, Mighty-God,
Eternal-Father, Prince-of-Peace.
Wide is his dominion
in a peace that has no end,
for the throne of David
and for his royal power,
which he establishes and makes secure
in justice and integrity.
From this time onwards and for ever,

CHRISTMAS DAY: MASS AT MIDNIGHT/A/B/C

the jealous love of the Lord of hosts will do this.

Responsorial Psalm   Psalm 95

℟ **Today a saviour has been born to us;
he is Christ the Lord.**

1. O sing a new song to the Lord,
   sing to the Lord all the earth.
   O sing to the Lord, bless his name. ℟

2. Proclaim his help day by day,
   tell among the nations his glory
   and his wonders among all the peoples. ℟

3. Let the heavens rejoice and earth be glad,
   let the sea and all within it thunder praise,
   let the land and all it bears rejoice,
   all the trees of the wood shout for joy
   at the presence of the Lord for he comes,
   he comes to rule the earth. ℟

4. With justice he will rule the world,
   he will judge the peoples with his truth. ℟

Second Reading   Titus 2:11-14
God's grace has been revealed to the whole human race.

God's grace has been revealed, and it has made salvation possible for the whole human race and taught us that what we have to do is to give up everything that does not lead to God, and all our worldly ambitions; we must be self-restrained and live good and religious lives here in this present world, while we are waiting in hope for the blessing which will come with the Appearing of the glory of our great God and saviour Christ Jesus. He sacrificed himself for us in order to set us free from all wickedness and to purify a people so that it could be his very own and would have no ambition except to do good.

Alleluia
Alleluia, alleluia! I bring you news of great joy: today a saviour has been born to us, Christ the Lord. Alleluia! Luke 2:10-11

Gospel   Luke 2:1-14
Today a saviour has been born to you.

Caesar Augustus issued a decree for a census of the whole world

CHRISTMAS DAY: MASS AT MIDNIGHT/A/B/C

to be taken. This census — the first — took place while Quirinius was governor of Syria, and everyone went to his own town to be registered. So Joseph set out from the town of Nazareth in Galilee and travelled up to Judaea, to the town of David called Bethlehem, since he was of David's House and line, in order to be registered together with Mary, his betrothed, who was with child. While they were there the time came for her to have her child, and she gave birth to a son, her first-born. She wrapped him in swaddling clothes, and laid him in a manger because there was no room for them at the inn. In the countryside close by there were shepherds who lived in the fields and took it in turns to watch their flocks during the night. The angel of the Lord appeared to them and the glory of the Lord shone round them. They were terrified, but the angel said, "Do not be afraid. Listen, I bring you news of great joy, a joy to be shared by the whole people. Today in the town of David a saviour has been born to you; he is Christ the Lord. And here is a sign for you: you will find a baby wrapped in swaddling clothes and lying in a manger." And suddenly with the angel was a great throng of the heavenly host, praising God and singing: "Glory to God in the highest heaven,
and peace to men who enjoy his favour".

Prayer over the Gifts
Lord,
accept our gifts on this joyful feast of our salvation.
By our communion with God made man,
may we become more like him
who joins our lives to yours,
for he is Lord for ever and ever.

Preface of Christmas I-III, page 559.

Communion Antiphon The Word of God became man; we have seen his glory. John 1:14.

Prayer after Communion
God our Father,
we rejoice in the birth of our Saviour.
May we share his life completely
by living as he has taught.

The priest may give the Solemn Blessing for Christmas on page 598.

CHRISTMAS DAY: MASS AT DAWN

The new light of the world!
Jesus Christ is born for us as the new light of the world. God takes pity on us and sends us his only Son to be our new leader. In the stable of Bethlehem with the shepherds we discover in this human baby the measure of God's compassionate love for us.

Entrance Antiphon A light will shine on us this day, the Lord is born for us: he shall be called Wonderful God, Prince of peace, Father of the world to come; and his kingship will never end. cf. Isaiah 9:2.6; Luke 1:33

Opening Prayer

Let us pray
  [that the love of Christ
  will be a light to the world]

Father,
we are filled with the new light
by the coming of your Word among us.
May the light of faith
shine in our words and actions.

or

Let us pray
  [for the peace
  that comes from the Prince of peace]

Almighty God and Father of light,
a child is born for us and a son is given to us.
Your eternal Word leaped down from heaven
in the silent watches of the night,

CHRISTMAS DAY: MASS AT DAWN/A/B/C

and now your Church is filled with wonder
at the nearness of her God.

Open our hearts to receive his life
and increase our vision with the rising of dawn,
that our lives may be filled with his glory and his peace,
who lives and reigns for ever and ever.

First Reading   Isaiah 62:11-12

Look, your saviour comes.

This the Lord proclaims
to the ends of the earth:

Say to the daughter of Zion, "Look,
your saviour comes,
the prize of his victory with him,
his trophies before him".

They shall be called "The Holy People",
"The Lord's Redeemed".
And you shall be called "The-sought-after",
"City-not-forsaken".

Responsorial Psalm   Psalm 96

℟ **This day new light will shine upon the earth:
the Lord is born for us.**

1. The Lord is king, let earth rejoice,
   the many coastlands be glad.
   The skies proclaim his justice;
   all peoples see his glory. ℟

2. Light shines forth for the just
   and joy for the upright of heart.
   Rejoice, you just, in the Lord:
   give glory to his holy name. ℟

Second Reading   Titus 3:4-7

It was for no reason except his own compassion that he saved us.

When the kindness and love of God our saviour for mankind were revealed, it was not because he was concerned with any righteous actions we might have done ourselves; it was for no reason except his own compassion that he saved us, by means of the cleansing water of rebirth and by renewing us with the Holy Spirit which he has so generously poured over us through Jesus

Christ our saviour. He did this so that we should be justified by his grace, to become heirs looking forward to inheriting eternal life.

Alleluia   Alleluia, alleluia! Glory to God in the highest heaven, and peace to men who enjoy his favour. Alleluia! Luke 2:14

Gospel   Luke 2:15-20

The shepherds found Mary and Joseph and the baby.

Now when the angels had gone from them into heaven, the shepherds said to one another, "Let us go to Bethlehem and see this thing that has happened which the Lord has made known to us". So they hurried away and found Mary and Joseph, and the baby lying in the manger. When they saw the child they repeated what they had been told about him, and everyone who heard it was astonished at what the shepherds had to say. As for Mary, she treasured all these things and pondered them in her heart. And the shepherds went back glorifying and praising God for all they had heard and seen; it was exactly as they had been told.

Prayer over the Gifts

Father,
may we follow the example of your Son
who became man and lived among us.
May we receive the gift of divine life
through these offerings here on earth.

Preface of Christmas I-III, page 559.

Communion Antiphon   Daughter of Zion, exult; shout aloud, daughter of Jerusalem! Your King is coming, the Holy One, the Saviour of the world.   cf. Zechariah 9:9

Prayer after Communion

Lord,
with faith and joy
we celebrate the birthday of your Son.
Increase our understanding and our love
of the riches you have revealed in him,
who is Lord for ever and ever.

The priest may give the Solemn Blessing for Christmas on page 598

CHRISTMAS DAY: MASS DURING THE DAY

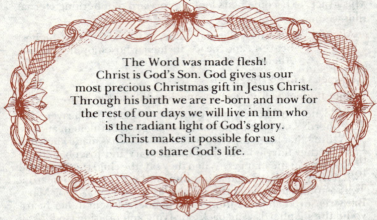

The Word was made flesh!
Christ is God's Son. God gives us our
most precious Christmas gift in Jesus Christ.
Through his birth we are re-born and now for
the rest of our days we will live in him who
is the radiant light of God's glory.
Christ makes it possible for us
to share God's life.

Entrance Antiphon A child is born for us, a son given to us; dominion is laid on his shoulder, and he shall be called Wonderful-Counsellor.

Isaiah 9:6

Opening Prayer

Let us pray
 [for the glory promised by the birth of Christ]

Lord God,
we praise you for creating man,
and still more for restoring him in Christ.
Your Son shared our weakness:
may we share his glory,
for he lives and reigns with you and the Holy Spirit,
one God, for ever and ever.

or

Let us pray
 [in the joy of Christmas
 because the Son of God lives among us]

God of love, Father of all,
the darkness that covered the earth
has given way to the bright dawn of your Word made flesh.

CHRISTMAS DAY: MASS DURING THE DAY/A/B/C

Make us a people of this light.
Make us faithful to your Word,
that we may bring your life to the waiting world.

First Reading   Isaiah 52:7-10

All the ends of the earth shall see the salvation of our God.

How beautiful on the mountains,
are the feet of one who brings good news,
who heralds peace, brings happiness,
proclaims salvation,
and tells Zion,
"Your God is king!"
Listen! Your watchmen raise their voices,
they shout for joy together,
for they see the Lord face to face,
as he returns to Zion.

Break into shouts of joy together,
you ruins of Jerusalem;
for the Lord is consoling his people,
redeeming Jerusalem.
The Lord bares his holy arm
in the sight of all the nations,
and all the ends of the earth shall see
the salvation of our God.

Responsorial Psalm   Psalm 97

℟ **All the ends of the earth have seen
the salvation of our God.**

1. Sing a new song to the Lord
   for he has worked wonders.
   His right hand and his holy arm
   have brought salvation. ℟

2. The Lord has made known his salvation;
   has shown his justice to the nations.
   He has remembered his truth and love
   for the house of Israel. ℟

3. All the ends of the earth have seen
   the salvation of our God.
   Shout to the Lord all the earth,
   ring out your joy. ℟

(continued)

CHRISTMAS DAY: MASS DURING THE DAY/A/B/C

4. Sing psalms to the Lord with the harp,
   with the sound of music.
   With trumpets and the sound of the horn
   acclaim the King, the Lord. ℟

Second Reading   Hebrews 1:1-6

God has spoken to us through his son.

At various times in the past and in various different ways, God spoke to our ancestors through the prophets; but in our own time, the last days, he has spoken to us through his Son, the Son that he has appointed to inherit everything and through whom he made everything there is. He is the radiant light of God's glory and the perfect copy of his nature, sustaining the universe by his powerful command; and now that he has destroyed the defilement of sin, he has gone to take his place in heaven at the right hand of divine Majesty. So he is now as far above the angels as the title which he has inherited is higher than their own name.

  God has never said to any angel: You are my Son, today I have become your father; or: I will be a father to him and he a son to me. Again, when he brings the First-born into the world, he says: Let all the angels of God worship him.

Alleluia   Alleluia, alleluia! A hallowed day has dawned upon us. Come, you nations, worship the Lord, for today a great light has shone down upon the earth. Alleluia!

Gospel   John 1:1-18

The Word was made flesh, and lived among us.

> In the beginning was the Word:
> the Word was with God
> and the Word was God.
> He was with God in the beginning.
> Through him all things came to be,
> not one thing had its being but through him.
> All that came to be had life in him
> and that life was the light of men,
> a light that shines in the dark,
> a light that darkness could not overpower.

A man came, sent by God.
His name was John.
He came as a witness,

CHRISTMAS DAY: MASS DURING THE DAY/A/B/C

as a witness to speak for the light,
so that every one might believe through him.
He was not the light,
only a witness to speak for the light.

> The Word was the true light
> that enlightens all men;
> and he was coming into the world.
> He was in the world
> that had its being through him,
> and the world did not know him.
> He came to his own domain
> and his own people did not accept him.
> But to all who did accept him
> he gave power to become children of God,
> to all who believe in the name of him
> who was born not out of human stock
> or urge of the flesh
> or will of man
> but of God himself.
> The Word was made flesh,
> he lived among us,
> and we saw his glory,
> the glory that is his as the only Son of the Father,
> full of grace and truth.

John appears as his witness. He proclaims:
"This is the one of whom I said:
He who comes after me
ranks before me
because he existed before me".
Indeed, from his fulness we have, all of us, received —
yes, grace in return for grace,
since, though the Law was given through Moses,
grace and truth have come through Jesus Christ.
No one has ever seen God;
it is the only Son, who is nearest to the Father's heart,
who has made him known.

Prayer over the Gifts

Almighty God,
the saving work of Christ
made our peace with you.

CHRISTMAS DAY: MASS DURING THE DAY A/B/C

May our offering today
renew that peace within us
and give you perfect praise.

Preface of Christmas I-III, page 559.

Communion Antiphon   All the ends of the earth have seen the saving power of God.   Psalm 97:3

Prayer after Communion

Father,
the child born today is the Saviour of the world.
He made us your children.
May he welcome us into your Kingdom
where he lives and reigns with you for ever and ever.

The priest may give the Solemn Blessing for Christmas on page 598.

SUNDAY IN THE OCTAVE OF CHRISTMAS
THE HOLY FAMILY OF JESUS, MARY AND JOSEPH/A

Christ in the human family.
God sets before us the Holy Family of Nazareth as the model for all families. The family unit is the basic structure on which human society is built. A good christian family life is a most powerful witness to our world of God's love for us revealed in Christ.

Entrance Antiphon The shepherds hastened to Bethlehem, where they found Mary and Joseph, and the baby lying in a manger. Luke 2:16

Opening Prayer

Let us pray
 [for peace in our families]
Father,
help us to live as the holy family,
united in respect and love.
Bring us to the joy and peace of your eternal home.
or
Let us pray
 [as the family of God,
 who share in his life]

Father in heaven, creator of all,
you ordered the earth to bring forth life
and crowned its goodness by creating the family of man.
In history's moment when all was ready,
you sent your Son to dwell in time,
obedient to the laws of life in our world.

THE HOLY FAMILY/A

Teach us the sanctity of human love,
show us the value of family life,
and help us to live in peace with all men
that we may share in your life for ever.

First Reading — Ecclesiasticus 3:2-6. 12-14
He who fears the Lord respects his parents.

The Lord honours the father in his children,
and upholds the rights of a mother over her sons.
Whoever respects his father is atoning for his sins,
he who honours his mother is like someone amassing a fortune.
Whoever respects his father will be happy with children of his own,
he shall be heard on the day when he prays.
Long life comes to him who honours his father,
he who sets his mother at ease is showing obedience to the Lord.
My son, support your father in his old age,
do not grieve him during his life.
Even if his mind should fail, show him sympathy,
do not despise him in your health and strength;
for kindness to a father shall not be forgotten
but will serve as reparation for your sins.

Responsorial Psalm — Psalm 127

℟ **O blessed are those who fear the Lord
and walk in his ways!**

1. O blessed are those who fear the Lord
   and walk in his ways!
   By the labour of your hands you shall eat.
   You will be happy and prosper. ℟

2. Your wife like a fruitful vine
   in the heart of your house;
   your children like shoots of the olive,
   around your table. ℟

3. Indeed thus shall be blessed
   the man who fears the Lord.
   May the Lord bless you from Zion
   all the days of your life! ℟

THE HOLY FAMILY/A

Second Reading Colossians 3:12-21
Family life in the Lord.

You are God's chosen race, his saints; he loves you, and you should be clothed in sincere compassion, in kindness and humility, gentleness and patience. Bear with one another; forgive each other as soon as a quarrel begins. The Lord has forgiven you; now you must do the same. Over all these clothes, to keep them together and complete them, put on love. And may the peace of Christ reign in your hearts, because it is for this that you were called together as parts of one body. Always be thankful.

Let the message of Christ, in all its richness, find a home with you. Teach each other, and advise each other, in all wisdom. With gratitude in your hearts sing psalms and hymns and inspired songs to God: and never say or do anything except in the name of the Lord Jesus, giving thanks to God the Father through him.

Wives, give way to your husbands, as you should in the Lord. Husbands, love your wives and treat them with gentleness. Children, be obedient to your parents always, because that is what will please the Lord. Parents, never drive your children to resentment or you will make them feel frustrated.

Alleluia Alleluia, alleluia! May the peace of Christ reign in your hearts; let the message of Christ find a home with you. Alleluia! Colossians 3:15.16

Gospel Matthew 2:13-15. 19-23
Take the child and his mother and escape into Egypt.

After the wise men had left, the angel of the Lord appeared to Joseph in a dream and said, "Get up, take the child and his mother with you, and escape into Egypt, and stay there until I tell you, because Herod intends to search for the child and do away with him." So Joseph got up and, taking the child and his mother with him, left that night for Egypt, where he stayed until Herod was dead. This was to fulfil what the Lord had spoken through the prophet:
I called my son out of Egypt.

THE HOLY FAMILY/A

After Herod's death, the angel of the Lord appeared in a dream to Joseph in Egypt and said, "Get up, take the child and his mother with you and go back to the land of Israel, for those who wanted to kill the child are dead." So Joseph got up and, taking the child and his mother with him, went back to the land of Israel. But when he learnt that Archelaus had succeeded his father Herod as ruler of Judaea he was afraid to go there, and being warned in a dream he left for the region of Galilee. There he settled in a town called Nazareth. In this way the words spoken through the prophets were to be fulfilled:
He will be called a Nazarene.

Prayer over the Gifts
Lord,
accept this sacrifice
and through the prayers of Mary, the virgin Mother of God,
and of her husband, Joseph,
unite our families in peace and love.

Preface of Christmas I-III, page 559.

Communion Antiphon
Our God has appeared on earth, and lived among men. Baruch 3:38.

Prayer after Communion
Eternal Father,
we want to live as Jesus, Mary, and Joseph,
in peace with you and one another.
May this communion strengthen us
to face the troubles of life.

The priest may give the Solemn Blessing of Christmas on page 598.

SUNDAY IN THE OCTAVE OF CHRISTMAS
THE HOLY FAMILY OF JESUS, MARY AND JOSEPH/B

Christ in the human family.
God sets before us the Holy Family of Nazareth as the model for all families. The family unit is the basic structure on which human society is built. A good christian family life is a most powerful witness to our world of God's love for us revealed in Christ.

Entrance Antiphon The shepherds hastened to Bethlehem, where they found Mary and Joseph, and the baby lying in a Manger. Luke 2:16.

Opening Prayer

Let us pray
  [for peace in our families]

Father,
help us to live as the holy family,
united in respect and love.
Bring us to the joy and peace of your eternal home.

or

Let us pray
  [as the family of God,
  who share in his life]

Father in heaven, creator of all,
you ordered the earth to bring forth life
and crowned its goodness by creating the family of man.
In history's moment when all was ready,
you sent your Son to dwell in time,

THE HOLY FAMILY/B

obedient to the laws of life in our world.

Teach us the sanctity of human love,
show us the value of human life,
and help us to live in peace with all men
that we may share in your life for ever.

First Reading   Genesis 15:1-6. 21:1-3.
'Your heir shall be of your own flesh and blood'

The word of the Lord was spoken to Abram in a vision. "Have no fear, Abram, I am your shield; your reward will be very great".

"My Lord God," Abram replied "what do you intend to give me? I go childless." Then Abram said, "See, you have given me no descendants; some man of my household will be my heir". And then this word of the Lord was spoken to him, 'He shall not be your heir; your heir shall be of your own flesh and blood'. Then taking him outside he said, 'Look up to heaven and count the stars if you can. Such will be your descendants' he told him. Abram put his faith in the Lord, who counted this as making him justified.

The Lord dealt kindly with Sarah as he had said and did what he had promised her. So Sarah conceived and bore a son to Abraham in his old age, at the time God had promised. Abraham named the son born to him Isaac, the son to whom Sarah had given birth.

Responsorial Psalm   Psalm 104
R/ **He, the Lord, is our God.
   He remember his covenant for ever.**

1 Give thanks to the Lord, tell his name,
   make known his deeds among the peoples.
   O sing to him, sing his praise;
   tell all his wonderful works! R/

2. Be proud of his holy name,
   let the hearts that seek the Lord rejoice.
   Consider the Lord and his strength;
   constantly seek his face. R/

THE HOLY FAMILY/B

3. Remember the wonders he has done,
   his miracles, the judgements he spoke.
   O children of Abraham, his servant,
   O sons of the Jacob he chose. R/

4. He remembers his covenant for ever,
   his promise for a thousand generations,
   the covenant he made with Abraham,
   the oath he swore to Isaac. R/

Second Reading   Hebrews 11:8. 11-12. 17-19.
The faith of Abraham, Sarah and Isaac.

It was by faith that Abraham obeyed the call to set out for a country that was the inheritance given to him and his descendants, and that he set out without knowing where he was going.

It was equally by faith that Sarah, in spite of being past the age, was made able to conceive, because she believed that he who had made the promise would be faithful to it. Because of this, there came from one man, and one who was already as good as dead himself, more descendants than could be counted, as many as the stars of heaven or the grains of sand on the seashore.

It was by faith that Abraham, when put to the test, offered up Isaac. He offered to sacrifice his only son even though the promises had been made to him and he had been told: It is through Isaac that your name will be carried on. He was confident that God had the power even to raise the dead; and so, figuratively speaking, he was given back Isaac from the dead.

Alleluia   Alleluia, alleluia! At various times in the past and in various different ways, God spoke to our ancestors through the prophets; but in our own time, the last days, he has spoken to us through his Son. Alleluia!
Hebrews 1:1-2.

Gospel   Luke 2.22-40.
The child grew, filled with wisdom.

When the day came for them to be purified as laid down by the Law of Moses, they took him up to Jerusalem to present him to the Lord

THE HOLY FAMILY/B

— observing what stands written in the Law of the Lord: Every first-born male must be consecrated to the Lord — and also to offer in sacrifice, in accordance with what is said in the Law of the Lord, a pair of turtledoves or two young pigeons. Now in Jerusalem there was a man named Simeon. He was an upright and devout man; he looked forward to Israel's comforting and the Holy Spirit rested on him. It had been revealed to him by the Holy Spirit that he would not see death until he had set eyes on the Christ of the Lord. Prompted by the Spirit he came to the Temple; and when the parents brought in the child Jesus to do for him what the Law required, he took him into his arms and blessed God; and he said:

"Now, Master, you can let your servant go in peace, just as you promised;
because my eyes have seen the salvation
which you have prepared for all the nations to see,
a light to enlighten the pagans
and the glory of your people Israel."

As the child's father and mother stood there wondering at the things that were being said about him, Simeon blessed them and said to Mary his mother, "You see this child: he is destined for the fall and for the rising of many in Israel, destined to be a sign that is rejected — and a sword will pierce your own soul too — so that the secret thoughts of many may be laid bare."

There was a prophetess also, Anna the daughter of Phanuel, of the tribe of Asher. She was well on in years. Her days of girlhood over, she had been married for seven years before becoming a widow. She was now eighty-four years old and never left the Temple, serving God night and day with fasting and prayer. She came by just at that moment and began to praise God; and she spoke of the child to all who looked forward to the deliverance of Jerusalem.

When they had done everything the Law of the Lord required, they went back to Galilee, to their own town of Nazareth. Meanwhile the child grew to maturity, and he was filled with wisdom; and God's favour was with him.

THE HOLY FAMILY/B

Prayer over the Gifts
Lord,
accept this sacrifice
and through the prayers of Mary, the virgin Mother of God,
and of her husband Joseph,
unite our families in peace and love.

Preface of Christmas I-III, page 559.

Communion Antiphon
Our God has appeared on earth, and lived among men. Baruch 3:38.

Prayer after Communion
Eternal Father,
we want to live as Jesus, Mary, and Joseph,
in peace with you and one another.
May this communion strengthen us
to face the troubles of life.

The priest may give the Solemn Blessing of Christmas on page 598.

SUNDAY IN THE OCTAVE OF CHRISTMAS
THE HOLY FAMILY OF JESUS, MARY AND JOSEPH/C

Christ in the human family.
God sets before us the Holy Family of Nazareth as the model for all families. The family unit is the basic structure on which human society is built. A good christian family is a most powerful witness to our world of God's love for us revealed in Christ.

Entrance Antiphon   The shepherds hastened to Bethlehem, where they found Mary and Joseph, and the baby lying in a manger. Luke 2:16.

Opening Prayer
Let us pray
  [for peace in our families]
Father,
help us to live as the holy family,
united in respect and love.
Bring us the joy and peace of your eternal home.

or

Let us pray
  [as the family of God,
  who share in his life]

THE HOLY FAMILY/C

Father in heaven, creator of all,
you ordered the earth to bring forth life
and crowned its goodness by creating the family of man.
In history's moment when all was ready,
you sent your Son to dwell in time,
obedient to the laws of life in our world.

Teach us the sanctity of human love,
show us the value of human life,
and help us to live in peace with all men
that we may share in your life for ever.

First Reading   1 Samuel 1:20-22. 24-28
Samuel is made over to the Lord for the whole of his life.

Hannah conceived and gave birth to a son, and called him Samuel "since" she said "I asked the Lord for him."

When a year had gone by, the husband Elkanah went up again with all his family to offer the annual sacrifice to the Lord and to fulfil his vow. Hannah, however, did not go up, having said to her husband, "Not before the child is weaned. Then I will bring him and present him before the Lord and he shall stay there for ever."

When she had weaned him, she took him up with her together with a three-year old bull, an ephah of flour and a skin of wine, and she brought him to the temple of the Lord at Shiloh; and the child was with them. They slaughtered the bull and the child's mother came to Eli. She said, "If you please, my Lord. As you live, my Lord, I am the woman who stood here beside you, praying to the Lord. This is the child I prayed for, and the Lord granted me what I asked him. Now I make him over to the Lord for the whole of his life. He is made over to the Lord."

There she left him, for the Lord.

Responsorial Psalm   Psalm 83
R/ **They are happy who dwell in your house, O Lord.**

1. How lovely is your dwelling place,
   Lord, God of hosts.
   My soul is longing and yearning,
   is yearning for the courts of the Lord.
   My heart and my soul ring out their joy
   to God, the living God. R/

THE HOLY FAMILY/C

2. They are happy, who dwell in your house,
   for ever singing your praise.
   They are happy, whose strength is in you,
   they walk with ever growing strength. R/
3. O Lord, God of hosts, hear my prayer,
   give ear, O God of Jacob.
   Turn your eyes, O God, our shield,
   look on the face of your anointed. R/

Second Reading 1 John 3:1-2. 21-24.
We are called God's children; and that is what we are.

Think of the love that the Father has lavished on us,
by letting us be called God's children;
and that is what we are.
Because the world refused to acknowledge him,
and therefore it does not acknowledge us.
My dear people, we are already the children of God
but what we are to be in the future has not yet been revealed;
all we know is, that when it is revealed
we shall all be like him
because we shall see him as he really is.

My dear people,
if we cannot be condemned by our own conscience,
we need not be afraid in God's presence,
and whatever we ask him,
We shall receive,
because we keep his commandments
and live the kind of life that he wants.
His commandments are these:
that we believe in the name of his Son Jesus Christ
and that we love one another as he told us to.
Whoever keeps his commandments
lives in God and God lives in him.
We know that he lives in us
by the Spirit that he has given us.

Alleluia!   Alleluia, alleluia! Open our heart, O Lord, to accept
the words of your Son. Alleluia! Acts 16:14b.

THE HOLY FAMILY/C

Gospel   Luke 2:41-52

Jesus is found by his parents sitting among the doctors.

Every year the parents of Jesus used to go to Jerusalem for the feast of the Passover. When he was twelve years old, they went up for the feast as usual. When they were on their way home after the feast, the boy Jesus stayed behind in Jerusalem without his parents knowing it. They assumed he was with the caravan, and it was only after a day's journey that they went to look for him among their relations and acquaintances. When they failed to find him they went back to Jerusalem looking for him everywhere.

Three days later, they found him in the Temple, sitting among the doctors, listening to them, and asking them questions; and all those who heard him were astounded at his intelligence and his replies. They were overcome when they saw him, and his mother said to him, "My child, why have you done this to us? See how worried your father and I have been, looking for you." "Why were you looking for me?" he replied. "Did you not know that I must be busy with my Father's affairs?" But they did not understand what he meant.

He then went down with them and came to Nazareth and lived under their authority. His mother stored up all these things in her heart. And Jesus increased in wisdom, in stature, and in favour with God and men.

Prayer over the Gifts

Lord,
accept this sacrifice
and through the prayers of Mary, the virgin Mother of God,
and of her husband Joseph,
unite our families in peace and love.

Preface of Christmas I-III, page 559.

Communion Antiphon   Our God has appeared on earth, and lived among men.   Baruch 3:38.

THE HOLY FAMILY/C

Prayer after Communion

Eternal Father,
we want to live as Jesus, Mary, and Joseph,
in peace with you and one another.
May this communion strengthen us
to face the troubles of life.

The priest may give the Solemn Blessing of Christmas on page 598.

JANUARY 1: OCTAVE OF CHRISTMAS
SOLEMNITY OF MARY, MOTHER OF GOD

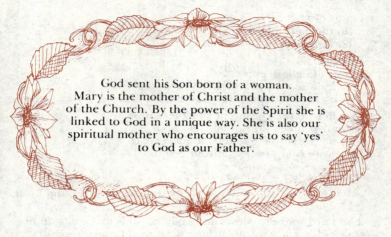

God sent his Son born of a woman. Mary is the mother of Christ and the mother of the Church. By the power of the Spirit she is linked to God in a unique way. She is also our spiritual mother who encourages us to say 'yes' to God as our Father.

Entrance Antiphon A light will shine on us this day, the Lord is born for us: he shall be called Wonderful God, Prince of peace, Father of the world to come; and his kingship will never end. cf. Isaiah 9:2.6; Luke 1:33.

or

Hail, holy Mother! The child to whom you gave birth is the King of heaven and earth for ever. Sedulius.

Opening Prayer

Let us pray
 [that Mary, the mother of the Lord,
  will help us by her prayers]

God our Father,
may we always profit by the prayers
of the Virgin Mother Mary,
for you bring us life and salvation
through Jesus Christ her Son
who lives and reigns with you and the Holy Spirit,
one God, for ever and ever.

MARY, MOTHER OF GOD/A/B/C

or

Let us pray
  [in the name of Jesus,
  born of a virgin and Son of God]

Father,
source of light in every age,
the virgin conceived and bore your Son
who is called Wonderful God, Prince of peace.

May her prayer, the gift of a mother's love,
be your people's joy through all ages.
May her response, born of a humble heart,
draw your Spirit to rest on your people.

First Reading   Numbers 6:22-27

They are to call down my name on the sons of Israel, and I will bless them.

The Lord spoke to Moses and said, "Say this to Aaron and his sons: 'This is how you are to bless the sons of Israel. You shall say to them:
May the Lord bless you and keep you.
May the Lord let his face shine on you and be gracious to you.
May the Lord uncover his face to you and bring you peace.'
   "This is how they are to call down my name on the sons of Israel, and I will bless them."

Responsorial Psalm   Psalm 66

℟ O God, be gracious and bless us.

1. God, be gracious and bless us
   and let your face shed its light upon us.
   So will your ways be known upon earth
   and all nations learn your saving help. ℟

2. Let the nations be glad and exult
   for you rule the world with justice.
   With fairness you rule the peoples,
   you guide the nations on earth. ℟

3. Let the peoples praise you, O God;
   let all the peoples praise you.
   May God still give us his blessing
   till the ends of the earth revere him. ℟

MARY, MOTHER OF GOD/A/B/C

Second Reading Galatians 4:4-7
God sent his Son, born of a woman.

When the appointed time came, God sent his Son, born of a woman, born a subject of the Law, to redeem the subjects of the Law and to enable us to be adopted as sons. The proof that you are sons is that God has sent the Spirit of his Son into our hearts: the Spirit that cries, "Abba, Father," and it is this that makes you a son, you are not a slave any more; and if God has made you son, then he has made you heir.

Alleluia
Alleluia, alleluia! At various times in the past and in various different ways, God spoke to our ancestors through the prophets; but in our own time, the last days, he has spoken to us through his Son. Alleluia!
Hebrews 1:1-2

Gospel Luke 2:16-21
They found Mary and Joseph and the baby ... When the eighth day came, they gave him the name Jesus.

The shepherds hurried away to Bethlehem and found Mary and Joseph, and the baby lying in the manger. When they saw the child they repeated what they had been told about him, and everyone who heard it was astonished at what the shepherds had to say. As for Mary, she treasured all these things and pondered them in her heart. And the shepherds went back glorifying and praising God, for all they had heard and seen; it was exactly as they had been told.

When the eighth day came and the child was to be circumcised they gave him the name Jesus, the name the angel had given him before his conception.

Prayer over the Gifts
God our Father,
we celebrate at this season
the beginning of our salvation.
On this feast of Mary, the Mother of God,
we ask that our salvation
will be brought to its fulfilment.

Preface
Father, all-powerful and ever-living God,

MARY, MOTHER OF GOD/A/B/C

we do well always and everywhere to give you thanks
as we celebrate the motherhood of the Blessed Virgin Mary.

Through the power of the Holy Spirit,
she became the virgin mother of your only Son,
our Lord Jesus Christ,
who is for ever the light of the world.

Through him the choirs of angels
and all the powers of heaven
praise and worship your glory.
May our voices blend with theirs
as we join in their unending hymn:

Holy, holy, holy . . .

Communion Antiphon

Jesus Christ is the same yesterday, today, and for ever. Hebrews 13:8

Prayer after Communion

Father,
as we proclaim the Virgin Mary
to be the mother of Christ and the mother of the Church,
may our communion with her Son
bring us to salvation.

Solemn Blessing

Bow your heads and pray for God's blessing.

Born of the Blessed Virgin Mary,
the Son of God redeemed mankind.
May he enrich you with his blessings.
R/ Amen.

You received the author of life through Mary.
May you always rejoice in her loving care.
R/ Amen.

You have come to rejoice at Mary's feast.
May you be filled with the joys of the Spirit
and the gifts of your eternal home.
R/ Amen.

May almighty God bless you,
the Father, and the Son, ✠ and the Holy Spirit.
R/ Amen.

SECOND SUNDAY AFTER CHRISTMAS

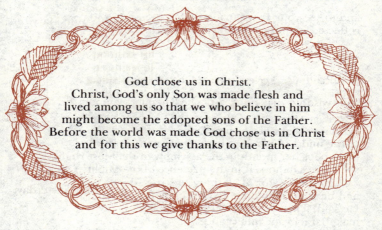

God chose us in Christ.
Christ, God's only Son was made flesh and
lived among us so that we who believe in him
might become the adopted sons of the Father.
Before the world was made God chose us in Christ
and for this we give thanks to the Father.

Entrance Antiphon   When peaceful silence lay over all, and night had run half of her swift course, your all-powerful word, O Lord, leaped down from heaven, from the royal throne. Wisdom 18:14-15

Opening Prayer

Let us pray
  [that all mankind may be enlightened by the gospel]

God of power and life,
glory of all who believe in you,
fill the world with your splendour
and show the nations the light of your truth.

or

Let us pray
  [aware of the dignity to which we are called
  by the love of Christ]

Father of our Lord Jesus Christ,
our glory is to stand before the world
as your own sons and daughters.

May the simple beauty of Jesus' birth
summon us always to love what is most deeply human,

SECOND SUNDAY AFTER CHRISTMAS/A/B/C

and to see your Word made flesh
reflected in those whose lives we touch.

First Reading   Ecclesiasticus 24:1-2. 8-12.

The wisdom of God has pitched her tent among the chosen people.

Wisdom speaks her own praises,
in the midst of her people she glories in herself.
She opens her mouth in the assembly of the Most High,
she glories in herself in the presence of the Mighty One;
"Then the creator of all things instructed me,
and he who created me fixed a place for my tent.
He said, 'Pitch your tent in Jacob,
make Israel your inheritance'.
From eternity, in the beginning, he created me,
and for eternity I shall remain.
I ministered before him in the holy tabernacle,
and thus was I established on Zion.
In the beloved city he has given me rest,
and in Jerusalem I wield my authority.
I have taken root in a privileged people,
in the Lord's property, in his inheritance."

Responsorial Psalm   Psalm 147

℟ **The Word was made flesh,
and lived among us.**

or ℟ **Alleluia!**

1. O praise the Lord, Jerusalem!
   Zion, praise your God!
   He has strengthened the bars of your gates,
   he has blessed the children within you. ℟

2. He established peace on your borders,
   he feeds you with finest wheat.
   He sends out his word to the earth
   and swiftly runs his command. ℟

SECOND SUNDAY AFTER CHRISTMAS/A/B/C

3. He makes his word known to Jacob,
to Israel his laws and decrees.
He has not dealt thus with other nations;
he has not taught them his decrees.
Alleluia! ℟

Second Reading   Ephesians 1:3-6. 15-18

He determined that we should become his adopted sons through Jesus.

Blessed be God the Father of our Lord Jesus Christ, who has blessed us with all the spiritual blessings of heaven in Christ. Before the world was made, he chose us, chose us in Christ, to be holy and spotless, and to live through love in his presence, determining that we should become his adopted sons, through Jesus Christ, for his own kind purposes, to make us praise the glory of his grace, his free gift to us in the Beloved.

That will explain why I, having once heard about your faith in the Lord Jesus, and the love that you show towards all the saints, have never failed to remember you in my prayers and to thank God for you. May the God of our Lord Jesus Christ, the Father of glory, give you a spirit of wisdom and perception of what is revealed, to bring you to full knowledge of him. May he enlighten the eyes of your mind so that you can see what hope his call holds for you, what rich glories he has promised the saints will inherit.

Alleluia
Alleluia, alleluia! Glory be to you, O Christ, proclaimed to the pagans; Glory be to you, O Christ, believed in by the world. Alleluia! 1 Timothy 3:16.

Gospel   John 1:1-18

The Word was made flesh, and lived among us.

In the beginning was the Word:
the Word was with God
and the Word was God.
He was with God in the beginning.
Through him all things came to be,
not one thing had its being but through him.
All that came to be had life in him
and that life was the light of men,

SECOND SUNDAY AFTER CHRISTMAS/A/B/C

> a light that shines in the dark,
> a light that darkness could not overpower.

A man came, sent by God.
His name was John.
He came as a witness,
as a witness to speak for the light,
so that everyone might believe through him.
He was not the light,
only a witness to speak for the light.

> The Word was the true light
> that enlightens all men;
> and he was coming into the world.
> He was in the world
> that had its being through him,
> and the world did not know him.
> He came to his own domain
> and his own people did not accept him.
> But to all who did accept him
> he gave power to become children of God,
> to all who believe in the name of him
> who was born not out of human stock
> or urge of the flesh
> or will of man
> but of God himself.
> The Word was made flesh,
> he lived among us,
> and we saw his glory,
> the glory that is his as the only Son of the Father,
> full of grace and truth.

John appears as his witness. He proclaims:
"This is the one of whom I said:
He who comes after me ·
ranks before me
because he existed before me."

Indeed, from his fulness we have, all of us, received —
yes, grace in return for grace,
since, though the Law was given through Moses,
grace and truth have come through Jesus Christ.

SECOND SUNDAY AFTER CHRISTMAS/A/B/C

No one has ever seen God;
it is the only Son, who is nearest to the Father's heart,
who has made him known.

Prayer over the Gifts

Lord,
make holy these gifts
through the coming of your Son,
who shows us the way of truth
and promises the life of your kingdom.

Preface of Christmas I-III, page 559.

Communion Antiphon

He gave to all who accepted him the power to become children of God.

John 1:12

Prayer after Communion

Lord,
hear our prayers.
By this eucharist free us from sin
and keep us faithful to your word.

The priest may give this Solemn Blessing.

Solemn Blessing

Bow your heads and pray for God's blessing.

Every good gift comes from the Father of light.
May he grant you his grace and every blessing
and keep you safe throughout the coming year.
R/ **Amen.**

May he grant you unwavering faith,
constant hope, and love that endures to the end.
R/ **Amen.**

May he order your days and work in his peace,
hear your every prayer,
and lead you to everlasting life and joy.
R/ **Amen.**

May almighty God bless you,
the Father, and the Son, ✠ and the Holy Spirit.
R/ **Amen.**

JANUARY 6
THE EPIPHANY OF THE LORD

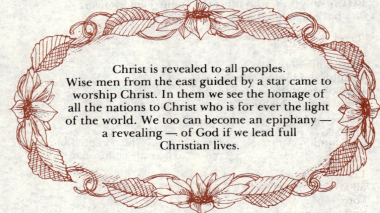

Christ is revealed to all peoples.
Wise men from the east guided by a star came to
worship Christ. In them we see the homage of
all the nations to Christ who is for ever the light
of the world. We too can become an epiphany —
a revealing — of God if we lead full
Christian lives.

Entrance Antiphon The Lord and ruler is coming; kingship is his, and government and power.
cf. Malachi 3:1; I Chronicles 19:12

Opening Prayer

Let us pray
 [that we will be guided by the light of faith]

Father,
you revealed your Son to the nations
by the guidance of a star.
Lead us to your glory in heaven
by the light of faith.

or

Let us pray
 [grateful for the glory revealed today
 through God made man]

Father of light, unchanging God,
today you reveal to men of faith
the resplendent fact of the Word made flesh.

Your light is strong,
your love is near;

THE EPIPHANY/A/B/C

draw us beyond the limits which this world imposes,
to the life where your Spirit makes all life complete.

First Reading   Isaiah 60:1-6

Above you the glory of the Lord appears.

Arise, shine out, for your light has come,
the glory of the Lord is rising on you,
though night still covers the earth
and darkness the peoples.

Above you the Lord now rises
and above you his glory appears.
The nations come to your light
and kings to your dawning brightness.

Lift up your eyes and look round:
all are assembling and coming towards you,
your sons from far away
and your daughters being tenderly carried.

At this sight you will grow radiant,
your heart throbbing and full;
since the riches of the sea will flow to you,
the wealth of the nations come to you;

camels in throngs will cover you,
and dromedaries of Midian and Ephah;
everyone in Sheba will come,
bringing gold and incense
and singing the praise of the Lord.

Responsorial Psalm   Psalm 71

R/ All nations shall fall prostrate before you, O Lord.

1. O God, give your judgement to the king,
   to a king's son your justice,
   that he may judge your people in justice
   and your poor in right judgement. R/

2. In his days justice shall flourish
   and peace till the moon fails.
   He shall rule from sea to sea,
   from the Great River to earth's bounds. R/

(continued)

THE EPIPHANY/A/B/C

3. The kings of Tarshish and the sea coasts
   shall pay him tribute.
   The kings of Sheba and Seba
   shall bring him gifts.
   Before him all kings shall fall prostrate,
   all nations shall serve him. R/

4. For he shall save the poor when they cry
   and the needy who are helpless.
   He will have pity on the weak
   and save the lives of the poor. R/

Second Reading   Ephesians 3:2-3a. 5-6

It has now been revealed that pagans share the same inheritance.

You have probably heard how I have been entrusted by God with the grace he meant for you, and that it was by a revelation that I was given the knowledge of the mystery.

   This mystery that has now been revealed through the Spirit to his holy apostles and prophets was unknown to any men in past generations; it means that pagans now share the same inheritance, that they are parts of the same body, and that the same promise has been made to them, in Christ Jesus, through the gospel.

Alleluia

Alleluia, alleluia! We saw his star as it rose and have come to do the Lord homage. Alleluia! Matthew 2:2

Gospel   Matthew 2:1-12

We came from the east to do the king homage.

After Jesus had been born at Bethlehem in Judaea during the reign of King Herod, some wise men came to Jerusalem from the east. "Where is the infant king of the Jews?" they asked. "We saw his star as it rose and have come to do him homage." When King Herod heard this he was perturbed, and so was the whole of Jerusalem. He called together all the chief priests and the scribes of the people, and enquired of them where the Christ was to be born. "At Bethlehem in Judaea," they told him "for this is what the prophet wrote:
And you, Bethlehem, in the land of Judah,
you are by no means least among the leaders of Judah,
for out of you will come a leader

THE EPIPHANY/A/B/C

who will shepherd my people Israel."
Then Herod summoned the wise men to see him privately. He asked them the exact date on which the star had appeared, and sent them on to Bethlehem. "Go and find out all about the child," he said "and when you have found him, let me know, so that I too may go and do him homage." Having listened to what the king had to say, they set out. And there in front of them was the star they had seen rising; it went forward and halted over the place where the child was. The sight of the star filled them with delight, and going into the house they saw the child with his mother Mary, and falling to their knees they did him homage. Then, opening their treasures, they offered him gifts of gold and frankincense and myrrh. But they were warned in a dream not to go back to Herod, and returned to their own country by a different way.

Prayer over the Gifts

Lord,
accept the offerings of your Church,
not gold, frankincense and myrrh,
but the sacrifice and food they symbolise:
Jesus Christ, who is Lord for ever and ever.

Preface

Father, all-powerful and ever-living God,
we do well always and everywhere to give you thanks.

Today you revealed in Christ your eternal plan of salvation
and showed him as the light of all peoples.
Now that his glory has shone among us
you have renewed humanity in his immortal image.

Now, with angels and archangels,
and the whole company of heaven,
we sing the unending hymn of your praise:

Holy, holy, holy ...

Communion Antiphon

We have seen his star in the east and have come with gifts to adore the Lord. cf. Matthew 2:2

THE EPIPHANY/A/B/C

Prayer after Communion

Father,
guide us with your light.
Help us to recognise Christ in this eucharist
and welcome him with love,
for he is Lord for ever and ever.

Solemn Blessing

The priest may give this Solemn Blessing, or another form on pages 598–599

Bow your heads and pray for God's blessing.

God has called you out of darkness,
into his wonderful light.
May you experience his kindness and blessings,
and be strong in faith, in hope, and in love.
℟ **Amen.**

Because you are followers of Christ,
who appeared on this day as a light shining in darkness,
may he make you a light to all your sisters and brothers.
℟ **Amen.**

The wise men followed the star,
and found Christ who is light from light.
May you too find the Lord
when your pilgrimage is ended.
℟ **Amen.**

May almighty God bless you,
the Father, and the Son, ✠ and the Holy Spirit.
℟ **Amen.**

SUNDAY AFTER JANUARY 6
THE BAPTISM OF THE LORD/A

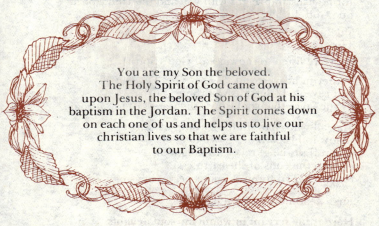

You are my Son the beloved.
The Holy Spirit of God came down
upon Jesus, the beloved Son of God at his
baptism in the Jordan. The Spirit comes down
on each one of us and helps us to live our
christian lives so that we are faithful
to our Baptism.

Entrance Antiphon When the Lord had been baptised, the heavens opened, and the Spirit came down like a dove to rest on him. Then the voice of the Father thundered: This is my beloved Son, with him I am well pleased.
cf. Matthew 3:16-17

Opening Prayer

Let us pray
   [that we will be faithful to our baptism]

Almighty, eternal God,
when the Spirit descended upon Jesus
at his baptism in the Jordan,
you revealed him as your own beloved Son.
Keep us, your children born of water and the Spirit,
faithful to our calling.

or

Father,
your only Son revealed himself to us by becoming man.
May we who share his humanity
come to share his divinity,

THE BAPTISM OF THE LORD/A

for he lives and reigns with you and the Holy Spirit,
one God, for ever and ever.

or

Let us pray
   [as we listen to the voice of God's Spirit]

Father in heaven,
you revealed Christ as your Son
by the voice that spoke over the waters of the Jordan.

May all who share in the sonship of Christ
follow in his path of service to man,
and reflect the glory of his kingdom
even to the ends of the earth,
for he is Lord for ever and ever.

First Reading   Isaiah 42:1-4, 6-7

Here is my servant in whom my soul delights.

Thus says the Lord:
Here is my servant whom I uphold,
my chosen one in whom my soul delights.
I have endowed him with my spirit
that he may bring true justice to the nations.

He does not cry out or shout aloud,
or make his voice heard in the streets.
He does not break the crushed reed,
nor quench the wavering flame.

Faithfully he brings true justice;
he will neither waver, nor be crushed
until true justice is established on earth,
for the islands are awaiting his law.

I, the Lord, have called you to serve the cause of right;
I have taken you by the hand and formed you;
I have appointed you as covenant of the people and light of
   nations,

to open the eyes of the blind,
to free captives from prison,
and those who live in darkness from the dungeon.

THE BAPTISM OF THE LORD/A

Responsorial Psalm   Psalm 28

℟ **The Lord will bless his people with peace.**

1. O give the Lord you sons of God,
   give the Lord glory and power;
   give the Lord the glory of his name.
   Adore the Lord in his holy court. ℟

2. The Lord's voice resounding on the waters,
   the Lord on the immensity of waters;
   the voice of the Lord, full of power,
   the voice of the Lord, full of splendour. ℟

3. The God of glory thunders.
   In his temple they all cry: "Glory!"
   The Lord sat enthroned over the flood;
   the Lord sits as king for ever. ℟

Second Reading   Acts 10:34-38

God anointed him with the Holy Spirit.

Peter addressed Cornelius and his household: "The truth I have now come to realise," he said "is that God does not have favourites, but that anybody of any nationality who fears God and does what is right is acceptable to him.

"It is true, God sent his word to the people of Israel, and it was to them that the good news of peace was brought by Jesus Christ — but Jesus Christ is Lord of all men. You must have heard about the recent happenings in Judaea; about Jesus of Nazareth and how he began in Galilee, after John had been preaching baptism. God had anointed him with the Holy Spirit and with power, and because God was with him, Jesus went about doing good and curing all who had fallen into the power of the devil."

Alleluia   Alleluia, alleluia! The heavens opened and the Father's voice resounded: "This is my Son, the Beloved. Listen to him." Alleluia! Mark 9:8

THE BAPTISM OF THE LORD/A

Gospel   Matthew 3:13-17

As soon as Jesus was baptised he saw the Spirit of God coming down on him.

Jesus came from Galilee to the Jordan to be baptised by John. John tried to dissuade him. "It is I who need baptism from you," he said "and yet you come to me!" But Jesus replied, "Leave it like this for the time being; it is fitting that we should, in this way, do all that righteousness demands." At this, John gave in to him.

As soon as Jesus was baptised he came up from the water, and suddenly the heavens opened and he saw the Spirit of God descending like a dove and coming down on him. And a voice spoke from heaven, "This is my Son, the Beloved; my favour rests on him."

Prayer over the Gifts

Lord,
we celebrate the revelation of Christ your Son
who takes away the sins of the world.
Accept our gifts
and let them become one with his sacrifice,
for he is Lord for ever and ever.

Preface

Father, all-powerful and ever-living God,
we do well always and everywhere to give you thanks.
You celebrated your new gift of baptism
by signs and wonders at the Jordan.
Your voice was heard from heaven
to awaken faith in the presence among us
of the Word made man.

Your Spirit was seen as a dove,
revealing Jesus as your servant,
and anointing him with joy as the Christ,
sent to bring to the poor
the good news of salvation.

In our unending joy we echo on earth
the song of the angels in heaven
as they praise your glory for ever:

THE BAPTISM OF THE LORD/A

Holy, holy, holy ...

Communion Antiphon   This is he of whom John said: I have seen and have given witness that this is the Son of God. John 1:32.34

Prayer after Communion

Lord,
you feed us with bread from heaven.
May we hear your Son with faith
and become your children in name and in fact.

The priest may give the Solemn Blessing as on page 153

The Cycle of Ordinary Sundays of the year now begins, and continues until the Season of Lent (see the Table of Movable Feasts on pages xii-xiii).

For the Ordinary Sundays of the Year, Cycle A, turn to page 609

SUNDAY AFTER JANUARY 6
THE BAPTISM OF THE LORD/B

> You are my Son the beloved.
> The Holy Spirit of God came down
> upon Jesus, the beloved Son of God at his
> baptism in the Jordan. The Spirit comes down
> on each one of us and helps us to live our
> christian lives so that we are faithful
> to our Baptism.

Entrance Antiphon

When the Lord had been baptised, the heavens opened, and the Spirit came down like a dove to rest on him. Then the voice of the Father thundered: This is my beloved Son, with him I am well pleased.
cf. Matthew 3:16-17.

Opening Prayer

Let us pray
  [that we will be faithful to our baptism]

Almighty, eternal God,
when the Spirit descended upon Jesus
at his baptism in the Jordan,
you revealed him as your own beloved Son.
Keep us, your children born of water and the Spirit,
faithful to our calling.

or

Father,
your only Son revealed himself to us by becoming man.
May we who share his humanity
come to share his divinity,
for he lives and reigns with you and the Holy Spirit, one God, for ever and ever.

THE BAPTISM OF THE LORD/B

or

Let us pray
   [as we listen to the voice of God's Spirit]

Father in heaven,
you revealed Christ as your Son
by the voice that spoke over the waters of Jordan.

May all who share in the sonship of Christ
follow in his path of service to man,
and reflect the glory of his kingdom
even to the ends of the earth,
for he is Lord for ever and ever.

First Reading   Isaiah 55:1-11.
Come to the water. Listen and your soul will live.

Oh, come to the water all you who are thirsty;
though you have no money, come!
Buy corn without money, and eat,
and, at no cost, wine and milk.
Why spend money on what is not bread,
your wages on what fails to satisfy?
Listen, listen to me, and you will have good things to eat
and rich food to enjoy.
Pay attention, come to me;
listen and your soul will live.

With you I will make an everlasting covenant
out of the favours promised to David.
See, I have made of you a witness to the peoples,
a leader and master of the nations.
See, you will summon a nation you never knew,
those unknown will come hurrying to you,
for the sake of the Lord your God,
of the Holy One of Israel who will glorify you.
Seek the Lord while he is still to be found,
call to him while he is still near.
Let the wicked man abandon his way,
the evil man his thoughts.
Let him turn back to the Lord who will take pity on him,
to our God who is rich in forgiving;
for my thoughts are not your thoughts,
my ways are not your ways — it is the Lord who speaks.

THE BAPTISM OF THE LORD/B

Yes, the heavens are as high above earth
as my ways are above your ways,
my thoughts above your thoughts.

Yes, as the rain and the snow come down from the heavens and do not return without watering the earth, making it yield and giving growth to provide seed for the sower and bread for the eating, so the word that goes from my mouth does not return to me empty, without carrying out my will and succeeding in what it was sent to do.

Responsorial Psalm   Isaiah 12:2-6.
R/ **With joy you will draw water from the wells of salvation.**

1. Truly God is my salvation,
   I trust, I shall not fear.
   For the Lord is my strength, my song,
   he became my saviour.
   With joy you will draw water
   from the wells of salvation. R/

2. Give thanks to the Lord, give praise to his name!
   make his mighty deeds known to the peoples,
   declare the greatness of his name. R/

3. Sing a Psalm to the Lord
   for he has done glorious deeds,
   make them known to all the earth!
   People of Zion, sing and shout for joy
   for great in your midst is the Holy One of Israel. R/

Second Reading   1 John 5:1-9
The Spirit and water and blood

Whoever believes that Jesus is the Christ
has been begotten by God;
and whoever loves the Father that begot him
loves the child whom he begets.
We can be sure that we love God's children
if we love God himself and do what he has commanded us;
this is what loving God is —
keeping his commandments;
and his commandments are not difficult,
because anyone who has been begotten by God
has already overcome the world;

THE BAPTISM OF THE LORD/B

this is the victory over the world —
our faith.
Who can overcome the world?
Only the man who believes that Jesus is the Son of God:
Jesus Christ who came by water and blood,
not with water only,
but with water and blood;
with the Spirit as another witness —
since the Spirit is the truth —
so that there are three witnesses,
the Spirit, the water and the blood,
and all three of them agree.
We accept the testimony of human witnesses,
but God's testimony is much greater,
and this is God's testimony,
given as evidence for his Son.

Alleluia Alleluia, alleluia! John saw Jesus coming towards him, and said, 'This is the Lamb of God that takes away the sins of the world.' Alleluia! John 1:29.

Gospel Mark 1:7-11

You are my Son, the Beloved; my favour rests on you.

In the course of his preaching, John the Baptist said, "Someone is following me, someone who is more powerful than I am, and I am not fit to kneel down and undo the strap of his sandals. I have baptised you with water, but he will baptise you with the Holy Spirit."

It was at this time that Jesus came from Nazareth in Galilee and was baptised in the Jordan by John. No sooner had he come up out of the water than he saw the heavens torn apart and the Spirit, like a dove, descending on him. And a voice came from heaven, "You are my Son, the Beloved; my favour rests on you."

Prayer over the Gifts

Lord,
we celebrate the revelation of Christ your Son
who takes away the sins of the world.
Accept our gifts
and let them become one with his sacrifice,
for he is Lord for ever and ever.

Preface as on page 162

THE BAPTISM OF THE LORD/B

Communion Antiphon This is he of whom John said: I have seen and have given witness that this is the Son of God. John 1:32-34.

Prayer after Communion

Lord,
you feed us with bread from heaven.
May we hear your Son with faith
and become your children in name and in fact.

The priest may give the Solemn Blessing of Christmas on page 153.

The Cycle of Ordinary Sundays of the Year now begins, and continues until the Season of Lent (see the Table of Movable Feasts on pages xii-xiii).

For the Ordinary Sundays of the Year, Cycle B, turn to page 737.

SUNDAY AFTER JANUARY 6
THE BAPTISM OF THE LORD/C

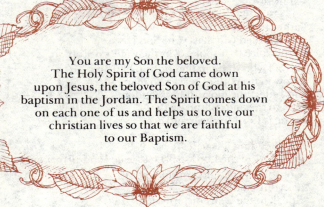

You are my Son the beloved.
The Holy Spirit of God came down
upon Jesus, the beloved Son of God at his
baptism in the Jordan. The Spirit comes down
on each one of us and helps us to live our
christian lives so that we are faithful
to our Baptism.

Entrance Antiphon   When the Lord had been baptised, the heavens opened, and the Spirit came down like a dove to rest on him. Then the voice of the Father thundered: This is my beloved Son, with him I am well pleased.
cf. Matthew 3:16-17.

Opening Prayer

Let us pray
   [that we will be faithful to our baptism]

Almighty, eternal God,
when the Spirit descended upon Jesus
at his baptism in the Jordan,
you revealed him as your own beloved Son.
Keep us, your children born of water and the Spirit,
faithful to our calling.

or

Father,
your only Son revealed himself to us by becoming man.
May we who share his humanity
come to share his divinity,
for he lives and reigns with you and the Holy Spirit, one God, for ever and ever.

THE BAPTISM OF THE LORD/C

or

Let us pray
> [as we listen to the voice of God's Spirit]

Father in heaven,
you revealed Christ as your Son
by the voice that spoke over the waters of Jordan.

May all who share in the sonship of Christ
follow in his path of service to man,
and reflect the glory of his kingdom
even to the ends of the earth,
for he is Lord for ever and ever.

First Reading   Isaiah 40:1-5. 9-11
The glory of the Lord shall be revealed and all mankind shall see it.

"Console my people, console them"
says your God.
"Speak to the heart of Jerusalem
and call to her
that her time of service is ended,
that her sin is atoned for,
that she has received from the hand of the Lord
double punishment for her crimes."

A voice cries, "Prepare in the wilderness
a way for the Lord.
Make a straight highway for our God
across the desert.
Let every valley be filled in,
every mountain and hill be laid low,
let every cliff become a plain,
and the ridges a valley;
then the glory of the Lord shall be revealed
and all mankind shall see it;
for the mouth of the Lord has spoken."

Go up on a high mountain,
joyful messenger to Zion.
Shout with a loud voice,
joyful messenger to Jerusalem.
Shout without fear,
say to the towns of Judah,
"here is your God".

THE BAPTISM OF THE LORD/C

Here is the Lord God coming with power,
his arms subduing all things to him.
The prize of his victory is with him,
his trophies all go before him.
He is like a shepherd feeding his flock,
gathering lambs in his arms,
holding them against his breast
and leading to their rest the mother ewes.

Responsorial Psalm   Psalm 103

R/ **Bless the Lord, my soul!
Lord God, how great you are!**

1. Lord God, how great you are,
   clothed in majesty and glory,
   wrapped in light as in a robe!
   You stretch out the heavens like a tent.   R/

2. Above the rains you build your dwelling.
   You make the clouds your chariot,
   you walk on the wings of the wind,
   you make the winds your messengers
   and flashing fire your servants.   R/

3. How many are your works, O Lord!
   In wisdom you have made them all.
   The earth is full of your riches.
   There is the sea, vast and wide,
   with its moving swarms past counting,
   living things great and small.   R/

4. All of these look to you
   to give them their food in due season.
   You give it, they gather it up:
   you open your hand, they have their fill.   R/

5. You take back your spirit, they die,
   returning to the dust from which they came.
   You send forth your spirit, they are created;
   and you renew the face of the earth.   R/

Second Reading   Titus 2:11-14; 3:4-7.

He saved us by means of the cleansing water of rebirth and by renewing us with the Holy Spirit.

God's grace has been revealed, and it has made salvation possible for the whole human race and taught us that what we have to do is

THE BAPTISM OF THE LORD/C

to give up everything that does not lead to God, and all our worldly ambitions; we must be self-restrained and live good and religious lives here in this present world, while we are waiting in hope for the blessing which will come from the Appearing of the glory of our great God and saviour Christ Jesus. He sacrificed himself for us in order to set us free from all wickedness and to purify a people so that it could be his very own and would have no ambition except to do good.

But when the kindness and love of God our saviour for mankind were revealed, it was not because he was concerned with any righteous actions we might have done ourselves; it was for no reason except his own compassion that he saved us, by means of the cleansing water of rebirth and by renewing us with the Holy Spirit which he has so generously poured over us through Jesus Christ our saviour. He did this so that we should be justified by his grace, to become heirs looking forward to inheriting eternal life.

Alleluia   Alleluia, alleluia! Someone is coming, said John, someone greater than I. He will baptise you with the Holy Spirit and with fire. Alleluia! Luke 3:16.

Gospel Luke 3:15-16. 21-22

While Jesus after his own baptism was at prayer, heaven opened.

A feeling of expectancy had grown among the people, who were beginning to think that John might be the Christ, so John declared before them all, "I baptise you with water, but someone is coming, someone who is more powerful than I am, and I am not fit to undo the strap of his sandals; he will baptise you with the Holy Spirit and fire."

Now when all the people had been baptised and while Jesus after his own baptism was at prayer, heaven opened and the Holy Spirit descended on him in bodily shape, like a dove. And a voice came from heaven. "You are my Son, the Beloved; my favour rests on you."

Prayer over the Gifts

Lord,
we celebrate the revelation of Christ your Son
who takes away the sins of the world.
Accept our gifts
and let them become one with his sacrifice,
for he is Lord for ever and ever.

THE BAPTISM OF THE LORD/C

Preface as on page 162.

Communion Antiphon   This is he of whom John said: I have seen and have given witness that this is the Son of God. John 1:32-34.

Prayer after Communion

Lord,
you feed us with bread from heaven.
May we hear your Son with faith
and become your children in name and in fact.

The priest may give the Solemn Blessing of Christmas on page 153.

The Cycle of Ordinary Sundays of the Year now begins, and continues until the Season of Lent (see the Table of Movable Feasts on pages xii-xiii).

For the Ordinary Sundays of the Year, Cycle C, turn to page 867.

The Season of Lent

The Season of Lent

LENT like Advent is a season of *preparation*. Its austerity motivated by our sorrow for sin is tempered by the joy we experience as people who have been redeemed by the passion, death and resurrection of the Lord Jesus. Lent puts before us the whole mystery of salvation through which God's merciful love has been revealed in Jesus Christ. 'God loved us with so much love that he was generous with his mercy: when we were dead through our sins, he brought us to life with Christ — it is through grace that you have been saved — and raised us up with him and gave us a place with him in heaven, in Christ Jesus. This was to show for all ages to come, through his goodness towards us in Christ Jesus, how infinitely rich he is in grace. Because it is by grace that you have been saved, through faith; not by anything of your own, but by a gift from God; not by anything that you have done, so that nobody can claim the credit. We are God's work of art, created in Christ Jesus to live the good life as from the beginning he had meant us to live it. Ephesians 2:4-10.

Lent is a time of *anticipation* and *waiting* for the coming Easter celebration. The full meaning of Lent is to be found in its consummation in the three days [triduum] of Holy Thursday, Good Friday and the Easter Vigil on Holy Saturday. The rigours of Lent are undergone to prepare us for the triumphant emergence of Christ from the tomb. In Lent we are reminded that we must die to ourselves if we are to rise with Christ. The Gospel message of Lent is clear: 'if we die with him we shall rise with him'.

Lent calls us to a renewed awareness of our vocation as christians. We have all fallen short of our ideal to follow him and we have each gone our own foolish ways. Now we have to look again at the fabric of our lives. We realise that the only true life and spiritual growth is through the cross. We are invited to take up our cross daily and follow him. Lent reminds us that this is not an easy way but it is the only one. We *renounce* our selfishness for material possessions which has clouded our vision of Christ in order to *announce* the power of his resurrection. Every renunciation is for annunciation. Our death to self is an ongoing process into the life of Christ.

In recent years the Church has relaxed its laws on the number of fast days during Lent but has insisted even more on the need

THE SEASON OF LENT

to develop our spiritual lives through the renunciation of those things which breed selfishness and spiritual apathy. Lent helps us to get our priorities right so that the hidden life of Christ within us may shine forth more fully. 'Out of his infinite glory, may he give you the power through his Spirit for your hidden self to grow strong, so that Christ may live in your hearts through faith, and then, planted in love and built on love, you will with all the saints have strength to grasp the breadth and the length, the height and the depth; until knowing the love of Christ, which is beyond all knowledge, you are filled with the utter fullness of God'. Ephesians 3:16-19.

Lent encourages us to undergo a *change of heart*. This change of heart is what the Jews meant by the word *repentance*. We have to change the direction of our lives and turn in trust and love to God who will receive us with the love of a father for his prodigal children. Even though we are reconciled to God in Christ nevertheless the effects of sin are still with us. We are a healed people who bear the scars of sin. The Lenten liturgy puts before us many stories of healing and through the Holy Spirit we come to our heavenly Father for healing so that we may renew our sorrow for sin and deepen our gratitude for all he has done for us. We have confidence that God will reshape our lives so that we may seek his kingdom first and his righteousness.

Lent is also a time of *forgiveness*. 'Have mercy on me, God, in your kindness'. Psalm 51:1. Our God is a Father who forgives us and gives us strength as his children to lead a new life. Our sorrow for sin is set against the background of God's loving forgiveness. We too must forgive each other from our hearts if we are to be sincere when we recite the words of the Lord's prayer 'forgive us our trespasses as we forgive those who trespass against us'. 'Bear with one another; forgive each other as soon as a quarrel begins. The Lord has forgiven you; now you must do the same.' Colossians 3:13.

Lent is a season of *concern for others*. We are encouraged by the Church's liturgy during Lent to remember that we are our brother's keeper. Lent is a season when we are taught to develop our social conscience not only about the Third World but also about those in need in our own neighbourhood. Almsgiving is a feature of Lent in which our christian concern for others is shown through compassionate service. We should really show that concern for others all through our lives but Lent comes

THE SEASON OF LENT

along to remind us of the kind of caring lives we should be living as christians.

Lent is a time of *prayer*. Prayer costs us nothing less than everything. We are invited to a more intense form of personal and communal prayer which finds its climax in the General Intercessions of the Good Friday Liturgy.

Through prayer we reflect on our lives in relation to the life of Christ. We offer our sufferings in union with his sufferings for it is by his wounds that we are healed. *Mortification* means dying to self in order to live in him. Each day we die a little bit more to self by mortifying our selfish appetites. In this way we conquer the temptations of the flesh in order to store up for ourselves a treasure in heaven. 'The troubles which are soon over, though they weigh little, train us for the carrying of a weight of eternal glory which is out of all proportion to them. And so we have no eyes for things that are visible, but only for things that are invisible; for visible things last only for a time, and the invisible things are eternal.' 2 Corinthians 4:17-18.

Above all Lent is a time for *renewing our baptismal life*. The christian life is initiated at baptism but the process will not be completed until we rise with Christ on the last day. Baptism is the great sacrament by which we undergo death to this world in order to live the life of the resurrection. In the early christian Church those to be baptised entered the waters of the baptistery from one end, were completely submerged, and rose to be clothed in white at the other end thus showing that they had left the old life behind them. 'You have been taught that when we were baptised in Christ Jesus we were baptised in his death; in other words, when we were baptised we went into the tomb with him and joined him in death, so that as Christ was raised from the dead by the Father's glory, we too might live a new life.' Romans 6:3-4. We have already undergone death and resurrection when we emerge from the baptismal font and we rejoice in the new life given to us in Christ.

Lent stresses the *public nature of baptism* because baptism is a public event. The reformed Roman liturgy highlights the baptismal elements in Lent and the Easter vigil is centred on the solemn celebration of adult baptism. The ancient practices of preparing catechumens during Lent and of baptising them at Easter is very much to the forefront of the Lenten liturgy. The reformed Roman liturgy makes provision on the third, fourth

THE SEASON OF LENT

and fifth Sundays of Lent for *scrutinies* when candidates for baptism can be examined on their progress in understanding and accepting the christian faith and practice.

During Lent the Church reminds us all of *renewal* by inviting us to renew our baptismal vows. Baptism is not a past event in our lives which is over and done with once we are baptised. Rather it places upon us the task of entering more deeply in our daily lives into Christ's death and resurrection and so gradually becoming what we are, brothers and sisters of him who is one with us.

Lent as well as being a period of preparation for the newly baptised was also a time when those who were guilty of serious crimes and were public sinners were expected to undergo a similar preparation for their *reconciliation* to the Church on Holy Thursday. We prepare also through prayer and fasting so that the renewal of our baptismal vows at the Easter Vigil may be a complete renewal of ourselves for the sake of the mission of the Church in the world. In this way the Church is renewed. 'This is the night when christians everywhere, washed clean of sin and freed from all defilement, are restored to grace and grow together in holiness.' Exultet.

Baptism therefore is not something which happens only to individuals but is above all a *public* event of *renewal* by which the Church reaffirms her reason for existence. 'Rejoice, O Mother Church, exult in glory! The risen Saviour shines upon you! Let this place resound with joy, echoing the mighty song of all God's people!' Exultet.

Lent is the time when the Church re-dedicates herself to the task of being the body of Christ. The Lenten readings are full of texts from the Old Testament which refer to the formation of God's people. They remind us that God is forever forming his people anew. Now in Lent the Church enters into the celebration of Christ's death and resurrection so that she too may be renewed. The spirit of Christ is constantly renewing us so that we can renew the face of the earth. When we as his people have fallen short of God's plan for us in Christ then we can trust that he will forgive us and renew us yet again.

The various aspects of Lent as a baptismal season are beautifully set out for us in the Gospels for the first and second Sundays of Lent. On the first Sunday, Christ in the desert refuses to seek his happiness in the riches of the world and affirms his trust and submission to the Father. On the second

Sunday the transfigured Christ accompanied by Moses and Elijah is revealed to his apostles as Israel's glory and ours. The life, death and resurrection of Christ are to become our life-style so that we may enter with him into glory. Our pilgrimage in the footsteps of the Master calls for constant vigilance, prayer and mortification as he leads us towards our heavenly Jerusalem. Our whole life is, like the season of Lent, waiting and preparing until the day when we will be with the Lord in his glory. This is the full meaning of christian baptism.

ASH WEDNESDAY

Turn away from sin and be faithful
to the Gospel.
The season of Lent reminds us that
we must change the direction of our lives,
turn away from sin and walk in the path of
the Gospel. Repentance means that
we must constantly take stock of our lives lest
we should become too complacent and so lose
our first fervour. Even though we have been
baptised we are still inclined to sin.
During the season of Lent we need to have
a change of heart and put the message of
Christ in the forefront of our lives.

Entrance Antiphon   Lord, you are merciful to all, and hate nothing you have created. You overlook the sins of men to bring them to repentance. You are the Lord our God.

cf. Wisdom 11:24-25.27

The penitential rite is replaced by the giving of ashes, and there is no Gloria.

Opening Prayer

Let us pray
   [for the grace to keep Lent faithfully]

Lord,
protect us in our struggle against evil.
As we begin the discipline of Lent,
make this season holy by our self-denial.

or

Let us pray
   [in quiet remembrance of our need for redemption]

Father in heaven,
the light of your truth bestows sight

ASH WEDNESDAY/A/B/C

to the darkness of sinful eyes.
May this season of repentance
bring us the blessing of your forgiveness
and the gift of your light.

First Reading   Joel 2:12-18
Let your hearts be broken, not your garments torn.

"Now, now — it is the Lord who speaks —
come back to me with all your heart,
fasting, weeping, mourning."
Let your hearts be broken, not your garments torn,
turn to the Lord your God again,
for he is all tenderness and compassion,
slow to anger, rich in graciousness,
and ready to relent.
Who knows if he will not turn again, will not relent,
will not leave a blessing as he passes,
oblation and libation
for the Lord your God?
Sound the trumpet in Zion!
Order a fast,
proclaim a solemn assembly,
call the people together,
summon the community,
assemble the elders,
gather the children,
even the infants at the breast.
Let the bridegroom leave his bedroom
and the bride her alcove.
Between vestibule and altar let the priests,
the ministers of the Lord, lament.
Let them say,
"Spare your people, Lord!
Do not make your heritage a thing of shame,
a byword for the nations.
Why should it be said among the nations,
'Where is their God?' "
Then the Lord, jealous on behalf of his land,
took pity on his people.

Responsorial Psalm   Psalm 50

℟ **Have mercy on us, O Lord, for we have sinned.**

ASH WEDNESDAY/A/B/C

1. Have mercy on me, God, in your kindness.
   In your compassion blot out my offence.
   O wash me more and more from my guilt
   and cleanse me from my sin. R/

2. My offences truly I know them;
   my sin is always before me.
   Against you, you alone, have I sinned:
   what is evil in your sight I have done. R/

3. A pure heart create for me, O God,
   put a steadfast spirit within me.
   Do not cast me away from your presence,
   nor deprive me of your holy spirit. R/

4. Give me again the joy of your help;
   with a spirit of fervour sustain me,
   O Lord, open my lips
   and my mouth shall declare your praise. R/

Second Reading 2 Corinthians 5:20-6:2

Be reconciled to God ... now is the favourable time.

We are ambassadors for Christ; it is as though God were appealing through us, and the appeal that we make in Christ's name is: be reconciled to God. For our sake God made the sinless one into sin, so that in him we might become the goodness of God. As his fellow workers, we beg you once again not to neglect the grace of God that you have received. For he says: At the favourable time, I have listened to you; on the day of salvation I came to your help. Well, now is the favourable time; this is the day of salvation.

Acclamation Praise to you, O Christ, king of eternal glory!
A pure heart create for me, O God, and give me again the joy of your help.
Praise to you, O Christ, king of eternal glory!
Psalm 56:12.14

Gospel Matthew 6:1-6.16-18

Your Father who sees all that is done in secret will reward you.

Jesus said to his disciples:

"Be careful not to parade your good deeds before men to attract their notice; by doing this you will lose all reward from your Father in heaven. So when you give alms, do not have it

ASH WEDNESDAY/A/B/C

trumpeted before you; this is what the hypocrites do in the synagogues and in the streets to win men's admiration. I tell you solemnly, they have had their reward. But when you give alms, your left hand must not know what your right is doing; your almsgiving must be secret, and your Father who sees all that is done in secret will reward you.

"And when you pray, do not imitate the hypocrites: they love to say their prayers standing up in the synagogues and at the street corners for people to see them. I tell you solemnly, they have had their reward. But when you pray, go to your private room and, when you have shut your door, pray to your Father who is in that secret place, and your Father who sees all that is done in secret will reward you.

"When you fast do not put on a gloomy look as the hypocrites do: they pull long faces to let men know they are fasting. I tell you solemnly, they have had their reward. But when you fast, put oil on your head and wash your face, so that no one will know you are fasting except your Father who sees all that is done in secret; and your Father who sees all that is done in secret will reward you."

Blessing and Giving of Ashes

After the homily the priest joins his hands and says:

Dear friends in Christ,
let us ask our Father
to bless these ashes
which we will use
as the mark of our repentance.

All pray silently.

Lord,
bless the sinner who asks for your forgiveness
and bless ✠ all those who receive these ashes.
May they keep this lenten season
in preparation for the joy of Easter.

or

Lord,
bless these ashes ✠
by which we show that we are dust.
Pardon our sins
and keep us faithful to the discipline of Lent,

ASH WEDNESDAY/A/B/C

for you do not want sinners to die
but to live with the risen Christ,
who reigns with you for ever and ever.

He sprinkles the ashes with holy water.
The priest then places ashes on those who come forward, saying to each:

Turn away from sin and be faithful to the gospel. Mark 1:15

or

Remember, man, you are dust
and to dust you will return. cf. Genesis 3:19

Meanwhile some of the following antiphons or other appropriate songs are sung.

Antiphon 1

Come back to the Lord with all your heart;
leave the past in ashes,
and turn to God with tears and fasting,
for he is slow to anger and ready to forgive. cf. Joel 2:13

Antiphon 2

Let the priests and ministers of the Lord
lament before his altar, and say:
Spare us, Lord; spare your people!
Do not let us die for we are crying out to you. cf. Joel 2:17;

Antiphon 3

Lord, take away our wickedness. Psalm 50:3

These may be repeated after each verse of Psalm 50, Have mercy on me, God, see page 185

Responsory

Direct our hearts to better things, O Lord;
heal our sin and ignorance.
Lord, do not face us suddenly with death,
but give us time to repent. Baruch 3:5

℟ **Turn to us with mercy, Lord; we have sinned against you.**

℣ Help us, God our saviour, rescue us for the honour of your name. Psalm 78:9

℟ **Turn to us with mercy, Lord; we have sinned against you.**

ASH WEDNESDAY/A/B/C

After the giving of ashes the priest washes his hands; the rite concludes with the prayer of the faithful.
The Creed is not said.

Prayer over the Gifts

Lord,
help us to resist temptation
by our lenten works of charity and penance.
By this sacrifice
may we be prepared to celebrate
the death and resurrection of Christ our Saviour
and be cleansed from sin and renewed in spirit.

Preface

Father, all-powerful and ever-living God,
we do well always and everywhere to give you thanks.

Through our observance of Lent
you correct our faults and raise our minds to you,
you help us to grow in holiness,
and offer us the reward of everlasting life
through Jesus Christ our Lord.

Through him the angels and all the choirs of heaven
worship in awe before your presence.
May our voices be one with theirs
as they sing with joy the hymn of your glory:

Holy, holy, holy ...

Communion Antiphon

The man who meditates day and night on the law of the Lord will yield fruit in due season. Psalm 1:2-3.

Prayer after Communion

Lord,
through this communion
may our lenten penance give you glory
and bring us your protection.

FIRST SUNDAY OF LENT/A

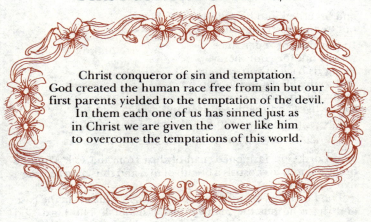

Christ conqueror of sin and temptation.
God created the human race free from sin but our
first parents yielded to the temptation of the devil.
In them each one of us has sinned just as
in Christ we are given the ower like him
to overcome the temptations of this world.

Entrance Antiphon   When he calls to me, I will answer; I will rescue him and give him honour. Long life and contentment will be his.

Psalm 90:15-16

There is no Gloria today.

Opening Prayer

Let us pray
   [that this Lent will help us reproduce in our lives
   the self-sacrificing love of Christ]

Father,
through our observance of Lent,
help us to understand the meaning
of your Son's death and resurrection,
and teach us to reflect it in our lives.

or

Let us pray
   [at the beginning of Lent
   for the spirit of repentance]

Lord our God,
you formed man from the clay of the earth

FIRST SUNDAY OF LENT/A

and breathed into him the spirit of life,
but he turned from your face and sinned.

In this time of repentance
we call out for your mercy.
Bring us back to you
and to the life your Son won for us
by his death on the cross,
for he lives and reigns for ever and ever.

First Reading   Genesis 2:7-9; 3:1-7
The creation and sin of our first parents.

The Lord God fashioned man of dust from the soil. Then he breathed into his nostrils a breath of life, and thus man became a living being.

The Lord God planted a garden in Eden which is in the east, and there he put the man he had fashioned. The Lord God caused to spring up from the soil every kind of tree enticing to look at and good to eat, with the tree of life and the tree of knowledge of good and evil in the middle of the garden.

The serpent was the most subtle of all the wild beasts that the Lord God had made. It asked the woman, "Did God really say you were not to eat from any of the trees in the garden?" The woman answered the serpent, "We may eat the fruit of the trees in the garden. But of the fruit of the tree in the middle of the garden God said, 'You must not eat it, nor touch it, under pain of death.'" Then the serpent said to the woman: "No! You will not die! God knows in fact that on the day you eat it your eyes will be opened and you will be like gods, knowing good and evil." The woman saw that the tree was good to eat and pleasing to the eye, and that it was desirable for the knowledge that it could give. So she took some of its fruit and ate it. She gave some also to her husband who was with her, and he ate it. Then the eyes of both of them were opened and they realised that they were naked. So they sewed fig-leaves together to make themselves loin-cloths.

Responsorial Psalm   Psalm 50

℟ **Have mercy on us, O Lord, for we have sinned.**

1. Have mercy on me, God, in your kindness.
   In your compassion blot out my offence.
   O wash me more and more from my guilt
   and cleanse me from my sin.   ℟

FIRST SUNDAY OF LENT/A

2 My offences truly I know them;
my sin is always before me.
Against you, you alone, have I sinned;
what is evil in your sight I have done. R/

3 A pure heart create for me, O God,
put a steadfast spirit within me.
Do not cast me away from your presence,
nor deprive me of your holy spirit. R/

4 Give me again the joy of your help;
with a spirit of fervour sustain me.
O Lord, open my lips
and my mouth shall declare your praise. R/

Second Reading   Romans 5:12-19
However great the number of sins committed, grace was even greater.

> Sin entered the world through one man, and through sin death, and thus death has spread through the whole human race because everyone has sinned.

Sin existed in the world long before the Law was given. There was no law and so no one could be accused of the sin of "law-breaking", yet death reigned over all from Adam to Moses, even though their sin, unlike that of Adam, was not a matter of breaking a law.

Adam prefigured the One to come, but the gift itself considerably outweighed the fall. If it is certain that through one man's fall so many died, it is even more certain that divine grace, coming through the one man, Jesus Christ, came to so many as an abundant free gift. The results of the gift also outweigh the results of one man's sin: for after one single fall came judgement with a verdict of condemnation, now after many falls comes grace with its verdict of acquittal.

> If it is certain that death reigned over everyone as the consequence of one man's fall, it is even more certain that one man, Jesus Christ, will cause everyone to reign in life who receives the free gift that he does not deserve, of being made righteous. Again, as one man's fall brought condemnation on everyone, so the good act of one man brings everyone life and

FIRST SUNDAY OF LENT/A

makes them justified. As by one man's disobedience many were made sinners, so by one man's obedience many will be made righteous.

Acclamation   Praise to you, O Christ, king of eternal glory!
Man does not live on bread alone but on every word that comes from the mouth of God.
Praise to you, O Christ, king of eternal glory!

Matthew 4:4.

Gospel   Matthew 4:1-11.

Jesus fasts for forty days and is tempted.

Jesus was led by the Spirit out into the wilderness to be tempted by the devil. He fasted for forty days and forty nights, after which he was very hungry, and the tempter came and said to him, "If you are the Son of God, tell these stones to turn into loaves". But he replied, "Scripture says:
Man does not live on bread alone
but on every word that comes from the mouth of God".
The devil then took him to the holy city and made him stand on the parapet of the Temple. "If you are the Son of God" he said "throw yourself down; for scripture says:
He will put you in his angels' charge,
and they will support you on their hands
in case you hurt your foot against a stone".
Jesus said to him, "Scripture also says:
You must not put the Lord your God to the test".
Next, taking him to a very high mountain, the devil showed him all the kingdoms of the world and their splendour. "I will give you all these," he said, "if you fall at my feet and worship me."
Then Jesus replied, "Be off, Satan! For scripture says:
You must worship the Lord your God,
and serve him alone."
Then the devil left him, and angels appeared and looked after him.

Prayer over the Gifts

Lord,
make us worthy to bring you these gifts.
May this sacrifice
help to change our lives.

FIRST SUNDAY OF LENT/A

Preface

The priest may use the following Preface, or Preface of Lent I or II, page 560.

Father, all-powerful and ever-living God,
we do well always and everywhere to give you thanks
through Jesus Christ our Lord.

His fast of forty days
makes this a holy season of self-denial.
By rejecting the devil's temptations
he has taught us
to rid ourselves of the hidden corruption of evil,
and so to share his paschal meal in purity of heart,
until we come to its fulfilment
in the promised land of heaven.

Now we join the angels and the saints
as they sing their unending hymn of praise:

Holy, holy, holy ..

Communion Antiphon

Man does not live on bread alone, but on every word that comes from the mouth of God. Matthew 4:4

or

The Lord will overshadow you, and you will find refuge under his wings. Psalm 90:4

Prayer after Communion

Father,
you increase our faith and hope,
you deepen our love in this communion.
Help us to live by your words
and to seek Christ, our bread of life,
who is Lord for ever and ever.

SECOND SUNDAY OF LENT/A

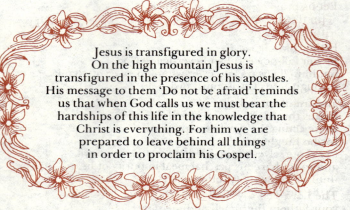

Jesus is transfigured in glory.
On the high mountain Jesus is
transfigured in the presence of his apostles.
His message to them 'Do not be afraid' reminds
us that when God calls us we must bear the
hardships of this life in the knowledge that
Christ is everything. For him we are
prepared to leave behind all things
in order to proclaim his Gospel.

Entrance Antiphon Remember your mercies, Lord, your tenderness from ages past. Do not let our enemies triumph over us; O God, deliver Israel from all her distress.
Psalm 24:6.3.22.

or

My heart has prompted me to seek your face; I seek it, Lord; do not hide from me.
Psalm 26:8-9.

There is no Gloria today.

Opening Prayer

Let us pray
   [for the grace to respond
   to the Word of God]

God our Father,
help us to hear your Son.
Enlighten us with your word,
that we may find the way to your glory.
or

SECOND SUNDAY OF LENT/A

Let us pray
  [in this season of Lent
  for the gift of integrity]
Father of light,
in you is found no shadow of change
but only the fullness of life and limitless truth.

Open our hearts to the voice of your Word
and free us from the original darkness that shadows our vision.
Return our sight that we may look upon your Son
who calls us to repentance and a change of heart,
for he lives and reigns with you for ever and ever.

First Reading   Genesis 12:1-4a
The call of Abraham, father of the People of God.

The Lord said to Abram, "Leave your country, your family and your father's house, for the land I will show you. I will make you a great nation; I will bless you and make your name so famous that it will be used as a blessing.
"I will bless those who bless you:
I will curse those who slight you.
All the tribes of the earth
shall bless themselves by you."
So Abram went as the Lord told him.

Responsorial Psalm   Psalm 32

℟ **May your love be upon us, O Lord,
as we place all our hope in you.**

1. The word of the Lord is faithful
   and all his works to be trusted.
   The Lord loves justice and right
   and fills the earth with his love. ℟
2. The Lord looks on those who revere him,
   on those who hope in his love,
   to rescue their souls from death,
   to keep them alive in famine. ℟
3. Our soul is waiting for the Lord.
   The Lord is our help and our shield.
   May your love be upon us, O Lord,
   as we place all our hope in you. ℟

SECOND SUNDAY OF LENT/A

Second Reading   2 Timothy 1:8-10
God calls and enlightens us.

With me, bear the hardships for the sake of the Good News, relying on the power of God who saved us and called us to be holy — not because of anything we ourselves have done but for his own purpose and by his own grace. This grace had already been granted to us, in Christ Jesus, before the beginning of time, but it has only been revealed by the Appearing of our saviour Christ Jesus. He abolished death, and he has proclaimed life and immortality through the Good News.

Acclamation
Glory and praise to you, O Christ!
From the bright cloud the Father's voice was heard: "This is my Son, the Beloved. Listen to him." Glory and praise to you, O Christ!

Matthew 17:5.

Gospel   Matthew 17:1-9

His face shone like the sun.

Jesus took with him Peter and James and his brother John and led them up a high mountain where they could be alone. There in their presence he was transfigured; his face shone like the sun and his clothes became as white as the light. Suddenly Moses and Elijah appeared to them; they were talking with him. Then Peter spoke to Jesus. "Lord," he said "it is wonderful for us to be here; if you wish, I will make three tents here, one for you, one for Moses and one for Elijah." He was still speaking when suddenly a bright cloud covered them with shadow, and from the cloud there came a voice which said, "This is my Son, the Beloved; he enjoys my favour. Listen to him." When they heard this, the disciples fell on their faces, overcome with fear. But Jesus came up and touched them. "Stand up," he said "do not be afraid." And when they raised their eyes they saw no one but only Jesus.

As they came down from the mountain Jesus gave them this order, "Tell no one about the vision until the Son of Man has risen from the dead."

SECOND SUNDAY OF LENT/A

Prayer over the Gifts

Lord,
make us holy.
May this eucharist take away our sins
that we may be prepared
to celebrate the resurrection.

Preface

The priest may use the following Preface, or Preface of Lent I or II, page 560.

Father, all-powerful and ever-living God,
we do well always and everywhere to give you thanks
through Jesus Christ our Lord.

On your holy mountain he revealed himself in glory
in the presence of his disciples.
He had already prepared them for his approaching death.
He wanted to teach them through the Law and the Prophets
that the promised Christ had first to suffer
and so come to the glory of his resurrection.

In our unending joy we echo on earth
the song of the angels in heaven
as they praise your glory for ever:

Holy, holy, holy . . .

Communion Antiphon

This is my Son, my beloved, in whom is all my delight: listen to him.

Matthew 17:5

Prayer after Communion

Lord,
we give thanks for these holy mysteries
which bring to us here on earth
a share in the life to come,
through Christ our Lord.

THIRD SUNDAY OF LENT/A

Christ, the Spring of Life.
Through baptism Christ becomes within us a source
of the living waters of grace. Through the
Holy Spirit the love of God is poured into
our hearts and our spiritual thirst is quenched.
We really come alive. We become in our turn
the wells of God's goodness at which
people will drink.

Entrance Antiphon My eyes are ever fixed on the Lord, for he releases my feet from the snare. O look at me and be merciful, for I am wretched and alone. Psalm 24:15-16.

or

I will prove my holiness through you. I will gather you from the ends of the earth; I will pour clean water on you and wash away all your sins. I will give you a new spirit within you, says the Lord.

Ezekiel 36:23-26

There is no Gloria today.

Opening Prayer
Let us pray
   [for confidence in the love of God
   and the strength to overcome all our weakness]

Father,
you have taught us to overcome our sins
by prayer, fasting and works of mercy.
When we are discouraged by our weakness,

THIRD SUNDAY OF LENT/A

give us confidence in your love.

or

Let us pray
[to the Father and ask him
to form a new heart within us]

God of all compassion, Father of all goodness,
to heal the wounds our sins and selfishness bring upon us
you bid us turn to fasting, prayer, and sharing with our
  brothers.
We acknowledge our sinfulness, our guilt is ever before us:
when our weakness causes discouragement,
let your compassion fill us with hope
and lead us through a Lent of repentance to the beauty of
  Easter joy.

First Reading Exodus 17:3-7
Give us water to drink.

Tormented by thirst, the people complained against Moses. "Why did you bring us out of Egypt?" they said. "Was it so that I should die of thirst, my children too, and my cattle?" Moses appealed to the Lord. "How am I to deal with this people?" he said. "A little more and they will stone me!" The Lord said to Moses, "Take with you some of the elders of Israel and move on to the forefront of the people; take in your hand the staff with which you struck the river, and go. I shall be standing before you there on the rock, at Horeb. You must strike the rock, and water will flow from it for the people to drink." This is what Moses did, in the sight of the elders of Israel. The place was named Massah and Meribah because of the grumbling of the sons of Israel and because they put the Lord to the test by saying, "Is the Lord with us, or not?"

Responsorial Psalm Psalm 94

R̸ **O that today you would listen to his voice:**
   'Harden not your hearts.'

1. Come, ring out our joy to the Lord;
   hail the rock who saves us.
   Let us come before him, giving thanks,
   with songs let us hail the Lord. R̸

THIRD SUNDAY OF LENT/A

2. Come in; let us bow and bend low;
   let us kneel before the God who made us
   for he is our God and we
   the people who belong to his pasture,
   the flock that is led by his hand. R⁄

3. O that today you would listen to his voice!
   "Harden not your hearts as at Meribah,
   as on that day at Massah in the desert
   when your fathers put me to the test;
   when they tried me, though they saw my work." R⁄

Second Reading   Romans 5:1-2. 5-8

The love of God has been poured into our hearts by the Holy Spirit which has been given us.

Through our Lord Jesus Christ by faith we are judged righteous and at peace with God, since it is by faith and through Jesus that we have entered this state of grace in which we can boast about looking forward to God's glory. This hope is not deceptive, because the love of God has been poured into our hearts by the Holy Spirit which has been given us. We were still helpless when at his appointed moment Christ died for sinful men. It is not easy to die even for a good man — though of course for someone really worthy, a man might be prepared to die — but what proves that God loves us is that Christ died for us while we were still sinners.

Acclamation   Glory to you, O Christ, you are the Word of God!
Lord, you are really the saviour of the world; give me the living water, so that I may never get thirsty.
Glory to you, O Christ, you are the Word of God!
                                                    John 4:42.15

Gospel   John 4:5-42

A spring of water welling up to eternal life.

Jesus came to the Samaritan town called Sychar, near the land that Jacob gave to his son Joseph. Joseph's well is there and Jesus, tired by the journey, sat straight down by the well. It was about the sixth hour. When a Samaritan woman came to draw water, Jesus said to her, "Give me a drink." His disciples had gone into the town to buy food. The Samaritan woman said to

THIRD SUNDAY OF LENT/A

him, "What? You are a Jew and you ask me, a Samaritan, for a drink?" — Jews, in fact, do not associate with Samaritans. Jesus replied:
"If you only knew what God is offering
and who it is that is saying to you:
'Give me a drink',
you would have been the one to ask,
and he would have given you living water."
"You have no bucket, sir," she answered, "and the well is deep: how would you get this living water? Are you a greater man than our father Jacob who gave us this well and drank from it himself with his sons and his cattle?" Jesus replied:
"Whoever drinks this water
will get thirsty again:
but anyone who drinks the water that I shall give
will never be thirsty again;
the water that I shall give
will turn into a spring inside him, welling up to eternal life."
 "Sir," said the woman, "give me some of that water, so that I may never get thirsty and never have to come here again to draw water."

"Go and call your husband," said Jesus to her "and come back here."

The woman answered, "I have no husband." He said to her, "You are right to say, 'I have no husband'; for although you have had five, the one you have now is not your husband. You spoke the truth there."

"I see you are a prophet, sir" said the woman. "Our fathers worshipped on this mountain, while you say that Jerusalem is the place where one ought to worship." Jesus said:
"Believe me, woman, the hour is coming
when you will worship the Father
neither on this mountain nor in Jerusalem.
You worship what you do not know;
we worship what we do know;
for salvation comes from the Jews.
But the hour will come — in fact it is here already —
when true worshippers will worship the Father in spirit and truth:

THIRD SUNDAY OF LENT/A

that is the kind of worshipper
the Father wants.
God is spirit,
and those who worship
must worship in spirit and truth."

The woman said to him, "I know that Messiah — that is, Christ — is coming; and when he comes he will tell us everything." "I who am speaking to you," said Jesus, "I am he." At this point his disciples returned, and were surprised to find him speaking to a woman, though none of them asked, "What do you want from her?" or, "Why are you talking to her?" The woman put down her water jar and hurried back to the town to tell the people, "Come and see a man who has told me everything I ever did; I wonder if he is the Christ?" This brought people out of the town and they started walking towards him.

Meanwhile, the disciples were urging him, "Rabbi, do have something to eat"; but he said, "I have food to eat that you do not know about." So the disciples asked one another. "Has someone been bringing him food?" But Jesus said:

"My food
is to do the will of the one who sent me,
and to complete his work.
Have you not got a saying:
Four months and then the harvest?
Well, I tell you:
Look around you, look at the fields;
already they are white, ready for harvest!
Already the reaper is being paid his wages,
already he is bringing in the grain for eternal life,
and thus sower and reaper rejoice together.
For here the proverb holds good:
one sows, another reaps;
I sent you to reap
a harvest you had not worked for.
Others worked for it;
and you have come into the rewards of their trouble."

Many Samaritans of that town had believed in him on the strength of the woman's testimony when she said, "He told me all I have ever done," so, when the Samaritans came up to him, they begged him to stay with them. He stayed for two days, and when he spoke to them many more came to believe; and they said to the woman, "Now we no longer believe because of what you told us; we have heard him ourselves and we know that he really is the saviour of the world."

Prayer over the Gifts

Lord,
by the grace of this sacrifice
may we who ask forgiveness
be ready to forgive one another.

Preface

Father, all-powerful and ever-living God,
we do well always and everywhere to give you thanks
through Jesus Christ our Lord.
When he asked the woman of Samaria for water to drink
Christ had already prepared for her the gift of faith.
In his thirst to receive her faith
he awakened in her heart the fire of your love.

With thankful praise,
in company with the angels,
we glorify the wonders of your power:

Holy, holy, holy . . .

Communion Antiphon

Whoever drinks the water that I shall give him, says the Lord, will have a spring inside him, welling up for eternal life. John 4:13-14.

Prayer after Communion

Lord,
in sharing this sacrament
may we receive your forgiveness
and be brought together in unity and peace.

FOURTH SUNDAY OF LENT/A

Christ our Shepherd and King.
Christ is descended from the line of David,
a shepherd, who was anointed King by Samuel.
Christ is our King who guides us with the
tender service of a shepherd.
With him by our side we shall want for nothing even
though we walk in the valley of darkness.

Entrance Antiphon   Rejoice, Jerusalem! Be glad for her, you who love her; rejoice with her, you who mourned for her, and you will find contentment at her consoling breasts.

cf. Isaiah 66:10-11.

There is no Gloria today.

Opening Prayer

Let us pray
  [for a greater faith and love]

Father of peace,
we are joyful in your Word,
your Son Jesus Christ,
who reconciles us to you.
Let us hasten toward Easter
with the eagerness of faith and love.

or

Let us pray
  [that by growing in love this Lenten season
  we may bring the peace of Christ to our world]

God our Father,
your Word, Jesus Christ, spoke peace to a sinful world

FOURTH SUNDAY OF LENT/A

and brought mankind the gift of reconciliation
by the suffering and death he endured.

Teach us, the people who bear his name,
to follow the example he gave us:
may our faith, hope, and charity
turn hatred to love, conflict to peace, death to eternal life.

First Reading   1 Samuel 16:1.6-7.10-13.
David is anointed king of Israel.

The Lord said to Samuel, "Fill your horn with oil and go. I am sending you to Jesse of Bethlehem, for I have chosen myself a king among his sons." When Samuel arrived, he caught sight of Eliab and thought, "Surely the Lord's anointed one stands there before him," but the Lord said to Samuel, "Take no notice of his appearance or his height for I have rejected him; God does not see as man sees; man looks at appearances but the Lord looks at the heart." Jesse presented his seven sons to Samuel, but Samuel said to Jesse, "The Lord has not chosen these." He then asked Jesse, "Are these all the sons you have?" He answered, "There is still one left, the youngest; he is out looking after the sheep." Then Samuel said to Jesse, 'Send for him; we will not sit down to eat until he comes." Jesse had him sent for, a boy of fresh complexion, with fine eyes and pleasant bearing. The Lord said, "Come, anoint him, for this is the one." At this, Samuel took the horn of oil and anointed him where he stood with his brothers; and the spirit of the Lord seized on David and stayed with him from that day on.

Responsorial Psalm   Psalm 22

℞ **The Lord is my shepherd;
there is nothing I shall want.**

1. The Lord is my shepherd;
   there is nothing I shall want.
   Fresh and green are the pastures
   where he gives me repose.
   Near restful waters he leads me,
   to revive my drooping spirit. ℞

2. He guides me along the right path;
   he is true to his name.
   If I should walk in the valley of darkness

FOURTH SUNDAY OF LENT/A

    no evil would I fear.
    You are there with your crook and your staff;
    with these you give me comfort. ℟

3. You have prepared a banquet for me
   in the sight of my foes.
   My head you have anointed with oil;
   my cup is overflowing. ℟

4. Surely goodness and kindness shall follow me
   all the days of my life.
   In the Lord's own house shall I dwell
   for ever and ever. ℟

Second Reading   Ephesians 5:8-14.

Rise from the dead and Christ will shine on you.

You were darkness once, but now you are light in the Lord; be like children of light, for the effects of the light are seen in complete goodness and right living and truth. Try to discover what the Lord wants of you, having nothing to do with the futile works of darkness but exposing them by contrast. The things which are done in secret are things that people are ashamed even to speak of; but anything exposed by the light will be illuminated and anything illuminated turns into light. That is why it is said:
Wake up from your sleep,
rise from the dead,
and Christ will shine on you.

Acclamation

Glory to you, O Christ, you are the Word of God!
I am the light of the world, says the Lord; anyone who follows me will have the light of life.
Glory to you, O Christ, you are the Word of God!

John 8:12.

Gospel   John 9:1-41.

The blind man went off and washed himself, and came away with his sight restored.

As Jesus went along, he saw a man who had been blind from birth.
His disciples asked him, "Rabbi, who sinned, this man or his parents, for him to have been born blind?" "Neither he nor his parents sinned," Jesus answered, "he was born blind so that the works of God might be displayed in him.

FOURTH SUNDAY OF LENT/A

"As long as the day lasts
I must carry out the work of the one who sent me;
the night will soon be here when no one can work.
As long as I am in the world
I am the light of the world."
Having said this,

> he spat on the ground, made a paste with the spittle, put this over the eyes of the blind man and said to him, "Go and wash in the Pool of Siloam" (a name that means "sent"). So the blind man went off and washed himself, and came away with his sight restored.
>
> His neighbours and people who earlier had seen him begging said, "Isn't this the man who used to sit and beg?" Some said, "Yes, it is the same one." Others said, "No, he only looks like him." The man himself said, "I am the man."

So they said to him, "Then how do your eyes come to be open?" "The man called Jesus," he answered, "made a paste, daubed my eyes with it and said to me, 'Go and wash at Siloam'; so I went, and when I washed I could see." They asked, "Where is he?" "I don't know," he answered.

> They brought the man who had been blind to the Pharisees. It had been a sabbath day when Jesus made the paste and opened the man's eyes, so when the Pharisees asked him how he had come to see, he said, "He put a paste on my eyes, and I washed, and I can see." Then some of the Pharisees said, "This man cannot be from God: he does not keep the sabbath." Others said, "How could a sinner produce signs like this?" And there was disagreement among them. So they spoke to the blind man again, "What have you to say about him yourself, now that he has opened your eyes?" "He is a prophet," replied the man.

However, the Jews would not believe that the man had been blind and had gained his sight, without first sending for his parents and asking them, "Is this man really your son who you say was born blind? If so, how is it that he is now able to see?" His parents answered, "We know he is our son and we know he was born blind, but we don't know how it is that he can see now, or who opened his eyes. He is old enough: let him speak for himself." His parents spoke like this out of fear of the Jews, who had already agreed to expel from the synagogue anyone who should acknowledge Jesus as the Christ. This was why his parents said, "He is old enough; ask him."

FOURTH SUNDAY OF LENT/A

So the Jews again sent for the man and said to him, "Give glory to God! For our part, we know that this man is a sinner." The man answered, "I don't know if he is a sinner; I only know that I was blind and now I can see." They said to him, "What did he do to you? How did he open your eyes?" He replied, "I have told you once and you wouldn't listen. Why do you want to hear it all again? Do you want to become his disciples too?" At this they hurled abuse at him: "You can be his disciple," they said, "we are disciples of Moses: we know that God spoke to Moses, but as for this man, we don't know where he comes from." The man replied, "Now here is an astonishing thing! He has opened my eyes, and you don't know where he comes from! We know that God doesn't listen to sinners, but God does listen to men who are devout and do his will. Ever since the world began it is unheard of for anyone to open the eyes of a man who was born blind; if this man were not from God, he couldn't do a thing."

"Are you trying to teach us," they replied, "and you a sinner through and through, since you were born!" And they drove him away.

Jesus heard they had driven him away, and when he found him he said to him, "Do you believe in the Son of Man?" "Sir," the man replied, "tell me who he is so that I may believe in him." Jesus said, "You are looking at him; he is speaking to you." The man said, "Lord, I believe," and worshipped him.

Jesus said:
"It is for judgement
that I have come into this world,
so that those without sight may see
and those with sight turn blind."

Hearing this, some Pharisees who were present said to him, "We are not blind surely?" Jesus replied:

"Blind? If you were,
you would not be guilty,
but since you say, 'We see,'
your guilt rer ains."

Prayer over the Gifts

Lord,
we offer you these gifts
which bring us peace and joy.
Increase our reverence by this eucharist,
and bring salvation to the world.

FOURTH SUNDAY OF LENT/A

Preface

Father, all-powerful and ever-living God,
we do well always and everywhere to give you thanks,
through Jesus Christ our Lord.

He came among us as a man,
to lead mankind from darkness
into the light of faith.

Through Adam's fall we were born as slaves of sin,
but now through baptism in Christ
we are reborn as your adopted children.

Earth unites with heaven
to sing the new song of creation,
as we adore and praise you for ever:

Holy, holy, holy . . .

Communion Antiphon

The Lord rubbed my eyes: I went away and washed; then I could see, and I believed in God. Cf. John 9:11.

Prayer after Communion

Father,
you enlighten all whom come into the world.
Fill our hearts with the light of your gospel,
that our thoughts may please you,
and our love be sincere.

FIFTH SUNDAY OF LENT/A

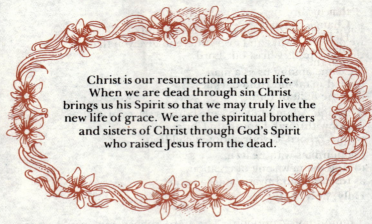

Christ is our resurrection and our life. When we are dead through sin Christ brings us his Spirit so that we may truly live the new life of grace. We are the spiritual brothers and sisters of Christ through God's Spirit who raised Jesus from the dead.

Entrance Antiphon Give me justice, O God, and defend my cause against the wicked; rescue me from deceitful and unjust men. You, O God, are my refuge. Psalm 42:1-2.

There is no Gloria today.

Opening Prayer

Let us pray
  [for the courage to follow Christ]

Father,
help us to be like Christ your Son,
who loved the world and died for our salvation.
Inspire us by his love,
guide us by his example,
who lives and reigns with you and the Holy Spirit,
one God, for ever and ever.

or

Let us pray
  [for the courage to embrace the world
  in the name of Christ]

Father in heaven,
the love of your Son led him to accept the suffering of the
  cross,

that his brothers might glory in new life.
Change our selfishness into self-giving.
Help us to embrace the world you have given us,
that we may transform the darkness of its pain
into the life and joy of Easter.

First Reading   Ezekiel 37:12-14.
I shall put my spirit in you, and you will live.

The Lord says this: I am now going to open your graves; I mean to raise you from your graves, my people, and lead you back to the soil of Israel. And you will know that I am the Lord, when I open your graves and raise you from your graves, my people. And I shall put my spirit in you, and you will live, and I shall resettle you on your own soil; and you will know that I, the Lord, have said and done this — it is the Lord God who speaks.

Responsorial Psalm   Psalm 129

R/ **With the Lord there is mercy
and fullness of redemption.**

1. Out of the depths I cry to you, O Lord,
   Lord, hear my voice!
   O let your ears be attentive
   to the voice of my pleading. R/

2. If you, O Lord, should mark our guilt,
   Lord, who would survive?
   But with you is found forgiveness:
   for this we revere you. R/

3. My soul is waiting for the Lord,
   I count on his word.
   My soul is longing for the Lord
   more than watchman for daybreak.
   (Let the watchman count on daybreak
   and Israel on the Lord.) R/

4. Because with the Lord there is mercy
   and fulness of redemption,
   Israel indeed he will redeem
   from all its iniquity. R/

FIFTH SUNDAY OF LENT/A

Second Reading Romans 8:8-11.

The Spirit of him who raised Jesus from the dead is living in you.

People who are interested only in unspiritual things can never be pleasing to God. Your interests, however, are not in the unspiritual, but in the spiritual, since the Spirit of God has made his home in you. In fact, unless you possessed the Spirit of Christ you would not belong to him. Though your body may be dead it is because of sin, but if Christ is in you then your spirit is life itself because you have been justified; and if the Spirit of him who raised Jesus from the dead is living in you, then he who raised Jesus from the dead will give life to your own mortal bodies through his Spirit living in you.

Acclamation Glory and praise to you, O Christ!
I am the resurrection and the life, says the Lord;
whoever believes in me will never die.
Glory and praise to you, O Christ! John 11:25,26

Gospel John 11:1-45

I am the resurrection and the life.

There was a man named Lazarus who lived in the village of Bethany with the two sisters, Mary and Martha, and he was ill. It was the same Mary, the sister of the sick man Lazarus, who anointed the Lord with ointment and wiped his feet with her hair.

The sisters, Martha and Mary, sent this message to Jesus, "Lord, the man you love is ill." On receiving the message, Jesus said, "This sickness will end not in death but in God's glory, and through it the Son of God will be glorified."

Jesus loved Martha and her sister and Lazarus, yet when he heard that Lazarus was ill he stayed where he was for two more days before saying to the disciples, "Let us go to Judea."

The disciples said, "Rabbi, it is not long since the Jews wanted to stone you; are you going back again?" Jesus replied:
"Are there not twelve hours in the day?
A man can walk in the daytime without stumbling
because he has the light of this world to see by;
but if he walks at night he stumbles,
because there is no light to guide him."

He said that and then added, "Our friend Lazarus is resting, I am going to wake him." The disciples said to him, "Lord, if he is

FIFTH SUNDAY OF LENT/A

able to rest he is sure to get better." The phrase Jesus used referred to the death of Lazarus, but they thought that by "rest" he meant "sleep", so Jesus put it plainly, "Lazarus is dead; and for your sake I am glad I was not there because now you will believe. But let us go to him." Then Thomas — known as the Twin — said to the other disciples, "Let us go too, and die with him."

On arriving, Jesus found that Lazarus had been in the tomb for four days already. Bethany is only about two miles from Jerusalem, and many Jews had come to Martha and Mary to sympathise with them over their brother. When Martha heard that Jesus had come she went to meet him. Mary remained sitting in the house. Martha said to Jesus, "If you had been here, my brother would not have died, but I know that, even now, whatever you ask of God, he will grant you." "Your brother," said Jesus to her "will rise again." Martha said, "I know he will rise again at the resurrection on the last day." Jesus said:
"I am the resurrection.
If anyone believes in me, even though he dies he will live,
and whoever lives and believes in me
will never die.
Do you believe this?"

"Yes, Lord," she said, "I believe that you are the Christ, the Son of God, the one who was to come into this world."

When she had said this, she went and called her sister Mary, saying in a low voice, "The Master is here and wants to see you." Hearing this, Mary got up quickly and went to him. Jesus had not yet come into the village; he was still at the place where Martha had met him. When the Jews who were in the house sympathising with Mary saw her get up so quickly and go out, they followed her, thinking that she was going to the tomb to weep there.

Mary went to Jesus, and as soon as she saw him she threw herself at his feet, saying, "Lord, if you had been here, my brother would not have died." At the sight of her tears, and those of the Jews who followed her,

Jesus said in great distress, with a sigh that came straight from the heart, "Where have you put him?" They said, "Lord, come and see." Jesus wept; and the Jews said, "See how much he loved him!" But there were some who remarked, "He opened

the eyes of the blind man, could he not have prevented this man's death?" Still sighing, Jesus reached the tomb: it was a cave with a stone to close the opening. Jesus said, "Take the stone away." Martha said to him, "Lord, by now he will smell; this is the fourth day." Jesus replied, "Have I not told you that if you believe you will see the glory of God?" So they took away the stone. Then Jesus lifted up his eyes and said:
"Father, I thank you for hearing my prayer.
I know indeed that you always hear me,
but I speak
for the sake of all these who stand round me,
so that they may believe it was you who sent me."

When he had said this, he cried in a loud voice, "Lazarus, here! Come out!" The dead man came out, his feet and hands bound with bands of stuff and a cloth round his face. Jesus said to them, "Unbind him, let him go free."

Many of the Jews who had come to visit Mary and had seen what he did believed in him.

Prayer over the Gifts

Almighty God,
may the sacrifice we offer
take away the sins of those
whom you enlighten with the Christian faith.

Preface

Father, all-powerful and ever-living God,
we do well always and everywhere to give you thanks
through Jesus Christ our Lord.

As a man like us, Jesus wept for Lazarus his friend.
As the eternal God, he raised Lazarus from the dead.
In his love for us all,
Christ gives us the sacraments
to lift us up to everlasting life.

Through him the angels of heaven offer their prayer of adoration
as they rejoice in your presence for ever.
May our voices be one with theirs
in their triumphant hymn of praise:

Holy, holy, holy ...

FIFTH SUNDAY OF LENT/A

Communion Antiphon He who lives and believes in me will not die for ever, said the Lord.
John 11:26

Prayer after Communion

Almighty Father,
by this sacrifice
may we always remain one with your Son, Jesus Christ,
whose body and blood we share,
for he is Lord for ever and ever.

The Liturgies of Holy Week will be found on pages 261 ff.

FIRST SUNDAY OF LENT/B

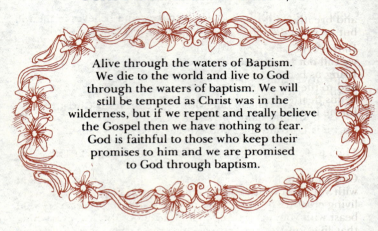

Alive through the waters of Baptism.
We die to the world and live to God
through the waters of baptism. We will
still be tempted as Christ was in the
wilderness, but if we repent and really believe
the Gospel then we have nothing to fear.
God is faithful to those who keep their
promises to him and we are promised
to God through baptism.

Entrance Antiphon   When he calls to me, I will answer; I will rescue him and give him honour. Long life and contentment will be his.
                                                        Psalm 90:15-16

The Gloria is not said today.

Opening Prayer

Let us pray
  [that this Lent will help us reproduce in our lives
  the self-sacrificing love of Christ]

Father,
through our observance of Lent,
help us to understand the meaning
of your Son's death and resurrection,
and teach us to reflect it in our lives.

or

Let us pray
  [at the beginning of Lent
  for the spirit of repentance]

Lord our God,
you formed man from the clay of the earth

FIRST SUNDAY OF LENT/B

and breathed into him the spirit of life,
but he turned from your face and sinned.

In this time of repentance
we call out for your mercy.
Bring us back to you
and to the life your Son won for us
by his death on the cross,
for he lives and reigns for ever and ever.

First Reading   Genesis 9:8-15.

God's covenant with Noah after he had saved him from the waters of the flood.

God spoke to Noah and his sons, "See, I establish my Covenant with you, and with your descendants after you; also with every living creature to be found with you, birds, cattle and every wild beast with you: everything that came out of the ark, everything that lives on the earth. I establish my Covenant with you: no thing of flesh shall be swept away again by the waters of the flood. There shall be no flood to destroy the earth again."

God said, "Here is the sign of the Covenant I make between myself and you and every living creature with you for all generations: I set my bow in the clouds and it shall be a sign of the Covenant between me and the earth. When I gather the clouds over the earth and the bow appears in the clouds, I will recall the Covenant between myself and you and every living creature of every kind. And so the waters shall never again become a flood to destroy all things of flesh."

Responsorial Psalm   Psalm 24.

℟ **Your ways, Lord, are faithfulness and love
for those who keep your covenant.**

1. Lord, make me know your ways.
   Lord, teach me your paths.
   Make me walk in your truth, and teach me:
   for you are God my saviour. ℟

2. Remember your mercy, Lord,
   and the love you have shown from of old.
   In your love remember me,
   because of your goodness, O Lord. ℟

FIRST SUNDAY OF LENT/B

3. The Lord is good and upright.
   He shows the path to those who stray,
   he guides the humble in the right path;
   he teaches his way to the poor. ℟

Second Reading   1 Peter 3:18-22.
That water is a type of the baptism which saves you now.

Christ himself, innocent though he was, died once for sins, died for the guilty, to lead us to God. In the body he was put to death, in the spirit he was raised to life, and, in the spirit, he went to preach to the spirits in prison. Now it was long ago, when Noah was still building that ark which saved only a small group of eight people "by water", and when God was still waiting patiently, that these spirits refused to believe. That water is a type of the baptism which saves you now, and which is not the washing off of physical dirt but a pledge made to God from a good conscience, through the resurrection of Jesus Christ, who has entered heaven and is at God's right hand, now that he has made the angels and Dominations and Powers his subjects.

Acclamation
Praise to you, O Christ, king of eternal glory!
Man does not live on bread alone, but on every word that comes from the mouth of God.
Praise to you, O Christ, king of eternal glory!

Matthew 4:4

Gospel   Mark 1:12-15.
Jesus was tempted by Satan, and the angels looked after him.

The Spirit drove Jesus out into the wilderness and he remained there for forty days, and was tempted by Satan. He was with the wild beasts, and the angels looked after him.

After John had been arrested Jesus went into Galilee. There he proclaimed the Good News from God. "The time has come" he said "and the kingdom of God is close at hand. Repent, and believe the Good News."

Prayer over the Gifts
Lord,
make us worthy to bring you these gifts.
May this sacrifice
help to change our lives.

FIRST SUNDAY OF LENT/B

Preface of First Sunday of Lent, page 193, Lent I or II, page 560.

Communion Antiphon   Man does not live on bread alone, but on every word that comes from the mouth of God. Matthew 4:4.

or

The Lord will overshadow you, and you will find refuge under his wings. Psalm 90:4

Prayer after Communion

Father,
you increase our faith and hope,
you deepen our love in this communion.
Help us to live by your words
and to seek Christ, our bread of life,
who is Lord for ever and ever.

SECOND SUNDAY OF LENT/B

God did not spare his own son.
Christ did not come to explain away
suffering. He came to fulfil it. Like
Abraham we must be prepared to sacrifice
everything to God and thus in turn we
find fulfilment. God will refuse us
nothing now that Christ, risen from
the dead, pleads our cause
before his Father in heaven.

Entrance Antiphon   Remember your mercies, Lord, your tenderness from ages past. Do not let our enemies triumph over us; O God, deliver Israel from all her distress.

Psalm 24:6.3.22

or

My heart has prompted me to seek your face; I seek it, Lord; do not hide from me.
Psalm 28:8-9

The Gloria is not said today.

Opening Prayer

Let us pray
  [for the grace to respond
  to the Word of God]

God our Father,
help us to hear your Son.
Enlighten us with your word,
that we may find the way to your glory.

or

SECOND SUNDAY OF LENT/B

Let us pray
 [in this season of Lent
 for the gift of integrity]

Father of light,
in you is found no shadow of change
but only the fullness of life and limitless truth.

Open our hearts to the voice of your Word
and free us from the original darkness that shadows our vision.
Restore our sight that we may look upon your Son
who calls us to repentance and a change of heart,
for he lives and reigns with you for ever and ever.

First Reading   Genesis 22:1-2.9-13.15-18.
The sacrifice of Abraham, our father in faith.

God put Abraham to the test. "Abraham, Abraham" he called. "Here I am" he replied. "Take your son," God said "your only child Isaac, whom you love, and go to the land of Moriah. There you shall offer him as a burnt offering, on a mountain I will point out to you."

When they arrived at the place God had pointed out to him, Abraham stretched out his hand and seized the knife to kill his son.

But the angel of the Lord called to him from heaven, "Abraham, Abraham" he said. "I am here" he replied. "Do not raise your hand against the boy" the angel said. "Do not harm him, for now I know you fear God. You have not refused me your son, your only son." Then looking up, Abraham saw a ram caught by its horns in a bush. Abraham took the ram and offered it as a burnt-offering in place of his son.

The angel of the Lord called Abraham a second time from heaven. "I swear by my own self — it is the Lord who speaks — because you have done this, because you have not refused me your son, your only son, I will shower blessings on you, I will make your descendants as many as the stars of heaven and the grains of sand on the seashore. Your descendants shall gain possession of the gates of their enemies. All the nations of the earth shall bless themselves by your descendants, as a reward for your obedience."

SECOND SUNDAY OF LENT/B

Responsional Psalm   Psalm 115.

℟ **I will walk in the presence of the Lord in the land of the living**

1. I trusted, even when I said:
   "I am sorely afflicted."
   O precious in the eyes of the Lord
   is the death of his faithful. ℟

2. Your servant, Lord, your servant am I;
   you have loosened my bonds.
   A thanksgiving sacrifice I make:
   I will call on the Lord's name. ℟

3. My vows to the Lord I will fulfil
   before all his people,
   in the courts of the house of the Lord,
   in your midst, O Jerusalem. ℟

Second Reading   Romans 8:31-34.

God did not spare his own Son.

With God on our side who can be against us? Since God did not spare his own Son, but gave him up to benefit us all, we may be certain, after such a gift, that he will not refuse anything he can give. Could anyone accuse those that God has chosen? When God acquits, could anyone condemn? Could Christ Jesus? No! He not only died for us — he rose from the dead, and there at God's right hand he stands and pleads for us.

Acclamation   Glory and praise to you, O Christ!
From the bright cloud the Father's voice was heard: "This is my Son, the Beloved. Listen to him". Glory and praise to you, O Christ!

Matthew 17:15.

Gospel   Mark 9:2-10.

This is my Son, the Beloved.

Jesus took with him Peter and James and John and led them up a high mountain where they could be alone by themselves. There in their presence he was transfigured: his clothes became dazzlingly white, whiter than any earthly bleacher could make them. Elijah appeared to them with Moses; and they were talking with Jesus.

SECOND SUNDAY OF LENT/B

Then Peter spoke to Jesus. "Rabbi", he said "it is wonderful for us to be here; so let us make three tents, one for you, one for Moses and one for Elijah." He did not know what to say; they were so frightened. And a cloud came, covering them in shadow; and there came a voice from the cloud, "This is my Son, the Beloved. Listen to him." Then suddenly, when they looked round, they saw no one with them any more but only Jesus.

As they came down the mountain he warned them to tell no one what they had seen, until after the Son of Man had risen from the dead. They observed the warning faithfully, though among themselves they discussed what "rising from the dead" could mean.

Prayer over the Gifts

Lord,
make us holy.
May this eucharist take away our sins
that we may be prepared
to celebrate the resurrection.

Preface of Second Sunday of Lent, page 197, or Preface of Lent I or II, page 560.

Communion Antiphon

This is my Son, my beloved, in whom is all my delight: listen to him.

Matthew 17:5

Prayer after Communion

Lord,
we give thanks for these holy mysteries
which bring to us here on earth
a share in the life to come,
through Christ our Lord.

THIRD SUNDAY OF LENT/B

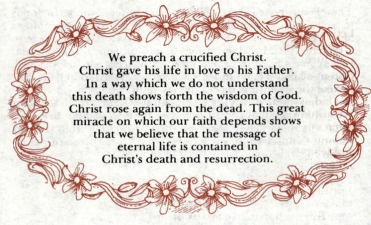

We preach a crucified Christ.
Christ gave his life in love to his Father.
In a way which we do not understand
this death shows forth the wisdom of God.
Christ rose again from the dead. This great
miracle on which our faith depends shows
that we believe that the message of
eternal life is contained in
Christ's death and resurrection.

Entrance Antiphon   My eyes are ever fixed on the Lord, for he releases my feet from the snare. O look at me and be merciful, for I am wretched and alone. Psalm 24:15-16.

or

I will prove my holiness through you. I will gather you from the ends of the earth; I will pour clean water on you and wash away all your sins. I will give you a new spirit within you, says the Lord.

Ezekiel 36:23-26

The Gloria is not said today.

Opening Prayer

Let us pray
  [for confidence in the love of God
  and the strength to overcome all our weakness]

Father,
you have taught us to overcome our sins
by prayer, fasting and works of mercy.
When we are discouraged by our weakness,
give us confidence in your love.

THIRD SUNDAY OF LENT/B

or

Let us pray
  [**to the Father and ask him**
  to form a new heart within us]

God of all compassion, Father of all goodness,
to heal the wounds our sins and selfishness bring upon us
you bid us turn to fasting, prayer, and sharing with our brothers.
We acknowledge our sinfulness, our guilt is ever before us:
when our weakness causes discouragement,
let your compassion fill us with hope
and lead us through a Lent of repentance to the beauty of
  Easter joy.

The readings for Cycle A on pages 199-203 may be used as alternative readings. If this is done, the Preface and Communion Antiphon of Cycle A are also used.

First Reading   Exodus 20:1-17.

The Law was given through Moses.

> God spoke all these words. He said, "I am the Lord your God who brought you out of the land of Egypt, out of the house of slavery.
>
> "You shall have no gods except me.
>
> "You shall not make yourself a carved image or any likeness of anything in heaven or on earth beneath or in the waters under the earth; you shall not bow down to them or serve them. For I, the Lord your God, am a jealous God and I punish the father's fault in the sons, the grandsons, and the great-grandsons of those who hate me; but I show kindness to thousands of those who love me and keep my commandments.
>
> "You shall not utter the name of the Lord your God to misuse it, for the Lord will not leave unpunished the man who utters his name to misuse it.
>
> "Remember the sabbath day and keep it holy.

For six days you shall labour and do all your work, but the seventh day is a sabbath for the Lord your God. You shall do no work that day, neither you nor your son nor your daughter nor your servants, men or women, nor your animals nor the stranger who lives with you. For in six days the Lord made the heavens and the earth and the sea and all that these hold, but on the seventh day he rested; that is why the Lord has blessed the sabbath and

THIRD SUNDAY OF LENT/B

made it sacred.

"Honour your father and your mother so that you may have a long life in the land that the Lord your God has given to you.

"You shall not kill.

"You shall not commit adultery.

"You shall not steal.

"You shall not bear false witness against your neighbour.

"You shall not covet your neighbour's house. You shall not covet your neighbour's wife, or his servant, man or woman, or his ox, or his donkey, or anything that is his."

Responsorial Psalm   Psalm 18.

℟ You, Lord, have the message of eternal life.

1. The law of the Lord is perfect,
   it revives the soul.
   The rule of the Lord is to be trusted,
   it gives wisdom to the simple. ℟

2. The precepts of the Lord are right,
   they gladden the heart.
   The command of the Lord is clear,
   it gives light to the eyes. ℟

3. The fear of the Lord is holy,
   abiding for ever.
   The decrees of the Lord are truth
   and all of them just. ℟

4. They are more to be desired than gold,
   than the purest of gold
   and sweeter are they than honey,
   than honey from the comb. ℟

Second Reading   1 Corinthians 1:22-25.

Here we are preaching a crucified Christ, an obstacle to men, but to those who are called, the wisdom of God.

While the Jews demand miracles and the Greeks look for wisdom, here are we preaching a crucified Christ; to the Jews an obstacle that they cannot get over, to the pagans madness, but to those who have been called, whether they are Jews or Greeks, a Christ who is the power and the wisdom of God. For God's foolishness is wiser than human wisdom, and God's weakness is stronger than human strength.

THIRD SUNDAY OF LENT/B

Acclamation Praise to you, O Christ, king of eternal glory!
I am the resurrection and the life, says the Lord,
whoever believes in me will never die.
Praise to you, O Christ, king of eternal glory!
John 11.25.26.

Gospel John 2:13-25.
Destroy this sanctuary, and in three days I will raise it up.

Just before the Jewish Passover Jesus went up to Jerusalem, and in the Temple he found people selling cattle and sheep and pigeons, and the money changers sitting at their counters there. Making a whip out of some cord, he drove them all out of the Temple, cattle and sheep as well, scattered the money changers' coins, knocked their tables over and said to the pigeon-sellers, "Take all this out of here and stop turning my Father's house into a market." Then his disciples remembered the words of scripture: Zeal for your house will devour me. The Jews intervened and said, "What sign can you show us to justify what you have done?" Jesus answered, "Destroy this sanctuary, and in three days I will raise it up." The Jews replied, "It has taken forty-six years to build this sanctuary: are you going to raise it up in three days?" But he was speaking of the sanctuary that was his body, and when Jesus rose from the dead, his disciples remembered that he had said this, and they believed the scripture and the words he had said.

During his stay in Jerusalem for the Passover many believed in his name when they saw the signs that he gave, but Jesus knew them all and did not trust himself to them; he never needed evidence about any man; he could tell what a man had in him.

Prayer over the Gifts

Lord,
by the grace of this sacrifice
may we who ask forgiveness
be ready to forgive one another.

Preface of Lent I or II, page 560.

THIRD SUNDAY OF LENT/B

Communion Antiphon

The sparrow even finds a home, the swallow finds a nest wherein to place her young, near to your altars, Lord of hosts, my King, my God! How happy they who dwell in your house! For ever they are praising you.

Psalm 83:4-5

Prayer after Communion

Lord,
in sharing this sacrament
may we receive your forgiveness
and be brought together in unity and peace.

FOURTH SUNDAY OF LENT/B

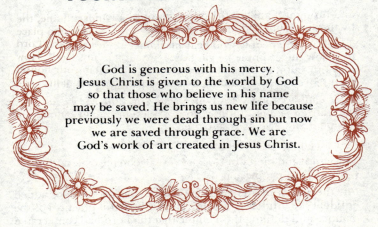

God is generous with his mercy.
Jesus Christ is given to the world by God
so that those who believe in his name
may be saved. He brings us new life because
previously we were dead through sin but now
we are saved through grace. We are
God's work of art created in Jesus Christ.

Entrance Antiphon   Rejoice, Jerusalem! Be glad for her, you who love her; rejoice with her, you who mourned for her, and you will find contentment at her consoling breasts.

cf. Isaiah 66:10-11

The Gloria is not said today.

Opening Prayer

Let us pray
   [for a greater faith and love]

Father of peace,
we are joyful in your Word,
your Son Jesus Christ,
who reconciles us to you.
Let us hasten toward Easter
with the eagerness of faith and love.

or

Let us pray
   [that by growing in love this Lenten season
   we may bring the peace of Christ to our world]

God our Father,
your Word, Jesus Christ, spoke peace to a sinful world

FOURTH SUNDAY OF LENT/B

and brought mankind the gift of reconciliation
by the suffering and death he endured.

Teach us, the people who bear his name,
to follow the example he gave us:
may our faith, hope, and charity
turn hatred to love, conflict to peace, death to eternal life.

The readings for Cycle A on pages 205-208 may be used as alternative readings. If this is done, the Preface and Communion Antiphon of Cycle A are also used.

First Reading   2 Chronicles 36:14-16.19-23.

The wrath and mercy of God are revealed in the exile and in the release of his people.

All the heads of the priesthood, and the people too, added infidelity to infidelity, copying all the shameful practices of the nations and defiling the Temple that the Lord had consecrated for himself in Jerusalem. The Lord, the God of their ancestors, tirelessly sent them messenger after messenger, since he wished to spare his people and his house. But they ridiculed the messengers of God, they despised his words, they laughed at his prophets, until at last the wrath of the Lord rose so high against his people that there was no further remedy.

Their enemies burned down the Temple of God, demolished the walls of Jerusalem, set fire to all its palaces, and destroyed everything of value in it. The survivors were deported by Nebuchadnezzar to Babylon; they were to serve him and his sons until the kingdom of Persia came to power. This is how the word of the Lord was fulfilled that he spoke through Jeremiah, "Until this land has enjoyed its sabbath rest, until seventy years have gone by, it will keep sabbath throughout the days of its desolation."

And in the first year of Cyrus king of Persia, to fulfil the word of the Lord that was spoken through Jeremiah, the Lord roused the spirit of Cyrus king of Persia to issue a proclamation and to have it publicly displayed throughout his kingdom: "Thus speaks Cyrus king of Persia, 'The Lord, the God of heaven, has given me all the kingdoms of the earth; he has ordered me to build him a Temple in Jerusalem, in Judah. Whoever there is among you of all his people, may his God be with him! Let him go up.'"

FOURTH SUNDAY OF LENT/B

Responsorial Psalm   Psalm 136.

℟ **O let my tongue
cleave to my mouth
if I remember you not!**

1. By the rivers of Babylon
   there we sat and wept,
   remembering Zion;
   on the poplars that grew there
   we hung up our harps.   ℟

2. For it was there that they asked us,
   our captors, for songs,
   our oppressors, for joy.
   "Sing to us," they said,
   "one of Zion's songs."   ℟

3. O how could we sing
   the song of the Lord
   on alien soil?
   If I forget you, Jerusalem,
   let my right hand wither!   ℟

4. O let my tongue
   cleave to my mouth
   if I remember you not,
   if I prize not Jerusalem
   above all my joys!   ℟

Second Reading   Ephesians 2:4-10.

You who were dead through your sins have been saved through grace.

God loved us with so much love that he was generous with his mercy: when we were dead through our sins, he brought us to life with Christ — it is through grace that you have been saved — and raised us up with him and gave us a place with him in heaven, in Christ Jesus.

This was to show for all ages to come, through his goodness towards us in Christ Jesus, how infinitely rich he is in grace. Because it is by grace that you have been saved, through faith; not by anything of your own, but by a gift from God; not by anything that you have done, so that nobody can claim the credit. We are God's work of art, created in Christ Jesus to live the good life as from the beginning he had meant us to live it.

FOURTH SUNDAY OF LENT/B

Acclamation Glory and praise to you, O Christ!
God loved the world so much that he gave his only Son; everyone who believes in him has eternal life.
Glory and praise to you, O Christ! John 3:16.

Gospel   John 3:14-21.

God sent his Son so that through him the world might be saved.

Jesus said to Nicodemus:
The Son of Man must be lifted up
as Moses lifted up the serpent in the desert,
so that everyone who believes may have eternal life in him.
Yes, God loved the world so much
that he gave his only Son,
so that everyone who believes in him may not be lost
but may have eternal life.
For God sent his Son into the world
not to condemn the world,
but so that through him the world might be saved.
No one who believes in him will be condemned;
but whoever refuses to believe is condemned already,
because he has refused to believe
in the name of God's only Son.
On these grounds is sentence pronounced:
that though the light has come into the world
men have shown they prefer darkness to the light
because their deeds were evil.
And indeed, everybody who does wrong
hates the light and avoids it,
for fear his actions should be exposed;
but the man who lives by the truth
comes out into the light,
so that it may be plainly seen that what he does is done in God.

Prayer over the Gifts

Lord,
we offer you these gifts
which bring us peace and joy.
Increase our reverence by this eucharist,
and bring salvation to the world.

Preface of Lent I or II, page 560.

FOURTH SUNDAY OF LENT/B

Communion Antiphon   To Jerusalem, that binds them together in unity, the tribes of the Lord go up to give him praise.

Psalm 121:3-4

Prayer after Communion

Father,
you enlighten all who come into the world.
Fill our hearts with the light of your gospel,
that our thoughts may please you,
and our love be sincere.

FIFTH SUNDAY OF LENT/B

I will write my law on their hearts. Christ, like the grain of wheat which dies in order to produce new life, dies for us. Following his example we must realise that if we want eternal life we must be prepared to give our lives to God. He writes his law in our hearts and we submit humbly to his will even when it causes us pain. We obey through suffering. There is no greater school in which to grow in holiness.

Entrance Antiphon Give me justice, O God, and defend my cause against the wicked; rescue me from deceitful and unjust men. You, O God, are my refuge. Psalm 42:1-2.

The Gloria is not said today.

Opening Prayer

Let us pray
 [for the courage to follow Christ]

Father,
help us to be like Christ your Son,
who loved the world and died for our salvation.
Inspire us by his love,
guide us by his example,
who lives and reigns with you and the Holy Spirit,
one God, for ever and ever.

or

Let us pray
 [for the courage to embrace the world
 in the name of Christ]

Father in heaven,
the love of your Son led him to accept the suffering of the cross

FIFTH SUNDAY OF LENT/B

that his brothers might glory in new life.
Change our selfishness into self-giving.
Help us to embrace the world you have given us,
that we may transform the darkness of its pain
into the life and joy of Easter.

The readings for Cycle A on pages 211-214 may be used as alternative readings. If this is done, the Preface and Communion Antiphon of Cycle A are also used.

First Reading   Jeremiah 31:31-34.

I will make a new covenant and never call their sin to mind.

See, the days are coming — it is the Lord who speaks — when I will make a new covenant with the House of Israel (and the House of Judah), but not a covenant like the one I made with their ancestors on the day I took them by the hand to bring them out of the land of Egypt. They broke that covenant of mine, so I had to show them who was master. It is the Lord who speaks. No, this is the covenant I will make with the House of Israel when those days arrive — it is the Lord who speaks. Deep within them I will plant my Law, writing it on their hearts. Then I will be their God and they shall be my people. There will be no further need for neighbour to try to teach neighbour, or brother to say to brother, "Learn to know the Lord!" No, they will all know me, the least no less than the greatest — it is the Lord who speaks — since I will forgive their iniquity and never call their sin to mind.

Responsorial Psalm   Psalm 50.

℟ **A pure heart create for me, O God.**

1. Have mercy on me, God, in your kindness.
   In your compassion blot out my offence.
   O wash me more and more from my guilt
   and cleanse me from my sin. ℟

2. A pure heart create for me, O God,
   put a steadfast spirit within me.
   Do not cast me away from your presence,
   nor deprive me of your holy spirit. ℟

3. Give me again the joy of your help;
   with a spirit of fervour sustain me,
   that I may teach transgressors your ways
   and sinners may return to you. ℟

FIFTH SUNDAY OF LENT/B

Second Reading   Hebrews 5:7-9.
He learnt to obey and became the source of eternal salvation.

During his life on earth, Christ offered up prayer and entreaty, aloud and in silent tears, to the one who had the power to save him out of death, and he submitted so humbly that his prayer was heard. Although he was Son, he learnt to obey through suffering; but having been made perfect, he became for all who obey him the source of eternal salvation.

Acclamation
Glory to you, O Christ, you are the Word of God!
If a man serves me, says the Lord, he must follow me, wherever I am, my servant will be there too.
Glory to you, O Christ, you are the Word of God!

John 12:26.

Gospel   John 12:20-30
If a grain of wheat falls on the ground and dies, it yields a rich harvest.

Among those who went up to worship at the festival were some Greeks. These approached Philip, who came from Bethsaida in Galilee, and put this request to him, "Sir, we should like to see Jesus." Philip went to tell Andrew, and Andrew and Philip together went to tell Jesus.

  Jesus replied to them:
"Now the hour has come
for the Son of Man to be glorified.
I tell you, most solemnly,
unless a wheat grain falls on the ground and dies,
it remains only a single grain;
but if it dies,
it yields a rich harvest.
Anyone who loves his life loses it;
anyone who hates his life in this world
will keep it for the eternal life.
If a man serves me, he must follow me,
wherever I am, my servant will be there too.
If anyone serves me, my Father will honour him.
Now my soul is troubled.
What shall I say:
Father, save me from this hour?
But it was for this very reason that I have come to this hour.

FIFTH SUNDAY OF LENT/B

Father, glorify your name!"

A voice came from heaven, "I have glorified it, and I will glorify it again."

People standing by, who heard this, said it was a clap of thunder; others said, "It was an angel speaking to him." Jesus answered, "It was not for my sake that this voice came, but for yours.
"Now sentence is being passed on this world;
now the prince of this world is to be overthrown.
And when I am lifted up from the earth,
I shall draw all men to myself."

By these words he indicated the kind of death he would die.

Prayer over the Gifts

Almighty God,
may the sacrifice we offer
take away the sins of those
whom you enlighten with the Christian faith.

Preface of Lent I or II, page 560.

Communion Antiphon   I tell you solemnly: Unless a grain of wheat falls on the ground and dies, it remains a single grain; but if it dies, it yields a rich harvest. John 12:24-25.

Prayer after Communion

Almighty Father,
by this sacrifice
may we always remain one with your Son, Jesus Christ,
whose body and blood we share,
for he is Lord for ever and ever.

The Liturgies of Holy Week will be found on pages 261 ff.

FIRST SUNDAY OF LENT/C

The Lord hears our voice.
In the midst of all our troubles God hears us and will lead us into a promised land of peace if only we are prepared to follow him. There is no temptation which cannot be overcome if we are open to the spirit who tells us Jesus is Lord whom God raised from the dead. God, through the risen Jesus is always with us just as in the Old Testament he rescued the Jews out of their bondage
in Egypt.

Entrance Antiphon When he calls to me, I will answer; I will rescue him and give him honour. Long life and contentment will be his.

Psalm 90:15-16.

There is no Gloria today.

Opening Prayer

Let us pray
 [that this Lent will help us reproduce in our lives
 the self-sacrificing love of Christ]

Father,
through our observance of Lent,
help us to understand the meaning
of your Son's death and resurrection,
and teach us to reflect it in our lives.

or

Let us pray
 [at the beginning of Lent
 for the spirit of repentance]

Lord our God,
you formed man from the clay of the earth

FIRST SUNDAY OF LENT/C

and breathed into him the spirit of life,
but he turned from your face and sinned.

In this time of repentance
we call out for your mercy.
Bring us back to you
and to the life your Son won for us
by his death on the cross,
for he lives and reigns for ever and ever.

First Reading Deuteronomy 26:4-10.

The creed of the chosen people.

Moses said to the people: "The priest shall take the pannier from your hand and lay it before the altar of the Lord your God. Then, in the sight of the Lord your God, you must make this pronouncement:

'My father was a wandering Aramaean. He went down into Egypt to find refuge there, few in numbers; but there he became a nation, great, mighty, and strong. The Egyptians ill-treated us, they gave us no peace and inflicted harsh slavery on us. But we called on the Lord, the God of our fathers. The Lord heard our voice and saw our misery, our toil and our oppression; and the Lord brought us out of Egypt with mighty hand and outstretched arm, with great terror, and with signs and wonders. He brought us here and gave us this land, a land where milk and honey flow. Here then I bring the first-fruits of the produce of the soil that you, Lord, have given me.' You must then lay them before the Lord your God, and bow down in the sight of the Lord your God."

Responsorial Psalm Psalm 90

℟ **Be with me, O Lord, in my distress.**

1. He who dwells in the shelter of the Most High
   and abides in the shade of the Almighty
   says to the Lord: "My refuge,
   my stronghold, my God in whom I trust! ℟

2. Upon you no evil shall fall,
   no plague approach where you dwell.
   For you has he commanded his angels,
   to keep you in all your ways. ℟

FIRST SUNDAY OF LENT/C

3. They shall bear you upon their hands
   lest you strike your foot against a stone.
   On the lion and the viper you will tread
   and trample the young lion and the dragon. ℟

4. His love he set on me, so I will rescue him;
   protect him for he knows my name.
   When he calls I shall answer: "I am with you."
   I will save him in distress and give him glory. ℟

Second Reading   Romans 10:8-13.

The creed of the Christian.

Scripture says: The word, that is the faith we proclaim, is very near to you, it is on your lips and in your heart. If your lips confess that Jesus is Lord and if you believe in your heart that God raised him from the dead, then you will be saved. By believing from the heart you are made righteous; by confessing with your lips you are saved. When scripture says: those who believe in him will have no cause for shame, it makes no distinction between Jew and Greek: all belong to the same Lord who is rich enough, however many ask for his help, for everyone who calls on the name of the Lord will be saved.

Acclamation   Praise to you, O Christ, king of eternal glory!
Man does not live on bread alone, but on every word that comes from the mouth of God.
Praise to you, O Christ, king of eternal glory!
                                                                        Matthew 4:4.

Gospel   Luke 4:1-13.

Jesus was led by the Spirit through the wilderness and was tempted there.

Filled with the Holy Spirit, Jesus left the Jordan and was led by the Spirit through the wilderness, being tempted there by the devil for forty days. During that time he ate nothing and at the end he was hungry. Then the devil said to him, "If you are the Son of God, tell this stone to turn into a loaf." But Jesus replied, "Scripture says: Man does not live on bread alone."

Then leading him to a height, the devil showed him in a moment of time all the kingdoms of the world and said to him, "I will give you all this power and the glory of these kingdoms, for it has been committed to me and I give it to anyone I choose. Worship me,

FIRST SUNDAY OF LENT/C

then, and it shall all be yours." But Jesus answered him, "Scripture says:
You must worship the Lord your God,
and serve him alone."

Then he led him to Jerusalem and made him stand on the parapet of the Temple. "If you are the Son of God," he said to him "throw yourself down from here; for scripture says:
He will put his angels in charge of you
to guard you,
and again:
They will hold you up on their hands
in case you hurt your foot against a stone."
But Jesus answered him, "It has been said:
You must not put the Lord your God to the test."
Having exhausted all these ways of tempting him, the devil left him, to return at the appointed time.

Prayer over the Gifts

Lord,
make us worthy to bring you these gifts.
May this sacrifice
help to change our lives.

Preface of First Sunday of Lent, page 193 or Lent I or II, page 560.

Communion Antiphon

Man does not live on bread alone, but on every word that comes from the mouth of God. **Matthew 4:4.**

or

The Lord will overshadow you, and you will find refuge under his wings. **Psalm 90:4.**

Prayer after Communion

Father,
you increase our faith and hope,
you deepen our love in this communion.
Help us to live by your words
and to seek Christ, our bread of life,
who is Lord for ever and ever.

SECOND SUNDAY OF LENT/C

The Lord Jesus Christ will transfigure us.
Jesus was transfigured in the presence of
his apostles and they realised how
wonderful it was to be with him.
Jesus is always with us ready to transform
our lives if through faith we believe in
his power. He is as faithful to us as God was
to Abraham who put his faith in the Lord.

Entrance Antiphon Remember your mercies, Lord, your tenderness from ages past. Do not let our enemies triumph over us; O God, deliver Israel from all her distress.

Psalm 24:6.3.22.

or

My heart has prompted me to seek your face; I seek it, Lord; do not hide from me.

Psalm 26:8-9.

There is no Gloria today.

Opening Prayer

Let us pray
   [for the grace to respond
   to the Word of God]

God our Father,
help us to hear your Son.
Enlighten us with your word,
that we may find the way to your glory.

or

Let us pray
   [in this season of Lent for the gift of integrity]

SECOND SUNDAY OF LENT/C

Father of light,
in you is found no shadow of change
but only the fullness of life and limitless truth.

Open our hearts to the voice of your Word
and free us from the original darkness that shadows our vision.
Restore our sight that we may look upon your Son
who calls us to repentance and a change of heart,
for he lives and reigns with you for ever and ever.

First Reading   Genesis 15:5-12. 17-18.
God enters into a Covenant with Abraham, the man of faith.

Taking Abram outside the Lord said, "Look up to heaven and count the stars if you can. Such will be your descendants" he told him. Abram put his faith in the Lord, who counted this as making him justified.

"I am the Lord" he said to him "who brought you out of Ur of the Chaldaeans to make you heir to this land." "My Lord, the Lord" Abram replied "how am I to know that I shall inherit it?" He said to him, "Get me a three-year-old heifer, a three-year-old goat, a three-year-old ram, a turtledove and a young pigeon." He brought him all these, cut them in half and put half on one side and half facing it on the other; but the birds he did not cut in half. Birds of prey came down on the carcasses but Abram drove them off.

Now as the sun was setting Abram fell into a deep sleep, and terror seized him. When the sun had set and darkness had fallen, there appeared a smoking furnace and a fire-brand that went between the halves. That day the Lord made a Covenant with Abram in these terms:
"To your descendants I give this land,
from the wadi of Egypt to the Great River."

Responsorial Psalm   Psalm 26

R/ The Lord is my light and my help.

1. The Lord is my light and my help;
   whom shall I fear?
   The Lord is the stronghold of my life;
   before whom shall I shrink?   R/

SECOND SUNDAY OF LENT/C

2. O Lord, hear my voice when I call;
   have mercy and answer.
   Of you my heart has spoken:
   "Seek his face." ℟

3. It is your face, O Lord, that I seek;
   hide not your face.
   Dismiss not your servant in anger;
   you have been my help. ℟

4. I am sure I shall see the Lord's goodness
   in the land of the living.
   Hope in him, hold firm and take heart.
   Hope in the Lord! ℟

Second Reading   Philippians 3:17 - 4:1.

Christ will transfigure our bodies into copies of his glorious body.

My brothers, be united in following my rule of life. Take as your models everybody who is already doing this and study them as you used to study us. I have told you often, and I repeat it today with tears, there are many who are behaving as the enemies of the cross of Christ. They are destined to be lost. They make foods into their god and they are proudest of something they ought to think shameful; the things they think important are earthly things.

For us, our homeland is in heaven, and from heaven comes the saviour we are waiting for, the Lord Jesus Christ, and he will transfigure these wretched bodies of ours into copies of his glorious body. He will do that by the same power with which he can subdue the whole universe.

So then, my brothers and dear friends, do not give way but remain faithful in the Lord. I miss you very much, dear friends; you are my joy and my crown.

Acclamation   Glory and praise to you, O Christ!
From the bright cloud the Father's voice was heard: "This is my Son, the Beloved. Listen to him". Glory and Praise to you, O Christ!

Matthew 17:5.

Gospel   Luke 9:28-36.

As Jesus prayed, the aspect of his face was changed.

Jesus took with him Peter and John and James and went up the

SECOND SUNDAY OF LENT/C

mountain to pray. As he prayed, the aspect of his face was changed and his clothing became brilliant as lightning. Suddenly there were two men there talking to him; they were Moses and Elijah appearing in glory, and they were speaking of his passing which he was to accomplish in Jerusalem. Peter and his companions were heavy with sleep, but they kept awake and saw his glory and the two men standing with him. As these were leaving him, Peter said to Jesus, "Master, it is wonderful for us to be here; so let us make three tents, one for you, one for Moses and one for Elijah." — He did not know what he was saying. As he spoke, a cloud came and covered them with shadow; and when they went into the cloud the disciples were afraid. And a voice came from the cloud saying, "This is my Son, the Chosen One. Listen to him." And after the voice had spoken, Jesus was found alone. The disciples kept silence and, at that time, told no one what they had seen.

Prayer over the Gifts

Lord,
make us holy.
May this eucharist take away our sins
that we may be prepared
to celebrate the resurrection.

Preface of Second Sunday of Lent, page 197, or Lent I or II, page 560.

Communion Antiphon

This is my Son, my beloved, in whom is all my delight: listen to him.

Matthew 17:5

Prayer after Communion

Lord,
we give thanks for these holy mysteries
which bring to us here on earth
a share in the life to come,
through Christ our Lord.

THIRD SUNDAY OF LENT/C

God said: "I am who I am".
God the creator of all things is faithful to his word. He is the one who acts, who intervenes in our lives, so that we turn to him in repentance. Despite God's goodness to the Jews in the desert many of them fell away from their belief. The events that happened to them in the Old Testament are a warning to us lest we make the same mistakes.

Entrance Antiphon My eyes are ever fixed on the Lord, for he releases my feet from the snare. O look at me and be merciful, for I am wretched and alone. Psalm 24:15-16.

or

I will prove my holiness through you. I will gather you from the ends of the earth; I will pour clean water on you and wash away all your sins. I will give you a new spirit within you, says the Lord.

Ezekiel 36:23-26

There is no Gloria today.

Opening Prayer
Let us pray
  [for confidence in the love of God
  and the strength to overcome all our weakness]

Father,
you have taught us to overcome our sins
by prayer, fasting and works of mercy.
When we are discouraged by our weakness,
give us confidence in your love.

THIRD SUNDAY OF LENT/C

or

Let us pray
  [to the Father and ask him
  to form a new heart within us]
God of all compassion, Father of all goodness,
to heal the wounds our sins and selfishness bring upon us
you bid us turn to fasting, prayer, and sharing with our
  brothers.
We acknowledge our sinfulness, our guilt is ever before us:
when our weakness causes discouragement,
let your compassion fill us with hope
and lead us through a Lent of repentance to the beauty of
Easter joy.

The readings for Cycle A on pages 199-203 may be used as alternative readings. If this is done, the Preface and Communion Antiphon of Cycle A are also used.

First Reading   Exodus 3:1-8.13-15.

I Am has sent me to you.

Moses was looking after the flock of Jethro, his father-in-law, priest of Midian. He led his flock to the far side of the wilderness and came to Horeb, the mountain of God. There the angel of the Lord appeared to him in the shape of a flame of fire, coming from the middle of a bush. Moses looked; there was a bush blazing but it was not being burnt up. "I must go and look at this strange sight," Moses said "and see why the bush is not burnt." Now the Lord saw him go forward to look, and God called to him from the middle of the bush. "Moses, Moses!" he said. "Here I am" he answered. "Come no nearer" he said. "Take off your shoes, for the place on which you stand is holy ground. I am the God of your father," he said "the God of Abraham, the God of Isaac and the God of Jacob." At this Moses covered his face, afraid to look at God.

And the Lord said, "I have seen the miserable state of my people in Egypt. I have heard their appeal to be free of their slave-drivers. Yes, I am well aware of their sufferings. I mean to deliver them out of the hands of the Egyptians and bring them up out of that land to a land rich and broad, a land where milk and honey flow."

Then Moses said to God, "I am to go, then, to the sons of Israel and say to them, 'The God of your fathers has sent me to you.' But

THIRD SUNDAY OF LENT/C

if they ask me what his name is, what am I to tell them?" And God said to Moses, "I Am who I Am. This" he added "is what you must say to the sons of Israel: 'I Am has sent me to you.'" And God also said to Moses, "You are to say to the sons of Israel: 'The Lord, the God of your fathers, the God of Abraham, the God of Isaac, and the God of Jacob, has sent me to you.' This is my name for all time; by this name I shall be invoked for all generations to come."

Responsorial Psalm   Psalm 102.

R/ **The Lord is compassion and love.**

1. My soul, give thanks to the Lord,
   all my being, bless his holy name.
   My soul give thanks to the Lord
   and never forget all his blessings. R/

2. It is he who forgives all your guilt,
   who heals every one of your ills,
   who redeems your life from the grave,
   who crowns you with love and compassion. R/

3. The Lord does deeds of justice,
   gives judgement for all who are oppressed.
   He made known his ways to Moses
   and his deeds to Israel's sons. R/

4. The Lord is compassion and love,
   slow to anger and rich in mercy.
   For as the heavens are high above the earth
   so strong is his love for those who fear him. R/

Second Reading   1 Corinthians 10:1-6.10-12.

The life of the people under Moses in the desert was written down to be a lesson for us.

I want to remind you, brothers, how our fathers were all guided by a cloud above them and how they all passed through the sea. They were all baptised into Moses in this cloud and in this sea; all ate the same spiritual food and all drank the same spiritual drink, since they all drank from the spiritual rock that followed them as they went, and that rock was Christ. In spite of this, most of them failed to please God and their corpses littered the desert.

THIRD SUNDAY OF LENT/C

These things all happened as warnings for us, not to have the wicked lusts for forbidden things that they had. You must never complain: some of them did, and they were killed by the Destroyer.

All this happened to them as a warning, and it was written down to be a lesson for us who are living at the end of the age. The man who thinks he is safe must be careful that he does not fall.

Acclamation Glory to you, O Christ, you are the Word of God! Repent, says the Lord, for the kingdom of heaven is close at hand. Glory to you, O Christ, you are the Word of God! Matthew 4:17.

Gospel Luke 13:1-9.

Unless you repent you will all perish as they did.

Some people arrived and told Jesus about the Galileans whose blood Pilate had mingled with that of their sacrifices. At this he said to them, "Do you suppose these Galileans who suffered like that were greater sinners than any other Galileans? They were not, I tell you. No; but unless you repent you will all perish as they did. Or those eighteen on whom the tower at Siloam fell and killed them? Do you suppose that they were more guilty than all the other people living in Jerusalem? They were not I tell you. No; but unless you repent you will all perish as they did."

He told this parable: "A man had a fig tree planted in his vineyard, and he came looking for fruit on it but found none. He said to the man who looked after the vineyard, 'Look here, for three years now I have been coming to look for fruit on this fig tree and finding none. Cut it down: why should it be taking up the ground?' 'Sir,' the man replied 'leave it one more year and give me time to dig round it and manure it: it may bear fruit next year; if not, then you can cut it down.'"

Prayer over the Gifts

Lord,
by the grace of this sacrifice
may we who ask forgiveness
be ready to forgive one another.

Preface of Lent I or II, page 560.

THIRD SUNDAY OF LENT/C

Communion Antiphon The sparrow even finds a home, the swallow finds a nest wherein to place her young, near to your altars, Lord of hosts, my King, my God! How happy they who dwell in your house! For ever they are praising you.

Psalm 83:4-5

Prayer after Communion

Lord,
in sharing this sacrament
may we receive your forgiveness
and be brought together in unity and peace.

FOURTH SUNDAY OF LENT/C

God reconciles us to himself in Christ.
Christ is our new creation. In him we are
re-born. When we were dead through sin
Christ came to reconcile us to the Father.
Now we are ambassadors for Christ and are
privileged to proclaim the Good News. Christ
takes away our shame if only we will return to
the Father's house as prodigal sons confessing
our weakness and waywardness.

Entrance Antiphon   Rejoice, Jerusalem! Be glad for her, you who love her; rejoice with her, you who mourned for her, and you will find contentment at her consoling breasts.

cf. Isaiah 66:10-11

There is no Gloria today.

Opening Prayer

Let us pray
  [for a greater faith and love

Father of peace,
we are joyful in your Word,
your Son Jesus Christ,
who reconciles us to you.
Let us hasten toward Easter
with the eagerness of faith and love.

or

Let us pray
  [that by growing in love this Lenten season
  we may bring the peace of Christ to our world]

FOURTH SUNDAY OF LENT/C

God our Father,
your Word, Jesus Christ, spoke peace to a sinful world
and brought mankind the gift of reconciliation
by the suffering and death he endured.

Teach us, the people who bear his name,
to follow the example he gave us:
may our faith, hope, and charity
turn hatred to love, conflict to peace, death to eternal life.

The readings for Cycle A on pages 205-208 may be used as alternative readings. If this is done, the Preface and Communion Antiphon of Cycle A are also used.

First Reading   Joshua 5:9-12.

The People of God keep the Passover on their entry into the promised land.

The Lord said to Joshua, "Today I have taken the shame of Egypt away from you."

The Israelites pitched their camp at Gilgal and kept the Passover there on the fourteenth day of the month, at evening in the plain of Jericho. On the morrow of the Passover they tasted the produce of that country, unleavened bread and roasted ears of corn, that same day. From that time, from their first eating of the produce of that country, the manna stopped falling. And having manna no longer, the Israelites fed from that year onwards on what the land of Canaan yielded.

Responsorial Psalm   Psalm 33.

℟ **Taste and see that the Lord is good.**

1. I will bless the Lord at all times,
   his praise always on my lips;
   in the Lord my soul shall make its boast.
   The humble shall hear and be glad. ℟

2. Glorify the Lord with me.
   Together let us praise his name.
   I sought the Lord and he answered me;
   from all my terrors he set me free. ℟

3. Look towards him and be radiant;
   let your faces not be abashed.

FOURTH SUNDAY OF LENT/C

This poor man called; the Lord heard him
and rescued him from all his distress. R/

Second Reading 2 Corinthians 5:17-21.
God reconciled us to himself through Christ.

For anyone who is in Christ, there is a new creation; the old creation has gone, and now the new one is here. It is all God's work. It was God who reconciled us to himself through Christ and gave us the work of handing on this reconciliation. In other words, God in Christ was reconciling the world to himself, not holding men's faults against them, and he has entrusted to us the news that they are reconciled. So we are ambassadors for Christ; it is as though God were appealing through us, and the appeal that we make in Christ's name is: be reconciled to God. For our sake God made the sinless one into sin, so that in him we might become the goodness of God.

Acclamation

Praise and honour to you, Lord Jesus!
I will leave this place and go to my father and say: "Father, I have sinned against heaven and against you." Praise and honour to you, Lord Jesus!
Luke 15:18.

Gospel Luke 15:1-3.11-32.
Your brother here was dead and has come to life.

The tax collectors and the sinners were all seeking the company of Jesus to hear what he had to say, and the Pharisees and the scribes complained. "This man" they said "welcomes sinners and eats with them." So he spoke this parable to them:

"A man had two sons. The younger said to his father, 'Father, let me have the share of the estate that would come to me.' So the father divided the property between them. A few days later, the younger son got together everything he had and left for a distant country where he squandered his money on a life of debauchery.

"When he had spent it all, that country experienced a severe famine, and now he began to feel the pinch, so he hired himself out to one of the local inhabitants who put him on his farm to feed the pigs. And he would willingly have filled his belly with the husks the pigs were eating but no one offered him anything. Then he came to his senses and said, 'How many of my father's paid servants have more food than they want, and here am I dying of

FOURTH SUNDAY OF LENT/C

hunger! I will leave this place and go to my father and say: Father, I have sinned against heaven and against you; I no longer deserve to be called your son; treat me as one of your paid servants.' So he left the place and went back to his father.

"While he was still a long way off, his father saw him and was moved with pity. He ran to the boy, clasped him in his arms and kissed him tenderly. Then his son said, 'Father, I have sinned against heaven and against you. I no longer deserve to be called your son.' But the father said to his servants, 'Quick! Bring out the best robe and put it on him; put a ring on his finger and sandals on his feet. Bring the calf we have been fattening, and kill it; we are going to have a feast, a celebration, because this son of mine was dead and has come back to life; he was lost and is found.' And they began to celebrate.

"Now the elder son was out in the fields, and on his way back, as he drew near the house, he could hear music and dancing. Calling one of the servants he asked what it was all about. 'Your brother has come' replied the servant 'and your father has killed the calf we had fattened because he has got him back safe and sound.' He was angry then and refused to go in, and his father came out to plead with him; but he answered his father, 'Look, all these years I have slaved for you and never once disobeyed your orders, yet you never offered me so much as a kid for me to celebrate with my friends. But, for this son of yours, when he comes back after swallowing up your property — he and his women — you kill the calf we had been fattening.'

"The father said, 'My son, you are with me always and all I have is yours. But it is only right we should celebrate and rejoice, because your brother here was dead and has come to life; he was lost and is found.'"

Prayer over the Gifts

Lord,
we offer you these gifts
which bring us peace and joy.
Increase our reverence by this eucharist,
and bring salvation to the world.

Preface of Lent I or II, page 560.

FOURTH SUNDAY OF LENT/C

Communion Antiphon My son, you should rejoice, because your brother was dead and has come back to life, he was lost and is found.

Luke 15:32

Prayer after Communion

Father,
you enlighten all who come into the world.
Fill our hearts with the light of your gospel,
that our thoughts may please you,
and our love be sincere.

FIFTH SUNDAY OF LENT/C

The Lord who forgives.
Christ came to show compassion and forgiveness for sinners. He condemned sin but let the woman guilty of adultery go free with the reminder that she was to sin no more. None of us is perfect since we can only hope that we will be saved. We suffer in this life but we can accept the loss of everything as so much rubbish if only we can have Christ and be given a share in his resurrection. In this way God, through Christ, is doing something new and is calling us from sinfulness to a life of service.

Entrance Antiphon Give me justice, O God, and defend my cause against the wicked; rescue me from deceitful and unjust men. You, O God, are my refuge. Psalm 42:1-2.

There is no Gloria today.

Opening Prayer

Let us pray
   [for the courage to follow Christ]

Father,
help us to be like Christ your Son,
who loved the world and died for our salvation.
Inspire us by his love,
guide us by his example,
who lives and reigns with you and the Holy Spirit,
one God, for ever and ever.

or

FIFTH SUNDAY OF LENT/C

Let us pray
  [for the courage to embrace the world
  in the name of Christ]

Father in heaven,
the love of your Son led him to accept the suffering of the cross
that his brothers might glory in new life.
Change our selfishness into self-giving.
Help us to embrace the world you have given us,
that we may transform the darkness of its pain
into the life and joy of Easter.

The readings for Cycle A on pages 211-214 may be used as alternative readings. If this is done, the Preface and Communion Antiphon of Cycle A are also used.

First Reading   Isaiah 43:16-21.

See, I am doing a new deed, and I will give my chosen people drink.

Thus says the Lord,
who made a way through the sea,
a path in the great waters;
who put chariots and horse in the field
and a powerful army,
which lay there never to rise again,
snuffed out, put out like a wick:

No need to recall the past,
no need to think about what was done before.
See, I am doing a new deed,
even now it comes to light; can you not see it?
Yes, I am making a road in the wilderness,
paths in the wilds.

The wild beasts will honour me,
jackals and ostriches,
because I am putting water in the wilderness
(rivers in the wild)
to give my chosen people drink.
The people I have formed for myself
will sing my praises.

FIFTH SUNDAY OF LENT/C

Responsorial Psalm   Psalm 125.

℟ **What marvels the Lord worked for us!
Indeed we were glad.**

1. When the Lord delivered Zion from bondage,
   it seemed like a dream.
   Then was our mouth filled with laughter,
   on our lips there were songs. ℟

2. The heathens themselves said: "What marvels
   the Lord worked for them!"
   What marvels the Lord worked for us!
   Indeed we were glad. ℟

3. Deliver us, O Lord, from our bondage
   as streams in dry land.
   Those who are sowing in tears
   will sing when they reap. ℟

4. They go out, they go out, full of tears,
   carrying seed for the sowing:
   they come back, they come back, full of song,
   carrying their sheaves. ℟

Second Reading   Philippians 3:8-14.

Reproducing the pattern of his death, I have accepted the loss of everything for Christ.

I believe nothing can happen that will outweigh the supreme advantage of knowing Christ Jesus my Lord. For him I have accepted the loss of everything, and I look on everything as so much rubbish if only I can have Christ and be given a place in him. I am no longer trying for perfection by my own efforts, the perfection that comes through faith in Christ, and is from God and based on faith. All I want is to know Christ and the power of his resurrection and to share his sufferings by reproducing the pattern of his death. That is the way I can hope to take my place in the resurrection of the dead. Not that I have become perfect yet: I have not yet won, but I am still running, trying to capture the prize for which Christ Jesus captured me. I can assure you my brothers, I am far from thinking that I have already won. All I can say is that

FIFTH SUNDAY OF LENT/C

I forget the past and I strain ahead for what is still to come; I am racing for the finish, for the prize to which God calls us upwards to receive in Christ Jesus.

Acclamation Praise to you, O Christ, king of eternal glory!
Seek good and not evil so that you may live, and that the Lord God of hosts may really be with you
Praise to you, O Christ, king of eternal glory!
Amos 5:14.

Gospel John 8:1-11.

If there is one of you who has not sinned, let him be the first to throw a stone at her.

Jesus went to the Mount of Olives. At daybreak he appeared in the Temple again; and as all the people came to him, he sat down and began to teach them.

The scribes and Pharisees brought a woman along who had been caught committing adultery; and making her stand there in full view of everybody, they said to Jesus, "Master, this woman was caught in the very act of committing adultery, and Moses has ordered us in the Law to condemn women like this to death by stoning. What have you to say?" They asked him this as a test, looking for something to use against him. But Jesus bent down and started writing on the ground with his finger. As they persisted with their question, he looked up and said, "If there is one of you who has not sinned, let him be the first to throw a stone at her." Then he bent down and wrote on the ground again. When they heard this they went away one by one, beginning with the eldest, until Jesus was left alone with the woman, who remained standing there. He looked up and said, "Woman, where are they? Has no one condemned you?" "No one, sir," she replied. "Neither do I condemn you," said Jesus "go away, and don't sin any more."

Prayer over the Gifts

Almighty God,
may the sacrifice we offer
take away the sins of those
whom you enlighten with the Christian faith.

Preface of Lent I or II, page 560.

FIFTH SUNDAY OF LENT/C

Communion Antiphon Has no one condemned you? The woman answered: No one, Lord. Neither do I condemn you: go and do not sin again. John 8:10-11.

Prayer after Communion

Almighty Father,
by this sacrifice
may we always remain one with your Son, Jesus Christ,
whose body and blood we share,
for he is Lord for ever and ever.

Holy Week

PASSION SUNDAY
PALM SUNDAY

Jesus is King!
The triumphal entry of Jesus into Jerusalem
gives way to his passion and death. Yet Jesus is King
and within a week will rise triumphant from
the dead. He is the firm ground of our hope
that all sufferings in this life are lost in
the power of his resurrection.

COMMEMORATION OF THE LORD'S ENTRANCE INTO JERUSALEM

First Form: The Procession

The congregation, holding palm branches, assembles in a place distinct from the church to which the procession will move. This antiphon, or another, is sung.

Hosanna to the Son of David,
the King of Israel.
Blessed is he who comes
in the name of the Lord.
Hosanna in the highest. Matthew 21:9

The priest then greets the people in the usual way and gives a brief introduction, inviting them to take a full part in the celebration. He may use these or similar words:

Dear friends in Christ, for five weeks of Lent we have been preparing, by works of charity and self-sacrifice, for the celebration of our Lord's paschal mystery. Today we come together to begin this solemn celebration in union with the whole Church throughout the world. Christ entered in triumph into his own city, to complete his work as our Messiah: to suffer, to die, and to rise again. Let us remember with devotion this entry which began his saving work and follow him with a lively faith. United with him in his suffering on the cross, may we share his resurrection and new life.

Afterwards the priest says one of the following payers:
Let us pray.

Almighty God,
we pray you
bless ✠ these branches
and make them holy.
Today we joyfully acclaim Jesus our Messiah and King.
May we reach one day the happiness of the new and everlasting Jerusalem
by faithfully following him
who lives and reigns for ever and ever.

or
Let us pray.

Lord, increase the faith of your people
and listen to our prayers.
Today we honour Christ our triumphant King
by carrying these branches.
May we honour you every day
by living always in him,
for he is Lord for ever and ever.

The priest sprinkles the palm branches with holy water. Then the account of the Lord's entrance is read from one of the four gospels.
Gospel A, B or C is read according to the Cycle for the Year.

A
Gospel   Matthew 21:1-11

Blessings on him who comes in the name of the Lord!

When they were near Jerusalem and had come in sight of Bethphage on the Mount of Olives, Jesus sent two disciples, saying to them, "Go to the village facing you, and you will immediately find a tethered donkey and a colt with her. Untie them and bring them to me. If anyone says anything to you, you

PASSION SUNDAY/A/B/C

are to say, 'The Master needs them and will send them back directly.' " This took place to fulfil the prophecy:

Say to the daughter of Zion:
Look, your king comes to you;
he is humble, he rides on a donkey
and on a colt, the foal of a beast of burden.

So the disciples went out and did as Jesus had told them. They brought the donkey and the colt, then they laid their cloaks on their backs and he sat on them. Great crowds of people spread their cloaks on the road, while others were cutting branches from the trees and spreading them in his path. The crowds who went in front of him and those who followed were all shouting:
"Hosanna to the Son of David!
Blessings on him who comes in the name of the Lord!
Hosanna in the highest heavens!"

And when he entered Jerusalem, the whole city was in turmoil. "Who is this?" people asked, and the crowds answered, "This is the prophet Jesus from Nazareth in Galilee."

B
Gospel   Mark 11:1-10

Blessings on him who comes in the name of the Lord.

When they were approaching Jerusalem, in sight of Bethphage and Bethany, close by the Mount of Olives, Jesus sent two of his disciples and said to them, "Go off to the village facing you, and as soon as you enter it you will find a tethered colt that no one has yet ridden. Untie it and bring it here. If anyone says to you, 'What are you doing?' say, 'The Master needs it and will send it back here directly.' They went off and found a colt tethered near a door in the open street. As they untied it, some men standing there said, "What are you doing, untying that colt?" They gave the answer Jesus had told them, and the men let them go. Then they took the colt to Jesus and threw their cloaks on its back, and he sat on it. Many people spread their cloaks on the road, others greenery which they had cut in the fields. And those who went in front and those who followed were all shouting, "Hosanna! Blessings on him who comes in the name of the Lord! Blessings on the coming kingdom of our father David! Hosanna in the highest heavens!"

or
B John 12:12-16
Blessings on him who comes in the name of the Lord.

The crowds who had come up for the festival heard that Jesus was on his way to Jerusalem. They took branches of palm and went out to meet him, shouting, "Hosanna! Blessings on the King of Israel, who comes in the name of the Lord." Jesus found a young donkey and mounted it — as scripture says: Do not be afraid, daughter of Zion; see, your king is coming, mounted on the colt of a donkey. At the time his disciples did not understand this, but later, after Jesus had been glorified, they remembered that this had been written about him and that this was in fact how they had received him.

C
Gospel Luke 19:28-40
Blessings on him who comes in the name of the Lord.

Jesus went on ahead, going up to Jerusalem. Now when he was near Bethphage and Bethany, close by the Mount of Olives as it is called, he sent two of the disciples, telling them, "Go off to the village opposite, and as you enter it you will find a tethered colt that no one has yet ridden. Untie it and bring it here. If anyone asks you, 'Why are you untying it?' you are to say this, 'The Master needs it.' " The messengers went off and found everything just as he had told them. As they were untying the colt, its owner said, "Why are you untying that colt?" and they answered, "The Master needs it."

So they took the colt to Jesus, and throwing their garments over its back they helped Jesus on to it. As he moved off, people spread their cloaks in the road, and now, as he was approaching the downward slope of the Mount of Olives, the whole group of disciples joyfully began to praise God at the top of their voices for all the miracles they had seen. They cried out:
"Blessings on the King who comes,
in the name of the Lord!
Peace in heaven
and glory in the highest heavens!"

Some Pharisees in the crowd said to him, "Master, check your disciples," but he answered, "I tell you, if these keep silence the stones will cry out."

PASSION SUNDAY/A/B/C

After the gospel a brief homily may be given. Before the procession begins, the celebrant or other suitable minister may address the people in these or similar words:

Let us go forth in peace,
praising Jesus our Messiah,
as did the crowds who welcomed him to Jerusalem.

The procession to the church where Mass will be celebrated then begins. During the procession, the choir and people sing the following or other appropriate songs:

Antiphon

The children of Jerusalem
welcomed Christ the King.
They carried olive branches
and loudly praised the Lord:
Hosanna in the highest.

The antiphon may be repeated between the verses of psalm 23.

Psalm 23

1. The Lord's is the earth and its fullness,
   the world and all its peoples.
   It is he who set it on the seas;
   on the waters he made it firm. (Ant.)

2. Who shall climb the mountain of the Lord?
   Who shall stand in his holy place?
   The man with clean hands and pure heart,
   who desires not worthless things,
   (who has not sworn so as to deceive his neighbour). (Ant.)

3. He shall receive blessings from the Lord
   and reward from the God who saves him.
   Such are the men who seek him,
   seek the face of the God of Jacob. (Ant.)

4. O gates, lift high your heads;
   grow higher, ancient doors.
   Let him enter, the king of glory. (Ant.)

5. Who is the king of glory?
   The Lord, the mighty, the valiant,
   the Lord, the valiant in war. (Ant.)

PASSION SUNDAY/A/B/C

6. O gates, lift high your heads;
grow higher, ancient doors.
Let him enter, the king of glory! (Ant.)

7. Who is he, the king of glory?
He, the Lord of armies.
he is the king of glory. (Ant.)

Antiphon

The children of Jerusalem
welcomed Christ the King.
They spread their cloaks before him
and loudly praised the Lord:
Hosanna to the Son of David!
Blessed is he who comes
in the name of the Lord!

The antiphon may be repeated between the verses of Psalm 46.

Psalm 46

1. All peoples, clap your hands,
cry to God with shouts of joy!
For the Lord, the Most High, we must fear,
great king over all the earth. (Ant.)

2. He subdues peoples under us
and nations under our feet.
Our inheritance, our glory, is from him,
given to Jacob out of love. (Ant.)

3. God goes up with shouts of joy;
the Lord goes up with trumpet blast.
Sing praise for God, sing praise,
sing praise to our king, sing praise. (Ant.)

4. God is king of all the earth.
Sing praise with all your skill.
God is king over the nations;
God reigns on his holy throne. (Ant.)

5. The princes of the peoples are assembled
with the people of Abraham's God.
The rulers of the earth belong to God,
to God who reigns over all. (Ant.)

PASSION SUNDAY/A/B/C

Hymn to Christ the King

**℟ All glory, laud and honour
To thee, Redeemer, King,
To whom the lips of children
Made sweet hosannas ring.**

Thou art the King of Israel,
Thou David's royal Son,
Who in the Lord's name comest,
The king and blessed one. ℟

The company of angels
Are praising thee on high,
And mortal men and all things
Created make reply. ℟

The people of the Hebrews
With palms before thee went;
Our praise and prayer and anthems
Before thee we present. ℟

To thee before thy Passion
They sang their hymns of praise;
To thee now high exalted
Our melody we raise. ℟

Thou didst accept their praises,
Accept the prayers we bring,
Who in all good delightest
Thou good and gracious king. ℟

Entry into the Church

As the procession enters the church, the following responsory or another song which refers to the Lord's entrance is sung.

**℟ The children of Jerusalem
welcomed Christ the King.
They proclaimed the resurrection of life,
and, waving olive branches,
they loudly praised the Lord:
Hosanna in the highest.**

℣ When the people heard that Jesus
was entering Jerusalem,
they went to meet him

and, waving olive branches,
they loudly praised the Lord:
Hosanna in the highest.

The Mass now begins with the Opening Prayer on page 271.

Second Form: The Solemn Entrance

If the procession cannot be held outside the church, the commemoration of the Lord's entrance may be celebrated before the principal Mass with the solemn entrance, which takes place within the church.

The congregation, holding palm branches, assembles either in front of the church door or inside the church. The priest and ministers, with a representative group of the faithful, go to a suitable place in the church outside the sanctuary, so that most of the people will be able to see the rite.

While the priest goes to the appointed place, the antiphon **Hosanna** or another suitable song is sung. Then the blessing of branches and proclamation of the gospel about the Lord's entrance into Jerusalem take place, as above. After the gospel the priest, with the ministers and the group of the faithful, moves solemnly through the church to the sanctuary, while the responsory **The Children of Jerusalem** or another appropriate song is sung.

The Mass then begins with the Opening Prayer on page 271.

Third Form: The Simple Entrance

At all other Masses on this Sunday, if the Solemn entrance is not held, the Lord's entrance is commemorated with the following simple entrance.

While the priest goes to the altar, the entrance antiphon (see below) with its psalm or another song with the same theme is sung, and the Mass continues in the usual way.

Entrance Antiphon Six days before the solemn passover the Lord came to Jerusalem, and children waving palm branches ran out to welcome him. They loudly praised the Lord: Hosanna in the highest. Blessed are you who have come to us so rich in love and mercy.

PASSION SUNDAY/A/B/C

Psalm 23:9-10

Open wide the doors and gates.
Lift high the ancient portals.
The King of glory enters.

Who is this King of glory?
He is God the mighty Lord.

Hosanna in the highest.
Blessed are you who have come to us
so rich in love and mercy.

PASSION SUNDAY/A/B/C

THE MASS

Opening Prayer

Let us pray
   [for a closer union with Christ
   during this holy season]

Almighty, ever-living God,
you have given the human race Jesus Christ our Saviour
as a model of humility.
He fulfilled your will
by becoming man and giving his life on the cross.
Help us to bear witness to you
by following his example of suffering
and make us worthy to share in his resurrection.

or

Let us pray
   [as we accompany our King to Jerusalem]

Almighty Father of our Lord Jesus Christ,
you sent your Son
to be born of woman and to die on a cross,
so that through the obedience of one man,
estrangement might be dissolved for all men.

Guide our minds by his truth
and strengthen our lives by the example of his death,
that we may live in union with you
in the kingdom of your promise.

First Reading   Isaiah 50:4-7

I did not cover my face against insult — I know I shall not be shamed.

The Lord has given me
a disciple's tongue.
So that I may know how to reply to the wearied
he provides me with speech.
Each morning he wakes me to hear,
to listen like a disciple.
The Lord has opened my ear.

PASSION SUNDAY/A/B/C

For my part, I made no resistance,
neither did I turn away.
I offered my back to those who struck me,
my cheeks to those who tore at my beard;
I did not cover my face
against insult and spittle.

The Lord comes to my help,
so that I am untouched by the insults.
So, too, I set my face like flint;
I know I shall not be shamed.

Responsorial Psalm   Psalm 21

R/ My God, my God, why have you forsaken me?

1. All who see me deride me.
   They curl their lips, they toss their heads.
   "He trusted in the Lord, let him save him;
   let him release him if this is his friend." R/

2. Many dogs have surrounded me,
   a band of the wicked beset me.
   They tear holes in my hands and my feet
   I can count every one of my bones. R/

3. They divide my clothing among them.
   They cast lots for my robe.
   O Lord, do not leave me alone,
   my strength, make haste to help me! R/

4. I will tell of your name to my brethren
   and praise you where they are assembled.
   "You who fear the Lord give him praise;
   all sons of Jacob, give him glory.
   Revere him, Israel's sons." R/

Second Reading   Philippians 2:6-11

He humbled himself, but God raised him high.

His state was divine,
yet Christ Jesus did not cling
to his equality with God
but emptied himself
to assume the condition of a slave,
and became as men are;

and being as all men are,
he was humbler yet,
even to accepting death,
death on a cross.
But God raised him high
and gave him the name
which is above all other names
so that all beings
in the heavens, on earth and in the underworld,
should bend the knee at the name of Jesus
and that every tongue should acclaim
Jesus Christ as Lord,
to the glory of God the Father.

Acclamation   Praise to you, O Christ, king of eternal glory! Christ was humbler yet, even to accepting death, death on a cross. But God raised him high and gave him the name which is above all names. Praise to you, O Christ, king of eternal glory!
Philippians 2:8-9.

Gospel A, B or C is read according to the Cycle for the year.

The Passion may be read by three people. One reads the narrative: his part is marked N; a deacon or priest reads the words of Christ (✠), and the third person reads the words of other speakers (C). The congregation may take the part of the crowd which is printed in bold type.

A
Gospel   Matthew 26:14-27.66
The passion of our Lord Jesus Christ according to Matthew.

N. One of the Twelve, the man called Judas Iscariot, went to the chief priests and said, C. "What are you prepared to give me if I hand him over to you?" N. They paid him thirty silver pieces, and from that moment he looked for an opportunity to betray him.

Now on the first day of Unleavened Bread the disciples came to Jesus to say, C. **"Where do you want us to make the preparations for you to eat the passover?"** N. He replied, ✠ "Go to

PASSION SUNDAY/A

so-and-so in the city and say to him, 'The Master says: My time is near. It is at your house that I am keeping Passover with my disciples'." N. The disciples did what Jesus told them and prepared the Passover.

When the evening came he was at table with the twelve disciples. And while they were eating he said, ✠ "I tell you solemnly, one of you is about to betray me." N. They were greatly distressed and started asking him in turn, C. "Not I, Lord, surely?" N. He answered, ✠ "Someone who has dipped his hand into the dish with me, will betray me. The Son of Man is going to his fate, as the scriptures say he will, but alas for that man by whom the Son of Man is betrayed! Better for that man if he had never been born!" N. Judas, who was to betray him, asked in his turn, C. "Not I, Rabbi surely?" N. Jesus answered, ✠ "They are your own words."

N. Now as they were eating, Jesus took some bread, and when he had said the blessing he broke it and gave it to the disciples and said, ✠ "Take it and eat; this is my body." N. Then he took a cup, and when he had returned thanks he gave it to them saying, ✠ "Drink all of you from this, for this is my blood, the blood of the covenant, which is to be poured out for many for the forgiveness of sins. From now on, I tell you, I shall not drink wine until the day I drink the new wine with you in the kingdom of my Father."

N. After psalms had been sung they left for the Mount of Olives. Then Jesus said to them, ✠ "You will all lose faith in me this night, for the scripture says: I shall strike the shepherd and the sheep of the flock will be scattered. But after my resurrection I shall go before you to Galilee." N. At this, Peter said, C. "Though all lose faith in you, I will never lose faith." N. Jesus answered him, ✠ "I tell you solemnly, this very night, before the cock crows, you will have disowned me three times." N. Peter said to him, C. "Even if I have to die with you, I will never disown you." N. And all the disciples said the same.

Then Jesus came with them to a small estate called Gethsemane; and he said to his disciples, ✠ "Stay here while I go over there to pray." N. He took Peter and the two sons of Zebedee with him. And sadness came over him, and great distress. Then he said to them, ✠ "My soul is sorrowful to the point of death. Wait here and keep awake with me." N. And going on a little further he fell on his face and prayed, ✠ "My

PASSION SUNDAY/A

Father, if it is possible let this cup pass me by. Nevertheless, let it be as you, not I, would have it." N. He came back to the disciples and found them sleeping, and he said to Peter, ✠ "So you had not the strength to keep awake with me one hour? You should be awake, and praying not to be put to the test. The Spirit is willing, but the flesh is weak." N. Again, a second time, he went away and prayed: ✠ "My Father, if this cup cannot pass by without my drinking it, your will be done!" N. And he came again back and found them sleeping, their eyes were so heavy. Leaving them there, he went away again and prayed for the third time, repeating the same words. Then he came back to the disciples and said to them, ✠ "You can sleep on now and take your rest. Now the hour has come when the Son of Man is to be betrayed into the hands of sinners. Get up! Let us go! My betrayer is already close at hand."

N. He was still speaking when Judas, one of the Twelve, appeared, and with him a large number of men armed with swords and clubs, sent by the chief priests and elders of the people. Now the traitor had arranged a sign with them. He had said, C. "The one I kiss, he is the man. Take him in charge." N. So he went straight up to Jesus and said, C. "Greetings, Rabbi," N. and kissed him. Jesus said to him, ✠ "My friend, do what you are here for." N. Then they came forward, seized Jesus and took him in charge. At that, one of the followers of Jesus grasped his sword and drew it; he struck out at the high priest's servant, and cut off his ear. Jesus then said, ✠ "Put your sword back, for all who draw the sword will die by the sword. Or do you think that I cannot appeal to my Father who would promptly send more than twelve legions of angels to my defence? But then, how would the scriptures be fulfilled that say this is the way it must be?" N. It was at this time that Jesus said to the crowds, ✠ "Am I a brigand, that you had to set out to capture me with swords and clubs? I sat teaching in the Temple day after day and you never laid hands on me." N. Now all this happened to fulfil the prophecies in scripture. Then all the disciples deserted him and ran away.

The men who had arrested Jesus led him off to Caiaphas the high priest, where the scribes and the elders were assembled. Peter followed him at a distance, and when he reached the high priest's palace, he went in and sat down with the attendants to see what the end would be.

PASSION SUNDAY/A

The chief priests and the whole Sanhedrin were looking for evidence against Jesus, however false, on which they might pass the death-sentence. But they could not find any, though several lying witnesses came forward. Eventually two stepped forward and made a statement, C. **"This man said, 'I have power to destroy the Temple of God and in three days build it up'."** N. The high priest then stood up and said to him, C. "Have you no answer to that? What is this evidence these men are bringing against you?" N. But Jesus was silent. And the high priest said to him, C. "I put you on oath by the living God to tell us if you are the Christ, the Son of God." N. Jesus answered, ✠ "The words are your own. Moreover, I tell you that from this time onward you will see the Son of Man seated at the right hand of the Power and coming on the clouds of heaven." N. At this, the high priest tore his clothes and said, C. "He has blasphemed. What need of witnesses have we now? There! You have just heard the blasphemy. What is your opinion?" N. They answered, C. **"He deserves to die".**

N. Then they spat in his face and hit him with their fists; others said as they struck him, C. **"Play the prophet, Christ! Who hit you then?".**

N. Meanwhile Peter was sitting outside in the courtyard, and a servant-girl came up to him and said, C. "You too were with Jesus the Galilean". N. But he denied it in front of them all, saying C. "I do not know what you are talking about". N. When he went out to the gateway another servant-girl saw him and said to the people there, C. "This man was with Jesus the Nazarene". N. And again, with an oath, he denied it, C. "I do not know the man". N. A little later the bystanders came up and said to Peter, C. **"You are one of them for sure! Why, your accent gives you away."** N. Then he started calling down curses on himself and swearing, C. "I do not know the man". N. At that moment the cock crew, and Peter remembered what Jesus had said, "Before the cock crows you will have disowned me three times". And he went outside and wept bitterly.

When morning came, all the chief priests and the elders of the people met in council to bring about the death of Jesus. They had him bound, and led him away to hand him over to Pilate, the governor.

When he found that Jesus had been condemned, Judas his betrayer was filled with remorse and took the thirty pieces of

PASSION SUNDAY/A

silver back to the chief priests and elders, saying, **C.** "I have sinned. I have betrayed innocent blood". **N.** They replied, **C. "What is that to us? That is your concern".** **N.** And flinging down the silver pieces in the sanctuary he made off, and went and hanged himself. The chief priests picked up the silver pieces and said, **C. "It is against the Law to put this into the treasury; it is blood money".** **N.** So they discussed the matter and bought the potter's field with it as a graveyard for foreigners, and this is why the field is called the Field of Blood today. The words of the prophet Jeremiah were then fulfilled: And they took the thirty silver pieces, the sum at which the precious One was priced by children of Israel, and they gave them for the potter's field, just as the Lord directed me.

Jesus, then, was brought before the governor, and the governor put to him this question, **C.** "Are you the king of the Jews?". **N.** Jesus replied, ✠ "It is you who say it". **N.** But when he was accused by the chief priests and the elders he refused to answer at all. Pilate then said to him, **C.** "Do you not hear how many charges they have brought against you?". **N.** But to the governor's complete amazement, he offered no reply to any of the charges.

At festival time it was the governor's practice to release a prisoner for the people, anyone they chose. Now there was at that time a notorious prisoner whose name was Barabbas. So when the crowd gathered, Pilate said to them, **C.** "Which do you want me to release for you: Barabbas or Jesus who is called Christ?". **N.** For Pilate knew it was out of jealousy that they had handed him over.

Now as he was seated in the chair of judgement, his wife sent him a message, **C.** "Have nothing to do with that man; I have been upset all day by a dream I had about him".

N. The chief priests and the elders, however, had persuaded the crowd to demand the release of Barabbas and the execution of Jesus. So when the governor spoke and asked them, **C.** "Which of the two do you want me to release for you?". **N.** They said, **C. "Barabbas".** **N.** Pilate said to them, **C.** "What am I to do with Jesus who is called Christ?". **N.** They all said, **C. "Let him be crucified!".** **N.** Pilate asked, **C.** "Why? What harm has he done?". **N.** But they all shouted the louder, **C. "Let him be crucified!".** **N.** Then Pilate saw that he was making no impression, that in fact a riot was imminent. So he took some water, washed his hands in front of the crowd and said, C. "I am innocent of this man's blood. It is your concern". N. And the people, to a man, shouted back, C. **"His blood be on us and on our children!"**. N. Then he released Barabbas for them. He ordered Jesus to be first scourged and then handed over to be crucified.

The governor's soldiers took Jesus with them into the Praetorium and collected the whole cohort round him. Then they stripped him and made him wear a scarlet cloak, and having twisted some thorns into a crown they put this on his head and placed a reed in his right hand. To make fun of him they knelt to him saying, C. **"Hail, king of the Jews!"**. N. And they spat on him and took the reed and struck him on the head with it. And when they had finished making fun of him, they took off the cloak and dressed him in his own clothes and led him away to crucify him.

On their way out, they came across a man from Cyrene, Simon by name, and enlisted him to carry his cross. When they had reached a place called Golgotha, that is, the place of the skull, they gave him wine to drink mixed with gall, which he tasted but refused to drink. When they had finished crucifying him they shared out his clothing by casting lots, and then sat down and stayed there keeping guard over him.

Above his head was placed the charge against him: it read: 'This is Jesus, the King of the Jews'. At the same time two robbers were crucified with him, one on the right and one on the left.

The passers-by jeered at him; they shook their heads and said, C. **"So you would destroy the Temple and rebuild it in three days! Then save yourself! If you are God's son, come down from the cross!"**. N. The chief priests, with the scribes and elders mocked him in the same way, saying, C. **"He saved others; he cannot save himself. He is the King of Israel; let him come down from the cross now, and we will believe in him. He put his trust in God; now let God rescue him if he wants him. For he did say, 'I am the son of God'."** N. Even the robbers who were crucified with him taunted him in the same way.

From the sixth hour there was darkness over all the land until the ninth hour. And about the ninth hour, Jesus cried out in a loud voice, ✠ "Eli, Eli, Lama sabachthani?". N. That is,

PASSION SUNDAY/A

✠ "My God, my God, why have you deserted me?". N. When some of those who stood there heard this, they said, C. **"The man is calling on Elijah,"** N. and one of them quickly ran to get a sponge which he dipped in vinegar and, putting it on a reed, gave it him to drink. The rest of them said, C. **"Wait! See if Elijah will come to save him".** N. But Jesus, again crying out in a loud voice, yielded up his spirit.

At that, the veil of the Temple was torn in two from top to bottom; the earth quaked; the rocks were split; the tombs opened and the bodies of many holy men rose from the dead, and these, after his resurrection, came out of the tombs, entered the Holy City and appeared to a number of people. Meanwhile the centurion, together with the others guarding Jesus, had seen the earthquake and all that was taking place, and they were terrified and said, C. **"In truth this was a son of God".**

N. And many women were there, watching from a distance, the same women who had followed Jesus from Galilee and looked after him. Among them were Mary of Magdala, Mary the mother of James and Joseph, the mother of Zebedee's sons.

When it was evening, there came a rich man of Arimathaea, called Joseph, who had himself become a disciple of Jesus. This man went to Pilate and asked for the body of Jesus. Pilate thereupon ordered it to be handed over. So Joseph took the body, wrapped it in a clean shroud and put it in his own new tomb which he had hewn out of the rock. He then rolled a large stone across the entrance of the tomb and went away. Now Mary of Magdala and the other Mary were there, sitting opposite the sepulchre.

Next day, that is, when Preparation Day was over, the chief priests and the Pharisees went in a body to Pilate and said to him, C. **"Your Excellency, we recall that this impostor said, while he was still alive, 'After three days I shall rise again'. Therefore give the order to have the sepulchre kept secure until the third day, for fear his disciples come and steal him away and tell the people, 'He has risen from the dead'. This last piece of fraud would be worse than what went before".** N. Pilate said to them, C. **"You may have your guards. Go and make all as secure as you know how".** N. So they went and made the sepulchre secure, putting seals on the stone and mounting a guard.

PASSION SUNDAY/B

B
Gospel   Mark 14:1-15.47

The passion of our Lord Jesus Christ according to Mark.

N. It was two days before the Passover and the feast of Unleavened Bread, and the chief priests and the scribes were looking for a way to arrest Jesus by some trick and have him put to death. For they said, C. **"It must not be during the festivities, or there will be a disturbance among the people."**

N. Jesus was at Bethany in the house of Simon the leper; he was at dinner when a woman came in with an alabaster jar of very costly ointment, pure nard. She broke the jar and poured the ointment on his head. Some who were there said to one another indignantly, C. **"Why this waste of ointment? Ointment like this could have been sold for over three hundred denarii and the money given to the poor;"** N. and they were angry with her. But Jesus said, ✠ "Leave her alone. Why are you upsetting her? What she has done for me is one of the good works. You have the poor with you always, and you can be kind to them whenever you wish, but you will not always have me. She has done what was in her power to do; she has anointed my body beforehand for its burial. I tell you solemnly, wherever throughout all the world the Good News is proclaimed, what she has done will be told also, in remembrance of her."

N. Judas Iscariot, one of the Twelve, approached the chief priests with an offer to hand Jesus over to them. They were delighted to hear it, and promised to give him money; and he looked for a way of betraying him when the opportunity should occur.

On the first day of Unleavened Bread, when the Passover lamb was sacrificed, his disciples said to him, C. **"Where do you want us to go and make the preparations for you to eat the passover?"** N. So he sent two of his disciples, saying to them, ✠ "Go into the city and you will meet a man carrying a pitcher of water. Follow him, and say to the owner of the house which he enters, "The Master says: Where is my dining room in which I can eat the passover with my disciples?' He will show you a large upper room furnished with couches, all prepared. Make the preparations for us there." N. The disciples set out and went to the city and found everything as he had told them, and prepared the Passover.

PASSION SUNDAY/B

When evening came he arrived with the Twelve. And while they were at table eating, Jesus said, ✠ "I tell you solemnly, one of you is about to betray me, one of you eating with me." N. They were distressed and asked him, one after another, C. "Not I, surely?" N. He said to them, ✠ "It is one of the Twelve, one who is dipping into the same dish with me. Yes, the Son of Man is going to his fate, as the scriptures say he will, but alas for that man by whom the Son of Man is betrayed! Better for that man if he had never been born!"

N. And as they were eating he took some bread, and when he had said the blessing he broke it and gave it to them, saying, ✠ "Take it; this is my body." N. Then he took a cup, and when he had returned thanks he gave it to them, and all drank from it, and he said to them, ✠ "This is my blood, the blood of the covenant, which is to be poured out for many. I tell you solemnly, I shall not drink any more wine until the day I drink the new wine in the kingdom of God."

N. After psalms had been sung they left for the Mount of Olives. And Jesus said to them, ✠ "You will all lose faith, for the scripture says, 'I shall strike the shepherd and the sheep will be scattered'. However after my resurrection I shall go before you to Galilee." N. Peter said, C. "Even if all lose faith, I will not." N. And Jesus said to him, ✠ "I tell you solemnly, this day, this very night, before the cock crows twice, you will have disowned me three times." N. But he repeated still more earnestly, C. "If I have to die with you, I will never disown you." N. And they all said the same.

They came to a small estate called Gethsemane, and Jesus said to his disciples, ✠ "Stay here while I pray." N. Then he took Peter and James and John with him. And a sudden fear came over him, and great distress. And he said to them, ✠ "My soul is sorrowful to the point of death. Wait here, and keep awake." N. And going on a little further he threw himself on the ground and prayed that, if it were possible, this hour might pass him by. He said, ✠ "Abba (Father)! Everything is possible for you. Take this cup away from me. But let it be as you, not I, would have it." N. He came back and found them sleeping, and he said to Peter, ✠ "Simon, are you asleep? Had you not the strength to keep awake one hour? You should be awake, and praying not to be put to the test. The spirit is willing but the flesh is weak." N. Again he went away and prayed, saying the same words. And once more

PASSION SUNDAY/B

he came back and found them sleeping, their eyes were so heavy; and they could find no answer for him. He came back a third time and said to them, ✠ "You can sleep on now and take your rest. It is all over. The hour has come. Now the Son of Man is to be betrayed into the hands of sinners. Get up! Let us go! My betrayer is close at hand already."

N. Even while he was still speaking, Judas, one of the Twelve, came up with a number of men armed with swords and clubs, sent by the chief priests and the scribes and the elders. Now the traitor had arranged a signal with them. He had said, C. "The one I kiss, he is the man. Take him in charge, and see he is well guarded when you lead him away." N. So when the traitor came, he went straight up to Jesus and said, C. "Rabbi!" N. and kissed him. The others seized him and took him in charge. Then one of the bystanders drew his sword and struck out at the high priest's servant, and cut off his ear.

Then Jesus spoke, ✠ "Am I a brigand that you had to set out to capture me with swords and clubs? I was among you teaching in the Temple day after day and you never laid hands on me. But this is to fulfil the scriptures." N. And they all deserted him and ran away. A young man who followed him had nothing on but a linen cloth. They caught hold of him, but he left the cloth in their hands and ran away naked.

They led Jesus off to the high priest; and all the chief priests and the elders and the scribes assembled there. Peter had followed him at a distance, right into the high priest's palace, and was sitting with the attendants warming himself at the fire.

The chief priests and the whole Sanhedrin were looking for evidence against Jesus on which they might pass the death-sentence. But they could not find any. Several, indeed, brought false evidence against him, but their evidence was conflicting. Some stood up and submitted this false evidence against him, C. **"We heard him say, 'I am going to destroy this Temple made by human hands, and in three days build another, not made by human hands'."** N. But even on this point their evidence was conflicting. The high priest then stood up before the whole assembly and put this question to Jesus, C. "Have you no answer to that? What is this evidence these men are bringing against you?" N. But he was silent and made no answer at all. The high priest put a second question to him, C. "Are you the Christ the Son of the Blessed One?". N. Jesus said, ✠ "I am, and you will see

PASSION SUNDAY/B

the Son of Man seated at the right hand of the Power and coming with the clouds of heaven". N. The high priest tore his robes, and said, C. "What need of witnesses have we now? You heard the blasphemy. What is your finding?". N. And they all gave their verdict: he deserved to die.

Some of them started spitting at him and, blindfolding him, began hitting him with their fists and shouting, C. **"Play the prophet!".** N. And the attendants rained blows on him.

While Peter was down below in the courtyard, one of the high-priest's servant-girls came up. She saw Peter warming himself there, stared at him and said, C. "You too were with Jesus, the man from Nazareth". N. But he denied it, saying C. "I do not know, I do not understand, what you are talking about". N. And he went out into the forecourt. The servant-girl saw him and again started telling bystanders, C. "This fellow is one of them". N. But he again denied it. A little later the bystanders themselves said to Peter, C. **"You are one of them for sure! Why, you are a Galilean".** N. But he started calling curses on himself and swearing, C. "I do not know the man you speak of". N. At that moment the cock crew for the second time, and Peter recalled how Jesus had said to him, 'Before the cock crows twice, you will have disowned me three times'. And he burst into tears.

First thing in the morning, the chief priests together with the elders and scribes, in short the whole Sanhedrin, had their plan ready. They had Jesus bound and took him away and handed him over to Pilate.

Pilate questioned him, C. "Are you the king of the Jews?". N. He answered, ✠ "It is you who say it". N. And the chief priests brought many accusations against him. Pilate questioned him again, C. "Have you no reply at all? See how many accusations they are bringing against you!". N. But to Pilate's amazement, Jesus made no further reply.

At festival time Pilate used to release a prisoner for them, anyone they asked for. Now a man called Barabbas was then in prison with the rioters who had committed murder during the uprising. When the crowd went up and began to ask Pilate the customary favour, Pilate answered them, C. "Do you want me to release for you the king of the Jews?". N. For he realised it was out of jealousy that the chief priests had handed Jesus over. The chief priests, however, had incited the crowd to demand that he should release Barabbas for them instead.

PASSION SUNDAY/B

Then Pilate spoke again. C. "But in that case, what am I to do with the man you call king of the Jews?". N. "They shouted back, C. **"Crucify him!"**. N. Pilate asked them, C. "Why? What harm has he done?". N. But they shouted all the louder, C. **"Crucify him!"**. N. So Pilate, anxious to placate the crowd, released Barabbas for them and, having ordered Jesus to be scourged, handed him over to be crucified.

The soldiers led him away to the inner part of the palace, that is, the Praetorium, and called the whole cohort together. They dressed him up in purple, twisted some thorns into a crown and put it on him. And they began saluting him, C. **"Hail, king of the Jews!"**. N. They struck his head with a reed and spat on him; and they went down on their knees to do him homage. And when they had finished making fun of him, they took off the purple and dressed him in his own clothes.

They led him out to crucify him. They enlisted a passer-by, Simon of Cyrene, father of Alexander and Rufus, who was coming in from the country, to carry his cross. They brought Jesus to the place called Golgotha, which means the place of the skull.

They offered him wine mixed with myrrh, but he refused it. Then they crucified him, and shared out his clothing, casting lots to decide what each should get. It was the third hour when they crucified him. The inscription giving the charge against him read: 'The King of the Jews'. And they crucified two robbers with him, one on his right and one on his left.

The passers-by jeered at him; they shook their heads and said, C. **"Aha! So you would destroy the Temple and rebuild it in three days! Then save yourself: come down from the cross!"**. N. The chief priests and the scribes mocked him among themselves in the same way. They said, C. **"He saved others, he cannot save himself. Let the Christ, the king of Israel, come down from the cross now, for us to see it and believe"**. N. Even those who were crucified with him taunted him.

When the sixth hour came there was darkness over the whole land until the ninth hour. And at the ninth hour Jesus cried out in a loud voice, ✠ "Eloi, Eloi, lama sabachthani?". N. This means ✠ "My God, my God, why have you deserted me?". N. When some of those who stood by heard this, they said, C. **"Listen, he is calling on Elijah"**. N. Someone ran and soaked a sponge in vinegar and, putting it on a reed, gave it him to drink, saying, C. "Wait and see if Elijah will come to take him down". N. But Jesus gave a loud cry and breathed his last. And the veil of the Temple was torn in two from top to bottom. The centurion, who was standing in front of him, had seen how he had died, and he said, C. "In truth this man was a son of God".

N. There were some women watching from a distance. Among them were Mary of Magdala, Mary who was the mother of James the younger and Joset, and Salome. These used to follow him and look after him when he was in Galilee. And there were many other women there who had come up to Jerusalem with him.

It was now evening, and since it was Preparation Day (that is, the vigil of the sabbath), there came Joseph of Arimathaea, a prominent member of the Council, who himself lived in the hope of seeing the kingdom of God, and he boldly went to Pilate and asked for the body of Jesus. Pilate, astonished that he should have died so soon, summoned the centurion and enquired if he was already dead. Having been assured of this by the centurion, he granted the corpse to Joseph who bought a shroud, took Jesus down from the cross, wrapped him in the shroud and laid him in a tomb which had been hewn out of the rock. He then rolled a stone against the entrance of the tomb. Mary of Magdala and Mary the mother of Joset were watching and took note of where he was laid.

C
Gospel Luke 22:14-23:56

The passion of our Lord Jesus Christ according to Luke.

N. When the hour came Jesus took his place at table, and the apostles with him. And he said to them, ✠ "I have longed to eat this passover with you before I suffer; because, I tell you, I shall not eat it again until it is fulfilled in the kingdom of God."

N. Then, taking a cup, he gave thanks and said, ✠ "Take this and share it among you, because from now on, I tell you, I shall not drink wine until the kingdom of God comes."

N. Then he took some bread, and when he had given thanks, broke it and gave it to them, saying, ✠ "This is my body which will be given for you; do this as a memorial of me." N. He did the

PASSION SUNDAY/C

same with the cup after supper, and said, ✠ "This cup is the new covenant in my blood which will be poured out for you.

"And yet, here with me on the table is the hand of the man who betrays me. The Son of Man does indeed go to his fate even as it has been decreed, but alas for that man by whom he is betrayed!" N. And they began to ask one another which of them it could be who was to do this thing.

A dispute arose also between them about which should be reckoned the greatest, but he said to them, ✠ "Among pagans it is the kings who lord it over them, and those who have authority over them are given the title Benefactor. This must not happen with you. No; the greatest among you must behave as if he were the youngest, the leader as if he were the one who serves. For who is the greater: the one at table or the one who serves? The one at table, surely? Yet here am I among you as one who serves!

"You are the men who have stood by me faithfully in my trials; and now I confer a kingdom on you, just as my Father conferred one on me: you will eat and drink at my table in my kingdom, and you will sit on thrones to judge the twelve tribes of Israel.

"Simon, Simon! Satan, you must know, has got his wish to sift you all like wheat; but I have prayed for you, Simon, that your faith may not fail, and once you have recovered, you in your turn must strengthen your brothers." N. He answered, C. "Lord, I would be ready to go to prison with you, and to death." N. Jesus replied, ✠ "I tell you, Peter, by the time the cock crows today you will have denied three times that you know me."

N. He said to them, ✠ "When I sent you out without purse or sandals, were you short of anything?" N. They answered, C. **"No."** N. He said to them, ✠ "But now if you have a purse, take it: if you have a haversack, do the same; if you have no sword, sell your cloak and buy one, because I tell you these words of scripture have to be fulfilled in me: He let himself be taken for a criminal. Yes, what scripture says about me is even now reaching its fulfilment." N. They said, C. **"Lord, there are two swords here now."** N. He said to them, ✠ "That is enough!" N. He then left the upper room to make his way as usual to the Mount of Olives, with the disciples following. When they reached the place he said to them, ✠ "Pray not to be put to the test."

N. Then he withdrew from them, about a stone's throw away, and knelt down and prayed, saying, ✠ "Father, if you are willing, take

PASSION SUNDAY/C

this cup away from me. Nevertheless, let your will be done, not mine." **N.** Then an angel appeared to him, coming from heaven to give him strength. In his anguish he prayed even more earnestly, and his sweat fell to the ground like great drops of blood.

When he rose from prayer he went to the disciples and found them sleeping for sheer grief. He said to them, ✠ "Why are you asleep? Get up and pray not to be put to the test."

N. He was still speaking when a number of men appeared, and at the head of them the man called Judas, one of the Twelve, who went up to Jesus to kiss him. Jesus said, ✠ "Judas, are you betraying the Son of Man with a kiss?" **N.** His followers, seeing what was happening, said, **C. "Lord, shall we use our swords?"** **N.** And one of them struck out at the high priest's servant, and cut off his right ear. But at this Jesus spoke, ✠ "Leave off! That will do!" **N.** And touching the man's ear he healed him.

Then Jesus spoke to the chief priests and captains of the Temple guard and elders who had come for him. He said, ✠ "Am I a brigand that you had to set out with swords and clubs? When I was among you in the Temple day after day you never moved to lay hands on me. But this is your hour; this is the reign of darkness."

N. They seized him then and led him away, and they took him to the high priest's house. Peter followed at a distance. They had lit a fire in the middle of the courtyard and Peter sat down among them, and as he was sitting there by the blaze a servant-girl saw him, peered at him and said, **C.** "This person was with him too." **N.** But he denied it, saying, **C.** "Woman, I do not know him." **N.** Shortly afterwards, someone else saw him and said, **C.** "You are another of them." **N.** But Peter replied, **C.** "I am not, my friend." **N.** About an hour later another man insisted saying, **C.** "This fellow was certainly with him. Why, he is a Galilean." **N.** Peter said, **C.** "My friend, I do not know what you are talking about." **N.** At that instant, while he was still speaking, the cock crew, and the Lord turned and looked straight at Peter, and Peter remembered what the Lord had said to him, ✠ 'Before the cock crows today, you will have disowned me three times'. And he went outside and wept bitterly.

Meanwhile the men who guarded Jesus were mocking and beating him. They blindfolded him and questioned him, saying, **C. "Play the prophet. Who hit you then?"** **N.** And they continued heaping insults on him.

PASSION SUNDAY/C

When day broke there was a meeting of the elders of the people, attended by the chief priests and scribes. He was brought before their council, and they said to him, C. **"If you are the Christ, tell us."** N. He replied, ✠ "If I tell you, you will not believe me, and if I question you, you will not answer. But from now on, the Son of Man will be seated at the right hand of the Power of God." N. Then they all said, C. **"So you are the Son of God then?"** N. He answered, ✠ "It is you who say I am." N. They said, C. **"What need of witnesses have we now? We have heard it for ourselves from his own lips."**

N. The whole assembly then rose, (the elders of the people and the chief priests and scribes rose,) and they brought him before Pilate. They began their accusation by saying, C. **"We found this man inciting our people to revolt, opposing payment of tribute to Caesar, and claiming to be Christ, a king."** N. Pilate put to him this question, C. "Are you the king of the Jews?" N. He replied, ✠ "It is you who say it." N. Pilate then said to the chief priests and the crowd, C. "I find no case against this man." N. But they persisted, C. **"He is inflaming the people with his teaching all over Judaea; it has come all the way from Galilee, where he started, down to here."** N. When Pilate heard this, he asked if the man were a Galilean; and finding that he came under Herod's jurisdiction he passed him over to Herod who was also in Jerusalem at that time.

Herod was delighted to see Jesus; he had heard about him and had been wanting for a long time to set eyes on him; moreover, he was hoping to see some miracle worked by him. So he questioned him at some length; but without getting any reply. Meanwhile the chief priests and the scribes were there, violently pressing their accusations. Then Herod, together with his guards, treated him with contempt and made fun of him; he put a rich cloak on him and sent him back to Pilate. And though Herod and Pilate had been enemies before, they were reconciled that same day.

Pilate then summoned the chief priests and the leading men and the people. He said, C. "You brought this man before me as a political agitator. Now I have gone into the matter myself in your presence and found no case against the man in respect of all the charges you bring against him. Nor has Herod either, since he has sent him back to us. As you can see, the man has

PASSION SUNDAY/C

done nothing that deserves death, so I shall have him flogged and then let him go." N. But as one man they howled, C. **"Away with him! Give us Barabbas!"** N. This man had been thrown into prison for causing a riot in the city and for murder.

Pilate was anxious to set Jesus free and addressed them again, but they shouted back. C. **"Crucify him! Crucify him!"**. N. And for the third time he spoke to them, C. "Why? What harm has this man done? I have found no case against him that deserves death, so I shall have him punished and then let him go." N. But they kept on shouting at the top of their voices, demanding that he should be crucified. And their shouts were growing louder.

Pilate then gave his verdict: their demand was to be granted. He released the man they asked for, who had been imprisoned for rioting and murder, and handed Jesus over to them to deal with as they pleased.

As they were leading him away they seized on a man, Simon from Cyrene, who was coming in from the country, and made him shoulder the cross and carry it behind Jesus. Large numbers of people followed him, and of women too, who mourned and lamented for him. But Jesus turned to them and said, ✠ "Daughters of Jerusalem, do not weep for me; weep rather for yourselves and for your children. For the days will surely come when people will say, 'Happy are those who are barren, the wombs that have never borne, the breasts that have never suckled!' Then they will begin to say to the mountains, 'Fall on us!'; to the hills, 'Cover us!' For if men use the green wood like this, what will happen when it is dry?" N. Now with him they were also leading out two other criminals to be executed.

When they reached the place called The Skull, they crucified him there and the two criminals also, one on the right, the other on the left. Jesus said, ✠ "Father, forgive them; they do not know what they are doing." N. Then they cast lots to share out his clothing.

The people stayed there watching him. As for the leaders, they jeered at him, saying, C. **"He saved others; let him save himself if he is the Christ of God, the Chosen One."** N. The soldiers mocked him too, and when they approached to offer him vinegar they said, C. **"If you are the king of the Jews, save yourself."** N. Above him there was an inscription: 'This is the

PASSION SUNDAY/C

King of the Jews.'

One of the criminals hanging there abused him, saying, C. "Are you not the Christ? Save yourself and us as well." N. But the other spoke up and rebuked him. C. "Have you no fear of God at all? You got the same sentence as he did, but in our case we deserved it: we are paying for what we did. But this man has done nothing wrong. Jesus, remember me when you come into your kingdom." N. He replied ✠ "Indeed, I promise you, today you will be with me in paradise."

N. It was now about the sixth hour and, with the sun eclipsed, a darkness came over the whole land until the ninth hour. The veil of the Temple was torn right down the middle; and when Jesus had cried out in a loud voice, he said, ✠ "Father, into your hands I commit my spirit." N. With these words he breathed his last.

When the centurion saw what had taken place, he gave praise to God and said, C. "This was a great and good man." N. And when all the people who had gathered for the spectacle saw what had happened, they went home beating their breasts.

All his friends stood at a distance; so also did the women who had accompanied him from Galilee, and they saw all this happen.

Then a member of the council arrived, an upright and virtuous man named Joseph. He had not consented to what the others had planned and carried out. He came from Arimathaea, a Jewish town, and he lived in the hope of seeing the kingdom of God. This man went to Pilate and asked for the body of Jesus. He then took it down, wrapped it in a shroud and put him in a tomb which was hewn in stone in which no one had yet been laid. It was Preparation Day and the sabbath was imminent.

Meanwhile the women who had come from Galilee with Jesus were following behind. They took note of the tomb and of the position of the body.

Then they returned and prepared spices and ointments. And on the sabbath day they rested, as the Law required.

Prayer over the Gifts

Lord,
may the suffering and death of Jesus, your only Son,

PASSION SUNDAY/C

make us pleasing to you.
Alone we can do nothing,
but may this perfect sacrifice
win us your mercy and love.

Preface

Father, all-powerful and ever-living God,
we do well always and everywhere to give you thanks
through Jesus Christ our Lord.

Though he was sinless, he suffered willingly for sinners.
Though innocent, he accepted death to save the guilty.
By his dying he has destroyed our sins.
By his rising, he has raised us up to holiness of life.

We praise you, Lord, with all the angels
in their song of joy:

Holy, holy, holy ...

Communion Antiphon

Father, if this cup may not pass, but I must drink it, then your will be done.
Matthew 26:42

Prayer after Communion

Lord,
you have satisfied our hunger with this eucharistic food.
The death of your Son gives us hope and strengthens our faith.
May his resurrection give us perseverance
and lead us to salvation.

The priest may give this Solemn Blessing or another form on pages 600-601.

Solemn Blessing

Bow your heads and pray for God's blessing.

The Father of mercies has given us an example of unselfish love
in the sufferings of his only Son.
Through your service of God and neighbour
may you receive his countless blessings.
℟ **Amen.**

You believe that by his dying
Christ destroyed death for ever.
May he give you everlasting life.
℟ **Amen.**

PASSION SUNDAY/C

He humbled himself for our sakes.
May you follow his example
and share in his resurrection.
R/ **Amen.**

May almighty God bless you,
the Father, and the Son, ✠ and the Holy Spirit.
R/ **Amen.**

The Paschal Triduum

THE next three days plunge us into the central mystery of our faith, the 'solemnity of solemnities', the event by which we are saved. The three days, Holy Thursday, Good Friday and Holy Saturday night are the climax of the whole christian year. It is the time when the mystery of the cross and resurrection brings us new life through the sacraments.

All the sacraments are consequences of Our Lord's death and resurrection. St. John saw blood and water flow from the wounded side of Jesus on the cross. Jesus gave his human life for us by pouring out his blood, a sacrifice for our sins, and the water was a symbol of the divine life which he calls us to share as christians. We are above all else a eucharistic community. All the other sacraments of the Church either prepare us for the eucharist or complete its effects. We are baptised 'in the waters of death' from which the living come forth as new christians on the night of the resurrection. Oils for the sacraments of confirmation, holy orders and the anointing of the sick are consecrated on Holy Thursday. The sacrament of marriage finds its model in the sacrifice of love by which Christ was united to his Church. Finally Easter plunges us into the mystery of life and death until we celebrate our final union in Christ with the Father whom one day we will see 'face to face'.

It is at Easter that we should eat the paschal lamb in preparation for our own deliverance and journey to the promised land. By laying down his life, Christ entered the glory of the resurrection to send forth his Spirit upon the world. Christ so loved us that he was obedient to his Father even to offering himself on the cross for our salvation 'and being as all men are, he was humbler yet, even to accepting death, death on a cross. But God raised him high and gave him the name which is above all other names so that all beings in the heavens, on earth and in the underworld, should bend the knee at the name of Jesus and that every tongue should acclaim Jesus Christ as Lord, to the glory of God the Father.' Philippians 2:8-11.

We speak of these three days as the time in which we celebrate the paschal mystery, a 'mystery' in so far as God intervenes in human history on behalf of his people and 'paschal' because these three days have their roots in the Jewish passover [pascha]

THE PASCHAL TRIDUUM

which celebrated Israel's deliverance from Egypt. The Church sees the Jewish passover festival as prefiguring [anticipating] its own deliverance by the saving power of Christ's death and resurrection.

The Jews used to celebrate the Passover as the greatest feast of their year. On that day the Jews at God's command sacrificed a lamb and the blood sprinkled on the doors of their homes protected them from the angel who slew the first-born of the Egyptians. In the following days the Jews were allowed to leave Egypt, the land of their slavery, and begin their journey to their promised land. So it is with us. Our paschal lamb is Christ. When we make our Easter communion we receive his flesh and blood and so are united to him in his death and 'pass over' with him to eternal life and resurrection. We are set by Christ on our way to salvation.

Before the season of Lent was instituted the paschal triduum was the Church's immediate preparation for Easter. Passover themes predominate in the liturgy of the triduum. On Holy Thursday we are reminded of Christ's command to remember him by the celebration of the eucharist in which we recall what Christ has done for us just as the Jewish passover reminds the Jews of what God did for them by delivering them out of the land of bondage. On Good Friday we celebrate Christ as our paschal lamb who takes away the sin of the world and on Easter Eve we celebrate the resurrection of our Lord and Saviour who has broken the bondage of sin and death to set us free.

Holy Thursday

CHRIST our leader came on earth as a servant. It was in the service of others that he lived and died. This evening at the Mass of the Lord's Supper we celebrate not only the institution of the eucharist but also our call as christians to the service of others as our witness to them of our love of Christ. Christ showed his love for his apostles when he washed their feed. 'When he had washed their feet and put on his clothes again he went back to the table. "Do you understand," he said "what I have done to you?. You call me Master and Lord, and rightly; so I am. If I, then, the Lord and Master, have washed your feet, you should wash each other's feet. I have given you an example so that you may copy what I have done to you." John 13:12-15.

Christ gave his life for our redemption in loving obedience to his Father. His farewell discourse to his apostles centred itself on the commandment of unselfish love. Our lives are to be motivated by this love. Just as Christ gave his life for us so we too must give our lives for the sake of our brethren. 'This is my commandment: love one another, as I have loved you. A man can have no greater love than to lay down his life for his friends.' John 15:12-13.

This morning at the eucharist celebrated by the bishop the holy oils are blessed. With them the ministry of Christ's service is continued in the Church: the oil of catechumens is a sign of the Church's strengthening of the weak; with the chrism the Church seals with the Spirit those who are to bear witness to him in the world [confirmation], commissions those whose lives are specially consecrated to his sacrificial service [ordination], and finally brings his ministry of healing to the sick [anointing of the sick].

Today priests all over the world renew their personal commitment to priestly service. So right at the beginning of the triduum the liturgy reminds us all that Christ wants us to give ourselves completely to him. Our whole lives will be spent in that service. For this we need his help and his grace.

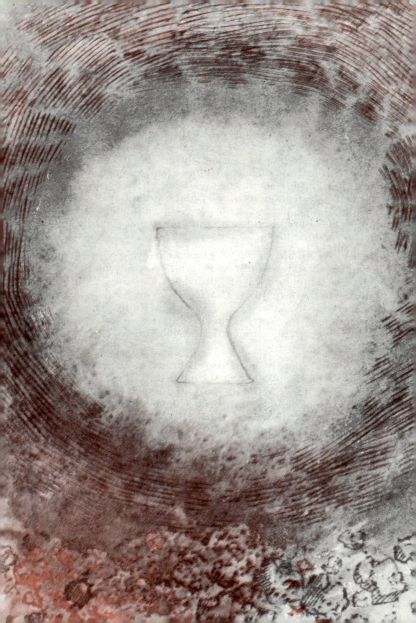

HOLY THURSDAY
EVENING MASS OF THE LORD'S SUPPER

Christ celebrated the Jewish Passover
with his apostles.
He gives them a new commandment that they
love one another as he loved them. This love is
shown in service. During the Supper Christ
washes the feet of his apostles. He institutes the
Sacrament of the Eucharist and so places himself
forever at the service of the Church. The Mass
makes effectively present the events which took
place on that night and is the source from which all
the other sacraments flow and towards which
they all lead. On this evening the old Jewish
rite gives way to the new sacrifice given to
the Church by Christ.

Entrance Antiphon   We should glory in the cross of our Lord Jesus Christ, for he is our salvation, our life and our resurrection; through him we are saved and made free.   see Gal. 6:14

During the singing of the Gloria the church bells are rung and then remain silent until the Easter Vigil, unless the conference of bishops or the Ordinary decrees otherwise.

Opening Prayer

God our Father,
we are gathered here to share in the supper
which your only Son left to his Church to reveal his love.
He gave it to us when he was about to die

HOLY THURSDAY/A/B/C

and commanded us to celebrate it as the new and eternal sacrifice.
We pray that in this eucharist
we may find the fullness of love and life.

First Reading Exodus 12:1-8, 11-14.

Instructions concerning the Passover meal.

The Lord said to Moses and Aaron in the land of Egypt, "This month is to be the first of all the others for you, the first month of your year. Speak to the whole community of Israel and say, 'On the tenth day of this month each man must take an animal from the flock, one for each family: one animal for each household. If the household is too small to eat the animal, a man must join with his neighbour, the nearest to his house, as the number of persons requires. You must take into account what each can eat in deciding the number for the animal. It must be an animal without blemish, a male one year old; you may take it from either sheep or goats. You must keep it till the fourteenth day of the month when the whole assembly of the community of Israel shall slaughter it between the two evenings. Some of the blood must then be taken and put on the two doorposts and the lintel of the houses where it is eaten. That night, the flesh is to be eaten, roasted over the fire; it must be eaten with unleavened bread and bitter herbs. You shall eat it like this: with a girdle round your waist, sandals on your feet, a staff in your hand. You shall eat it hastily: it is a passover in honour of the Lord. That night, I will go through the land of Egypt and strike down all the first-born in the land of Egypt, man and beast alike, and I shall deal out punishment to all the gods of Egypt, I am the Lord. The blood shall serve to mark the houses that you live in. When I see the blood I will pass over you and you shall escape the destroying plague when I strike the land of Egypt. This day is to be a day of remembrance for you, and you must celebrate it as a feast in the Lord's honour. For all generations you are to declare it a day of festival, for ever'."

Responsorial Psalm Psalm 115

℟. **The blessing-cup that we bless
is a communion with the blood of Christ.**

HOLY THURSDAY/A/B/C

1. How can I repay the Lord
   for his goodness to me?
   The cup of salvation I will raise;
   I will call on the Lord's name. ℟

2. O precious in the eyes of the Lord
   is the death of his faithful.
   Your servant, Lord, your servant I am;
   you have loosened my bonds. ℟

3. A thanksgiving sacrifice I make:
   I will call on the Lord's name.
   My vows to the Lord I will fulfil
   before all his people. ℟

Second Reading   1 Corinthians 11:23-26

Every time you eat this bread and drink this cup, you are proclaiming the death of the Lord.

This is what I received from the Lord, and in turn passed on to you: that on the same night that he was betrayed, the Lord Jesus took some bread, and thanked God for it and broke it, and he said, "This is my body, which is for you; do this as a memorial of me". In the same way he took the cup after supper, and said, "This cup is the new covenant in my blood. Whenever you drink it, do this as a memorial of me". Until the Lord comes, therefore, every time you eat this bread and drink this cup, you are proclaiming his death.

Acclamation

Praise and honour to you, Lord Jesus!
I give you a new commandment: love one another
just as I have loved you, says the Lord.
Praise and honour to you, Lord Jesus! John 13:34.

Gospel   John 13:1-15.

Now he showed how perfect his love was.

It was before the festival of the Passover, and Jesus knew that the hour had come for him to pass from this world to the Father. He had always loved those who were his in the world, but now he showed how perfect his love was.

HOLY THURSDAY/A/B/C

They were at supper, and the devil had already put it into the mind of Judas Iscariot son of Simon, to betray him. Jesus knew that the Father had put everything into his hands, and that he had come from God and was returning to God, and he got up from table, removed his outer garment and, taking a towel, wrapped it round his waist; he then poured water into a basin and began to wash the disciples' feet and to wipe them with the towel he was wearing.

He came to Simon Peter, who said to him, "Lord, are you going to wash my feet?". Jesus answered, "At the moment you do not know what I am doing, but later you will understand". "Never!" said Peter "You shall never wash my feet." Jesus replied, "If I do not wash you, you can have nothing in common with me." "Then, Lord," said Simon Peter "not only my feet, but my hands and my head as well!" Jesus said, "No one who has taken a bath needs washing, he is clean all over. You too are clean, though not all of you are." He knew who was going to betray him, that was why he said, "though not all of you are."

When he had washed their feet and put on his clothes again he went back to the table. "Do you understand," he said, "what I have done to you? You call me Master and Lord, and rightly; so I am. If I, then, the Lord and Master, have washed your feet, you should wash each other's feet. I have given you an example so that you may copy what I have done to you."

Washing of Feet

The washing of feet may follow the homily. The men who have been chosen are led by the ministers to chairs prepared in a suitable place. Then the priest goes to each man. He pours water over each one's feet and dries them.

Meanwhile some of the following antiphons or other appropriate songs are sung.

Antiphon 1

The Lord Jesus,
when he had eaten with his disciples,
poured water into a basin
and began to wash their feet, saying:
This example I leave you.   cf. John 13:4.5.15

HOLY THURSDAY/A/B/C

Antiphon 2

Lord, do you wash my feet?
Jesus said to him:
If I do not wash your feet,
you can have no part with me.

℣ So he came to Simon Peter,
who said to him:
Lord, do you wash my feet?

℣ Now you do not know what I am doing,
but later you will understand.
Lord, do you wash my feet? John 13:6.7.8

Antiphon 3

If I, your Lord and Teacher, have washed your feet,
then surely you must wash one another's feet. cf. John 13:14

Antiphon 4

If there is this love among you,
all will know that you are my disciples.

℣ Jesus said to his disciples:
If there is this love among you,
all will know that you are my disciples. John 13:35

Antiphon 5

I give you a new commandment:
love one another as I have loved you, says the Lord. John 13:34

Antiphon 6

Faith, hope, and love,
let these endure among you;
and the greatest of these is love. 1 Corinthians 13:13

There is no Creed today. The Mass continues with the Prayer of the Faithful.

THE LITURGY OF THE EUCHARIST

At the beginning of the liturgy of the eucharist, there may be a procession of the faithful with gifts for the poor.
During the procession the following may be sung, or another appropriate song.

Antiphon

Where charity and love are found, there is God.

℣ The love of Christ has gathered us together into one.
℣ Let us rejoice and be glad in him.
℣ Let us fear and love the living God,
℣ and love each other from the depths of our heart.

℟ Where charity and love are found, there is God.

℣ Therefore when we are together,
℣ let us take heed not to be divided in mind.
℣ Let there be an end to bitterness and quarrels, an end to strife,
℣ and in our midst be Christ our God.

℟ Where charity and love are found, there is God.

℣ And, in company with the blessed, may we see
℣ your face in glory, Christ our God,
℣ pure and unbounded joy
℣ for ever and for ever.

℟ Where charity and love are found, there is God.

Prayer over the Gifts

Lord,
make us worthy to celebrate these mysteries.
Each time we offer this memorial sacrifice
the work of our redemption is accomplished.

Preface

Father, all-powerful and ever-living God,
we do well always and everywhere to give you thanks
through Jesus Christ our Lord.

He is the true and eternal priest
who established this unending sacrifice.
He offered himself as a victim for our deliverance
and taught us to make this offering in his memory.
As we eat his body which he gave for us,

HOLY THURSDAY/A/B/C

we grow in strength.
As we drink his blood which he poured out for us,
we are washed clean.

Now, with angels and archangels,
and the whole company of heaven,
we sing the unending hymn of your praise:

Holy, holy, holy . . .

Communion Antiphon   This body will be given for you. This is the cup of the new covenant in my blood; whenever you receive them, do so in remembrance of me.
1 Corinthians 11:24-25

Prayer after Communion

Almighty God,
we receive new life
from the supper your Son gave us in this world.
May we find full contentment
in the meal we hope to share
in your eternal kingdom.

TRANSFER OF THE HOLY EUCHARIST

After the prayer the priest accompanied by the ministers carries the Blessed Sacrament in procession to the place where it is to be kept until tomorrow. During the procession, the Pange lingua or another suitable hymn is sung.

Hymn: Pange Lingua

1. Of the glorious Body telling,
   O my tongue, its mysteries sing,
   And the Blood, all price excelling,
   Which the world's eternal King,
   In a noble womb once dwelling,
   Shed for the world's ransoming.

2. Given for us, for us descending,
   Of a Virgin to proceed,
   Man with man in converse blending,
   Scattered he the Gospel seed,
   Till his sojourn drew to ending,
   Which he closed in wondrous deed.

3. At the last great Supper lying
   Circled by his brethren's band,
   Meekly with the law complying,
   First he finished its command,
   Then, immortal Food supplying,
   Gave himself with his own hand.

4. Word made Flesh, by word he maketh
   Very bread his Flesh to be;
   Man in wine Christ's Blood partaketh:
   And if senses fail to see,
   Faith alone the true heart waketh
   To behold the mystery.

When the procession reaches the place of reposition the singing is concluded with these verses:

5. Therefore we, before him bending,
   This great Sacrament revere;
   Types and shadows have their ending,
   For the newer rite is here;
   Faith, our outward sense befriending,
   Makes the inward vision clear.

HOLY THURSDAY/A/B/C

6. Glory let us give, and blessing
   To the Father and the Son;
   Honour, might, and praise addressing,
   While eternal ages run;
   Ever too his love confessing,
   Who, from both, with both is one.
   Amen.

After a period of silent adoration, the priest and ministers return to the sacristy.

Then the altar is stripped and, if possible, the crosses are removed from the church or covered.

Adoration of the Blessed Sacrament should continue until midnight.

Good Friday

GOOD Friday is not simply the anniversary of a past event. The afternoon's solemn service takes us right into the mystery of what the Lord has done and is doing for us through his passion and death. Today we reflect on Christ the high priest offering himself to his Father on the cross. 'But now Christ has come, as the high priest of all the blessings which were to come. He has passed through the greater, the more perfect tent, which is better than the one made by men's hands because it is not of this created order; and he has entered the sanctuary once and for all, taking with him not the blood of goats and bull calves, but his own blood, having won an eternal redemption for us.' Hebrews 9:11-12.

We know that the day can be called good because on that day Christ by his death brought life to all who believe in his name. Accordingly the stress in today's liturgy is not only on the supreme sacrifice of Christ's love tested in suffering with its atmosphere of sadness but we also should be full of joy and hope as we think deeply on the Lord's triumph on the cross. Red vestments are worn as a sign of Christ's victory and the reading of the passion from John's Gospel stresses that Christ is the conqueror of sin and death. When we venerate the cross we are already aware of the triumph of the resurrection.

Today we listen to the beautiful reading from Isaiah which tells of the suffering servant 'so will the crowds be astonished at seeing him, and kings stand speechless before him; for they shall see something never told and witness something never heard before.' Isaiah 52:15. We try to understand the wonderful self-giving of Christ for our sake. We pray in the shadow of the cross for the needs of the world which he has redeemed. We venerate the cross which is everything to us and is our banner of hope. Finally in communion we enter into Christ's life-giving sacrifice. This indeed is Good Friday when Christ died so that we might live.

GOOD FRIDAY
CELEBRATION OF THE LORD'S PASSION

It is accomplished.
We celebrate the Passion and death of Our Lord Jesus Christ. Christ died that we might live and by his wounds we are healed. He transforms the Cross of shame into a symbol of triumph. On the Cross he offers the perfect prayer for all peoples to the end of time. We join in his sufferings through the giving of our lives to him, knowing that if we die with him we will also rise with him.

The ministers, wearing red vestments, go to the altar, where they kneel or prostrate in silence. When the celebrant faces the people he says one of the following prayers.

Prayer

Lord,
by shedding his blood for us,
your Son, Jesus Christ,
established the paschal mystery.
In your goodness, make us holy
and watch over us always.

or

Lord,
by the suffering of Christ your Son
you have saved us all from the death
we inherited from sinful Adam.
By the law of nature
we have borne the likeness of his manhood.
May the sanctifying power of grace
help us to put on the likeness of our Lord in heaven,
who lives and reigns for ever and ever.

FIRST PART: LITURGY OF THE WORD

First Reading   Isaiah 52:13-53:12.
He was pierced through for our faults.

See, my servant will prosper,
he shall be lifted up, exalted, rise to great heights.

As the crowds were appalled on seeing him
— so disfigured did he look
that he seemed no longer human —
so will the crowds be astonished at him,
and kings stand speechless before him;
for they shall see something never told
and witness something never heard before:
"Who could believe what we have heard,
and to whom has the power of the Lord been revealed?"

Like a sapling he grew up in front of us,
like a root in arid ground.
Without beauty, without majesty (we saw him),
no looks to attract our eyes;
a thing despised and rejected by men,
a man of sorrows and familiar with suffering,
a man to make people screen their faces;
he was despised and we took no account of him.

And yet ours were the sufferings he bore,
ours the sorrows he carried.
But we, we thought of him as someone punished,
struck by God, and brought low.
Yet he was pierced through for our faults,
crushed for our sins.

On him lies a punishment that brings us peace,
and through his wounds we are healed.
We had all gone astray like sheep,
each taking his own way,
and the Lord burdened him
with the sins of all of us.

Harshly dealt with, he bore it humbly,
he never opened his mouth,
like a lamb that is led to the slaughter-house,
like a sheep that is dumb before its shearers
never opening its mouth.

GOOD FRIDAY/A/B/C

By force and by law he was taken;
would anyone plead his cause?
Yes, he was torn away from the land of the living;
for our faults struck down in death.
They gave him a grave with the wicked,
a tomb with the rich,
though he had done no wrong
and there had been no perjury in his mouth.
The Lord has been pleased to crush him with suffering.
If he offers his life in atonement,
he shall see his heirs, he shall have a long life
and through him what the Lord wishes will be done.

His soul's anguish over
he shall see the light and be content.
By his sufferings shall my servant justify many,
taking their faults on himself.

Hence I will grant whole hordes for his tribute,
he shall divide the spoil with the mighty,
for surrendering himself to death
and letting himself be taken for a sinner,
while he was bearing the faults of many
and praying all the time for sinners.

Responsorial Psalm   Psalm 30.

℟ **Father, into your hands I commend my spirit.**

1. In you, O Lord, I take refuge.
   Let me never be put to shame.
   In your justice, set me free.
   Into your hands I commend my spirit.
   It is you who will redeem me, Lord.   ℟

2. In the face of all my foes
   I am a reproach,
   an object of scorn to my neighbours
   and of fear to my friends.   ℟

3. Those who see me in the street
   run far away from me.
   I am like a dead man, forgotten in men's hearts,
   like a thing thrown away.   ℟

4. But as for me, I trust in you, Lord,

GOOD FRIDAY/A/B/C

I say: "You are my God."
My life is in your hands, deliver me
from the hands of those who hate me. R/

5. Let your face shine on your servant.
Save me in your love.
Be strong, let your heart take courage,
all who hope in the Lord. R/

Second Reading   Hebrews 4:14-16; 5:7-9.

He learnt to obey through suffering and became for all who obey him the source of eternal salvation.

Since in Jesus, the Son of God, we have the supreme high priest who has gone through to the highest heaven, we must never let go of the faith that we have professed. For it is not as if we had a high priest who was incapable of feeling our weaknesses with us; but we have one who has been tempted in every way that we are, though he is without sin. Let us be confident, then, in approaching the throne of grace, that we shall have mercy from him and find grace when we are in need of help.

During his life on earth, he offered up prayer and entreaty, aloud and in silent tears, to the one who had the power to save him out of death, and he submitted so humbly that his prayer was heard. Although he was a Son, he learnt to obey through suffering; but having been made perfect, he became for all who obey him the source of eternal salvation.

Acclamation   Glory and praise to you, O Christ!
Christ was humbler yet, even to accepting death, death on a cross. But God raised him high and gave him the name which is above all names.
Glory and praise to you, O Christ!

Philippians 2:8-9

Gospel   John 18:1-19:42.

The passion of our Lord Jesus Christ according to John.

N. Jesus left with his disciples and crossed the Kedron valley. There was a garden there, and he went into it with his disciples. Judas the traitor knew the place well, since Jesus had often met his disciples there, and he brought the cohort to this place together with a detachment of guards sent by the chief priests and the Pharisees, all with lanterns and torches and weapons. Knowing everything that was going to happen to him, Jesus then came forward and said, ✠ "Who are you looking for?" N. They answered, C. **"Jesus the Nazarene".** N. He said, ✠ "I am he". N. Now Judas the traitor was standing among them. When Jesus said, 'I am he', they moved back and fell to the ground. He asked them a second time, ✠ "Who are you looking for?" N. They said, C. **"Jesus the Nazarene".** N. Jesus replied ✠ "I have told you that I am he. If I am the one you are looking for, let these others go". N. This was to fulfil the words he had spoken: "Not one of those you gave me have I lost".

Simon Peter, who carried a sword, drew it and wounded the high priest's servant, cutting off his right ear. The servant's name was Malchus. Jesus said to Peter, ✠ "Put your sword back in its scabbard; am I not to drink the cup that the Father has given me?".

N. The cohort and its captain and the Jewish guards seized Jesus and bound him. They took him first to Annas, because Annas was the father-in-law of Caiaphas, who was high priest that year. It was Caiaphas who had suggested to the Jews, 'It is better for one man to die for the people'.

Simon Peter, with another disciple, followed Jesus. This disciple, who was known to the high priest, went with Jesus into the high priest's palace, but Peter stayed outside the door. So the other disciple, the one known to the high priest, went out, spoke to the woman who was keeping the door and brought Peter in. The maid on duty at the door said to Peter, C. "Aren't you another of that man's disciples?". N. He answered, C. "I am not". N. Now it was cold, and the servants and guards had lit a charcoal fire and were standing there warming themselves, so Peter stood there too, warming himself with the others.

The high priest questioned Jesus about his disciples and his teaching. Jesus answered, ✠ "I have spoken openly for all the world to hear; I have always taught in the synagogue and in the Temple where all the Jews meet together: I have said nothing in secret. But why ask me? Ask my hearers what I taught: they know what I said". N. At these words, one of the guards standing by gave Jesus a slap in the face, saying, C. "Is that the way to answer the high priest?" N. Jesus replied, ✠ "If there is something wrong in what I said, point it out; but if there is no offence in it, why do you strike me?". N. Then Annas sent him, still bound, to Caiaphas, the high priest.

GOOD FRIDAY/A/B/C

As Simon Peter stood there warming himself, someone said to him, **C.** "Aren't you another of his disciples?". **N.** He denied it saying, **C.** "I am not". **N.** One of the high priest's servants, a relation of the man whose ear Peter had cut off, said, **C.** "Didn't I see you in the garden with him?". **N.** Again Peter denied it; and at once a cock crew.

They then led Jesus from the house of Caiaphas to the Praetorium. It was now morning. They did not go into the Praetorium themselves or they would be defiled and unable to eat the passover. So Pilate came outside to them and said, **C.** "What charge do you bring against this man?" **N.** They replied, **C. "If he were not a criminal, we should not be handing him over to you".** **N.** Pilate said, **C.** "Take him yourselves, and try him by your own Law". **N.** The Jews answered, **C. "We are not allowed to put a man to death".** **N.** This was to fulfil the words Jesus had spoken indicating the way he was going to die.

So Pilate went back into the Praetorium and called Jesus to him, and asked, **C.** "Are you the king of the Jews?". **N.** Jesus replied, ✠ "Do you ask this of your own accord, or have others spoken to you about me?". **N.** Pilate answered, **C.** "Am I a Jew? It is your own people and the chief priests who have handed you over to me: what have you done?" **N.** Jesus replied, ✠ "Mine is not a kingdom of this world; if my kingdom were of this world, my men would have fought to prevent me being surrendered to the Jews. But my kingdom is not of this kind". **N.** Pilate said, **C.** "So you are a king then?". **N.** Jesus answered, ✠ "It is you who say it. Yes, I am a king. I was born for this, I came into the world for this; to bear witness to the truth, and all who are on the side of truth listen to my voice". **N.** Pilate said **C.** "Truth? What is that?". **N.** And with that he went out again to the Jews and said, **C.** "I find no case against him. But according to a custom of yours I should release one prisoner at the Passover; would you like me, then, to release the king of the Jews?". **N.** At this they shouted: **C. "Not this man, but Barabbas".**
N. Barabbas was a brigand.

Pilate then had Jesus taken away and scourged; and after this, the soldiers twisted some thorns into a crown and put it on his head, and dressed him in a purple robe. They kept coming up to him and saying, **C. "Hail, king of the Jews!"** **N.** and they slapped him in the face.

GOOD FRIDAY/A/B/C

Pilate came outside again and said to them, C. "Look, I am going to bring him out to you to let you see that I find no case." N. Jesus then came out wearing the crown of thorns and the purple robe. Pilate said, C. "Here is the man." N. When they saw him the chief priests and the guards shouted, C. **"Crucify him! Crucify him!"** N. Pilate said, C. "Take him yourselves and crucify him: I can find no case against him." N. The Jews replied, C. **We have a Law, and according to the Law he ought to die, because he has claimed to be the Son of God."**

N. When Pilate heard them say this his fears increased. Re-entering the Praetorium, he said to Jesus, C. "Where do you come from?" N. But Jesus made no answer. Pilate then said to him, C. "Are you refusing to speak to me? Surely you know I have power to release you and I have power to crucify you?" N. Jesus replied ✠ "You would have no power over me if it had not been given you from above; that is why the one who handed me over to you has the greater guilt."

N. From that moment Pilate was anxious to set him free, but the Jews shouted. C. **"If you set him free you are no friend of Caesar's; anyone who makes himself king is defying Caesar."** N. Hearing these words, Pilate had Jesus brought out, and seated himself on the chair of judgement at a place called the Pavement, in Hebrew Gabbatha. It was Passover Preparation Day, about the sixth hour. Pilate said to the Jews, C. "Here is your king." N. They said, C. **"Take him away, take him away. Crucify him!"** N. Pilate said, C. "Do you want me to crucify your king?" N. The chief priests answered, C. **"We have no king except Caesar."** N. So in the end Pilate handed him over to them to be crucified.

They then took charge of Jesus, and carrying his own cross he went out of the city to the place of the skull or, as it was called in Hebrew, Golgotha, where they crucified him with two others, one on either side with Jesus in the middle. Pilate wrote out a notice and had it fixed to the cross; it ran: 'Jesus the Nazarene, King of the Jews.' This notice was read by many of the Jews, because the place where Jesus was crucified was not far from the city, and the writing was in Hebrew, Latin and Greek. So the Jewish chief priests said to Pilate, C. **"You should not write 'King of the Jews', but 'This man said: I am King of the Jews'."** N. Pilate answered, C. "What I have written, I have written."

N. When the soldiers had finished crucifying Jesus they took

GOOD FRIDAY/A/B/C

his clothing and divided it into four shares, one for each soldier. His undergarment was seamless, woven in one piece from neck to hem; so they said to one another, C. **"Instead of tearing it, let's throw dice to decide who is to have it."** N. In this way the words of scripture were fulfilled:
They shared out my clothing among them.
They cast lots for my clothes.

This is exactly what the soldiers did.

Near the cross of Jesus stood his mother and his mother's sister, Mary the wife of Clopas, and Mary of Magdala. Seeing his mother and the disciple he loved standing near her, Jesus said to his mother, ✠ "Woman, this is your son." N. Then to the disciple he said, ✠ "This is your mother." N. And from that moment the disciple made a place for her in his home.

After this, Jesus knew that everything had now been completed, and to fulfil the scripture perfectly he said: ✠ "I am thirsty."

N. A jar full of vinegar stood there, so putting a sponge soaked in vinegar on a hyssop stick they held it up to his mouth. After Jesus had taken the vinegar he said, ✠ "It is accomplished;" N. and bowing his head he gave up the spirit.

All kneel and pause a moment.

It was Preparation Day, and to prevent the bodies remaining on the cross during the sabbath — since that sabbath was a day of special solemnity — the Jews asked Pilate to have the legs broken and the bodies taken away. Consequently the soldiers came and broke the legs of the first man who had been crucified with him and then of the other. When they came to Jesus, they found he was already dead, and so instead of breaking his legs one of the soldiers pierced his side with a lance; and immediately there came out blood and water. This is the evidence of one who saw it — trustworthy evidence, and he knows he speaks the truth — and he gives it so that you may believe as well. Because all this happened to fulfil the words of scripture:
Not one bone of his will be broken,
and again, in another place scripture says:
They will look on the one whom they have pierced.

After this, Joseph of Arimathaea, who was a disciple of Jesus — though a secret one because he was afraid of the Jews — asked Pilate to let him remove the body of Jesus. Pilate gave permission, so they came and took it away. Nicodemus came as well — the same one who had first come to Jesus at night-time — and he brought a mixture of myrrh and aloes weighing about a hundred pounds. They took the body of Jesus and wrapped it with the spices in linen cloths, following the Jewish burial custom. At the place where he had been crucified there was a garden, and in this garden a new tomb in which no one had yet been buried. Since it was the Jewish Day of Preparation and the tomb was near at hand, they laid Jesus there.

General Intercessions

The general intercessions conclude the liturgy of the word. The priest introduces each intention and there follows a period of silent prayer.

The people may either kneel or stand throughout the entire period of the general intercessions according to custom.

1. For the Church

Let us pray, dear friends,
for the holy Church of God throughout the world,
that God the almighty Father
guide it and gather it together
so that we may worship him
in peace and tranquillity.

Silent prayer. Then the priest says:

Almighty and eternal God,
you have shown your glory to all nations
in Christ, your Son.
Guide the work of your Church.
Help it to persevere in faith,
proclaim your name,
and bring your salvation to people everywhere.
We ask this through Christ our Lord.

R/ **Amen.**

2.

Let us pray
for our Holy Father, Pope N.,
that God who chose him to be bishop
may give him health and strength
to guide and govern God's holy people.

GOOD FRIDAY/A/B/C

Silent prayer. Then the priest says:

Almighty and eternal God,
you guide all things by your word,
you govern all Christian people.
In your love protect the Pope you have chosen for us.
Under his leadership deepen our faith
and make us better Christians.

We ask this through Christ our Lord.

℟ **Amen.**

3. For the clergy and laity of the Church

Let us pray
for N., our bishop,
for all bishops, priests, and deacons;
for all who have a special ministry in the Church;
and for all God's people.

Silent prayer. Then the priest says:

Almighty and eternal God,
your Spirit guides the Church
and makes it holy.
Listen to our prayers
and help each of us
in his vocation
to do your work more faithfully.

We ask this through Christ our Lord.

℟ **Amen.**

4. For those preparing for baptism

Let us pray
for those (among us) preparing for baptism,
that God in his mercy
make them responsive to his love,
forgive their sins through the waters of new birth,
and give them life in Jesus Christ our Lord.

Silent prayer. Then the priest says:

Almighty and eternal God,
you continually bless your Church with new members.
Increase the faith and understanding

of those (among us) preparing for baptism.
Give them a new birth in these living waters
and make them members of your chosen family.

We ask this through Christ our Lord.

℟ **Amen.**

5. For the unity of Christians

Let us pray
for all our brothers and sisters
who share our faith in Jesus Christ,
that God may gather and keep together in one Church
all those who seek the truth with sincerity.

Silent prayer. Then the priest says:

Almighty and eternal God,
you keep together those you have united.
Look kindly on all who follow Jesus your Son.
We are all consecrated to you by our common baptism.
Make us one in the fullness of faith,
and keep us one in the fellowship of love.

We ask this through Christ our Lord.

℟ **Amen.**

6. For the Jewish people

Let us pray
for the Jewish people,
the first to hear the word of God,
that they may continue to grow in the love of his name
and in faithfulness to his covenant.

Silent prayer. Then the priest says:

Almighty and eternal God,
long ago you gave your promise to Abraham and his posterity.
Listen to your Church as we pray
that the people you first made your own
may arrive at the fullness of redemption.

We ask this through Christ our Lord.

℟ **Amen.**

GOOD FRIDAY/A/B/C

7. For those who do not believe in Christ

Let us pray
for those who do not believe in Christ,
that the light of the Holy Spirit
may show them the way to salvation.

Silent prayer. Then the priest says:

Almighty and eternal God,
enable those who do not acknowledge Christ to find the truth
as they walk before you in sincerity of heart.
Help us to grow in love for one another,
to grasp more fully the mystery of your godhead,
and to become more perfect witnesses of your love in the sight of men.

We ask this through Christ our Lord.

℟ **Amen.**

8. For those who do not believe in God

Let us pray
for those who do not believe in God,
that they may find him
by sincerely following all that is right.

Silent prayer. Then the priest says:

Almighty and eternal God,
you created mankind
so that all might long to find you
and have peace when you are found.
Grant that, in spite of the hurtful things
that stand in their way,
they may all recognise in the lives of Christians
the tokens of your love and mercy,
and gladly acknowledge you
as the one true God and Father of us all.

We ask this through Christ our Lord.

℟ **Amen.**

GOOD FRIDAY/A/B/C

9. For all in public office

Let us pray
for those who serve us in public office,
that God may guide their minds and hearts,
so that all men may live in true peace and freedom.

Silent prayer. Then the priest says:

Almighty and eternal God,
you know the longings of men's hearts
and you protect their rights.
In your goodness
watch over those in authority,
so that people everywhere may enjoy
religious freedom, security, and peace.

We ask this through Christ our Lord.

℟ **Amen.**

10. For those in special need

Let us pray, dear friends,
that God the almighty Father
may heal the sick,
comfort the dying,
give safety to travellers,
free those unjustly deprived of liberty,
and rid the world of falsehood,
hunger, and disease.

Silent prayer. Then the priest says:

Almighty, ever-living God,
you give strength to the weary
and new courage to those who have lost heart.
Hear the prayers of all who call on you in any trouble
that they may have the joy of receiving your help in their need.

We ask this through Christ our Lord.

℟ **Amen.**

SECOND PART: VENERATION OF THE CROSS

The Invitation
The cross is shown to the people three times, either from the altar, while it is unveiled, or as it is carried in procession through the Church to the sanctuary. Each time the priest sings.

This is the wood of the cross, on which hung the Saviour of the world.

and the people reply:

℟ **Come, let us worship.**

After each response, all kneel and venerate the cross briefly in silence. Then the cross and candles are placed at the entrance to the sanctuary.

Veneration of the Cross
The priest, clergy, and faithful approach to venerate the cross in a kind of procession. They make a simple genuflection or perform some other appropriate sign of reverence according to local custom, for example, kissing the cross.

Songs at the Veneration of the Cross
During the Veneration these or other suitable songs may be sung.

Individual parts are indicated by no. 1 (first choir) and no. 2 (second choir); parts sung by both choirs together are indicated by nos. 1 and 2.

1. Antiphon

1 and 2: Antiphon
We worship you, Lord,
we venerate your cross,
we praise your resurrection.
Through the cross you brought joy to the world.

1: Psalm 66:2
May God be gracious and bless us;
and let his face shed its light upon us.

1 and 2: Antiphon
We worship you, Lord,
we venerate your cross,

GOOD FRIDAY/A/B/C

we praise your resurrection.
Through the cross you brought joy to the world.

2. The Reproaches

I

1 and 2: My people, what have I done to you?
How have I offended you? Answer me!

1: I led you out of Egypt, from slavery to freedom,
but you led your Saviour to the cross.

2: My people, what have I done to you?
How have I offended you? Answer me!

1: Holy is God!

2: Holy and strong!

1: Holy immortal One,
have mercy on us!

1 and 2: For forty years I led you safely through the desert.
I fed you with manna from heaven,
and brought you to a land of plenty;
but you led your Saviour to the cross.

1: Holy is God!

2: Holy and strong!

1: Holy immortal One,
have mercy on us!

1 and 2: What more could I have done for you?
I planted you as my fairest vine,
but you yielded only bitterness:
when I was thirsty you gave me vinegar to drink,
and you pierced your Saviour with a lance.

1: Holy is God!

2: Holy and strong!

1: Holy immortal One,
have mercy on us!

II

1: For your sake I scourged your captors and their
firstborn sons,
but you brought your scourges down on me.

GOOD FRIDAY/A/B/C

2: My people, what have I done to you?
How have I offended you? Answer me!

1: I led you from slavery to freedom
and drowned your captors in the sea,
but you handed me over to your high priests

2: My people, what have I done to you?
How have I offended you? Answer me!

1: I opened the sea before you,
but you opened my side with a spear.

2: My people, what have I done to you?
How have I offended you? Answer me!

1: I led you on your way in a pillar of cloud,
but you led me to Pilate's court.

2: My people, what have I done to you?
How have I offended you? Answer me!

1: I bore you up with manna in the desert,
but you struck me down and scourged me.

2: My people, what have I done to you?
How have I offended you? Answer me!

1: I gave you saving water from the rock,
but you gave me gall and vinegar to drink.

2: My people, what have I done to you?
How have I offended you? Answer me!

1: For you I struck down the kings of Canaan,
but you struck my head with a reed.

2: My people, what have I done to you?
How have I offended you? Answer me!

1: I gave you a royal sceptre,
but you gave me a crown of thorns.

2: My people, what have I done to you?
How have I offended you? Answer me!

1: I raised you to the height of majesty,
but you have raised me high on a cross.

2: My people, what have I done to you?
How have I offended you? Answer me!

GOOD FRIDAY/A/B/C

3. **Hymn**

1. Faithful Cross! above all other
   One and only noble tree!
   None in foliage, none in blossom,
   None in fruit thy peer may be;
   Dearest wood and dearest iron!
   Dearest weight is hung on thee.

2. Sing, my tongue, the glorious battle,
   Sing the ending of the fray;
   Now above the Cross, the trophy,
   Sound the loud triumphant lay:
   Tell how Christ the world's Redeemer,
   As a Victim won the day.

3. God in pity saw man fallen,
   Shamed and sunk in misery,
   When he fell on death by tasting
   Fruit of the forbidden tree;
   Then another tree was chosen
   Which the world from death should free.

4. Thus the scheme of our salvation
   Was of old in order laid,
   That the manifold deceiver's
   Art by art might be outweighed,
   And the lure the foe put forward
   Into means of healing made.

5. Therefore when the appointed fullness
   Of the holy time was come,
   He was sent who maketh all things
   Forth from God's eternal home;
   Thus he came to earth, incarnate,
   Offspring of a maiden's womb.

6. Hear the helpless baby crying
   Where the narrow manger stands;
   See how she, his Virgin Mother,
   Ties his limbs with slender bands,
   Swaddling clothes she wraps about him,
   And confines God's feet and hands!

GOOD FRIDAY/A/B/C

7. Thirty years among us dwelling,
   His appointed time fulfilled,
   Born for this, he meets his Passion,
   For that this he freely willed,
   On the Cross the Lamb is lifted
   Where his life-blood shall be spilled.

8. He endured the nails, the spitting,
   Vinegar, and spear, and reed;
   From that holy Body broken
   Blood and water forth proceed:
   Earth, and stars, and sky, and ocean
   By that flood from stain are freed.

9. Bend thy boughs, O Tree of Glory!
   Thy relaxing sinews bend;
   For a while the ancient rigour
   That thy birth bestowed, suspend;
   And the King of heavenly beauty
   On thy bosom gently tend!

10. Thou alone wast counted worthy
    This world's ransom to uphold;
    For a ship-wreck'd race preparing
    Harbour, like the Ark of old;
    With the sacred Blood anointed
    From the smitten Lamb that rolled.

11. To the Trinity be glory
    Everlasting, as is meet;
    Equal to the Father, equal
    To the Son, and Paraclete:
    Trinal Unity, whose praises
    All created things repeat. Amen.

THIRD PART: HOLY COMMUNION

The altar is prepared and the priest brings the Blessed Sacrament from the place of reposition to the altar while all stand in silence. He then says:

Let us pray with confidence to the Father
in the words our Saviour gave us:
Our Father . . .

Deliver us, Lord, from every evil,
and grant us peace in our day.
In your mercy keep us free from sin
and protect us from all anxiety
as we wait in joyful hope
for the coming of our Saviour, Jesus Christ.
For the kingdom, the power, and the glory are yours,
now and for ever.

The priest says quietly:

Lord Jesus Christ, with faith in your love and mercy I eat your
 body and drink your blood.
Let it not bring me condemnation, but health in mind and body.

He then says aloud:

This is the Lamb of God
who takes away the sins of the world.
Happy are those who are called to his supper.
**Lord, I am not worthy to receive you,
but only say the word and I shall be healed.**
Then communion is distributed to the faithful.

Prayer after Communion

Let us pray.
Almighty and eternal God,
you have restored us to life
by the triumphant death and resurrection of Christ.
Continue this healing work within us.
May we who participate in this mystery
never cease to serve you.

Dismissing the people, the priest says:

GOOD FRIDAY/A/B/C

Prayer over the People

Lord,
send down your abundant blessing
upon your people who have devoutly recalled the death of
 your Son
in the sure hope of the resurrection.
Grant them pardon; bring them comfort.
May their faith grow stronger
and their eternal salvation be assured.

All depart in silence.

The Season of Easter

The Season of Easter

THE Church celebrates the entire season of fifty days from Easter to Pentecost as a very special time of great christian joy. Ceaselessly she proclaims the triumphant Alleluia as a sign of our joy that Christ, now risen from the dead, cannot die again. We share in the joy of his resurrection through baptism. In the eucharist we anticipate the triumphant feast in the world to come. We live with joy in a world redeemed and restored to unity with the Father.

The apostles rejoiced in the company of the Risen Lord. We do the same as Christ moves amongst us, his presence proclaimed in word and sacrament. The Easter candle lightens our darkness and proclaims to us all that Christ really has won and has risen as he said. Christ's triumph is the promise of our own redemption and so we rejoice in hope.

The season of Easter closes with the two great feasts of the Ascension and Pentecost. The Ascension does not mark the beginning of Christ's absence but rather highlights the resurrection as understood under the aspect of Christ's exaltation at the right hand of the Father. Christ rose, not to ordinary life, but to the glory of the Father. It is through the risen and exalted humanity of Christ that the Spirit is sent upon us. The feast of Pentecost is the climax of a season which continually rejoices in the sending of the Spirit by the Risen Lord. We live today in the age of the Spirit and it is he who is renewing us, the Church, and the face of the earth.

Holy Saturday

THIS night of passover, when Christ passed from death to the glory of the resurrection, is the most important moment in the entire liturgical year. We celebrate our own passing over from sin and death to newness of live in the Risen Lord. Christ passed from darkness to light and if we have kept Lent well according to the spirit of renewal put forward by the Church then this night will reveal to us in a special way what the splendour of God's life in us really means.

From the earliest times christians devoted this night of the resurrection to watching and waiting. As faithful people we keep the lamps of our faith alight so that when Christ emerges from the tomb he will find us awake and ready to celebrate his victory. The resurrection of the Lord is the climax of history towards which God our Father has been directing us all from the beginning of time.

The night vigil is arranged in four parts.

1. The Church begins the liturgy with a *service of light* to remind us that the darkness of the past is over. Now we live in the full light of the resurrection.

2. During the *liturgy of the word* we meditate on all the wonderful things which God did for his people.

3. During the *liturgy of baptism* new members of the Church are reborn in the sacrament of baptism. We all promote the spiritual renewal of the Church through the renewal of our own baptismal vows. Each one in renewing himself helps the Church's mission of salvation.

4. In the *liturgy of the eucharist* we participate in Easter communion and witness to the eucharist as the focal point of our christian worship and spirituality.

In the earliest days the Church held no feasts at all but celebrated the resurrection and nothing but the resurrection. She did so every week of the year, on the Sunday. In the risen Christ we proclaim even more loudly that we are a new creation. In and through Christ the whole purpose of creation is fulfilled. We are a people called to proclaim the wonders of our God in the Risen Lord. Alleluia!

DURING THE NIGHT
THE EASTER VIGIL

Most Blessed of all nights!
This night of the Passover when Christ passed from death to life is the most important moment in the entire christian year. We celebrate our passing over through baptism from the death of sin to the life of grace. Christians, from the earliest times, devoted this night to watching and waiting. We too keep our vigil knowing that the Lord will rise triumphant from the tomb to establish his Church among us. The tiny grain of seed, the humanity of Christ, has died and now the Church is born which will give shelter to countless millions to the end of time.

In accord with ancient tradition, this night is one of vigil for the Lord (Exodus 12:42). The Gospel of Luke (12:35ff) is a reminder to the faithful to have their lamps burning ready, to be like men awaiting their master's return, so that when he arrives he will find them wide awake and seat them at his table.

The Vigil is arranged in four parts.
The first part begins the Vigil with a brief service of light.

This is followed by the liturgy of the word when the Church meditates on all the wonderful things God has done for his people from the beginning.

The third part is the liturgy of baptism when new members of the Church are re-born as the day of resurrection approaches.

Finally, there is the liturgy of the eucharist when the whole Church is called to the table which the Lord has prepared for his people through his death and resurrection.

Part One
THE SERVICE OF LIGHT

Blessing of the Fire and Lighting of the Candle.

The church is in darkness. A large fire is prepared outside the church and everyone assembles round it. If the weather is intemperate or it is not possible to have a fire outside the church the blessing of the fire is adapted to the circumstances.

The priest greets the people and says a brief word of explanation about the Vigil in these or similar words:

Dear friends in Christ,
on this most holy night,
when our Lord Jesus Christ passed from death to life,
the Church invites her children throughout the world
to come together in vigil and prayer.
This is the passover of the Lord:
if we honour the memory of his death and resurrection
by hearing his word and celebrating his mysteries,
then we may be confident
that we shall share his victory over death
and live with him for ever in God.

Then the fire is blessed.

Let us pray.
Father,
we share in the light of your glory
through your Son, the light of the world.
Make this new fire ✠ holy, and inflame us with new hope.
Purify our minds by this Easter celebration,
and bring us one day to the feast of eternal light.
We ask this through Christ our Lord.
℟ **Amen.**

The Easter candle is lighted from the new fire.

The procession may follow immediately (see facing page) or the optional blessing of the candle may follow.

Blessing of the Candle (Optional)

After the blessing of the new fire the celebrant cuts a cross in the wax with a stylus. Then he traces the Greek letter alpha (meaning 'the first') above the cross, the letter omega (meaning 'the last') below, and the numerals of the current year between the arms of the cross. Meanwhile he says:

THE EASTER VIGIL/A/B/C

1. Christ yesterday and today
2. the beginning and the end
3. Alpha
4. and Omega
5. all time belongs to him
6. and all the ages
7. to him be glory and power
8. through every age and for ever. Amen.

When the cross and other marks have been made, the priest may insert five grains of incense in the candle. He does this in the form of a cross, saying:

1. By his holy   1
2. and glorious wounds
3. may Christ our Lord   4   2   5
4. guard us
5. and keep us. Amen.   3

The priest lights the candle from the new fire, saying:

May the light of Christ, rising in glory,
dispel the darkness of our hearts and minds.

Procession

Then the priest takes the Easter candle, lifts it high, and sings:

Christ our light.
R/ **Thanks be to God.**

Everyone enters the church, led by the deacon or priest with the Easter candle. At the church door the deacon or priest lifts the candle high and sings a second time:

Christ our light.
R/ **Thanks be to God.**

THE EASTER VIGIL/A/B/C

All light their candles from the Easter candle and continue in the procession. When the deacon or priest arrives before the altar, he faces the people and sings a third time:

Christ our light.
R/ **Thanks be to God.**

Then the lights in the church are put on.

The candle is placed on a stand in the middle of the sanctuary or near the lectern. Then the Easter proclamation is sung.

1. Long Form

Rejoice, heavenly powers! Sing, choirs of angels!
    Exult, all creation around God's throne!
    Jesus Christ, our King, is risen!
    Sound the trumpet of salvation!

Rejoice, O earth, in shining splendour,
    radiant in the brightness of your King!
    Christ has conquered! Glory fills you!
    Darkness vanishes for ever!

Rejoice, O Mother Church! Exult in glory!
    The risen Saviour shines upon you!
    Let this place resound with joy,
    echoing the mighty song of all God's people!

(My dearest friends, standing with me in this holy light,
    join me in asking God for mercy,
    that he may give his unworthy minister
    grace to sing his Easter praises.)*

(V/ The Lord be with you.
R/ **And also with you.**)*
V/ Lift up your hearts.
R/ **We lift them up to the Lord.**
V/ Let us give thanks to the Lord our God.
R/ **It is right to give him thanks and praise.**

It is truly right
that with full hearts and minds and voices
we should praise the unseen God, the all-powerful Father,
and his only Son, our Lord Jesus Christ.

*These words are omitted if the proclamation is sung by one who is not a deacon.

THE EASTER VIGIL/A/B/C

For Christ has ransomed us with his blood,
  and paid for us the price of Adam's sin
  to our eternal Father!

This is our passover feast,
  when Christ, the true Lamb, is slain,
  whose blood consecrates the homes of all believers.

This is the night when first you saved our fathers:
  you freed the people of Israel from their slavery
  and led them dry-shod through the sea.

This is the night when the pillar of fire
  destroyed the darkness of sin!

This is the night when Christians everywhere,
  washed clean of sin
  and freed from all defilement,
  are restored to grace and grow together in holiness.

This is the night when Jesus Christ
  broke the chains of death
  and rose triumphant from the grave.

What good would life have been to us,
  had Christ not come as our Redeemer?

Father, how wonderful your care for us!
  How boundless your merciful love!
  To ransom a slave
  you gave away your Son.

O happy fault, O necessary sin of Adam,
  which gained for us so great a Redeemer!

Most blessed of all nights, chosen by God
  to see Christ rising from the dead!

Of this night scripture says:
  "The night will be as clear as day:
  it will become my light, my joy."

The power of this holy night
  dispels all evil, washes guilt away,
  restores lost innocence, brings mourners joy;
  it casts out hatred, brings us peace, and humbles earthly pride.

Night truly blessed when heaven is wedded to earth
  and man is reconciled with God!

THE EASTER VIGIL/A/B/C

Therefore, heavenly Father, in the joy of this night,
    receive our evening sacrifice of praise,
    your Church's solemn offering.

Accept this Easter candle,
    a flame divided but undimmed,
    a pillar of fire that glows to the honour of God.

Let it mingle with the lights of heaven
    and continue bravely burning
    to dispel the darkness of this night!

May the Morning Star which never sets find this flame still burning:
    Christ, that Morning Star, who came back from the dead,
    and shed his peaceful light on all mankind,
    your Son who lives and reigns for ever and ever.

℟ **Amen.**

or

2. Short Form

Rejoice, heavenly powers! Sing, choirs of angels!
    Exult, all creation around God's throne!
    Jesus Christ, our King, is risen!
    Sound the trumpet of salvation!

Rejoice, O earth, in shining splendour,
    radiant in the brightness of your King!
    Christ has conquered! Glory fills you!
    Darkness vanishes for ever!

Rejoice, O Mother Church! Exult in glory!
    The risen Saviour shines upon you!
    Let this place resound with joy,
    echoing the mighty song of all God's people!

(℣ The Lord be with you
℟ **And also with you.**)*
℣ Lift up your hearts.
℟ **We lift them up to the Lord.**
℣ Let us give thanks to the Lord our God.
℟ **It is right to give him thanks and praise.**

*These words are omitted if the proclamation is sung by one who is not a deacon.

THE EASTER VIGIL/A/B/C

It is truly right
that with full hearts and minds and voices
we should praise the unseen God, the all-powerful Father,
and his only Son, our Lord Jesus Christ.

For Christ has ransomed us with his blood,
and paid for us the price of Adam's sin
to our eternal Father!

This is our passover feast,
when Christ, the true Lamb, is slain,
whose blood consecrates the homes of all believers.

This is the night when first you saved our fathers:
you freed the people of Israel from their slavery
and led them dry-shod through the sea.

This is the night when Christians everywhere,
washed clean of sin
and freed from all defilement,
are restored to grace and grow together in holiness.

This is the night when Jesus Christ
broke the chains of death
and rose triumphant from the grave.

Father, how wonderful your care for us!
How boundless your merciful love!
To ransom a slave
you gave away your Son.

O happy fault, O necessary sin of Adam,
which gained for us so great a Redeemer!

The power of this holy night
dispels all evil, washes guilt away,
restores lost innocence, brings mourners joy.

Night truly blessed when heaven is wedded to earth
and man is reconciled with God!

Therefore, heavenly Father, in the joy of this night,
receive our evening sacrifice of praise,
your Church's solemn offering.

Accept this Easter candle.
May it always dispel the darkness of this night!

May the Morning Star which never sets find this flame still burning:

THE EASTER VIGIL/A/B/C

Christ, that Morning Star, who came back from the dead,
and shed his peaceful light on all mankind,
your Son who lives and reigns for ever and ever.
℟ **Amen.**

Part Two
LITURGY OF THE WORD

In this vigil, nine readings are provided, seven from the Old Testament and two from the New Testament (the epistle and gospel).

After the Easter proclamation, the candles are put aside and all sit down. Before the readings begin, the priest speaks to the people in these or similar words:

Dear friends in Christ,
we have begun our solemn vigil.
Let us now listen attentively to the word of God,
recalling how he saved his people throughout history
and, in the fullness of time,
sent his own Son to be our Redeemer.

Through this Easter celebration,
may God bring to perfection
the saving work he has begun in us.

First Reading   Genesis 1:1-2:2

God saw all he had made, and indeed it was very good.

In the beginning God created the heavens and the earth. Now the earth was a formless void, there was darkness over the deep, and God's spirit hovered over the water.

God said, "Let there be light," and there was light. God saw that light was good, and God divided light from darkness. God called light "day", and darkness he called "night". Evening came and morning came: the first day.

God said, "Let there be a vault in the waters to divide the waters in two." And so it was. God made the vault, and it divided the waters above the vault from the waters under the vault. God called the vault "heaven". Evening came and morning came: the second day.

God said, "Let the waters under heaven come together into a single mass, and let dry land appear." And so it was. God called the dry land "earth" and the mass of water "seas", and God saw that it was good.

God said, "Let the earth produce vegetation: seed-bearing plants, and fruit trees bearing fruit with their seed inside, on the earth." And so it was. The earth produced vegetation: plants bearing seed in their several kinds and trees bearing fruit with their seed inside in their several kinds, God saw that it was good. Evening came and morning came; the third day.

God said, "Let there be lights in the vault of heaven to divide day from night, and let them indicate festivals, days and years. Let them be lights in the vault of heaven to shine on the earth." And so it was. God made the two great lights: the greater light to govern the day, the smaller light to govern the night, and the stars. God set them in the vault of heaven to shine on the earth, to govern the day and the night and to divide light from darkness. God saw that it was good. Evening came and morning came: the fourth day.

God said, "Let the waters teem with living creatures, and let birds fly above the earth within the vault of heaven." And so it was. God created great sea-serpents and every kind of living creature with which the waters teem, and every kind of winged creature. God saw that it was good. God blessed them, saying "Be fruitful, multiply, and fill the waters of the seas; and let the birds multiply upon the earth." Evening came and morning came: the fifth day.

God said, "Let the earth produce every kind of living creature: cattle, reptiles, and every kind of wild beast." And so it was. God made every kind of wild beast, every kind of cattle, and every kind of land reptile. God saw that it was good.

God said, "Let us make man in our own image, in the likeness of ourselves, and let them be masters of the fish of the sea, the birds of heaven, the cattle, all the wild beasts and all the reptiles that crawl upon the earth."
God created man in the image of himself,
in the image of God he created him,
male and female he created them.

God blessed them, saying to them, "Be fruitful, multiply, fill the earth and conquer it. Be masters of the fish of the sea, the birds of heaven and all living animals on the earth." God said, "See, I give you all the seed-bearing plants that are upon the whole earth, and all the trees with seed-bearing fruit; this shall be your food. To all wild beasts, all birds of heaven and all living reptiles on the earth I give all the foliage of plants for food." And so it was. God saw all he had made, and indeed it was very good. Evening came and morning came: the sixth day.

Thus heaven and earth were completed with all their array. On the seventh day God completed the work he had been

THE EASTER VIGIL/A/B/C

doing. He rested on the seventh day after all the work he had been doing.

The psalm or a period of silence follows.

Responsorial Psalm   Psalm 103

℟ **Send forth your spirit, O Lord,
and renew the face of the earth.**

1. Bless the Lord, my soul!
   Lord God, how great you are,
   clothed in majesty and glory,
   wrapped in light as in a robe! ℟

2. You founded the earth on its base,
   to stand firm from age to age.
   You wrapped it with the ocean like a cloak:
   the waters stood higher than the mountains. ℟

3. You make springs gush forth in the valleys:
   they flow in between the hills.
   On their banks dwell the birds of heaven;
   from the branches they sing their song. ℟

4. From your dwelling you water the hills;
   earth drinks its fill of your gift.
   You make the grass grow for the cattle
   and the plants to serve man's needs. ℟

5. How many are your works, O Lord!
   In wisdom you have made them all.
   The earth is full of your riches.
   Bless the Lord, my soul! ℟

or

Psalm 32

℟ **The Lord fills the earth with his love.**

1. The word of the Lord is faithful
   and all his works to be trusted.
   The Lord loves justice and right
   and fills the earth with his love. ℟

2. By his word the heavens were made,
   by the breath of his mouth all the stars.
   He collects the waves of the ocean;
   he stores up the depths of the sea. ℟

THE EASTER VIGIL/A/B/C

3. They are happy, whose God is the Lord,
   the people he has chosen as his own.
   From the heavens the Lord look forth,
   he sees all the children of men. ℞

4. Our soul is waiting for the Lord.
   The Lord is our help and our shield.
   May your love be upon us, O Lord,
   as we place all our hope in you. ℞

All stand

Prayer

Let us pray.
Almighty and eternal God,
you created all things in wonderful beauty and order.
Help us now to perceive
how still more wonderful is the new creation
by which in the fullness of time
you redeemed your people
through the sacrifice of our passover, Jesus Christ,
who lives and reigns for ever and ever.

or

Let us pray.
Lord God, the creation of man was a wonderful work,
his redemption still more wonderful.
May we persevere in right reason
against all that entices to sin
and so attain to everlasting joy.

Second Reading Genesis 22:1-18

The sacrifice of Abraham, our father in faith.

> God put Abraham to the test, "Abraham, Abraham," he called. "Here I am," he replied. "Take your son," God said "your only child Isaac, whom you love, and go to the land of Moriah. There you shall offer him as a burnt offering, on a mountain I will point out to you."

Rising early next morning Abraham saddled his ass and took with him two of his servants and his son Isaac. He chopped wood for the burnt offering and started on his journey to the place God had pointed out to him. On the third day Abraham looked up and saw the place in the distance. Then Abraham said to his

THE EASTER VIGIL/A/B/C

servants, "Stay here with the donkey. The boy and I will go over there, we will worship and come back to you."

Abraham took the wood for the burnt offering, loaded it on Isaac, and carried in his own hands the fire and the knife. Then the two of them set out together. Isaac spoke to his father Abraham. "Father," he said. "Yes, my son," he replied. "Look," he said, "here are the fire and the wood, but where is the lamb for the burnt offering?" Abraham answered, "My son, God himself will provide the lamb for the burnt offering." Then the two of them went on together.

> When they arrived at the place God had pointed out to him, Abraham built an altar there, and arranged the wood. Then he bound his son Isaac and put him on the altar on top of the wood. Abraham stretched out his hand and seized the knife to kill his son.

But the angel of the Lord called to him from heaven.

"Abraham, Abraham," he said. "I am here," he replied. "Do not harm him, for now I know you fear God. You have not refused me your son, your only son." Then looking up, Abraham saw a ram caught by its horns in a bush. Abraham took the ram and offered it as a burnt-offering in place of his son.

Abraham called this place "The Lord provides", and hence the saying today: On the mountain the Lord provides.

> The angel of the Lord called Abraham a second time from heaven. "I swear by my own self — it is the Lord who speaks — because you have done this, because you have not refused me your son, your only son, I will shower blessings on you, I will make your descendants as many as the stars of heaven and the grains of sand on the seashore. Your descendants shall gain possession of the gates of their enemies. All the nations of the earth shall bless themselves by your descendants, as a reward for your obedience."

The psalm or a period of silence follows.

Responsorial Psalm   Psalm 15

R/ Preserve me, God I take refuge in you.

1. O Lord, it is you who are my portion and cup;
   it is you yourself who are my prize.
   I keep the Lord ever in my sight:
   since he is at my right hand, I shall stand firm. **R/**

THE EASTER VIGIL/A/B/C

2. And so my heart rejoices, my soul is glad;
even my body shall rest in safety.
For you will not leave my soul among the dead,
nor let your beloved know decay. ℟

3. You will show me the path of life,
the fullness of joy in your presence,
at you right hand happiness for ever. ℟

All stand

Prayer

Let us pray.
God and Father of all who believe in you,
you promised Abraham that he would become the father of all nations,
and through the death and resurrection of Christ
you fulfil that promise:
everywhere throughout the world you increase your chosen people.
May we respond to your call
by joyfully accepting your invitation to the new life of grace.

The following reading is obligatory.

Third Reading Exodus 14:15-15:1

The sons of Israel went on dry ground right into the sea.

The Lord said to Moses, "Why do you cry to me so? Tell the sons of Israel to march on. For yourself, raise your staff and stretch out your hand over the sea and part it for the sons of Israel to walk through the sea on dry ground. I for my part will make the heart of the Egyptians so stubborn that they will follow them. So shall I win myself glory at the expense of Pharaoh, of all his army, his chariots, his horsemen. And when I have won glory for myself, at the expense of Pharaoh and his chariots and his army, the Egyptians will learn that I am the Lord."

Then the angel of the Lord, who marched at the front of the army of Israel, changed station and moved to their rear. The pillar of cloud changed station from the front to the rear of them, and remained there. It came between the camp of the Egyptians and the camp of Israel. The cloud was dark, and the night passed without the armies drawing any closer the whole night long. Moses stretched out his hand over the sea. The Lord drove back the sea with a strong easterly wind all night, and he made dry land of the sea. The waters parted and the sons of Israel went on dry ground right into the sea, walls of water to right and to left of them. The Egyptians gave chase: after them they went, right into the sea, all Pharaoh's horses, his chariots, and his horsemen. In the morning watch, the Lord looked down on the army of the Egyptians from the pillar of fire and cloud, and threw the army into confusion. He so clogged their chariot wheels that they could scarcely make headway. "Let us flee from the Israelites," the Egyptians cried "the Lord is fighting for them against the Egyptians!" "Stretch out your hand over the sea," the Lord said to Moses "that the waters may flow back on the Egyptians and their chariots and their horsemen." Moses stretched out his hand over the sea and, as day broke, the sea returned to its bed. The fleeing Egyptians marched right into it, and the Lord overthrew the Egyptians in the very middle of the sea. The returning waters overwhelmed the chariots and the horsemen of Pharaoh's whole army, which had followed the Israelites into the sea; not a single one of them was left. But the sons of Israel had marched through the sea on dry ground, walls of water to right and to left of them. That day, the Lord rescued Israel from the Egyptians, and Israel saw the Egyptians lying dead on the shore. Israel witnessed the great act that the Lord had performed against the Egyptians, and the people venerated the Lord; they put their faith in the Lord and in Moses, his servant.

It was then that Moses and the sons of Israel sang this song in honour of the Lord:

The Responsional Psalm is taken up immediately.

Responsorial Psalm   Exodus 15:1-6.17-18

℟ **I will sing to the Lord, glorious his triumph!**

1. I will sing to the Lord, glorious his triumph!
   Horse and rider he has thrown into the sea!
   The Lord is my strength, my song, my salvation.
   This is my God and I extol him,
   my father's God and I gave him praise. ℟

2. The Lord is a warrior! The Lord is his name.
   The chariots of Pharaoh he hurled into the sea,

THE EASTER VIGIL/A/B/C

    the flower of his army is drowned in the sea.
    The deeps hide them; they sank like a stone. ℟

3. Your right hand, Lord, glorious in its power,
   your right hand, Lord, has shattered the enemy.
   In the greatness of your glory you crushed the foe. ℟

4. You will lead them and plant them on your mountain,
   the place, O Lord, where you have made your home,
   the sanctuary, Lord, which your hands have made.
   The Lord will reign for ever and ever. ℟

All stand

Prayer

Let us pray.
Father,
even today we see the wonders
of the miracles you worked long ago.
You once saved a single nation from slavery,
and now you offer that salvation to all through baptism.
May the peoples of the world become true sons of Abraham
and prove worthy of the heritage of Israel.

or

Let us pray.
Lord God,
in the new covenant
you shed light on the miracles you worked in ancient times:
the Red Sea is a symbol of our baptism,
and the nation you freed from slavery
is a sign of your Christian people.
May every nation
share the faith and privilege of Israel,
and come to new birth in the Holy Spirit.

Fourth Reading   Isaiah 54:5-14

With everlasting love the Lord your redeemer has taken pity on you.

Now your creator will be your husband,
his name, the Lord of hosts;
your redeemer will be the Holy One of Israel,
he is called the God of the whole earth.

THE EASTER VIGIL/A/B/C

Yes, like a forsaken wife, distressed in spirit,
the Lord calls you back.
Does a man cast off the wife of his youth?
says your God.
I did forsake you for a brief moment,
but with great love will I take you back.
In excess of anger, for a moment
I hid my face from you.
But with everlasting love I have taken pity on you,
says the Lord, your redeemer.

I am now as I was in the days of Noah
when I swore that Noah's waters
should never flood the world again.
So now I swear concerning my anger with you
and the threats I made against you;

for the mountains may depart,
the hills be shaken,
but my love for you will never leave you
and my covenant of peace with you will never be shaken,
says the Lord who takes pity on you.

Unhappy creature, storm-tossed, disconsolate,
see, I will set your stones on carbuncles
and your foundations on sapphires.
I will make rubies your battlements,
your gates crystal,
and your entire wall precious stones.
Your sons will all be taught by the Lord.
The prosperity of your sons will be great.
You will be founded on integrity;
remote from oppression, you will have nothing to fear;
remote from terror, it will not approach you.

The psalm or a period of silence follows.

Responsorial Psalm   Psalm 29

℟ **I will praise you, Lord, you have rescued me.**

1. I will praise you, Lord, you have rescued me
   and have not let my enemies rejoice over me.
   O Lord, you have raised my soul from the dead,
   restored me to life from those who sink into the grave. ℟

THE EASTER VIGIL/A/B/C

2. Sing psalms to the Lord, you who love him,
give thanks to his holy name.
His anger lasts but a moment; his favour through life.
At night there are tears, but joy comes with dawn. ℟

3. The Lord listened and had pity.
The Lord came to my help.
For me you have changed my mourning into dancing,
O Lord my God, I will thank you for ever. ℟

All stand

Prayer

Let us pray.
Almighty and eternal God,
glorify your name by increasing your chosen people
as you promised long ago.
In reward for their trust,
may we see in the Church the fulfilment of your promise.

Prayers may also be chosen from those given after the following readings, if the readings are omitted.

Fifth Reading   Isaiah 55:1-11

Come to me and your soul will live, and I will make an everlasting covenant with you.

Thus says the Lord:
Oh, come to the water all you who are thirsty;
though you have no money, come!
Buy corn without money, and eat,
and, at no cost, wine and milk.
Why spend money on what is not bread,
your wages on what fails to satisfy?
Listen, listen to me, and you will have good things to eat
and rich food to enjoy.
Pay attention, come to me;
listen, and your soul will live.

With you I will make an everlasting covenant
out of the favours promised to David.
See, I have made of you a witness to the peoples,
a leader and a master of the nations.
See, you will summon a nation you never knew,

those unknown will come hurrying to you,
for the sake of the Lord your God,
of the Holy One of Israel who will glorify you.
Seek the Lord while he is still to be found,
call to him while he is still near.
Let the wicked man abandon his way,
the evil man his thoughts.
Let him turn back to the Lord who will take pity on him,
to our God who is rich in forgiving;
for my thoughts are not your thoughts,
my ways are not your ways — it is the Lord who speaks.
Yes, the heavens are as high above earth
as my ways are above your ways,
my thoughts above your thoughts.

Yes, as the rain and the snow come down from the heavens and do not return without watering the earth, making it yield and giving growth to provide seed for the sower and bread for the eating, so the word that goes from my mouth does not return to me empty, without carrying out my will and succeeding in what it was sent to do.

The psalm or a period of silence follows.

Responsorial Psalm   Isaiah 12:2-6

℟ **With joy you will draw water from the wells of salvation.**

1. Truly God is my salvation,
   I trust, I shall not fear.
   For the Lord is my strength, my song,
   he became my saviour.
   With joy you will draw water
   from the wells of salvation. ℟

2. Give thanks to the Lord, give praise to his name!
   make his mighty deeds known to the peoples,
   declare the greatness of his name. ℟

3. Sing a psalm to the Lord
   for he has done glorious deeds,
   make them known to all the earth!
   People of Zion, sing and shout for joy
   for great in your midst is the Holy One of Israel. ℟

THE EASTER VIGIL/A/B/C

All stand

Prayer

Let us pray.
Almighty, ever-living God,
only hope of the world,
by the preaching of the prophets
you proclaimed the mysteries we are celebrating tonight.
Help us to be your faithful people,
for it is by your inspiration alone
that we can grow in goodness.

Sixth Reading   Baruch 3:9-15.32-4:4

In the radiance of the Lord make your way to light.

Listen, Israel, to commands that bring life;
hear, and learn what knowledge means.
Why, Israel, why are you in the country of your enemies,
growing older and older in an alien land,
sharing defilement with the dead,
reckoned with those who go to Sheol?
Because you have forsaken the fountain of wisdom.
Had you walked in the way of God,
you would have lived in peace for ever.
Learn where knowledge is, where strength,
where understanding, and so learn
where length of days is, where life,
where the light of the eyes and where peace.
But who has found out where she lives,
who has entered her treasure house?

But the One who knows all knows her,
he has grasped her with his own intellect,
he has set the earth firm for ever
and filled it with four-footed beasts,
he sends the light — and it goes,
he recalls it — and trembling it obeys;
the stars shine joyfully at their set times:
when he calls them, they answer, "Here we are";
they gladly shine for their creator.
It is he who is our God,
no other can compare with him.
He has grasped the whole way of knowledge,

THE EASTER VIGIL/A/B/C

and confided it to his servant Jacob,
to Israel his well-beloved;
so causing her to appear on earth
and move among men.
This is the book of the commandments of God,
the Law that stands for ever;
those who keep her live,
those who desert her die.
Turn back, Jacob, seize her,
in her radiance make your way to light:
do not yield your glory to another,
your privilege to a people not your own.
Israel, blessed are we:
what pleases God has been revealed to us.

The psalm or a period of silence follows.

Responsorial Psalm   Psalm 18

R/ **You have the message of eternal life, O Lord.**

1. The law of the Lord is perfect,
   it revives the soul.
   The rule of the Lord is to be trusted,
   it gives wisdom to the simple. R/

2. The precepts of the Lord are right,
   they gladden the heart.
   The command of the Lord is clear,
   it gives light to the eyes. R/

3. The fear of the Lord is holy,
   abiding for ever.
   The decrees of the Lord are truth
   and all of them just. R/

4. They are more to be desired than gold,
   than the purest of gold
   and sweeter are they than honey,
   than honey from the comb. R/

All stand.

Prayer

Let us pray.
Father,
you increase your Church

THE EASTER VIGIL/A/B/C

by continuing to call all people to salvation.
Listen to our prayers
and always watch over those you cleanse in baptism.

Seventh Reading   Ezekiel 36:16-17a, 18-28

I shall pour clean water over you, and I shall give you a new heart.

The word of the Lord was addressed to me as follows: "Son of man, the members of the House of Israel used to live in their own land, but they defiled it by their conduct and actions.

"I then discharged my fury at them because of the blood they shed in their land and the idols with which they defiled it. I scattered them among the nations and dispersed them in foreign countries. I sentenced them as their conduct and actions deserved. And now they have profaned my holy name among the nations where they have gone, so that people say of them, 'These are the people of the Lord; they have been exiled from his land.' But I have been concerned about my holy name, which the House of Israel has profaned among the nations where they have gone. And so, say to the House of Israel, 'The Lord says this: I am not doing this for your sake, House of Israel, but for the sake of my holy name, which you have profaned among the nations where you have gone. I mean to display the holiness of my great name, which has been profaned among the nations, which you have profaned among them. And the nations will learn that I am the Lord — it is the Lord who speaks — when I display my holiness for your sake before their eyes. Then I am going to take you from among the nations and gather you together from all the foreign countries, and bring you home to your own land. I shall cleanse you of all your defilement and all your idols. I shall give you a new heart, and put a new spirit in you; I shall remove the heart of stone from your bodies and give you a heart of flesh instead. I shall put my spirit in you, and make you keep my laws and sincerely respect my observances. You will live in the land which I gave your ancestors. You shall be my people and I will be your God.'"

The psalm or a period of silence follows.

THE EASTER VIGIL/A/B/C

Responsorial Psalm   Psalms 41 and 42

**R/ Like the deer that yearns for running streams,
so my soul is yearning for you, my God.**

1. My soul is thirsting for God.
   the God of my life;
   when can I enter and see
   the face of God? R/

2. These things will I remember
   as I pour out my soul:
   how I would lead the rejoicing crowd
   into the house of God,
   amid cries of gladness and thanksgiving,
   the throng wild with joy. R/

3. O send forth your light and your truth;
   let these be my guide.
   Let them bring me to your holy mountain
   to the place where you dwell. R/

4. And I will come to the altar of God,
   the God of my joy.
   My redeemer, I will thank you on the harp,
   O God, my God. R/

If a Baptism takes place, the Responsorial Psalm which follows the Fifth Reading (page 353) is used, or Psalm 50 as follows:

Responsorial Psalm   Psalm 50

R/ A pure heart create for me, O God.

1. A pure heart create for me, O God.
   put a steadfast spirit within me.
   Do not cast me away from your presence,
   nor deprive me of your holy spirit. R/

2. Give me again the joy of your help;
   with a spirit of fervour sustain me,
   that I may teach transgressors your ways
   and sinners may return to you. R/

3. For in sacrifice you take no delight,
   burnt offering from me you would refuse,
   my sacrifice, a contrite spirit.
   A humbled, contrite heart you will not spurn. R/

THE EASTER VIGIL/A/B/C

All stand.
Prayer
Let us pray.
God of unchanging power and light,
look with mercy and favour on your entire Church.
Bring lasting salvation to mankind,
so that the world may see
the fallen lifted up,
the old made new,
and all things brought to perfection,
through him who is their origin,
our Lord Jesus Christ,
who lives and reigns for ever and ever.

or

Let us pray.
Father,
you teach us in both the Old and the New Testament
to celebrate this passover mystery.
Help us to understand your great love for us.
May the goodness you now show us
confirm our hope in your future mercy.

or (if there are candidates to be baptised):

Let us pray.
Almighty and eternal God,
be present in this sacrament of your love.
Send your Spirit of adoption
on those to be born again in baptism.
And may the work of our humble ministry
be brought to perfection by your mighty power.

After the last reading from the Old Testament with its psalm and prayer, the altar candles are lighted, and the priest intones the Gloria, which is taken up by all present. The church bells are rung, according to local custom. At the end of the Gloria, the priest sings or says the opening prayer in the usual way.

Opening Prayer
Let us pray.
Lord God,
you have brightened this night

THE EASTER VIGIL/A/B/C

with the radiance of the risen Christ.
Quicken the spirit of sonship in your Church;
renew us in mind and body
to give you whole-hearted service.

New Testament Reading   Romans 6:3-11
Christ, having been raised from the dead, will never die again.

When we were baptised in Christ Jesus we were baptised in his death; in other words, when we were baptised we went into the tomb with him and joined him in death, so that as Christ was raised from the dead by the Father's glory, we too might live a new life.

If in union with Christ we have imitated his death, we shall also imitate him in his resurrection. We must realise that our former selves have been crucified with him to destroy this sinful body and to free us from the slavery of sin. When a man dies, of course, he has finished with sin.

But we believe that having died with Christ we shall return to life with him: Christ, as we know, having been raised from the dead will never die again. Death has no power over him any more. When he died, he died, once for all, to sin, so his life now is life with God; and in that way, you too must consider yourselves to be dead to sin but alive for God in Christ Jesus.

After the epistle all rise, and the priest or cantor solemnly intones the Alleluia which is repeated by all present.

Responsorial Psalm   Psalm 117
℟ **Alleluia, alleluia, alleluia!**

1. Give thanks to the Lord for he is good,
   for his love has no end.
   Let the sons of Israel say:
   "His love has no end." ℟

2. The Lord's right hand has triumphed;
   his right hand raised me up.
   I shall not die, I shall live
   and recount his deeds. ℟

THE EASTER VIGIL/A/B/C

3. The stone which the builders rejected
   has become the corner stone.
   This is the work of the Lord,
   a marvel in our eyes. ℟

The Gospel follows. Either A, B or C is read, according to the Cycle for the Year.

A
Gospel   Matthew 28:1-10

He has risen from the dead and now he is going before you into Galilee.

After the sabbath, and towards dawn on the first day of the week, Mary of Magdala and the other Mary went to visit the sepulchre. And all at once there was a violent earthquake, for the angel of the Lord, descended from heaven, came and rolled away the stone and sat on it. His face was like lightning, his robe white as snow. The guards were so shaken, so frightened of him, that they were like dead men. But the angel spoke; and he said to the women, "There is no need for you to be afraid. I know you are looking for Jesus, who was crucified. He is not here, for he has risen, as he said he would. Come and see the place where he lay, then go quickly and tell his disciples, 'He has risen from the dead and now he is going before you to Galilee; it is there you will see him.' Now I have told you." Filled with awe and great joy the women came quickly away from the tomb and ran to tell the disciples.

And there, coming to meet them, was Jesus. "Greetings," he said. And the women came up to him and, falling down before him, clasped his feet. Then Jesus said to them, "Do not be afraid; go and tell my brothers that they must leave for Galilee; they will see me there."

Turn to page 362.

B
Gospel   Mark 16:1-7

Jesus of Nazareth, who was crucified, has risen.

When the sabbath was over, Mary of Magdala, Mary the mother of James, and Salome, brought spices with which to go and anoint him. And very early in the morning on the first day of the week they went to the tomb, just as the sun was rising.

THE EASTER VIGIL/A/B/C

They had been saying to one another, "Who will roll away the stone for us from the entrance to the tomb?" But when they looked they could see that the stone — which was very big — had already been rolled back. On entering the tomb they saw a young man in a white robe seated on the right-hand side, and they were struck with amazement. But he said to them, "There is no need for alarm. You are looking for Jesus of Nazareth, who was crucified: he has risen, he is not here. See, here is the place where they laid him. But you must go and tell his disciples and Peter, 'He is going before you to Galilee; it is there you will see him, just as he told you.' "

Turn to page 362.

C
Gospel Luke 24:1-12

Why look among the dead for someone who is alive?

On the first day of the week, at the first sign of dawn, they went to the tomb with the spices they had prepared. They found that the stone had been rolled away from the tomb, but on entering discovered that the body of the Lord Jesus was not there. As they stood there not knowing what to think, two men in brilliant clothes suddenly appeared at their side. Terrified, the women lowered their eyes. But the two men said to them, "Why look among the dead for someone who is alive? He is not here; he has risen. Remember what he told you when he was still in Galilee: that the Son of Man had to be handed over into the power of sinful men and be crucified, and rise again on the third day?" And they remembered his words.

When the women returned from the tomb they told all this to the Eleven and to all the others. The women were Mary of Magdala, Joanna, and Mary the mother of James. The other women with them also told the apostles, but this story of theirs seemed pure nonsense, and they did not believe them.

Peter, however, went running to the tomb. He bent down and saw the binding cloths, but nothing else; he then went back home, amazed at what had happened.

The Homily follows.

Part Three
LITURGY OF BAPTISM

The priest goes with the ministers to the baptismal font, if this can be seen by the congregation. Otherwise a vessel of water is placed in the sanctuary.

If there are candidates to be baptised, they are called forward and presented by their godparents. If they are children, the parents and godparents bring them forward in front of the congregation.

Then the priest speaks to the people in these or similar words:

If there are candidates to be baptised
Dear friends in Christ,
as our brothers and sisters approach the waters of rebirth,
let us help them by our prayers
and ask God, our almighty Father,
to support them with his mercy and love.

If the font is to be blessed, but there is no one to be baptised
Dear friends in Christ,
let us ask God, the almighty Father,
to bless this font,
that those reborn in it
may be made one with his adopted children in Christ.

Litany of Saints

Lord, have mercy	Lord, have mercy
Christ, have mercy	Christ, have mercy
Lord, have mercy	Lord, have mercy
Holy Mary, Mother of God	pray for us
Saint Michael	pray for us
Holy angels of God	pray for us
Saint John the Baptist	pray for us
Saint Joseph	pray for us
Saint Peter and Saint Paul	pray for us
Saint Andrew	pray for us
Saint John	pray for us
Saint Mary Magdalene	pray for us
Saint Stephen	pray for us
Saint Ignatius	pray for us

THE EASTER VIGIL/A/B/C

Saint Lawrence	pray for us
Saint Perpetua and Saint Felicity	pray for us
Saint Agnes	pray for us
Saint Gregory	pray for us
Saint Augustine	pray for us
Saint Athanasius	pray for us
Saint Basil	pray for us
Saint Martin	pray for us
Saint Benedict	pray for us
Saint Francis and Saint Dominic	pray for us
Saint Francis Xavier	pray for us
Saint John Vianney	pray for us
Saint Catherine	pray for us
Saint Teresa	pray for us
All holy men and women	pray for us
Lord, be merciful	Lord, save your people
From all evil	Lord, save your people
From every sin	Lord, save your people
From everlasting death	Lord, save your people
By your coming as man	Lord, save your people
By your death and rising to new life	Lord, save your people
By your gift of the Holy Spirit	Lord, save your people
Be merciful to us sinners	Lord, hear our prayer

If there are candidates to be baptised

Give new life to these chosen ones by the grace of baptism	Lord, hear our prayer

If there is no one to be baptised

By your grace bless this font where your children will be reborn	Lord, hear our prayer

THE EASTER VIGIL/A/B/C

Jesus Son of the
  living God
Christ, hear us
Lord Jesus, hear
  our prayer

Lord, hear our prayer
Christ, hear us

Lord Jesus, hear our prayer

Blessing of Water
The priest then blesses the baptismal water.

Father, you give us grace through sacramental signs,
  which tell us of the wonders of your unseen power.

In baptism we use your gift of water,
  which you have made a rich symbol
  of the grace you give us in this sacrament.

At the very dawn of creation
  your Spirit breathed on the waters,
  making them the wellspring of all holiness.

The waters of the great flood
  you made a sign of the waters of baptism,
  that make an end of sin and a new beginning of goodness.

Through the waters of the Red Sea
  you led Israel out of slavery,
  to be an image of God's holy people,
  set free from sin by baptism.

In the waters of the Jordan
  your Son was baptised by John
  and anointed with the Spirit.

Your Son willed that water and blood
  should flow from his side
  as he hung upon the cross.

After his resurrection he told his disciples:
  "Go out and teach all nations,
  baptising them in the name of the Father
  and of the Son and of the Holy Spirit."

Father, look now with love upon your Church,
  and unseal for her the fountain of baptism.

By the power of the Spirit
  give to the water of this font
  the grace of your Son.

You created man in your own likeness:
   cleanse him from sin in a new birth of innocence
   by water and the Spirit.

The priest may lower the Easter candle into the water either once or three times, as he continues:

We ask you, Father, with your Son
   to send the Holy Spirit upon the waters of this font.

He holds the candle in the water:

May all who are buried with Christ
   in the death of baptism
   rise also with him to newness of life.

We ask this through Christ our Lord.
℟ **Amen.**

Then the candle is taken out of the water as the people sing this acclamation or another:

Springs of water, bless the Lord.
Give him glory and praise for ever.

Blessing of Water

If no one is to be baptized and the font is not to be blessed, the priest blesses the water with this prayer:

My brothers and sisters,
let us ask the Lord our God
to bless this water he has created,
which we shall use to recall our baptism.
May he renew us
and keep us faithful to the Spirit
we have all received.

All pray silently for a short while. The priest continues:

Lord our God,
this night your people keep prayerful vigil.
Be with us as we recall the wonder of our creation
and the great wonder of our redemption.
Bless this water: it makes the seed to grow,

THE EASTER VIGIL/A/B/C

it refreshes us and makes us clean.
You have made of it a servant of your loving kindness:
through water you set your people free,
and quenched their thirst in the desert.
With water the prophets announced a new covenant
that you would make with man.
By water, made holy by Christ in the Jordan,
you made our sinful nature new
in the bath that gives rebirth.
Let this water remind us of our baptism;
let us share the joys of our brothers
who are baptised this Easter.

We ask this through Christ our Lord.

R/ **Amen.**

Renewal of Baptismal Promises

All present stand with lighted candles and renew their baptismal profession of faith. The priest speaks to the people in these or similar words:

Dear friends,
through the paschal mystery
we have been buried with Christ in baptism,
so that we may rise with him to a new life.
Now that we have completed our lenten observance,
let us renew the promises we made in baptism
when we rejected Satan and his works,
and promised to serve God faithfully,
in his holy Catholic Church.

And so:

Priest	Do you reject Satan?
All	**I do.**
Priest	And all his works?
All	**I do.**
Priest	And all his empty promises?
All	**I do.**

or

Priest	Do you reject sin, so as to live in the freedom of God's children?
All	**I do.**

THE EASTER VIGIL/A/B/C

Priest — Do you reject the glamour of evil, and refuse to be mastered by sin?
All — **I do.**
Priest — Do you reject Satan, father of sin and prince of darkness?
All — **I do.**

Then the priest continues:

Priest — Do you believe in God, the Father almighty, creator of heaven and earth?
All — **I do.**
Priest — Do you believe in Jesus Christ, his only Son, our Lord,
who was born of the Virgin Mary,
was crucified, died, and was buried,
rose from the dead,
and is now seated at the right hand of the Father?
All — **I do.**
Priest — Do you believe in the Holy Spirit,
the holy Catholic Church, the communion of saints,
the forgiveness of sins, the resurrection of the body,
and life everlasting?
All — **I do.**

The priest concludes:

God, the all-powerful Father of our Lord Jesus Christ,
has given us a new birth by water and the Holy Spirit,
and forgiven all our sins.

May he also keep us faithful to our Lord Jesus Christ for ever and ever.

℟ **Amen.**

The priest sprinkles the people with the blessed water, while all sing a song which is baptismal in character, such as:

I saw water flowing
from the right side of the temple, alleluia.
It brought God's life and his salvation,
and the people sang in joyful praise:
alleluia, alleluia. cf. Ezekiel 47:1-2,9

THE EASTER VIGIL/A/B/C

Meanwhile the newly baptised are led to their place among the faithful.

If the blessing of the baptismal water does not take place in the baptistery, the ministers reverently carry the vessel of water to the font.

If the blessing of the font does not take place, the blessed water is put in a convenient place.

After the people have been sprinkled, the priest returns to the chair. The profession of faith is omitted, and the priest directs the general intercessions, (bidding prayers) in which the newly baptised take part for the first time.

Part Four

LITURGY OF THE EUCHARIST

The priest goes to the altar and begins the liturgy of the eucharist in the usual way. (Turn to page 553 for the Order of Mass.)

It is fitting that the bread and wine be brought forward by the newly baptised.

Prayer over the Gifts

Lord,
accept the prayers and offerings of your people.
With your help
may this Easter mystery of our redemption
bring to perfection the saving work you have begun in us.

Preface

Father, all-powerful and ever-living God,
we do well always and everywhere to give you thanks
through Jesus Christ our Lord.

We praise you with greater joy than ever
on this Easter night (day),
when Christ became our paschal sacrifice.

He is the true Lamb who took away the sins of the world.
By dying he destroyed our death;
by rising he restored our life.

And so, with all the choirs of angels in heaven
we proclaim your glory
and join in their unending hymn of praise:

Holy, holy, holy . . .

If Eucharistic Prayer I is used, the following special forms are said:

Easter and octave:

In union with the whole Church
we celebrate that day (night)
when Jesus Christ, our Lord,
rose from the dead in his human body.
We honour Mary,
the ever-virgin mother of Jesus Christ our Lord and God

THE EASTER VIGIL/A/B/C

Father, accept this offering
from your whole family
and from those born into the new life
of water and the Holy Spirit,
with all their sins forgiven.
Grant us your peace. . . . . . .

Communion Antiphon   Christ has become our paschal sacrifice; let us feast with the unleavened bread of sincerity and truth, alleluia. 1 Corinthians 5:7-8.

Prayer after Communion
Lord,
you have nourished us with your Easter sacraments.
Fill us with your Spirit
and make us all one in peace and love.

The deacon (or the priest) sings or says the dismissal as follows
Go in the peace of Christ, alleluia, alleluia.

or

The Mass is ended, go in peace, alleluia, alleluia.

or

Go in peace to love and serve the Lord, alleluia, alleluia.

R/ **Thanks be to God, alleluia, alleluia.**

EASTER SUNDAY

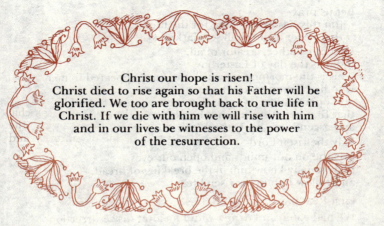

Christ our hope is risen!
Christ died to rise again so that his Father will be glorified. We too are brought back to true life in Christ. If we die with him we will rise with him and in our lives be witnesses to the power of the resurrection.

Entrance Antiphon I have risen: I am with you once more; you placed your hand on me to keep me safe. How great is the depth of your wisdom, alleluia! Psalm 138:18.5-6

or

The Lord has indeed risen, alleluia. Glory and kingship be his for ever and ever.
Luke 24:34; cf. Revelation 1:6

Opening Prayer

Let us pray
 [that the risen Christ will raise us up
 and renew our lives]

God our Father,
by raising Christ your Son
you conquered the power of death
and opened for us the way to eternal life.
Let our celebration today
raise us up and renew our lives
by the Spirit that is within us.

or

EASTER SUNDAY/A/B/C

Let us pray
  [on this Easter morning for the life
  that never again shall see darkness]

God our Father, creator of all,
today is the day of Easter joy.
This is the morning on which the Lord appeared to men
who had begun to lose hope
and opened their eyes to what the scriptures foretold:
that first he must die, and then he would rise
and ascend into his Father's glorious presence.

May the risen Lord
breathe on our minds and open our eyes
that we may know him in the breaking of bread,
and follow him in his risen life.

First Reading   Acts 10:34.37-43.

We had eaten and drunk with him after his resurrection

Peter addressed Cornelius and his household: "You must have heard about the recent happenings in Judaea; about Jesus of Nazareth and how he began in Galilee, after John had been preaching baptism. God had anointed him with the Holy Spirit and with power, and because God was with him, Jesus went about doing good and curing all who had fallen into the power of the devil. Now I, and those with me, can witness to everything he did throughout the countryside of Judaea and in Jerusalem itself: and also to the fact that they killed him by hanging him on a tree, yet three days afterwards God raised him to life and allowed him to be seen, not by the whole people but only by certain witnesses God had chosen beforehand. Now we are those witnesses — we have eaten and drunk with him after his resurrection from the dead — and he has ordered us to proclaim this to his people and to tell them that God has appointed him to judge everyone, alive or dead. It is to him that all the prophets bear this witness: that all who believe in Jesus will have their sins forgiven through his name."

Responsorial Psalm   Psalm 117

R/ **This day was made by the Lord;
  we rejoice and are glad.**

or

  Alleluia, alleluia, alleluia!

1. Give thanks to the Lord for he is good,
   for his love has no end.
   Let the sons of Israel say:
   "His love has no end". R/

2. The Lord's right hand has triumphed;
   his right hand raised me up.
   I shall not die, I shall live
   and recount his deeds. R/

3. The stone which the builders rejected
   has become the corner stone.
   This is the work of the Lord,
   a marvel in our eyes. R/

Second Reading   Colossians 3:1-4

You must look for the things that are in heaven, where Christ is.

Since you have been brought back to true life with Christ, you must look for the things that are in heaven, where Christ is, sitting at God's right hand. Let your thoughts be on heavenly things, not on the things that are on the earth, because you have died, and now the life you have is hidden with Christ in God. But when Christ is revealed — and he is your life — you too will be revealed in all your glory with him.

or

Alternative Reading   1 Corinthians 5:6-8

Get rid of the old yeast, make yourselves into a completely new batch of bread.

You must know how even a small amount of yeast is enough to leaven all the dough, so get rid of all the old yeast, and make yourselves into a completely new batch of bread, unleavened as you are meant to be. Christ, our passover, has been sacrificed; let us celebrate the feast, then, by getting rid of all the old yeast of evil and wickedness, having only the unleavened bread of sincerity and truth.

Sequence

Christians, to the Paschal Victim offer sacrifice and praise.
The sheep are ransomed by the Lamb;

EASTER SUNDAY/A/B/C

and Christ, the undefiled,
hath sinners to his Father reconciled.
Death with life contended: combat strangely ended!
Life's own Champion, slain, yet lives to reign.
Tell us, Mary: say what thou didst see upon the way.
The tomb the Living did enclose;
I saw Christ's glory as he rose!
The angels there attesting;
shroud with grave-clothes resting.
Christ, my hope, has risen: he goes before you into Galilee.
That Christ is truly risen from the dead we know.
Victorious king, thy mercy show!

Alleluia   Alleluia, alleluia! Christ, our passover, has been sacrificed; let us celebrate the feast then, in the Lord. Alleluia! I Corinthians 5:7-8

Gospel   John 20:1-9

He must rise from the dead.

It was very early on the first day of the week and still dark, when Mary of Magdala came to the tomb. She saw that the stone had been moved away from the tomb and came running to Simon Peter and the other disciple, the one Jesus loved. "They have taken the Lord out of the tomb," she said "and we don't know where they have put him."

So Peter set out with the other disciples to go to the tomb. They ran together, but the other disciple, running faster than Peter, reached the tomb first; he bent down and saw the linen cloths lying on the ground, but did not go in. Simon Peter who was following now came up, went right into the tomb, saw the linen cloths on the ground, and also the cloth that had been over his head; this was not with the linen cloths but rolled up in a place by itself. Then the other disciple who had reached the tomb first also went in; he saw and he believed. Till this moment they had failed to understand the teaching of scripture, that he must rise from the dead.

As an alternative, the gospel of the Mass of Easter Night, pages 360-361, may be read.

At evening Mass on Easter Sunday the Gospel of Third Sunday of Easter, Cycle A, page 383, may be read.

EASTER SUNDAY/A/B/C

Renewal of Baptismal Promises

In Easter Sunday Masses the rite of the renewal of baptismal promises may be repeated after the homily. Turn to pages 366-367.

The Creed is not said.

Prayer over the Gifts

Lord,
with Easter joy we offer you the sacrifice
by which your Church is reborn and nourished
through Christ our Lord.

Preface of Easter I, page 369.

Communion Antiphon

Christ has become our paschal sacrifice; let us feast with the unleavened bread of sincerity and truth, alleluia.

1 Corinthians 5:7-8

Prayer after Communion

Father of love,
watch over your Church
and bring us to the glory of the resurrection
promised by this Easter sacrament.

Solemn Blessing

The priest may give this blessing.

Bow your heads and pray for God's blessing.
May almighty God bless you on this solemn feast of Easter,
and may he protect you against all sin.
℟ **Amen.**

Through the resurrection of his Son
God has granted us healing.
May he fulfil his promises,
and bless you with eternal life.
℟ **Amen.**

You have mourned for Christ's sufferings;
now you celebrate the joy of his resurrection.
May you come with joy to the feast which lasts for ever.
℟ **Amen.**

May almighty God bless you,
the Father, and the Son, ✠ and the Holy Spirit.
℟ **Amen.**

SECOND SUNDAY OF EASTER/A

We do not see yet we believe!
God has created a new human family through his
raising of Jesus Christ from the dead. It is our belief
in the resurrection of Jesus Christ which becomes
the source of Christ's life within us. We do not
see yet we believe. Our faith overcomes our
doubts and we acknowledge the power of
the risen Christ.

Entrance Antiphon   Like newborn children you should thirst for milk, on which your spirit can grow to strength, alleluia. 1 Peter 2:2.

or

Rejoice to the full in the glory that is yours, and give thanks to God who called you to his kingdom, alleluia.

4 Ezra 2:36-37

Opening Prayer

Let us pray
 [for a deeper awareness of our Christian baptism]

God of mercy,
 you wash away our sins in water,
 you give us new birth in the Spirit,
 and redeem us in the blood of Christ.
As we celebrate Christ's resurrection
increase our awareness of these blessings,
and renew your gift of life within us.

or

Let us pray
 [as Christians thirsting for the risen life]

SECOND SUNDAY OF EASTER/A

Heavenly Father and God of mercy,
we no longer look for Jesus among the dead,
for he is alive and has become the Lord of life.
From the waters of death you raise us with him
and renew your gift of life within us.

Increase in our minds and hearts
the risen life we share with Christ
and help us to grow as your people
towards the fullness of eternal life with you.

First Reading   Acts 2:42-47

The faithful all lived together and owned everything in common.

The whole community remained faithful to the teaching of the apostles, to the brotherhood, to the breaking of bread and to the prayers.

The many miracles and signs worked through the apostles made a deep impression on everyone.

The faithful all lived together, and owned everything in common; they sold their goods and possessions and shared out the proceeds among themselves according to what each one needed.

They went as a body to the Temple every day but met in their houses for the breaking of bread; they shared their food gladly and generously; they praised God and were looked up to by everyone. Day by day the Lord added to their community those destined to be saved.

Responsorial Psalm   Psalm 117

R/ **Give thanks to the Lord for he is good,
for his love has no end.**

1. Let the sons of Israel say:
   "His love has no end."
   Let the sons of Aaron say:
   "His love has no end."
   Let those who fear the Lord say:
   "His love has no end."   R/

2. I was thrust, thrust down and falling
   but the Lord was my helper.

SECOND SUNDAY OF EASTER/A

The Lord is my strength and my song;
he was my saviour.
There are shouts of joy and victory
in the tents of the just. ℟

3. The stone which the builders rejected
has become the corner stone.
This is the work of the Lord,
a marvel in our eyes.
This day was made by the Lord;
we rejoice and are glad. ℟

Second Reading   1 Peter 1:3-9

In his great mercy he has given us a new birth as his sons by raising Jesus from the dead.

Blessed be God the Father of our Lord Jesus Christ, who in his great mercy has given us a new birth as his sons, by raising Jesus Christ from the dead, so that we have a sure hope and the promise of an inheritance that can never be spoilt or soiled and never fade away, because it is being kept for you in the heavens. Through your faith God's power will guard you until the salvation which has been prepared is revealed at the end of time. This is a cause of great joy for you, even though you may for a short time have to bear being plagued by all sorts of trials; so that, when Jesus Christ is revealed, your faith will have been tested and proved like gold — only it is more precious than gold, which is corruptible even though it bears testing by fire — and then you will have praise and glory and honour. You did not see him, yet you loved him; and still without seeing him, you are already filled with a joy so glorious, that it cannot be described, because you believe; and you are sure of the end to which your faith looks forward, that is, the salvation of your souls.

Alleluia

Alleluia, alleluia! Jesus said: "You believe because you can see me. Happy are those who have not seen and yet believe." Alleluia! John 20:29

Gospel   John 20:19-31

Eight days later, Jesus came.

In the evening of that same day, the first day of the week, the doors were closed in the room where the disciples were, for fear of the Jews. Jesus came and stood among them. He said to them,

SECOND SUNDAY OF EASTER/A

"Peace be with you," and showed them his hands and his side. The disciples were filled with joy when they saw the Lord, and he said to them again, "Peace be with you.
"As the Father sent me,
so am I sending you."
After saying this he breathed on them and said:
"Receive the Holy Spirit.
For those whose sins you forgive,
they are forgiven;
for those whose sins you retain,
they are retained."

Thomas, called the Twin, who was one of the Twelve, was not with them when Jesus came. When the disciples said, "We have seen the Lord," he answered, "Unless I see the holes that the nails made in his hands and can put my finger into the holes they made, and unless I can put my hand into his side, I refuse to believe." Eight days later the disciples were in the house again and Thomas was with them. The doors were closed, but Jesus came in and stood among them. "Peace be with you," he said. Then he spoke to Thomas, "Put your finger here; look, here are my hands. Give me your hand; put it into my side. Doubt no longer but believe." Thomas replied, "My Lord and my God!" Jesus said to him:
"You believe because you can see me.
Happy are those who have not seen and yet believe."

There were many other signs that Jesus worked and the disciples saw, but they are not recorded in this book. These are recorded so that you may believe that Jesus is the Christ, the Son of God, and that believing this you may have life through his name.

Prayer over the Gifts
Lord,
through faith and baptism
we have become a new creation.
Accept the offerings of your people
(and of those born again in baptism)
and bring us to eternal happiness.

Preface of Easter I, page 369.

SECOND SUNDAY OF EASTER/A

Communion Antiphon   Jesus spoke to Thomas: Put your hand here, and see the place of the nails. Doubt no longer, but believe, alleluia! cf. John 20:27

Prayer after Communion

Almighty God,
may the Easter sacraments we have received
live for ever in our minds and hearts.

The priest may give the Solemn Blessing for Easter on page 375, or another form on page 599.

THIRD SUNDAY OF EASTER/A

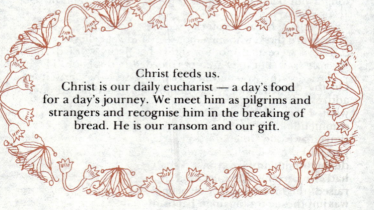

Christ feeds us.
Christ is our daily eucharist — a day's food for a day's journey. We meet him as pilgrims and strangers and recognise him in the breaking of bread. He is our ransom and our gift.

Entrance Antiphon   Let all the earth cry out to God with joy; praise the glory of his name; proclaim his glorious praise, alleluia. Psalm 65:1-2

THIRD SUNDAY OF EASTER/A

Opening Prayer

Let us pray
   [that Christ will give us
   a share in the glory of his unending life]

God our Father,
may we look forward with hope to our resurrection,
for you have made us your sons and daughters,
and restored the joy of our youth.

or

Let us pray
   [in confident peace and Easter hope]

Father in heaven, author of all truth,
a people once in darkness has listened to your Word
and followed your Son as he rose from the tomb.

Hear the prayer of this newborn people
and strengthen your Church to answer your call.
May we rise and come forth into the light of day
to stand in your presence until eternity dawns.

First Reading   Acts 2:14. 22-28.

It was impossible for him to be held in the power of Hades.

On the day of Pentecost Peter stood up with the Eleven and addressed the crowd in a loud voice: "Men of Israel, listen to what I am going to say: Jesus the Nazarene was a man commended to you by God by the miracles and portents and signs that God worked through him when he was among you, as you all know. This man, who was put into your power by the deliberate intention and foreknowledge of God, you took and had crucified by men outside the Law. You killed him, but God raised him to life, freeing him from the pangs of Hades; for it was impossible for him to be held in its power since, as David says of him:
I saw the Lord before me always,
for with him at my right hand nothing can shake me.

THIRD SUNDAY OF EASTER/A

So my heart was glad
and my tongue cried out with joy;
my body, too, will rest in the hope
that you will not abandon my soul to Hades
nor allow your holy one to experience corruption.
You have made known the way of life to me,
you will fill me with gladness through your presence."

"Brothers, no one can deny that the patriarch David himself is dead and buried: his tomb is still with us. But since he was a prophet, and knew that God had sworn him an oath to make one of his descendants succeed him on the throne, what he foresaw and spoke about was the resurrection of the Christ: he is the one who was not abandoned to Hades, and whose body did not experience corruption. God raised this man Jesus to life, and all of us are witnesses to that. Now raised to the heights by God's right hand, he has received from the Father the Holy Spirit, who was promised, and what you see and hear is the outpouring of that Spirit."

Responsorial Psalm   Psalm 15

R/ **Show us, Lord the path of life.**

or

Alleluia!

1. Preserve me, God, I take refuge in you.
   I say to the Lord: "You are my God.
   O Lord, it is you who are my portion and cup;
   it is you yourself who are my prize." R/

2. I will bless the Lord who gives me counsel,
   who even at night directs my heart.
   I keep the Lord ever in my sight:
   since he is at my right hand, I shall stand firm. R/

3. And so my heart rejoices, my soul is glad;
   even my body shall rest in safety.
   For you will not leave my soul among the dead,
   nor let your beloved know decay. R/

4. You will show me the path of life,
   the fullness of joy in your presence,
   at your right hand happiness for ever. R/

THIRD SUNDAY OF EASTER/A

Second Reading   1 Peter 1:17-21.

Your ransom was paid in the precious blood of a lamb without spot or stain, namely, Christ.

If you are acknowledging as your Father one who has no favourites and judges every one according to what he has done, you must be scrupulously careful as long as you are living away from your home. Remember, the ransom that was paid to free you from the useless way of life your ancestors handed down was not paid in anything corruptible, neither in silver nor gold, but in the precious blood of a lamb without spot or stain, namely Christ; who, though known since before the world was made, has been revealed only in our time, the end of the ages, for your sake. Through him you now have faith in God, who raised him from the dead and gave him glory for that very reason — so that you would have faith and hope in God.

Alleluia   Alleluia, alleluia! Lord Jesus, explain the scriptures to us. Make our hearts burn within us as you talk to us. Alleluia! cf. Luke 24:32.

Gospel   Luke 24:13-35.

They recognised him at the breaking of bread.

Two of the disciples of Jesus were on their way to a village called Emmaus, seven miles from Jerusalem, and they were talking together about all that had happened. Now as they talked this over, Jesus himself came up and walked by their side; but something prevented them from recognising him. He said to them, "What matters are you discussing as you walk along?" They stopped short, their faces downcast.

Then one of them called Cleopas, answered him, "You must be the only person staying in Jerusalem who does not know the things that have been happening there these last few days." "What things?" he asked. "All about Jesus of Nazareth," they answered, "who proved he was a great prophet by the things he said and did in the sight of God and of the whole people; and how our chief priests and our leaders handed him over to be sentenced to death, and had him crucified. Our own hope had been that he would be the one to set Israel free. And this is not

THIRD SUNDAY OF EASTER/A

all: two whole days have gone by since it all happened; and some women from our group have astounded us: they went to the tomb in the early morning, and when they did not find the body, they came back to tell us they had seen a vision of angels who declared he was alive. Some of our friends went to the tomb and found everything exactly as the women had reported, but of him they saw nothing."

Then he said to them, "You foolish men! So slow to believe the full message of the prophets! Was it not ordained that the Christ should suffer and so enter into his glory?" Then, starting with Moses and going through all the prophets, he explained to them the passages throughout the scriptures that were about himself.

When they drew near to the village to which they were going, he made as if to go on; but they pressed him to stay with them. "It is nearly evening," they said, "and the day is almost over." So he went in to stay with them. Now while he was with them at table, he took the bread and said the blessing; then he broke it and handed it to them. And their eyes were opened and they recognised him; but he had vanished from their sight. Then they said to each other, "Did not our hearts burn within us as he talked to us on the road and explained the scriptures to us?"

They set out that instant and returned to Jerusalem. There they found the Eleven assembled together with their companions, who said to them, "Yes, it is true. The Lord has risen and has appeared to Simon." Then they told their story of what had happened on the road and how they had recognised him at the breaking of bread.

Prayer over the Gifts
Lord,
receive these gifts from your Church.
May the great joy you give us
come to perfection in heaven.

Preface of Easter II-V, pages 561-562.

Communion Antiphon
The disciples recognised the Lord Jesus in the breaking of bread, alleluia. Luke 24:35.

THIRD SUNDAY OF EASTER/A

Prayer after Communion

Lord,
look on your people with kindness
and by these Easter mysteries
bring us to the glory of the resurrection.

The priest may give the Solemn Blessing for Easter on page 375, or another form on page 599.

FOURTH SUNDAY OF EASTER/A

Christ the Shepherd brings us life.
God has appointed Christ as the Shepherd of
the whole human race. He has become our
gateway to eternal life because he lays down
his life for us. Even though we have gone astray
through sin, nevertheless by his wounds we are
healed and given a new direction in our lives.

Entrance Antiphon The earth is full of the goodness of the Lord; by the word of the Lord the heavens were made, alleluia. Psalm 32:5-6

Opening Prayer

Let us pray
 [that Christ our shepherd
 will lead us through the difficulties of this life]

Almighty and ever-living God,
give us new strength
from the courage of Christ our shepherd,
and lead us to join the saints in heaven,
where he lives and reigns with you and the Holy Spirit,
one God, for ever and ever.

or

Let us pray
 [to God our helper in time of distress]

God and Father of our Lord Jesus Christ,
though your people walk in the valley of darkness,
no evil should they fear;
for they follow in faith the call of the shepherd
whom you have sent for their hope and strength.
Attune our minds to the sound of his voice,

FOURTH SUNDAY OF EASTER/A

lead our steps in the path he has shown,
that we may know the strength of his outstretched arm
and enjoy the light of your presence for ever.

First Reading   Acts 2:14. 36-41.
God has made him both Lord and Christ.

On the day of Pentecost Peter stood up with the Eleven and addressed the crowd with a loud voice: "The whole House of Israel can be certain that God has made this Jesus whom you crucified both Lord and Christ."

Hearing this, they were cut to the heart and said to Peter and the apostles, "What must we do, brothers?" "You must repent," Peter answered, "and every one of you must be baptised in the name of Jesus Christ for the forgiveness of your sins, and you will receive the gift of the Holy Spirit. The promise that was made is for you and your children, and for all those who are far away, for all those whom the Lord our God will call to himself." He spoke to them for a long time using many arguments, and he urged them, "Save yourselves from this perverse generation." They were convinced by his arguments, and they accepted what he said and were baptised. That very day about three thousand were added to their number.

Responsorial Psalm   Psalm 22

℟ **The Lord is my Shepherd;
there is nothing I shall want.**

or

   Alleluia!

1. The Lord is my shepherd;
   there is nothing I shall want.
   Fresh and green are the pastures
   where he gives me repose.
   Near restful waters he leads me,
   to revive my drooping spirit. ℟

2. He guides me along the right path;
   he is true to his name.
   If I should walk in the valley of darkness
   no evil would I fear.
   You are there with your crook and your staff;
   with these you give me comfort. ℟

FOURTH SUNDAY OF EASTER/A

3 You have prepared a banquet for me
in the sight of my foes.
My head you have anointed with oil;
my cup is overflowing ℟

4 Surely goodness and kindness shall follow me
all the days of my life.
In the Lord's own house shall I dwell
for ever and ever. ℟

Second Reading   1 Peter 2:20-25.
You have come back to the shepherd of your souls.

The merit, in the sight of God, is in bearing punishment patiently when you are punished after doing your duty.

This, in fact, is what you were called to do, because Christ suffered for you and left an example for you to follow the way he took. He had not done anything wrong, and there had been no perjury in his mouth. He was insulted and did not retaliate with insults; when he was tortured he made no threats but he put his trust in the righteous judge. He was bearing our faults in his own body on the cross, so that we might die to our faults and live for holiness; through his wounds you have been healed. You had gone astray like sheep but now you have come back to the shepherd and guardian of your souls.

Alleluia   Alleluia, alleluia! I am the good shepherd, says the Lord; I know my own sheep and my own know me. Alleluia! John 10:14.

Gospel   John 10:1-10
I am the gate of the sheepfold.

Jesus said: "I tell you most solemnly, anyone who does not enter the sheepfold through the gate, but gets in some other way is a thief and a brigand. The one who enters through the gate is the shepherd of the flock; the gate-keeper lets him in, the sheep hear his voice, one by one he calls his own sheep and leads them out. When he has brought out his flock, he goes ahead of them, and the sheep follow because they know his voice. They never follow a stranger but run away from him: they do not recognise the voice of strangers."

FOURTH SUNDAY OF EASTER/A

Jesus told them this parable but they failed to understand what he meant by telling it to them.
So Jesus spoke to them again:
"I tell you most solemnly,
I am the gate of the sheepfold.
All others who have come
are thieves and brigands;
but the sheep took no notice of them.
I am the gate.
Anyone who enters through me will be safe:
he will go freely in and out
and be sure of finding pasture.
The thief comes
only to steal and kill and destroy.
I have come
so that they may have life
and have it to the full."

Prayer over the Gifts

Lord,
restore us by these Easter mysteries.
May the continuing work of our Redeemer
bring us eternal joy.

Preface of Easter II-V, pages 561-562.

Communion Antiphon

The Good Shepherd is risen! He who laid down his life for his sheep, who died for his flock, he is risen, alleluia.

Prayer after Communion

Father, eternal shepherd,
watch over the flock redeemed by the blood of Christ
and lead us to the promised land.

The priest may give the Solemn Blessing for Easter on page 375, or another form on page 599.

FIFTH SUNDAY OF EASTER/A

Christ is our Way, Truth and Life.
We are a chosen race, a royal priesthood, a
consecrated nation, a people set apart to sing
the praises of God. God has poured out all these
gifts on us through the Holy Spirit. We are to
devote ourselves to proclaiming God's Word
revealed in Christ, and to trust that Christ
always has a special love and care for us.

Entrance Antiphon   Sing to the Lord a new song, for he has done marvellous deeds; he has revealed to the nations his saving power, alleluia.
Psalm 97:1-2

Opening Prayer

Let us pray
  [that we may enjoy true freedom]

God our Father,
look upon us with love.
You redeem us and make us your children in Christ.
Give us true freedom
and bring us to the inheritance you promised.

or

Let us pray
  [in the freedom of the sons of God]

Father of our Lord Jesus Christ,
you have revealed to the nations your saving power
and filled all ages with the words of a new song.
Hear the echo of this hymn.
Give us voice to sing your praise
throughout this season of joy.

FIFTH SUNDAY OF EASTER/A

First Reading   Acts 6:1-7
They elected seven men full of the Holy Spirit.

About this time, when the number of disciples was increasing, the Hellenists made a complaint against the Hebrews: in the daily distribution their own widows were being overlooked. So the Twelve called a full meeting of the disciples and addressed them, "It would not be right for us to neglect the word of God so as to give out food; you, brothers, must select from among yourselves seven men of good reputation, filled with the Spirit and with wisdom; we will hand over this duty to them, and continue to devote ourselves to prayer and to the service of the word." The whole assembly approved of this proposal and elected Stephen, a man full of faith and of the Holy Spirit, together with Philip, Prochorus, Nicanor, Timon, Parmenas, and Nicolaus of Antioch, a convert to Judaism. They presented these to the apostles, who prayed and laid their hands on them.

The word of the Lord continued to spread: the number of disciples in Jerusalem was greatly increased, and a large group of priests made their submission to the faith.

Responsorial Psalm   Psalm 32

℟ **May your love be upon us, O Lord,
  as we place all our hope in you.**

or

  Alleluia!

1. Ring out your joy to the Lord, O you just;
   for praise is fitting for loyal hearts.
   Give thanks to the Lord upon the harp,
   with a ten-stringed lute sing him songs. ℟

2. For the word of the Lord is faithful
   and all his works to be trusted.
   The Lord loves justice and right
   and fills the earth with his love. ℟

3. The Lord looks on those who revere him,
   on those who hope in his love,
   to rescue their souls from death,
   to keep them alive in famine. ℟

Second Reading   1 Peter 2:4-9
But you are a chosen race, a royal priesthood.

FIFTH SUNDAY OF EASTER/A

The Lord is the living stone, rejected by men but chosen by God and precious to him; set yourselves close to him so that you too, the holy priesthood that offers the spiritual sacrifices which Jesus Christ has made acceptable to God, may be living stones making a spiritual house. As scripture says: See how I lay in Zion a precious cornerstone that I have chosen and the man who rests his trust on it will not be disappointed. That means that for you who are believers, it is precious; but for unbelievers, the stone rejected by the builders has proved to be the keystone, a stone to stumble over, a rock to bring men down. They stumble over it because they do not believe in the word; it was the fate in store for them.

But you are a chosen race, a royal priesthood, a consecrated nation, a people set apart to sing the praises of God who called you out of the darkness into his wonderful light.

Alleluia   Alleluia, alleluia! Jesus said: "I am the Way, the Truth and the Life. No one can come to the Father except through me." Alleluia! John 14:6.

Gospel   John 14:1-12
I am the Way, the Truth and the Life.

Jesus said to his disciples:
"Do not let your hearts be troubled.
Trust in God still, and trust in me.
There are many rooms in my Father's house;
if there were not, I should have told you.
I am now going to prepare a place for you,
and after I have gone and prepared you a place,
I shall return to take you with me;
so that where I am
you may be too.
You know the way to the place where I am going."
    Thomas said, "Lord, we do not know where you are going, so how can we know the way?" Jesus said:
"I am the Way, the Truth and the Life.
No one can come to the Father except through me.
If you know me, you know my Father too.
From this moment you know him and have seen him."

FIFTH SUNDAY OF EASTER/A

Philip said, "Lord, let us see the Father and then we shall be satisfied." "Have I been with you all this time, Philip," said Jesus to him "and you still do not know me?
"To have seen me is to have seen the Father,
so how can you say, 'Let us see the Father'?
Do you not believe
that I am in the Father and the Father is in me?
The words I say to you I do not speak as from myself:
It is the Father, living in me, who is doing this work.
You must believe me when I say
that I am in the Father and the Father is in me;
believe it on the evidence of this work, if for no other reason.
I tell you most solemnly,
whoever believes in me
will perform the same works as I do myself,
he will perform even greater works,
because I am going to the Father."

Prayer over the Gifts

Lord God,
by this holy exchange of gifts
you share with us your divine life.
Grant that everything we do
may be directed by the knowledge of your truth.

Preface of Easter II-V, pages 561-562.

Communion Antiphon

I am the vine and you are the branches, says the Lord; he who lives in me, and I in him, will bear much fruit, alleluia. John 15:5.

Prayer after Communion

Merciful Father,
may these mysteries give us new purpose
and bring us to a new life in you.

The priest may give the Solemn Blessing for Easter on page 375, or another form on page 599.

SIXTH SUNDAY OF EASTER/A

The Holy Spirit restores us to life.
After his resurrection Christ promised that he
would send the Holy Spirit on his Church.
It is the Spirit of Christ which is the source of
our joy and helps us to do great things in
the Lord's Name. We are healed by
the Spirit and are called to take
part in the healing mission of
the Church.

Entrance Antiphon   Speak out with a voice of joy; let it be heard to the ends of the earth: The Lord has set his people free, alleluia.

cf. Isaiah 48:20.

Opening Prayer

Let us pray
   [that we may practise in our lives
   the faith we profess]

Ever-living God,
help us to celebrate our joy
in the resurrection of the Lord
and to express in our lives
the love we celebrate.

or
Let us pray
   [in silence, reflecting on the joy of Easter]

God our Father, maker of all,
the crown of your creation was the Son of Man,
born of a woman, but without beginning;
he suffered for us but lives for ever.
May our mortal lives be crowned with the ultimate joy
of rising with him,
who is Lord for ever and ever.

SIXTH SUNDAY OF EASTER/A

First Reading   Acts 8:5-8.14-17

They laid hands on them, and they received the Holy Spirit.

Philip went to a Samaritan town and proclaimed the Christ to them. The people united in welcoming the message Philip preached, either because they had heard of the miracles he worked or because they saw them for themselves. There were, for example, unclean spirits that came shrieking out of many who were possessed, and several paralytics and cripples were cured. As a result there was great rejoicing in that town.

When the apostles in Jerusalem heard that Samaria had accepted the word of God, they sent Peter and John to them, and they went down there, and prayed for the Samaritans to receive the Holy Spirit, for as yet he had not come down on any of them: they had only been baptised in the name of the Lord Jesus. Then they laid hands on them, and they received the Holy Spirit.

Responsorial Psalm   Psalm 65

℟ **Cry out with joy to God all the earth.**

or

    Alleluia!

1. Cry out with joy to God all the earth,
   O sing to the glory of his name.
   O render him glorious praise.
   Say to God: "How tremendous your deeds!" ℟

2. "Before you all the earth shall bow;
   shall sing to you, sing to your name!"
   Come and see the works of God,
   tremendous his deeds among men. ℟

3. He turned the sea into dry land,
   they passed through the river dry-shod.
   Let our joy then be in him;
   he rules for ever by his might. ℟

4. Come and hear, all who fear God.
   I will tell what he did for my soul:
   Blessed be God who did not reject my prayer
   nor withhold his love from me. ℟

SIXTH SUNDAY OF EASTER/A

Second Reading   1 Peter 3:15-18
In the body he was put to death, in the spirit he was raised to life.

Reverence the Lord Christ in your hearts, and always have your answer ready for people who ask you the reason for the hope that you all have. But give it with courtesy and respect and with a clear conscience, so that those who slander you when you are living a good life in Christ may be proved wrong in the accusations that they bring. And if it is the will of God that you should suffer, it is better to suffer for doing right than for doing wrong.

Why, Christ himself, innocent though he was, had died once for sins, died for the guilty, to lead us to God. In the body he was put to death, in the spirit he was raised to life.

Alleluia
Alleluia, alleluia! Jesus said: "If anyone loves me he will keep my word, and my Father will love him, and we shall come to him." Alleluia! John 14:23

Gospel   John 14:15-21
I shall ask the Father, and he will give you another Advocate.

Jesus said to his disciples:
"If you love me you will keep my commandments.
I shall ask the Father,
and he will give you another Advocate
to be with you for ever,
that Spirit of truth
whom the world can never receive
since it neither sees nor knows him;
but you know him,
because he is with you, he is in you.
I will not leave you orphans;
I will come back to you.
In a short time the world will no longer see me;
but you will see me,
because I live and you will live.
On that day
you will understand that I am in my Father

SIXTH SUNDAY OF EASTER/A

and you in me and I in you.
Anybody who receives my commandments and keeps them
will be one who loves me;
and anybody who loves me will be loved by my Father,
and I shall love him and show myself to him."

Prayer over the Gifts

Lord,
accept our prayers and offerings.
Make us worthy of your sacraments of love
by granting us your forgiveness.

Preface of Easter II-V, pages 561-562.

Communion Antiphon

If you love me, keep my commandments says the Lord. The Father will send you the Holy Spirit, to be with you for ever, alleluia. John 14:15-16.

Prayer after Communion

Almighty and ever-living Lord,
you restored us to life
by raising Christ from death.
Strengthen us by this Easter sacrament; may we feel its saving power in our daily life.

The priest may give the Solemn Blessing for Easter on page 375, or another form on page 599.

THURSDAY OF THE SIXTH WEEK OF EASTER
THE ASCENSION OF THE LORD

Christ ascends to his Father!
Christ's Ascension is our guarantee
that one day we will be with him in heaven
to praise the glory of God our Father.
The Ascension is our hope of the great
inheritance which awaits those of us who
believe in the power of the risen Christ.

Entrance Antiphon Men of Galilee, why do you stand looking in the sky? The Lord will return, just as you have seen him ascend, alleluia.
Acts 1:11

Let us pray
 [that the risen Christ
 will lead us to eternal life]

God our Father,
make us joyful in the ascension of your Son Jesus Christ.
May we follow him into the new creation,
for his ascension is our glory and our hope.

or

Let us pray
 [on this day of Ascension
 as we watch and wait for Jesus' return]

Father in heaven,
our minds were prepared for the coming of your kingdom
when you took Christ beyond our sight
so that we might seek him in his glory.

May we follow where he has led
and find our hope in his glory,
for he is Lord for ever.

THE ASCENSION OF THE LORD/A

First Reading   Acts 1:1-11
He was lifted up while they looked on.

In my earlier work, Theophilus, I dealt with everything Jesus had done and taught from the beginning until the day he gave his instructions to the apostles he had chosen through the Holy Spirit, and was taken up to heaven. He had shown himself alive to them after his Passion by many demonstrations: for forty days he had continued to appear to them and tell them about the kingdom of God. When he had been at table with them, he had told them not to leave Jerusalem, but to wait there for what the Father had promised. "It is," he had said, "what you have heard me speak about: John baptised with water but you, not many days from now, will be baptised with the Holy Spirit."

Now having met together, they asked him, "Lord, has the time come? Are you going to restore the kingdom to Israel?" He replied, "It is not for you to know times or dates that the Father has decided by his own authority, but you will receive power when the Holy Spirit comes on you, and then you will be my witnesses not only in Jerusalem but throughout Judaea and Samaria, and indeed to the ends of the earth."

As he said this he was lifted up while they looked on, and a cloud took him from their sight. They were still staring into the sky when suddenly two men in white were standing near them and they said, "Why are you men from Galilee standing here looking into the sky? Jesus who has been taken up from you into heaven, this same Jesus will come back in the same way as you have seen him go there."

Responsorial Psalm   Psalm 46

℟ **God goes up with shouts of joy;**
   the Lord goes up with trumpet blast.

or

   Alleluia!

1. All peoples, clap your hands,
   cry to God with shouts of joy!
   For the Lord, the Most High, we must fear,
   great king over all the earth. ℟

THE ASCENSION OF THE LORD/A

2. God goes up with shouts of joy;
   the Lord goes up with trumpet blast.
   Sing praise for God, sing praise,
   sing praise to our king, sing praise. ℟

3. God is king of all the earth.
   Sing praise with all your skill.
   God is king over the nations;
   God reigns on his holy throne. ℟

Second Reading   Ephesians 1:17-23

He made him sit at his right hand in heaven.

May the God of our Lord Jesus Christ, the Father of glory, give you a spirit of wisdom and perception of what is revealed, to bring you to full knowledge of him. May he enlighten the eyes of your mind so that you can see what hope his call holds for you, what rich glories he has promised the saints will inherit and how infinitely great is the power that he has exercised for us believers. This you can tell from the strength of his power at work in Christ, when he used it to raise him from the dead and to make him sit at his right hand in heaven, far above every Sovereignty, Authority, Power, or Domination, or any other name that can be named, not only in this age, but also in the age to come. He has put all things under his feet, and made him, as the ruler of everything, the head of the Church; which is his body, the fullness of him who fills the whole creation.

Alleluia   Alleluia, alleluia! Go, make disciples of all the nations; I am with you always; yes, to the end of time. Alleluia! Matthew 28:19-20.

Gospel   Matthew 28:16-20

All authority in heaven and on earth has been given to me.

The eleven disciples set out for Galilee, to the mountain where Jesus had arranged to meet them. When they saw him they fell down before him, though some hesitated. Jesus came up and spoke to them. He said, "All authority in heaven and on earth has been given to me. Go, therefore, make disciples of all the nations; baptise them in the name of the Father and of the Son and of the Holy Spirit, and teach them to observe all the

THE ASCENSION OF THE LORD/A

commands I gave you. And know that I am with you always; yes, to the end of time."

Prayer over the Gifts

Lord,
receive our offering
as we celebrate the ascension of Christ your Son.
May his gifts help us rise with him
to the joys of heaven,
where he lives and reigns for ever and ever.

Preface

I

Father, all-powerful and ever-living God,
we do well always and everywhere to give you thanks.

[Today] the Lord Jesus, the king of glory,
the conqueror of sin and death,
ascended to heaven while the angels sang his praises.

Christ, the mediator between God and man,
judge of the world and Lord of all,
has passed beyond our sight,
not to abandon us but to be our hope.
Christ is the beginning, the head of the Church;
where he has gone, we hope to follow.

The joy of the resurrection and ascension renews the whole world, while the choirs of heaven sing for ever to your glory:
Holy, holy, holy ...

or

II

Father, all-powerful and ever-living God,
we do well always and everywhere to give you thanks
through Jesus Christ our Lord.

In his risen body he plainly showed himself to his disciples
and was taken up to heaven in their sight
to claim for us a share in his divine life.

And so, with all the choirs of angels in heaven
we proclaim your glory
and join in their unending hymn of praise:

Holy, holy, holy ...

THE ASCENSION OF THE LORD/A

Communion Antiphon I, the Lord, am with you always, until the end of the world, alleluia.

Matthew 28:20.

Prayer after communion
Father,
in this eucharist
we touch the divine life you give to the world.
Help us to follow Christ with love
to eternal life where he is Lord for ever and ever.

Solemn Blessing
Bow your heads and pray for God's blessing.

May almighty God bless you on this day
when his only Son ascended into heaven
to prepare a place for you.

℟ **Amen.**

After his resurrection, Christ was seen by his disciples.
When he appears as judge
may you be pleasing for ever in his sight.

℟ **Amen.**

You believe that Jesus has taken his seat in majesty
at the right hand of the Father.
May you have the joy of experiencing
that he is also with you to the end of time,
according to his promise.

℟ **Amen.**

May almighty God bless you,
the Father, and the Son, ✠ and the Holy Spirit.

℟ **Amen.**

SEVENTH SUNDAY OF EASTER/A

Christ our model of prayer and suffering. Prayer is the birthright of every christian. It is natural to us as the air we breathe. The early christians were people of deep prayer and suffered for their faith. Prayer and suffering are two sides of the same coin by which Christ gives glory to God in me.

Entrance Antiphon Lord, hear my voice when I call to you. My heart has prompted me to seek your face; I seek it, Lord; do not hide from me, alleluia. Psalm 26:7-9

Opening Prayer

Let us pray
  [that we may recognise
  the presence of Christ in our midst]

Father,
help us keep in mind that Christ our Saviour
lives with you in glory
and promised to remain with us until the end of time.

or

Let us pray
  [to our Father
  who has raised us to life in Christ]

Eternal Father,
reaching from end to end of the universe,
and ordering all things with your mighty arm:
for you, time is the unfolding of truth that already is,
the unveiling of beauty that is yet to be.

Your Son has saved us in history

SEVENTH SUNDAY OF EASTER/A

by rising from the dead,
so that transcending time he might free us from death.
May his presence among us
lead to the vision of unlimited truth
and unfold the beauty of your love.

First Reading   Acts 1:12-14
All joined in continuous prayer.

After Jesus was taken up into heaven, the apostles went back from the Mount of Olives, as it is called to Jerusalem, a short distance away, no more than a sabbath walk; and when they reached the city they went to the upper room where they were staying; there were Peter and John, James and Andrew, Philip and Thomas, Bartholomew and Matthew, James son of Alphaeus and Simon the Zealot, and Jude son of James. All these joined in continuous prayer, together with several women, including Mary the mother of Jesus, and with his brothers.

Responsorial Psalm   Psalm 26

℟ **I am sure I shall see the Lord's goodness
in the land of the living.**

or

Alleluia!

1. The Lord is my light and my help;
   whom shall I fear?
   The Lord is the stronghold of my life;
   before whom shall I shrink? ℟

2. There is one thing I ask of the Lord,
   for this I long,
   to live in the house of the Lord,
   all the days of my life,
   to savour the sweetness of the Lord,
   to behold his temple. ℟

3. O Lord, hear my voice when I call;
   have mercy and answer.
   Of you my heart has spoken:
   "Seek his face." ℟

SEVENTH SUNDAY OF EASTER/A

Second Reading 1 Peter 4:13-16

It is a blessing for you when they insult you for bearing the name of Christ.

If you can have some share in the sufferings of Christ, be glad, because you will enjoy a much greater gladness when his glory is revealed. It is a blessing for you when they insult you for bearing the name of Christ, because it means that you have the Spirit of glory, the Spirit of God resting on you. None of you should ever deserve to suffer for being a murderer, a thief, a criminal or an informer; but if anyone of you should suffer for being a Christian, then he is not to be ashamed of it; he should thank God that he has been called one.

Alleluia Alleluia, alleluia! I will not leave you orphans, says the Lord; I will come back to you, and your hearts will be full of joy. Alleluia! John 14:18

Gospel John 17:1-11

Father, glorify your Son.

Jesus raised his eyes to heaven and said:
"Father, the hour has come:
glorify your Son
so that your Son may glorify you;
and, through the power over all mankind that you have given him,
let him give eternal life to all those you have entrusted to him.
And eternal life is this:
to know you,
the only true God,
and Jesus Christ whom you have sent.
I have glorified you on earth
and finished the work
that you gave me to do.
Now, Father, it is time for you to glorify me
with that glory I had with you
before ever the world was.
I have made your name known
to the men you took from the world to give me.
They were yours and you gave them to me,

SEVENTH SUNDAY OF EASTER/A

and they have kept your word.
Now at last they know
that all you have given me comes indeed from you;
for I have given them
the teaching you gave to me,
and they have truly accepted this, that I came from you,
and have believed that it was you who sent me.
I pray for them;
I am not praying for the world
but for those you have given me,
because they belong to you:
all I have is yours
and all you have is mine,
and in them I am glorified.
I am not in the world any longer,
but they are in the world,
and I am coming to you."

Prayer over the Gifts

Lord,
accept the prayers and gifts
we offer in faith and love.
May this eucharist
bring us to your glory.

Preface of Ascension I or II, page 401.

Communion Antiphon

This is the prayer of Jesus: that his believers may become one as he is one with the Father, alleluia. John 17:22.

Prayer after Communion

God our Saviour,
hear us,
and through this holy mystery give us hope
that the glory you have given Christ
will be given to the Church, his body,
for he is Lord for ever and ever.

The priest may give the Solemn Blessing of Easter on page 375, or another form on page 599.

The Mass for Pentecost Sunday will be found on page 469.

SECOND SUNDAY OF EASTER/B

Our faith is the victory over the world.
We believe that Jesus Christ rose from
the dead. It is this faith that Jesus is
the Son of God which helps us
to overcome the world with its
temptations and doubts. We have
not seen yet we believe.
We acknowledge that Christ is our Lord
and our God.

Entrance Antiphon Like newborn children you should thirst for milk, on which your spirit can grow to strength, alleluia. 1 Peter 2:2.

or

Rejoice to the full in the glory that is yours, and give thanks to God who called you to his kingdom, alleluia.
4 Ezra 2:36-37

Opening Prayer
Let us pray
  [for a deeper awareness of our Christian baptism]

God of mercy,
you wash away our sins in water,
you give us new birth in the Spirit,
and redeem us in the blood of Christ.
As we celebrate Christ's resurrection
increase our awareness of these blessings,
and renew your gift of life within us.

or

SECOND SUNDAY OF EASTER/B

Let us pray
   [as Christians thirsting for the risen life]
Heavenly Father and God of mercy,
we no longer look for Jesus among the dead,
for he is alive and has become the Lord of life.
From the waters of death you raise us with him
and renew your gift of life within us.

Increase in our minds and hearts
the risen life we share with Christ
and help us to grow as your people
towards the fullness of eternal life with you.

First Reading   Acts 4:32-35.
United, heart and soul.

The whole group of believers was united, heart and soul; no one claimed for his own use anything that he had, as everything they owned was held in common.

The apostles continued to testify to the resurrection of the Lord Jesus with great power, and they were all given great respect.

None of their members was ever in want, as all those who owned land or houses would sell them, and bring the money from them, to present it to the apostles; it was then distributed to any members who might be in need.

Responsorial Psalm   Psalm 117.

℟ **Give thanks to the Lord for he is good,
for his love has no end.**

or

   Alleluia, alleluia, alleluia!

1. Let the sons of Israel say:
"His love has no end."
Let the sons of Aaron say:
"His love has no end."
Let those who fear the Lord say:
"His love has no end." ℟

SECOND SUNDAY OF EASTER/B

2. The Lord's right hand has triumphed;
   his right hand raised me up.
   I shall not die, I shall live
   and recount his deeds.
   I was punished, I was punished by the Lord,
   but not doomed to die. R/

3. The stone which the builders rejected
   has become the corner stone.
   This is the work of the Lord,
   a marvel in our eyes.
   This day was made by the Lord;
   we rejoice and are glad. R/

Second Reading   John 5:1-6.

Anyone who has been begotten by God has already overcome the world.

Whoever believes that Jesus is the Christ
has been begotten by God;
and whoever loves the Father that begot him
loves the child whom he begets.
We can be sure that we love God's children
if we love God himself and do what he has commanded us,
this is what loving God is —
keeping his commandments;
and his commandments are not difficult,
because anyone who has been begotten by God
has already overcome the world;
this is the victory over the world —
our faith.
Who can overcome the world?
Only the man who believes that Jesus is the Son of God;
Jesus Christ who came by water and blood,
not with water only,
but with water and blood;
with the Spirit as another witness —
since the Spirit is the truth.

SECOND SUNDAY OF EASTER/B

Alleluia Alleluia, alleluia! Jesus said: "You believe because you can see me. Happy are those who have not seen and yet believe." Alleluia! John 20:29.

Gospel   John 20:19-31.
Eight days later, Jesus came.

In the evening of that same day, the first day of the week, the doors were closed in the room where the disciples were, for fear of the Jews. Jesus came and stood among them. He said to them, "Peace be with you," and showed them his hands and his side. The disciples were filled with joy when they saw the Lord, and he said to them again, "Peace be with you.
"As the Father sent me,
so am I sending you."
After saying this he breathed on them and said:
"Receive the Holy Spirit.
For those whose sins you forgive,
they are forgiven;
for those whose sins you retain,
they are retained."

Thomas, called the Twin, who was one of the Twelve, was not with them when Jesus came. When the disciples said, "We have seen the Lord", he answered, "Unless I see the holes that the nails made in his hands and can put my finger into the holes they made, and unless I can put my hand into his side, I refuse to believe." Eight days later the disciples were in the house again and Thomas was with them. The doors were closed, but Jesus came in and stood among them. "Peace be with you" he said. Then he spoke to Thomas, "Put your finger here: look, here are my hands. Give me your hand; put it into my side. Doubt no longer but believe." Thomas replied, "My Lord and my God!" Jesus said to him:
"You believe because you can see me.
Happy are those who have not seen and yet believe."

There were many other signs that Jesus worked and the disciples saw, but they are not recorded in this book. These are recorded so that you may believe that Jesus is the Christ, the Son of God, and that believing this you may have life through his name.

SECOND SUNDAY OF EASTER/B

Prayer over the Gifts
Lord,
through faith and baptism
we have become a new creation.
Accept the offerings of your people
(and of those born again in baptism)
and bring us to eternal happiness.

Preface of Easter I, as for Easter Vigil, page 369.

Communion Antiphon
Jesus spoke to Thomas: Put your hand here, and see the place of the nails. Doubt no longer, but believe, alleluia. cf. John 20:27.

Prayer after Communion
Almighty God,
may the Easter sacraments we have received
live for ever in our minds and hearts.

The priest may give the Solemn Blessing for Easter on page 375, or another form on page 599.

THIRD SUNDAY OF EASTER/B

Christ is the sacrifice that takes our sins away. Christ died for the sins of the world. God the Father raises him to life and in his resurrection we too find life. In the light of Easter we turn away from sin and discover the peace of Christ. We are witnesses to God's saving power by living out Christ's resurrection in our daily lives.

Entrance Antiphon Let all the earth cry out to God with joy; praise the glory of his name; proclaim his glorious praise, alleluia. Psalm 65:1-2.

Opening Prayer

Let us pray
 [that Christ will give us
 a share in the glory of his unending life]

God our Father,
may we look forward with hope to our resurrection,
for you have made us your sons and daughters,
and restored the joy of our youth.

or

Let us pray
 [in confident peace and Easter hope]

Father in heaven, author of all truth,
a people once in darkness has listened to your Word
and followed your Son as he rose from the tomb.

Hear the prayer of this newborn people
and strengthen your Church to answer your call.
May we rise and come forth into the light of day
to stand in your presence until eternity dawns.

THIRD SUNDAY OF EASTER/B

First Reading   Acts 3:13-15.17-19.

You killed the prince of life. God, however, raised him from the dead.

Peter said to the people: "You are Israelites, and it is the God of Abraham, Isaac and Jacob, the God of our ancestors, who has glorified his servant Jesus, the same Jesus you handed over and then disowned in the presence of Pilate, after Pilate had decided to release him. It was you who accused the Holy One, the Just One, you who demanded the reprieve of a murderer while you killed the prince of life. God, however, raised him from the dead, and to that fact we are the witnesses.

"Now I know, brothers, that neither you nor your leaders had any idea what you were really doing; this was the way God carried out what he had foretold, when he said through all his prophets that his Christ would suffer. Now you must repent and turn to God, so that your sins may be wiped out."

Responsorial Psalm   Psalm 4.

℟ **Lift up the light of your face on us, O Lord.**

or

   Alleluia!

1. When I call, answer me, O God of justice;
   from anguish you released me, have mercy and hear me! ℟

2. It is the Lord who grants favours to those whom he loves;
   the Lord hears me whenever I call him. ℟

3. "What can bring us happiness?" many say.
   Lift up the light of your face on us, O Lord. ℟

4. I will lie down in peace and sleep comes at once
   for you alone, Lord, make me dwell in safety. ℟

Second Reading   1 John 2:1-5.

He is the sacrifice that takes our sins away, and not only ours, but the whole world's.

I am writing this, my children,
to stop you sinning;
but if anyone should sin
we have our advocate with the Father,
Jesus Christ, who is just;

THIRD SUNDAY OF EASTER/B

he is the sacrifice that takes our sins away,
and not only ours,
but the whole world's.
We can be sure that we know God
only by keeping his commandments.
Anyone who says, "I know him",
and does not keep his commandments,
is a liar,
refusing to admit the truth.
But when anyone does obey what he has said,
God's love comes to perfection in him.

Alleluia Alleluia, alleluia! Lord Jesus, explain the scriptures to us. Make our hearts burn within us as you talk to us. Alleluia. cf. Luke 24:32.

Gospel Luke 24:35-48.

So you see how it is written that the Christ would suffer and on the third day rise from the dead.

The disciples told their story of what had happened on the road and how they had recognised Jesus at the breaking of bread.

They were still talking about all this when Jesus himself stood among them and said to them, "Peace be with you!" In a state of alarm and fright, they thought they were seeing a ghost. But he said, "Why are you so agitated, and why are these doubts rising in your hearts? Look at my hands and feet; yes, it is I indeed Touch me and see for yourselves; a ghost has no flesh and bones as you can see I have." And as he said this he showed them his hands and feet. Their joy was so great that they could not believe it, and they stood dumbfounded; so he said to them, "Have you anything here to eat?" And they offered him a piece of grilled fish, which he took and ate before their eyes.

Then he told them, "This is what I meant when I said, while I was still with you, that everything written about me in the Law of Moses, in the Prophets and in the Psalms, has to be fulfilled." He then opened their minds to understand the scriptures, and he said to them, "So you see how it is written that the Christ would suffer and on the third day rise from the dead, and that, in his name, repentance for the forgiveness of sins would be preached to all the nations, beginning from Jerusalem. You are witnesses to this."

THIRD SUNDAY OF EASTER/B

Prayer over the Gifts

Lord,
receive these gifts from your Church.
May the great joy you give us
come to perfection in heaven.

Preface of Easter II-V, page 561.

Communion Antiphon

Christ had to suffer and to rise from the dead on the third day. In his name penance for the remission of sins is to be preached to all nations, alleluia. Luke 24:46-47.

Prayer after Communion

Lord,
look on your people with kindness
and by these Easter mysteries
bring us to the glory of the resurrection.

The priest may give the Solemn Blessing for Easter on page 375, or another form on page 599.

FOURTH SUNDAY OF EASTER/B

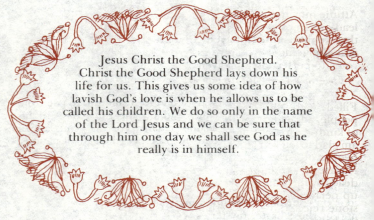

Jesus Christ the Good Shepherd.
Christ the Good Shepherd lays down his
life for us. This gives us some idea of how
lavish God's love is when he allows us to be
called his children. We do so only in the name
of the Lord Jesus and we can be sure that
through him one day we shall see God as he
really is in himself.

Entrance Antiphon   The earth is full of the goodness of the Lord; by the word of the Lord the heavens were made, alleluia.

Psalm 32:5-6

Opening Prayer
Let us pray
   [that Christ our shepherd
   will lead us through the difficulties of this life]

Almighty and ever-living God,
give us new strength
from the courage of Christ our shepherd,
and lead us to join the saints in heaven,
where he lives and reigns with you and the Holy Spirit
one God, for ever and ever.

or
Let us pray
   [to God our helper in time of distress]

God and Father of our Lord Jesus Christ,
though your people walk in the valley of darkness,
no evil should they fear;
for they follow in faith the call of the shepherd
whom you have sent for their hope and strength.

FOURTH SUNDAY OF EASTER/B

Attune our minds to the sound of his voice,
lead our steps in the path he has shown,
that we may know the strength of his outstretched arm
and enjoy the light of your presence for ever.

First Reading   Acts 4:8-12.
This is the only name by which we can be saved.

Filled with the Holy Spirit, Peter said: "Rulers of the people, and elders! If you are questioning us today about an act of kindness to a cripple, and asking us how he was healed, then I am glad to tell you all, and would indeed be glad to tell the whole people of Israel, that it was by the name of Jesus Christ the Nazarene, the one you crucified, whom God raised from the dead, by this name and by no other that this man is able to stand up perfectly healthy, here in your presence, today. This is the stone rejected by you the builders, but which has proved to be the keystone. For of all the names in the world given to men, this is the only one by which we can be saved."

Responsorial Psalm   Psalm 117.

℟ **The stone which the builders rejected
has become the corner stone.**

or
   Alleluia!

1. Give thanks to the Lord for he is good,
   for his love has no end.
   It is better to take refuge in the Lord
   than to trust in men:
   it is better to take refuge in the Lord
   than to trust in princes. ℟

2. I will thank you for you have given answer
   and you are my saviour.
   The stone which the builders rejected
   has become the corner stone.
   This is the work of the Lord,
   a marvel in our eyes. ℟

3. Blessed in the name of the Lord
   is he who comes.

FOURTH SUNDAY OF EASTER/B

We bless you from the house of the Lord;
I will thank you for you have given answer
and you are my saviour.
Give thanks to the Lord for he is good;
for his love has no end. ℟

Second Reading   1 John 3:1-2.

We shall see God as he really is.

Think of the love that the Father has lavished on us,
by letting us be called God's children;
and that is what we are.
Because the world refused to acknowledge him,
therefore it does not acknowledge us.
My dear people, we are already the children of God
but what we are to be in the future has not yet been revealed;
all we know is, that when it is revealed
we shall be like him
because we shall see him as he really is.

Alleluia   Alleluia, alleluia! I am the good shepherd, says the Lord; I know my own sheep and my own know me. Alleluia! John 10:14.

Gospel   John 10:11-18.

The good shepherd is one who lays down his life for his sheep.

Jesus said:
"I am the good shepherd:
the good shepherd is one who lays down his life for his sheep.
The hired man, since he is not the shepherd
and the sheep do not belong to him,
abandons the sheep and runs away
as soon as he sees a wolf coming,
and then the wolf attacks and scatters the sheep;
this is because he is only a hired man
and has no concern for the sheep.
I am the good shepherd;
I know my own
and my own know me,
just as the Father knows me
and I know the Father;
and I lay down my life for my sheep.

FOURTH SUNDAY OF EASTER/B

And there are other sheep I have
 that are not of this fold,
and these I have to lead as well.
They too will listen to my voice,
and there will be only one flock,
and one shepherd.
The Father loves me,
because I lay down my life
in order to take it up again.
No one takes it from me;
I lay it down of my own free will,
and as it is in my power to lay it down,
so it is in my power to take it up again;
and this is the command I have been given by my Father."

Prayer over the Gifts

Lord,
restore us by these Easter mysteries.
May the continuing work of our Redeemer
bring us eternal joy.

Preface of Easter II-V, pages 561-562.

Communion Antiphon

The Good Shepherd is risen! He who laid down his life for his sheep, who died for his flock, he is risen, alleluia.

Prayer after Communion

Father, eternal shepherd,
watch over the flock redeemed by the blood of Christ
and lead us to the promised land.

The priest may give the Solemn Blessing for Easter on page 375, or another form on page 599.

FIFTH SUNDAY OF EASTER/B

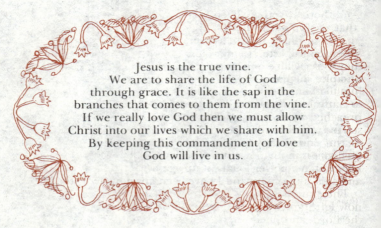

Jesus is the true vine.
We are to share the life of God
through grace. It is like the sap in the
branches that comes to them from the vine.
If we really love God then we must allow
Christ into our lives which we share with him.
By keeping this commandment of love
God will live in us.

Entrance Antiphon   Sing to the Lord a new song, for he has done marvellous deeds; he has revealed to the nations his saving power, alleluia.

Psalm 97:1-2

Opening Prayer

Let us pray
   [that we may enjoy true freedom]

God our Father,
look upon us with love.
You redeem us and make us your children in Christ.
Give us true freedom
and bring us to the inheritance you promised.

or

Let us pray
   [in the freedom of the sons of God]

Father of our Lord Jesus Christ,
you have revealed to the nations your saving power
and filled all ages with the words of a new song.
Hear the echo of this hymn.
Give us voice to sing your praise
throughout this season of joy.

FIFTH SUNDAY OF EASTER/B

First Reading   Acts 9:26-31.

Barnabas explained how the Lord had appeared to Saul on his journey.

When Saul got to Jerusalem he tried to join the disciples, but they were all afraid of him: they could not believe he was really a disciple. Barnabas, however, took charge of him, introduced him to the apostles, and explained how the Lord had appeared to Saul and spoken to him on his journey, and how he had preached boldly at Damascus in the name of Jesus. Saul now started to go round with them in Jerusalem, preaching fearlessly in the name of the Lord. But after he had spoken to the Hellenists, and argued with them, they became determined to kill him. When the brothers knew, they took him to Caesarea, and sent him off from there to Tarsus.

The churches throughout Judaea, Galilee and Samaria were now left in peace, building themselves up, living in the fear of the Lord, and filled with the consolation of the Holy Spirit.

Responsorial Psalm   Psalm 21.

℟ **You, Lord, are my praise in the great assembly.**

or

Alleluia!

1. My vows I will pay before those who fear him.
   The poor shall eat and shall have their fill.
   They shall praise the Lord, those who seek him.
   May their hearts live for ever and ever! ℟

2. All the earth shall remember and return to the Lord,
   all families of the nations worship before him.
   They shall worship him, all the mighty of the earth;
   before him shall bow all who go down to the dust. ℟

3. And my soul shall live for him, my children serve him.
   They shall tell of the Lord to generations yet to come,
   declare his faithfulness to peoples yet unborn:
   "These things the Lord has done." ℟

Second Reading   1 John 3:18-24.

His commandments are these: that we believe in his Son and that we love one another.

FIFTH SUNDAY OF EASTER/B

My children,
our love is not to be just words or mere talk,
but something real and active;
only by this can we be certain
that we are the children of the truth
and be able to quieten our conscience in his presence,
whatever accusations it may raise against us,
because God is greater than our conscience and he knows everything.
My dear people,
if we cannot be condemned by our own conscience,
we need not be afraid in God's presence,
and whatever we ask him,
we shall receive,
because we keep his commandments
and live the kind of life that he wants.
His commandments are these:
that we believe in the name of his Son Jesus Christ
and that we love one another
as he told us to.
Whoever keeps his commandments
lives in God and God lives in him.
We know that he lives in us
by the Spirit that he has given us.

Alleluia   Alleluia, alleluia! Make your home in me, as I make mine in you. Whoever remains in me bears fruit in plenty. Alleluia! John 15:4-5.

Gospel   John 15:1-8.
Whoever remains in me, with me in him, bears fruit in plenty.

Jesus said to his disciples:
"I am the true vine,
and my Father is the vinedresser.
Every branch in me that bears no fruit
he cuts away,
and every branch that does bear fruit he prunes
to make it bear even more.
You are pruned already,
by means of the word that I have spoken to you.

FIFTH SUNDAY OF EASTER/B

Make your home in me, as I make mine in you.
As a branch cannot bear fruit all by itself,
but must remain part of the vine,
neither can you unless you remain in me.
I am the vine,
you are the branches.
Whoever remains in me, with me in him,
bears fruit in plenty;
for cut off from me you can do nothing.
Anyone who does not remain in me
is like a branch that has been thrown away
— he withers;
these branches are collected and thrown on the fire,
and they are burnt.
If you remain in me
and my words remain in you,
you may ask what you will
and you shall get it.
It is to the glory of my Father that you should bear much fruit,
and then you will be my disciples."

Prayer over the Gifts

Lord God,
by this holy exchange of gifts
you share with us your divine life.
Grant that everything we do
may be directed by the knowledge of your truth.

Preface of Easter II-V, pages 561-562.

Communion Antiphon

I am the vine and you are the branches, says the Lord; he who lives in me, and I in him, will bear much fruit. John 15:5.

Prayer after Communion

Merciful Father,
may these mysteries give us new purpose
and bring us to a new life in you.

The priest may give the Solemn Blessing for Easter on page 375, or another form on page 599.

SIXTH SUNDAY OF EASTER/B

God is love.
True love is from God. The Holy Spirit
comes not only to us but to many outside
the visible Church. In these people we too
praise the wonderful saving power of God.
We prove we are christians by the generous
love which we show to one another and
to all people irrespective of race,
colour or creed.

Entrance Antiphon Speak out with a voice of joy; let it be heard to the ends of the earth: The Lord has set his people free, alleluia.

cf. Isaiah 48:20

Opening Prayer

Let us pray
  [that we may practise in our lives
  the faith we profess]

Ever-living God,
help us to celebrate our joy
in the resurrection of the Lord
and to express in our lives
the love we celebrate.

or

Let us pray
  [in silence, reflecting on the joy of Easter]

God our Father, maker of all,
the crown of your creation was the Son of Man,
born of a woman, but without beginning;
he suffered for us but lives for ever.

SIXTH SUNDAY OF EASTER/B

May our mortal lives be crowned with the ultimate joy
of rising with him,
who is Lord for ever and ever.

First Reading   Acts 10:25-26.34-35.44-48.

The Holy Spirit has been poured out on the pagans too.

As Peter reached the house Cornelius went out to meet him, knelt at his feet and prostrated himself. But Peter helped him up. "Stand up," he said "I am only a man after all!"

Then Peter addressed them: "The truth I have now come to realise" he said "is that God does not have favourites, but that anybody of any nationality who fears God and does what is right is acceptable to him."

While Peter was still speaking the Holy Spirit came down on all the listeners. Jewish believers who had accompanied Peter were all astonished that the gift of the Holy Spirit should be poured out on the pagans too, since they could hear them speaking strange languages and proclaiming the greatness of God. Peter himself then said, "Could anyone refuse the water of Baptism to these people, now they have received the Holy Spirit just as much as we have?" He then gave orders for them to be baptised in the name of Jesus Christ. Afterwards they begged him to stay on for some days.

Responsorial Psalm   Psalm 97.

℟ **The Lord has shown his salvation to the nations.**

or

   Alleluia!

1. Sing a new song to the Lord
   for he has worked wonders.
   His right hand and his holy arm
   have brought salvation. ℟

2. The Lord has made known his salvation;
   has shown his justice to the nations.
   He has remembered his truth and love
   for the house of Israel. ℟

3. All the ends of the earth have seen
   the salvation of our God.
   Shout to the Lord all the earth,
   ring out your joy. ℟

SIXTH SUNDAY OF EASTER/B

Second Reading 1 John 4:7-10.

God is love.

My dear people,
let us love one another
since love comes from God
and everyone who loves is begotten by God and knows God.
Anyone who fails to love can never have known God,
because God is love.
God's love for us was revealed
when God sent into the world his only Son
so that we could have life through him;
this is the love I mean:
not our love for God,
but God's love for us when he sent his Son
to be the sacrifice that takes our sins away.

Alleluia Alleluia, alleluia! Jesus said: "If anyone loves me he will keep my word, and my Father will love him, and we shall come to him." Alleluia! John 14:23.

Gospel John 15:9-17.

A man can have no greater love than to lay down his life for his friends.

Jesus said to his disciples:
"As the Father has loved me,
so I have loved you.
Remain in my love.
If you keep my commandments
you will remain in my love,
just as I have kept my Father's commandments
and remain in his love.
I have told you this
so that my own joy may be in you
and your joy be complete.
This is my commandment:
Love one another,
as I have loved you.
A man can have no greater love
than to lay down his life for his friends.
You are my friends,
if you do what I command you.

SIXTH SUNDAY OF EASTER/B

I shall not call you servants any more,
because a servant does not know
his master's business;
I call you friends,
because I have made known to you
everything I have learnt from my Father.
You did not choose me,
no, I chose you;
and I commissioned you
to go out and to bear fruit,
fruit that will last;
and then the Father will give you
anything you ask him in my name.
What I command you
is to love one another."

Prayer over the Gifts
Lord,,
accept our prayers and offerings.
Make us worthy of your sacraments of love
by granting us your forgiveness.

Preface of Easter II-V, pages 561-562.

Communion Antiphon
If you love me, keep my commandments, says the Lord. The Father will send you the Holy Spirit, to be with you for ever, alleluia. John 14:15-16.

Prayer after Communion
Almighty and ever-living Lord,
you restored us to life
by raising Christ from death.
Strengthen us by this Easter sacrament;
may we feel its saving power in our daily life.

The priest may give the Solemn Blessing of Easter on page 375, or another form on page 599.

THURSDAY OF THE SIXTH WEEK OF EASTER
THE ASCENSION OF THE LORD

Christ ascends to his Father!
Christ's Ascension is our guarantee
that one day we will be with him in heaven
to praise the glory of God our Father.
The Ascension is our hope of the great
inheritance which awaits those of us who
believe in the power of the risen Christ.

Entrance Antiphon Men of Galilee, why do you stand looking in the sky? The Lord will return, just as you have seen him ascend, alleluia.

Acts 1:11

Let us pray
 [that the risen Christ
 will lead us to eternal life]

God our Father,
make us joyful in the ascension of your Son Jesus Christ.
May we follow him into the new creation,
for his ascension is our glory and our hope.

or

Let us pray
 [on this day of Ascension
 as we watch and wait for Jesus' return]

Father in heaven,
our minds were prepared for the coming of your kingdom
when you took Christ beyond our sight
so that we might seek him in his glory.

May we follow where he has led
and find our hope in his glory,
for he is Lord for ever.

THE ASCENSION OF THE LORD/B

First Reading   Acts 1:1-11
He was lifted up while they looked on.

In my earlier work, Theophilus, I dealt with everything Jesus had done and taught from the beginning until the day he gave his instructions to the apostles he had chosen through the Holy Spirit, and was taken up to heaven. He had shown himself alive to them after his Passion by many demonstrations: for forty days he had continued to appear to them and tell them about the kingdom of God. When he had been at table with them, he had told them not to leave Jerusalem, but to wait there for what the Father had promised. "It is," he had said, "what you have heard me speak about: John baptised with water but you, not many days from now, will be baptised with the Holy Spirit."

Now having met together, they asked him, "Lord, has the time come? Are you going to restore the kingdom to Israel?" He replied, "It is not for you to know times or dates that the Father has decided by his own authority, but you will receive power when the Holy Spirit comes on you, and then you will be my witnesses not only in Jerusalem but throughout Judaea and Samaria, and indeed to the ends of the earth."

As he said this he was lifted up while they looked on, and a cloud took him from their sight. They were still staring into the sky when suddenly two men in white were standing near them and they said, "Why are you men from Galilee standing here looking into the sky? Jesus who has been taken up from you into heaven, this same Jesus will come back in the same way as you have seen him go there."

Responsorial Psalm   Psalm 46

℟ **God goes up with shouts of joy;
the Lord goes up with trumpet blast.**

or

Alleluia!

1. All peoples, clap your hands,
   cry to God with shouts of joy!
   For the Lord, the Most High, we must fear,
   great king over all the earth. ℟

THE ASCENSION OF THE LORD/B

2. God goes up with shouts of joy;
   the Lord goes up with trumpet blast.
   Sing praise for God, sing praise,
   sing praise to our king, sing praise. ℟

3. God is king of all the earth.
   Sing praise with all your skill.
   God is king over the nations;
   God reigns on his holy throne. ℟

Second Reading   Ephesians 1:17-23
He made him sit at his right hand in heaven.

May the God of our Lord Jesus Christ, the Father of glory, give you a spirit of wisdom and perception of what is revealed, to bring you to full knowledge of him. May he enlighten the eyes of your mind so that you can see what hope his call holds for you, what rich glories he has promised the saints will inherit and how infinitely great is the power that he has exercised for us believers. This you can tell from the strength of his power at work in Christ, when he used it to raise him from the dead and to make him sit at his right hand in heaven, far above every Sovereignty, Authority, Power, or Domination, or any other name that can be named, not only in this age, but also in the age to come. He has put all things under his feet, and made him, as the ruler of everything, the head of the Church; which is his body, the fullness of him who fills the whole creation.

or

Second Reading   Ephesians 4:1-13
Fully mature with the fullness of Christ.

I, the prisoner in the Lord, implore you therefore to lead a life worthy of your vocation. Bear with one another charitably, in complete selflessness, gentleness and patience. Do all you can to preserve the unity of the Spirit by the peace that binds you together. There is one Body, one Spirit, just as you were all called into one and the same hope when you were called. There is one Lord, one faith, one baptism, and one God who is Father of all, over all, through all and within all.

Each one of us, however, has been given his own share of grace, given as Christ allotted it.

THE ASCENSION OF THE LORD/B

It was said that he would:
When he ascended to the height, he captured prisoners,
he gave gifts to men.

When it says, 'he ascended', what can it mean if not that he descended right down to the lower regions of the earth?

The one who rose higher than all the heavens to fill all things is none other than the one who descended.

And to some, his gift was that they should be apostles; to some, prophets; to some, evangelists; to some, pastors and teachers; so that the saints together make a unity in the work of service, building up the body of Christ. In this way we are all to come to unity in our faith and in our knowledge of the Son of God, until we become the perfect Man, fully mature with the fullness of Christ himself.

Alleluia   Alleluia, alleluia! Go, make disciples of all the nations; I am with you always; yes, to the end of time. Alleluia! Matthew 28:19-20.

Gospel   Mark 16:15-20

He was taken up into heaven: there at the right hand of God he took his place.

Jesus showed himself to the Eleven, and said to them, "Go out to the whole world, proclaim the Good News to all creation. He who believes and is baptised will be saved; he who does not believe will be condemned. These are the signs that will be associated with believers: in my name they will cast out devils; they will have the gift of tongues; they will pick up snakes in their hands, and be unharmed should they drink deadly poison; they will lay their hands on the sick, who will recover."

And so the Lord Jesus, after he had spoken to them, was taken up into heaven: there at the right hand of God he took his place, while they, going out, preached everywhere, the Lord working with them and confirming the word by the signs that accompanied it.

Prayer over the Gifts

Lord,
receive our offering
as we celebrate the ascension of Christ your Son.

THE ASCENSION OF THE LORD/B

May his gifts help us rise with him
to the joys of heaven,
where he lives and reigns for ever and ever.

Preface of Ascension I or II page 401

Communion Antiphon   I, the Lord, am with you always, until
the end of the world, alleluia.
Matthew 28:20.

Prayer after communion

Father,
in this eucharist
we touch the divine life you give to the world.
Help us to follow Christ with love
to eternal life where he is Lord for ever and ever.

Solemn Blessing

Bow your heads and pray for God's blessing.

May almighty God bless you on this day
when his only Son ascended into heaven
to prepare a place for you.
R/ Amen.

After his resurrection, Christ was seen by his disciples.
When he appears as judge
may you be pleasing for ever in his sight.
R/ Amen.

You believe that Jesus has taken his seat in majesty
at the right hand of the Father.
May you have the joy of experiencing
that he is also with you to the end of time,
according to his promise.
R/ Amen.

May almighty God bless you,
the Father, and the Son, ✠ and the Holy Spirit.
R/ Amen.

SEVENTH SUNDAY OF EASTER/B

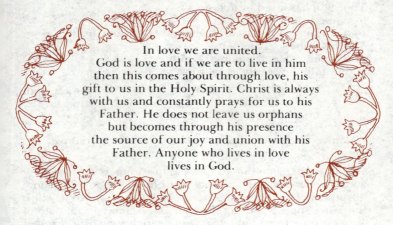

In love we are united.
God is love and if we are to live in him
then this comes about through love, his
gift to us in the Holy Spirit. Christ is always
with us and constantly prays for us to his
Father. He does not leave us orphans
but becomes through his presence
the source of our joy and union with his
Father. Anyone who lives in love
lives in God.

Entrance Antiphon Lord, hear my voice when I call to you. My heart has prompted me to seek your face; I seek it, Lord; do not hide from me, alleluia. Psalm 26:7-9.

Opening Prayer
Let us pray
  [that we may recognise
  the presence of Christ in our midst]

Father,
help us keep in mind that Christ our Saviour
lives with you in glory
and promised to remain with us until the end of time.

or
Let us pray
  [to our Father
  who has raised us to life in Christ]

Eternal Father,
reaching from end to end of the universe,
and ordering all things with your mighty arm:
for you, time is the unfolding of truth that already is,
the unveiling of beauty that is yet to be.

SEVENTH SUNDAY OF EASTER/B

Your Son has saved us in history
by rising from the dead,
so that transcending time he might free us from death.
May his presence among us
lead to the vision of unlimited truth
and unfold the beauty of your love.

First Reading   Acts 1:15-17.20-26.

We must choose one of these to be a witness to his resurrection with us.

One day Peter stood up to speak to the brothers — there were about a hundred and twenty persons in the congregation: "Brothers, the passage of scripture had to be fulfilled in which the Holy Spirit, speaking through David, foretells the fate of Judas, who offered himself as a guide to the men who arrested Jesus — after having been one of our number and actually sharing this ministry of ours.

In the Book of Psalms it says: Let someone else take his office.

"We must therefore choose someone who has been with us the whole time that the Lord Jesus was travelling round with us, someone who was with us right from the time when John was baptising until the day when he was taken up from us — and he can act with us as a witness to his resurrection."

Having nominated two candidates, Joseph known as Barsabbas, whose surname was Justus, and Matthias, they prayed, "Lord, you can read everyone's heart; show us therefore which of these two you have chosen to take over this ministry and apostolate, which Judas abandoned to go to his proper place." They then drew lots for them, and as the lot fell to Matthias, he was listed as one of the twelve apostles.

Responsorial Psalm   Psalm 102.

℟ **The Lord has set his sway in heaven.**

or

   Alleluia!

SEVENTH SUNDAY OF EASTER/B

1. My soul, give thanks to the Lord,
   all my being, bless his holy name.
   My soul, give thanks to the Lord
   and never forget all his blessings. ℟

2. For as the heavens are high above the earth
   so strong is his love for those who fear him.
   As far as the east is from the west
   so far does he remove our sins. ℟

3. The Lord has set his sway in heaven
   and his kingdom is ruling over all.
   Give thanks to the Lord, all his angels,
   mighty in power, fulfilling his word. ℟

Second Reading 1 John 4:11-16.

Anyone who lives in love lives in God, and God lives in him.

My dear people,
since God has loved us so much,
we too should love one another.
No one has ever seen God;
but as long as we love one another
God will live in us
and his love will be complete in us.
We can know that we are living in him
and he is living in us
because he lets us share his Spirit.
We ourselves saw and we testify
that the Father sent his Son
as saviour of the world.
If ayone acknowledges that Jesus is the Son of God,
God lives in him, and he in God.
We ourselves have known and put our faith in
God's love towards ourselves.
God is love
and anyone who lives in love lives in God,
and God lives in him.

Alleluia   Alleluia, alleluia! I will not leave you orphans, says the Lord; I will come back to you, and your hearts will be full of joy. Alleluia! John 14:18.

SEVENTH SUNDAY OF EASTER/B

Gospel   John 17:11-19.
That they may be one like us!

Jesus raised his eyes to heaven and said:
"Holy Father,
keep those you have given me true to your name,
so that they may be one like us.
While I was with them,
 I kept those you had given me true to your name.
I have watched over them and not one is lost
except the one who chose to be lost,
and this was to fulfil the scriptures.
But now I am coming to you
and while still in the world I say these things
to share my joy with them to the full.
I passed your word on to them,
and the world hated them,
because they belong to the world
no more than I belong to the world.
I am not asking you to remove them from the world,
but to protect them from the evil one.
They do not belong to the world
any more than I belong to the world.
Consecrate them in the truth;
your word is truth.
As you sent me into the world,
I have sent them into the world,
and for their sake I consecrate myself
so that they too may be consecrated in truth."

Prayer over the Gifts

Lord,
accept the prayers and gifts
we offer in faith and love.
May this eucharist
bring us to your glory.

Preface of the Ascension I or II, page 401.

Communion Antiphon
This is the prayer of Jesus: that his believers may become one as he is one with the Father, alleluia. John 17:22.

SEVENTH SUNDAY OF EASTER/B

Prayer after Communion

God our Saviour,
hear us,
and through this holy mystery give us hope
that the glory you have given Christ
will be given to the Church, his body,
for he is Lord for ever and ever.

The priest may give the Solemn Blessing for Easter on page 375, or another form on page 599.

The Mass for Pentecost Sunday will be found on page 469.

SECOND SUNDAY OF EASTER/C

Entrance Antiphon Receive the Holy Spirit.
Jesus, our risen Lord, bestows his spirit on us.
We believe even though we have not seen that
he is our Lord and our God. We are apostles of
the resurrection and we now live the life of the
spirit. This spirit is for mission. As the Father
sent Christ so now we are sent to preach the
Good News to all men.

or

Like newborn children you should thirst
for milk, on which your spirit can grow to
strength, alleluia. 1 Peter 2:2.

or

Rejoice to the full in the glory that is yours,
and give thanks to God who called you to
his kingdom, alleluia. 4 Ezra 2:36-37.

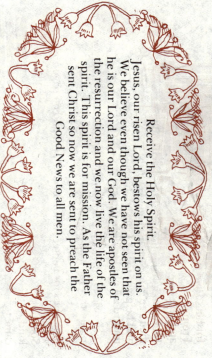

Opening Prayer

Let us pray
[for a deeper awareness of our Christian baptism]
God of mercy,
you wash away our sins in water,
you give us new birth in the Spirit,
and redeem us in the blood of Christ.
As we celebrate Christ's resurrection
increase our awareness of these blessings,
and renew your gift of life within us.

or

Let us pray
[as Christians thirsting for the risen life]
Heavenly Father and God of mercy,
we no longer look for Jesus among the dead,

SECOND SUNDAY OF EASTER/C

for he is alive and has become the Lord of life.
From the waters of death you raise us with him
and renew your gift of life within us.

Increase in our minds and hearts
the risen life we share with Christ
and help us to grow as your people
towards the fullness of eternal life with you.

First Reading   Acts 5:12-16.

The numbers of men and women who came to believe in the Lord increased steadily.

The faithful all used to meet by common consent in the Portico of Solomon. No one else ever dared to join them, but the people were loud in their praise and the numbers of men and women who came to believe in the Lord increased steadily. So many signs and wonders were worked among the people at the hands of the apostles that the sick were even taken out into the streets and laid on beds and sleeping-mats in the hope that at least the shadow of Peter might fall across some of them as he went past. People even came crowding in from the towns round about Jerusalem, bringing with them their sick and those tormented by unclean spirits, and all of them were cured.

Responsorial Psalm   Psalm 117:2-4.22-27.

℟ **Give thanks to the Lord for he is good,
for his love has no end.**

or

    Alleluia, alleluia, alleluia!

1. Let the sons of Israel say:
"His love has no end."
Let the sons of Aaron say:
"His love has no end."
Let those who fear the Lord say:
"His love has no end." ℟

2. The stone which the builders rejected
has become the corner stone.
This is the work of the Lord,
a marvel in our eyes.
This day was made by the Lord;
we rejoice and are glad. ℟

SECOND SUNDAY OF EASTER/C

3. O Lord, grant us salvation;
   O Lord, grant success.
   Blessed in the name of the Lord
   is he who comes.
   We bless you from the house of the Lord;
   the Lord God is our light. ℟

Second Reading   Apocalypse 1:9-13.17-19.

I was dead and now I am to live for ever and ever.

My name is John, and through our union in Jesus I am your brother and share your sufferings, your kingdom, and all you endure. I was on the island of Patmos for having preached God's word and witnessed for Jesus; it was the Lord's day and the Spirit possessed me, and I heard a voice behind me, shouting like a trumpet, "Write down all that you see in a book." I turned round to see who had spoken to me, and when I turned I saw seven golden lampstands and, surrounded by them, a figure like a Son of man, dressed in a long robe tied at the waist with a golden girdle.

   When I saw him, I fell in a dead faint at his feet, but he touched me with his right hand and said, "Do not be afraid; it is I, the First and the Last; I am the Living One. I was dead and now I am to live for ever and ever, and I hold the keys of death and of the underworld. Now write down all that you see of present happenings and things that are still to come."

Alleluia   Alleluia, alleluia! Jesus said: "You believe because you can see me. Happy are those who have not seen and yet believe."   John 20:29.

Gospel   John 20:19-31.

Eight days later, Jesus came.

In the evening of that same day, the first day of the week, the doors were closed in the room where the disciples were, for fear of the Jews. Jesus came and stood among them. He said to them, "Peace be with you," and showed them his hands and his side. The disciples were filled with joy when they saw the Lord, and he said to them again, "Peace be with you.
"As the Father sent me,
so am I sending you."
After saying this he breathed on them and said:
"Receive the Holy Spirit.

SECOND SUNDAY OF EASTER/C

For those whose sins you forgive,
they are forgiven;
for those whose sins you retain,
they are retained."

Thomas, called the Twin, who was one of the Twelve, was not with them when Jesus came. When the disciples said, "We have seen the Lord," he answered, "Unless I see the holes that the nails made in his hands and can put my finger into the holes they made, and unless I can put my hand into his side, I refuse to believe." Eight days later the disciples were in the house again and Thomas was with them. The doors were closed, but Jesus came in and stood among them. "Peace be with you" he said. Then he spoke to Thomas, "Put your finger here; look, here are my hands. Give me your hand; put it into his side. Doubt no longer but believe." Thomas replied, "My Lord and my God!" Jesus said to him:
"You believe because you can see me.
Happy are those who have not seen and yet believe."

There were many other signs that Jesus worked and the disciples saw, but they are not recorded in this book. These are recorded so that you may believe that Jesus is the Christ, the Son of God, and that believing this you may have life through his name.

Prayer over the Gifts

Lord,
through faith and baptism
we have become a new creation.
Accept the offerings of your people
(and of those born again in baptism)
and bring us to eternal happiness.

Preface of Easter I, page 369.

Communion Antiphon

Jesus spoke to Thomas: Put your hand here, and see the place of the nails. Doubt no longer, but believe, alleluia.
cf. John 20:27

Prayer after Communion

Almighty God,
may the Easter sacraments we have received
live for ever in our minds and hearts.

The priest may give the Solemn Blessing for Easter on page 375, or another form on page 599.

THIRD SUNDAY OF EASTER/C

We are witnesses to the resurrection. The Holy Spirit gives us the courage to witness to the power of Christ's resurrection. He is the lamb to whom all praise, honour, glory and power must be given for ever and ever. We will suffer opposition and misunderstanding because of our belief but Christ is always with us once we dare to follow him.

Entrance Antiphon Let all the earth cry out to God with joy; praise the glory of his name; proclaim his glorious praise, alleluia. Psalm 65:1-2.

Opening Prayer

Let us pray
 [that Christ will give us
 a share in the glory of his unending life]

God our Father,
may we look forward with hope to our resurrection,
for you have made us your sons and daughters,
and restored the joy of our youth.

or

Let us pray
 [in confident peace and Easter hope]

Father in heaven, author of all truth,
a people once in darkness has listened to your Word
and followed your Son as he rose from the tomb.

Hear the prayer of this newborn people
and strengthen your Church to answer your call.
May we rise and come forth into the light of day
to stand in your presence until eternity dawns.

THIRD SUNDAY OF EASTER/C

First Reading   Acts 5:27-32.40-41.
We are witnesses of all this, we and the Holy Spirit.

The high priest demanded an explanation of the apostles. "We gave you a formal warning," he said "not to preach in this name, and what have you done? You have filled Jerusalem with your teaching, and seem determined to fix the guilt of this man's death on us." In reply Peter and the apostles said, "Obedience to God comes before obedience to men; it was the God of our ancestors who raised up Jesus, but it was you who had him executed by hanging on a tree. By his own right hand God has now raised him up to be leader and saviour, to give repentance and forgiveness of sins through him to Israel. We are witnesses to all this, we and the Holy Spirit whom God has given to those who obey him." They warned the apostles not to speak in the name of Jesus and released them. And so they left the presence of the Sanhedrin glad to have had the honour of suffering humiliation for the sake of the name.

Responsorial Psalm   Psalm 29.

℟ **I will praise you, Lord,
    you have rescued me.**

or

   Alleluia!

1. I will praise you, Lord, you have rescued me
   and have not let my enemies rejoice over me.
   O Lord, you have raised my soul from the dead,
   restored me to life from those who sink into the grave.   ℟

2. Sing psalms to the Lord, you who love him,
   give thanks to his holy name.
   His anger lasts but a moment; his favour through life.
   At night there are tears, but joy comes with dawn.   ℟

3. The Lord listened and had pity.
   The Lord came to my help.
   For me you have changed my mourning into dancing,
   O Lord my God, I will thank you for ever.   ℟

THIRD SUNDAY OF EASTER/C

Second Reading   Apocalypse 5:11-14.

The Lamb that was sacrificed is worthy to be given riches and power.

In my vision, I, John, heard the sound of an immense number of angels gathered round the throne and the animals and the elders; there were ten thousand times ten thousand of them and thousands upon thousands, shouting, "The Lamb that was sacrificed is worthy to be given power, riches, wisdom, strength, honour, glory and blessing." Then I heard all the living things in creation — everything that lives in the air, and on the ground, and under the ground, and in the sea, crying, "To the One who is sitting on the throne and to the Lamb, be all praise, honour, glory and power, for ever and ever." And the four animals said, "Amen"; and the elders prostrated themselves to worship.

Alleluia   Alleluia, alleluia! Lord Jesus, explain the scriptures to us. Make our hearts burn within us as you talk to us. Alleluia! cf. Luke 24:32.

or

Alleluia, alleluia! Christ has risen: he who created all things, and has granted his mercy to men. Alleluia!

Gospel   John 21:1-19.

Jesus stepped forward, took the bread and gave it to them, and the same with the fish.

> Jesus showed himself again to the disciples. It was by the Sea of Tiberias, and it happened like this: Simon Peter, Thomas called the Twin, Nathanael from Cana in Galilee, the sons of Zebedee and two more of his disciples were together. Simon Peter said, "I'm going fishing." They replied, "We'll come with you." They went out and got into the boat but caught nothing that night.
>
> It was light by now and there stood Jesus on the shore, though the disciples did not realise that it was Jesus. Jesus called out, "Have you caught anything, friends?" And when they answered, "No", he said, "Throw the net out to starboard and you'll find something." So they dropped the net, and there were so many fish that they could not haul it in. The disciple Jesus loved said to Peter, "It is the Lord." At these words "It is the Lord", Simon Peter, who had practically nothing on, wrapped

THIRD SUNDAY OF EASTER/C

his cloak round him and jumped into the water. The other disciples came on in the boat, towing the net and the fish; they were only about a hundred yards from land.

As soon as they came ashore they saw that there was some bread there, and a charcoal fire with fish cooking on it. Jesus said, "Bring some of the fish you have just caught." Simon Peter went aboard and dragged the net to the shore, full of big fish, one hundred and fifty-three of them; and in spite of there being so many the net was not broken. Jesus said to them, "Come and have breakfast." None of the disciples was bold enough to ask, "Who are you?"; they knew quite well it was the Lord. Jesus then stepped forward, took the bread and gave it to them, and the same with the fish. This was the third time that Jesus showed himself to the disciples after rising from the dead.

After the meal Jesus said to Simon Peter, "Simon son of John, do you love me more than these others do?" He answered, "Yes Lord, you know I love you." Jesus said to him, "Feed my lambs." A second time he said to him, "Simon son of John, do you love me?" He replied, "Yes, Lord, you know I love you." Jesus said to him, "Look after my sheep." Then he said to him a third time, "Simon son of John, do you love me?" Peter was upset that he asked him the third time, "Do you love me?" and said, "Lord, you know everything; you know I love you." Jesus said to him, "Feed my sheep.

"I tell you most solemnly,
when you were young
you put on your belt
and walked where you liked;
but when you grow old
you will stretch out your hands,
and somebody else will put a belt round you
and take you where you would rather not go."
In these words he indicated the kind of death by which Peter would give glory to God. After this he said, "Follow me."

Prayer over the Gifts

Lord,
receive these gifts from your Church.
May the great joy you give us
come to perfection in heaven.

Preface of Easter II-V, pages 561-562.

THIRD SUNDAY OF EASTER/C

Communion Antiphon Jesus said to his disciples: Come and eat. And he took the bread, and gave it to them, alleluia. cf. John 21:12-13.

Prayer after Communion
Lord,
look on your people with kindness
and by these Easter mysteries
bring us to the glory of the resurrection.

The priest may give the Solemn Blessing for Easter on page 375, or another form on page 599.

FOURTH SUNDAY OF EASTER/C

Christ gives eternal life to all who listen to his voice. Christ is the good shepherd who will lead us to springs of living water where God will wipe away all tears from our eyes. We are a light for the nations so that the salvation of Christ may be preached to the ends of the earth. We have a mission to everyone even though at times people will turn against us because of our belief. We remain full of joy in the Holy Spirit.

Entrance Antiphon The earth is full of the goodness of the Lord; by the word of the Lord the heavens were made, alleluia. **Psalm 32:5-6.**

Opening Prayer

Let us pray
   [that Christ our shepherd
   will lead us through the difficulties of this life]

Almighty and ever-living God,
give us new strength
from the courage of Christ our shepherd,
and lead us to join the saints in heaven,
where he lives and reigns with you and the Holy Spirit,
one God, for ever and ever.

or

Let us pray
   [to God our helper in time of distress]

God and Father of our Lord Jesus Christ,
though your people walk in the valley of darkness,
no evil should they fear;
for they follow in faith the call of the shepherd
whom you have sent for their hope and strength.

FOURTH SUNDAY OF EASTER/C

Attune our minds to the sound of his voice,
lead our steps in the path he has shown,
that we may know the strength of his outstretched arm
and enjoy the light of your presence for ever.

First Reading   Acts 13:14.43-52.
We must turn to the pagans.

Paul and Barnabas carried on from Perga till they reached Antioch in Pisidia. Here they went to synagogue on the sabbath and took their seats.

When the meeting broke up, many Jews and devout converts joined Paul and Barnabas, and in their talks with them Paul and Barnabas urged them to remain faithful to the grace God had given them.

The next sabbath almost the whole town assembled to hear the word of God. When they saw the crowds, the Jews, prompted by jealousy, used blasphemies and contradicted everything Paul said. Then Paul and Barnabas spoke out boldly. "We had to proclaim the word of God to you first, but since you have rejected it, since you do not think yourselves worthy of eternal life, we must turn to the pagans. For this is what the Lord commanded us to do when he said:
I have made you a light for the nations,
so that my salvation may reach the ends of the earth."

It made the pagans very happy to hear this and they thanked the Lord for his message; all who were destined for eternal life became believers. Thus the word of the Lord spread through the whole countryside.

But the Jews worked upon some of the devout women of the upper classes and the leading men of the city and persuaded them to turn against Paul and Barnabas and expel them from their territory. So they shook the dust from their feet in defiance and went off to Iconium; but the disciples were filled with joy and the Holy Spirit.

Responsorial Psalm   Psalm 99.
R/ **We are his people, the sheep of his flock.**

or

Alleluia!

FOURTH SUNDAY OF EASTER/C

1. Cry out with joy to the Lord, all the earth.
   Serve the Lord with gladness.
   Come before him, singing for joy. ℟

2. Know that he, the Lord, is God.
   He made us, we belong to him,
   we are his people, the sheep of his flock. ℟

3. Indeed, how good is the Lord,
   eternal his merciful love.
   He is faithful from age to age. ℟

Second Reading   Apocalypse 7:9.14-17.

The Lamb will be their shepherd and will lead them to springs of living water.

I, John, saw a huge number, impossible to count, of people from every nation, race, tribe and language; they were standing in front of the throne and in front of the Lamb, dressed in white robes and holding palms in their hands. One of the elders said to me, "These are the people who have been through the great persecution, and because they have washed their robes white again in the blood of the Lamb, they now stand in front of God's throne and serve him day and night in his sanctuary; and the One who sits on the throne will spread his tent over them. They will never hunger or thirst again; neither the sun nor scorching wind will ever plague them, because the Lamb who is at the throne will be their shepherd and will lead them to springs of living water; and God will wipe away all tears from their eyes."

Alleluia

Alleluia, alleluia! I am the good shepherd, says the Lord; I know my own sheep and my own know me. Alleluia! John 10:14.

Gospel   John 10:27-30.

I give eternal life to the sheep that belong to me.

Jesus said:
"The sheep that belong to me listen to my voice;
I know them and they follow me.
I give them eternal life;
they will never be lost

FOURTH SUNDAY OF EASTER/C

and no one will ever steal them from me.
The Father who gave them to me is greater than anyone
and no one can steal from the Father.
The Father and I are one."

Prayer over the Gifts

Lord,
restore us by these Easter mysteries.
May the continuing work of our Redeemer
bring us eternal joy.

Preface of Easter II-V, pages 561-562.

Communion Antiphon

The Good Shepherd is risen! He who laid down his life for his sheep, who died for his flock, he is risen, alleluia.

Prayer after Communion

Father, eternal shepherd,
watch over the flock redeemed by the blood of Christ
and lead us to the promised land.

The priest may give the Solemn Blessing for Easter on page 375, or another form on page 599.

FIFTH SUNDAY OF EASTER/C

You must love one another.
Jesus tells us that we are known as his disciples
by the caring love that we show for one
another. We have to love one another as he has
loved us. In this way we will open the door of
faith to the pagans and give them the
opportunity to praise God who makes
all things new.

Entrance Antiphon Sing to the Lord a new song, for he has done marvellous deeds; he has revealed to the nations his saving power, alleluia.

Psalm 97:1-2

Opening Prayer

Let us pray
   [that we may enjoy true freedom]

God our Father,
look upon us with love.
You redeem us and make us your children in Christ.
Give us true freedom
and bring us to the inheritance you promised.

or

Let us pray
   [in the freedom of the sons of God]

Father of our Lord Jesus Christ,
you have revealed to the nations your saving power
and filled all ages with the words of a new song.
Hear the echo of this hymn.
Give us voice to sing your praise
throughout this season of joy.

FIFTH SUNDAY OF EASTER/C

First Reading   Acts 14:21-27.

They gave an account to the church of all that God had done with them.

Paul and Barnabas went back through Lystra and Iconium to Antioch. They put fresh heart into the disciples, encouraging them to persevere in the faith. "We all have to experience many hardships" they said "before we enter the kingdom of God." In each of these churches they appointed elders, and with prayer and fasting they commended them to the Lord in whom they had come to believe.

They passed through Pisidia and reached Pamphylia. Then after proclaiming the word at Perga they went down to Attalia and from there sailed for Antioch, where they had originally been commended to the grace of God for the work they had now completed.

On their arrival they assembled the church and gave an account of all that God had done with them, and how he had opened the door of faith to the pagans.

Responsorial Psalm   Psalm 144.

℟ **I will bless your name for ever, O God my King.**

or

Alleluia!

1. The Lord is kind and full of compassion,
   slow to anger, abounding in love.
   How good is the Lord to all,
   compassionate to all his creatures. ℟

2. All your creatures shall thank you, O Lord,
   and your friends shall repeat their blessing.
   They shall speak of the glory of your reign
   and declare your might, O God,
   to make known to men your mighty deeds
   and the glorious splendour of your reign. ℟

3. Yours is an everlasting kingdom;
   your rule lasts from age to age. ℟

FIFTH SUNDAY OF EASTER/C

Second Reading Apocalypse 21:1-5.

God will wipe away all tears from their eyes.

I, John, saw a new heaven and a new earth; the first heaven and the first earth had disappeared now, and there was no longer any sea. I saw the holy city, and the new Jerusalem, coming down from God out of heaven, as beautiful as a bride all dressed for her husband. Then I heard a loud voice call from the throne, "You see this city? Here God lives among men. He will make his home among them; they shall be his people, and he will be their God; his name is God-with-them. He will wipe away all tears from their eyes; there will be no more death, and no more mourning or sadness. The world of the past has gone."

Then the One sitting on the throne spoke: "Now I am making the whole of creation new" he said.

Alleluia Alleluia, alleluia! Jesus said: "I give you a new commandment: love one another, just as I have loved you." Alleluia! John 14:6.

Gospel John 13:31-35.

I give you a new commandment: love one another.

When Judas had gone Jesus said:
"Now has the Son of Man been glorified,
and in him God has been glorified.
If God has been glorified in him,
God will in turn glorify him in himself,
and will glorify him very soon.
My little children,
I shall not be with you much longer.
I give you a new commandment:
love one another;
just as I have loved you,
you also must love one another.
By this love you have for one another,
every one will know that you are my disciples."

FIFTH SUNDAY OF EASTER/C

Prayer over the Gifts

Lord God,
by this holy exchange of gifts
you share with us your divine life.
Grant that everything we do
may be directed by the knowledge of your truth.

Preface of Easter II-V, pages 561-562.

Communion Antiphon

I am the vine and you are the branches, says the Lord; he who lives in me, and I in him, will bear much fruit, Alleluia. **John 15:5.**

Prayer after Communion

Merciful Father,
may these mysteries give us new purpose
and bring us to a new life in you.

The priest may give the Solemn Blessing for Easter on page 375, or aother form on page 599.

SIXTH SUNDAY OF EASTER/C

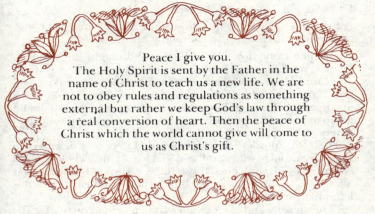

Peace I give you.
The Holy Spirit is sent by the Father in the name of Christ to teach us a new life. We are not to obey rules and regulations as something external but rather we keep God's law through a real conversion of heart. Then the peace of Christ which the world cannot give will come to us as Christ's gift.

Entrance Antiphon Speak out with a voice of joy; let it be heard to the ends of the earth: The Lord has set his people free, alleluia. cf. Isaiah 48:20.

Opening Prayer

Let us pray
 [that we may practise in our lives
 the faith we profess]

Ever-living God,
help us to celebrate our joy
in the resurrection of the Lord
and to express in our lives
the love we celebrate.

or

Let us pray
 [in silence, reflecting on the joy of Easter]

God our Father, maker of all,
the crown of your creation was the Son of Man,
born of a woman, but without beginning;
he suffered for us but lives for ever.

May our mortal lives be crowned with the ultimate joy
of rising with him,
who is Lord for ever and ever.

SIXTH SUNDAY OF EASTER/C

First Reading   Acts 15:1-2.22-29.

It has been decided by the Holy Spirit and by ourselves not to saddle you with any burden beyond these essentials.

Some men came down from Judaea and taught the brothers, "Unless you have yourselves circumcised in the tradition of Moses you cannot be saved." This led to disagreement, and after Paul and Barnabas had had a long argument with these men it was arranged that Paul and Barnabas and others of the church should go up to Jerusalem and discuss the problem with the apostles and elders.

Then the apostles and elders decided to choose delegates to send to Antioch with Paul and Barnabas; the whole church concurred with this. They chose Judas known as Barsabbas and Silas, both leading men in the brotherhood, and gave them this letter to take with them.

"The apostles and elders, your brothers, send greetings to the brothers of pagan birth in Antioch, Syria and Cilicia. We hear that some of our members have disturbed you with their demands and have unsettled your minds. They acted without any authority from us, and so we have decided unanimously to elect delegates and to send them to you with Barnabas and Paul, men we highly respect who have dedicated their lives to the name of our Lord Jesus Christ. Accordingly we are sending you Judas and Silas, who will confirm by word of mouth what we have written in this letter. It has been decided by the Holy Spirit and by ourselves not to saddle you with any burden beyond these essentials: you are to abstain from food sacrificed to idols, from blood, from the meat of strangled animals and from fornication. Avoid these, and you will do what is right. Farewell."

Responsional Psalm   Psalm 66.

R/ **Let the peoples praise you, O God;
let all the peoples praise you.**

or

   Alleluia!

1. O God, be gracious and bless us
   and let your face shed its light upon us.
   So will your ways be known upon earth
   and all nations learn your saving help.   R/

SIXTH SUNDAY OF EASTER/C

2. Let the nations be glad and exult
   for you rule the world with justice.
   With fairness you rule the peoples,
   you guide the nations on earth. ℟

3. Let the peoples praise you, O God;
   let all the peoples praise you.
   May God still give us his blessing
   till the ends of the earth revere him. ℟

Second Reading   Apocalypse 21:10-14.22-23.
He showed me the holy city coming down out of heaven.

In the spirit, the angel took me to the top of an enormous high mountain and showed me Jerusalem, the holy city, coming down from God out of heaven. It had all the radiant glory of God and glittered like some precious jewel of crystal-clear diamond. The walls of it were of a great height, and had twelve gates; at each of the twelve gates there was an angel, and over the gates were written the names of the twelve tribes of Israel; on the east there were three gates, on the north three gates, on the south three gates, and on the west three gates. The city walls stood on twelve foundation stones, each one of which bore the name of one of the twelve apostles of the Lamb.

I saw that there was no temple in the city since the Lord God Almighty and the Lamb were themselves the temple, and the city did not need the sun or the moon for light, since it was lit by the radiant glory of God and the Lamb was a lighted torch for it.

Alleluia
Alleluia, alleluia! Jesus said: "If anyone loves me he will keep my word, and my Father will love him, and we shall come to him. Alleluia! John 14:23.

Gospel   John 14:23-29.
The Holy Spirit will remind you of all I have said to you.

Jesus said to his disciples:
"If anyone loves me he will keep my word,
and my Father will love him,
and we shall come to him
and make our home with him.
Those who do not love me do not keep my words.
And my word is not my own:

SIXTH SUNDAY OF EASTER/C

it is the word of the one who sent me.
I have said these things to you
while still with you;
but the Advocate, the Holy Spirit,
whom the Father will send in my name,
will teach you everything
and remind you of all I have said to you.
Peace I bequeath to you,
my own peace I give you,
a peace the world cannot give, this is my gift to you.
Do not let your hearts be troubled or afraid.
You heard me say:
I am going away, and shall return.
If you loved me you would have been glad to know that I am
 going to the Father,
for the Father is greater than I.
I have told you this now before it happens,
so that when it does happen you may believe."

Prayer over the Gifts

Lord,
accept our prayers and offerings.
Make us worthy of your sacraments of love
by granting us your forgiveness.

Preface of Easter II-V, pages 561-562.

Communion Antiphon

If you love me, keep my commandments, says the Lord. The Father will send you the Holy Spirit, to be with you for ever, alleluia. John 14:15-16.

Prayer after Communion

Almighty and ever-living Lord,
you restored us to life
by raising Christ from death.
Strengthen us by this Easter sacrament.
may we feel its saving power in our daily life.

The priest may give the Solemn Blessing for Easter, on page 375, or another form on page 599.

THURSDAY OF THE SIXTH WEEK OF EASTER
THE ASCENSION OF THE LORD

Christ ascends to his Father!
Christ's Ascension is our guarantee
that one day we will be with him in heaven
to praise the glory of God our Father.
The Ascension is our hope of the great
inheritance which awaits those of us who
believe in the power of the risen Christ.

Entrance Antiphon Men of Galilee, why do you stand looking in the sky? The Lord will return, just as you have seen him ascend, alleluia.
Acts 1:11

Let us pray
  [that the risen Christ
  will lead us to eternal life]

God our Father,
make us joyful in the ascension of your Son Jesus Christ.
May we follow him into the new creation,
for his ascension is our glory and our hope.

or

Let us pray
  [on this day of Ascension
  as we watch and wait for Jesus' return]

Father in heaven,
our minds were prepared for the coming of your kingdom
when you took Christ beyond our sight
so that we might seek him in his glory.

May we follow where he has led
and find our hope in his glory,
for he is Lord for ever.

THE ASCENSION OF THE LORD/C

First Reading   Acts 1:1-11
He was lifted up while they looked on.

In my earlier work, Theophilus, I dealt with everything Jesus had done and taught from the beginning until the day he gave his instructions to the apostles he had chosen through the Holy Spirit, and was taken up to heaven. He had shown himself alive to them after his Passion by many demonstrations: for forty days he had continued to appear to them and tell them about the kingdom of God. When he had been at table with them, he had told them not to leave Jerusalem, but to wait there for what the Father had promised. "It is," he had said, "what you have heard me speak about: John baptised with water but you, not many days from now, will be baptised with the Holy Spirit."

Now having met together, they asked him, "Lord, has the time come? Are you going to restore the kingdom to Israel?" He replied, "It is not for you to know times or dates that the Father has decided by his own authority, but you will receive power when the Holy Spirit comes on you, and then you will be my witnesses not only in Jerusalem but throughout Judaea and Samaria, and indeed to the ends of the earth."

As he said this he was lifted up while they looked on, and a cloud took him from their sight. They were still staring into the sky when suddenly two men in white were standing near them and they said, "Why are you men from Galilee standing here looking into the sky? Jesus who has been taken up from you into heaven, this same Jesus will come back in the same way as you have seen him go there."

Responsorial Psalm   Psalm 46
℟ **God goes up with shouts of joy;**
  the Lord goes up with trumpet blast.

or

  Alleluia!

1. All peoples, clap your hands,
   cry to God with shouts of joy!
   For the Lord, the Most High, we must fear,
   great king over all the earth.   ℟

THE ASCENSION OF THE LORD/C

2. God goes up with shouts of joy;
   the Lord goes up with trumpet blast.
   Sing praise for God, sing praise,
   sing praise to our king, sing praise. ℟

3. God is king of all the earth.
   Sing praise with all your skill.
   God is king over the nations;
   God reigns on his holy throne. ℟

Second Reading   Ephesians 1:17-23
He made him sit at his right hand in heaven.

May the God of our Lord Jesus Christ, the Father of glory, give you a spirit of wisdom and perception of what is revealed, to bring you to full knowledge of him. May he enlighten the eyes of your mind so that you can see what hope his call holds for you, what rich glories he has promised the saints will inherit and how infinitely great is the power that he has exercised for us believers. This you can tell from the strength of his power at work in Christ, when he used it to raise him from the dead and to make him sit at his right hand in heaven, far above every Sovereignty, Authority, Power, or Domination, or any other name that can be named, not only in this age, but also in the age to come. He has put all things under his feet, and made him, as the ruler of everything, the head of the Church; which is his body, the fullness of him who fills the whole creation.

or

Second Reading   Hebrews 9:24-28. 10:19-23
Christ has entered heaven itself.

It is not as though Christ has entered a man-made sanctuary which was only modelled on the real one; but it was heaven itself, so that he could appear in the actual presence of God on our behalf. And he does not have to offer himself again and again, like the high priest going into the sanctuary year after year with the blood that is not his own, or else he would have had to suffer over and over again since the world began. Instead of that, he has made his appearance once and for all, now at the end of the last age, to do away with sin by sacrificing himself. Since men only die once, and after that comes judgement, so Christ, too, offers himself only

THE ASCENSION OF THE LORD/C

once to take the faults of many on himself, and when he appears a second time, it will not be to deal with sin but to reward with salvation those who are waiting for him.

In other words, brothers, through the blood of Jesus we have the right to enter the sanctuary, by a new way which he has opened for us, a living opening through the curtain, that is to say, his body. And we have the supreme high priest over all the house of God. So as we go in, let us be sincere in heart and filled with faith, our minds sprinkled and free from any trace of bad conscience and our bodies washed with pure water. Let us keep firm in the hope we profess, because the one who made the promise is faithful.

Alleluia

Alleluia, alleluia! Go, make disciples of all the nations; I am with you always; yes, to the end of time. Alleluia! Matthew 28:19-20.

Gospel   Luke 24:46-53

As he blessed them he was carried up to heaven.

Jesus said to his disciples: "You see how it is written that the Christ would suffer and on the third day rise from the dead, and that, in his name, repentance for the forgiveness of sins would be preached to all the nations, beginning from Jerusalem. You are witnesses to this.

"And now I am sending down to you what the Father has promised. Stay in the city then, until you are clothed with the power from on high."

Then he took them out as far as the outskirts of Bethany, and lifting up his hands he blessed them. Now as he blessed them, he withdrew from them and was carried up to heaven. They worshipped him and then went back to Jerusalem full of joy; and they were continually in the Temple praising God.

Prayer over the Gifts

Lord,
receive our offering
as we celebrate the ascension of Christ your Son.
May his gifts help us rise with him
to the joys of heaven,
where he lives and reigns for ever and ever.

THE ASCENSION OF THE LORD/C

Preface of Ascension I or II page 401

Communion Antiphon   I, the Lord, am with you always, until the end of the world, alleluia.
Matthew 28:20.

Prayer after communion

Father,
in this eucharist
we touch the divine life you give to the world.
Help us to follow Christ with love
to eternal life where he is Lord for ever and ever.

Solemn Blessing

Bow your heads and pray for God's blessing.

May almighty God bless you on this day
when his only Son ascended into heaven
to prepare a place for you.
℟ **Amen.**

After his resurrection, Christ was seen by his disciples.
When he appears as judge
may you be pleasing for ever in his sight.
℟ **Amen.**

You believe that Jesus has taken his seat in majesty
at the right hand of the Father.
May you have the joy of experiencing
that he is also with you to the end of time,
according to his promise.
℟ **Amen.**

May almighty God bless you,
the Father, and the Son, ✠ and the Holy Spirit.
℟ **Amen.**

SEVENTH SUNDAY OF EASTER/C

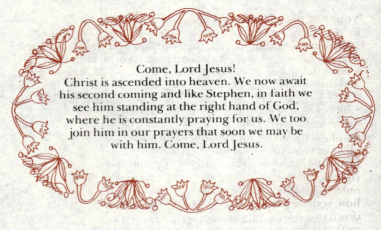

Come, Lord Jesus!
Christ is ascended into heaven. We now await
his second coming and like Stephen, in faith we
see him standing at the right hand of God,
where he is constantly praying for us. We too
join him in our prayers that soon we may be
with him. Come, Lord Jesus.

Entrance Antiphon Lord, hear my voice when I call to you. My heart has prompted me to seek your face; I seek it, Lord; do not hide from me, alleluia.

Psalm 26:7-9

Opening Prayer

Let us pray
  [that we may recognise
  the presence of Christ in our midst]

Father,
help us keep in mind that Christ our Saviour
lives with you in glory
and promised to remain with us until the end of time.

or

Let us pray
  [to our Father
  who has raised us to life in Christ]

Eternal Father,
reaching from end to end of the universe,
and ordering all things with your mighty arm:
for you, time is the unfolding of truth that already is,
the unveiling of beauty that is yet to be.

SEVENTH SUNDAY OF EASTER/C

Your Son has saved us in history
by rising from the dead,
so that transcending time he might free us from death.
May his presence among us
lead to the vision of unlimited truth
and unfold the beauty of your love.

First Reading   Acts 7:55-60.
I can see the Son of Man standing at the right hand of God.

Stephen, filled with the Holy Spirit, gazed into heaven and saw the glory of God, and Jesus standing at God's right hand. "I can see heaven thrown open" he said "and the Son of Man standing at the right hand of God." At this all the members of the council shouted out and stopped their ears with their hands; then they all rushed at him, sent him out of the city and stoned him. The witnesses put down their clothes at the feet of a young man called Saul. As they were stoning him, Stephen said in invocation, "Lord Jesus, receive my spirit." Then he knelt down and said aloud, "Lord, do not hold this sin against them"; and with these words he fell asleep.

Responsorial Psalm   Psalm 96.

R/ **The Lord is king, most high above all the earth.**

or

   Alleluia!

1. The Lord is king, let earth rejoice,
   the many coastlands be glad.
   His throne is justice and right. R/
2. The skies proclaim his justice;
   all peoples see his glory.
   All you spirits, worship him. R/
3. For you indeed are the Lord
   most high above all the earth
   exalted far above all spirits. R/

Second Reading   Apocalypse 22:12-14.16-17.20.
Come, Lord Jesus.

I, John, heard a voice speaking to me: "Very soon now, I shall be with you again, bringing the reward to be given to every man

SEVENTH SUNDAY OF EASTER/C

according to what he deserves. I am the Alpha and the Omega, the First and the Last, the Beginning and the End. Happy are those who will have washed their robes clean, so that they will have the right to feed on the tree of life and can come through the gates into the city."

I, Jesus, have sent my angel to make these revelations to you for the sake of the churches. I am of David's line, the root of David and the bright star of the morning.

The Spirit and the Bride say, "Come." Let everyone who listens answer, "Come." Then let all who are thirsty come; all who want it may have the water of life, and have it free.

The one who guarantees these revelations repeats his promise: I shall indeed be with you. Amen; come, Lord Jesus.

Alleluia Alleluia, alleluia! I will not leave you orphans, says the Lord; I will come back to you, and your hearts will be full of joy. Alleluia! John 14:18.

Gospel John 17:20-26.

May they be completely one.

Jesus raised his eyes to heaven and said:
"Holy Father,
I pray not only for these,
but for those also
who through their words will believe in me.
May they all be one.
Father, may they be one in us,
as you are in me and I am in you,
so that the world may believe it was you who sent me.
I have given them the glory you gave to me,
that they may be one as we are one.
With me in them and you in me,
may they be so completely one
that the world will realise that it was you who sent me
and that I have loved them as much as you loved me.
Father,
I want those you have given me
to be with me where I am,
so that they may always see the glory
you have given me
because you loved me

SEVENTH SUNDAY OF EASTER/C

before the foundation of the world.
Father, Righteous One,
the world has not known you,
but I have known you,
and these have known
that you have sent me.
I have made your name known to them
and will continue to make it known,
so that the love with which you loved me may be in them,
and so that I may be in them."

Prayer over the Gifts

Lord,
accept the prayers and gifts
we offer in faith and love.
May this eucharist
bring us to your glory.

Preface of the Ascension, page 401.

Communion Antiphon

This is the prayer of Jesus: that his believers may become one as he is one with the Father, alleluia. John 17:22.

Prayer after Communion

God our Saviour,
hear us,
and through this holy mystery give us hope
that the glory you have given Christ
will be given to the Church, his body,
for he is Lord for ever and ever.

The priest may give the Solemn Blessing for Easter on page 375, or another form on page 599.

PENTECOST SUNDAY

The coming of the Holy Spirit on the Church. The message 'Jesus is Lord' must be preached to every corner of the earth. We cannot do this unless we receive the Holy Spirit. Today we pray that we may be open to the power of the Spirit and that he will come and fill the hearts of the faithful.

Entrance Antiphon The Spirit of the Lord fills the whole world. It holds all things together and knows every word spoken by man, alleluia. Wisdom 1:7.

or

The love of God has been poured into our hearts by his Spirit living in us, alleluia.
cf. Romans 5:5;8:11

Opening Prayer

Let us pray
 [that the Spirit will work through our lives
 to bring Christ to the world]

God our Father,
let the Spirit you sent on your Church
to begin the teaching of the gospel
continue to work in the world
through the hearts of all who believe.

or

Let us pray
 [in the Spirit who dwells within us]

Father of light, from whom every good gift comes,

PENTECOST SUNDAY /A/B/C/

send your Spirit into our lives
with the power of a mighty wind,
and by the flame of your wisdom
open the horizons of our minds.

Loosen our tongues to sing your praise
in words beyond the power of speech,
for without your Spirit
man could never raise his voice in words of peace
or announce the truth that Jesus is Lord,
who lives and reigns with you and the Holy Spirit,
one God, for ever and ever.

The First Reading and Psalm are used in all three years

First Reading   Acts 2:1-11
They were all filled with the Holy Spirit and began to speak.

When Pentecost day came round, the apostles had all met in one room, when suddenly they heard what sounded like a powerful wind from heaven, the noise of which filled the entire house in which they were sitting; and something appeared to them that seemed like tongues of fire; these separated and came to rest on the head of each of them. They were all filled with the Holy Spirit, and began to speak foreign languages as the Spirit gave them the gift of speech.

Now there were devout men living in Jerusalem from every nation under heaven, and at this sound they all assembled, each one bewildered to hear these men speaking his own language. They were amazed and astonished. "Surely," they said, "all these men speaking are Galileans? How does it happen that each of us hears them in his own native language? Parthians, Medes and Elamites; people from Mesopotamia, Judaea and Cappadocia, Pontus and Asia, Phrygia and Pamphylia, Egypt and the parts of Libya round Cyrene; as well as visitors from Rome — Jews and proselytes alike — Cretans and Arabs; we hear them preaching in our own language about the marvels of God."

Responsorial Psalm   Psalm 103

R/ **Send forth your Spirit, O Lord,
and renew the face of the earth.**
or
   Alleluia!

PENTECOST SUNDAY A/B/C

1. Bless the Lord, my soul!
   Lord God, how great you are,
   How many are your works, O Lord!
   The earth is full of your riches. ℟

2. You take back your spirit, they die,
   returning to the dust from which they came.
   You send forth your spirit, they are created;
   and you renew the face of the earth. ℟

3. May the glory of the Lord last for ever!
   May the Lord rejoice in his works!
   May my thoughts be pleasing to him.
   I find my joy in the Lord. ℟

The Second Reading and Gospel A, B or C follow according to the year of the Cycle: Cycle A readings may be used in any year.

A

Second Reading   1 Corinthians 12:3-7.12-13

In the one Spirit we were all baptised.

No one can say, "Jesus is Lord" unless he is under the influence of the Holy Spirit.

There is a variety of gifts but always the same Spirit; there are all sorts of service to be done, but always to the same Lord; working in all sorts of different ways in different people, it is the same God who is working in all of them. The particular way in which the Spirit is given to each person is for a good purpose.

Just as a human body, though it is made up of many parts, is a single unit because all these parts, though many, make one body, so it is with Christ. In the one Spirit we were all baptized, Jews as well as Greeks, slaves as well as citizens, and one Spirit was given to us all to drink.

Sequence
The Sequence may be said or sung

Holy Spirit, Lord of Light,
From the clear celestial height
Thy pure beaming radiance give.
Come, thou Father of the poor,
Come with treasures which endure:
Come, thou light of all that live!

PENTECOST SUNDAY A/B/C

Thou, of all consoler's best,
Thou, the soul's delightful guest,
Dost refreshing peace bestow;
Thou in toil art comfort sweet;
Pleasant coolness in the heat;
Solace in the midst of woe.

Light immortal, light divine,
Visit thou these hearts of thine,
And our inmost being fill:
If thou take thy grace away,
Nothing pure in man will stay;
All his good is turned to ill.

Heal our wounds, our strength renew;
On our dryness pour thy dew;
Wash the stains of guilt away:
Bend the stubborn heart and will;
Melt the frozen, warm the chill;
Guide the steps that go astray.

Thou, on us who evermore
Thee confess and thee adore,
With thy sevenfold gifts descend:
Give us comfort when we die;
Give us life with thee on high;
Give us joys that never end.

Alleluia Alleluia, alleluia! Come, Holy Spirit, fill the hearts of your faithful, and kindle in them the fire of your love. Alleluia!

Gospel John 20:19-23

As the Father sent me, so am I sending you: receive the Holy Spirit.

In the evening of that same day, the first day of the week, the doors were closed in the room where the disciples were, for fear of the Jews. Jesus came and stood among them. He said to them, "Peace be with you," and showed them his hands and his side. The disciples were filled with joy when they saw the Lord, and he said to them again. "Peace be with you.
"As the Father sent me,
so am I sending you."

PENTECOST SUNDAY A/B/C

After saying this he breathed on them and said:
"Receive the Holy Spirit.
For those whose sins you forgive,
they are forgiven;
for those whose sins you retain,
they are retained."

B
Second Reading   Galatians 5:16-25
The fruit of the Spirit.

If you are guided by the Spirit you will be in no danger of yielding to self-indulgence, since self-indulgence is the opposite of the Spirit, the Spirit is totally against such a thing, and it is precisely because the two are so opposed that you do not always carry out your good intentions. If you are led by the Spirit, no law can touch you. When self-indulgence is at work the results are obvious: fornication, gross indecency and sexual irresponsibility; idolatry and sorcery; feuds and wrangling, jealousy, bad temper and quarrels; disagreements, factions, envy; drunkenness, orgies and similar things. I warn you now, as I warned you before: those who behave like this will not inherit the kingdom of God. What the Spirit brings is very different: love, joy, peace, patience, kindness, goodness, trustfulness, gentleness and self-control. There can be no law against things like that, of course. You cannot belong to Christ Jesus unless you crucify all self-indulgent passions and desire.

   Since the Spirit is our life, let us be directed by the Spirit.

Sequence on page 471

Alleluia   Alleluia, alleluia! Come, Holy Spirit, fill the hearts of your faithful and kindle in them the fire of your love. Alleluia!

Gospel   John 15:26-27; 16:12-15
The Spirit of truth will lead you to the complete truth.

Jesus said to his disciples:
"When the Advocate comes,
whom I shall send to you from the Father,
the Spirit of truth who issues from the Father,
he will be my witness.

PENTECOST SUNDAY A/B/C

And you will be my witnesses,
because you have been with me from the outset.
I still have many things to say to you
but they would be too much for you now.
But when the Spirit of truth comes
he will lead you to the complete truth,
since he will not be speaking as from himself
but will say only what he has learnt;
and he will tell you of the things to come.
He will glorify me,
since all he tells you
will be taken from what is mine.
Everything the Father has is mine;
that is why I said:
All he tells you
will be taken from what is mine."

C
Second Reading   Romans 8:8-17.
Everyone moved by the Spirit is a son of God.

People who are interested only in unspiritual things can never be pleasing to God. Your interests, however, are not in the unspiritual, since the Spirit of God has made his home in you. In fact, unless you possessed the Spirit of Christ you would not belong to him. Though your body may be dead it is because of sin, but if Christ is in you then your spirit is life itself because you have been justified; and if the Spirit of him who raised Jesus from the dead is living in you, then he who raised Jesus from the dead will give life to your own mortal bodies through his Spirit living in you.

So then, my brothers, there is no necessity for us to obey our unspiritual selves or to live unspiritual lives. If you do live in that way, you are doomed to die; but if by the Spirit you put an end to the misdeeds of the body you will live.

Everyone moved by the Spirit is a son of God. The spirit you received is not the spirit of slaves bringing fear into your lives again; it is the spirit of sons, and it makes us cry out, "Abba, Father!" The Spirit himself and our spirit bear united witness that we are children of God. And if we are children we are heirs as well: heirs of God and coheirs with Christ, suffering so as to share his glory.

PENTECOST SUNDAY/A/B/C

Alleluia Alleluia, alleluia! Come, Holy Spirit, fill the hearts of your faithful and kindle in them the fire of your love. Alleluia!

Gospel John 14:15-16. 23-26.
The Holy Spirit will teach you everything.
Jesus said to his disciples
"If you love me you will keep my commandments.
I shall ask the Father
and he will give you another Advocate
to be with you forever.
"If anyone loves me he will keep my word,
and my Father will love him,
and we shall come to him
and make our home with him.
Those who do not love me do not keep my words.
And my word is not my own;
it is the word of the one who sent me.
I have said these things to you
while still with you;
but the Advocate, the Holy Spirit,
whom the Father will send in my name,
will teach you everything
and remind you of all I have said to you."

Prayer over the Gifts

Lord,
may the Spirit you promised
lead us into all truth
and reveal to us the full meaning of this sacrifice.

Preface

Father, all-powerful and ever-living God,
we do well always and everywhere to give you thanks.

Today you sent the Holy Spirit
on those marked out to be your children
by sharing the life of your only Son,
and so you brought the paschal mystery to its completion.

PENTECOST SUNDAY A/B/C

Today we celebrate the great beginning of your Church
when the Holy Spirit made known to all peoples the one true God,
and created from the many languages of man
one voice to profess one faith.

The joy of the resurrection renews the whole world,
while the choirs of heaven sing for ever to your glory:
Holy, holy, holy ...

Communion Antiphon   They were all filled with the Holy Spirit, and they spoke of the great things God had done, alleluia.

Acts 2:4.11

Prayer after Communion

Father,
may the food we receive in the eucharist
help our eternal redemption.
Keep within us the vigour of your Spirit
and protect the gifts you have given to your Church.

Solemn Blessing

Bow your heads and pray for God's blessing.

This day the Father of light
has enlightened the minds of the disciples
by the outpouring of the Holy Spirit.
May he bless you
and give you the gifts of the Spirit for ever.
℟ **Amen.**

May that fire which hovered over the disciples
as tongues of flame
burn out all evil from your hearts
and make them glow with pure light.
℟ **Amen.**

God inspired speech in different tongues
to proclaim one faith.
May he strengthen your faith
and fulfil your hope to see him face to face.
℟ **Amen.**

May almighty God bless you,
the Father, and the Son, ✠ and the Holy Spirit.
℟ **Amen.**

SUNDAY AFTER PENTECOST
THE MOST HOLY TRINITY/A

Father, Son and Holy Spirit.
Through our life in Christ we live the
life of the Trinity. God is a perfect community
and if we model our lives on the Trinity
then the God of love and peace
will be with us.

Entrance Antiphon Blessed be God the Father and his only-begotten Son and the Holy Spirit: for he has shown that he loves us.

Opening Prayer

Let us pray
   [to the one God, Father, Son and Spirit,
   that our lives may bear witness to our faith]

Father,
you sent your Word to bring us truth
and your Spirit to make us holy.
Through them we come to know the mystery of your life.
Help us to worship you, one God in three Persons,
by proclaiming and living our faith in you.

or

Let us pray
[to our God who is Father, Son, and Holy Spirit]
God, we praise you:
Father all-powerful, Christ Lord and Saviour, Spirit of love.
You reveal yourself in the depths of our being,
drawing us to share in your life and your love.
One God, three Persons,
be near to the people formed in your image,
close to the world your love brings to life.

THE MOST HOLY TRINITY/A

First Reading   Exodus 34:4-6.8-9

Lord, Lord, a God of tenderness and compassion.

With the two tablets of stone in his hands, Moses went up the mountain of Sinai in the early morning as the Lord had commanded him. And the Lord descended in the form of a cloud, and Moses stood with him there.

He called on the name of the Lord. The Lord passed before him and proclaimed, "Lord, Lord, a God of tenderness and compassion, slow to anger, rich in kindness and faithfulness." And Moses bowed down to the ground at once and worshipped. "If I have indeed won your favour, Lord," he said, "let my Lord come with us, I beg. True, they are a headstrong people, but forgive us our faults and our sins, and adopt us as your heritage."

Responsorial Psalm   Daniel 3:52-56

1. You are blest, Lord God of our fathers.
   R/ To you glory and praise for evermore.
   Blest your glorious holy name.
   R/ To you glory and praise for evermore.

2. You are blest in the temple of your glory.
   R/ To you glory and praise for evermore.
   You are blest on the throne of your kingdom.
   R/ To you glory and praise for evermore.

3. You are blest who gaze into the depths.
   R/ To you glory and praise for evermore.
   You are blest in the firmament of heaven.
   R/ To you glory and praise for evermore.

Second Reading   2 Corinthians 13:11-13

The grace of Jesus Christ, the love of God, and the fellowship of the Holy Spirit.

Brothers, we wish you happiness; try to grow perfect; help one another. Be united; live in peace, and the God of love and peace will be with you.

Greet one another with the holy kiss. All the saints send you greetings.

The grace of the Lord Jesus Christ, the love of God and the fellowship of the Holy Spirit be with you all.

THE MOST HOLY TRINITY/A

Alleluia Alleluia, alleluia! Glory be to the Father, and to the Son, and to the Holy Spirit, the God who is, who was, and who is to come. Alleluia! Revelation 1:8.

Gospel John 3:16-18

God sent his Son so that through him the world might be saved.

Jesus said to Nicodemus,
"God loved the world so much
that he gave his only Son,
so that everyone who believes in him may not be lost
but may have eternal life.
For God sent his Son into the world
not to condemn the world,
but so that through him the world might be saved.
No one who believes in him will be condemned;
but whoever refuses to believe is condemned already,
because he has refused to believe
in the name of God's only Son."

Prayer over the Gifts

Lord our God,
make these gifts holy,
and through them
make us a perfect offering to you.

Preface

Father, all-powerful and ever-living God,
we do well always and everywhere to give you thanks.

We joyfully proclaim our faith
in the mystery of your Godhead.
You have revealed your glory
as the glory also of your Son
and of the Holy Spirit:
three Persons equal in majesty,
undivided in splendour,
yet one Lord, one God,
ever to be adored in your everlasting glory.

And so, with all the choirs of angels in heaven
we proclaim your glory
and join in their unending hymn of praise:
Holy, holy, holy ...

THE MOST HOLY TRINITY/A

Communion Antiphon — You are the sons of God, so God has given you the Spirit of his Son to form your hearts and make you cry out: Abba, Father. Galatians 4:6.

Prayer after Communion
Lord God,
we worship you, a Trinity of Persons, one eternal God.
May our faith and the sacrament we receive
bring us health of mind and body.

SUNDAY AFTER PENTECOST
THE MOST HOLY TRINITY/B

> You received the spirit of sons.
> We have received the Holy Spirit
> who makes us aware that we are truly
> God's children and not his slaves. We are free
> with the unique freedom of those whom
> God has chosen as his own. Our spirit
> and God's spirit become one as
> we call God 'Abba, Father'.

Entrance Antiphon Blessed be God the Father and his only-begotten Son and the Holy Spirit: for he has shown that he loves us.

Opening Prayer

Let us pray
 [to the one God, Father, Son and Spirit,
 that our lives may bear witness to our faith]

Father,
you sent your Word to bring us truth
and your Spirit to make us holy.
Through them we come to know the mystery of your life.
Help us to worship you, one God in three Persons,
by proclaiming and living our faith in you.

or

Let us pray
 [to our God who is Father, Son, and Holy Spirit]

God, we praise you:
Father all-powerful, Christ Lord and Saviour, Spirit of love.
You reveal yourself in the depths of our being,
drawing us to share in your life and your love.
One God, three Persons,

THE MOST HOLY TRINITY/B

be near to the people formed in your image,
close to the world your love brings to life.

First Reading   Deuteronomy 4:32-34.39-40.

The Lord is God indeed, in heaven above as on earth beneath, he and no other.

Moses said to the people: "Put this question, then, to the ages that are past, that went before you, from the time God created man on earth: Was there ever a word so majestic, from one end of heaven to the other? Was anything ever heard? Did ever a people hear the voice of the living God speaking from the heart of the fire, as you heard it, and remain alive? Has any god ventured to take to himself one nation from the midst of another by ordeals, signs, wonders, war with mighty hand and outstretched arm, by fearsome terrors — all this that the Lord your God did for you before your eyes in Egypt?

"Understand this today, therefore, and take it to heart: The Lord is God indeed, in heaven above as on earth beneath, he and no other. Keep his laws and commandments as I give them to you today, so that you and your children may prosper and live long in the land that the Lord your God gives you for ever."

Responsorial Psalm   Psalm 32.

R/ **Happy the people the Lord has chosen as his own.**

1. The word of the Lord is faithful
   and all his works to be trusted.
   The Lord loves justice and right
   and fills the earth with his love. R/

2. By his word the heavens were made,
   by the breath of his mouth all the stars.
   He spoke; and they came to be.
   He commanded; they sprang into being. R/

3. The Lord looks on those who revere him,
   on those who hope in his love,
   to rescue their souls from death,
   to keep them alive in famine. R/

4. Our soul is waiting for the Lord.
   The Lord is our help and our shield.
   May your love be upon us, O Lord,
   as we place all our hope in you. R/

THE MOST HOLY TRINITY/B

Second Reading   Romans 8:14-17.

You received the spirit of sons, and it makes us cry out, "Abba, Father!"

Everyone moved by the Spirit is a son of God. The spirit you received is not the spirit of slaves bringing fear into your lives again; it is the spirit of sons, and it makes us cry out, "Abba, Father!" The Spirit himself and our spirit bear united witness that we are children of God. And if we are children we are heirs as well: heirs of God and coheirs with Christ, sharing his sufferings so as to share his glory.

Alleluia

Alleluia, alleluia! Glory be to the Father, and to the Son, and to the Holy Spirit, the God who is, who was, and who is to come. Alleluia! Revelation 1:8.

Gospel   Matthew 28:16-20.

Baptise them in the name of the Father and of the Son and of the Holy Spirit.

The eleven disciples set out for Galilee, to the mountain where Jesus had arranged to meet them. When they saw him they fell down before him, though some hesitated. Jesus came up and spoke to them. He said, "All authority in heaven and on earth has been given to me. Go, therefore, make disciples of all the nations; baptise them in the name of the Father and of the Son and of the Holy Spirit, and teach them to observe all the commands I gave you. And know that I am with you always; yes, to the end of time."

Prayer over the Gifts

Lord our God,
make these gifts holy,
and through them
make us a perfect offering to you.

Preface

Father, all-powerful and ever-living God,
we do well always and everywhere to give you thanks.

We joyfully proclaim our faith
in the mystery of your Godhead.
You have revealed your glory

THE MOST HOLY TRINITY/B

as the glory also of your Son
and of the Holy Spirit:
three Persons equal in majesty,
undivided in splendour,
yet one Lord, one God,
ever to be adored in your everlasting glory.

And so, with all the choirs of angels in heaven
we proclaim your glory
and join in their unending hymn of praise:

Holy, holy, holy ...

Communion Antiphon   You are the sons of God, so God has given you the Spirit of his Son to form your hearts and make you cry out: Abba, Father. Galatians 4:6.

Prayer after Communion

Lord God,
we worship you, a Trinity of Persons, one eternal God.
May our faith and the sacrament we receive
bring us health of mind and body.

SUNDAY AFTER PENTECOST
THE MOST HOLY TRINITY/C

The Spirit will lead you to the complete truth. The spirit of truth existed before the earth came into being. Jesus promises us the Holy Spirit who will lead us into the fulness of truth provided we are prepared to pay the price. We persevere in hope knowing that the love of God has been poured out into our heart by the Holy Spirit. The Spirit leads us into a deeper understanding of what the Gospel of Christ really means.

Entrance Antiphon   Blessed be God the Father and his only-begotten Son and the Holy Spirit: for he has shown that he loves us.

Opening Prayer
Let us pray
  [to the one God, Father, Son and Spirit,
   that our lives may bear witness to our faith]

Father,
you sent your Word to bring us truth
and your Spirit to make us holy.
Through them we come to know the mystery of your life.
Help us to worship you, one God in three Persons,
by proclaiming and living our faith in you.

or

Let us pray
  [to our God who is Father, Son, and Holy Spirit]

God, we praise you:
Father all-powerful, Christ Lord and Saviour, Spirit of love.
You reveal yourself in the depths of our being,

THE MOST HOLY TRINITY/C

drawing us to share in your life and your love.
One God, three Persons,
be near to the people formed in your image,
close to the world your love brings to life.

First Reading   Proverbs 8:22-31.
Before the earth came into being, Wisdom was born.

The Wisdom of God cries aloud,
The Lord created me when his purpose first unfolded,
before the oldest of his works.
From everlasting I was firmly set,
from the beginning, before earth came into being.
The deep was not, when I was born,
there were no springs to gush with water.
Before the mountains were settled,
before the hills, I came to birth;
before he made the earth, the countryside,
or the first grains of the world's dust.
When he fixed the heavens firm, I was there,
when he drew a ring on the surface of the deep,
when he thickened the clouds above,
when he fixed fast the springs of the deep,
when he assigned the sea its boundaries
— and the waters will not invade the shore —
when he laid down the foundations of the earth,
I was by his side, a master craftsman,
delighting him day after day,
ever at play in his presence,
at play everywhere in his world,
delighting to be with the sons of men.

Responsorial Psalm   Psalm 8.

R/ **How great is your name, O Lord our God,
through all the earth!**

1. When I see the heavens, the work of your hands,
   the moon and the stars which you arranged,
   what is man that you should keep him in mind,
   mortal man that you care for him?   R/

THE MOST HOLY TRINITY/C

2. Yet you have made him little less than a god;
   with glory and honour you crowned him,
   gave him power over the works of your hand,
   put all things under his feet. R/

3. All of them, sheep and cattle,
   yes, even the savage beasts,
   birds of the air, and fish
   that make their way through the waters. R/

Second Reading   Romans 5:1-5.

To God, through Christ, in the love poured out by the Spirit.

Through our Lord Jesus Christ, by faith we are judged righteous and at peace with God, since it is by faith and through Jesus that we have entered this state of grace in which we can boast about looking forward to God's glory. But that is not all we can boast about; we can boast about our sufferings. These sufferings bring patience, as we know, and patience brings perseverance, and perseverance brings hope, and this hope is not deceptive, because the love of God has been poured into our hearts by the Holy Spirit which has been given us.

Alleluia   Alleluia, alleluia! Glory be to the Father, and to the Son, and to the Holy Spirit, the God who is, who was, and who is to come. Alleluia! Revelation 1:8.

Gospel   John 16:12-15.

Everything the Father has is mine; all the Spirit tells you will be taken from what is mine.

Jesus said to his disciples:
"I still have many things to say to you
but they would be too much for you now.
But when the Spirit of truth comes
he will lead you to the complete truth,
since he will not be speaking as from himself
but will say only what he has learnt;
and he will tell you of the things to come.
He will glorify me,
since all he tells you
will be taken from what is mine.
Everything the Father has is mine;

THE MOST HOLY TRINITY/C

that is why I said:
All he tells you
will be taken from what is mine."

Prayer over the Gifts

Lord our God,
make these gifts holy,
and through them
make us a perfect offering to you.

Preface of the Holy Trinity, page 479.

Communion Antiphon

You are the sons of God, so God has given you the Spirit of his Son to form your hearts and make you cry out: Abba, Father. Galatians 4:6.

Prayer after Communion

Lord God,
we worship you, a Trinity of Persons, one eternal God.
May our faith and the sacrament we receive
bring us health of mind and body.

THURSDAY AFTER TRINITY SUNDAY
CORPUS CHRISTI/A
THE BODY AND BLOOD OF CHRIST

Christ is our food and drink.
Just as in human life we need food and
drink so we need Christ to sustain us in our
spiritual lives. He feeds us with himself just as
God fed the Jews with manna in the
wilderness. Our sharing of the one Body
and Blood of Christ means that we share
with each other Christ's eternal life.

Entrance Antiphon   The Lord fed his people with the finest wheat and honey; their hunger was satisfied. Psalm 80:17.

Opening Prayer

Let us pray
  [to the Lord who gives himself in the eucharist,
   that this sacrament may bring us salvation
   and peace]

Lord Jesus Christ,
you gave us this eucharist
as the memorial of your suffering and death.
May our worship of this sacrament of your body and blood
help us to experience the salvation you won for us
and the peace of the kingdom
where you live with the Father and the Holy Spirit,
one God, for ever and ever.

or

Let us pray
  [for the willingness to make present in our world
   the love of Christ shown to us in the eucharist]

CORPUS CHRISTI/A

Lord Jesus Christ,
we worship you living among us
in the sacrament of your body and blood.

May we offer to our Father in heaven
a solemn pledge of undivided love.
May we offer to our brothers and sisters
a life poured out in loving service of that kingdom
where you live with the Father and the Holy Spirit,
one God, for ever and ever.

First Reading   Deuteronomy 8:2-3.14-16

He fed you with manna which neither you nor your fathers had known.

Moses said to the people: "Remember how the Lord your God led you for forty years in the wilderness, to humble you, to test you and know your inmost heart — whether you would keep his commandments or not. He humbled you, he made you feel hunger, he fed you with manna which neither you nor your fathers had known, to make you understand that man does not live on bread alone but that man lives on everything that comes from the mouth of the Lord.

"Do not then forget the Lord your God who brought you out of the land of Egypt, out of the house of slavery: who guided you through this vast and dreadful wilderness, a land of fiery serpents, scorpions, thirst; who in this waterless place brought you water from the hardest rock; who in this wilderness fed you with manna that your fathers had not known."

Responsorial Psalm   Psalm 147

℟ **O praise the Lord, Jerusalem!**
or
   Alleluia!

1. O praise the Lord, Jerusalem!
   Zion, praise your God!
   He has strenghtened the bars of your gates,
   he has blessed the children within you.   ℟

2. He established peace on your borders,
   he feeds you with finest wheat.
   He sends out his word to the earth
   and swiftly runs his command.   ℟

CORPUS CHRISTI/A

3. He makes his work known to Jacob,
   to Israel his laws and decrees.
   He has not dealt thus with other nations;
   he has not taught them his decrees.
   Alleluia! ℟

Second Reading   1 Corinthians 10:16-17

That there is only one loaf means that, though there are many of us, we form a single body.

The blessing-cup that we bless is a communion with the blood of Christ, and the bread that we break is a communion with the body of Christ. The fact that there is only one loaf means that, though there are many of us, we form a single body because we all have a share in this one loaf.

Sequence

Behold the bread of angels, sent
For the pilgrims in their banishment,
The bread for God's true children meant,
   That may not unto dogs be given:
Oft in the olden types foreshadowed;
In Isaac on the altar bowed,
And in the ancient paschal food,
   And in the manna sent from heaven.

Come then, good shepherd, bread divine,
Still to us show they mercy sign;
Oh, feed us still, still keep us thine;
So we may see thy glories shine;
   In the fields of immortality;
O thou, the wisest, mightiest best,
Our present food, our future rest,
Come, make us each thy chosen guest,
Co-heirs of thine, and comrades blest
   With saints whose dwelling is with thee.

Alleluia   Alleluia, alleluia! I am the living bread which has come down from heaven, says the Lord. Anyone who eats this bread will live for ever. Alleluia!
                                                         John 6:51-52.

CORPUS CHRISTI/A

Gospel John 6:51-58

My flesh is real food and my blood is real drink.

Jesus said to the Jews:
"I am the living bread which has come down from heaven.
Anyone who eats this bread will live for ever;
and the bread that I shall give
is my flesh, for the life of the world."

  Then the Jews started arguing with one another: "How can this man give us his flesh to eat?" they said. Jesus replied:
"I tell you most solemnly,
if you do not eat the flesh of the Son of Man
and drink his blood,
you will not have life in you.
Anyone who does eat my flesh and drink my blood
has eternal life,
and I shall raise him up on the last day.
For my flesh is real food
and my blood is real drink.
He who eats my flesh and drinks my blood
lives in me
and I live in him.
As I, who am sent by the living Father,
myself draw life from the Father,
so whoever eats me will draw life from me.
This is the bread come down from heaven;
not like the bread our ancestors ate:
they are dead,
but anyone who eats this bread will live for ever."

Prayer over the Gifts

Lord,
may the bread and cup we offer
bring your Church the unity and peace they signify.

Preface

The priest may use the Preface which follows or the Preface of Holy Thursday, page 302.

Father, all-powerful and ever-living God,
we do well always and everywhere to give you thanks
through Jesus Christ our Lord.

CORPUS CHRISTI/A

At the last supper,
as he sat at table with his apostles,
he offered himself to you as the spotless lamb,
the acceptable gift that gives you perfect praise.
Christ has given us this memorial of his passion
to bring us its saving power until the end of time.

In this great sacrament you feed your people
and strengthen them in holiness,
so that the family of mankind
may come to walk in the light of one faith,
in one communion of love.
We come then to this wonderful sacrament
to be fed at your table
and grow into the likeness of the risen Christ.

Earth unites with heaven
to sing the new song of creation
as we adore and praise you for ever:

Holy, holy, holy ...

Communion Antiphon

Whoever eats my flesh and drinks my blood will live in me and I in him, says the Lord. **John 6:57**.

Prayer after Communion

Lord Jesus Christ,
you give us your body and blood in the eucharist
as a sign that even now we share your life.
May we come to possess it completely in the kingdom
where you live for ever and ever.

THURSDAY AFTER TRINITY SUNDAY
CORPUS CHRISTI/B

This is My Body. This is My Blood. Christ is our high priest who constantly makes intercession for us. He offers himself to his Father as an atonement for our sins and establishes a new covenant or pact with God which is his own body and blood. This is far greater than the old Jewish sacrifice of goats and bull calves. It wins for us the eternal inheritance which we have been promised.

Entrance Antiphon   The Lord fed his people with the finest wheat and honey; their hunger was satisfied. Psalm 80:17.

Opening Prayer

Let us pray
  [to the Lord who gives himself in the eucharist,
   that this sacrament may bring us salvation and peace]

Lord Jesus Christ,
you gave us the eucharist
as the memorial of your suffering and death.
May our worship of this sacrament of your body and blood
help us to experience the salvation you won for us
and the peace of the kingdom
where you live with the Father and the Holy Spirit,
one God, for ever and ever.

or

Let us pray
  [for the willingness to make present in our world
   the love of Christ shown to us in the eucharist]

Lord Jesus Christ,

CORPUS CHRISTI/B

we worship you living among us
in the sacrament of your body and blood.

May we offer to our Father in heaven
a solemn pledge of undivided love.
May we offer to our brothers and sisters
a life poured out in loving service of that kingdom
where you live with the Father and the Holy Spirit,
one God, for ever and ever.

First Reading   Exodus 24:3-8.

This is the blood of the Covenant that the Lord has made with you.

Moses went and told the people all the commands of the Lord and all the ordinances. In answer, all the people said with one voice, "We will observe all the commands that the Lord has decreed." Moses put all the commands of the Lord into writing, and early next morning he built an altar at the foot of the mountain, with twelve standing-stones for the twelve tribes of Israel. Then he directed certain young Israelites to offer holocausts and to immolate bullocks to the Lord as communion sacrifices. Half of the blood Moses took up and put into basins, the other half he cast on the altar. And taking the Book of the Covenant he read it to the listening people, and they said, "We will observe all that the Lord has decreed; we will obey." Then Moses took the blood and cast it towards the people. "This" he said "is the blood of the Covenant that the Lord has made with you, containing all these rules."

Responsorial Psalm   Psalm 115.

℟ **The cup of salvation I will raise;
I will call on the Lord's name.**

1. How can I repay the Lord
   for his goodness to me?
   The cup of salvation I will raise;
   I will call on the Lord's name.   ℟

2. O precious in the eyes of the Lord
   is the death of his faithful.
   Your servant, Lord, your servant am I;
   you have loosened my bonds.   ℟

CORPUS CHRISTI/B

3. A thanksgiving sacrifice I make:
   I will call on the Lord's name.
   My vows to the Lord I will fulfil
   before all his people. ℟

Second Reading Hebrews 9:11-15.

The blood of Christ can purify our inner self from dead actions.

Now Christ has come, as the high priest of all the blessings which were to come. He has passed through the greater, the more perfect tent, which is better than one made by men's hands because it is not of this created order; and he has entered the sanctuary once and for all, taking with him not the blood of goats and bull calves, but his own blood, having won an eternal redemption for us. The blood of goats and bulls and the ashes of a heifer are sprinkled on those who have incurred defilement and they restore the holiness of their outward lives; how much more effectively the blood of Christ, who offered himself as the perfect sacrifice to God through the eternal Spirit, can purify our inner self from dead actions so that we do our service to the living God.

He brings a new covenant, as the mediator, only so that the people who were called to an eternal inheritance may actually receive what was promised: his death took place to cancel the sins that infringed the earlier covenant.

The Sequence may be sung or said: see page 491

Alleluia Alleluia, alleluia! I am the living bread which has come down from heaven, says the Lord. Anyone who eats this bread will live for ever. Alleluia!

John 6:51-52

Gospel Mark 14:12-16.22-26.

This is my body. This is my blood.

On the first day of Unleavened Bread, when the Passover lamb was sacrificed, his disciples said to Jesus, "Where do you want us to go and make the preparations for you to eat the passover?" So he sent two of his disciples, saying to them, "Go into the city and you will meet a man carrying a pitcher of water. Follow him, and say to the owner of the house which he enters, 'The Master says: Where is my dining room in which I can eat the passover with my disciples?' He will show you a large upper room furnished with couches, all prepared. Make the preparations for us there." The

CORPUS CHRISTI/B

disciples set out and went to the city and found everything as he had told them, and prepared the Passover.

And as they were eating he took some bread, and when he had said the blessing he broke it and gave it to them, "Take it," he said "this is my body." Then he took a cup, and when he had returned thanks he gave it to them, and all drank from it, and he said to them, "This is my blood, the blood of the covenant, which is to be poured out for many. I tell you solemnly, I shall not drink any more wine until the day I drink the new wine in the kingdom of God."

After psalms had been sung they left for the Mount of Olives.

Prayer over the Gifts

Lord,
may the bread and cup we offer
bring your Church the unity and peace they signify.

Preface

Father, all-powerful and ever-living God,
we do well always and everywhere to give you thanks
through Jesus Christ our Lord.

At the last supper,
as he sat at table with his apostles,
he offered himself to you as the spotless lamb,
the acceptable gift that gives you perfect praise.
Christ has given us this memorial of his passion
to bring us its saving power until the end of time.

In this great sacrament you feed your people
and strengthen them in holiness,
so that the family of mankind
may come to walk in the light of one faith,
in one communion of love.
We come then to this wonderful sacrament
to be fed at your table
and grow into the likeness of the risen Christ.

Earth unites with heaven
to sing the new song of creation
as we adore and praise you for ever:

Holy, holy, holy ...

CORPUS CHRISTI/B

or the Preface of the Holy Eucharist I, as at Holy Thursday, may be said, page 302.

Communion Antiphon

Whoever eats my flesh and drinks my blood will live in me and I in him, says the Lord. John 6:57.

Prayer after Communion

Lord Jesus Christ,
you give us your body and blood in the eucharist
as a sign that even now we share your life.
May we come to possess it completely in the kingdom
where you live for ever and ever.

THURSDAY AFTER TRINITY SUNDAY
CORPUS CHRISTI/C

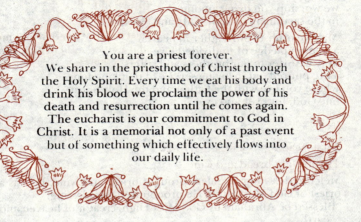

You are a priest forever.
We share in the priesthood of Christ through
the Holy Spirit. Every time we eat his body and
drink his blood we proclaim the power of his
death and resurrection until he comes again.
The eucharist is our commitment to God in
Christ. It is a memorial not only of a past event
but of something which effectively flows into
our daily life.

Entrance Antiphon   The Lord fed his people with the finest wheat and honey; their hunger was satisfied. Psalm 80:17.

Opening Prayer

Let us pray
   [to the Lord who gives himself in the eucharist,
   that this sacrament may bring us salvation
   and peace]

Lord Jesus Christ,
you gave us the eucharist
as the memorial of your suffering and death.
May our worship of this sacrament of your body and blood
help us to experience the salvation you won for us
and the peace of the kingdom
where you live with the Father and the Holy Spirit,
one God, for ever and ever.

or

Let us pray
   [for the willingness to make present in our world
   the love of Christ shown to us in the eucharist]

CORPUS CHRISTI/C

Lord Jesus Christ,
we worship you living among us
in the sacrament of your body and blood.

May we offer to our Father in heaven
a solemn pledge of undivided love.
May we offer to our brothers and sisters
a life poured out in loving service of that kingdom
where you live with the Father and the Holy Spirit,
one God, for ever and ever.

First Reading   Genesis 14:18-20.
He brought bread and wine.

Melchizedek king of Salem brought bread and wine; he was a priest of God Most High. He pronounced this blessing:
"Blessed be Abraham by God Most High, creator of heaven and earth,
and blessed be God Most High for handing over your enemies to you."
And Abraham gave him a tithe of everything.

Responsorial Psalm   Psalm 109.

**R/ You are a priest for ever,
a priest like Melchizedek of old.**

1. The Lord's revelation to my Master:
   "Sit on my right:
   I will put your foes beneath your feet."   R/

2. The Lord will send from Zion
   your sceptre of power:
   rule in the midst of all your foes.   R/

3. A prince from the day of your birth
   on the holy mountains;
   from the womb before the daybreak I begot you.   R/

4. The Lord has sworn an oath he will not change.
   "You are a priest for ever,
   a priest like Melchizedek of old."   R/

CORPUS CHRISTI/C

Second Reading 1 Corinthians 11:23-26.

Every time you eat this bread and drink this cup, you are proclaiming the Lord's death.

This is what I received from the Lord, and in turn passed on to you: that on the same night that he was betrayed, the Lord Jesus took some bread, and thanked God for it and broke it, and he said, "This is my body, which is for you; do this as a memorial of me." In the same way he took the cup after supper, and said, "This cup is the new covenant in my blood. Whenever you drink it, do this as a memorial of me." Until the Lord comes, therefore, every time you eat this bread and drink this cup, you are proclaiming his death.

The Sequence may be sung or said: see page 491.

Alleluia   Alleluia, alleluia! I am the living bread which has come down from heaven, says the Lord. Anyone who eats this bread will live for ever. Alleluia!

John 6:51-52

Gospel Luke 9:11-17.

They all ate as much as they wanted.

Jesus made the crowds welcome and talked to them about the kingdom of God; and he cured those who were in need of healing.

It was late afternoon when the Twelve came to him and said, "Send the people away, and they can go to the villages and farms round about to find lodging and food; for we are in a lonely place here." He replied, "Give them something to eat yourselves." But they said, "We have no more than five loaves and two fish, unless we are to go ourselves and buy food for all these people." For there were about five thousand men. But he said to his disciples, "Get them to sit down in parties of about fifty." They did so and made them all sit down. Then he took the five loaves and the two fish, raised his eyes to heaven, and said the blessing over them; then he broke them and handed them to his disciples to distribute among the crowd. They all ate as much as they wanted, and when the scraps remaining were collected they filled twelve baskets.

Prayer over the Gifts

Lord,
may the bread and cup we offer
bring your Church the unity and peace they signify.

CORPUS CHRISTI/C

Preface of the Holy Eucharist page 492: or the Preface of Holy Thursday, page 302, may be said.

Communion Antiphon Whoever eats my flesh and drinks my blood will live in me and I in him, says the Lord. John 6:57.

Prayer after Communion
Lord Jesus Christ,
you give us your body and blood in the eucharist
as a sign that even now we share your life.
May we come to possess it completely in the kingdom
where you live for ever and ever.

FRIDAY AFTER THE SECOND SUNDAY OF PENTECOST
THE SACRED HEART OF JESUS/A

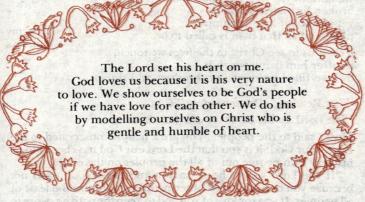

The Lord set his heart on me.
God loves us because it is his very nature
to love. We show ourselves to be God's people
if we have love for each other. We do this
by modelling ourselves on Christ who is
gentle and humble of heart.

Entrance Antiphon The thoughts of his heart last through every generation, that he will rescue them from death and feed them in time of famine. **Psalm 32:11.19.**

Opening Prayer

Let us pray
  [that we will respond to the love of Christ]

Father,
we rejoice in the gifts of love
we have received from the heart of Jesus your Son.
Open our hearts to share his life
and continue to bless us with his love.

or

Father,
we have wounded the heart of Jesus your Son,
but he brings us forgiveness and grace.
Help us to prove our grateful love
and make amends for our sins.

or

Let us pray
  [that the love of Christ's heart
  may touch the world with healing and peace]

THE SACRED HEART/A

Father,
we honour the heart of your Son
broken by man's cruelty,
yet symbol of love's triumph,
pledge of all that man is called to be.

Teach us to see Christ in the lives we touch,
to offer him living worship
by love-filled service to our brothers and sisters.

First Reading   Deuteronomy 7:6-11
The Lord set his heart on you and chose you.

Moses said to the people: "You are a people consecrated to the Lord your God; it is you that the Lord our God has chosen to be his very own people out of all the peoples on the earth.

"If the Lord set his heart on you and chose you, it was not because you outnumbered other peoples: you were the least of all peoples. It was for love of you and to keep the oath he swore to your fathers that the Lord brought you out with his mighty hand and redeemed you from the house of slavery, from the power of Pharaoh king of Egypt. Know then that the Lord your God is God indeed, the faithful God who is true to his covenant and his graciousness for a thousand generations towards those who love him and keep his commandments, but who punishes in their own persons those that hate him. He makes him work out his punishment in person. You are therefore to keep and observe the commandments and statutes and ordinances that I lay down for you today."

Responsional Psalm   Psalm 102

℟ **The love of the Lord is everlasting
  upon those who hold him in fear.**

1. My soul, give thanks to the Lord,
   all my being, bless his holy name.
   My soul, give thanks to the Lord
   and never forget all his blessings.   ℟

2. It is he who forgives all your guilt,
   who heals every one of your ills,
   who redeems your life from the grave,
   who crowns you with love and compassion.   ℟   (continued)

THE SACRED HEART/A

³The Lord does deeds of justice,
gives judgement for all who are oppressed.
He made known his ways to Moses
and his deeds to Israel's sons. ℟

⁴The Lord is compassion and love,
slow to anger and rich in mercy.
He does not treat us according to our sins
nor repay us according to our faults. ℟

Second Reading 1 John 4:7-16.

Love comes from God.

My dear people,
let us love one another
since love comes from God
and everyone who loves is begotten by God and knows God.
Anyone who fails to love can never have known God,
because God is love.
God's love for us was revealed
when God sent into the world his only Son
so that we could have life through him;
this is the love I mean:
not our love for God,
but God's love for us when he sent his Son
to be the sacrifice that takes our sins away.
My dear people,
since God has loved us so much,
we too should love one another.
No one has ever seen God;
but as long as we love one another
God will live in us
and his love will be complete in us.
We can know that we are living in him
and he is living in us
because he lets us share his spirit.
We ourselves saw and we testify
that the Father sent his son
as saviour of the world.
If anyone acknowledges that Jesus is the Son of God,
God lives in him, and he in God.
We ourselves have known and put our faith in God's love
   towards ourselves.

THE SACRED HEART/A

God is love
and anyone who lives in love lives in God,
and God lives in him.

Alleluia Alleluia, alleluia! Shoulder my yoke and learn from me, for I am gentle and humble in heart. Alleluia.

Matthew 11:29

Gospel Matthew 11:25-30
I am gentle and humble in heart.

Jesus exclaimed, "I bless you, Father, Lord of heaven and of earth, for hiding these things from the learned and the clever and revealing them to mere children. Yes, Father, for that is what it pleased you to do. Everything has been entrusted to me by my Father; and no one knows the Son except the Father, just as no one knows the Father except the Son and those to whom the Son chooses to reveal him.

"Come to me, all you who labour and are overburdened and I will give you rest. Shoulder my yoke and learn from me, for I am gentle and humble in heart, and you will find rest for your souls. Yes, my yoke is easy and my burden light."

Prayer over the Gifts

Lord,
look on the heart of Christ your Son
filled with love for us.
Because of his love
accept our eucharist and forgive our sins.

Preface

Father, all-powerful and ever-living God,
we do well always and everywhere to give you thanks
through Jesus Christ our Lord.

Lifted high on the cross,
Christ gave his life for us,
so much did he love us.
From his wounded side flowed blood and water,
the fountain of sacramental life in the Church.
To his open heart the Saviour invites all men,

THE SACRED HEART/A

to draw water in joy from the springs of salvation.
Now, with all the saints and angels,
we praise you for ever:
Holy, holy, holy . . .

Communion Antiphon The Lord says: If anyone is thirsty, let him come to me; whoever believes in me, let him drink. Streams of living water shall flow out from within him.
John 7:37-38
or
One of the soldiers pierced Jesus' side with a lance, and at once there flowed out blood and water.
John 19:34.

Prayer after Communion
Father,
may this sacrament fill us with love.
Draw us closer to Christ your Son
and help us to recognise him in others.

FRIDAY AFTER THE SECOND SUNDAY OF PENTECOST
THE SACRED HEART OF JESUS/B

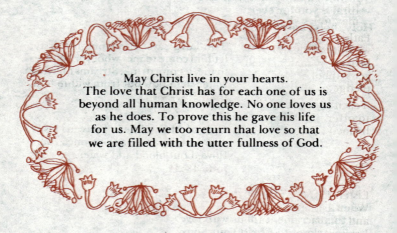

May Christ live in your hearts. The love that Christ has for each one of us is beyond all human knowledge. No one loves us as he does. To prove this he gave his life for us. May we too return that love so that we are filled with the utter fullness of God.

Entrance Antiphon The thoughts of his heart last through every generation, that he will rescue them from death and feed them in time of famine. **Psalm 32:11.19.**

Opening Prayer

Let us pray
  [that we will respond to the love of Christ]

Father,
we rejoice in the gifts of love
we have received from the heart of Jesus your Son.
Open our hearts to share his life
and continue to bless us with his love.

or

Father,
we have wounded the heart of Jesus your Son,
but he brings us forgiveness and grace.
Help us to prove our grateful love
and make amends for our sins.

THE SACRED HEART/B

or

Let us pray
   [that the love of Christ's heart
   may touch the world with healing and peace]

Father,
we honour the heart of your Son
broken by man's cruelty,
yet symbol of love's triumph,
pledge of all that man is called to be.

Teach us to see Christ in the lives we touch,
to offer him living worship
by love-filled service to our brothers and sisters.

First Reading   Hosea 11:1.3-4.8-9.

My heart recoils from it.

Listen to the word of the Lord:
When Israel was a child I loved him,
and I called my son out of Egypt.
I myself taught Ephraim to walk,
I took them in my arms;
yet they have not understood that I was the one looking after
   them.
I led them with reins of kindness,
with leading-strings of love.
I was like someone who lifts an infant close against his cheek;
stooping down to him I gave him his food.
How could I treat you like Admah,
or deal with you like Zeboiim?
My heart recoils from it,
my whole being trembles at the thought.
I will not give rein to my fierce anger,
I will not destroy Ephraim again,
for I am God, not man:
I am the Holy One in your midst
and have no wish to destroy.

Responsorial Psalm   Isaiah 12:2-6.

℟ **With joy you will draw water
   from the wells of the Saviour.**

THE SACRED HEART/B

1. Truly God is my salvation,
   I trust, I shall not fear.
   For the Lord is my strength, my song,
   he became my saviour.
   With joy you will draw water
   from the wells of salvation. ℟

2. Give thanks to the Lord, give praise to his name!
   make his mighty deeds known to the peoples!
   Declare the greatness of his name. ℟

3. Sing a psalm to the Lord
   for he has done glorious deeds;
   make them known to all the earth!
   People of Zion, sing and shout for joy
   for great in your midst is the Holy One of Israel. ℟

Second Reading   Ephesians 3:8-12.14-19.

The love of Christ is beyond all knowledge.

I, Paul, who am less than the least of all the saints, have been entrusted with this special grace, not only of proclaiming to the pagans the infinite treasure of Christ but also of explaining how the mystery is to be dispensed. Through all the ages, this has been kept hidden in God, the creator of everything. Why? So that the Sovereignties and Powers should learn only now, through the Church, how comprehensive God's wisdom really is, exactly according to the plan which he had had from all eternity in Christ Jesus our Lord. This is why we are bold enough to approach God in complete confidence, through our faith in him.

This, then, is what I pray, kneeling before the Father, from whom every family, whether spiritual or natural, takes its name:

Out of his infinite glory, may he give you the power through his Spirit for your hidden self to grow strong, so that Christ may *live in* your hearts through faith, and then, planted in love and built on love, you will with all the saints have strength to grasp the breadth and the length, the height and the depth; until, knowing the love of Christ, which is beyond all knowledge, you are filled with the utter fullness of God.

THE SACRED HEART/B

Alleluia Alleluia, alleluia! Shoulder my yoke and learn from me, for I am gentle and humble in heart. Alleluia!
Matthew 11:29.

or

Alleluia, alleluia! This is the love I mean: God's love for us when he sent his Son to be the sacrifice that takes our sins away. Alleluia!   1 John 4:10.

Gospel   John 19:31-37.

One of the soldiers pierced his side and there came out blood and water.

It was Preparation Day, and to prevent the bodies remaining on the cross during the sabbath — since that sabbath was a day of special solemnity — the Jews asked Pilate to have the legs broken and the bodies taken away. Consequently the soldiers came and broke the legs of the first man who had been crucified with him and then of the other. When they came to Jesus, they found he was already dead, and so instead of breaking his legs one of the soldiers pierced his side with a lance; and immediately there came out blood and water. This is the evidence of one who saw it — trustworthy evidence, and he knows he speaks the truth — and he gives it so that you may believe as well. Because all this happened to fulfil the words of scripture:
Not one bone of his will be broken;
and again, in another place scripture says:
They will look on the one whom they have pierced.

Prayer over the Gifts

Lord,
look on the heart of Christ your Son
filled with love for us.
Because of his love
accept our eucharist and forgive our sins.

THE SACRED HEART/B

Preface

Father, all powerful and ever-living God,
we do well always and everywhere to give you thanks
through Jesus Christ our Lord.

Lifted high on the cross,
Christ gave his life for us,
so much did he love us.
From his wounded side flowed blood and water,
the fountain of sacramental life in the Church.
To his open heart the Saviour invites all men,
to draw water in joy from the springs of salvation.

Now, with all the saints and angels,
we praise you for ever:

Holy, holy, holy ...

Communion Antiphon

The Lord says: If anyone is thirsty, let him come to me; whoever believes in me, let him drink. Streams of living water shall flow out from within him.
John 7:37-38

or

One of the soldiers pierced Jesus' side with a lance, and at once there flowed out blood and water.
John 19:34

Prayer after Communion

Father,
may this sacrament fill us with love.
Draw us closer to Christ your Son
and help us to recognise him in others.

FRIDAY AFTER THE SECOND SUNDAY OF PENTECOST
THE SACRED HEART OF JESUS/C

The love of Christ reconciles us to God. Christ died for us while we were still sinners. He gave his life as a shepherd so that we as his sheep might find new pastures. He will not abandon us but constantly looks for the lost one, bandages the wounded and makes the weak strong. He watches over us himself.

Entrance Antiphon The thoughts of his heart last through every generation, that he will rescue them from death and feed them in time of famine. **Psalm 32:11.19.**

Opening Prayer

Let us pray
 [that we will respond to the love of Christ]

Father,
we rejoice in the gifts of love
we have received from the heart of Jesus your Son.
Open our hearts to share his life
and continue to bless us with his love.

or

Father,
we have wounded the heart of Jesus your Son,
but he brings us forgiveness and grace.
Help us to prove our grateful love
and make amends for our sins.

or

THE SACRED HEART/C

Let us pray
  [that the love of Christ's heart
  may touch the world with healing and peace]
Father,
we honour the heart of your Son
broken by man's cruelty,
yet symbol of love's triumph,
pledge of all that man is called to be.

Teach us to see Christ in the lives we touch,
to offer him living worship
by love-filled service to our brothers and sisters.

First Reading   Ezekiel 34:11-6.
I myself will pasture my sheep, I myself will show them where to rest.

The Lord God says this: I am going to look after my flock myself and keep all of it in view. As a shepherd keeps all his flock in view when he stands up in the middle of his scattered sheep, so shall I keep my sheep in view. I shall rescue them from wherever they have been scattered during the mist and darkness. I shall bring them out of the countries where they are; I shall gather them together from foreign countries and bring them back to their own land. I shall pasture them on the mountains of Israel, in the ravines and in every inhabited place in the land. I shall feed them in good pasturage; the high mountains of Israel will be their grazing ground. There they will rest in good grazing ground; they will browse in rich pastures on the mountains of Israel. I myself will pasture my sheep, I myself will show them were to rest — it is the Lord who speaks. I shall look for the lost one, bring back the stray, bandage the wounded and make the weak strong. I shall watch over the fat and healthy. I shall be a true shepherd to them.

Responsorial Psalm   Psalm 22.
R/ **The Lord is my shepherd;
  there is nothing I shall want.**

1. The Lord is my shepherd;
  there is nothing I shall want.
  Fresh and green are the pastures
  where he gives me repose.

(continued)

THE SACRED HEART/C

Near restful waters he leads me,
to revive my drooping spirit. R̸

2. He guides me along the right path;
he is true to his name.
If I should walk in the valley of darkness
no evil would I fear.
You are there with your crook and your staff;
with these you give me comfort. R̸

3. You have prepared a banquet for me
in the sight of my foes.
My head you have anointed with oil;
my cup is overflowing. R̸

4. Surely goodness and kindness shall follow me
all the days of my life.
In the Lord's own house shall I dwell
for ever and ever. R̸

Second Reading   Romans 5:5-11.

What proves that God loves us is that Christ died for us.

The love of God has been poured into our hearts by the Holy Spirit which has been given us. We were still helpless when at his appointed moment Christ died for sinful men. It is not easy to die even for a good man — though of course for someone really worthy, a man might be prepared to die — but what proved that God loves us is that Christ died for us while we were still sinners. Having died to make us righteous, is it likely that he would now fail to save us from God's anger? When we were reconciled to God by the death of his Son, we were still enemies; now that we have been reconciled, surely we may count on being saved by the life of his Son? Not merely because we have been reconciled but because we are filled with joyful trust in God, through our Lord Jesus Christ, through whom we have already gained our reconciliation.

Alleluia   Alleluia, alleluia! Shoulder my yoke and learn from me, for I am gentle and humble in heart. Alleluia!
                                                                Matthew 11:29.

or

THE SACRED HEART/C

Alleluia, alleluia! I am the good shepherd, says the Lord; I know my own sheep and my own know me. Alleluia! John 10:14.

Gospel   Luke 15:3-7.
Rejoice with me, I have found my sheep that was lost.

Jesus spoke this parable to the scribes and Pharisees:

"What man among you with a hundred sheep, losing one, would not leave the ninety-nine in the wilderness and go after the missing one till he found it? And when he found it, would he not joyfully take it on his shoulders and then, when he got home, call together his friends and neighbours? 'Rejoice with me,' he would say, 'I have found my sheep that was lost.' In the same way, I tell you, there will be more rejoicing in heaven over one repentant sinner than over ninety-nine virtuous men who have no need of repentance."

Prayer over the Gifts

Lord,
look on the heart of Christ your Son
filled with love for us.
Because of his love
accept our eucharist and forgive our sins.
Preface of the Sacred Heart, page 506.

Communion Antiphon

The Lord says: If anyone is thirsty, let him come to me; whoever believes in me, let him drink. Streams of living water shall flow out from within him. **or** John 7:37-38

One of the soldiers pierced Jesus' side with a lance, and at once there flowed out blood and water. John 19:34.

Prayer after Communion

Father,
may this sacrament fill us with love.
Draw us closer to Christ your Son
and help us to recognise him in others.

The Order of Mass

The Order of Mass

WHEN we get accustomed to anything it is hard to change. The Mass had become so familiar to us that any alteration however small tended to disturb us. The Mass like our faith had become unchangeable. It is very necessary for us therefore to understand the meaning and significance of the changes that have taken place. Basically very little has been changed by the Second Vatican Council. There has been a greater emphasis on the need for a fuller participation in the liturgy and a deeper understanding of the word of God which we call the Liturgy of the Word. Before there can be any gathering of christians the Gospel has to be preached so that our faith in Jesus Christ may be strengthened and increased. The Gospel leads us to the action of the eucharist [Liturgy of the Eucharist] so that the word and sacrament are closely linked in the eucharist.

Up to the Second Vatican Council's famous document on the liturgy *[Sacrosanctum Concilium]* we usually described the Mass as having three principal parts: offertory, consecration and communion. They are now, more or less, to be found in the Liturgy of the Eucharist. The eucharist is structured as follows and it will help us to keep these parts in mind when we participate in worship as members of Christ's family.

1. Introductory Rites.
2. Liturgy of the Word.
3. Liturgy of the Eucharist.
4. Concluding Rites.

1. INTRODUCTORY RITES

The purpose of these rites is to help the assembled people to become a worshipping community and to prepare them for listening to God's word and celebrating the eucharist. The assembly forms as it were a new person, the Church, whom, Christ has chosen and loves as a bride. As a bride of Christ the Church is the partner in the worship which the Bridegroom gives to our Father in heaven. He wants her to be 'holy and spotless' and that is why the priest sprinkles the congregation with holy water. We have to be cleansed from any defilements which come between us and God. The water is used to remind us of our baptism by which we died to sin in order to live the new life

THE ORDER OF MASS

of grace. We ask God our Father to renew the living spring of his life within us so that we may be freed from our sins and so come into his presence to receive his gift of salvation.

However our salvation as individuals has not yet been achieved and is a task which has to be worked at to the end of time. We are conscious of the many ways we have personally failed to live out our baptismal commitment and so we come together as a christian family to ask Our Father's forgiveness knowing that he is full of gentleness and compassion. We have sinned in thought, word and deed. Full of good resolutions we have succumbed to temptations and so have disorientated the relationship between ourselves and God as well as placing barriers between each other as a community. We remember the Lord's words: 'You must therefore be perfect just as your heavenly Father is perfect'. Matthew 5:48. and again: 'If you are bringing your offering to the altar and there remember that your brother has something against you leave your offering there before the altar, go and be reconciled with your brother first, and then come back and present your offering.' Matthew 5:23-24. Our confession of sin is in no way tinged with fear or servility because we know that if we are sincerely sorry then the Lord will have mercy on us.

The Introductory Rite concludes with a hymn to God's glory who brings peace to his people on earth. We worship, praise and thank him through Jesus Christ who takes away our sins and presents our prayer to the Father who alone is holy and whose life we are called to share. We respond 'Amen' to the special prayer of the day thus showing our belief that the world in which we live is still being redeemed by our Saviour whose word we will receive with joy and gladness.

2. THE LITURGY OF THE WORD

We are a Gospel-filled people. The promise made to Abraham, our father in faith, now finds its fulfilment in us as the new people of God. Among biblical scholars especially over the past fifty years there has been an upsurge of interest in the Bible as the living word of God. 'The word of God is something alive and active: it cuts like any double-edged sword but more finely: it can slip through the place where the soul is divided from the spirit or joints from the marrow; it can judge the secret emotions and thoughts. No created thing can hide from him; everything is

THE ORDER OF MASS

uncovered and open to the eyes of the one to whom we must give account of ourselves.' Hebrews 4:12-13. It is only to be expected that this reawakening of our consciousness of the Bible should find visible expression in our worship and in our daily lives as christians. One of our main functions as a eucharistic community is to proclaim the Gospel. Through our acceptance of God's living word we testify that the world has been redeemed through the saving power of Christ.

The readings from the lectionary with its wide range of selected passages appropriate to every situation in which a christian finds himself have now woven themselves into the daily fabric of our lives. That lay people are actively encouraged to read lessons from the Bible for the instruction of the eucharistic congregation shows quite clearly that all, priests and people, have as their task and privilege the *proclamation* of God's saving word. We are instructed and instruct so that we may be better equipped to preach the Gospel 'in season and out of season'.

God is the maker of history past and present. Just as truly as he spoke to Moses, Abraham and the early Church so now he speaks to us today in Christ as he reveals to us the pattern of our lives. 'At various times in the past and in various ways God spoke to our ancestors through the prophets; but in our own time, the last days, he has spoken to us through his Son . . .' Hebrews 1:1-2. the Old Testament God has revealed himself as a loving Father through the inspired reflections of wise men, revelations of prophets, the lives of his people etc. and shown us what he expects of his people in return. He chose the human voices of his prophets and people to speak to us. The Bible is really a dialogue between God and us. Christ is God's word made flesh. He is the perfect and final word in whom and through whom we grow in our relationship with God and with one another.

Christ, as we know, is the beginning of a new humanity. 'He is the image of the unseen God, and the first born of all creation'. Colossians 1:15. He is the peace between us and God because he has taken away our sins. In the Liturgy of the Word we recall the long *centuries of waiting for the coming* of the Messiah which reminds us how we too should live our lives as we are called to follow Christ into the splendour of God's Kingdom. We must become one with him. We hear the voices of the prophets warning us to be patient and in the New Testament we rejoice at Christ's coming among us to forgive us our sins and promising us

THE ORDER OF MASS

a share in his kingdom. We marvel at a world made whole by Christ's redeeming power and we share in the Church's triumph that its Lord has risen from the dead and is still with us. We stand between the ages for 'Christ has come' and we are now called to respond more fully to his saving love so that we may move forward in his footsteps until 'he comes again'. In this way we prepare for the celebration of the eucharist for while we proclaim Christ's death and resurrection we still wait for his coming in glory.

The Liturgy of the Word is as much prayer and reflection as it is instruction. Along with the readings there are prayers, responsorial psalms and general intercessions as we plead for the Church and the world. We use periods of *silence* after the readings especially after the Gospel to let God's message have time and space to sink into our minds and hearts. We are to become a people saturated with the truth of his Word made flesh so that in turn we can become other Christs to our world.

3. THE LITURGY OF THE EUCHARIST

In our desire to understand this very important part of the eucharistic celebration we can do no better than quote in full the General Instruction laid down in the official English Text of the Roman Missal revised by the decree of the Second Vatican Council and published by the authority of Pope Paul VI:

'At the Last Supper Christ instituted the paschal sacrifice and meal. In this meal the sacrifice of the cross is continually made present in the Church when the priest, representing Christ, carries out what the Lord did and handed over to his disciples to do in his memory.

Christ took bread and the cup, gave thanks, broke, gave to his disciples, saying: 'Take and eat, this is my body. Take and drink, this is the cup of my blood. Do this in memory of me.' The Church has arranged the celebration of the eucharistic liturgy to correspond to these words and actions of Christ.

1) In the preparation of the gifts, bread, wine and water are brought to the altar, the same elements which Christ used.

2) The eucharistic prayer is the hymn of thanksgiving to God for the whole work of salvation; the offerings become the body and blood of Christ.

3) The breaking of the one bread is a sign of the unity of the

THE ORDER OF MASS

faithful, and in communion they receive the body and blood of Christ as the apostles did from his hands.'

In obedience to its Lord the Church does what he commands: *takes* bread and wine [preparation of the altar and gifts], *gives* praise and thanks [eucharistic prayer], and *breaks* the bread *and presents* the chalice to be received [communion]. These are the three main parts of the Liturgy of the Eucharist.

1. Preparation of the altar and gifts. The term 'preparation of the altar and gifts' more accurately reflects the meaning of what we formerly called the 'Offertory' since it is really the action of *preparing* for the offering of the eucharist, rather than the offering itself which now takes place within the eucharistic prayer. The Latin word *offertorium* did not mean the offering but simply the bringing up of the gifts. It is for this reason that offertory processions from the body of the congregation now form a significant part of our liturgical celebration as a christian community. These gifts not only of bread and wine but of money also bring us back to the ancient custom when the people brought bread and wine for the liturgy from their homes.

2. Eucharistic Prayer. The eucharistic prayer, a prayer of thanksgiving and sanctification, is the centre and high point of the entire celebration. In an introductory dialogue the priest invites the people to lift their hearts to God in prayer and thanks; he unites them with himself in the prayer he addresses in their name to the Father through Jesus Christ. The meaning of the prayer is that the whole congregation joins Christ in acknowledging the works of God and in offering the sacrifice.

The chief elements of the eucharistic prayer are these:

a) Thanksgiving [expressed especially in the preface]: in the name of the entire people of God, the priest praises the Father and gives him thanks for the work of salvation or for some special aspect of it in keeping with the day, feast, or season.

b) Acclamation: united with the angels, the congregation sings or recites the *Sanctus*. This acclamation forms part of the eucharistic prayer, and all the people join with the priest in singing or reciting it.

c) Epiclesis: in special invocations the Church calls on God's power and asks that the gifts offered by men be consecrated, that is, become the body and blood of Christ and that the victim may

THE ORDER OF MASS

become a source of salvation for those who are to share in common.

d) Narrative of the institution and consecration: in the words and actions of Christ, the sacrifice he instituted at the Last Supper is celebrated when under the appearances of bread and wine he offered his body and blood, gave them to his apostles to eat and drink and commanded them to carry on this mystery.

e) Anamnesis: in fulfilment of the command received from Christ through the apostles, the Church keeps his memorial by recalling especially his passion, resurrection and ascension.

f) Offering: in this memorial, the Church — and in particular the Church here and now assembled — offers the victim to the Father in the Holy Spirit. The Church's intention is that the faithful not only offer the spotless victim but also learn to offer themselves and daily to be drawn into ever more perfect union, through Christ the Mediator, with the Father and with each other, so that at last God may be all in all.

g) Intercessions: the intercessions make it clear that the eucharist is celebrated in communion with the whole Church of heaven and all its members, living and dead, who are called to share in the salvation and redemption acquired by the body and blood of Christ.

h) Final doxology: the praise of God is expressed in the doxology which is confirmed and concluded by the acclamation of the people.

All should listen to the eucharistic prayer in silent reverence and share in it by making the acclamations.'

The term 'eucharistic prayer' is preferred to 'consecration' with which we were familiar. The reason for the change is quite simply that 'eucharistic prayer' expresses more adequately that part of the Mass which signifies not only the coming of Christ to be present under the appearances of bread and wine, but also the Church's offering of itself to God the Father through Christ the High Priest and Victim present in our midst.

The words 'in memory' are perhaps the most important and least understood in the Gospel narrative at the heart of the eucharistic prayer. Yet they are in fact the key to its meaning. The liturgy often speaks of remembering, calling to mind, commemorating, doing 'in memory'. In the scriptures, as in the prayers of the liturgy, words which speak of our remembering what God has done, or of God remembering us, mean far more than thinking of a past event which is over and done with and a thing of the past. When God remembers his people it means that he acts on their behalf *here and now*. Similarly, when his people remember what God has done his activity continues in the present. Like the Passover of the Israelites the eucharist is a memorial [anamnesis]. But, like the Passover, it is no mere recalling of a past event. It is *making effective in the present a past saving event in a ritual memorial of it:* 'Do this in memory of me'. It is God himself remembering and making present when we remember what Christ has commanded us to do. This effective actualization is traditionally associated with the real presence of Christ's body and blood in the eucharist. Thus the eucharistic memorial is a real renewal or *re-presentation* of what God has done for us through Christ. We enter again into the passion, death, resurrection and ascension of the Lord.

We must also emphasise the role of the Holy Spirit in the eucharistic prayer. It is he who is given to us in baptism and whose spirit we share as he calls us together into a living, loving, praying community. The eucharist is his action as well as being the action of the risen Christ among us. In the three new eucharistic prayers special emphasis is given to the 'epiclesis' or invocation of the Holy Spirit.

Characteristic of the new eucharistic prayers are the *acclamations* in which the whole Church expresses its share in the eucharistic offering. The three most important of these are the Sanctus, the memorial acclamation and the Great Amen, all of which should preferably be sung. The *Sanctus* acknowledges in awe and wonder the splendour of God to whom it is right and fitting that we should give praise. It is preceded by reminding us of the worship of the Church in heaven. In the Sanctus we join the priest, the whole of creation and the whole company of heaven in praising our loving Father. The *memorial acclamation* reminds us that while the eucharist is a proclamation of Christ's death and resurrection it is also an expression of our waiting in hope until he comes again. The *Great Amen* is our liturgical answer to all that has happened in the eucharistic prayer. It is our *yes,* our assent as believers in a christian community to all that has taken place in our presence and in our name.

4. THE COMMUNION RITE

'Since the eucharistic celebration is the paschal meal, in accord with his command, the body and the blood of the Lord should be received as spiritual food by the faithful who are properly disposed. This is the purpose of the breaking of the bread and the other preparatory rites which lead directly to the communion of the people.

a) Lord's Prayer: this is a petition both for daily food, which for christians means also the eucharistic bread, and for forgiveness from sin, so that what is holy may be given to those who are holy. The priest invites all the faithful to sing or say the Lord's Prayer with him. He alone adds the embolism, *Deliver us;* and the people conclude this with the doxology. The addition to the Lord's Prayer develops the last petition and begs in the name of the community deliverance from the power of evil. The invitation, the prayer itself, the embolism, and the people's doxology are sung or spoken aloud.

b) Rite of peace: before they share in the same bread, the people express their love for one another and beg for peace and unity in the Church and with all mankind.

The form of this rite is left to the conference of bishops to decide in accord with the customs and mentality of the people.

c) Breaking of bread: this gesture of Christ at the Last Supper gave the entire eucharistic action its name in apostolic times. In addition to its practical aspect, it signifies that in communion we who are many are made one body in the one bread of life which is Christ [cf. 1 Corinthians 10:17].

d) Commingling: the celebrant drops a part of the host into the chalice.

e) Agnus Dei: during the breaking of the bread and the commingling the Agnus Dei is ordinarily sung by the choir or cantor with the people responding; or it may be said aloud. This invocation may be repeated as often as necessary to accompany the breaking of the bread, and is brought to a close by the words, *grant us peace.*

f) Private preparation of the priest: the priest prepares himself to receive the body and blood of Christ by praying quietly. The faithful also do this by praying in silence.

g) The priest then shows the eucharistic bread to the faithful.

THE ORDER OF MASS

He invites them to participate in the meal and leads them in an act of humility, using words from the Gospel.

h) It is most desirable that the faithful should receive the body of the Lord in hosts consecrated at the same Mass and should share the cup when it is permitted. Communion is thus a clearer sign of sharing in the sacrifice that is actually being celebrated.

i) The song during the communion of the priest and people expresses the spiritual union of the communicants who join their voices in a single song, shows the joy of all, and makes the communion procession an act of brotherhood.'

Beginning with the Lord's prayer, the communion rite emphasises our fellowship in community through its sincere signs of peace, unity and prayer for forgiveness. The communion rite is not only communion, the receiving of Christ. It also acknowledges that we are one with Christ and with each other. In his name we call God our Father, we wish to be healed by peace in the community and when we say 'Lord, I am not worthy' we do so, not to refuse his gift, but to acknowledge that God's love for us revealed in Christ overcomes our sinfulness. We praise him who is Lord of all.

5. CONCLUDING RITE

'The concluding rite consists of:

a) The priest's greeting and blessing which is on certain days and occasions expanded by the prayer over the people or other solemn form;

b) the dismissal which sends each member of the congregation to do good works, praising and blessing the Lord.'

The eucharist penetrates every moment of our lives. It transforms them into a continual encounter with God the Father through Jesus Christ. He is with us always and we pray in his Spirit. In the 'now' of time, at each stage in every situation in which we find ourselves, we live the new and wonderful life of grace. Each of us is called to mediate the saving love of Christ for everyone. The eucharist is the source of our mission as we move outwards into a world which needs our joy and hope. The more difficult the situation the more necessary it is to call on our loving Father who wills nothing but the best for us. At the very centre of

THE ORDER OF MASS

our unshakable faith stands an event, an historic fact, the death and resurrection of Christ.

We live and preach the resurrection of the Lord. In the eucharist 'we have heard and we have seen with our own eyes; that we have watched and touched with our hands: the Word, who is life.' 1 John 1:1.We are the new people of God. In the eucharist we give praise and thanks that our Lord comes amongst us in a loving way until one day he will finally come in glory. Of all the people on this earth we are the most fortunate. 'The Word was made flesh, he lived among us, and we saw his glory, the glory that is his as the only Son of the Father, full of grace and truth.' John 1:14.

Table of the Order of Mass

INTRODUCTORY RITES	LITURGY OF THE WORD
Entrance Procession	First Reading
Greeting	Responsorial Psalm
Penitential Rite or Rite of Sprinkling Kyrie	Second Reading
(Gloria)	Gospel
Opening Prayer	(Gospel Acclamation). Proclamation of the Gospel
	Homily
	(Profession of Faith)
	Bidding Prayer

TABLE OF ORDER OF MASS

LITURGY OF THE EUCHARIST

PREPARATION OF THE ALTAR AND GIFTS

Procession with Gifts
(Incensing of Altar and Assembly)
Invitation to prayer
Prayer over the Gifts

THE EUCHARISTIC PRAYER

Introductory Dialogue
Preface
Sanctus
Epiclesis (Invocation of the Spirit)
Last Supper Narrative
Memorial Acclamation
Memorial Offering (Anamnesis)
Intercessions
Doxology and Great Amen

THE COMMUNION RITE

Lord's Prayer
Rite of Peace
Breaking of Bread
Communion
(Silent Prayer)
Prayer after Communion

CONCLUDING RITES

Blessing
Dismissal

Prayers before Mass

Gratitude for Sunday, a day of worship

O God, our Father, we give you thanks that today
  you are calling us to worship you and to learn of you.
You know the needs with which we will go to your
  house.
Grant that in it we may find comfort for sorrow, and
  soothing for the hearts that are sore.
Grant that in it we may find guidance for problems,
  and light for minds which are perplexed.
Grant that in it we may find strength for our temptations,
  and grace to overcome the fascination of the
  wrong things.
Grant that in it we may meet Jesus, and to go out, not
  to forget him any more.
Remember those who cannot go to Church today;
  those who are ill; those who are aged; those who
  are too sad to come; those who have the care of
  children and of family things; those who are nursing
  invalids; those who must work even today. And grant
  that in their own homes, in the hospitals, the
  infirmaries, the nursing-homes they may know the
  unseen fellowship of the worshipping company of those
  who love you: through Jesus Christ our Lord. Amen.

William Barclay (adapted)

The Song of Ascent

How I rejoiced when they said to me,
  'Let us go to the house of Yahweh!'
And now our feet are standing
  in your gateways, Jerusalem.

Jerusalem restored! The city,
  one united whole!
Here the tribes come up,
  the tribes of Yahweh,

PRAYERS BEFORE MASS

they come to praise Yahweh's name,
    as he ordered Israel,
here where the tribunals of justice are,
    the royal tribunals of David.

Pray for peace in Jerusalem,
    'Prosperity to your houses!
Peace inside your city walls!
    Prosperity to your palaces!

Since all are my brothers and friends,
    I say, 'Peace be with you!'
Since Yahweh our God lives here,
    I pray for your happiness.

Psalm 122

Invitation to praise God

Acclaim Yahweh, all the earth,
    serve Yahweh gladly,
    come into his presence with songs of joy!

Know that he, Yahweh, is God,
    he made us and we belong to him,
    we are his people, the flock that he pastures.

Walk through his porticos giving thanks,
    enter his courts praising him,
    give thanks to him, bless his name!

Yes, Yahweh is good,
    his love is everlasting,
    his faithfulness endures from age to age.

Psalm 100

Prayer of St. Thomas Aquinas

Almighty and ever-living God,
I approach the sacrament of your only-begotten Son, our Lord Jesus Christ.
I come sick to the doctor of life,
    unclean to the fountain of mercy,
    blind to the radiance of eternal light,
    and poor and needy to the Lord of heaven and earth.
Lord, in your great generosity,
    heal my sickness, wash away my defilement,

PRAYERS BEFORE MASS

enlighten my blindness, enrich my poverty,
and clothe my nakedness.
May I receive the bread of angels,
the King of kings and Lord of lords,
with humble reverence,
with the purity and faith,
the repentance and love, and the determined purpose
that will help to bring me to salvation.
May I receive the sacrament of the Lord's body and blood,
and its reality and power.
Kind God,
may I receive the body of your only-begotten Son,
our Lord Jesus Christ,
born from the womb of the Virgin Mary,
and so be received into his mystical body,
and numbered among his members.
Loving Father,
as on my earthly pilgrimage
I now receive your beloved Son
under the veil of a sacrament,
may I one day see him face to face in glory,
who lives and reigns with you for ever. Amen.

Roman Missal

A loving prayer

My God, I love thee: not because
I hope for Heaven thereby,
nor yet because who love thee not
are lost eternally.

Thou, O my Jesus, thou didst me
upon the cross embrace;
for me didst bear the nails and spear
and manifold disgrace.

And griefs and torments numberless
and sweat of agony;
even death itself — and all for one
who was thine enemy.

Then why, O blessed Jesu Christ,
should I not love thee well;

PRAYERS BEFORE MASS

    not for the sake of winning Heaven
    or of escaping Hell;
    not with the hope of gaining aught,
    nor seeking a reward:
    but as thyself has loved me,
    O ever-loving Lord!

Even so I love thee, and will love
    and in thy praise will sing,
    solely because thou art my God,
    and my eternal King.

St. Francis Xavier

Invitation to the altar

Draw nigh and take the Body of the Lord,
    and drink the holy Blood for you outpoured.
Saved by that Body and that holy Blood,
    with souls refreshed, we render thanks to God.

Mankind is ransomed from eternal loss
    by flesh and blood offered upon the cross.

Salvation's giver, Christ, the only Son,
    by his dear cross and Blood the victory won.

Offered was he for greatest and for least,
    himself the victim, and himself the priest.

Victims are offered by the law of old,
    which in a type this heavenly mystery told.

He, ransomer from death, and light from shade,
    now gives his holy grace his saints to aid.

Approach ye then with faithful hearts sincere,
    and take the safeguard of salvation here.

He, that his saints in this world rules and shields,
    to all believers life eternal yields;

With heavenly bread makes then that hunger whole,
    gives living waters to the thirsting soul. Amen.

Bangor Antiphonary, 7th Century

PRAYERS BEFORE MASS

Eucharistic Offering

O Lord, to whom belongs all that is in heaven and earth,
I desire to consecrate myself wholly to you and to be
yours for evermore. This day I offer myself to you,
O Lord, in singleness of heart, to serve and obey you always,
and I offer you without ceasing a sacrifice of praise and
thanksgiving. Receive me, O my Saviour, in union with the
holy oblation of your precious blood which I offer to you
this day, in the presence of angels, that this sacrifice may
avail unto my salvation and that of the whole world.

Imitation of Christ

Act of Humility

Master, I daily betray thee,
Unworthy I am to kneel at thy feet;
Neither goodness is there, nor purity in me;
Nought but disloyalty, meanness, self-serving.
All things lie open to thee:
Dumbly I show thee the worst,
All my shame and sorrowful weakness,
All my baseness and cowardice, failure, folly and sin.
O Master, beautiful, stainless, and holy,
Thou knowest it all;
I am thine, take thou again
This worthless gift of my life,
Ah! take me again.
Only, Master, O Christ,
Only, I love thee so:
O Saviour, O Lover, O King
I love thee so.

J. S. Hoyland

Adoro Te Devote

Godhead here in hiding, whom I do adore
Masked by these bare shadows, shape and
    nothing more,
See, Lord, at thy service low lies here a heart
Lost, all lost in wonder at the God thou art.

PRAYERS BEFORE MASS

Seeing, touching, tasting are in thee deceived;
How says trusty hearing? That shall be believed;
What God's Son has told me, take for truth I do;
Truth himself speaks truly or there's nothing true.

On the cross thy godhead made no sign to men;
Here thy very manhood steals from human ken:
Both are my confession, both are my belief,
And I pray the prayer of the dying thief.

I am not like Thomas, wounds I cannot see,
But can plainly call thee Lord and God as he:
This faith each day deeper be my holding of,
Daily make me harder hope and dearer love.

O thou our reminder of Christ crucified,
Living Bread the life of us for whom he died,
Lend this life to me then: feed and feast my mind,
There be thou the sweetness man was meant to find.

Bring the tender tale true of the Pelican;
Bath me, Jesu Lord, in what thy bosom ran —
Blood that but one drop of has the worth to win
All the world forgiveness of its world of sin.

Jesu whom I look at shrouded here below,
I beseech thee send me what I thirst for so,
Some day to gaze on thee face to face in light
And be blest for ever with thy glory's sight.
Amen.

tr. Gerard Manley Hopkins

Psalm 23

Yahweh is my shepherd,
   I lack nothing.
In meadows of green grass he lets me lie.
To the waters of repose he leads me;
   there he revives my soul.

He guides me by paths of virtue
   for the sake of his name.

Though I pass through a gloomy valley,
   I fear no harm;
   beside me your rod and your staff
   are there, to hearten me.

PRAYERS BEFORE MASS

You prepare a table before me
  under the eyes of my enemies;
  you anoint my head with oil,
  my cup brims over.

Ah, how goodness and kindness pursue me,
  every day of my life;
  my home, the house of Yahweh,
  as long as I live!

THE ORDER OF MASS

Introductory Rites

The purpose of these rites is to help the assembled people to become a worshipping community and to prepare us to listen to God's work and to celebrate the eucharist.

The introductory rite is omitted entirely on some occasions such as Passion Sunday (Palm Sunday) when there is a procession, at the Easter Vigil, when a sacrament is celebrated, or when part of morning or evening prayer precedes the Mass.

ENTRANCE PROCESSION

All stand

Through the entrance song and the priest's greeting we become aware of the saving presence of Christ. We acknowledge that we are assembled in his name to worship the Father in his Spirit. The altar is a symbol of Christ himself. The priest kisses the altar before greeting the congregation and thus signifies the union between Christ and his members. He may incense the altar as a symbol of our prayer which goes up to God like the smoke of the sacrifices of old.

The entrance song is chosen in accordance with the season and occasion. If there is no singing then all say the entrance antiphon.

Entrance Song: *turn to the Proper of the Day*

After the entrance song we all remain standing and make the sign of the cross as the celebrant sings or says:

In the name of the Father, and of the Son ✠ and of the Holy Spirit.

Amen.

THE ORDER OF THE MASS

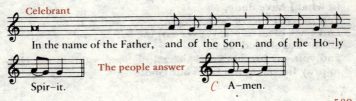

Celebrant: In the name of the Father, and of the Son, and of the Holy Spirit.

The people answer: Amen.

THE ORDER OF THE MASS

GREETING

The priest, facing the people, extends his hands and greets the people with one of the following greetings:

1. The grace of our Lord Jesus Christ and the love of God and the fellowship of the Holy Spirit be with you all.
   And also with you.

or

2. The grace and peace of God our Father and the Lord Jesus Christ be with you.
   Blessed be God, the Father of our Lord Jesus Christ.

or **And also with you.**

or

3. The Lord be with you.
   And also with you.

THEME OF THE MASS
The priest may introduce briefly the theme of the Mass.

PENITENTIAL RITE
The priest invites us to acknowledge our sinfulness before the forgiving Lord in these or similar words

My brothers and sisters,
to prepare ourselves to celebrate the sacred mysteries,
let us call to mind our sins.

A pause for silent reflection is followed by one of the three forms of the penitential rite.

1. **I confess to almighty God,
    and to you, my brothers and sisters,
    that I have sinned through my own fault**
    All strike their breast
    **in my thoughts and in my words,
    in what I have done,
    and in what I have failed to do;
    and I ask blessed Mary, ever virgin,
    all the angels and saints,
    and you, my brothers and sisters,
    to pray for me to the Lord our God.**

or

THE ORDER OF MASS

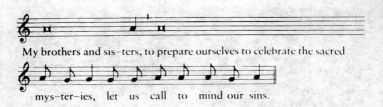

THE ORDER OF MASS

2. Lord, we have sinned against you:
Lord, have mercy.
   Lord, have mercy.
Lord, show us your mercy and love.
   And grant us your salvation.

or

3. You were sent to heal the contrite:
Lord, have mercy.
   Lord, have mercy.
You came to call sinners:
Christ have mercy.
   Christ, have mercy.

You plead for us at the right hand of the Father:
Lord, have mercy.
   Lord, have mercy.

Similar invocations may be used in place of these but the people's response always remains the same.

The priest sings or says the absolution

May almighty God have mercy on us,
forgive us our sins,
and bring us to everlasting life.
   Amen.

RITE OF BLESSING AND SPRINKLING OF HOLY WATER

This Rite may be celebrated instead of the Penitential Rite.

After greeting the people the priest blesses the water using these or similar words:

Dear friends,
this water will be used
to remind us of our baptism.
Ask God to bless it,
and to keep us faithful
to the Spirit he has given us.

1. God our Father,
your gift of water
brings life and freshness to the earth;

THE ORDER OF MASS

THE ORDER OF MASS

it washes away our sins
and brings us eternal life.

We ask you now
to bless ✠ this water,
and to give us your protection on this day
which you have made your own.
Renew the living spring of your life within us
and protect us in spirit and body,
that we may be free from sin
and come into your presence
to receive your gift of salvation.

or

2. Lord God almighty,
creator of all life,
of body and soul,
we ask you to bless ✠ this water:
as we use it in faith
forgive our sins .
and save us from all illness
and the power of evil.

Lord,
in your mercy
give us living water,
always springing up as a fountain of salvation:
free us, body and soul, from every danger,
and admit us to your presence
in purity of heart.

or

3. During the Easter season

Lord God almighty,
hear the prayers of your people:
we celebrate our creation and redemption.
Hear our prayers and bless ✠ this water
which gives fruitfulness to the fields,
and refreshment and cleansing to man.
You chose water to show your goodness
when you led your people to freedom
through the Red Sea

THE ORDER OF MASS

and satisfied their thirst in the desert
with water from the rock.
Water was the symbol used by the prophets
to foretell your new covenant with man.
You made the water of baptism holy
by Christ's baptism in the Jordan:
by it you gave us a new birth
and renew us in holiness.
May this water remind us of our baptism,
and let us share the joy
of all who have been baptised at Easter.

Where it is necessary, salt may be mixed with the holy water. The priest blesses the salt, saying:

Almighty God,
we ask you to bless ✠ this salt
as once you blessed the salt scattered over the water
by the prophet Elisha.
Wherever this salt and water is sprinkled,
drive away the power of evil,
and protect us always
in the presence of your Holy Spirit.

While the priest sprinkles himself, his ministers and the people, an appropriate hymn or antiphon is sung. When he returns to his place he concludes the rite with the following prayer:

May almighty God cleanse us of our sins,
and through the eucharist we celebrate
make us worthy to sit at his table
in his heavenly kingdom.

Amen.

THE ORDER OF MASS

THE KYRIE

This is not only a plea for forgiveness but also a joyful acknowledgement of the saving presence of the risen Christ in our midst.

It is not said here if it has already been used in form 3 of the penitential rite or when the blessing and sprinkling of holy water takes place.

Lord, have mercy.
    Lord, have mercy.
Christ, have mercy.
    Christ, have mercy.
Lord, have mercy.
    Lord, have mercy.

THE GLORIA

This triumphant hymn of praise is sung or said on Sundays outside of the Seasons of Advent and Lent, on solemnities and feasts, and on some other occasions of special importance.

Glory to God in the highest,
    and peace to his people on earth.

Lord God, heavenly King,
almighty God and Father,
    we worship you, we give you thanks,
    we praise you for your glory.
Lord Jesus Christ, only Son of the Father,
Lord God, Lamb of God,
you take away the sin of the world:
    have mercy on us;
you are seated at the right hand of the Father:
    receive our prayer.
For you alone are the Holy One,
you alone are the Lord,
you alone are the Most High,
    Jesus Christ,
    with the Holy Spirit,
    in the glory of God the Father. Amen.

THE ORDER OF MASS

OPENING PRAYER: *turn to the Proper of the Day.*

The priest invites us to pray. Together we spend a few moments in reverent silence realising that we are in the presence of God our Father to whom we make our petitions.

The priest 'collects' the prayerful thoughts of all in this Opening Prayer. We should make this prayer our own and so we give our assent by responding:

Amen.

THE ORDER OF MASS

Liturgy of the Word

God speaks to us of redemption and salvation and nourishes us with his word. We are not just listening to past history. The God who speaks to Israel and the early Church speaks to us today and reveals the pattern of his plan for our lives.

Reading, Responsorial Psalm, Alleluia verse: turn to the Proper of the Day.

FIRST READING
All sit
On Sundays there are three readings. The first, which is generally related to the Gospel of the day, is from the Old Testament or, during Eastertide, from the Acts of the Apostles.

At the end of the reading:

Reader: This is the Word of the Lord.
Thanks be to God.

RESPONSORIAL PSALM
The responsorial psalm and silent pauses between the readings enable us to meditate on the word of God in prayer and praise.

The Cantor (Reader) sings or recites the psalm to which the people make the response.

SECOND READING
This reading generally comes from one of the New Testament letters, although it is sometimes taken from the Acts of the Apostles or the Apocalypse.

At the end of the reading:

Reader: This is the Word of the Lord.
Thanks be to God.

PROCLAMATION OF THE GOSPEL
All stand

Procession
Christ is present among us through his saving Word. We stand for the proclamation of the good news and so acknowledge that we are a people with a mission through the sacrament of his word.

THE ORDER OF MASS

At the end of the reading

At the beginning of the gospel

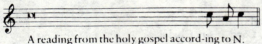

At the end of the gospel

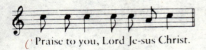

THE ORDER OF MASS

The Book of the Gospels may be carried in solemn procession accompanied by a thurifer and two acolytes emphasizing the presence of Christ through his Word. During the procession the Alleluia or Acclamation may be sung or said by all the congregation.

ALLELUIA OR ACCLAMATION: *Turn to the Proper of the Day.*

The Lord be with you.
  And also with you.
A reading from the holy Gospel according to N.
  Glory to you, Lord.

The Book of the Gospels may be incensed.

At the end of the Gospel:
This is the Gospel of the Lord.
  Praise to you, Lord Jesus Christ.

HOMILY

All sit

We are a eucharistic community in word as well as sacrament. The priest or deacon therefore reflects with us on the readings of the day, relating them to the eucharistic celebration and to ordinary life.

A period of silent reflection may follow the homily.

PROFESSION OF FAITH

All stand

We stand to profess our faith in response to the word of God written in the Gospel and spoken in the homily. We testify that God is our Father who gives us new life through his Son and who calls us together as a people, a living community of his abiding love and care.

THE ORDER OF MASS

The profession of our faith is used on Sundays and solemnities.
We believe in one God,
  the Father, the Almighty,
  maker of heaven and earth,
  of all that is, seen and unseen.

We believe in one Lord, Jesus Christ,
  the only Son of God,
  eternally begotten of the Father,
  God from God, Light from Light,
  true God from true God,
  begotten, not made,
  of one Being with the Father.
  Through him all things were made.
  For us men and for our salvation
    he came down from heaven: *All bow*
  by the power of the Holy Spirit
    he became incarnate from the Virgin Mary, and was made man.
  For our sake he was crucified under Pontius Pilate;
    he suffered death and was buried.
    On the third day he rose again
      in accordance with the Scriptures;
    he ascended into heaven
      and is seated at the right hand of the Father.
  He will come again in glory to judge the living and the dead,
    and his kingdom will have no end.

We believe in the Holy Spirit, the Lord, the giver of life,
  who proceeds from the Father and the Son.
  With the Father and the Son he is worshipped and glorified.
  He has spoken through the Prophets.
  We believe in one holy catholic and apostolic Church.
  We acknowledge one baptism for the forgiveness of sins.
  We look for the resurrection of the dead,
    and the life of the world to come. Amen.

THE ORDER OF MASS

Where approved the following may be said:

I believe in God, the Father almighty,
  creator of heaven and earth.
I believe in Jesus Christ, his only Son, our Lord.
  He was conceived by the power of the Holy Spirit
    and born of the Virgin Mary.
  He suffered under Pontius Pilate,
    was crucified, died, and was buried.
  He descended to the dead.
  On the third day he rose again.
  He ascended into heaven,
    and is seated at the right hand of the Father.
  He will come again to judge the living and the dead.
I believe in the Holy Spirit,
  the holy catholic Church,
  the communion of saints,
  the forgiveness of sins,
  the resurrection of the body,
  and the life everlasting. Amen.

THE PRAYER OF THE FAITHFUL

Through baptism we have been made one with Christ, our high priest, and we share in his intercessions before the Father for the needs of mankind, of the Church and of all people. Our intercessions flow from our listening to the Gospel and homily by which we have been made more aware of our christian commitment.

The Bidding Prayer (or General Intercessions), which now follows, is preceded by the invitation and consists of a series of intentions, announced by a reader, each of which ends:

Lord hear us (or similar words). The people answer:
  Lord graciously hear us (or appropriate response).

After the last intention there is a pause for silent prayer when we pray for our own personal intentions. The priest says the concluding prayer to which we give our assent by responding
  Amen.

Liturgy of the Eucharist

At the Last Supper Christ took bread and the cup, gave thanks, broke and gave to his disciples. In the eucharist we take our gifts to the altar and when the priest, in the name of us all, has given thanks to God, the bread is broken and we receive in communion the body of the Lord. In this way the Church carries out what the Lord did and handed over to his disciples to do in his memory.

Preparation of the Altar and Gifts

PROCESSION WITH GIFTS

The altar is now prepared for the eucharistic sacrifice. The gifts of bread and wine together with the offerings of the people are taken to the altar. During the procession an appropriate song may be sung as a symbol of our joy in bringing our gifts to the Lord. If there is no song then the people may join in by making their responses to the prayers.

Blessed are you, Lord, God of all creation.
Through your goodness we have this bread to offer,
which earth has given and human hands have made.
It will become for us the bread of life.
   Blessed be God for ever.

The priest pours wine and water into the chalice as a symbol of our union with Christ

Blessed are you, Lord, God of all creation.
Through your goodness we have this wine to offer
which earth has given and human hands have made.
It will become our spiritual drink.
   Blessed be God for ever.

The priest bows and says quietly:

Lord God, we ask you to receive us and be pleased with the sacrifice we offer you with humble and contrite hearts.

Incense may be used to honour the gifts and the altar, as well as the priest and people, as a symbol of preparing the Church to bring the offering and prayer before God.

The priest washes his hands as an expression of his desire for inward purification, saying quietly:

Lord, wash away my iniquity; cleanse me from my sin.

THE ORDER OF MASS

PRAYER OVER THE GIFTS
All stand
The priest invites us to join him in prayer.
Pray, brethren, that our sacrifice
may be acceptable to God, the almighty Father.

> **May the Lord accept the sacrifice at your hands
> for the praise and glory of his name,
> for our good, and the good of all his Church.**

The priest in his prayer sets aside our gifts to the service of the Lord.

Prayer over the Gifts: *turn to the Proper of the Day.*

Once again with the celebrant we make the prayers our own and signify our assent by saying:
> **Amen.**

The Eucharistic Prayer

The great prayer of praise and thanksgiving proclaims the wonderful works of God. Even though it is the priest's prayer nevertheless it is offered in the name of us all and so through our reflective attention we join ourselves with Christ in praise to the Father. We express our share in the prayer and eucharistic offering by joining in the acclamation (joyful shouts or chants) the Sanctus which concludes the preface, the memorial acclamation, and the great Amen which concludes the eucharistic prayer.

INTRODUCTORY DIALOGUE

The eucharistic prayer is the centre and high point of the whole celebration. The priest invites us to lift up our hearts to God.
The Lord be with you.
> **And also with you.**

Lift up your hearts.
> **We lift them up to the Lord.**

Let us give thanks to the Lord our God.
> **It is right to give him thanks and praise.**

THE ORDER OF MASS

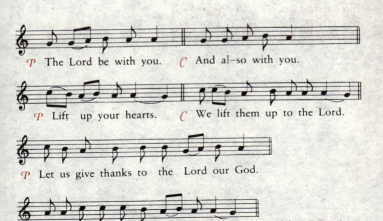

𝒫 The Lord be with you. 𝒞 And al-so with you.

𝒫 Lift up your hearts. 𝒞 We lift them up to the Lord.

𝒫 Let us give thanks to the Lord our God.

𝒞 It is right to give him thanks and praise.

THE ORDER OF MASS

THE PREFACE

The priest now sings or says the Preface, a prayer of thanksgiving.

The Preface for some feast days is found in the Proper of the Day, otherwise turn to the seasonal Prefaces on pages 558-565.

At the end of the Preface all join in the following acclamation:

**Holy, holy, holy Lord, God of power and might,
heaven and earth are full of your glory.
Hosanna in the highest.**

**Blessed is he who comes in the name of the Lord.
Hosanna in the highest.**

*All kneel**

We never grasp the full meaning of the eucharist in a single form of the eucharistic prayer. Variety is a feature of the new eucharistic liturgy since there are many ways of thanking God for all he has accomplished for us through the redeeming work of Christ.

Eucharistic Prayer I see page 566.
Eucharistic Prayer II see page 573.
Eucharistic Prayer III see page 579.
Eucharistic Prayer IV see page 584.

---

* In some places it is the custom to remain standing for the entire eucharistic prayer.

THE ORDER OF MASS

Prefaces

Season of Advent

PREFACE OF ADVENT I
From the First Sunday of Advent until 16 December

Father, all-powerful and ever-living God,
we do well always and everywhere to give you thanks
through Jesus Christ our Lord.

When he humbled himself to come among us as a man,
he fulfilled the plan you formed long ago
and opened for us the way to salvation.

Now we watch for the day,
hoping that the salvation promised us will be ours
when Christ our Lord will come again in his glory.

And so, with all the choirs of angels in heaven
we proclaim your glory
and join in their unending hymn of praise:
Holy, holy, holy ...

PREFACE OF ADVENT II
17 December–24 December

Father, all-powerful and ever-living God,
we do well always and everywhere to give you thanks
through Jesus Christ our Lord.

His future coming was proclaimed by all the prophets.
The virgin mother bore him in her womb with love beyond all telling.
John the Baptist was his herald
and made him known when at last he came.
In his love Christ has filled us with joy
as we prepare to celebrate his birth,
so that when he comes he may find us watching in prayer,
our hearts filled with wonder and praise.
And so, with all the choirs of angels in heaven
we proclaim your glory
and join in their unending hymn of praise:
Holy, holy, holy ...

Season of Christmas
PREFACE OF CHRISTMAS I
Father, all-powerful and ever-living God,
we do well always and everywhere to give you thanks
through Jesus Christ our Lord.
In the wonder of the incarnation
your eternal Word has brought to the eyes of faith
a new and radiant vision of your glory.
In him we see our God made visible
and so are caught up in love of the God we cannot see.
And so, with all the choirs of angels in heaven
we proclaim your glory
and join in their unending hymn of praise:
Holy, holy, holy ...

PREFACE OF CHRISTMAS II
Father, all-powerful and ever-living God,
we do well always and everywhere to give you thanks
through Jesus Christ our Lord.
Today you fill our hearts with joy
as we recognise in Christ the revelation of your love.
No eye can see his glory as our God,
yet now he is seen as one like us.
Christ is your Son before all ages,
yet now he is born in time.
He has come to lift up all things to himself,
to restore unity to creation,
and to lead mankind from exile into your heavenly kingdom.
With all the angels of heaven
we sing our joyful hymn of praise:
Holy, holy, holy ...

PREFACE OF CHRISTMAS III
Father, all-powerful and ever-living God,
we do well always and everywhere to give you thanks
through Jesus Christ our Lord.
Today in him a new light has dawned upon the world:
God has become one with man,
and man has become one again with God.
Your eternal Word has taken upon himself our human weakness,

PREFACES

giving our mortal nature immortal value.
So marvellous is this oneness between God and man
that in Christ man restores to man the gift of everlasting life.
In our joy we sing to your glory
with all the choirs of angels:
Holy, holy, holy ...

Season of Lent

The Prefaces of Lent are said especially on Sundays of Lent which have no preface of their own.

PREFACE OF LENT I

Father, all-powerful and ever-living God,
we do well always and everwhere to give you thanks
through Jesus Christ our Lord.
Each year you give us this joyful season
when we prepare to celebrate the paschal mystery
with mind and heart renewed.
You give us a spirit of loving reverence for you, our Father,
and of willing service to our neighbour.
As we recall the great events that gave us a new life in Christ,
you bring the image of your Son to perfection within us.
Now, with angels and archangels,
and the whole company of heaven,
we sing the unending hymn of your praise:
Holy, holy, holy ...

PREFACE OF LENT II

Father, all-powerful and ever-living God,
we do well always and everywhere to give you thanks.
This great season of grace is your gift to your family
to renew us in spirit.
You give us strength to purify our hearts,
to control our desires,
and so to serve you in freedom.
You teach us how to live in this passing world,
with our heart set on the world that will never end.
Now, with all the saints and angels,
we praise you for ever:
Holy, holy, holy ...

PREFACES

Season of Easter

The Prefaces of Easter are said during the Easter Season. The Preface of Easter I is given with the Easter Vigil, see above, page 369.

PREFACE OF EASTER II

Father, all-powerful and ever-living God,
we do well always and everywhere to give you thanks
through Jesus Christ our Lord.
We praise you with greater joy than ever in this Easter season,
when Christ became our paschal sacrifice.
He has made us children of the light,
rising to new and everlasting life.
He has opened the gates of heaven
to receive his faithful people.
His death is our ransom from death:
his resurrection is our rising to life.
The joy of the resurrection renews the whole world,
while the choirs of heaven sing for ever to your glory:
Holy, holy, holy ...

PREFACE OF EASTER III

Father, all-powerful and ever-living God,
we do well always and everywhere to give you thanks
through Jesus Christ our Lord.
We praise you with greater joy than ever in this Easter season,
when Christ became our paschal sacrifice.
He is still our priest,
our advocate who always pleads our cause.
Christ is the victim who dies no more,
the Lamb, once slain, who lives for ever.
The joy of the resurrection renews the whole world,
while the choirs of heaven sing for ever to your glory:
Holy, holy, holy ...

PREFACE OF EASTER IV

Father, all-powerful and ever-living God,
we do well always and everywhere to give you thanks
through Jesus Christ our Lord.
We praise you with greater joy than ever in this Easter season,
when Christ became our paschal sacrifice.

PREFACES

In him a new age has dawned,
the long reign of sin is ended,
a broken world has been renewed,
and man is once again made whole.
The joy of the resurrection renews the whole world,
while the choirs of heaven sing for ever to your glory:
Holy, holy, holy ...

PREFACE OF EASTER V

Father, all-powerful and ever-living God,
we do well always and everywhere to give you thanks
through Jesus Christ our Lord.
We praise you with greater joy than ever in this Easter season,
when Christ became our paschal sacrifice.
As he offered his body on the cross,
his perfect sacrifice fulfilled all others.
As he gave himself into your hands for our salvation,
he showed himself to be the priest, the altar, and the lamb of
  sacrifice.
The joy of the resurrection renews the whole world,
while the choirs of heaven sing for ever to your glory:
Holy, holy, holy ...

Sundays in Ordinary Time

The Sunday Prefaces are said on the Ordinary Sundays of the
Year.

PREFACE OF SUNDAYS I

Father, all-powerful and ever-living God,
we do well always and everywhere to give you thanks
through Jesus Christ our Lord.
Through his cross and resurrection
he freed us from sin and death
and called us to the glory that has made us
a chosen race, a royal priesthood,
a holy nation, a people set apart.
Everywhere we proclaim your mighty works
for you have called us out of darkness
into your own wonderful light.
And so, with all the choirs of angels in heaven

PREFACES

we proclaim your glory
and join in their unending hymn of praise:
Holy, holy, holy ...

PREFACE OF SUNDAYS II

Father, all-powerful and ever-living God,
we do well always and everywhere to give you thanks
through Jesus Christ our Lord.
Out of love for sinful man,
he humbled himself to be born of the Virgin.
By suffering on the cross
he freed us from unending death,
and by rising from the dead
he gave us eternal life.
And so, with all the choirs of angels in heaven
we proclaim your glory
and join in their unending hymn of praise:
Holy, holy, holy ...

PREFACE OF SUNDAYS III

Father, all-powerful and ever-living God,
we do well always and everywhere to give you thanks.
We see your infinite power
in your loving plan of salvation.
You came to our rescue by your power as God,
but you wanted us to be saved by one like us.
Man refused your friendship,
but man himself was to restore it
through Jesus Christ our Lord.
Through him the angels of heaven offer their prayer of adoration
as they rejoice in your presence for ever.
May our voices be one with theirs
in their triumphant hymn of praise:
Holy, holy, holy ...

PREFACE OF SUNDAYS IV

Father, all-powerful and ever-living God,
we do well always and everywhere to give you thanks
through Jesus Christ our Lord.
By his birth we are reborn.
In his suffering we are freed from sin.

PREFACES

By his rising from the dead we rise to everlasting life.
In his return to you in glory
we enter into your heavenly kingdom.
And so, we join the angels and the saints
as they sing their unending hymn of praise:
Holy, holy, holy ...

PREFACE OF SUNDAYS V

Father, all-powerful and ever-living God,
we do well always and everywhere to give you thanks.
All things are of your making,
all times and seasons obey your laws,
but you chose to create man in your own image,
setting him over the whole world in all its wonder.
You made man the steward of creation,
to praise you day by day for the marvels of your wisdom and
  power,
through Jesus Christ our Lord.
We praise you, Lord, with all the angels
in their song of joy:
Holy, holy, holy ...

PREFACE OF SUNDAYS VI

Father, all-powerful and ever-living God,
we do well always and everywhere to give you thanks.
In you we live and move and have our being.
Each day you show us a Father's love;
your Holy Spirit, dwelling within us,
gives us on earth the hope of unending joy.
Your gift of the Spirit,
who raised Jesus from the dead,
is the foretaste and promise
of the paschal feast of heaven.
With thankful praise,
in company with the angels,
we glorify the wonders of your power:
Holy, holy, holy ...

PREFACE OF SUNDAYS VII

Father, all-powerful and ever-living God,
we do well always and everywhere to give you thanks.

So great was your love
that you gave us your Son as our redeemer.
You sent him as one like ourselves,
though free from sin,
that you might see and love in us
what you see and love in Christ.
Your gifts of grace, lost by disobedience,
are now restored by the obedience of your Son.
We praise you, Lord, with all the angels and saints
in their song of joy:
Holy, holy, holy …

PREFACE OF SUNDAYS VIII

Father, all-powerful and ever-living God,
we do well always and everywhere to give you thanks.
When your children sinned
and wandered far from your friendship,
you reunited them with yourself
through the blood of your Son
and the power of the Holy Spirit.
You gather them into your Church,
to be one as you, Father, are one
with your Son and the Holy Spirit.
You call them to be your people,
to praise your wisdom in all your works.
You make them the body of Christ
and the dwelling-place of the Holy Spirit.
In our joy we sing to your glory
with all the choirs of angels:
Holy, holy, holy …

THE ORDER OF MASS

Eucharistic Prayer I

The passages within the brackets may be omitted if the celebrant wishes.

We come to you, Father,
with praise and thanksgiving,
through Jesus Christ your Son.
Through him we ask you to accept and bless
these gifts we offer you in sacrifice.

We pray for the Church.

We offer them for your holy catholic Church,
watch over it, Lord, and guide it;
grant it peace and unity throughout the world.
We offer them for N. our Pope,
for N. our bishop,
and for all who hold and teach the catholic faith
that comes to us from the apostles.

For the living.

Remember, Lord, your people,
especially those for whom we now pray, N. and N.
Remember all of us gathered here before you.
You know how firmly we believe in you
and dedicate ourselves to you.
We offer you this sacrifice of praise
for ourselves and those who are dear to us.
We pray to you, our living and true God,
for our well-being and redemption.

To honour the saints.

In union with the whole Church
we honour Mary,
the ever-virgin mother of Jesus Christ our Lord and God.
We honour Joseph, her husband,
the apostles and martyrs
Peter and Paul, Andrew,
(James, John, Thomas,
James, Philip,
Bartholomew, Matthew, Simon and Jude;
we honour Linus, Cletus, Clement, Sixtus,
Cornelius, Cyprian, Lawrence, Chrysogonus,
John and Paul, Cosmas and Damian)

THE ORDER OF MASS

and all the saints.
May their merits and prayers
gain us your constant help and protection.
(Through Christ our Lord. Amen.)

For acceptance of this offering.
Father, accept this offering
from your whole family.
Grant us your peace in this life,
save us from final damnation,
and count us among those you have chosen.
(Through Christ our Lord. Amen.)

Bless and approve our offering;
make it acceptable to you,
an offering in spirit and in truth.
Let it become for us
the body and blood of Jesus Christ,
your only Son, our Lord.
(Through Christ our Lord. Amen.)

The Lord's supper: the consecration.
The day before he suffered
he took bread in his sacred hands
and looking up to heaven,
to you, his almighty Father,
he gave you thanks and praise.
He broke the bread,
gave it to his disciples, and said:

Take this, all of you, and eat it:
this is my body which will be given up for you.

When supper was ended,
he took the cup.
Again he gave you thanks and praise,
gave the cup to his disciples, and said:
Take this, all of you, and drink from it:
this is the cup of my blood,
the blood of the new and everlasting covenant.
It will be shed for you and for all men
so that sins may be forgiven.
Do this in memory of me.

THE ORDER OF MASS

Memorial acclamation of the people

Let us proclaim the mystery of faith:

1. **Christ has died,
   Christ is risen,
   Christ will come again.**

2. **Dying you destroyed our death,
   rising you restored our life.
   Lord Jesus, come in glory.**

3. **When we eat this bread and drink this cup,
   we proclaim your death, Lord Jesus,
   until you come in glory.**

4. **Lord, by your cross and resurrection
   you have set us free.
   You are the Saviour of the world.**

5. *(In Ireland:)* **My Lord and my God.**

Memorial of the paschal mystery and offering.

Father, we celebrate the memory of Christ, your Son.
We, your people and your ministers,
recall his passion,
his resurrection from the dead,
and his ascension into glory;
and from the many gifts you have given us
we offer to you, God of glory and majesty,
this holy and perfect sacrifice:
the bread of life
and the cup of eternal salvation.

Look with favour on these offerings
and accept them as once you accepted
the gifts of your servant Abel,
the sacrifice of Abraham, our father in faith,
and the bread and wine offered by your priest Melchisedech.
Almighty God,
we pray that your angel may take this sacrifice
to your altar in heaven.
Then, as we receive from this altar
the sacred body and blood of your Son,
let us be filled with every grace and blessing.
(Through Christ our Lord. Amen.)

THE ORDER OF MASS

Let us proclaim the mystery of faith:

1. Christ has died, Christ is risen, Christ will come again.

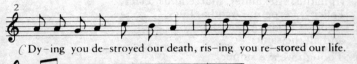

2. Dying you destroyed our death, rising you restored our life. Lord Jesus, come in glory.

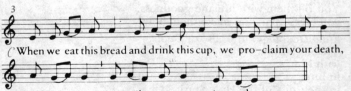
3. When we eat this bread and drink this cup, we proclaim your death, Lord Jesus, until you come in glory.

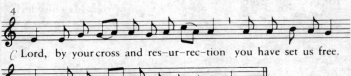

4. Lord, by your cross and resurrection you have set us free. You are the Saviour of the world.

THE ORDER OF MASS

For the dead.
Remember, Lord, those who have died
and have gone before us marked with the sign of faith,
especially those for whom we now pray, N. and N.
May these, and all who sleep in Christ,
find in your presence
light, happiness, and peace.
(Through Christ our Lord. Amen.)

For us sinners.
For ourselves, too, we ask
some share in the fellowship of your apostles and martyrs,
with John the Baptist, Stephen, Matthias, Barnabas,
(Ignatius, Alexander, Marcellinus, Peter,
Felicity, Perpetua, Agatha, Lucy,
Agnes, Cecilia, Anastasia)
and all the saints.

Though we are sinners,
we trust in your mercy and love.
Do not consider what we truly deserve,
but grant us your forgiveness.

Through Christ our Lord
you give us all these gifts.
You fill them with life and goodness,
you bless them and make them holy.

Final Doxology: in praise of God.
Through him,
with him,
in him,
in the unity of the Holy Spirit,
all glory and honour is yours,
almighty Father,
for ever and ever.
   Amen.

Turn to page 590.

THE ORDER OF MASS

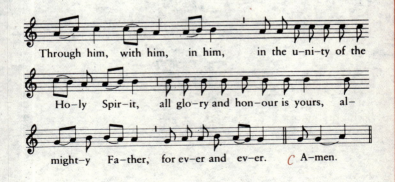

THE ORDER OF MASS

Eucharistic Prayer II

Preface
This may be replaced by another preface.

Father, it is our duty and our salvation,
always and everywhere
to give you thanks
through your beloved Son, Jesus Christ.

He is the Word through whom you made the universe,
the Saviour you sent to redeem us.
By the power of the Holy Spirit
he took flesh and was born of the Virgin Mary.

For our sake he opened his arms on the cross;
he put an end to death
and revealed the resurrection.
In this he fulfilled your will
and won for you a holy people.

And so we join the angels and the saints
in proclaiming your glory
as we sing (say):

> **Holy, holy, holy Lord, God of power and might,
> heaven and earth are full of your glory.**
> > **Hosanna in the highest.**
>
> **Blessed is he who comes in the name of the Lord.**
> > **Hosanna in the highest.**

Invocation of the Holy Spirit.
Lord, you are holy indeed,
the fountain of all holiness.
Let your Spirit come upon these gifts to make them holy,
so that they may become for us
the body and blood of our Lord, Jesus Christ.

The Lord's Supper.
Before he was given up to death,
a death he freely accepted,
he took bread and gave you thanks.
He broke the bread,
gave it to his disciples, and said:
Take this, all of you, and eat it:
this is my body which will be given up for you.

THE ORDER OF MASS

When supper was ended, he took the cup.
Again he gave you thanks and praise,
gave the cup to his disciples, and said:

Take this, all of you, and drink from it:
this is the cup of my blood,
the blood of the new and everlasting covenant.
It will be shed for you and for all men
so that sins may be forgiven.
Do this in memory of me.

Memorial acclamation of the people

Let us proclaim the mystery of faith:

1. **Christ has died,
   Christ is risen,
   Christ will come again.**
2. **Dying you destroyed our death,
   rising you restored our life.
   Lord Jesus, come in glory.**
3. **When we eat this bread and drink this cup,
   we proclaim your death, Lord Jesus,
   until you come in glory.**
4. **Lord, by your cross and resurrection
   you have set us free.
   You are the Saviour of the world.**
5. *(In Ireland:)* **My Lord and my God.**

The memorial prayer.

In memory of his death and resurrection,
we offer you, Father, this life-giving bread,
this saving cup.
We thank you for counting us worthy
to stand in your presence and serve you.
May all of us who share in the body and blood of Christ
be brought together in unity by the Holy Spirit.

Intercessions for the Church.

Lord, remember your Church throughout the world;
make us grow in love,
together with N. our Pope,
N. our bishop, and all the clergy.

THE ORDER OF MASS

Let us pro-claim the mys-te-ry of faith:

1. Christ has died, Christ is ris-en, Christ will come a-gain.

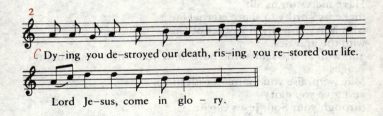

2. Dy-ing you de-stroyed our death, ris-ing you re-stored our life. Lord Je-sus, come in glo-ry.

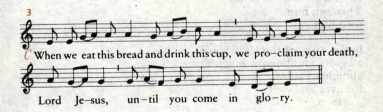

3. When we eat this bread and drink this cup, we pro-claim your death, Lord Je-sus, un-til you come in glo-ry.

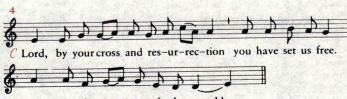

4. Lord, by your cross and res-ur-rec-tion you have set us free. You are the Sav-iour of the world.

THE ORDER OF MASS

For the dead.
(In Masses for the Dead the following may be added:
Remember N., whom you have called from this life.
In baptism he [she] died with Christ:
may he [she] also share his resurrection.)

Remember our brothers and sisters
who have gone to their rest
in the hope of rising again;
bring them and all the departed
into the light of your presence.

In communion with the saints.
Have mercy on us all;
make us worthy to share eternal life
with Mary, the virgin mother of God,
with the apostles,
and with all the saints who have done your will throughout the
  ages.
May we praise you in union with them,
and give you glory
through your Son, Jesus Christ.

Final doxology: in praise of God.
Through him,
with him,
in him,
in the unity of the Holy Spirit,
all glory and honour is yours,
almighty Father,
for ever and ever.
  Amen.

Turn to page 590.

THE ORDER OF MASS

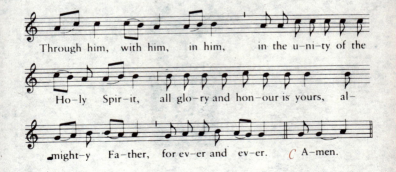

Eucharistic Prayer III

Praise to the Father.
Father, you are holy indeed,
and all creation rightly gives you praise.
All life, all holiness comes from you
through your Son, Jesus Christ our Lord,
by the working of the Holy Spirit.
From age to age you gather a people to yourself,
so that from east to west
a perfect offering may be made
to the glory of your name.

Invocation of the Holy Spirit.
And so, Father, we bring you these gifts.
We ask you to make them holy by the power of your Spirit,
that they may become the body and blood
of your Son, our Lord Jesus Christ,
at whose command we celebrate this eucharist.

The Lord's Supper.
On the night he was betrayed,
he took bread and gave you thanks and praise.
He broke the bread, gave it to his disciples, and said:
Take this, all of you, and eat it:
this is my body which will be given up for you.

When supper was ended, he took the cup.
Again he gave you thanks and praise,
gave the cup to his disciples, and said:

Take this, all of you, and drink from it:
this is the cup of my blood,
the blood of the new and everlasting covenant.
It will be shed for you and for all men
so that sins may be forgiven.
Do this in memory of me.

THE ORDER OF MASS

Memorial acclamation of the people
Let us proclaim the mystery of faith:
1. **Christ has died,
   Christ is risen,
   Christ will come again.**
2. **Dying you destroyed our death,
   rising you restored our life.
   Lord Jesus, come in glory.**
3. **When we eat this bread and drink this cup,
   we proclaim your death, Lord Jesus,
   until you come in glory.**
4. **Lord, by your cross and resurrection
   you have set us free.
   You are the Saviour of the world.**
5. *(In Ireland:)* **My Lord and my God.**

The memorial prayer
Father, calling to mind the death your Son endured for our salvation,
his glorious resurrection and ascension into heaven,
and ready to greet him when he comes again,
we offer you in thanksgiving this holy and living sacrifice.

Look with favour on your Church's offering,
and see the Victim whose death has reconciled us to yourself.
Grant that we, who are nourished by his body and blood,
may be filled with his Holy Spirit,
and become one body, one spirit in Christ.

In Communion with the Saints
May he make us an everlasting gift to you
and enable us to share in the inheritance of your saints,
with Mary, the virgin Mother of God;
with the apostles, the martyrs,
(Saint N. — the saint of the day or patron saint) and all your saints,
on whose constant intercession we rely for help.

Intercession for the Church
Lord, may this sacrifice,
which has made our peace with you,
advance the peace and salvation of all the world.

THE ORDER OF MASS

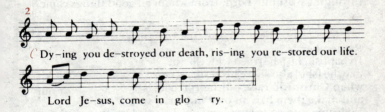

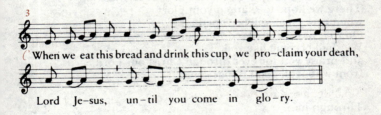

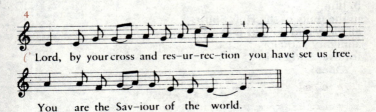

581

THE ORDER OF MASS

Strengthen in faith and love your pilgrim Church on earth;
your servant, Pope N., our bishop N.,
and all the bishops,
with the clergy and the entire people your Son has gained for you.
Father, hear the prayers of the family you have gathered here
  before you.
In mercy and love unite all your children wherever they may be.*

For the dead
Welcome into your kingdom our departed brothers and sisters,
and all who have left this world in your friendship.
We hope to enjoy for ever the vision of your glory,
through Christ our Lord, from whom all good things come.

Or:

*In Masses for the dead, the following may be said:
Remember N.
In baptism he [she] died with Christ:
may he [she] also share his resurrection,
when Christ will raise our mortal bodies
and make them like his own in glory.
Welcome into your kingdom our departed brothers and sisters,
and all who have left this world in your friendship.
There we hope to share in your glory
when every tear will be wiped away.
On that day we shall see you, our God, as you are.
We shall become like you
and praise you for ever through Christ our Lord,
from whom all good things come.

Final doxology: in praise of God.
Through him,
with him,
in him,
in the unity of the Holy Spirit,
all glory and honour is yours,
almighty Father,
for ever and ever.
  Amen.

Turn to page 590.

THE ORDER OF MASS

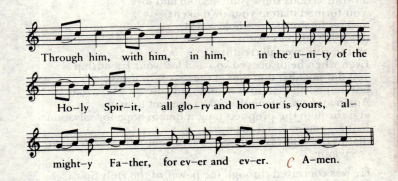

Through him, with him, in him, in the unity of the Holy Spirit, all glory and honour is yours, almighty Father, for ever and ever. C A-men.

THE ORDER OF MASS

Eucharistic Prayer IV
Preface

Father in heaven,
it is right that we should give you thanks and glory:
you alone are God, living and true.
Through all eternity you live in unapproachable light.
Source of life and goodness, you have created all things,
to fill your creatures with every blessing
and lead all men to the joyful vision of your light.
Countless hosts of angels stand before you to do your will;
they look upon your splendour
and praise you, night and day.
United with them,
and in the name of every creature under heaven,
we too praise your glory as we say:

> **Holy, holy, holy Lord, God of power and might,**
> **heaven and earth are full of your glory.**
>> **Hosanna in the highest.**
>
> **Blessed is he who comes in the name of the Lord.**
>> **Hosanna in the highest.**

Praise to the Father.

Father, we acknowledge your greatness:
all your actions show your wisdom and love.
You formed man in your own likeness
and set him over the whole world
to serve you, his creator,
and to rule over all creatures.
Even when he disobeyed you and lost your friendship
you did not abandon him to the power of death,
but helped all men to seek and find you.
Again and again you offered a covenant to man,
and through the prophets taught him to hope for salvation.
Father, you so loved the world
that in the fullness of time you sent your only Son to be our
  Saviour.

He was conceived through the power of the Holy Spirit,
and born of the Virgin Mary,
a man like us in all things but sin.
To the poor he proclaimed the good news of salvation,

THE ORDER OF MASS

to prisoners, freedom,
and to those in sorrow, joy.
In fulfilment of your will
he gave himself up to death;
but by rising from the dead,
he destroyed death and restored life.
And that we might live no longer for ourselves but for him,
he sent the Holy Spirit from you, Father,
as his first gift to those who believe,
to complete his work on earth
and bring us the fullness of grace.

Invocation of the Holy Spirit
Father, may this Holy Spirit sanctify these offerings.
Let them become the body and blood of Jesus Christ our Lord
as we celebrate the great mystery
which he left us as an everlasting covenant.

The Lord's Supper
He always loved those who were his own in the world.
When the time came for him to be glorified by you, his heavenly
   Father,
he showed the depth of his love.

While they were at supper,
he took bread, said the blessing, broke the bread
and gave it to his disciples, saying:
Take this, all of you, and eat it:
this is my body which will be given up for you.

In the same way, he took the cup, filled with wine.
He gave you thanks, and giving the cup to his disciples, said:

Take this, all of you, and drink from it:
this is the cup of my blood,
the blood of the new and everlasting covenant.
It will be shed for you and for all men
so that sins may be forgiven.
Do this in memory of me.

THE ORDER OF MASS

Memorial acclamation of the people

Let us proclaim the mystery of faith:

1. **Christ has died,
   Christ is risen,
   Christ will come again.**
2. **Dying you destroyed our death,
   rising your restored our life.
   Lord Jesus, come in glory.**
3. **When we eat this bread and drink this cup,
   we proclaim your death, Lord Jesus,
   until you come in glory.**
4. **Lord, by your cross and resurrection
   you have set us free.
   You are the Saviour of the world.**
5. *(In Ireland:)* **My Lord and my God.**

The memorial prayer.

Father, we now celebrate this memorial of our redemption.
We recall Christ's death, his descent among the dead,
his resurrection, and his ascension to your right hand;
and, looking forward to his coming in glory,
we offer you his body and blood,
the acceptable sacrifice
which brings salvation to the whole world.

Intercessions: for the Church.

Lord, look upon this sacrifice which you have given to your
  Church;
and by your Holy Spirit, gather all who share* this bread and
  wine
into the one body of Christ, a living sacrifice of praise.

Lord, remember those for whom we offer this sacrifice,
especially N. our Pope,
 N. our bishop, and bishops and clergy everywhere.
Remember those who take part in this offering,
those here present and all your people,
and all who seek you with a sincere heart.

* In England & Wales: 'who share this one bread and one cup'.

THE ORDER OF MASS

Let us proclaim the mystery of faith:

1. Christ has died, Christ is risen, Christ will come again.

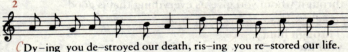
2. Dying you destroyed our death, rising you restored our life.

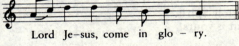
Lord Jesus, come in glory.

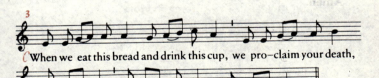
3. When we eat this bread and drink this cup, we proclaim your death, Lord Jesus, until you come in glory.

4. Lord, by your cross and resurrection you have set us free.

You are the Saviour of the world.

THE ORDER OF MASS

For the dead.
Remember those who have died in the peace of Christ
and all the dead whose faith is known to you alone.

In communion with the saints.
Father, in your mercy grant also to us, your children,
to enter into our heavenly inheritance
in the company of the Virgin Mary, the Mother of God,
and your apostles and saints.
Then, in your kingdom, freed from the corruption of sin and death,
we shall sing your glory with every creature through Christ our Lord,
through whom you give us everything that is good.

Final doxology: in praise of God.
Through him,
with him,
in him,
in the unity of the Holy Spirit,
all glory and honour is yours,
almighty Father,
for ever and ever.
Amen.

THE ORDER OF MASS

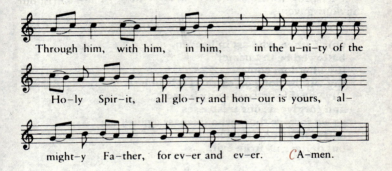

THE ORDER OF MASS

Communion Rite

All stand

The communion rite lays strong emphasis on peace, unity and our prayer for forgiveness. We come together to the Lord's table as a community bound together by love. We are confident in Christ's mercy as we respond to his call to come to his table.

THE LORD'S PRAYER

The priest invites us to join him in saying the Lord's prayer, using the following or similar words.

Let us pray with confidence to the Father in the words our Saviour gave us.

> **Our Father, who art in heaven,**
> **hallowed be thy name;**
> **thy kingdom come;**
> **thy will be done on earth as it is in heaven.**
> **Give us this day our daily bread;**
> **and forgive us our trespasses**
> **as we forgive those who trespass against us;**
> **and lead us not into temptation,**
> **but deliver us from evil.**

The priest continues alone.
Deliver us, Lord, from every evil,
and grant us peace in our day.
In your mercy keep us free from sin
and protect us from all anxiety
as we wait in joyful hope
for the coming of our Saviour, Jesus Christ.

We give our assent to the prayer by joining in the acclamation.

> **For the kingdom, the power, and the glory are yours,**
> **now and forever.**

THE ORDER OF MASS

Celebrant: Let us pray with confidence to the Father in the words our Saviour gave us:

All: Our Father, who art in heaven, hallowed be thy name. Thy kingdom come. Thy will be done on earth, as it is in heaven. Give us this day our daily bread, and forgive us our trespasses, as we forgive those who trespass against us, and lead us not into temptation, but deliver us from evil.

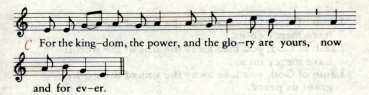

C. For the kingdom, the power, and the glory are yours, now and for ever.

THE ORDER OF MASS

THE RITE OF PEACE

We acknowledge our unity with one another in Christ which his death and resurrection have brought to us. He is the peace between us. The sign of peace echoes Christ's own resurrection greeting to his disciples.

Lord Jesus Christ, you said to your apostles:
I leave you peace, my peace I give you.
Look not on our sins, but on the faith of your Church,
and grant us the peace and unity of your kingdom
where you live for ever and ever.
   Amen.
The peace of the Lord be with you always.
   And also with you.

The priest (or deacon) may add these or similar words.

Let us offer each other the sign of peace.

All make an appropriate sign of peace according to local custom.

THE BREAKING OF BREAD

Christ's gesture of breaking bread with his disciples at the Last Supper gave the entire eucharist the name of the "breaking of bread" (fractio panis). This gesture signifies that we who share one bread and one cup are made one. Through the breaking of the host the eucharist is seen more clearly as a sign of unity and charity since the one bread is being distributed among the members of one family.

The priest breaks the host and places a small piece in the chalice, saying quietly:

May this mingling of the body and blood of our Lord
Jesus Christ
bring eternal life to us who receive it.

During the breaking of bread the Lamb of God is either sung or said.

> **Lamb of God, you take away the sins of the world:**
>   **have mercy on us.**
> **Lamb of God, you take away the sins of the world:**
>   **have mercy on us.**
> **Lamb of God, you take away the sins of the world:**
>   **grant us peace.**

THE ORDER OF MASS

The peace of the Lord be with you al-ways.

And al-so with you.

Then the celebrant may add

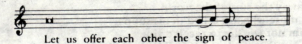
Let us offer each other the sign of peace.

THE ORDER OF MASS

PREPARATION FOR COMMUNION

The priest prepares privately for communion. We should do the same through one or other of the following prayers.

Lord Jesus Christ, Son of the living God, by the will of the Father and the work of the Holy Spirit your death brought life to the world. By your holy body and blood free me from all my sins and from every evil. Keep me faithful to your teaching, and never let me be parted from you.

or

Lord Jesus Christ, with faith in your love and mercy I eat your body and drink your blood. Let it not bring me condemnation, but health in mind and body.

INVITATION TO COMMUNION

The priest lifts up the sacred host and invites us to share in the eucharistic banquet with these words:

This is the Lamb of God
who takes away the sins of the world.
Happy are those who are called to his supper.
Lord, I am not worthy to receive you,
but only say the word and I shall be healed.

THE PRIEST'S COMMUNION

The priest receives the body and blood of Christ

THE PEOPLE'S COMMUNION

The congregation in procession approach the altar to communicate. The communion hymn or antiphon may be sung or said during communion.

COMMUNION SONG: *turn to the Proper of the Day.*

The priest goes to the communicants and for each one he takes a host, raises it a little and shows it saying:

The body of Christ.
Amen.

THE ORDER OF MASS

The sign of communion is more complete when given under both kinds since the sign of the eucharistic meal of food and drink appears more clearly. Our earthly meal is a foretaste of the heavenly banquet to which we are all invited through baptism. The priest presents the chalice to the communicant saying:

The blood of Christ:
  Amen.

SILENCE or SONG

After communion a period of silence may be observed. A psalm or song of praise may be sung through which we express our gratitude to the Lord for all he has given to us.

PRAYER AFTER COMMUNION: *turn to the Proper of the Day.*
All stand

The priest invites us all to pray that the eucharist will have its effect in our lives and bring us to God's kingdom. Priest and people pray for a short while in silence unless the silence has already been observed after communion. We show our assent by responding:
  Amen.

THE ORDER OF MASS

Concluding Rite

The priest greets us once more and invokes God's blessing upon us. Brief announcements, if any, are made at this time. If any liturgical service follows immediately, the rite of dismissal is omitted.

Greeting

The Lord be with you.
And also with you.

Blessing

Simple form:
May almighty God bless you,
The Father, and the Son ✠ and the Holy Spirit.
Amen.

or

Solemn Blessing
On certain days another more solemn form of blessing or prayer over the people may be used.

Solemn Blessing: *turn to the Proper of the Day.*
or
Prayer over the People

This special prayer always ends with this blessing:
And may almighty God bless you,
the Father, and the Son ✠ and the Holy Spirit.
Amen

Dismissal

The priest may make some concluding comments to remind us of the theme of the Mass. The priest or deacon then sends us out to do good works, praising and blessing the Lord.
Go in the peace of Christ.
or
The Mass is ended, go in peace.
or
Go in peace to love and serve the Lord.
Thanks be to God.

THE ORDER OF MASS

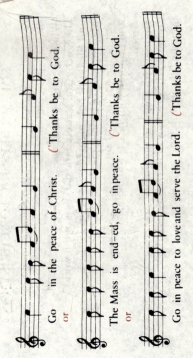

Solemn Blessings

SOLEMN BLESSING FOR ADVENT

During the Season of Advent the priest may give this Solemn Blessing at the end of Mass.

You believe that the Son of God once came to us;
you look for him to come again.
May his coming bring you the light of his holiness
and free you with his blessing.
Amen.

May God make you steadfast in faith,
joyful in hope, and untiring in love
all the days of your life.
Amen.

You rejoice that our Redeemer came to live with us as man.
When he comes again in glory,
may he reward you with endless life.
Amen.

May almighty God bless you,
the Father, and the Son, ✠ and the Holy Spirit.
Amen.

SOLEMN BLESSING FOR CHRISTMAS

During the Season of Christmas the priest may give this Solemn Blessing at the end of Mass.

When he came to us as man,
the Son of God scattered the darkness of this world,
and filled this holy night [day] with his glory.
May the God of infinite goodness
scatter the darkness of sin
and brighten your hearts with holiness.
Amen.

God sent his angels to shepherds
to herald the great joy of our Saviour's birth.
May he fill you with joy

and make you heralds of his gospel.
Amen.
When the Word became man,
earth was joined to heaven.
May he give you his peace and good will,
and fellowship with all the heavenly host.
Amen.
May almighty God bless you,
the Father, and the Son, ✠ and the Holy Spirit.
Amen.

SOLEMN BLESSING FOR EASTERTIME

During the Season of Easter the priest may give this Solemn Blessing at the end of Mass.

Through the resurrection of his Son
God has redeemed you and made you his children.
May he bless you with joy.
Amen.
The Redeemer has given you lasting freedom.
May you inherit his everlasting life.
Amen.
By faith you rose with him in baptism.
May your lives be holy,
so that you will be united with him for ever.
Amen.
May almighty God bless you,
the Father, and the Son, ✠ and the Holy Spirit.
Amen.

SOLEMN BLESSINGS FOR ORDINARY TIME

During Ordinary Time the priest may give one of these Solemn Blessings at the end of Mass.

ONE Blessing of Aaron Numbers 6:24-26

May the Lord bless you and keep you.
Amen.
May his face shine upon you,
and be gracious to you.
Amen.
May he look upon you with kindness,
and give you his peace.
Amen.
May almighty God bless you,
the Father, and the Son, ✠ and the Holy Spirit.
Amen.

TWO Philippians 4:7

May the peace of God
which is beyond all understanding
keep your hearts and minds
in the knowledge and love of God
and of his Son, our Lord Jesus Christ.
Amen.
May almighty God bless you,
the Father, and the Son, ✠ and the Holy Spirit.
Amen.

THREE

May almighty God bless you in his mercy,
and make you always aware of his saving wisdom.
Amen.
May he strengthen your faith with proofs of his love,
so that you will persevere in good works.
Amen.
May he direct your steps to himself,
and show you how to walk in charity and peace.
Amen.
May almighty God bless you,
the Father, and the Son, ✠ and the Holy Spirit.
Amen.

SOLEMN BLESSING

FOUR
May the God of all consolation
bless you in every way
and grant you peace all the days of your life.
Amen.
May he free you from all anxiety
and strengthen your hearts in his love.
Amen.
May he enrich you with his gifts of faith, hope, and
  love,
so that what you do in this life
will bring you to the happiness of everlasting life.
Amen.
May almighty God bless you,
the Father, and the Son, ✠ and the Holy Spirit.
Amen.

FIVE
May almighty God keep you from all harm
and bless you with every good gift.
Amen.
May he set his Word in your heart
and fill you with lasting joy.
Amen.
May you walk in his ways,
always knowing what is right and good,
until you enter your heavenly inheritance.
Amen.
May almighty God bless you,
the Father, the Son, ✠ and the Holy Spirit.
Amen.

Thanksgiving After Mass

Prayers of thanksgiving to God the Father

We thank you, holy Father,
for your holy name
which you have made dwell in our hearts,
and for the knowledge, faith and immortality
which you have made known to us through your
servant Jesus.
    Glory be to you for ever.

You, almighty Lord,
created all things for your glory,
and you give food and drink to men
that they may enjoy it and give thanks to you.
But to us you give spiritual food and drink
and life eternal through your Servant.
Above all we thank you for your power.
    Glory be to you for ever.

Be mindful of your Church, Lord,
deliver her from all evil,
perfect her in your love,
gather her, your holy Church, from the four winds
into the kingdom you have prepared for her.
For yours is the power and the glory
for ever and ever.
Let grace come, and this world pass away!
Hosanna to the God of David!
If anyone is holy, let him draw near;
if anyone is not holy, let him repent.
      COME, LORD! AMEN!

The Didache

We bless and praise you, Father, for you have
    accepted from our hands
these simple gifts and made them holy,
a sign of your endless love.
Make us also signs that we are your children.
May we live as the broken bread passing among men.

THANKSGIVING AFTER MASS

We thank you, Father, for your Son
in this meal we have shared.
It is he who transforms us,
makes us new men,
a living promise of your hope to all men.
May we live as witnesses to your Son,
who has come and who will come again,
and so we give you, your Son and your Holy Spirit,
glory and praise, now and for ever.

Father, we are your chosen people.
May we live with compassion, kindness, humility and patience.
May we forgive each other, as you forgive us.
May we live with love, which brings all men together
    into perfect harmony.
May the peace of Christ reign in our hearts.
May the words we speak and the deeds we perform
    in your Son's name
tell you of our thanks and praise.

Psalm 136 vv. 1-16; 23-26

Alleluia!
Give thanks to Yahweh, for he is good,
    his love is everlasting!
Give thanks to the God of gods,
    his love is everlasting!
Give thanks to the Lord of lords,
    his love is everlasting!

He alone performs great marvels,
    his love is everlasting!
His wisdom made the heavens,
    his love is everlasting!
He set the earth on the waters,
    his love is everlasting!

He made the great lights,
    his love is everlasting!
The sun to govern the day,
    his love is everlasting!

THANKSGIVING AFTER MASS

Moon and stars to govern the night,
 his love is everlasting!

He struck down the first-born of Egypt,
 his love is everlasting!
And brought Israel out,
 his love is everlasting!
With mighty hand and outstretched arm,
 his love is everlasting!

He split the Sea of Reeds,
 his love is everlasting!
Led Israel through the middle,
 his love is everlasting!
Drowned Pharaoh and his army,
 his love is everlasting!

He led his people through the wilderness,
 his love is everlasting!
He remembered us when we were down,
 his love is everlasting!
And snatched us from our oppressors,
 his love is everlasting!

He provides for all living creatures,
 his love is everlasting!
Give thanks to the God of Heaven,
 his love is everlasting!

Magnificat Luke 1: 46-55

My soul proclaims the greatness of the Lord
and my spirit exults in God my saviour;
because he has looked upon his lowly handmaid.
Yes, from this day forward all generations will call me blessed,
for the Almighty has done great things for me.
Holy is his name,
and his mercy reaches from age to age for those who fear him.
He has shown the power of his arm,
he has routed the proud of heart.
He has pulled down princes from their thrones and exalted the
 lowly.
The hungry he has filled with good things, the rich sent empty
 away.

THANKSGIVING AFTER MASS

He has come to the help of Israel his servant, mindful of **his mercy**
   according to the promise he made to our ancestors —
of his mercy to Abraham and to his descendants for ever.

Prayer to Jesus Christ Crucified

My good and dear Jesus
I kneel before you,
asking you most earnestly
to engrave upon my heart
a deep and lively faith, hope and charity,
with true repentance for my sins,
and a firm resolve to make amends.
As I reflect upon your five wounds,
and dwell upon them with deep compassion and grief,
I recall, good Jesus, the words the prophet David spoke
long ago concerning yourself:
they have pierced my hands and my feet,
they have counted all my bones!

Prayer to our Redeemer

Soul of Christ, make me holy,
Body of Christ, be my salvation.
Blood of Christ, let me drink your wine.
Water flowing from the side of Christ, wash me clean.
Passion of Christ, strengthen me.
Kind Jesus, hear my prayer;
hide me within your wounds
and keep me close to you.
Defend me from the evil enemy.
Call me at my death
to the fellowship of your saints,
that I may sing your praise with them
through all eternity. Amen.

Prayer of self-dedication to Jesus Christ

Lord Jesus Christ,
take all my freedom,
my memory, my understanding, and my will.
All that I have and cherish
you have given me.

THANKSGIVING AFTER MASS

I surrender it all to be guided by your will.
Your grace and your love
are wealth enough for me.
Give me these, Lord Jesus,
and I ask for nothing more.

Thanksgiving for Sunday

O God, our Father, we thank you for this your own day.

We thank you for this day's rest, in which we lay aside our daily work and tasks to relax our bodies, to refresh our minds, and to strengthen our spirits.

We thank you for this day's worship, in which we lay aside our cares and our anxieties to concentrate our every thought on you alone.

We thank you for your Church. We thank you for the fellowship we enjoy within it; for the teaching which is given to us; for the guidance for life and living which we receive.

We thank you for the reading of your word, for the preaching of your truth, for the singing of your praise, for the prayers of your people, and for the sacraments of your grace.

Grant that in this day given to you we may receive such strength and guidance, that we shall be enabled to go out to walk with you, and not to fall from you, in all the days of this week which lies ahead: through Jesus Christ our Lord. Amen.

William Barclay

The Universal Prayer

Lord, I believe in you: increase my faith.
I trust in you: strengthen my trust.
I love you: let me love you *more* and more.
I *am sorry* for my sins: deepen my sorrow.

I worship you as my first beginning,
I long for you as my last end,
I praise you as my constant helper,
and call on you as my loving protector.

THANKSGIVING AFTER MASS

Guide me by your wisdom,
correct me with your justice,
comfort me with your mercy,
protect me with your power.

I offer you, Lord, my thoughts: to be fixed on you;
my words: to have you for their theme;
my actions: to reflect my love for you;
my sufferings: to be endured for your greater glory.

I want to do what you ask of me:
in the way you ask,
for as long as you ask,
because you ask it.

Lord, enlighten my understanding,
strengthen my will,
purify my heart,
and make me holy.
Help me to repent of my past sins
and to resist temptation in the future.
Help me to rise above my human weaknesses
and to grow stronger as a Christian.

Let me love you, my Lord and my God,
and see myself as I really am:
a pilgrim in this world,
a Christian called to respect and love
all whose lives I touch,
those in authority over me
or those under my authority,
my friends and my enemies.

Help me to conquer anger with gentleness,
greed by generosity,
apathy by fervour.
Help me to forget myself
and reach out to others.

Make me prudent in planning,
courageous in taking risks.
Make me patient in suffering, unassuming in prosperity.

Keep me, Lord, attentive at prayer,
temperate in food and drink,
diligent in my work,

THANKSGIVING AFTER MASS

firm in my intentions.

Let my conscience be clear,
my conduct without fault,
my speech blameless,
my life well-ordered.

Put me on my guard against my human weaknesses.
Let me cherish your love for me,
keep your law,
and come at last to your salvation.

Teach me to realise that this world is passing,
that my true future is the happiness of heaven,
that life on earth is short,
and the life to come eternal.

Help me to prepare for death
with a proper fear of judgment,
but a greater trust in your goodness.
Lead me safely through death
to the endless joy of heaven.

Grant this through Christ our Lord. Amen.

Pope Clement XI

Sundays in Ordinary Time/A

Year A: The Year of Matthew

THE new series of readings from Scripture which we hear every sunday at Mass has rightly been called the catechism of the Church. The Second Vatican Council stressed the centrality of scripture as the perpetual source of our spiritual life. Saint Jerome reminds us that 'ignorance of the Scriptures is ignorance of Christ'. The composers of the new lectionary (readings) opted for a three-year cycle with each year being characterized by one of the synoptic Gospels:

> Year A: the year of Matthew
> Year B: the year of Mark
> Year C: the year of Luke

Each of these Gospels is read in semi-continuous form throughout the liturgical year on the sundays in ordinary time. Each evangelist gives us his own special insights into the life of Christ. John's Gospel deals with the seasons of Lent and Easter while the Gospels of Matthew and Luke are used for the season of Advent. We have, therefore, in the liturgy over the three-year cycle a comprehensive presentation of christian doctrine.

What distinguishes Matthew's account of the Gospel story from the others is his concentration on the *words* of Jesus. His portrait of Christ is basically that of the master, the teacher of the new law. His technique is simple. He gathers the sayings of Jesus into five major discourses or 'sermons' and uses them as the skeleton round which he builds his Gospel. The five sermons are:

> The sermon on the mount Chs. 5-7
> The mission sermon Ch. 10
> The parable sermon Ch. 13
> The community sermon Ch. 18
> The final sermon Chs. 23-25

The 'sermons' represent the core of the catechetical instruction of the liturgy in the first year of the cycle. Matthew's Gospel underlines his conviction that the Lord is with His Church, "always to the end of time". This is the theology which Matthew offers us. The abiding presence of the Lord has guided the evangelist in his choice of themes. Each theme gives us an insight

YEAR A: YEAR OF MATTHEW

into the nature of the Church and Christ's activity through it. The mystery of the Church is the centre of Matthew's theology and this leads us to the theology of the Church and the theology of the sacraments.

The narrative parts of the Gospel are intertwined with the five discourses to give us a carefully worked-out catechetical construction of the whole Gospel. From a very early stage Matthew's Gospel was recognised as 'the ecclesiastical Gospel'. He starts with a principle in theology, 'Christ the sacrament of the encounter with God' and develops it in line with the present experience of the Lord's abiding presence and activity in the Church, namely through the sacraments. The Gospel of Matthew, therefore, essentially deals with the mystery of the Church and the sacramental life.

With these principles before us we can begin to appreciate the riches of the Gospel which the Church puts before us. Our lives are intimately linked with the Church and we share the life of Our Lord through the life-giving power of the sacraments. We realise even more that the Church, through the sunday readings of the Gospel, has built its own programme of catechetical instruction into the framework of the liturgy when we all come together as a community to worship God.

STAGE ONE:
THE FIGURE OF JESUS THE MESSIAH — SUNDAYS 1-2

1. The baptism of Jesus — Matthew 3, 13-17
2. The witness of John the Baptist — John 1, 29-34

STAGE TWO:
CHRIST'S DESIGN FOR LIFE IN GOD'S KINGDOM — SUNDAYS 3-9

3. The call of the first disciples — Matthew 4:12-23
4. The sermon on the mount (1) — 5:1-12
5. The sermon on the mount (2) — 5:13-16
6. The sermon on the mount (3) — 5:17-37
7. The sermon on the mount (4) — 5:38-48
8. The sermon on the mount (5) — 6:24-34
9. The sermon on the mount (6) — 7:21-27

YEAR A: YEAR OF MATTHEW

STAGE THREE:
THE SPREAD OF GOD'S KINGDOM — SUNDAYS 10-13

10. The call of Levi — Matthew 9:9-13
11. The mission sermon (1) — 9:36-10:8
12. The mission sermon (2) — 10:26-33
13. The mission sermon (3) — 10:37-42

STAGE FOUR:
THE MYSTERY OF GOD'S KINGDOM — SUNDAYS 14-17

14. The revelation of the simple — Matthew 11:25-30
15. The parable sermon (1) — 13:1-23
16. The parable sermon (2) — 13:23-42
17. The parable sermon (3) — 13:44-52

STAGE FIVE:
GOD'S KINGDOM ON EARTH — CHRIST'S CHURCH — SUNDAYS 18-24

18. The feeding of five thousand — Matthew 14:13-21
19. Jesus walks on the waters — 14:22-23
20. The Canaanite woman — 15:21-28
21. Peter's confession: primacy conferred — 16:13-20
22. The passion prophesied: discipleship — 16:21-27
23. The community sermon (1) — 18:15-20
24. The community sermon (2) — 18:21-35

STAGE SIX:
AUTHORITY AND INVITATION — THE MINISTRY ENDS — SUNDAYS 25-33

25. The parable of the labourers — Matthew 20:1-16
26. The parable of the two sons — 21:28-32
27. The parable of the wicked vinedressers — 21:33-43
28. The parable of the marriage feast — 22:1-14
29. Paying tribute to Caesar — 22:15-21
30. The greatest commandment — 22:34-40
31. Hypocrisy and ambition — 23:1-12
32. The final sermon (1) — 25:1-13
33. The final sermon (2) — 25:14-30

STAGE SEVEN:
GOD'S KINGDOM FULFILLED — SUNDAY 34

34. The solemnity of Christ the King — Matthew 25:31-46

2nd SUNDAY IN ORDINARY TIME/A

Christ the Light of the Nations!
The Spirit of God rested on Christ when he
was baptised by John the Baptist. Through the
giving of the Spirit John recognises Christ as
the Lamb of God who takes away the sins of
the world. We too through the gift of the
Holy Spirit are to become the light of the world
proclaiming salvation to the ends of the earth.

Entrance Antiphon May all the earth give you worship and praise, and break into song to your name, O God, Most High. Psalm 65:4.

Opening Prayer

Let us pray
  [to our Father for the gift of peace]

Father of heaven and earth,
hear our prayers,
and show us the way to peace in the world.

or

Let us pray
  [for the gift of peace]

Almighty and ever-present Father,
your watchful care reaches from end to end
and orders all things in such power
that even the tensions and the tragedies of sin
cannot frustrate your loving plans.

Help us to embrace your will,
give us the strength to follow your call,
so that your truth may live in our hearts
and reflect peace to those who believe in your love.

SECOND SUNDAY IN ORDINARY TIME/A

First Reading   Isaiah 49:3. 5-6
I will make you the light of the nations so that my salvation may reach to the ends of the earth.

The Lord said to me, "You are my servant, Israel,
in whom I shall be glorified";
I was honoured in the eyes of the Lord,
my God was my strength.

And now the Lord has spoken,
he who formed me in the womb to be his servant,
to bring Jacob back to him,
to gather Israel to him:
"It is not enough for you to be my servant,
to restore the tribes of Jacob and bring back the survivors of Israel;
I will make you the light of the nations
so that my salvation may reach to the ends of the earth."

Responsorial Psalm   Psalm 39

℟ **Here I am Lord!
I come to do your will.**

1. I waited, I waited for the Lord
   and he stooped down to me;
   he heard my cry.
   He put a new song into my mouth,
   praise of our God.

2. You do not ask for sacrifice and offerings,
   but an open ear.
   You do not ask for holocaust and victim.
   Instead, here am I. ℟

3. In the scroll of the book it stands written
   that I should do your will.
   My God, I delight in your law
   in the depth of my heart. ℟

4. Your justice I have proclaimed
   in the great assembly.
   My lips I have not sealed;
   you know it, O Lord. ℟

SECOND SUNDAY IN ORDINARY TIME/A

Second Reading 1 Corinthians 1:1-3

May God our Father and the Lord Jesus Christ send you grace and peace.

I, Paul, appointed by God to be an apostle, together with brother Sosthenes, send greetings to the church of God in Corinth, to the holy people of Jesus Christ, who are called to take their place among all the saints everywhere who pray to our Lord Jesus Christ; for he is their Lord no less than ours. May God our Father and the Lord Jesus Christ send you grace and peace.

Alleluia   Alleluia, alleluia! Blessings on the King who comes, in the name of the Lord! Peace in heaven and glory in the highest heavens! Alleluia! Luke 19:38.

or   Alleluia, alleluia! The Word was made flesh and lived among us; to all who did accept him he gave power to become children to God. Alleluia! John 1:14.12.

Gospel John 1:29-34.

Look, there is the lamb of God that takes away the sin of the world.

Seeing Jesus coming towards him, John said, "Look, there is the lamb of God that takes away the sin of the world. This is the one I spoke of when I said: A man is coming after me who ranks before me because he existed before me. I did not know him myself, and yet it was to reveal him to Israel that I came baptising with water." John also declared, "I saw the Spirit coming down on him from heaven like a dove and resting on him. I did not know him myself, but he who sent me to baptise with water had said to me, 'The man on whom you see the Spirit come down and rest is the one who is going to baptise with the Holy Spirit.' Yes, I have seen and I am the witness that he is the Chosen One of God."

Prayer over the Gifts

Father,
may we celebrate the eucharist
with reverence and love,
for when we proclaim the death of the Lord
you continue the work of his redemption,
who is Lord for ever and ever.

Preface of Sundays I-VIII, pages 562-565.

THIRD SUNDAY IN ORDINARY TIME/A

Communion Antiphon — The Lord has prepared a feast for me: given wine in plenty for me to drink. Psalm 22:5.

or

We know and believe in God's love for us. 1 John 4:16.

Prayer after Communion

Lord,
you have nourished us with bread from heaven.
Fill us with your Spirit,
and make us one in peace and love.

3rd SUNDAY IN ORDINARY TIME/A

> Christ is our light and our help!
> Christ lightens our darkness and helps us to see the real meaning of life. When he calls us to follow him we must learn to put aside our differences. It is in true christian charity that we are able to proclaim the good news of the kingdom, and it is for this purpose that Christ calls us to follow him.

Entrance Antiphon — Sing a new song to the Lord! Sing to the Lord, all the earth. Truth and beauty surround him, he lives in holiness and glory. Psalm 95:1.6.

Opening Prayer

Let us pray
  [for unity and peace]

All-powerful and ever-living God,

THIRD SUNDAY IN ORDINARY TIME/A

direct your love that is within us,
that our efforts in the name of your Son
may bring mankind to unity and peace.

or
>Let us pray
>>[pleading that our vision
>>may overcome our weakness]

>Almighty Father,
>the love you offer
>always exceeds the furthest expression of our human longing,
>for you are greater than the human heart.

>Direct each thought, each effort of our life,
>so that the limits of our faults and weaknesses
>may not obscure the vision of your glory
>or keep us from the peace you have promised.

First Reading   Isaiah 8:23-9:3.
In Galilee of the nations the people has seen a great light.

In days past the Lord humbled the land of Zebulum and the land of Naphtali, but in days to come he will confer glory on the Way of the Sea on the far side of Jordan, province of the nations.
The people that walked in darkness
has seen a great light;
on those who live in a land of deep shadow
a light has shone.
You have made their gladness greater,
you have made their joy increase;
they rejoice in your presence
as men rejoice at harvest time,
as men are happy when they are dividing the spoils.

For the yoke that was weighing on him,
the bar across his shoulders,
the rod of his oppressor,
these you break as on the day of Midian.

Responsorial Psalm   Psalm 26
℟ **The Lord is my light and my help.**

1. The Lord is my light and my help;
   whom shall I fear?

THIRD SUNDAY IN ORDINARY TIME/A

The Lord is the stronghold of my life;
before whom shall I shrink? ℟

2. There is one thing I ask of the Lord,
for this I long,
to live in the house of the Lord,
all the days of my life,
to savour the sweetness of the Lord,
to behold his temple. ℟

3. I am sure I shall see the Lord's goodness
in the land of the living.
Hope in him, hold firm and take heart.
Hope in the Lord! ℟

Second Reading   1 Corinthians 1:10-13. 17

Make up the differences between you instead of disagreeing among yourselves.

I appeal to you, brothers, for the sake of our Lord Jesus Christ, to make up the differences between you, and instead of disagreeing among yourselves, to be united again in your belief and practice. From what Chloe's people have been telling me, my dear brothers, it is clear that there are serious differences among you. What I mean are all these slogans that you have, like: "I am for Paul", "I am for Apollos", "I am for Cephas", "I am for Christ". Has Christ been parcelled out? Was it Paul that was crucified for you? Were you baptised in the name of Paul?

For Christ did not send me to baptise, but to preach the Good News, and not to preach that in the terms of philosophy in which the crucifixion of Christ cannot be expressed.

Alleluia   Alleluia, alleluia! Jesus proclaimed the Good News of the kingdom, and cured all kinds of sickness among the people. Alleluia! Matthew 4:23.

Gospel   Matthew 4:12-23.

He went and settled in Capernaum: in this way the prophecy of Isaiah was to be fulfilled.

Hearing that John had been arrested Jesus went back to Galilee, and leaving Nazareth he went and settled in Capernaum, a lakeside town on the borders of Zebulun and

> Naphtali. In this way the prophecy of Isaiah was to be fulfilled:
> Land of Zebulun! Land of Naphtali!
> Way of the sea on the far side of Jordan,
> Galilee of the nations!
> The people that lived in darkness
> has seen a great light;
> on those who dwell in the land and shadow of death
> a light has dawned.
> From that moment Jesus began his preaching with the message, "Repent, for the kingdom of heaven is close at hand."

As he was walking by the Sea of Galilee he saw two brothers, Simon, who was called Peter, and his brother Andrew; they were making a cast in the lake with their net, for they were fishermen. And he said to them, "Follow me and I will make you fishers of men." And they left their nets at once and followed him.

Going on from there he saw another pair of brothers, James son of Zebedee and his brother John; they were in their boat with their father Zebedee, mending their nets, and he called them. At once, leaving the boat and their father, they followed him.

He went round the whole of Galilee teaching in their synagogues, proclaiming the Good News of the kingdom and curing all kinds of diseases and sickness among the people.

Prayer over the Gifts

Lord,
receive our gifts.
Let our offerings make us holy
and bring us salvation.

Preface of Sundays I-VIII, pages 562-565.

Communion Antiphon

Look up at the Lord with gladness and smile; your face will never be ashamed. Psalm 33:6.

or

I am the light of the world, says the Lord; the man who follows me will have the light of life. John 8:12.

FOURTH SUNDAY IN ORDINARY TIME/A

Prayer after Communion
God, all-powerful Father,
may the new life you give us increase our love
and keep us in the joy of your kingdom.

4th SUNDAY IN ORDINARY TIME/A

> How happy are the poor in spirit!
> Jesus gives us the beatitudes and tells us how
> happy we would be if we were poor in spirit
> because then the kingdom of heaven would
> be ours. Poverty of spirit means having a correct
> standard of values in which we put Christ first
> and everything else is sub-ordinate to him.
> We are rich in Christ because we know that
> everything of lasting value comes from him.

Entrance Antiphon Save us, Lord our God, and gather us together from the nations, that we may proclaim your holy name and glory in your praise. Psalm 105:47.

Opening Prayer
Let us pray
  [for a greater love of God
  and of our fellow men]

Lord our God,
help us to love you with all our hearts
and to love all men as you love them.

or

Let us pray
  [joining in the praise of the living God
  for we are his people]

FOURTH SUNDAY IN ORDINARY TIME/A

Father in heaven,
from the days of Abraham and Moses
until this gathering of your Church in prayer,
you have formed a people in the image of your Son.

Bless this people with the gift of your kingdom.
May we serve you with our every desire
and show love for one another
even as you have loved us.

First Reading   Zephaniah 2:3; 3:12-13.

In your midst I will leave a humble and lowly people.

Seek the Lord
all you, the humble of the earth,
who obey his commands.
Seek integrity,
seek humility:
you may perhaps find shelter
on the day of the anger of the Lord.
In your midst I will leave
a humble and lowly people,
and those who are left in Israel will seek refuge in the name of
   the Lord.
They will do no wrong,
will tell no lies;
and the perjured tongue will no longer
be found in their mouths.
But they will be able to graze and rest
with no one to disturb them.

Responsorial Psalm   Psalm 145

℟ **How happy are the poor in spirit;**   or ℟ Alleluia!
theirs is the kingdom of heaven.

1. It is the Lord who keeps faith for ever,
   who is just to those who are oppressed.
   It is he who gives bread to the hungry,
   the Lord, who sets prisoners free.   ℟

2. It is the Lord who gives sight to the blind,
   who raises up those who are bowed down,
   the Lord, who protects the stranger
   and upholds the widow and orphan.   ℟

FOURTH SUNDAY IN ORDINARY TIME/A

3. It is the Lord who loves the just
but thwarts the path of the wicked.
The Lord will reign for ever,
Zion's God, from age to age. R/

Second Reading   1 Corinthians 1:26-31.

God chose what is foolish by human reckoning.

Take yourselves for instance, brothers, at the time when you were called: how many of you were wise in the ordinary sense of the word, how many were influential people, or came from noble families? No, it was to shame the wise that God chose what is foolish by human reckoning, and to shame what is strong that he chose what is weak by human reckoning; those whom the world thinks common and contemptible are the ones that God has chosen — those who are nothing at all to show up those who are everything. The human race has nothing to boast about to God, but you, God has made members of Christ Jesus and by God's doing he has become our wisdom, and our virtue, and our holiness, and our freedom. As scripture says: if anyone wants to boast, let him boast about the Lord.

Alleluia   Alleluia, alleluia! Blessed are you, Father, Lord of heaven and earth, for revealing the mysteries of the kingdom to mere children. Alleluia! Matthew 11:25.

or   Alleluia, alleluia! Rejoice and be glad: your reward will be great in heaven. Alleluia! Matthew 5:12.

Gospel   Matthew 5:1-12.

How happy are the poor in spirit.

Seeing the crowds, Jesus went up the hill. There he sat down and was joined by his disciples. Then he began to speak. This is what he taught them:
"How happy are the poor in spirit;
theirs is the kingdom of heaven.
Happy the gentle:
they shall have the earth for their heritage.
Happy those who mourn:
they shall be comforted.
Happy those who hunger and thirst for what is right:
they shall be satisfied.
Happy the merciful:

they shall have mercy shown them.
Happy the pure in heart:
they shall see God.
Happy the peacemakers:
they shall be called sons of God.
Happy those who are persecuted in the cause of right:
theirs is the kingdom of heaven.
"Happy are you when people abuse you and persecute you and speak all kinds of calumny against you on my account. Rejoice and be glad, for your reward will be great in heaven."

Prayer over the Gifts

Lord,
be pleased with the gifts we bring to your altar,
and make them the sacrament of our salvation.

Preface of Sundays I-VIII, pages 562-565.

Communion Antiphon

Let your face shine on your servant, and save me by your love. Lord, keep me from shame, for I have called to you. **Psalm 30:17-18.**

or

Happy are the poor in spirit; the kingdom of heaven is theirs!
Happy are the lowly; they shall inherit the land. **Matthew 5:3-4.**

Prayer after Communion

Lord,
you invigorate us with this help to our salvation.
By this eucharist give the true faith continued growth throughout the world.

5th SUNDAY IN ORDINARY TIME/A

Salt of the earth and light of the world!
Jesus calls us to be the salt of the
earth and gives us an example in his own
crucifixion. We are also, through our good
works, a light shining in the darkness so
that others may be guided on their
journey to God.

Entrance Antiphon Come, let us worship the Lord. Let us bow down in the presence of our maker, for he is the Lord our God. Psalm 94:6-7.

Opening Prayer

Let us pray
 [that God will watch over us and protect us]

Father,
watch over your family
and keep us safe in your care,
for all our hope is in you.

or

Let us pray
 [with reverence in the presence of the living God]

In faith and love we ask you, Father,
to watch over your family gathered here.
In your mercy and loving kindness
no thought of ours is left unguarded,
no tear unheeded, no joy unnoticed.

Through the prayer of Jesus
may the blessings promised to the poor in spirit
lead us to the treasures of your heavenly kingdom.

FIFTH SUNDAY IN ORDINARY TIME/A

First Reading   Isaiah 58:7-10

Then will your light shine like the dawn.

Thus says the Lord:
Share your bread with the hungry,
and shelter the homeless poor,
clothe the man you see to be naked
and turn not from your own kin.
Then will your light shine like the dawn
and your wound be quickly healed over.

Your integrity will go before you
and the glory of the Lord behind you.
Cry, and the Lord will answer;
call, and he will say, "I am here."

If you do away with the yoke,
the clenched fist, the wicked word,
if you give your bread to the hungry,
and relief to the oppressed,
your light will rise in the darkness,
and your shadows become like noon.

Responsorial Psalm   Psalm 111

℟ **The good man is a light in the darkness for the upright.**

or ℟ Alleluia!

1. He is a light in the darkness for the upright:
   he is generous, merciful and just.
   The good man takes pity and lends,
   he conducts his affairs with honour. ℟

2. The just man will never waver:
   he will be remembered for ever.
   He has no fear of evil news;
   with a firm heart he trusts in the Lord. ℟

3. With a steadfast heart he will not fear;
   Open-handed, he gives to the poor;
   his justice stands firm for ever.
   His head will be raised in glory. ℟

Second Reading   1 Corinthians 2:1-5

During my stay with you, the only knowledge I claimed to have was about Jesus as the crucified Christ.

FIFTH SUNDAY IN ORDINARY TIME/A

When I came to you, brothers, it was not with any show of oratory or philosophy, but simply to tell you what God had guaranteed. During my stay with you, the only knowledge I claimed to have was about Jesus, and only about him as the crucified Christ. Far from relying on any power of my own, I came among you in great "fear and trembling" and in my speeches and the sermons that I gave, there were none of the arguments that belong to philosophy; only a demonstration of the power of the Spirit. And I did this so that your faith should not depend on human philosophy but on the power of God.

Alleluia   Alleluia, alleluia! I am the light of the world, says the Lord, anyone who follows me will have the light of life. Alleluia! John 8:12.

Alternative Alleluias will be found on pages 1004-1006

Gospel   Matthew 5:13-16
You are the light of the world.

Jesus said to his disciples: "You are the salt of the earth. But if salt becomes tasteless, what can make it salty again? It is good for nothing, and can only be thrown out to be trampled underfoot by men.

"You are the light of the world. A city built on a hill-top cannot be hidden. No one lights a lamp to put it under a tub; they put it on the lamp-stand where it shines for everyone in the house. In the same way your light must shine in the sight of men, so that, seeing your good works, they may give the praise to your Father in heaven."

Prayer over the Gifts

Lord our God,
may the bread and wine
you give us for our nourishment on earth
become the sacrament of our eternal life.

Preface of Sundays I-VIII, pages 562-565.

Communion Antiphon   Give praise to the Lord for his kindness, for his wonderful deeds toward men. He has filled the hungry with good things, he has satisfied the thirsty. Psalm 106:8-9.

SIXTH SUNDAY IN ORDINARY TIME/A

or

Happy are the sorrowing; they shall be consoled. Happy those who hunger and thirst for what is right; they shall be satisfied. Matthew 5:5-6.

Prayer after Communion

God our Father,
you give us a share in the one bread and the one cup
and make us one in Christ.
Help us to bring your salvation and joy
to all the world.

6th SUNDAY IN ORDINARY TIME/A

> The law of God is for man's happiness.
> God's ways are other than ours. When
> we try to penetrate deeper into the meaning
> of his laws we realise that it is only his Spirit
> which will help us to plumb the depths of
> what he commands us. Jesus by his
> life-style is the fulfilment of the law.
> If we follow him we will keep
> God's word.

Entrance Antiphon Lord, be my rock of safety, the stronghold that saves me. For the honour of your name, lead me and guide me.
Psalm 30:3-4.

Opening Prayer

Let us pray
[that everything we do
will be guided by God's law of love]

SIXTH SUNDAY IN ORDINARY TIME/A

God our Father,
you have promised to remain for ever
with those who do what is just and right.
Help us to live in your presence.

or

Let us pray
  [for the wisdom that is greater than human words]

Father in heaven,
the loving plan of your wisdom took flesh in Jesus Christ,
and changed mankind's history
by his command of perfect love.

May our fulfilment of his command reflect your wisdom
and bring your salvation to the ends of the earth.

First Reading   Ecclesiasticus 15:15-20

He never commanded anyone to be godless.

If you wish, you can keep the commandments,
to behave faithfully is within your power.
He has set fire and water before you;
put out your hand to whichever you prefer.
Man has life and death before him;
whichever a man likes better will be given him.
For vast is the wisdom of the Lord;
he is almighty and all-seeing.
His eyes are on those who fear him,
he notes every action of man.
He never commanded anyone to be godless,
he has given no one permission to sin.

Responsorial Psalm   Psalm 118

℟ They are happy who follow God's law!

1. They are happy whose life is blameless,
   who follow God's law!
   They are happy those who do his will,
   seeking him with all their hearts. ℟

2. You have laid down your precepts
   to be obeyed with care.
   May my footsteps be firm
   to obey your statutes. ℟

SIXTH SUNDAY IN ORDINARY TIME/A

3. Bless your servant and I shall live
   and obey your word.
   Open my eyes that I may consider
   the wonders of your law. R/

4. Teach me the demands of your statutes
   and I will keep them to the end.
   Train me to observe your law,
   to keep it with my heart. R/

Second Reading   1 Corinthians 2:6-10

God predestined wisdom to be for our glory before the ages began.

We have a wisdom to offer those who have reached maturity: not a philosophy of our age, it is true, still less of the masters of our age, which are coming to their end. The hidden wisdom of God which we teach in our mysteries is the wisdom that God predestined to be for our glory before the ages began. It is a wisdom that none of the masters of this age have ever known, or they would not have crucified the Lord of Glory; we teach what scripture calls: the things that no eye has seen and no ear has heard, things beyond the mind of man, all that God has prepared for those who love him.

These are the very things that God has revealed to us through the Spirit, for the Spirit reaches the depths of everything, even the depths of God.

Alleluia	Alleluia, alleluia! Speak, Lord, your servant is listening: you have the message of eternal life. Alleluia! 1 Samuel 3:9; John 6:68.
or	Alleluia, alleluia! Blessed are you, Father, Lord of heaven and earth, for revealing the mysteries of the Kingdom to mere children. Alleluia! Matthew 11:25.

Gospel   Matthew 5:17-37

You have learnt how it was said to our ancestors; but I say this to you.

Jesus said to his disciples:

"Do not imagine that I have come to abolish the Law or the Prophets. I have come not to abolish them but to complete them. I tell you solemnly, till heaven and earth disappear, not one

SIXTH SUNDAY IN ORDINARY TIME/A

dot, one little stroke, shall disappear from the Law until its purpose is achieved. Therefore, the man who infringes even one of the least of these commandments and teaches others to do the same will be considered the least in the kingdom of heaven; but the man who keeps them and teaches them will be considered great in the kingdom of heaven.

"For I tell you, if your virtue goes no deeper than that of the scribes and Pharisees, you will never get into the kingdom of heaven.

"You have learnt how it was said to our ancestors: You must not kill; and if anyone does kill he must answer for it before the court. But I say this to you: anyone who is angry with his brother will answer for it before the court;

if a man calls his brother 'Fool' he will answer for it before the Sanhedrin; and if a man calls him 'Renegade' he will answer for it in hell fire. So then, if you are bringing your offering to the altar and there remember that your brother has something against you, leave your offering there before the altar, go and be reconciled with your brother first, and then come back and present your offering. Come to terms with your opponent in good time while you are still on the way to the court with him, or he may hand you over to the judge and the judge to the officer, and you will be thrown into prison. I tell you solemnly, you will not get out till you have paid the last penny.

"You have learnt how it was said: You must not commit adultery. But I say this to you: if a man looks at a woman lustfully, he has already committed adultery with her in his heart.

If your right eye should cause you to sin, tear it out and throw it away; for it will do you less harm to lose one part of you than to have your whole body thrown into hell. And if your right hand should cause you to sin, cut it off and throw it away; for it will do you less harm to lose one part of you than to have your whole body go to hell.

"It has also been said: Anyone who divorces his wife must give her a writ of dismissal. But I say this to you: everyone who divorces his wife, except for the case of fornication, makes her an adulteress; and anyone who marries a divorced woman commits adultery.

"Again, you have learnt how it was said to our ancestors: You must not break your oath, but must fulfil your oaths to the

SIXTH SUNDAY IN ORDINARY TIME/A

Lord. But I say this to you: do not swear at all,
either by heaven, since that is God's throne; or by the earth, since that is his footstool; or by Jerusalem, since that is the city of the great king. Do not swear by your own head either, since you cannot turn a single hair white or black.

All you need say is 'Yes' if you mean yes, 'No' if you mean no; anything more than this comes from the evil one."

Prayer over the Gifts

Lord,
we make this offering in obedience to your word.
May it cleanse and renew us,
and lead us to our eternal reward.

Preface of Sundays I-VIII, pages 562-565.

Communion Antiphon

They ate and were filled; the Lord gave them what they wanted: they were not deprived of their desire.
Psalm 77:29-30.

or

God loved the world so much, he gave his only Son, that all who believe in him might not perish, but might have eternal life. John 3:16.

Prayer after Communion

Lord,
you give us food from heaven.
May we always hunger
for the bread of life.

7th SUNDAY IN ORDINARY TIME/A

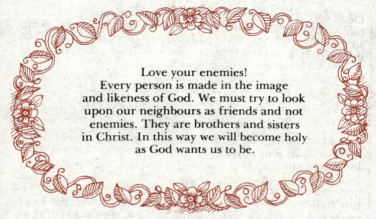

Love your enemies!
Every person is made in the image
and likeness of God. We must try to look
upon our neighbours as friends and not
enemies. They are brothers and sisters
in Christ. In this way we will become holy
as God wants us to be.

Entrance Antiphon   Lord, your mercy is my hope, my heart rejoices in your saving power. I will sing to the Lord, for his goodness to me.

Psalm 12:6

Opening Prayer

Let us pray
  [that God will make us more like Christ, his Son]

Father,
keep before us the wisdom and love
you have revealed in your Son.
Help us to be like him
in word and deed,
for he lives and reigns with you and the Holy Spirit,
one God, for ever and ever.

or

Let us pray
  [to the God of power and might,
  for his mercy is our hope]

Almighty God,
Father of our Lord Jesus Christ,
faith in your word is the way to wisdom,
and to ponder your divine plan is to grow in the truth.

SEVENTH SUNDAY IN ORDINARY TIME/A

Open our eyes to your deeds,
our ears to the sound of your call,
so that our every act may increase our sharing
in the life you have offered us.

First Reading Leviticus 19:1-2.17-18
You must love your neighbour as yourself.

The Lord spoke to Moses; he said: "Speak to the whole community of the sons of Israel and say to them: 'Be holy, for I, the Lord your God, am holy.'

"You must not bear hatred for your brother in your heart. You must openly tell him, your neighbour, of his offence: this way you will not take a sin upon yourself. You must not exact vengeance, nor must you bear a grudge against the children of your people. You must love your neighbour as yourself. I am the Lord."

Responsorial Psalm Psalm 102

℟ **The Lord is compassion and love.**

1. My soul, give thanks to the Lord,
all my being, bless his holy name.
My soul, give thanks to the Lord
and never forget all his blessings. ℟

2. It is he who forgives all your guilt,
who heals every one of your ills,
who redeems your life from the grave,
who crowns you with love and compassion. ℟

3. The Lord is compassion and love,
slow to anger and rich in mercy.
He does not treat us according to our sins
nor repay us according to our faults. ℟

4. As far as the east is from the west
so far does he remove our sins.
As a father has compassion on his sons,
the Lord has pity on those who fear him. ℟

SEVENTH SUNDAY IN ORDINARY TIME/A

Second Reading 1 Corinthians 3:16-23

All are your servants, but you belong to Christ and Christ belongs to God.

Didn't you realise that you were God's temple and that the Spirit of God was living among you? If anybody should destroy the temple of God, God will destroy him, because the temple of God is sacred; and you are that temple.

Make no mistake about it: if any one of you think of himself as wise, in the ordinary sense of the word, then he must learn to be a fool before he really can be wise. Why? Because the wisdom of this world is foolishness to God. As scripture says: The Lord knows wise men's thoughts: he knows how useless they are, or again: God is not convinced by the arguments of the wise. So there is nothing to boast about in anything human: Paul, Apollos, Cephas, the world, life and death, the present and the future, are all your servants; but you belong to Christ and Christ belongs to God.

Alleluia	Alleluia, alleluia! If anyone loves me he will keep my word, and my Father will love him, and we shall come to him. Alleluia! John 14:23.
or	Alleluia, alleluia! When anyone obeys what Christ has said, God's love comes to perfection in him. Alleluia!
	1 John 2:5

Gospel Matthew 5:38:48.

Love your enemies.

Jesus said to his disciples: "You have learnt how it was said: Eye for eye and tooth for tooth. But I say this to you: offer the wicked man no resistance. On the contrary, if anyone hits you on the right cheek, offer him the other as well; if a man takes you to law and would have your tunic, let him have your cloak as well. And if anyone orders you to one mile, go two miles with him. Give to anyone who asks, and if anyone wants to borrow, do not turn away.

"You have learnt how it was said: You must love your neighbour and hate your enemy. But I say this to you: love your enemies and pray for those who persecute you; in this way you will be sons of your Father in heaven, for he causes his sun to rise on bad men as well as good, and his rain to fall on honest and dishonest men alike. For if you love those who love you, what

SEVENTH SUNDAY IN ORDINARY TIME/A

right have you to claim any credit? Even the tax collectors do as much, do they not? And if you save your greetings for your brothers, are you doing anything exceptional? Even the pagans do as much, do they not? You must therefore be perfect just as your heavenly Father is perfect."

Prayer over the Gifts

Lord,
as we make this offering,
may our worship in Spirit and truth
bring us salvation.

Preface of Sundays I-VIII, pages 562-565.

Communion Antiphon

I will tell all your marvellous works. I will rejoice and be glad in you, and sing to your name, Most High.
Psalm 9:2-3

or

Lord, I believe that you are the Christ, the Son of God, who was to come into this world. John 11:27.

Prayer after Communion

Almighty God,
help us to live the example of love
we celebrate in this eucharist,
that we may come to its fulfilment in your presence.

8th SUNDAY IN ORDINARY TIME/A

Do not worry about tomorrow. The philosophy of Jesus penetrates to the nerve-centre of all our fears and worries. The past is dead and the future yet to come. We have to live every moment to the full since we only have today. God never abandons us and knows the deepest desires and intentions of our hearts.

Entrance Antiphon

The Lord has been my strength; he has led me into freedom. He saved me because he loves me. Psalm 17:19-20.

Opening Prayer

Let us pray
  [that God will bring peace to the world
  and freedom to his Church]

Lord,
guide the course of world events
and give your Church the joy and peace
of serving you in freedom.

or

Let us pray
  [that the peace of Christ
  may find welcome in the world]

Father in heaven,
form in us the likeness of your Son
and deepen his life within us.
Send us as witnesses of gospel joy
into a world of fragile peace and broken promises.
Touch the hearts of all men with your love
that they in turn may love one another.

EIGHTH SUNDAY IN ORDINARY TIME/A

First Reading   Isaiah 49:14-15
I will never forget you.

Zion was saying, "The Lord has abandoned me,
the Lord has forgotten me."
Does a woman forget her baby at the breast,
or fail to cherish the son of her womb?
Yet even if these forget,
I will never forget you.

Responsorial Psalm   Psalm 61

℟ **In God alone is my soul at rest.**

1. In God alone is my soul at rest;
   my help comes from him.
   He alone is my rock, my stronghold,
   my fortress: I stand firm. ℟

2. In God alone be at rest, my soul;
   for my hope comes from him.
   He alone is my rock, my stronghold
   my fortress: I stand firm. ℟

3. In God is my safety and glory,
   the rock of my strength.
   Take refuge in God all you people.
   Trust him at all times.
   Pour out your hearts before him. ℟

Second Reading   1 Corinthians 4:1-5
The Lord will reveal the secret intentions of men's hearts.

People must think of us as Christ's servants, stewards entrusted with the mysteries of God. What is expected of stewards is that each one should be found worthy of his trust. Not that it makes the slightest difference to me whether you, or indeed any human tribunal, find we worthy or not. I will not even pass judgement on myself. True, my conscience does not reproach me at all, but that does not prove that I am acquitted: the Lord alone is my judge. There must be no passing of premature judgement. Leave that until the Lord comes: he will light up all that is hidden in the dark and reveal the secret intentions of men's hearts. Then will be the time for each one to have whatever praise he deserves, from God.

EIGHTH SUNDAY IN ORDINARY TIME/A

Alleluia Alleluia, alleluia! Your word is truth, O Lord, consecrate us in the truth. Alleluia! John 17:17.

or Alleluia, alleluia! The word of God is something alive and active; it can judge secret emotions and thoughts. Alleluia! Hebrews 4:12.

Gospel Matthew 6:24-34.
Do not worry about tomorrow.

Jesus said to his disciples: "No one can be the slave of two masters: he will either hate the first and love the second, or treat the first with respect and the second with scorn. You cannot be the slave both of God and money.

"That is why I am telling you not to worry about your life and what you are to eat, nor about your body and how you are to clothe it. Surely life means more than food, and the body more than clothing! Look at the birds in the sky. They do not sow or reap or gather into barns; yet your heavenly Father feeds them. Are you not worth much more than they are? Can any of you, for all his worrying, add one single cubit to his span of life? And why worry about clothing? Think of the flowers growing in the fields; they never have to work or spin; yet I assure you that not even Solomon in all his regalia was robed like one of these. Now if that is how God clothes the grass in the field which is there today and thrown into the furnace tomorrow, will he not much more look after you, you men of little faith? So do not worry; do not say, 'What are we to eat? What are we to drink? How are we to be clothed?' It is the pagans who set their hearts on all these things. Your heavenly Father knows you need them all. Set your hearts on his kingdom first, and on his righteousness, and all these other things will be given you as well. So do not worry about tomorrow: tomorrow will take care of itself. Each day has enough trouble of its own."

Prayer over the Gifts

God our Creator,
may this bread and wine we offer
as a sign of our love and worship
lead us to salvation.

Preface of Sundays I-VIII, pages 562-565.

Communion Antiphon I will sing to the Lord for his goodness to me, I will sing the name of the Lord, Most High. Psalm 12:6.

or I, the Lord, am with you always, until the end of the world. Matthew 28:30

Prayer after Communion

God of salvation,
may this sacrament which strengthens us here on earth
bring us to eternal life.

9th SUNDAY IN ORDINARY TIME/A

Faith is as strong as a rock!
Faith is God's gift to us and we must let it
penetrate into our hearts and souls. All our
actions must spring from the deep well of faith
rather than from the external observance of law.
In times of trouble and temptation our faith will
stand firm like a house built on a rock.

Entrance Antiphon O look at me and be merciful, for I am wretched and alone. See my hardship and my poverty, and pardon all my sins.
Psalm 24:16-18

Opening Prayer

Let us pray
  [for God's care and protection]

Father,
your love never fails.
Hear our call.
Keep us from danger
and provide for all our needs.

NINTH SUNDAY IN ORDINARY TIME/A

or Let us pray
  [for the confidence born of faith]
  God our Father,
  teach us to cherish the gifts that surround us.
  Increase our faith in you
  and bring our trust to its promised fulfilment
  in the joy of your kingdom.

First Reading Deuteronomy 11:18. 26-28. 32

See, I set before you today a blessing and a curse.

Moses said to the people: "Let these words of mine remain in your heart and in your soul; fasten them on your hand as a sign and on your forehead as a circlet.

"See, I set before you today a blessing and a curse: a blessing, if you obey the commandments of the Lord our God that I enjoin on you today; a curse, if you disobey the commandments of the Lord your God and leave the way I have marked out for you today, by going after other gods you have not known. You must keep and observe all the laws and customs that I set before you today."

Responsional Psalm Psalm 30.

R/ **Be a rock of refuge for me, O Lord.**

1. In you, O Lord, I take refuge.
   Let me never be put to shame.
   In your justice, set me free,
   hear me and speedily rescue me. R/

2. Be a rock of refuge for me,
   a mighty stronghold to save me,
   for you are my rock, my stronghold.
   For your name's sake, lead me and guide me. R/

3. Let your face shine on your servant.
   Save me in your love.
   Be strong, let your heart take courage,
   all who hope in the Lord. R/

Second Reading Romans 3:21-25. 28.

A man is justified by faith and not by doing something the Law tells him to do.

God's justice that was made known through the Law and the

NINTH SUNDAY IN ORDINARY TIME/A

Prophets has now been revealed outside the Law, since it is the same justice of God that comes through faith to everyone, Jew and pagan alike, who believes in Jesus Christ. Both Jew and pagan sinned and forfeited God's glory, and both are justified through the free gift of his grace by being redeemed in Christ Jesus who was appointed by God to sacrifice his life so as to win reconciliation through faith since, as we see it, a man is justified by faith and not by doing something the Law tells him to do.

Alleluia Alleluia, alleluia! If anyone loves me he will keep my word, and my Father will love him, and we shall come to him. Alleluia! John 14:23.

or Alleluia, alleluia! I am the vine, you are the branches, says the Lord. Whoever remains in me, with me in him, bears fruit in plenty. Alleluia! John 15:5

Gospel Matthew 7:21-27.

The house built on rock and the house built on sand.

Jesus said to his disciples: "It is not those who say to me, 'Lord, Lord', who will enter the kingdom of heaven, but the person who does the will of my Father in heaven. When the day comes many will say to me, 'Lord, Lord, did we not prophesy in your name, cast out demons in your name, work many miracles in your name?' Then I shall tell them to their faces: I have never known you; away from me, you evil men!'

"Therefore, everyone who listens to these words of mine and acts on them will be like a sensible man who built his house on rock. Rain came down, floods rose, gales blew and hurled themselves against that house, and it did not fall: it was founded on rock. But everyone who listens to these words of mine and does not act on them will be like a stupid man who built his house on sand. Rain came down, floods rose, gales blew and struck that house, and it fell; and what a fall it had!"

Prayer over the Gifts

Lord,
as we gather to offer our gifts
confident in your love,
make us holy by sharing your life with us
and by this eucharist forgive our sins.

Preface of Sundays I-VIII, pages 562-565.

TENTH SUNDAY IN ORDINARY TIME/A

Communion Antiphon

I call upon you, God, for you will answer me; bend your ear and hear my prayer. **Psalm 16:6.**

or

I tell you solemnly, whatever you ask for in prayer, believe that you have received it, and it will be yours, says the Lord. **Mark 11:23,24.**

Prayer after Communion

Lord,
as you give us the body and blood of your Son,
guide us with your Spirit
that we may honour you
not only with our lips,
but also with the lives we lead,
and so enter your kingdom.

10th SUNDAY IN ORDINARY TIME/A

What I want is mercy not sacrifice. God tells us that love must be sincere and flow from our deep faith in him. He does not want the mere externals of sacrifice. Faith and love show themselves in action. We must be merciful like Christ towards sinners because it is those who are sick who have need of a doctor.

Entrance Antiphon

The Lord is my light and my salvation. Who shall frighten me? The Lord is the defender of my life. Who shall make me tremble? **Psalm 26:1-2.**

TENTH SUNDAY IN ORDINARY TIME/A

Opening Prayer

Let us pray
   [for the guidance of the Holy Spirit]

God of wisdom and love,
source of all good,
send your Spirit to teach us your truth
and guide our actions
in your way of peace.

or

Let us pray,
   [to our Father
   who calls us to freedom in Jesus his Son]

Father in heaven,
words cannot measure the boundaries of love
for those born to new life in Christ Jesus.
Raise us beyond the limits this world imposes,
so that we may be free to love as Christ teaches
and find our joy in your glory.

First Reading   Hosea 6:3-6.

What I want is love, not sacrifice.

Let us set ourselves to know the Lord;
that he will come is as certain as the dawn
his judgement will rise like the light,
he will come to us as showers come,
like spring rains watering the earth.

What am I to do with you, Ephraim?
What am I to do with you, Judah?
This love of yours is like a morning cloud,
like the dew that quickly disappears.
This is why I have torn them to pieces by the prophets,
why I slaughtered them with the words from my mouth,
since what I want is love, not sacrifice;
knowledge of God, not holocausts.

TENTH SUNDAY IN ORDINARY TIME/A

Responsorial Psalm Psalm 49.

℟ **I will show God's salvation to the upright.**

1. The God of gods, the Lord,
   has spoken and summoned the earth,
   from the rising of the sun to its setting,
   "I find no fault with your sacrifices,
   your offerings are always before me. ℟

2. "Were I hungry, I would not tell you,
   for I own the world and all it holds.
   Do you think I eat the flesh of bulls,
   or drink the blood of goats? ℟

3. "Pay your sacrifice of thanksgiving to God
   and render him your votive offerings.
   Call on me in the day of distress.
   I will free you and you shall honour me." ℟

Second Reading Romans 4:18-25.

Abraham drew strength from faith and gave glory to God.

Though it seemed Abraham's hope could not be fulfilled, he hoped and he believed, and through doing so he did become the father of many nations exactly as he had been promised: Your descendants will be as many as the stars. Even the thought that his body was past fatherhood — he was about a hundred years old — and Sarah too old to become a mother, did not shake his belief. Since God had promised it, Abraham refused either to deny it or even to doubt it, but drew strength from faith and gave glory to God, convinced that God had power to do what he had promised. This is the faith that was "considered as justifying him". Scripture however does not refer only to him but to us as well when it says that his faith was thus "considered"; our faith too will be "considered" if we believe in him who raised Jesus our Lord from the dead, Jesus who was put to death for our sins and raised to life to justify us.

Alleluia   Alleluia, alleluia! Open our heart, O Lord, to accept the words of your Son. Alleluia! Acts 16:14.

or   Alleluia, alleluia! The Lord has sent me to bring the good news to the poor, to proclaim liberty to the captives. Alleluia! Luke 4:18

TENTH SUNDAY IN ORDINARY TIME/A

Gospel   Matthew 9:9-13.

I did not come to call the virtuous, but sinners.

As Jesus was walking on he saw a man named Matthew sitting by the customs house, and he said to him, "Follow me." And he got up and followed him.

   While he was at dinner in the house it happened that a number of tax collectors and sinners came to sit at the table with Jesus and his disciples. When the Pharisees saw this, they said to his disciples, "Why does your master eat with tax collectors and sinners?" When he heard this he replied, "It is not the healthy who need the doctor, but the sick. Go and learn the meaning of the words: What I want is mercy, not sacrifice. And indeed I did not come to call the virtuous, but sinners."

Prayer over the Gifts

Lord,
look with love on our service.
Accept the gifts we bring
and help us grow in Christian love.

Preface of Sundays I-VIII, pages 562-565.

Communion Antiphon
I can rely on the Lord; I can always turn to him for shelter. It was he who gave me my freedom. My God, you are always there to help me!
Psalm 17:3

or

God is love, and he who lives in love, lives in God, and God in him.
1 John 4:16

Prayer after Communion

Lord,
may your healing love
turn us from sin
and keep us on the way that leads to you.

11th SUNDAY IN ORDINARY TIME/A

> Christ our reconciliation and our mission.
> We are reconciled to God by the death of his Son
> and we trust that God will give us new life
> through Christ's resurrection. We share in his
> Gospel and proclaim to everyone that the
> kingdom of heaven is close at hand.
> That is the mission which we share with all the
> followers of Christ.

Entrance Antiphon   Lord, hear my voice when I call to you.
You are my help; do not cast me off, do
not desert me, my Saviour God.
Psalm 26:7.9

Opening Prayer

Let us pray
  [for the grace to follow Christ more closely]

Almighty God,
our hope and our strength,
without you we falter.
Help us to follow Christ
and to live according to your will.

or

Let us pray
  [to the Father
  whose love gives us strength to follow his Son]

God our Father,
we rejoice in the faith that draws us together,
aware that selfishness can drive us apart.
Let your encouragement be our constant strength.
Keep us one in the love that has sealed our lives,
help us to live as one family
the gospel we profess.

ELEVENTH SUNDAY IN ORDINARY TIME/A

First Reading   Exodus 19:2-6.

I will count you a kingdom of priests, a consecrated nation.

From Rephidim the Israelites set out again; and when they reached the wilderness of Sinai, there in the wilderness they pitched their camp; there facing the mountain Israel pitched camp.

   Moses then went up to God, and the Lord called to him from the mountain, saying, "Say this to the House of Jacob, declare this to the sons of Israel, 'You yourselves have seen what I did with the Egyptians, how I carried you on eagle's wings and brought you to myself. From this you know that now, if you obey my voice and hold fast to my covenant, you of all the nations shall be my very own for all the earth is mine. I will count you a kingdom of priests, a consecrated nation.'"

Responsorial Psalm   Psalm 99.

℟ **We are his people: the sheep of his flock.**

1. Cry out with joy to the Lord, all the earth.
   Serve the Lord with gladness.
   Come before him, singing for joy. ℟

2. Know that he, the Lord, is God.
   He made us, we belong to him,
   we are his people, the sheep of his flock. ℟

3. Indeed, how good is the Lord,
   eternal his merciful love.
   He is faithful from age to age. ℟

Second Reading   Romans 5:6-11.

Now that we have been reconciled by the death of his Son, surely we may count on being saved by the life of his Son.

We were still helpless when at his appointed moment Christ died for sinful men. It is not easy to die even for a good man — though of course for someone really worthy, a man might be prepared to die — but what proves that God loves us is that Christ died for us while we were still sinners. Having died to make us righteous, is it likely that he would now fail to save us from God's anger? When we were reconciled to God by the death of his Son, we were still enemies; now that we have been reconciled, surely we may count on being saved by the life of his Son? Not merely because we have been reconciled but because

ELEVENTH SUNDAY IN ORDINARY TIME/A

we are filled with joyful trust in God, through our Lord Jesus Christ, through whom we have already gained our reconciliation.

Alleluia   Alleluia, alleluia! The sheep that belong to me listen to my voice, says the Lord, I know them and they follow me. Alleluia! John 10:27.

or   Alleluia, alleluia! The kingdom of God is close at hand. Repent, and believe the good news. Alleluia!
Mark 1:15.

Gospel   Matthew 9:36 — 10:8.
He summoned his twelve disciples and sent them out.

When Jesus saw the crowds he felt sorry for them because they were harassed and dejected, like sheep without a shepherd. Then he said to his disciples, "The harvest is rich but the labourers are few, so ask the Lord of the harvest to send labourers to his harvest."

He summoned his twelve disciples, and gave them authority over unclean spirits with power to cast them out and to cure all kinds of diseases and sickness.

These are the names of the twelve apostles: first, Simon who is called Peter, and his brother Andrew; James the son of Zebedee, and his brother John; Philip and Bartholomew; Thomas, and Matthew the tax collector; James the son of Alphaeus, and Thaddaeus; Simon the Zealot and Judas Iscariot, the one who was to betray him. These twelve Jesus sent out, instructing them as follows:

"Do not turn your steps to pagan territory, and do not enter any Samaritan town; go rather to the lost sheep of the House of Israel. And as you go, proclaim that the kingdom of heaven is close at hand. Cure the sick, raise the dead, cleanse the lepers, cast out devils. You received without charge, give without charge."

Prayer over the Gifts

Lord God,
in this bread and wine
you give us food for body and spirit.
May the eucharist renew our strength
and bring us health of mind and body.

Preface of Sundays I-VIII, pages 562-565.

TWELFTH SUNDAY IN ORDINARY TIME/A

Communion Antiphon

One thing I seek: to dwell in the house of the Lord all the days of my life. Psalm 26:4.

or

Father, keep in your name those you have given me, that they may be one as we are one, says the Lord.
John 17:11

Prayer after Communion

Lord,
may this eucharist
accomplish in your Church
the unity and peace it signifies.

12th SUNDAY IN ORDINARY TIME/A

Do not be afraid!
We have no need to be afraid since God is always at our side supporting and strengthening us in times of weakness and temptation. The evil effects of sin are swallowed up in the victory of Christ. He is the life of our souls and with him within us we have no cause for fear.

Entrance Antiphon

God is the strength of his people. In him, we his chosen live in safety. Save us, Lord, who share in your life, and give us your blessing; be our shepherd for ever.
Psalm 27:8-9

TWELFTH SUNDAY IN ORDINARY TIME/A

Opening Prayer

Let us pray
  [that we may grow in the love of God]
Father,
guide and protector of your people,
grant us an unfailing respect for your name,
and keep us always in your love.

Let us pray
  [to God whose fatherly love keeps us safe]
God of the universe,
we worship you as Lord.
God, ever close to us,
we rejoice to call you Father.
From this world's uncertainty we look to your covenant.
Keep us one in your peace, secure in your love.

First Reading   Jeremiah 20:10-13.
He has delivered the soul of the needy from the hands of evil men.

Jeremiah said:
I hear so many disparaging me,
" 'Terror from every side!'
denounce him! Let us denounce him!"
All those who used to be my friends
watched for my downfall,
"Perhaps he will be seduced into error.
Then we will master him
and take our revenge!"
But the Lord is at my side, a mighty hero;
my opponents will stumble, mastered,
confounded by their failure;
everlasting, unforgettable disgrace will be theirs.
But you, Lord of Hosts, you who probe with justice,
who scrutinise the loins and heart,
let me see the vengeance you will take on them,
for I have committed my cause to you.
Sing to the Lord,
praise the Lord,
for he has delivered the soul of the needy
from the hands of evil men.

TWELFTH SUNDAY IN ORDINARY TIME/A

Responsorial Psalm   Psalm 68.

℟ **In your great love, answer me, O God.**

1. It is for you that I suffer taunts,
   that shame covers my face,
   that I have become a stranger to my brothers,
   an alien to my own mother's sons.
   I burn with zeal for your house
   and taunts against you fall on me. ℟

2. This is my prayer to you,
   my prayer for your favour.
   In your great love, answer me, O God,
   with your help that never fails:
   Lord, answer, for your love is kind;
   in your compassion, turn towards me. ℟

3. The poor when they see it will be glad
   and God-seeking hearts will revive;
   for the Lord listens to the needy
   and does not spurn his servants in their chains.
   Let the heavens and the earth give him praise,
   the sea and all its living creatures. ℟

Second Reading   Romans 5:12-15.

The gift considerably outweighed the fall.

Sin entered the world through one man, and through sin death, and thus death has spread through the whole human race because everyone has sinned. Sin existed in the world long before the Law was given. There was no law and so no one could be accused of the sin of "law-breaking", yet death reigned over all from Adam to Moses, even though their sin, unlike that of Adam, was not a matter of breaking a law.

   Adam prefigured the One to come, but the gift itself considerably outweighed the fall. If it is certain that through one man's fall so many died, it is even more certain that divine grace, coming through the one man, Jesus Christ, came to so many as an abundant free gift.

Alleluia   Alleluia, alleluia! The Word was made flesh and lived among us; to all who did accept him he gave power to become children of God. Alleluia!
                                                John 1:12.14

TWELFTH SUNDAY IN ORDINARY TIME/A

or Alleluia, alleluia! The Spirit of truth will be my witness; and you too will be my witnesses. Alleluia!
John 15:26.27.

Gospel Matthew 10:26-33.

Do not be afraid of those who kill the body.

Jesus instructed the Twelve as follows: "Do not be afraid. For everything that is now covered will be uncovered, and everything now hidden will be made clear. What I say to you in the dark, tell in the daylight; what you hear in whispers, proclaim from the housetops.

"Do not be afraid of those who kill the body but cannot kill the soul; fear him rather who can destroy both body and soul in hell. Can you not buy two sparrows for a penny? And yet not one falls to the ground without your Father knowing. Why, every hair on your head has been counted. So there is no need to be afraid; you are worth more than hundreds of sparrows.

"So if anyone declares himself for me in the presence of men, I will declare myself for him in the presence of my Father in heaven. But the one who disowns me in the presence of men, I will disown in the presence of my Father in heaven."

Prayer over the Gifts

Lord,
receive our offering,
and may this sacrifice of praise
purify us in mind and heart
and make us always eager to serve you.

Preface of Sundays I-VIII, pages 562-565.

Communion Antiphon

The eyes of all look to you, O Lord, and you give them food in due season. Psalm 144:15.

or I am the Good Shepherd; I give my life for my sheep, says the Lord.
John 10:11. 15.

Prayer after Communion

Lord,
you give us the body and blood of your Son
to renew your life within us.
In your mercy, assure our redemption

and bring us to the eternal life
we celebrate in this eucharist.

13th SUNDAY IN ORDINARY TIME/A

> If we die with Christ we shall live with him.
> In our daily lives we take up our Cross
> and follow Christ, knowing that through
> suffering we are securing a place in the
> resurrection. We are dead to sin and alive
> to God. In our holiness there is within us
> a new creation as we welcome Christ
> daily within us as our new life.

Entrance Antiphon All nations, clap your hands. Shout with a voice of joy to God. Psalm 46:2.

Opening Prayer

Let us pray
   [that Christ may be our light]

Father,
you call your children
to walk in the light of Christ.
Free us from darkness
and keep us in the radiance of your truth.

or

Let us pray
   [for the strength to reject the darkness of sin]

Father in heaven,
the light of Jesus
has scattered the darkness of hatred and sin.
Called to that light

THIRTEENTH SUNDAY IN ORDINARY TIME/A

we ask for your guidance.
Form our lives in your truth, our hearts in your love.

First Reading   2 Kings 4:8-11.14-16.
This is a holy man of God, let him rest there.

One day as Elisha was on his way to Shunem, a woman of rank who lived there pressed him to stay and eat there. After this he always broke his journey for a meal when he passed that way. She said to her husband, "Look, I am sure the man who is constantly passing our way must be a holy man of God. Let us build him a small room on the roof, and put him a bed in it, and a table and chair and lamp; whenever he comes to us he can rest there." One day when he came, he retired to the upper room and lay down. "What can be done for her then?" he asked. Gehazi answered, "Well, she has no son and her husband is old." Elisha said, "Call her." The servant called her and she stood at the door. "This time next year," he said, "you will hold a son in your arms."

Responsorial Psalm   Psalm 88

R/ I will sing for ever of your love, O Lord.

1. I will sing for ever of your love, O Lord;
   through all ages my mouth will proclaim your truth.
   Of this I am sure, that your love lasts for ever,
   that your truth is firmly established as the heavens. R/
2. Happy the people who acclaim such a king,
   who walk, O Lord, in the light of your face,
   who find their joy every day in your name,
   who make your justice the source of their bliss. R/
3. For it is you, O Lord, who are the glory of their strength;
   it is by your favour that our might is exalted:
   for our ruler is in the keeping of the Lord;
   our king in the keeping of the Holy One of Israel. R/

Second Reading   Romans 6:3-4.8-11
When we were baptised we went into the tomb with Christ, so that we too might live a new life.

When we were baptised in Christ Jesus we were baptised in his death; in other words, when we were baptised we went into the tomb with him and joined him in death, so that as Christ was raised from the dead by the Father's glory, we too might live a new life.

THIRTEENTH SUNDAY IN ORDINARY TIME/A

But we believe that having died with Christ we shall return to life with him: Christ, as we know, having been raised from the dead will never die again. Death has no power over him any more. When he died, he died, once for all, to sin, so his life now is life with God; and in that way, you too must consider yourselves to be dead to sin but alive for God in Christ Jesus.

Alleluia   Alleluia, alleluia! Open our heart, O Lord, to accept the words of your Son. Alleluia! **Acts 16:14.**

or   Alleluia, alleluia! You are a chosen race, a royal priesthood, a people set apart to sing the praises of God who called you out of darkness into his wonderful light. Alleluia! **1 Peter 2:9.**

Gospel   **Matthew 10:37-42.**

Anyone who does not take his cross is not worthy of me. Anyone who welcomes you welcomes me.

Jesus instructed the Twelve as follows: "Anyone who prefers father or mother to me is not worthy of me. Anyone who prefers son or daughter to me is not worthy of me. Anyone who does not take his cross and follow in my footsteps is not worthy of me. Anyone who finds his life will lose it; anyone who loses his life for my sake will find it.

"Anyone who welcomes you welcomes me; and those who welcome me welcome the one who sent me.

"Anyone who welcomes a prophet because he is a prophet will have a prophet's reward; and anyone who welcomes a holy man because he is a holy man will have a holy man's reward.

"If anyone gives so much as a cup of cold water to one of these little ones because he is a disciple, then I tell you solemnly, he will most certainly not lose his reward."

Prayer over the Gifts

Lord God,
through your sacraments
you give us the power of your grace.
May this eucharist
help us to serve you faithfully.

Preface of Sundays I-VIII, pages 562-565.

Communion Antiphon   O, bless the Lord, my soul, and all that is within me bless his holy name.
Psalm 102:1

FOURTEENTH SUNDAY IN ORDINARY TIME/A

or

Father, I pray for them: may they be one in us, so that the world may believe it was you who sent me.

John 17:20-21

Prayer after Communion

Lord,
may this sacrifice and communion
give us a share in your life
and help us bring your love to the world.

14th SUNDAY IN ORDINARY TIME/A

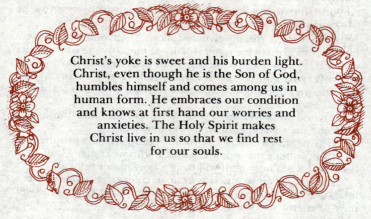

Christ's yoke is sweet and his burden light. Christ, even though he is the Son of God, humbles himself and comes among us in human form. He embraces our condition and knows at first hand our worries and anxieties. The Holy Spirit makes Christ live in us so that we find rest for our souls.

Entrance Antiphon Within your temple, we ponder your loving kindness, O God. As your name, so also your praise reaches to the ends of the earth; your right hand is filled with justice. Psalm 47:10-11

Opening Prayer

Let us pray
  [for forgiveness through the grace of Jesus Christ]
Father,

FOURTEENTH SUNDAY IN ORDINARY TIME/A

through the obedience of Jesus,
your servant and your Son,
you raised a fallen world.
Free us from sin
and bring us the joy that lasts for ever.

or

Let us pray
  [for greater willingness
  to serve God and our fellow man]

Father,
in the rising of your Son
death gives birth to new life.
The sufferings he endured restored hope to a fallen world.
Let sin never ensnare us
with empty promises of passing joy.
Make us one with you always,
so that our joy may be holy,
and our love may give life.

First Reading   Zechariah 9:9-10
See now, your king comes humbly to you.

The Lord says this:
"Rejoice heart and soul, daughter of Zion!
Shout with gladness, daughter of Jerusalem!
See now, your king comes to you;
he is victorious, he is triumphant,
humble and riding on a donkey,
on a colt, the foal of a donkey.
He will banish chariots from Ephraim
and horses from Jerusalem;
the bow of war will be banished.
He will proclaim peace for the nations.
His empire shall stretch from sea to sea,
from the River to the ends of the earth."

FOURTEENTH SUNDAY IN ORDINARY TIME/A

Responsorial Psalm Psalm 144

℟ **I will bless your name for ever,
O God my King.**

1. I will give you glory, O God my King,
   I will bless your name for ever.
   I will bless you day after day
   and praise your name for ever. ℟

2. The Lord is kind and full of compassion,
   slow to anger, abounding in love.
   How good is the Lord to all,
   compassionate to all his creatures. ℟

3. All your creatures shall thank you, O Lord,
   and your friends shall repeat their blessing.
   They shall speak of the glory of your reign
   and declare your might, O God. ℟

4. The Lord is faithful in all his words
   and loving in all his deeds.
   The Lord supports all who fall
   and raises all who are bowed down. ℟

Second Reading Romans 8:9.11-13

If by the Spirit you put an end to the misdeeds of the body, you will live.

Your interests are not in the unspiritual, but in the spiritual, since the Spirit of God has made his home in you. In fact, unless you possessed the Spirit of Christ you would not belong to him, and if the Spirit of him who raised Jesus from the dead is living in you, then he who raised Jesus from the dead will give life to your own mortal bodies through his Spirit living in you.

So then, my brothers, there is no necessity for us to obey our unspiritual selves or to live unspiritual lives. If you do live in that way, you are doomed to die; but if by the Spirit you put an end to the misdeeds of the body you will live.

Alleluia   Alleluia, alleluia! Blessed are you, Father, Lord of heaven and earth, for revealing the mysteries of the kingdom to mere children. Alleluia! Matthew 11:25.

Alternative Alleluias, pages 1004-1006.

FOURTEENTH SUNDAY IN ORDINARY TIME/A

Gospel   Matthew 11:25-30
I am gentle and humble in heart.

Jesus exclaimed, "I bless you, Father, Lord of heaven and of earth, for hiding these things from the learned and the clever and revealing them to mere children. Yes, Father, for that is what it pleased you to do. Everything has been entrusted to me by my Father; and no one knows the Son except the Father, just as no one knows the Father except the Son and those to whom the Son chooses to reveal him.

"Come to me, all you who labour and are overburdened, and I will give you rest. Shoulder my yoke and learn from me, for I am gentle and humble in heart, and you will find rest for your souls. Yes, my yoke is easy and my burden light."

Prayer over the Gifts

Lord,
let this offering to the glory of your name
purify us and bring us closer to eternal life.

Preface of Sundays I-VIII, pages 562-565.

Communion Antiphon   Taste and see the goodness of the Lord; blessed is he who hopes in God. **Psalm 33:9**

or

Come to me, all you that labour and are burdened, and I will give you rest, says the Lord. **Matthew 11:28**

Prayer after Communion

Lord,
may we never fail to praise you
for the fullness of life and salvation
you give us in this eucharist.

15th SUNDAY IN ORDINARY TIME/A

The seed of faith must grow in our lives. God does nothing in vain. All our suffering has a meaning and through it we are so deepened in our spiritual lives that we yield a rich harvest. The world longs for the Spirit of Christ to come and set us free from clinging to the things of this world.

Entrance Antiphon In my justice I shall see your face, O Lord; when your glory appears, my joy will be full. **Psalm 16:15.**

Opening Prayer

Let us pray
  [that the gospel may be our rule of life]

God our Father,
your light of truth
guides us to the way of Christ.
May all who follow him
reject what is contrary to the gospel.

or

Let us pray
  [to be faithful to the light we have received,
  to the name we bear]

Father,
let the light of your truth
guide us to your kingdom
through a world filled with lights contrary to your own.
Christian is the name and the gospel we glory in.
May your love make us what you have called us to be.

FIFTEENTH SUNDAY IN ORDINARY TIME/A

First Reading   Isaiah 55:10-11
The rain makes the earth give growth.
Thus says the Lord: "Yes, as the rain and the snow come down from the heavens and do not return without watering the earth, making it yield and giving growth to provide seed for the sower and bread for the eating, so the word that goes from my mouth does not return to me empty, without carrying out my will and succeeding in what it was sent to do."

Responsorial Psalm   Psalm 64
R/ **Some seed fell into rich soil,
and produced its crop.**

1. You care for the earth, give it water,
   you fill it with riches.
   Your river in heaven brims over
   to provide its grain. R/

2. And thus you provide for the earth;
   you drench its furrows,
   you level it, soften it with showers,
   you bless its growth. R/

3. You crown the year with your goodness.
   Abundance flows in your steps,
   in the pastures of the wilderness it flows. R/

4. The hills are girded with joy,
   the meadows covered with flocks,
   the valleys are decked with wheat.
   They shout for joy, yes, they sing. R/

Second Reading   Romans 8:18-23
The whole creation is eagerly waiting for God to reveal his sons.
I think that what we suffer in this life can never be compared to the glory, as yet unrevealed, which is waiting for us. The whole creation is eagerly waiting for God to reveal his sons. It was not for any fault on the part of creation that it was made unable to attain its purpose, it was made so by God; but creation still retains the hope of being freed, like us, from its slavery to decadence, to enjoy the same freedom and glory as the children of God. From the beginning till now the entire creation, as we know, has been groaning in one great act of giving birth; and not only creation, but all of us who possess the first-fruits of the Spirit, we too groan inwardly as we wait for our bodies to be set free.

FIFTEENTH SUNDAY IN ORDINARY TIME/A

Alleluia — Alleluia, alleluia! Speak, Lord, your servant is listening; you have the message of eternal life. Alleluia! 1 Samuel 3:9; John 6:68.

or — Alleluia, alleluia! The seed is the word of God, Christ the sower; whoever finds this seed will remain for ever. Alleluia!

Gospel Matthew 13:1-23

A sower went out to sow.

> Jesus left the house and sat by the lakeside, but such crowds gathered round him that he got into a boat and sat there. The people all stood on the beach, and he told them many things in parables.
>
> He said, "Imagine a sower going out to sow. As he sowed, some seeds fell on the edge of the path, and the birds came and ate them up. Others fell on patches of rock where they found little soil and sprang up straight away, because there was no depth of earth; but as soon as the sun came up they were scorched and, not having any roots, they withered away. Others fell among thorns, and the thorns grew up and choked them. Others fell on rich soil and produced their crop, some a hundredfold, some sixty, some thirty. Listen, anyone who has ears!"

Then the disciples went up to him and asked, "Why do you talk to them in parables?" "Because," he replied, "the mysteries of the kingdom of heaven are revealed to you, but they are not revealed to them. For anyone who has will be given more, and he will have more than enough; but from anyone who has not, even what he has will be taken away. The reason I talk to them in parables is that they look without seeing and listen without hearing or understanding. So in their case this prophecy of Isaiah is being fulfilled:
You will listen and listen again, but not understand,
see and see again, but not perceive.
For the heart of this nation has grown coarse,
their ears are dull of hearing, and they have shut their eyes,
for fear they should see with their eyes,
hear with their ears,
understand with their heart,
and be converted
and be healed by me.

FIFTEENTH SUNDAY IN ORDINARY TIME/A

"But happy are your eyes because they see, your ears because they hear! I tell you solemnly, many prophets and holy men longed to see what you see, and never saw it; to hear what you hear, and never heard it.

"You, therefore, are to hear the parable of the sower. When anyone hears the word of the kingdom without understanding, the evil one comes and carries off what was sown in his heart: this is the man who received the seed on the edge of the path. The one who received it on patches of rock is the man who hears the word and welcomes it at once with joy. But he has no root in him, he does not last; let some trial come, or some persecution on account of the word, and he falls away at once. The one who received the seed in thorns is the man who hears the word, but the worries of this world and the lure of riches choke the word and so he produces nothing. And the one who received the seed in rich soil is the man who hears the word and understands it; he is the one who yields a harvest and produces now a hundredfold, now sixty, now thirty."

Prayer over the Gifts

Lord,
accept the gifts of your Church.
May this eucharist
help us grow in holiness and faith.

Preface of Sundays I-VIII, pages 562-565.

Communion Antiphon

The sparrow even finds a home, the swallow finds a nest wherein to place her young, near to your altars, Lord of hosts, my King, my God! How happy they who dwell in your house! For ever they are praising you.
Psalm 83:4-5

or

Whoever eats my flesh and drinks my blood will live in me and I in him, says the Lord. *John 6:57.*

Prayer after Communion

Lord,
by our sharing in the mystery of this eucharist,
let your saving love grow within us.

16th SUNDAY IN ORDINARY TIME/A

*The Spirit is our help!
We are a people full of weaknesses
due to sin. We cannot pray for repentance
unless the Spirit comes to help us in our
weakness. Our God is mild in judgement
and we pray that his mercy will be with us
so that like wheat we will be gathered
into his barn.*

Entrance Antiphon God himself is my help. The Lord upholds my life. I will offer you a willing sacrifice; I will praise your name, O Lord, for its goodness. Psalm 53:6.8.

Opening Prayer

Let us pray
   [to be kept faithful in the service of God]
Lord,
be merciful to your people.
Fill us with your gifts
and make us always eager to serve you
in faith, hope, and love.

or

Let us pray
   [that God will continue to bless us
   with his compassion and love]
Father,
let the gift of your life
continue to grow in us,
drawing us from death to faith, hope, and love.
Keep us alive in Christ Jesus.
Keep us watchful in prayer
and true to his teaching
till your glory is revealed in us.

SIXTEENTH SUNDAY IN ORDINARY TIME/A

First Reading Wisdom 12:13. 16-19.

After sin you will grant repentance.

There is no god, other than you, who cares for everything,
to whom you might have to prove that you never judged
  unjustly.
Your justice has its source in strength,
your sovereignty over all makes you lenient to all.
You show your strength when your sovereign power is
  questioned
and you expose the insolence of those who know it;
but, disposing of such strength, you are mild in judgement,
you govern us with great lenience,
for you have only to will, and your power is there.
By acting thus you have taught a lesson to your people
how the virtuous man must be kindly to his fellow men,
and you have given your sons the good hope
that after sin you will grant repentance.

Responsorial Psalm Psalm 85

℟ **O Lord, you are good and forgiving.**

1. O Lord, you are good and forgiving,
   full of love to all who call.
   Give heed, O Lord, to my prayer
   and attend to the sound of my voice. ℟

2. All the nations shall come to adore you
   and glorify your name, O Lord:
   for you are great and do marvellous deeds,
   you who alone are God. ℟

3. But you, God of mercy and compassion,
   slow to anger, O Lord,
   abounding in love and truth,
   turn and take pity on me. ℟

Second Reading Romans 8:26-27.

The Spirit expresses our plea in a way that could never be put into words.

The Spirit comes to help us in our weakness. For when we cannot choose words in order to pray properly, the Spirit himself expresses our plea in a way that could never be put into words,

SIXTEENTH SUNDAY IN ORDINARY TIME/A

and God who knows everything in our hearts knows perfectly well what he means, and that the pleas of the saints expressed by the Spirit are according to the mind of God.

Alleluia Alleluia, alleluia! May the Father of our Lord Jesus Christ enlighten the eyes of our mind, so that we can see what hope his call holds for us. Alleluia!
Ephesians 1:17.18

or Alleluia, alleluia! Blessed are you, Father, Lord of heaven and earth, for revealing the mysteries of the kingdom to mere children. Alleluia! **Matthew 11:25.**

Gospel Matthew 13:24-43.

Let them both grow till the harvest.

> Jesus put a parable before the crowds, "The kingdom of heaven may be compared to a man who sowed good seed in his field. While everybody was asleep his enemy came, sowed darnel all among the wheat, and made off. When the new wheat sprouted and ripened, the darnel appeared as well. The owner's servant went to him and said, 'Sir, was it not good seed that you sowed in your field? If so, where does the darnel come from?' 'Some enemy has done this,' he answered. And the servant said, 'Do you want us to go and weed it out?' But he said, 'No, because when you weed out the darnel you might pull up the wheat with it. Let them both grow till the harvest; and at harvest time I shall say to the reapers: First collect the darnel and tie it in bundles to be burnt, then gather the wheat into my barn.'

He put another parable before them, "The kingdom of heaven is like a mustard seed which a man took and sowed in his field. It is the smallest of all the seeds, but when it has grown it is the biggest shrub of all and becomes a tree so that the birds of the air come and shelter in its branches."

He told them another parable, "The kingdom of heaven is like the yeast a woman took and mixed in with three measures of flour till it was leavened all through."

In all this Jesus spoke to the crowds in parables; indeed, he would never speak to them except in parables. This was to fulfil the prophecy: I will speak to you in parables
and expound things hidden
since the foundation of the world.

SIXTEENTH SUNDAY IN ORDINARY TIME/A

Then, leaving the crowds, he went to the house; and his disciples came to him and said, "Explain the parable about the darnel in the field to us." He said in reply, "The sower of the good seed is the Son of Man. The field is the world; the good seed is the subjects of the kingdom; the darnel, the subjects of the evil one; the enemy who sowed them, the devil; the harvest is the end of the world; the reapers are the angels. Well then, just as the darnel is gathered up and burnt in the fire, so it will be at the end of time. The Son of Man will send his angels and they will gather out of his kingdom all things that provoke offences and all who do evil, and throw them into the blazing furnace, where there will be weeping and grinding of teeth. Then the virtuous will shine like the sun in the kingdom of their Father. Listen, anyone who has ears!"

Prayer over the Gifts
Lord,
bring us closer to salvation
through these gifts which we bring in your honour.
Accept the perfect sacrifice you have given us,
bless it as you blessed the gifts of Abel.

Preface of Sundays I-VIII, pages 562-565.

Communion Antiphon
The Lord keeps in our minds the wonderful things he has done. He is compassion and love; he always provides for his faithful.
Psalm 110: 4-5.

or

I stand at the door and knock, says the Lord. If anyone hears my voice and opens the door, I will come in and sit down to supper with him, and he with me. **Apocalypse 3:20.**

Prayer after Communion
Merciful Father,
may these mysteries
give us new purpose
and bring us to a new life in you.

17th SUNDAY IN ORDINARY TIME/A

Faith is a priceless treasure.
God turns everything to our good. He gives us a wisdom by which we discern true values in the world around us. Our greatest gift is faith which gives us a deeper wisdom even than that of Solomon.

Entrance Antiphon God is in his holy dwelling; he will give a home to the lonely, he gives power and strength to his people. Psalm 67:6-7. 36.

Opening Prayer

Let us pray
   [that we will make good use of the gifts
   that God has given us]

God our Father and protector,
without you nothing is holy,
nothing has value.
Guide us to everlasting life
by helping us to use wisely
the blessings you have given to the world.

or

Let us pray
   [for the faith to recognize God's presence
   in our world]

SEVENTEENTH SUNDAY IN ORDINARY TIME/A

God our Father,
open our eyes to see your hand at work
in the splendour of creation,
in the beauty of human life.
Touched by your hand our world is holy.
Help us to cherish the gifts that surround us,
to share your blessings with our brothers and sisters,
and to experience the joy of life in your presence.

First Reading   1 Kings 3:5. 7-12.
You have asked for a discerning judgement for yourself.

The Lord appeared to Solomon in a dream and said, "Ask what you would like me to give you." Solomon replied, "Lord, my God, you have made. your servant king in succession to David my father. But I am a very young man, unskilled in leadership. Your servant finds himself in the midst of this people of yours that you have chosen, a people so many its numbers cannot be counted or reckoned. Give your servant a heart to understand how to discern between good and evil, for who could govern this people of yours that is so great?" It pleased the Lord that Solomon should have asked for this. "Since you have asked for this," the Lord said, "and not asked for long life for yourself or riches or the lives of your enemies, but have asked for a discerning judgement for yourself, here and now I do what you ask. I give you a heart wise and shrewd as none before you has had and none will have after you."

Responsorial Psalm   Psalm 118

R/ **Lord, how I love your law!**

1. My part, I have resolved, O Lord,
   is to obey your word.
   The law from your mouth means more to me
   than silver and gold. R/

2. Let your love be ready to console me
   by your promise to your servant.
   Let your love come to me and I shall live
   for your law is my delight. R/

SEVENTEENTH SUNDAY IN ORDINARY TIME/A

3. That is why I love your commands
   more than finest gold.
   That is why I rule my life by your precepts:
   I hate false ways. ℟
4. Your will is wonderful indeed;
   therefore I obey it.
   The unfolding of your word gives light
   and teaches the simple. ℟

Second Reading   Romans 8:28-30
God intended us to become true images of his Son.

We know that by turning everything to their good God co-operates with all those who love him, with all those that he has called according to his purpose. They are the ones he chose specially long ago and intended to become true images of his Son, so that his Son might be the eldest of many brothers. He called those he intended for this; those he called he justified, and with those he justified he shared his glory.

Alleluia	Alleluia, alleluia! I call you friends, says the Lord, because I have made known to you everything I have learnt from my Father. Alleluia! John 15:15.
or	Alleluia, alleluia! Blessed are you, Father, Lord of heaven and earth, for revealing the mysteries of the kingdom to mere children. Alleluia! Matthew 11:25.

Gospel Matthew 13:44-52
He sells everything he owns and buys the field.

Jesus said to the crowds, "The kingdom of heaven is like treasure hidden in a field which someone has found; he hides it again, goes off happy, sells everything he owns and buys the field.

"Again, the kingdom of heaven is like a merchant looking for fine pearls; when he finds one of great value he goes and sells everything he owns and buys it.

"Again, the kingdom of heaven is like a dragnet cast into the sea that brings in a haul of all kinds. When it is full, the fishermen haul it ashore; then, sitting down, they collect the good ones in a basket and throw away those that are no use. This is how it

SEVENTEENTH SUNDAY IN ORDINARY TIME/A

will be at the end of time: the angels will appear and separate the wicked from the just to throw them into the blazing furnace where there will be weeping and grinding of teeth.

"Have you understood all this?" They said, "Yes." And he said to them, "Well, then, every scribe who becomes a disciple of the kingdom of heaven is like a householder who brings out from his storeroom things both new and old."

Prayer over the Gifts

Lord,
receive these offerings
chosen from your many gifts.
May these mysteries make us holy
and lead us to eternal joy.

Preface of Sundays I-VIII, pages 562-565.

Communion Antiphon

O, bless the Lord, my soul, and remember all his kindness.
Psalm 102:2

or

Happy are those who show mercy; mercy shall be theirs. Happy are the pure of heart, for they shall see God.
Matthew 5:7-8

Prayer after Communion

Lord,
we receive the sacrament
which celebrates the memory
of the death and resurrection of Christ your Son.
May this gift bring us closer to our eternal salvation.

18th SUNDAY IN ORDINARY TIME/A

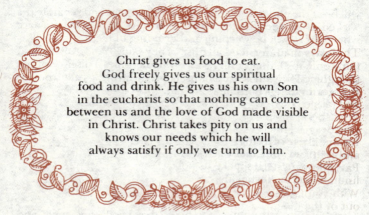

Christ gives us food to eat.
God freely gives us our spiritual
food and drink. He gives us his own Son
in the eucharist so that nothing can come
between us and the love of God made visible
in Christ. Christ takes pity on us and
knows our needs which he will
always satisfy if only we turn to him.

Entrance Antiphon God, come to my help. Lord, quickly give me assistance. You are the one who helps me and sets me free: Lord, do not be long in coming. Psalm 69:2.6

Opening Prayer

Let us pray
   [for the gift of God's forgiveness and love]

Father of everlasting goodness,
our origin and guide,
be close to us
and hear the prayers of all who praise you.
Forgive our sins and restore us to life.
Keep us safe in your love.

or

Let us pray
   [to the Father whose kindness never fails]

God our Father,
gifts without measure flow from your goodness
to bring us your peace.
Our life is your gift.
Guide our life's journey,
for only your love makes us whole.
Keep us strong in your love.

EIGHTEENTH SUNDAY IN ORDINARY TIME/A

First Reading — Isaiah 55:1-3

Come and eat.

Thus says the Lord:
Oh, come to the water all you who are thirsty;
though you have no money, come!
Buy corn without money, and eat,
and, at no cost, wine and milk.
Why spend money on what is not bread,
your wages on what fails to satisfy?
Listen, listen to me and you will have good things to eat
and rich food to enjoy.
Pay attention, come to me;
listen, and your soul will live.
With you I will make an everlasting covenant
out of the favours promised to David.

Responsorial Psalm — Psalm 144

**R/ You open wide your hand, O Lord,
you grant our desires.**

1. The Lord is kind and full of compassion,
   slow to anger, abounding in love.
   How good is the Lord to all,
   compassionate to all his creatures. R/

2. The eyes of all creatures look to you
   and you give them their food in due time.
   You open wide your hand,
   grant the desires of all who live. R/

3. The Lord is just in all his ways
   and loving in all his deeds.
   He is close to all who call him,
   who call on him from their hearts. R/

Second Reading — Romans 8:35.37-39

No created thing can ever come between us and the love of God made visible in Christ.

Nothing can come between us and the love of Christ, even if we are troubled or worried, or being persecuted, or lacking food or clothes, or being threatened or even attacked. These are the trials through which we triumph, by the power of him who loved us.

EIGHTEENTH SUNDAY IN ORDINARY TIME/A

For I am certain of this: neither death nor life, no angel, no prince, nothing that exists, nothing still to come, not any power, or height or depth, nor any created thing, can ever come between us and the love of God made visible in Christ Jesus our Lord.

Alleluia	Alleluia, alleluia! Blessings on the King who comes, in the name of the Lord! Peace in heaven and glory in the highest heavens! Alleluia! Luke 19:38.
or	Alleluia, alleluia! Man does not live on bread alone, but on every word that comes from the mouth of God. Alleluia! Matthew 4:4.

Gospel Matthew 14:13-21.

They all ate as much as they wanted.

When Jesus received the news of John the Baptist's death he withdrew by boat to a lonely place where they could be by themselves. But the people heard of this and, leaving the towns, went after him on foot. So as he stepped ashore he saw a large crowd; and he took pity on them and healed their sick.

When evening came, the disciples went to him and said, "This is a lonely place, and the time has slipped by; so send the people away, and they can go to the villages to buy themselves some food." Jesus replied, "There is no need for them to go: give them something to eat yourselves." But they answered, "All we have with us is five loaves and two fish." "Bring them here to me," he said. He gave orders that the people were to sit down on the grass; then he took the five loaves and the two fish, raised his eyes to heaven and said the blessing. And breaking the loaves he handed them to his disciples who gave them to the crowds. They all ate as much as they wanted, and they collected the scraps remaining, twelve baskets full. Those who ate numbered about five thousand men, to say nothing of women and children.

Prayer over the Gifts

Merciful Lord,
make holy these gifts,
and let our spiritual sacrifice
make us an everlasting gift to you.

Preface of Sundays I-VIII, pages 562-565.

EIGHTEENTH SUNDAY IN ORDINARY TIME/A

Communion Antiphon
You gave us bread from heaven, Lord: a sweet-tasting bread that was very good to eat. Wisdom 16:20.

or

The Lord says: I am the bread of life. A man who comes to me will not go away hungry, and no one who believes in me will thirst. John 6:35.

Prayer after Communion
Lord,
you give us the strength of new life
by the gift of the eucharist.
Protect us with your love
and prepare us for eternal redemption.

19th SUNDAY IN ORDINARY TIME/A

*God speaks in a gentle breeze.
Jesus spoke to the storm and there
followed a great calm. God spoke to
Elijah in the whisper of a gentle breeze.
In every aspect of our life, especially in
moments of great trial, God speaks
to us in Christ if only we will listen
to his voice.*

Entrance Antiphon   Lord, be true to your covenant, forget not the life of your poor ones for ever. Rise up, O God, and defend your cause, do not ignore the shouts of your enemies.
Psalm 73:20.19.22.23

Opening Prayer

Let us pray
   [in the Spirit
   that we may grow in the love of God]

Almighty and ever-living God,
your Spirit made us your children,
confident to call you Father.
Increase your Spirit within us
and bring us to our promised inheritance.

or

Let us pray
   [that through us
   others may find the way to life in Christ]

Father,
we come, reborn in the Spirit,
to celebrate our sonship in the Lord Jesus Christ.
Touch our hearts,

NINETEENTH SUNDAY IN ORDINARY TIME/A

help them grow towards the life you have promised.
Touch our lives,
make them signs of your love for all men.

First Reading   1 Kings 19:9.11-13
Stand on the mountain before the Lord.

When Elijah reached Horelo, the mountain of God, he went into the cave and spent the night in it. Then he was told, "Go out and stand on the mountain before the Lord." Then the Lord himself went by. There came a mighty wind, so strong it tore the mountains and shattered the rocks before the Lord. But the Lord was not in the wind. After the wind came an earthquake. But the Lord was not in the earthquake. After the earthquake came a fire. But the Lord was not in the fire. And after the fire there came the sound of a gentle breeze. And when Elijah heard this, he covered his face with his cloak and went out and stood at the entrance of the cave.

Responsorial Psalm   Psalm 84

R/ **Let us see, O Lord, your mercy
and give us your saving help.**

1. I will hear what the Lord God has to say,
   a voice that speaks of peace.
   His help is near for those who fear him
   and his glory will dwell in our land. R/

2. Mercy and faithfulness have met;
   justice and peace have embraced.
   Faithfulness shall spring from the earth
   and justice look down from heaven. R/

3. The Lord will make us prosper
   and our earth shall yield its fruit.
   Justice shall march before him
   and peace shall follow his steps. R/

Second Reading   Romans 9:1-5
I would willingly be condemned if it could help my brothers.

What I want to say is no pretence; I say it in union with Christ — it is the truth — my conscience in union with the Holy Spirit assures me of it too. What I want to say is this: my sorrow is so great, my mental anguish so endless, I would willingly be con-

NINETEENTH SUNDAY IN ORDINARY TIME/A

demned and be cut off from Christ if it could help my brothers of Israel, my own flesh and blood. They were adopted as sons, they were given the glory and the covenants; the Law and the ritual were drawn up for them, and the promises were made to them. They are descended from the patriarchs and from their flesh and blood came Christ who is above all, God for ever blessed! Amen.

Alleluia   Alleluia, alleluia! Blessings on the King who comes, in the name of the Lord! Peace in heaven and glory in the highest heavens! Alleluia! Luke 19:38.

or   Alleluia, alleluia! My soul is waiting for the Lord, I count on his word. Alleluia! Psalm 129:5.

Gospel   Matthew 14:22-33.

Tell me to come to you across the water.

Jesus made the disciples get into the boat and go on ahead to the other side while he would send the crowds away. After sending the crowds away he went up into the hills by himself to pray. When evening came, he was there alone, while the boat, by now far out on the lake, was battling with a heavy sea, for there was a headwind. In the fourth watch of the night he went towards them, walking on the lake, and when the disciples saw him walking on the lake they were terrified. "It is a ghost," they said, and cried out in fear. But at once Jesus called out to them, saying, "Courage! It is I! Do not be afraid." It was Peter who answered. "Lord," he said, "if it is you, tell me to come to you across the water." "Come," said Jesus. Then Peter got out of the boat and started walking towards Jesus across the water, but as soon as he felt the force of the wind, he took fright and began to sink. "Lord! Save me!" he cried. Jesus put out his hand at once and held him. "Man of little faith," he said, "why did you doubt?" And as they got into the boat the wind dropped. The men in the boat bowed down before him and said, "Truly, you are the Son of God"

Prayer over the Gifts

God of power,
giver of the gifts we bring,
accept the offering of your Church
and make it the sacrament of our salvation.

Preface of Sundays I-VIII, pages 562-565.

TWENTIETH SUNDAY IN ORDINARY TIME/A

Communion Antiphon Praise the Lord, Jerusalem; he feeds you with the finest wheat.

Psalm 147:12.14

or

The bread I shall give is my flesh for the life of the world, says the Lord.

John 6:52

Prayer after Communion

Lord,
may the eucharist you give us
bring us to salvation
and keep us faithful to the light of your truth.

20th SUNDAY IN ORDINARY TIME/A

God shows mercy to all mankind.
God named the Jews as his chosen race but many of them failed to recognise Christ. In his own lifetime Jesus acknowledged that he discovered faith in many people who were pagans. We realise how many people in the world around us seem to have a deeper faith than we have as christians. This should make us more aware of God's generosity to all men and give us a deeper appreciation of the great gift of faith which is given to us.

Entrance Antiphon God, our protector, keep us in mind; always give strength to your people. For if we can be with you even one day, it is better than a thousand without you.

Psalm 83:10-11

TWENTIETH SUNDAY IN ORDINARY TIME/A

Opening Prayer

Let us pray
   [that the love of God
   may raise us beyond what we see
   to the unseen glory of his kingdom]

God our Father,
may we love you in all things and above all things
and reach the joy you have prepared for us
beyond all our imagining.

or

Let us pray
   [with humility and persistence]

Almighty God, ever-loving Father,
your care extends beyond the boundaries of race and nation
to the hearts of all who live.

May the walls, which prejudice raises between us,
crumble beneath the shadow of your outstretched arm.

First Reading   Isaiah 56:1.6-7.
I will bring foreigners to my holy mountain.

Thus says the Lord: Have a care for justice, act with integrity, for soon my salvation will come and my integrity be manifest.

Foreigners who have attached themselves to the Lord to serve him and to love his name and be his servants — all who observe the sabbath, not profaning it, and cling to my covenant — these I will bring to my holy mountain. I will make them joyful in my house of prayer. Their holocausts and their sacrifices will be accepted on my altar, for my house will be called a house of prayer for all the peoples.

Responsorial Psalm   Psalm 66

℟ **Let the peoples praise you, O God;
   let all the peoples praise you.**

1. O God, be gracious and bless us
   and let your face shed its light upon us.
   So will your ways be known upon earth
   and all nations learn your saving help.   ℟

TWENTIETH SUNDAY IN ORDINARY TIME/A

2. Let the nations be glad and exult
for you rule the world with justice.
With fairness you rule the peoples,
you guide the nations on earth. ℟

3. Let the peoples praise you, O God;
let all the peoples praise you.
May God still give us his blessing
till the ends of the earth revere him. ℟

Second Reading Romans 11:13-15.29-32.

With Israel, God never takes back his gifts or revokes his choice.

Let me tell you pagans this: I have been sent to the pagans as their apostle, and I am proud of being sent, but the purpose of it is to make my own people envious of you, and in this way save some of them. Since their rejection meant the reconciliation of the world, do you know what their admission will mean? Nothing less than a resurrection from the dead! God never takes back his gifts or revokes his choice.

Just as you changed from being disobedient to God, and now enjoy mercy because of their disobedience, so those who are disobedient now — and only because of the mercy shown to you — will also enjoy mercy eventually. God has imprisoned all men in their own disobedience only to show mercy to all mankind.

Alleluia   Alleluia, alleluia! The sheep that belong to me listen to my voice, says the Lord, I know them and they follow me. Alleluia! John 10:27.

or   Alleluia, Alleluia! Jesus proclaimed the Good News of the kingdom, and cured all kinds of sickness among the people. Alleluia! Matthew 4:23.

Gospel Matthew 15:21-28.

Woman, you have great faith.

Jesus left Gennesaret and withdrew to the region of Tyre and Sidon. Then out came a Canaanite woman from that district and started shouting, "Sir, Son of David, take pity on me. My daughter is tormented by a devil." But he answered her not a word. And his disciples went and pleaded with him. "Give her what she wants," they said, "because she is shouting after us." He said in reply, "I was sent only to the lost sheep of the House of

TWENTIETH SUNDAY IN ORDINARY TIME/A

Israel." But the woman had come up and was kneeling at his feet. "Lord," she said, "help me." He replied, "It is not fair to take the children's food and throw it to the house-dogs." She retorted, "Ah yes, sir; but even house-dogs can eat the scraps that fall from their master's table." Then Jesus answered her, "Woman, you have great faith. Let your wish be granted." And from that moment her daughter was well again.

Prayer over the Gifts

Lord,
accept our sacrifice
as a holy exchange of gifts.
By offering what you have given us
may we receive the gift of yourself.

Preface of Sundays I-VIII, pages 562-565.

Communion Antiphon

With the Lord there is mercy, and fullness of redemption. Psalm 129:7.

or

I am the living bread from heaven, says the Lord; if anyone eats this bread he will live for ever.

John 6:51-52

Prayer after Communion

God of mercy,
by this sacrament you make us one with Christ.
By becoming more like him on earth,
may we come to share his glory in heaven,
where he lives and reigns for ever and ever.

21st SUNDAY IN ORDINARY TIME/A

Peter and the keys of the Kingdom. Christ chose Peter as the rock on which he would build his church. Peter was a man of faith and it is upon faith that Christ always builds. When we proclaim: 'You are the Christ' we also ask for a deepening of our faith. Through faith we fix our eyes on God who is infinite wisdom and it is for his good purposes that we were chosen to be members of Christ's Church on earth.

Entrance Antiphon Listen, Lord, and answer me. Save your servant who trusts in you. I call to you all day long, have mercy on me, O Lord.
Psalm 85:1-3

Opening Prayer

Let us pray
 [that God will make us one in mind and heart]

Father,
help us to seek the values
that will bring us lasting joy in this changing world.
In our desire for what you promise
make us one in mind and heart.

or

Let us pray
 [with minds fixed on eternal truth]

Lord our God,
all truth is from you,
and you alone bring oneness of heart.
Give your people the joy
of hearing your word in every sound
and of longing for your presence more than for life itself.
May all the attractions of a changing world

TWENTY-FIRST SUNDAY IN ORDINARY TIME/A

serve only to bring us
the peace of your kingdom which this world does not give.

First Reading   Isaiah 22:19-23.

I place the key of the House of David on his shoulder.

Thus says the Lord of hosts to Shebna, the master of the palace:
I dismiss you from your office,
I remove you from your post,
and the same day I call on my servant
Eliakim son of Hilkiah.
I invest him with your robe,
gird him with your sash,
entrust him with your authority;
and he shall be a father
to the inhabitants of Jerusalem
and to the House of Judah.
I place the key of the House of David
on his shoulder;
should he open, no one shall close,
should he close, no one shall open.
I drive him like a peg
into a firm place;
he will become a throne of glory
for his father's house.

Responsorial Psalm   Psalm 137

**R/ Your love, O Lord, is eternal,
discard not the work of your hands.**

1. I thank you, Lord, with all my heart,
   you have heard the words of my mouth.
   Before the angels I will bless you.
   I will adore before your holy temple.   R/

2. I thank you for your faithfulness and love
   which excel all we ever knew of you.
   On the day I called, you answered;
   you increased the strength of my soul.   R/

3. The Lord is high yet he looks on the lowly
   and the haughty he knows from afar.
   Your love, O Lord, is eternal,
   discard not the work of your hands.   R/

TWENTY-FIRST SUNDAY IN ORDINARY TIME/A

Second Reading   Romans 11:33-36
All that exists comes from him; all is by him and for him.

How rich are the depths of God — how deep his wisdom and knowledge — and how impossible to penetrate his motives or understand his methods! Who could ever know the mind of the Lord? Who could ever be his counsellor? Who could ever give him anything or lend him anything? All that exists comes from him; all is by him and for him. To him be glory for ever! Amen.

Alleluia	Alleluia, alleluia! God in Christ was reconciling the world to himself, and he has entrusted to us the news that they are reconciled. Alleluia!
	2 Corinthians 5:19
or	Alleluia, alleluia! You are Peter and on this rock I will build my Church. And the gates of the underworld can never hold out against it. Alleluia! Matthew 16:18.

Gospel   Matthew 16:13-20.
You are Peter, and I will give you the keys of the kingdom of heaven.

When Jesus came to the region of Caesarea Philippi he put this question to his disciples, "Who do people say the Son of Man is?" And they said, "Some say he is John the Baptist, some Elijah, and others Jeremiah or one of the prophets." "But you," he said, "who do you say I am?" Then Simon Peter spoke up, "You are the Christ," he said, "the Son of the living God." Jesus replied, "Simon son of Jonah, you are a happy man! Because it was not flesh and blood that revealed this to you but my Father in heaven. So I now say to you: You are Peter and on this rock I will build my Church. And the gates of the underworld can never hold out against it. I will give you the keys of the kingdom of heaven: whatever you bind on earth shall be considered bound in heaven; whatever you loose on earth shall be considered loosed in heaven." Then he gave the disciples strict orders not to tell anyone that he was the Christ.

Prayer over the Gifts

Merciful God,
the perfect sacrifice of Jesus Christ
made us your people.
In your love,
grant peace and unity to your Church.

TWENTY-SECOND SUNDAY IN ORDINARY TIME/A

Preface of Sundays I-VIII, pages 562-565.

Communion Antiphon

Lord, the earth is filled with your gift from heaven; man grows bread from earth, and wine to cheer his heart.
Psalm 103:13-15

or

The Lord says: The man who eats my flesh and drinks my blood will live for ever; I shall raise him to life on the last day. *John 6:55.*

Prayer after Communion

Lord,
may this eucharist increase within us
the healing power of your love.
May it guide and direct our efforts
to please you in all things.

22nd SUNDAY IN ORDINARY TIME/A

Take up your daily cross. Suffering shows us how much we are prepared to sacrifice in our following of Christ. He tells us to take up our cross daily and follow him. It is in apparently losing our lives that we will find them in a newer, deeper way and then we shall be rewarded according to our behaviour. This approach will never be easy but it is the only path to real holiness and happiness.

Entrance Antiphon

I call to you all day long, have mercy on me, O Lord. You are good and forgiving, full of love for all who call to you.
Psalm 85:3.5

TWENTY-SECOND SUNDAY IN ORDINARY TIME/A

Opening Prayer

Let us pray
   [that God will increase our faith
   and bring to perfection the gifts he has given us]

Almighty God,
every good thing comes from you.
Fill our hearts with love for you,
increase our faith,
and by your constant care
protect the good you have given us.

or

Let us pray
   [to God who forgives all who call upon him]

Lord God of power and might,
nothing is good which is against your will,
and all is of value which comes from your hand.
Place in our hearts a desire to please you
and fill our minds with insight into love,
so that every thought may grow in wisdom
and all our efforts may be filled with your peace.

First Reading   Jeremiah 20:7-9

The word of the Lord has meant insult for me.

You have seduced me, Lord, and I have let myself be seduced;
you have overpowered me: you were the stronger.
I am a daily laughing-stock,
everybody's butt.
Each time I speak the word, I have to howl
and proclaim: "Violence and ruin!"
The word of the Lord has meant for me
insult, derision, all day long.
I used to say, "I will not think about him,
I will not speak in his name any more."
Then there seemed to be a fire burning in my heart,
imprisoned in my bones.
The effort to restrain it wearied me,
I could not bear it.

TWENTY-SECOND SUNDAY IN ORDINARY TIME/A

Responsorial Psalm   Psalm 62

℟ **For you my soul is thirsting, O Lord my God.**

1. O God, you are my God, for you I long;
   for you my soul is thirsting.
   My body pines for you
   like a dry, weary land without water. ℟

2. So I gaze on you in the sanctuary
   to see your strength and your glory.
   For your love is better than life,
   my lips will speak your praise. ℟

3. So I will bless you all my life,
   in your name I will lift up my hands.
   My soul shall be filled as with a banquet,
   my mouth shall praise you with joy. ℟

4. For you have been my help;
   in the shadow of your wings I rejoice.
   My soul clings to you;
   your right hand holds me fast. ℟

Second Reading   Romans 12:1-2

Offer your bodies as a living sacrifice.

Think of God's mercy, my brothers, and worship him, I beg you, in a way that is worthy of thinking beings, by offering your living bodies as a holy sacrifice, truly pleasing to God. Do not model yourselves on the behaviour of the world around you, but let your behaviour change, modelled by your new mind. This is the only way to discover the will of God and know what is good, what it is that God wants, what is the perfect thing to do.

Alleluia   Alleluia, alleluia! May the Father of our Lord Jesus Christ enlighten the eyes of our mind, so that we can see what hope his call holds for us. Alleluia!

Ephesians 1:17.18

Alternative Alleluias, pages 1004-1006.

Gospel   Matthew 16:21-27

If anyone wants to be a follower of mine, let him renounce himself.

Jesus began to make it clear to his disciples that he was destined

TWENTY-SECOND SUNDAY IN ORDINARY TIME/A

to go to Jerusalem and suffer grievously at the hands of the elders and chief priests and scribes, to be put to death and to be raised up on the third day. Then, taking him aside, Peter started to remonstrate with him. "Heaven preserve you, Lord," he said. "This must not happen to you." But he turned and said to Peter, "Get behind me, Satan! You are an obstacle in my path, because the way you think is not God's way but man's."

Then Jesus said to his disciples, "If anyone wants to be a follower of mine, let him renounce himself and take up his cross and follow me. For anyone who wants to save his life will lose it; but anyone who loses his life for my sake will find it. What, then, will a man gain if he wins the whole world and ruins his life? Or what has a man to offer in exchange for his life?

"For the Son of Man is going to come in the glory of his Father with his angels, and, when he does, he will reward each one according to his behaviour."

Prayer over the Gifts

Lord,
may this holy offering
bring us your blessing
and accomplish within us
its promise of salvation.

Preface of Sundays I-VIII, pages 562-565.

Communion Antiphon

O Lord, how great is the depth of the kindness which you have shown to those who love you. Psalm 30:20.

or

Happy are the peacemakers; they shall be called sons of God. Happy are they who suffer persecution for justice's sake; the kingdom of heaven is theirs. Matthew 5:9-10.

Prayer after Communion

Lord,
you renew us at your table with the bread of life.
May this food strengthen us in love
and help us to serve you in each other.

23rd SUNDAY IN ORDINARY TIME/A

Correct each other in charity.
We live together in society and we
must be prepared to correct and
encourage each other. No man is an island.
If Christ be among us then we will help
each other in true christian charity.
Love is the one thing that cannot hurt
your neighbour.

Entrance Antiphon   Lord, you are just, and the judgements you make are right. Show mercy when you judge me, your servant.

Psalm 118:137.124

Opening Prayer

Let us pray
 [that we may realise the freedom God has given us
 in making us his sons and daughters]

God our Father,
you redeem us
and make us your children in Christ.
Look upon us,
give us true freedom
and bring us to the inheritance you promised.

or

Let us pray
 [to our just and merciful God]

Lord our God,
in you justice and mercy meet.
With unparalleled love you have saved us from death
and drawn us into the circle of your life.

Open our eyes to the wonders this life sets before us,

TWENTY-THIRD SUNDAY IN ORDINARY TIME/A

that we may serve you free from fear
and address you as God our Father.

First Reading   Ezekiel 33:7-9

If you do not speak to the wicked man, I will hold you responsible for his death.

The word of the Lord was addressed to me as follows, "Son of man, I have appointed you as sentry to the House of Israel. When you hear a word from my mouth, warn them in my name. If I say to a wicked man: Wicked wretch, you are to die, and you do not speak to warn the wicked man to renounce his ways, then he shall die for his sin, but I will hold you responsible for his death. If, however, you do warn a wicked man to renounce his ways and repent, and he does not repent, then he shall die for his sin, but you yourself will have saved your life."

Responsorial Psalm   Psalm 94

℟ **O that today you would listen to his voice!
Harden not your hearts.**

1. Come, ring out our joy to the Lord;
hail the rock who saves us.
Let us come before him, giving thanks,
with songs let us hail the Lord.   ℟

2. Come in; let us bow and bend low;
let us kneel before the God who made us
for he is our God and we
the people who belong to his pasture,
the flock that is led by his hand.   ℟

3. O that today you would listen to his voice!
"Harden not your hearts as at Meribah,
as on that day at Massah in the desert
when your fathers put me to the test;
when they tried me, though they saw my work."   ℟

Second Reading   Romans 13:8-10

Love is the answer to every one of the commandments.

Avoid getting into debt, except the debt of mutual love. If you love your fellow men you have carried out your obligations. All the commandments: You shall not commit adultery, you shall not kill, you shall not steal, you shall not covet, and so on, are

TWENTY-THIRD SUNDAY IN ORDINARY TIME/A

summed up in this single command: You must love your neighbour as yourself. Love is the one thing that cannot hurt your neighbour; that is why it is the answer to every one of the commandments.

Alleluia Alleluia, alleluia! Your word is truth, O Lord, consecrate us in the truth. Alleluia! John 17:17.

or Alleluia, alleluia! God in Christ was reconciling the world to himself, and he has entrusted to us the news that they are reconciled. Alleluia! 2 Corinthians 5:19.

Gospel Matthew 18:15-20

If he listens to you, you have won back your brother.

Jesus said to his disciples: "If your brother does something wrong go and have it out with him alone, between your two selves. If he listens to you, you have won back your brother. If he does not listen, take one or two others along with you: the evidence of two or three witnesses is required to sustain any charge. But if he refuses to listen to these, report it to the community and if he refuses to listen to the community, treat him like a pagan or a tax collector.

"I tell you solemnly, whatever you bind on earth shall be considered bound in heaven; whatever you loose on earth shall be considered loosed in heaven.

"I tell you solemnly once again, if two of you on earth agree to ask anything at all, it will be granted to you by my Father in heaven. For where two or three meet in my name, I shall be there with them."

Prayer over the Gifts

God of peace and love,
may our offering bring you true worship
and make us one with you.

Preface of Sundays I-VIII, pages 562-565.

Communion Antiphon Like a deer that longs for running streams, my soul longs for you, my God. My soul is thirsting for the living God. Psalm 41:2-3.

TWENTY-FOURTH SUNDAY IN ORDINARY TIME/A

Prayer after Communion

Lord,
your word and your sacrament
give us food and life.
May this gift of your Son
lead us to share his life for ever.

24th SUNDAY IN ORDINARY TIME/A

> Forgive from your heart.
> Christ is the perfect example of
> forgiveness. He died for us when
> we were still his enemies by sin and
> through his death we are brought to life.
> His life and death have an influence on all
> of us. Now we must forgive each other as
> Christ forgives us since we ask God to
> forgive us our trespasses as we
> forgive those who trespass against us.

Entrance Antiphon Give peace, Lord, to those who wait for you, and your prophets will proclaim you as you deserve. Hear the prayers of your servant and of your people Israel.

cf. Ecclesiasticus 36:18.

Opening Prayer

Let us pray
  [that God will keep us faithful in his service]

Almighty God,
our creator and guide,
may we serve you with all our heart
and know your forgiveness in our lives.

TWENTY-FOURTH SUNDAY IN ORDINARY TIME/A

or

Let us pray
  [for the peace which is born of faith and hope]

Father in heaven, Creator of all,
look down upon your people in their moments of need,
for you alone are the source of our peace.
Bring us to the dignity which distinguishes the poor in spirit
and show us how great is the call to serve,
that we may share in the peace of Christ
who offered his life in the service of all.

First Reading   Ecclesiasticus 27:30 - 28:7.

**Forgive your neighbour the hurt he does you,
and when you pray, your sins will be forgiven.**

Resentment and anger, these are foul things,
and both are found with the sinner.
He who exacts vengeance will experience the vengeance of the
  Lord,
who keeps strict account of sin.
Forgive your neighbour the hurt he does you,
and when you pray, your sins will be forgiven.
If a man nurses anger against another,
can he then demand compassion from the Lord?
Showing no pity for a man like himself,
can he then plead for his own sins?
Mere creature of flesh, he cherishes resentment;
who will forgive him his sins?
Remember the last things, and stop hating,
remember dissolution and death, and live by the
  commandments.
Remember the commandments, and do not bear your
  neighbour ill-will;
remember the covenant of the Most High, and overlook the
  offence.

Responsorial Psalm   Psalm 102.

R/ **The Lord is compassion and love,
slow to anger and rich in mercy.**

TWENTY-FOURTH SUNDAY IN ORDINARY TIME/A

1. My soul, give thanks to the Lord,
   all my being, bless his holy name.
   My soul, give thanks to the Lord
   and never forget all his blessings. ℟

2. It is he who forgives all your guilt,
   who heals every one of your ills,
   who redeems your life from the grave,
   who crowns you with love and compassion. ℟

3. His wrath will come to an end;
   he will not be angry for ever.
   He does not treat us according to our sins
   nor repay us according to our faults. ℟

4. For as the heavens are high above the earth
   so strong is his love for those who fear him.
   As far as the east is from the west
   so far does he remove our sins. ℟

Second Reading Romans 14:7-9.

Alive or dead we belong to the Lord.

The life and death of each of us has its influence on others; if we live, we live for the Lord; and if we die, we die for the Lord, so that alive or dead we belong to the Lord. This explains why Christ both died and came to life, it was so that he might be Lord both of the dead and of the living.

Alleluia   Alleluia, alleluia! Speak, Lord, your servant is listening: you have the message of eternal life. Alleluia! 1 Samuel 3:9; John 6:68.

or   Alleluia, alleluia! I give you a new commandment: love one another, just as I have loved you, says the Lord. Alleluia. John 13:34.

Gospel Matthew 18:21-35.

I do not tell you to forgive seven times, but seventy-seven times.

Peter went up to Jesus and said, "Lord, how often must I forgive my brother if he wrongs me? As often as seven times?" Jesus answered, "Not seven, I tell you, but seventy-seven times.

"And so the kingdom of heaven may be compared to a king who decided to settle his accounts with his servants. When the reckoning began, they brought him a man who owed ten

TWENTY-FOURTH SUNDAY IN ORDINARY TIME/A

thousand talents; but he had no means of paying, so his master gave orders that he should be sold, together with his wife and children and all his possessions, to meet the debt. At this, the servant threw himself down at his master's feet. 'Give me time,' he said, 'and I will pay the whole sum.' And the servant's master felt so sorry for him that he let him go and cancelled the debt. Now as this servant went out, he happened to meet a fellow servant who owed him one hundred denarii; and he seized him by the throat and began to throttle him. 'Pay what you owe me,' he said. His fellow servant fell at his feet and implored him, saying, 'Give me time and I will pay you.' But the other would not agree; on the contrary, he had him thrown into prison till he should pay the debt. His fellow servants were deeply distressed when they saw what had happened, and they went to their master and reported the whole affair to him. Then the master sent for him. 'You wicked servant,' he said. 'I cancelled all that debt of yours when you appealed to me. Were you not bound, then, to have pity on your fellow servant just as I had pity on you?' And in his anger the master handed him over to the torturers till he should pay all his debt. And that is how my heavenly Father will deal with you unless you each forgive your brother from your heart."

Prayer over the Gifts
Lord,
hear the prayers of your people
and receive our gifts.
May the worship of each one here
bring salvation to all.

Preface of Sundays I-VIII, pages 562-565.

Communion Antiphon

O God, how much we value your mercy! All mankind can gather under your protection. Psalm 35:8.

or

The cup that we bless is a communion with the blood of Christ; and the bread that we break is a communion with the body of the Lord.

cf. 1 Corinthians 10:16

Prayer after Communion

Lord,
may the eucharist you have given us
influence our thoughts and actions.
May your Spirit guide and direct us in your way.

25th SUNDAY IN ORDINARY TIME/A

> God's ways are not our ways.
> We judge by human standards. If we
> want our judgements to be the right ones
> then we must pray for guidance so that we
> may always judge generously. God rewards
> everyone individually according to his
> judgement and not ours. We need,
> therefore, to see people
> through God's eyes.

Entrance Antiphon

I am the Saviour of all people, says the Lord. Whatever their troubles, I will answer their cry, and I will always be their Lord.

Opening Prayer

Let us pray
  [that we will grow in the love of God
  and of one another]

Father,
guide us, as you guide creation
according to your law of love.
May we love one another
and come to perfection
in the eternal life prepared for us.

TWENTY-FIFTH SUNDAY IN ORDINARY TIME/A

or

Let us pray
   [to the Lord who is a God of love to all peoples]

Father in heaven,
the perfection of justice is found in your love
and all mankind is in need of your law.

Help us to find this love in each other
that justice may be attained
through obedience to your law.

First Reading   Isaiah 55:6-9.
My thoughts are not your thoughts.

Seek the Lord while he is still to be found,
call to him while he is still near.
Let the wicked man abandon his way,
the evil man his thoughts.
Let him turn back to the Lord who will take pity on him,
to our God who is rich in forgiving;
for my thoughts are not your thoughts,
my ways not your ways — it is the Lord who speaks.
Yes, the heavens are as high above earth
as my ways are above your ways,
my thoughts above your thoughts.

Responsorial Psalm   Psalm 144

℟ **The Lord is close to all who call him.**

1. I will bless you day after day
   and praise your name for ever.
   The Lord is great, highly to be praised,
   his greatness cannot be measured. ℟

2. The Lord is kind and full of compassion,
   slow to anger, abounding in love.
   How good is the Lord to all,
   compassionate to all his creatures. ℟

3. The Lord is just in all his ways
   and loving in all his deeds.
   He is close to all who call him,
   who call on him from their hearts. ℟

TWENTY-FIFTH SUNDAY IN ORDINARY TIME/A

Second Reading Philippians 1:20-24.27
Life to me is Christ.

Christ will be glorified in my body, whether by my life or by my death. Life to me, of course, is Christ, but then death would bring me something more; but then again, if living in this body means doing work which is having good results — I do not know what I should choose. I am caught in this dilemma: I want to be gone and be with Christ, which would be very much better, but for me to stay alive in this body is a more urgent need for your sake.

Avoid anything in your everyday lives that would be unworthy of the gospel of Christ.

Alleluia Alleluia, alleluia! Blessings on the King who comes, in the name of the Lord! Peace in heaven and glory in the highest heavens! Alleluia! Luke 19:38.

or Alleluia, alleluia! Open our heart, O Lord, to accept the words of your Son. Alleluia! Acts 16:14.

Gospel Matthew 20:1-16
Why be envious because I am generous?

Jesus said to his disciples: "The kingdom of heaven is like a landowner going out at daybreak to hire workers for his vineyard. He made an agreement with the workers for one denarius a day, and sent them to his vineyard. Going out at about the third hour he saw others standing idle in the market place and said to them, 'You go to my vineyard too and I will give you a fair wage.' So they went. At about the sixth hour and again at about the ninth hour, he went out and did the same. Then at about the eleventh hour he went out and found more men standing round, and he said to them, 'Why have you been standing here idle all day?' 'Because no one has hired us,' they answered. He said to them, 'You go into my vineyard too.' In the evening, the owner of the vineyard said to his bailiff, 'Call the workers and pay them their wages, starting with the last arrivals and ending with the first.' So those who were hired at about the eleventh hour came forward and received one denarius each. When the first came, they expected to get more, but they too received one denarius each. They took it, but grumbled at the land-owner. 'The men who came last' they said, 'have done only one hour, and you have

TWENTY-FIFTH SUNDAY IN ORDINARY TIME/A

treated them the same as us, though we have done a heavy day's work in all the heat.' He answered one of them and said, 'My friend, I am not being unjust to you; did we not agree on one denarius? Take your earnings and go. I choose to pay the last-comer as much as I pay you. Have I no right to do what I like with my own? Why be envious because I am generous?' Thus the last will be first, and the first, last."

Prayer over the Gifts

Lord,
may these gifts which we now offer
to show our belief and our love
be pleasing to you.
May they become for us
the eucharist of Jesus Christ your Son,
who is Lord for ever and ever.

Preface of Sundays I-VIII, pages 562-565.

Communion Antiphon

You have laid down your precepts to be faithfully kept. May my footsteps be firm in keeping your commands. Psalm 118:4-5

or

I am the Good Shepherd, says the Lord; I know my sheep, and mine know me. John 10:14.

Prayer after Communion

Lord,
help us with your kindness.
Make us strong through the eucharist.
May we put into action
the saving mystery we celebrate.

26th SUNDAY IN ORDINARY TIME/A

*Christ came to forgive sinners.
We all need God's forgiveness and
it was for this reason that Christ came
humbling himself to the death of a cross.
When we renounce sin we will truly live. We
remember that we are in constant need
of forgiveness and so we must never
take our salvation for granted.*

Entrance Antiphon   O Lord, you had just cause to judge men as you did: because we sinned against you and disobeyed your will. But now show us your greatness of heart, and treat us with your unbounded kindness.

Daniel 3:31.29.30.43.42

Opening Prayer

Let us pray
  [for God's forgiveness
  and for the happiness it brings]

Father,
you show your almighty power
in your mercy and forgiveness.
Continue to fill us with your gifts of love.
Help us to hurry towards the eternal life you promise
and come to share in the joys of your kingdom.

or

Let us pray
  [for the peace of the kingdom
  which we have been promised]

Father of our Lord Jesus Christ,
in your unbounded mercy

TWENTY-SIXTH SUNDAY IN ORDINARY TIME/A

you have revealed the beauty of your power
through your constant forgiveness of our sins.

May the power of this love be in our hearts
to bring your pardon and your kingdom to all we meet.

First Reading   Ezekiel 18:25-28
When the sinner renounces sin, he shall certainly live.

The word of the Lord was addressed to me as follows: "You object, 'What the Lord does is unjust.' Listen, you House of Israel: is what I do unjust? Is it not what you do that is unjust? When the upright man renounces his integrity to commit sin and dies because of this, he dies because of the evil that he himself has committed. When the sinner renounces sin to become law-abiding and honest, he deserves to live. He has chosen to renounce all his previous sins; he shall certainly live; he shall not die."

Responsorial Psalm   Psalm 24

℟ **Remember your mercy, Lord.**

1. Lord, make me know your ways.
   Lord, teach me your paths.
   Make me walk in your truth, and teach me:
   for you are God my saviour. ℟

2. Remember your mercy, Lord,
   and the love you have shown from of old.
   Do not remember the sins of my youth.
   In your love remember me,
   because of your goodness, O Lord. ℟

3. The Lord is good and upright.
   He shows the path to those who stray,
   he guides the humble in the right path;
   he teaches his way to the poor. ℟

Second Reading   Philippians 2:1-11
In your minds you must be the same as Christ Jesus.

If our life in Christ means anything to you, if love can persuade at all, or the Spirit that we have in common, or any tenderness and sympathy, then be united in your convictions and united in your love, with a common purpose and a common mind. That is the one thing which would make me

TWENTY-SIXTH SUNDAY IN ORDINARY TIME/A

completely happy. There must be no competition among you, no conceit; but everybody is to be self-effacing. Always consider the other person to be better than yourself, so that nobody thinks of his own interests first but everybody thinks of other people's interests instead. In your minds you must be the same as Christ Jesus:

His state was divine,
yet he did not cling
to his equality with God
but emptied himself
to assume the condition of a slave,
and became as men are;
and being as all men are,
he was humbler yet,
even to accepting death,
death on a cross.
But God raised him high
and gave him the name
which is above all other names .
so that all beings
in the heavens, on earth and in the underworld,
should bend the knee at the name of Jesus
and that every tongue should acclaim
Jesus Christ as Lord,
to the glory of God the Father.

Alleluia Alleluia, alleluia! If anyone loves me he will keep my word, and my Father will love him, and we shall come to him. Alleluia! John 14:23.

or Alleluia, alleluia! The sheep that belong to me listen to my voice, says the Lord, I know them and they follow me. Alleluia! John 10:27.

Gospel Matthew 21:28-32
He thought better of it and went. Tax collectors and prostitutes are making their way into the kingdom of God before you.

Jesus said to the chief priests and the elders of the people, "What is your opinion? A man had two sons. He went and said to the first, 'My boy, you go and work in the vineyard today.' He answered, 'I will not go,' but afterwards thought better of it and went. The man then went and said the same thing to the second who answered, 'Certainly, sir,' but did not go. Which of the two

TWENTY-SIXTH SUNDAY IN ORDINARY TIME/A

did the father's will?" "The first," they said. Jesus said to them, "I tell you solemnly, tax collectors and prostitutes are making their way into the kingdom of God before you. For John came to you, a pattern of true righteousness, but you did not believe him, and yet the tax collectors and prostitutes did. Even after seeing that, you refused to think better of it and believe in him."

Prayer over the Gifts
God of mercy,
accept our offering
and make it a source of blessing for us.

Preface of Sundays I-VIII, pages 562-565.

Communion Antiphon
O Lord, remember the words you spoke to me, your servant, which made me live in hope and consoled me when I was downcast.

Psalm 118:49-50

or

This is how we know what love is: Christ gave up his life for us; and we too must give up our lives for our brothers. I John 3:16.

Prayer after Communion
Lord,
may this eucharist
in which we proclaim the death of Christ
bring us salvation
and make us one with him in glory,
for he is Lord for ever and ever.

27th SUNDAY IN ORDINARY TIME/A

The Lord of the vineyard.
God is master of all creation and giver of all gifts. If we do not use these gifts properly he will take them away from us. If our lives are full of prayer and thanksgiving then the God of peace will be always with us.

Entrance Antiphon O Lord, you have given everything its place in the world, and no one can make it otherwise. For it is your creation, the heavens and the earth and the stars: you are the Lord of all. Esther 13:9.10-11.

Opening Prayer

Let us pray
  [that God will forgive our failings
  and bring us peace]

Father,
your love for us
surpasses all our hopes and desires.
Forgive our failings,
keep us in your peace
and lead us in the way of salvation.

or

Let us pray
  [before the face of God,
  in trusting faith]

Almighty and eternal God,
Father of the world to come,

TWENTY-SEVENTH SUNDAY IN ORDINARY TIME/A

your goodness is beyond what our spirit can touch
and your strength is more than the mind can bear.
Lead us to seek beyond our reach
and give us the courage to stand before your truth.

First Reading   Isaiah 5:1-7
The vineyard of the Lord of hosts is the House of Israel.

Let me sing to my friend
the song of his love for his vineyard.

My friend had a vineyard
on a fertile hillside.
He dug the soil, cleared it of stones,
and planted choice vines in it.
In the middle he built a tower,
he dug a press there too.
He expected it to yield grapes,
but sour grapes were all that it gave.

And now, inhabitants of Jerusalem
and men of Judah,
I ask you to judge
between my vineyard and me.
What could I have done for my vineyard
that I have not done?
I expected it to yield grapes.
Why did it yield sour grapes instead?

Very well, I will tell you
what I am going to do to my vineyard;
I will take away its hedge for it to be grazed on,
and knock down its wall for it to be trampled on.
I will lay it waste, unpruned, undug;
overgrown by the briar and the thorn.
I will command the clouds
to rain no rain on it.
Yes, the vineyard of the Lord of hosts
is the House of Israel,
and the men of Judah
that chosen plant.
He expected justice, but found bloodshed,
integrity, but only a cry of distress.

TWENTY-SEVENTH SUNDAY IN ORDINARY TIME/A

Responsorial Psalm   Psalm 79

**℟ The vineyard of the Lord
is the House of Israel.**

1. You brought a vine out of Egypt;
   to plant it you drove out the nations.
   It stretched out its branches to the sea,
   to the Great River it stretched out its shoots. ℟

2. Then why have you broken down its walls?
   It is plucked by all who pass by.
   It is ravaged by the boar of the forest,
   devoured by the beasts of the field. ℟

3. God of hosts, turn again, we implore,
   look down from heaven and see.
   Visit this vine and protect it,
   the vine your right hand has planted. ℟

4. And we shall never forsake you again:
   give us life that we may call upon your name.
   God of hosts, bring us back;
   let your face shine on us and we shall be saved. ℟

Second Reading   Philippians 4:6-9

The God of peace will be with you.

There is no need to worry; but if there is anything you need, pray for it, asking God for it with prayer and thanksgiving, and that peace of God, which is so much greater than we can understand, will guard your hearts and your thoughts, in Christ Jesus. Finally, brothers, fill your minds with everything that is true, everything that is noble, everything that is good and pure, everything that we love and honour, and everything that can be thought virtuous or worthy of praise. Keep doing all the things that you learnt from me and have been taught by me and have heard or seen that I do. Then the God of peace will be with you.

Alleluia   Alleluia, alleluia! I call you friends, says the Lord, because I have made known to you everything I have learnt from my Father. Alleluia! John 15:15.

or   Alleluia, alleluia! I chose you from the world to go out and bear fruit, fruit that will last, says the Lord. Alleluia! John 15:18.

TWENTY-SEVENTH SUNDAY IN ORDINARY TIME/A

Gospel   Matthew 21:33-43
He will lease the vineyard to other tenants.

Jesus said to the chief priests and the elders of the people, "Listen to another parable. There was a man, a landowner, who planted a vineyard; he fenced it round, dug a winepress in it and built a tower; then he leased it to tenants and went abroad. When vintage time drew near he sent his servants to the tenants to collect his produce. But the tenants seized his servants, thrashed one, killed another and stoned a third. Next he sent some more servants, this time a larger number, and they dealt with them in the same way. Finally he sent his son to them. 'They will respect my son,' he said. But when the tenants saw the son, they said to each other, 'This is the heir. Come on, let us kill him and take over his inheritance.' So they seized him and threw him out of the vineyard and killed him. Now when the owner of the vineyard comes, what will he do to those tenants?" They answered, "He will bring those wretches to a wretched end and lease the vineyard to other tenants who will deliver the produce to him when the season arrives." Jesus said to them, "Have you never read in the scriptures:

"It was the stone rejected by the builders
that became the keystone.
This was the Lord's doing
and it is wonderful to see?

  "I tell you, then, that the kingdom of God will be taken from you and given to a people who will produce its fruit."

Prayer over the Gifts

Father,
receive these gifts
which our Lord Jesus Christ
has asked us to offer in his memory.
May our obedient service
bring us to the fullness of your redemption.
Preface of Sundays I-VIII, pages 562-565.

Communion Antiphon

The Lord is good to those who hope in him, to those who are searching for his love: Lamentations 3:25.

or

Because there is one bread, we, though many, are one body, for we all share in the one loaf and in the one cup. cf. 1 Corinthians 10:17.

Prayer after Communion
Almighty God,
let the eucharist we share
fill us with your life.
May the love of Christ
which we celebrate here
touch our lives and lead us to you.

28th SUNDAY IN ORDINARY TIME/A

The Lord has prepared a banquet for me. God invites us all to share in the wedding feast of his son. He knows our poverty and wants to share his riches with us. In this banquet we will be happy and every tear will be wiped away from our eyes.

Entrance Antiphon If you, O Lord, laid bare our guilt, who could endure it? But you are forgiving, God of Israel. Psalm 129:3-4.

Opening Prayer
Let us pray
 [that God will help us to love one another]
Lord,

TWENTY-EIGHTH SUNDAY IN ORDINARY TIME/A

our help and guide,
make your love the foundation of our lives.
May our love for you express itself
in our eagerness to do good for others.

or

Let us pray
   [in quiet for the grace of sincerity]

Father in heaven,
the hand of your loving kindness
powerfully yet gently guides all the moments of our day.

Go before us in our pilgrimage of life,
anticipate our needs and prevent our falling.
Send your Spirit to unite us in faith,
that sharing in your service,
we may rejoice in your presence.

First Reading   Isaiah 25:6-10

The Lord will prepare a banquet, and will wipe away tears from every cheek.

On this mountain,
the Lord of hosts will prepare for all peoples
a banquet of rich food, a banquet of fine wines,
of food rich and juicy, of fine strained wines.
On this mountain he will remove
the mourning veil covering all peoples,
and the shroud enwrapping all nations,
he will destroy Death for ever.
The Lord will wipe away
the tears from every cheek;
he will take away his people's shame
everywhere on earth,
for the Lord has said so.
That day, it will be said: See, this is our God
in whom we hoped for salvation;
the Lord is the one in whom we hoped.
We exult and we rejoice

TWENTY-EIGHTH SUNDAY IN ORDINARY TIME/A

that he has saved us;
for the hand of the Lord
rests on this mountain.

Responsorial Psalm   Psalm 22

℟ **In the Lord's own house shall I dwell
for ever and ever.**

1. The Lord is my shepherd;
   there is nothing I shall want.
   Fresh and green are the pastures
   where he gives me repose.
   Near restful waters he leads me,
   to revive my drooping spirit.

2. He guides me along the right path;
   he is true to his name.
   If I should walk in the valley of darkness
   no evil would I fear.
   You are there with your crook and your staff;
   with these you give me comfort. ℟

3. You have prepared a banquet for me
   in the sight of my foes.
   My head you have anointed with oil;
   my cup is overflowing. ℟

4. Surely goodness and kindness shall follow me
   all the days of my life.
   In the Lord's own house shall I dwell
   for ever and ever. ℟

Second Reading   Philippians 4:12-14.19-20.

There is nothing I cannot master with the help of the One who gives me strength.

I know how to be poor and I know how to be rich too. I have been through my initiation and now I am ready for anything anywhere: full stomach or empty stomach, poverty or plenty. There is nothing I cannot master with the help of the One who gives me strength. All the same, it was good of you to share with me in my hardships. In return my God will fulfil all your needs, in Christ Jesus, as lavishly as only God can. Glory to God, our Father, for ever and ever. Amen.

TWENTY-EIGHTH SUNDAY IN ORDINARY TIME/A

Alleluia Alleluia, alleluia! The Word was made flesh and lived among us; to all who did accept him he gave power to become children of God. Alleluia!

John 1:12.14

or Alleluia, alleluia! May the Father of our Lord Jesus Christ enlighten the eyes of our mind, so that we can see what hope his call holds for us. Alleluia!

Ephesians 1:17-18.

Gospel Matthew 22:1-14.

Invite everyone you can find to the wedding.

> Jesus said to the chief priests and elders of the people: "The kingdom of heaven may be compared to a king who gave a feast for his son's wedding. He sent his servants to call those who had been invited, but they would not come. Next he sent some more servants. 'Tell those who have been invited,' he said, 'that I have my banquet all prepared, my oxen and fattened cattle have been slaughtered, everything is ready. Come to the wedding.' But they were not interested: one went off to his farm, another to his business, and the rest seized his servants, maltreated them and killed them. The king was furious. He despatched his troops, destroyed those murderers and burnt their town. Then he said to his servants, 'The wedding is ready; but as those who were invited proved to be unworthy, go to the crossroads in the town and invite everyone you can find to the wedding.' So these servants went out on to the roads and collected together everyone they could find, bad and good alike; and the wedding hall was filled with guests.

"When the king came in to look at the guests he noticed one man who was not wearing a wedding garment, and said to him, 'How did you get in here, my friend, without a wedding garment?' And the man was silent. Then the king said to the attendants, 'Bind him hand and foot and throw him out into the dark, where there will be weeping and grinding of teeth.' For many are called, but few are chosen."

Prayer over the Gifts

Lord,
accept the prayers and gifts
we offer in faith and love.
May this eucharist bring us to your glory.

Preface of Sundays I-VIII, pages 562-565.

TWENTY-NINTH SUNDAY IN ORDINARY TIME/A

Communion Antiphon The rich suffer want and go hungry, but nothing shall be lacking to those who fear the Lord. **Psalm 33.11.**

or

When the Lord is revealed we shall be like him, for we shall see him as he is.
1 John 3:2.

Prayer after Communion

Almighty Father,
may the body and blood of your Son
give us a share in his life,
for he is Lord for ever and ever.

29th SUNDAY IN ORDINARY TIME/A

Give the Lord glory and power.
God alone is king and to him we must give the homage of our love and obedience.
All temporal power is subordinate to God's rule over the universe. We must get our priorities right — God first; all others only in relation to him.

Entrance Antiphon I call upon you, God, for you will answer me; bend your ear and hear my prayer. Guard me as the pupil of your eye; hide me in the shade of your wings.
Psalm 16:6.8

TWENTY-NINTH SUNDAY IN ORDINARY TIME/A

Opening Prayer

Let us pray
   [for the gift of simplicity and joy
   in our service of God and man]

Almighty and ever-living God,
our source of power and inspiration,
give us strength and joy
in serving you as followers of Christ,
who lives and reigns with you and the Holy Spirit,
one God, for ever and ever.

or

Let us pray
   [to the Lord who bends close to hear our prayer]

Lord our God, Father of all,
you guard us under the shadow of your wings
and search into the depths of our hearts.
Remove the blindness that cannot know you
and relieve the fear that would hide us from your sight.

First Reading   Isaiah 45:1.4-6.

I have taken Cyrus by his right hand to subdue nations before him.

Thus says the Lord to his anointed, to Cyrus.
whom he has taken by his right hand
to subdue nations before him
and strip the loins of kings,
to force gateways before him
that their gates be closed no more:
It is for the sake of my servant Jacob,
of Israel my chosen one,
that I have called you by your name,
conferring a title though you do not know me.
I am the Lord, unrivalled;
there is no other God besides me.
Though you do not know me, I arm you
that men may know from the rising to the setting of the sun
that, apart from me, all is nothing.

TWENTY-NINTH SUNDAY IN ORDINARY TIME/A

Responsorial Psalm   Psalm 95

℟**Give the Lord glory and power.**

1. O sing a new song to the Lord,
   sing to the Lord all the earth.
   Tell among the nations his glory
   and his wonders among all the peoples.   ℟

2. The Lord is great and worthy of praise,
   to be feared above all gods;
   the gods of the heathens are naught.
   It was the Lord who made the heavens.   ℟

3. Give the Lord, you families of peoples,
   give the Lord glory and power,
   give the Lord the glory of his name.
   Bring an offering and enter his courts.   ℟

4. Worship the Lord in his temple.
   O earth, tremble before him.
   Proclaim to the nations: "God is king."
   He will judge the peoples in fairness.   ℟

Second Reading   Thessalonians 1:1-5.

We constantly remember your faith, your love and your hope.

From Paul, Silvanus and Timothy, to the Church in Thessalonika which is in God the Father and the Lord Jesus Christ; wishing you grace and peace.

We always mention you in our prayers and thank God for you all, and constantly remember before God our Father how you have shown your faith in action, worked for love and persevered through hope in our Lord Jesus Christ.

We know, brothers, that God loves you and that you have been chosen, because when we brought the Good News to you, it came to you not only as words, but as power and as the Holy Spirit and as utter conviction.

Alleluia	Alleluia, alleluia! Your word is truth, O Lord, consecrate us in the truth, Alleluia! John 17:17.
or	Alleluia, alleluia! You will shine in the world like bright stars because you are offering it the word of life. Alleluia! Philippians 2:15-16.

TWENTY-NINTH SUNDAY IN ORDINARY TIME/A

Gospel Matthew 22:15-21.

Give back to Caesar what belongs to Caesar — and to God what belongs to God.

The Pharisees went away to work out between them how to trap Jesus in what he said. And they sent their disciples to him, together with the Herodians, to say, "Master, we know that you are an honest man and teach the way of God in an honest way, and that you are not afraid of anyone, because a man's rank means nothing to you. Tell us your opinion, then. Is it permissible to pay taxes to Caesar or not?" But Jesus was aware of their malice and replied, "You hypocrites! Why do you set this trap for me? Let me see the money you pay the tax with." They handed him a denarius, and he said, "Whose head is this? Whose name?" "Caesar's," they replied. He then said to them, "Very well, give back to Caesar what belongs to Caesar — and to God what belongs to God."

Prayer over the Gifts

Lord God,
may the gifts we offer
bring us your love and forgiveness
and give us freedom to serve you with our lives.

Preface of Sundays I-VIII, pages 562-565.

Communion Antiphon See how the eyes of the Lord are on those who fear him, on those who hope in his love, that he may rescue them from death and feed them in time of famine. Psalm 32:18-19.

or

The Son of Man came to give his life as a ransom for many. Mark 10:45.

Prayer after Communion

Lord,
may this eucharist help us to remain faithful.
May it teach us the way to eternal life.

30th SUNDAY IN ORDINARY TIME/A

Love God and your neighbour.
God is love and he made us in his own image.
We love him with all our heart, soul and mind
because through his grace the pattern of
our life-style is changed. We love our neighbour
knowing that God lives in him also. We must
help him in every way to show the quality
of our love.

Entrance Antiphon Let hearts rejoice who search for the Lord. Seek the Lord and his strength, seek always the face of the Lord.

Psalm 104:3-4.

Opening Prayer

Let us pray
 [for the strength to do God's will]

Almighty and ever-living God,
strengthen our faith, hope, and love.
May we do with loving hearts
what you ask of us
and come to share the life you promise.

or

Let us pray
 [in humble hope for salvation]

Praised be you, God and Father of our Lord Jesus Christ.
There is no power for good
which does not come from your covenant,
and no promise to hope in
that your love has not offered.
Strengthen our faith to accept your covenant
and give us the love to carry out your command.

THIRTIETH SUNDAY IN ORDINARY TIME/A

First Reading Exodus 22:20-26.

If you are harsh with the widow, or with the orphan, my anger will flare against you.

The Lord said to Moses, "Tell the sons of Israel this, 'You must not molest the stranger or oppress him, for you lived as strangers in the land of Egypt. You must not be harsh with the widow, or with the orphan; if you are harsh with them, they will surely cry out to me, and be sure I shall hear their cry; my anger will flare and I shall kill you with the sword, your own wives will be widows, your own children orphans.

" 'If you lend money to any of my people, to any poor man among you, you must not play the usurer with him: you must not demand interest from him.

" 'If you take another's cloak as a pledge, you must give it back to him before sunset. It is all the covering he has; it is the cloak he wraps his body in; what else would he sleep in? If he cries to me, I will listen, for I am full of pity.' "

Responsorial Psalm Psalm 17

℟ **I love you, Lord my strength.**

1. I love you, Lord, my strength,
   my rock, my fortress, my saviour.
   My God is the rock where I take refuge;
   my shield, my mighty help, my stronghold.
   The Lord is worthy of all praise:
   when I call I am saved from my foes. ℟

2. Long life to the Lord, my rock!
   Praised be the God who saves me.
   He has given great victories to his king
   and shown his love for his anointed. ℟

Second Reading 1 Thessalonians 1:5-10.

You broke with idolatry and became servants of God; you are now waiting for his Son.

You observed the sort of life we lived when we were with you, which was for your instruction, and you were led to become

THIRTIETH SUNDAY IN ORDINARY TIME/A

imitators of us, and of the Lord; and it was with the joy of the Holy Spirit that you took to the gospel, in spite of the great opposition all round you. This has made you the great example to all believers in Macedonia and Achaia since it was from you that the word of the Lord started to spread — and not only throughout Macedonia and Achaia, for the news of your faith in God has spread everywhere. We do not need to tell other people about it: other people tell us how we started the work among you, how you broke with idolatry when you were converted to God and became servants of the real, living God; and how you are now waiting for Jesus, his Son, whom he raised from the dead, to come from heaven to save us from the retribution which is coming.

Alleluia Alleluia, alleluia! Open our heart, O Lord, to accept the words of your Son. Alleluia! Acts 16:14.

or Alleluia, alleluia! If anyone loves me he will keep my word, and my Father will love him, and we shall come to him. Alleluia! John 14:23.

Gospel Matthew 22:34-40.

You must love the Lord your God and your neighbour as yourself.

When the Pharisees heard that Jesus had silenced the Sadducees they got together and, to disconcert him, one of them put a question, "Master, which is the greatest commandment of the Law?" Jesus said, "You must love the Lord your God with all your heart, with all your soul, and with all your mind. This is the greatest and the first commandment. The second resembles it: You must love your neighbour as yourself. On these two commandments hang the whole Law, and the Prophets also."

Prayer over the Gifts

Lord God of power and might,
receive the gifts we offer
and let our service give you glory.

Preface of Sundays I-VIII, pages 562-565.

Communion Antiphon We will rejoice at the victory of God and make our boast in his great name.
Psalm 19:6.

THIRTY-FIRST SUNDAY IN ORDINARY TIME/A

or Christ loved us and gave himself up for us as a fragrant offering to God. Ephesians 5:2.

Prayer after Communion

Lord,
bring to perfection within us
the communion we share in this sacrament.
May our celebration have an effect in our lives.

31st SUNDAY IN ORDINARY TIME/A

Practise what you preach!
The Pharisees were singled out by Christ as being hypocrites and frauds. They were not humble enough to ease the burdens of others and so became a stumbling block to the faith of many people. We preach the Gospel or Good News not so much by what we say but by the way in which we live our lives.

Entrance Antiphon

Do not abandon me, Lord. My God, do not go away from me! Hurry to help me, Lord, my Saviour. Psalm 37:22-23.

Opening Prayer

Let us pray
 [that our lives will reflect our faith]

God of power and mercy,
only with your help
can we offer you fitting service and praise.
May we live the faith we profess
and trust your promise of eternal life.

THIRTY-FIRST SUNDAY IN ORDINARY TIME/A

or

Let us pray
  [in the presence of God, the source of every good]

Father in heaven, God of power and Lord of mercy,
from whose fullness we have received,
direct our steps in our everyday efforts.
May the changing moods of the human heart
and the limits which our failings impose on hope
never blind us to you, source of every good.

Faith gives us the promise of peace
and makes known the demands of love.
Remove the selfishness that blurs the vision of faith.

First Reading   Malachi 1:14-2:2. 8-10.

You have strayed from the way; you have caused many to stumble by your teaching.

I am a great king, says the Lord of hosts, and my name is feared throughout the nations. And now, priests, this warning is for you. If you do not listen, if you do not find it in your heart to glorify my name, says the Lord of hosts, I will send the curse on you and curse your very blessing. You have strayed from the way; you have caused many to stumble by your teaching. You have destroyed the covenant of Levi, says the Lord of hosts. And so I in my turn have made you contemptible and vile in the eyes of the whole people in repayment for the way you have not kept to my paths but have shown partiality in your administration.

Have we not all one Father? Did not God create us? Why, then, do we break faith with one another, profaning the covenant of our ancestors?

Responsorial Psalm   Psalm 130

℟ **Keep my soul in peace before you, O Lord.**

1. O Lord, my heart is not proud
   nor haughty my eyes.
   I have not gone after things too great
   nor marvels beyond me. ℟

THIRTY-FIRST SUNDAY IN ORDINARY TIME/A

2. Truly I have set my soul
in silence and peace.
A weaned child on its mother's breast,
even so is my soul. R/

3. O Israel, hope in the Lord
both now and for ever. R/

Second Reading   1 Thessalonians 2:7-9. 13.

We were eager to hand over to you not only the Good News but our whole lives as well.

Like a mother feeding and looking after her own children, we felt so devoted and protective towards you, and had come to love you so much, that we were eager to hand over to you not only the Good News but our whole lives as well. Let me remind you, brothers, how hard we used to work, slaving night and day so as not to be a burden on any one of you while we were proclaiming God's Good News to you.

    Another reason why we constantly thank God for you is that as soon as you heard the message that we brought you as God's message, you accepted it for what it really is, God's message and not some human thinking; and it is still a living power among you who believe it.

Alleluia   Alleluia, alleluia! Speak, Lord, your servant is listening: you have the message of eternal life. Alleluia! 1 Samuel 3:9; John 6:68.

or   Alleluia, alleluia! You have only one Father, and he is in heaven; you have only one Teacher, the Christ! Alleluia! Matthew 23:9.10.

Gospel   Matthew 23:1-12.

They do not practise what they preach.

Addressing the people and his disciples Jesus said, "The scribes and the Pharisees occupy the chair of Moses. You must therefore do what they tell you and listen to what they say; but do not be guided by what they do: since they do not practise what they preach. They tie up heavy burdens and lay them on men's shoulders, but will they lift a finger to move them? Not they! Everything they do is done to attract attention, like wearing broader phylacteries and longer tassels, like wanting to take the place of honour at banquets and the front seats in the synagogues, being greeted obsequiously in the market squares and having people call them Rabbi.

"You, however, must not allow yourselves to be called Rabbi, since you have only one Master, and you are all brothers. You must call no one on earth your father, since you have only one Father, and he is in heaven. Nor must you allow yourselves to be called teachers, for you have only one Teacher, the Christ. The greatest among you must be your servant. Anyone who exalts himself will be humbled, and anyone who humbles himself will be exalted."

Prayer over the Gifts

God of mercy,
may we offer a pure sacrifice
for the forgiveness of our sins.

Preface of Sundays I-VIII, pages 562-565.

Communion Antiphon

Lord, you will show me the path of life and fill me with joy in your presence. Psalm 15:11.

or

As the living Father sent me, and I live because of the Father, so he who eats my flesh and drinks my blood will live because of me. John 6:58.

Prayer after Communion

Lord,
you give us new hope in this eucharist.
May the power of your love
continue its saving work among us
and bring us to the joy you promise.

32nd SUNDAY IN ORDINARY TIME/A

The **Bridegroom** is here!
We await the second coming of Christ just as the
ten bridesmaids waited for the bridegroom.
We must be awake and patient at all times so we
are always ready when the shout goes up
'He is here'. We have no need to worry about
those who have **died** before us as they too will
rise from the dead with Christ in glory.

Entrance Antiphon Let my prayer come before you, Lord; listen, and answer me. **Psalm 87:3.**

Opening Prayer

Let us pray
 [for health of mind and body]

God of power and mercy,
protect us from all harm.
Give us freedom of spirit
and health in mind and body
to do your work on earth.

or

Let us pray
 [that our prayer rise like incense
 in the presence of the Lord]

Almighty Father,
strong is your justice and great is your mercy.
Protect us in the burdens and challenges of life.
Shield our minds from the distortion of pride
and enfold our desire with the beauty of truth.

Help us to become more aware of your loving design
so that we may more willingly give our lives in service to all.

THIRTY-SECOND SUNDAY IN ORDINARY TIME/A

First Reading   Wisdom 6:12-16.
Wisdom is found by those who look for her.

Wisdom is bright, and does not grow dim.
By those who love her she is readily seen,
and found by those who look for her.
Quick to anticipate those who desire her, she makes herself
  known to them.
Watch for her early and you will have no trouble;
you will find her sitting at your gates.
Even to think about her is understanding fully grown;
be on the alert for her and anxiety will quickly leave you.
She herself walks about looking for those who are worthy of
  her
and graciously shows herself to them as they go,
in every thought of theirs coming to meet them.

Responsorial Psalm   Psalm 62

R/ **For you my soul is thirsting, O God, my God.**

1. O God, you are my God, for you I long;
   for you my soul is thirsting.
   My body pines for you
   like a dry, weary land without water. R/

2. So I gaze on you in the sanctuary
   to see your strength and your glory.
   For your love is better than life,
   my lips will speak your praise. R/

3. So I will bless you all my life,
   in your name I will lift up my hands.
   My soul shall be filled as with a banquet,
   my mouth shall praise you with joy. R/

4. On my bed I remember you.
   On you I muse through the night
   for you have been my help;
   in the shadow of your wings I rejoice. R/

Second Reading   1 Thessalonians 4:13-18.
God will bring with him those who have died in Jesus.

We want you to be quite certain, brothers, about those who

THIRTY-SECOND SUNDAY IN ORDINARY TIME/A

> have died, to make sure that you do not grieve about them, like the other people who have no hope. We believe that Jesus died and rose again, and that it will be the same for those who have died in Jesus: God will bring them with him.

We can tell you this from the Lord's own teaching, that any of us who are left alive until the Lord's coming will not have any advantage over those who have died. At the trumpet of God, the voice of the archangel will call out the command and the Lord himself will come down from heaven; those who have died in Christ will be the first to rise, and then those of us who are still alive will be taken up in the clouds, together with them, to meet the Lord in the air. So we shall stay with the Lord for ever. With such thoughts as these you should comfort one another.

Alleluia — Alleluia, alleluia! Stay awake and stand ready, because you do not know the hour when the Son of Man is coming. Alleluia! Matthew 24:42.44.

Alternative Alleluias, pages 1004-1006, nos. 14, 15, 16

Gospel Matthew 25:1-13.

The bridegroom is here! Go out and meet him.

Jesus told this parable to his disciples: "The kingdom of heaven will be like this: Ten bridesmaids took their lamps and went to meet the bridegroom. Five of them were foolish and five were sensible: the foolish ones did take their lamps, but they brought no oil, whereas the sensible ones took flasks of oil as well as their lamps. The bridegroom was late, and they all grew drowsy and fell asleep. But at midnight there was a cry, 'The bridegroom is here! Go out and meet him.' At this, all those bridesmaids woke up and trimmed their lamps, and the foolish ones said to the sensible ones, 'Give us some of your oil: our lamps are going out.' But they replied, 'There may not be enough for us and for you; you had better go to those who sell it and buy some for yourselves.' They had gone off to buy it when the bridegroom arrived. Those who were ready went in with him to the wedding hall and the door was closed. The other bridesmaids arrived later. 'Lord, Lord,' they said 'open the door for us.' But he replied, 'I tell you solemnly, I do not know you.' So stay awake, because you do not know either the day or the hour."

THIRTY-SECOND SUNDAY IN ORDINARY TIME/A

Prayer over the Gifts

God of mercy,
in this eucharist we proclaim the death of the Lord.
Accept the gifts we present
and help us follow him with love,
for he is Lord for ever and ever.

Preface of Sundays I-VIII, pages 562-565.

Communion Antiphon The Lord is my shepherd; there is nothing I shall want. In green pastures he gives me rest, he leads me beside the waters of peace.

Psalm 22:1-2.

or

The disciples recognised the Lord Jesus in the breaking of bread.

Luke 24:35.

Prayer after Communion

Lord,
we thank you for the nourishment you give us
through your holy gift.
Pour out your Spirit upon us
and in the strength of this food from heaven
keep us single-minded in your service.

33rd SUNDAY IN ORDINARY TIME/A

Work for the Lord!
God gives talents to each one of us and
they must be used in his name. We cannot
relax our efforts but must continually
do all in our power to work as children
of the light. A good wife is a blessing in
the family. We should all be a blessing
in the family of God.

Entrance Antiphon   The Lord says: my plans for you are peace and not disaster; when you call to me, I will listen to you, and I will bring you back to the place from which I exiled you. Jeremiah 29:11.12.14.

Opening Prayer

Let us pray
  [that God will help us to be faithful]

Father of all that is good,
keep us faithful in serving you,
for to serve you is our lasting joy.

or

Let us pray
  [with hearts that long for peace]

Father in heaven,
ever-living source of all that is good,
from the beginning of time you promised man salvation
through the future coming of your Son, our Lord Jesus Christ.

Help us to drink of his truth
and expand our hearts with the joy of his promises,
so that we may serve you in faith and in love
and know for ever the joy of your presence.

THIRTY-THIRD SUNDAY IN ORDINARY TIME/A

First Reading   Proverbs 31:10-13. 19-20. 30-31.

A perfect wife — who can find her?

A perfect wife — who can find her?
She is far beyond the price of pearls.
Her husband's heart has confidence in her,
from her he will derive no little profit.
Advantage and not hurt she brings him
all the days of her life.
She is always busy with wool and with flax,
she does her work with eager hands.
She sets her hands to the distaff,
her fingers grasp the spindle.
She holds out her hand to the poor,
she opens her arms to the needy.
Charm is deceitful, and beauty empty;
the woman who is wise is the one to praise.
Give her a share in what her hands have worked for,
and let her works tell her praises at the city gates.

Responsorial Psalm   Psalm 127

℟ **O blessed are those who fear the Lord.**

1. O blessed are those who fear the Lord
   and walk in his ways!
   By the labour of your hands you shall eat.
   You will be happy and prosper. ℟

2. Your wife like a fruitful vine
   in the heart of your house;
   your children like shoots of the olive,
   around your table. ℟

3. Indeed thus shall be blessed
   the man who fears the Lord.
   May the Lord bless you from Zion
   in a happy Jerusalem
   all the days of your life. ℟

Second Reading   1 Thessalonians 5:1-6.

Let not the Day of the Lord overtake you like a thief.

You will not be expecting us to write anything to you, brothers, about "times and seasons", since you know very well that the Day

THIRTY-THIRD SUNDAY IN ORDINARY TIME/A

of the Lord is going to come like a thief in the night. It is when people are saying, "How quiet and peaceful it is" that the worst suddenly happens, as suddenly as labour pains come on a pregnant woman; and there will be no way for anybody to evade it.

But it is not as if you live in the dark, my brothers, for that Day to overtake you like a thief. No, you are all sons of light and sons of the day: we do not belong to the night or to darkness, so we should not go on sleeping, as everyone else does, but stay wide awake and sober.

Alleluia   Alleluia, alleluia! Even if you have to die, says the Lord, keep faithful, and I will give you the crown of life. Alleluia! Revelation 2:10.

or   Alleluia, alleluia! Make your home in me, as I make mine in you, says the Lord. Whoever remains in me bears fruit in plenty. Alleluia! John 15:4.5.

Gospel   Matthew 25:14-30.

You have been faithful in small things; come and join in your master's happiness.

> Jesus spoke this parable to his disciples: "The kingdom of heaven is like a man on his way abroad who summoned his servants and entrusted his property to them. To one he gave five talents, to another two, to a third one; each in proportion to his ability. Then he set out.

"The man who had received the five talents promptly went and traded with them and made five more. The man who had received two made two more in the same way. But the man who had received one went off and dug a hole in the ground and hid his master's money.

> "Now a long time after, the master of those servants came back and went through his accounts with them. The man who had received the five talents came forward bringing five more. 'Sir,' he said, 'you entrusted me with five talents; here are five more that I have made'.

"His master said to him, 'Well done, good and faithful servant; you have shown you can be faithful in small things, I will trust you with greater; come and join in your master's happiness.' Next the man with two talents came forward. 'Sir,' he said, 'you entrusted me with two talents; here are two more that I have

THIRTY-THIRD SUNDAY IN ORDINARY TIME/A

made.' His master said to him, 'Well done, good and faithful servant; you have shown you can be faithful in small things, I will trust you with greater; come and join in your master's happiness.' Last came forward the man who had the one talent. 'Sir,' said he, 'I had heard you were a hard man, reaping where you have not sown and gathering where you have not scattered; so I was afraid, and I went off and hid your talent in the ground. Here it is; it was yours, you have it back.' But his master answered him, 'You wicked and lazy servant! So you knew that I reap where I have not sown and gather where I have not scattered? Well then, you should have deposited my money with the bankers, and on my return I would have recovered my capital with interest. So now, take the talent from him and give it to the man who has the five talents. For to everyone who has will be given more, and he will have more than enough; but from the man who has not, even what he has will be taken away. As for this good-for-nothing servant, throw him out into the dark, where there will be weeping and grinding of teeth.' "

Prayer over the Gifts

Lord God,
may the gifts we offer
increase our love for you
and bring us to eternal life.

Preface of Sundays I-VIII, pages 562-565.

Communion Antiphon

It is good for me to be with the Lord and to put my hope in him.
Psalm 72:28.

or

I tell you solemnly, whatever you ask for in prayer, believe that you have received it, and it will be yours, says the Lord. **Mark 11:23.24.**

Prayer after Communion

Father,
may we grow in love
by the eucharist we have celebrated
in memory of the Lord Jesus,
who is Lord for ever and ever.

LAST SUNDAY IN ORDINARY TIME
OUR LORD JESUS CHRIST, UNIVERSAL KING/A

Christ the King!
God looks after his sheep through Jesus Christ
his shepherd and king. Christ is anointed king
of the universe by his Father. We will be judged
by our actions and finally Christ will present
us to his Father. We must live our lives for
our king so that we may enter with him
into glory.

Entrance Antiphon   The Lamb who was slain is worthy to receive strength and divinity, wisdom and power and honour: to him be glory and power for ever. Revelation 5:12; 1:6.

Opening Prayer

Let us pray
  [that all men will acclaim Jesus as Lord]

Almighty and merciful God,
you break the power of evil
and make all things new
in your Son Jesus Christ, the King of the universe.
May all in heaven and earth acclaim your glory
and never cease to praise you.

or

Let us pray
  [that the kingdom of Christ
  may live in our hearts and come to our world]

Father all-powerful, God of love,
you have raised our Lord Jesus Christ from death to life,

THIRTY-FOURTH SUNDAY IN ORDINARY TIME/A

resplendent in glory as King of creation.
Open our hearts,
free all the world to rejoice in his peace,
to glory in his justice, to live in his love.
Bring all mankind together in Jesus Christ your Son,
whose kingdom is with you and the Holy Spirit,
one God, for ever and ever.

First Reading   Ezekiel 34:11-12. 15-17.

As for you, my sheep, I will judge between sheep and sheep.

The Lord says this: I am going to look after my flock myself and keep all of it in view. As a shepherd keeps all his flock in view when he stands up in the middle of his scattered sheep, so shall I keep my sheep in view. I shall rescue them from wherever they have been scattered during the mist and darkness. I myself will pasture my sheep, I myself will show them where to rest — it is the Lord who speaks. I shall look for the lost one, bring back the stray, bandage the wounded and make the weak strong. I shall watch over the fat and healthy. I shall be a true shepherd to them.

As for you, my sheep, the Lord says this: I will judge between sheep and sheep, between rams and he-goats.

Responsorial Psalm   Psalm 22

℟ **The Lord is my shepherd
   there is nothing I shall want.**

1. The Lord is my shepherd;
   there is nothing I shall want.
   Fresh and green are the pastures
   where he gives me repose. ℟

2. Near restful waters he leads me,
   to revive my drooping spirit.
   He guides me along the right path;
   he is true to his name. ℟

3. You have prepared a banquet for me
   in the sight of my foes.
   My head you have anointed with oil;
   my cup is overflowing.
   Surely goodness and kindness shall follow me

THIRTY-FOURTH SUNDAY IN ORDINARY TIME/A

all the days of my life.
In the Lord's own house shall I dwell
for ever and ever. ℟

Second Reading   1 Corinthians 15:20-26. 28.

He will hand over the kingdom to God the Father, so that God may be all in all.

Christ has been raised from the dead, the first-fruits of all who have fallen asleep. Death came through one man and in the same way the resurrection of the dead has come through one man. Just as all men die in Adam, so all men will be brought to life in Christ; but all of them in their proper order: Christ as the first-fruits and then, after the coming of Christ, those who belong to him. After that will come the end, when he hands over the kingdom to God the Father, having done away with every sovereignty, authority and power. For he must be king until he has put all his enemies under his feet and the last of the enemies to be destroyed is death. And when everything is subjected to him, then the Son himself will be subject in his turn to the One who subjected all things to him, so that God may be all in all.

Alleluia   Alleluia, alleluia! Blessings on him who comes in the name of the Lord! Blessings on the coming kingdom of our father David! Alleluia! Mark 11:10.

Gospel   Matthew 25:31-46.

He will take his seat on his throne of glory, and he will separate men one from another.

Jesus said to his disciples: "When the Son of Man comes in his glory, escorted by all the angels, then he will take his seat on his throne of glory. All the nations will be assembled before him and he will separate men one from another as the shepherd separates sheep from goats. He will place the sheep on his right hand the goats on his left. Then the King will say to those on his right hand, 'Come, you whom my Father has blessed, take for your heritage the kingdom prepared for you since the foundation of the world. For I was hungry and you gave me food; I was thirsty and you gave me drink; I was a stranger and you made me welcome; naked and you clothed me, sick and you visited me, in prison and you came to see me.' Then the virtuous will say to him in reply, 'Lord, when did we see you hungry and

THIRTY-FOURTH SUNDAY IN ORDINARY TIME/A

feed you; or thirsty and give you drink? When did we see you a stranger and make you welcome; naked and clothed you; sick or in prison and go to see you?' And the King will answer, 'I tell you solemnly, in so far as you did this to one of the least of these brothers of mine, you did it to me.' Next he will say to those on his left hand, 'Go away from me, with your curse upon you, to the eternal fire prepared for the devil and his angels. For I was hungry and you never gave me food; I was thirsty and you never gave me anything to drink; I was a stranger and you never made me welcome, naked and you never clothed me, sick and in prison and you never visited me.' Then it will be their turn to ask, 'Lord, when did we see you hungry or thirsty, a stranger or naked, sick or in prison, and did not come to your help?' Then he will answer, 'I tell you solemnly, in so far as you neglected to do this to one of the least of these, you neglected to do it to me.' And they will go away to eternal punishment, and the virtuous to eternal life."

Prayer over the Gifts

Lord,
we offer you the sacrifice
by which your Son reconciles mankind.
May it bring unity and peace to the world.

Preface

Father, all-powerful and ever-living God,
we do well always and everywhere to give you thanks.

You anointed Jesus Christ, your only Son, with the oil of
   gladness,
as the eternal priest and universal king.

As priest he offered his life on the altar of the cross
and redeemed the human race
by this one perfect sacrifice of peace.

As king he claims dominion over all creation,
that he may present to you, his almighty Father,
an eternal and universal kingdom:
a kingdom of truth and life,
a kingdom of holiness and grace,
a kingdom of justice, love, and peace.

And so, with all the choirs of angels in heaven

THIRTY-FOURTH SUNDAY IN ORDINARY TIME/A

we proclaim your glory
and join in their unending hymn of praise:
Holy, holy, holy . . .

Communion Antiphon

The Lord will reign for ever and will give his people the gift of peace.

Psalm 28:10-11.

Prayer after Communion

Lord,
you give us Christ, the King of all creation,
as food for everlasting life.
Help us to live by his gospel
and bring us to the joy of his kingdom,
where he lives and reigns for ever and ever.

Sundays in Ordinary Time/B

Year B: The Year of Mark

THE Gospel of Mark confronts us with the *person* of Jesus Christ. Theologians rely heavily on his writing as their source for their tract on Christology, the study of Christ. Mark faces us with the mystery of Christ and asks us for a response. Each reader must pose this question to himself or herself: "Who is this person?" He or she will respond that Jesus Christ is the Son of God and also the Son of Man. It is round the two natures of the unique person of our Saviour that Mark's Gospel revolves.

Mark was not only Peter's companion, he was also his interpreter or catechist. Mark keeps close to Peter who remains the original, if not the only, source of his story. It is this fact which explains why we are given so many episodes in Mark which can only be described as 'eye-witness accounts' or 'narratives based on personal testimony'. Mark begins by introducing his main interest — the person of Jesus himself — and he follows Jesus through his public ministry in Galilee, outside of Galilee and in Jerusalem immediately before his passion. The 'confession of Peter' is the crisis or turning point of his Gospel so that the rest of the Gospel moves from the theme of the 'kingdom of God' to that of personal attachment to Jesus. After the 'confession' there follows the 'first prophecy of the passion' and the whole emphasis of Jesus' teaching is that the Son of Man must suffer. Jesus directs his teaching exclusively to his disciples so that Mark's Gospel becomes a catechism of the christian life even to the point of suffering and death. We have to take up our cross daily and follow him. Mark so stresses the suffering, death and resurrection of Christ that his Gospel has been described as a 'Passion Story with an introduction'. The main theological theme is, therefore, on the mystery of Christ while the secondary theological themes deal with faith, discipleship and mission.

Mark's Gospel is short and his way of telling a story is direct and simple. He leads his readers directly to the person of Jesus Christ and in doing so is not afraid to depict in all its starkness the humanity of Jesus. While he does not dwell on the Incarnation, he is at pains to show us that God is present and at work in the person and ministry of Jesus. Everything else that he has to say is directed towards our understanding of this basic notion.

YEAR B: YEAR OF MARK

There is a series of five Sundays (17-21) when the readings are taken from John 6 to complete and fill out the eucharistic doctrine of Mark. Mark tells us of the compassion of Jesus for the crowds (16) and this is followed by the feeding of the five thousand (17). The expression of the compassion of Jesus is found in the multiplication of the loaves and fishes: at this stage the Gospel of John takes over and presents us with the feeding of the five thousand as a 'sign' of Jesus as the Bread of Life. We move then from faith in the person of Jesus to the place which the eucharist has in the life of the disciples and of the community. The teaching of Jesus on the eucharist causes a split in the community and some walked no more with him. We see Peter's confession of faith as our own. Jesus asked "who do you say I am?" Peter spoke up and said to him, "You are the Christ". The difference which it makes to Peter's life marks out the life that we are destined to live. Mark asks us to concentrate on Jesus, Son of God and Son of Man, so that we will follow him because we know he has the words of eternal life.

STAGE ONE:

THE MYSTERY OF THE SON OF GOD — SUNDAYS 1-24

1. The baptism of Jesus — Mark 1:6b-11
2. The call of Andrew and friend — John 1:35-42
3. The call of the first apostles — Mark 1:14-20
4. A day in Capernaum (1) — 1:21-28
5. A day in Capernaum (2) — 1:29-39
6. The cure of a leper — 1:40-45
7. The cure of a paralytic — 2:1-12
8. The question of fasting — 2:18-22
9. Violation of the sabbath — 2:23-3:6
10. Serious criticism of Jesus — 3:20-35
11. Parables of the kingdom — 4:26-34
12. The calming of the storm — 4:35-41
13. Jairus' daughter and the woman in the crowd — 5:21-43
14. Jesus rejected at Nazareth — 6:1-6
15. The mission of the Twelve — 6:7,13
16. Compassion for the crowds — 6:30-34
17. Feeding of five thousand — John 6:1-15
18. The bread of life (1) — 6:24-35
19. The bread of life (2) — 6:41-52

YEAR B: YEAR OF MARK

20.	The eucharist	6:51-58
21.	Incredulity and faith	6:61-70
22.	Jewish customs	Mark 7:1-8,14-15,21
23.	Cure of a deaf-mute	7:31-37
24.	Peter's confession	8:27-35

STAGE TWO:
THE MYSTERY OF THE SON OF MAN — SUNDAYS 25-34

25.	Passion and resurrection prophesied	Mark 9:29-36
26.	Instructions for disciples	9:37-42,44,46-47
27.	What God has joined together	10:2-16
28.	The problem of wealth	10:17-30
29.	The sons of Zebedee	10:35-46
30.	The cure of Bartimaeus	10:46-52
31.	The first commandment	12:28b-34
32.	The scribes; the widow's mite	12:38-44
33.	The last things	13:24-32
34.	Solemnity of Christ the King	John 18:33b-37

2nd SUNDAY IN ORDINARY TIME/B

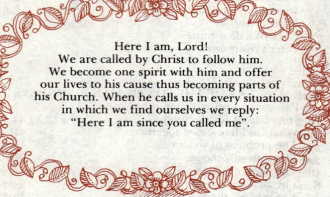

Here I am, Lord!
We are called by Christ to follow him.
We become one spirit with him and offer
our lives to his cause thus becoming parts of
his Church. When he calls us in every situation
in which we find ourselves we reply:
"Here I am since you called me".

Entrance Antiphon May all the earth give you worship and praise, and break into song to your name, O God, Most High. Psalm 65:4.

Opening Prayer

Let us pray
 [to our Father for the gift of peace]

Father of heaven and earth,
hear our prayers,
and show us the way to peace in the world.

or

Let us pray
 [for the gift of peace]

Almighty and ever-present Father,
your watchful care reaches from end to end
and orders all things in such power
that even the tensions and the tragedies of sin
cannot frustrate your loving plans.

Help us to embrace your will,
give us the strength to follow your call,
so that your truth may live in our hearts
and reflect peace to those who believe in your love.

SECOND SUNDAY IN ORDINARY TIME/B

First Reading   1 Samuel 3:3-10.19.

Speak, Lord, your servant is listening.

Samuel was lying in the sanctuary of the Lord where the ark of God was, when the Lord called, "Samuel! Samuel!" He answered, "Here I am." Then he ran to Eli and said, "Here I am, since you called me." Eli said, "I did not call. Go back and lie down." So he went and lay down. Once again the Lord called, "Samuel! Samuel!" Samuel got up and went to Eli and said, "Here I am, since you called me." He replied, "I did not call you, my son; go back and lie down." Samuel had as yet no knowledge of the Lord and the word of the Lord had not yet been revealed to him. Once again the Lord called, the third time. He got up and went to Eli and said, "Here I am, since you called me." Eli then understood that it was the Lord who was calling the boy, and he said to Samuel, "Go and lie down, and if someone calls say, 'Speak, Lord, your servant is listening.'" So Samuel went and lay down in his place.

The Lord then came and stood by, calling as he had done before, "Samuel! Samuel!" Samuel answered, "Speak, Lord, your servant is listening."

Samuel grew up and the Lord was with him and let no word of his fall to the ground.

Responsorial Psalm   Psalm 39.

℟ **Here I am Lord!**
  I come to do your will.

1. I waited, I waited for the Lord
   and he stooped down to me;
   he heard my cry.
   He put a new song into my mouth,
   praise of our God. ℟

2. You do not ask for sacrifice and offerings,
   but an open ear.
   You do not ask for holocaust and victim.
   Instead, here am I. ℟

3. In the scroll of the book it stands written
   that I should do your will.
   My God, I delight in your law
   in the depth of my heart. ℟

SECOND SUNDAY IN ORDINARY TIME/B

4. Your justice I have proclaimed
in the great assembly.
My lips I have not sealed;
you know it, O Lord. ℟

Second Reading 1 Corinthians 6:13-15.17-20.

Your bodies are members making up the body of Christ.

The body is not meant for fornication; it is for the Lord, and the Lord for the body. God who raised the Lord from the dead, will by his power raise us up too.

You know, surely, that your bodies are members making up the body of Christ; anyone who is joined to the Lord is one spirit with him.

Keep away from fornication. All the other sins are committed outside the body; but to fornicate is to sin against your own body. Your body, you know, is the temple of the Holy Spirit, who is in you since you received him from God. You are not your own property; you have been bought and paid for. That is why you should use your body for the glory of God.

Alleluia Alleluia, alleluia! Speak, Lord, your servant is listening: you have the message of eternal life. Alleluia! 1 Samuel 3:9; John 6:68.

or Alleluia, alleluia! We have found the Messiah — which means the Christ — grace and truth have come through him. Alleluia! John 1:41.17.

Gospel John 1:35-42.

They saw where he lived, and stayed with him.

As John stood with two of his disciples, Jesus passed, and John stared hard at him and said, "Look, there is the lamb of God." Hearing this, the two disciples followed Jesus. Jesus turned round, saw them following and said, "What do you want?" They answered, "Rabbi," — which means Teacher — "where do you live?" "Come and see" he replied; so they went and saw where he lived, and stayed with him the rest of that day. It was about the tenth hour.

One of these two who became followers of Jesus after hearing what John had said was Andrew, the brother of Simon Peter. Early next morning, Andrew met his brother and said to him, "We have found the Messiah" — which means the Christ — and

SECOND SUNDAY IN ORDINARY TIME/B

he took Simon to Jesus. Jesus looked hard at him and said, "You are Simon son of John; you are to be called Cephas" — meaning Rock.

Prayer over the Gifts

Father,
may we celebrate the eucharist
with reverence and love,
for when we proclaim the death of the Lord
you continue the work of his redemption,
who is Lord for ever and ever.

Preface of Sundays I-VIII, pages 562-565.

Communion Antiphon   The Lord has prepared a feast for me: given wine in plenty for me to drink. Psalm 22:5.

or

We know and believe in God's love for us. 1 John 4:16.

Prayer after Communion

Lord,
you have nourished us with bread from heaven.
Fill us with your Spirit,
and make us one in peace and love.

3rd SUNDAY IN ORDINARY TIME/B

> Repent and believe the Good News!
> As christians we have to review our lives in the light of the Gospel. This process goes on in our daily lives and we ask God to show his ways so that we may choose the right path. The world as we know it is passing away and therefore we should not be engrossed in it.

Entrance Antiphon Sing a new song to the Lord! Sing to the Lord, all the earth. Truth and beauty surround him, he lives in holiness and glory. **Psalm 95:1.6.**

Opening Prayer

Let us pray
   [for unity and peace]

All-powerful and ever-living God,
direct your love that is within us,
that our efforts in the name of your Son
may bring mankind to unity and peace.

or

Let us pray
   [pleading that our vision
   may overcome our weakness]

Almighty Father,
the love you offer
always exceeds the furthest expression of our human longing,
for you are greater than the human heart.

Direct each thought, each effort of our life,
so that the limits of our faults and weaknesses

may not obscure the vision of your glory
or keep us from the peace you have promised.

First Reading Jonah 3:1-5.10.
The people of Nineveh renounce their evil behaviour.

The word of the Lord was addressed a second time to Jonah: "Up!" he said "Go to Nineveh, the great city, and preach to them as I told you to." Jonah set out and went to Nineveh in obedience to the word of the Lord. Now Nineveh was a city great beyond compare: it took three days to cross it. Jonah went on into the city, making a day's journey. He preached in these words, "Only forty days more and Nineveh is going to be destroyed." And the people of Nineveh believed in God; they proclaimed a fast and put on sackcloth, from the greatest to the least.

God saw their efforts to renounce their evil behaviour. And God relented: he did not inflict on them the disaster which he had threatened.

Responsorial Psalm Psalm 24.

R/ **Lord, make me know your ways.**

1. Lord, make me know your ways.
   Lord, teach me your paths.
   Make me walk in your truth, and teach me:
   for you are God my saviour. R/

2. Remember your mercy, Lord,
   and the love you have shown from of old.
   In your love remember me,
   because of your goodness, O Lord. R/

3. The Lord is good and upright.
   He shows the path to those who stray,
   he guides the humble in the right path;
   he teaches his way to the poor. R/

Second Reading 1 Corinthians 7:29-31.
The world as we know it is passing away.

Brothers, our time is growing short. Those who have wives should live as though they had none, and those who mourn should live as though they had nothing to mourn for; those who are enjoying life should live as though there were nothing to laugh about; those

THIRD SUNDAY IN ORDINARY TIME/B

whose life is buying things should live as though they had nothing of their own; and those who have to deal with the world should not become engrossed in it. I say this because the world as we know it is passing away.

Alleluia   Alleluia, alleluia! The kingdom of God is close at hand; believe the Good News. Alleluia! Mark 1:15.

Gospel   Mark 1:14-20.
Repent, and believe the Good News.

After John had been arrested, Jesus went into Galilee. There he proclaimed the Good News from God. "The time has come" he said "and the kingdom of God is close at hand. Repent, and believe the Good News."

As he was walking along by the sea of Galilee he saw Simon and his brother Andrew casting a net in the lake — for they were fishermen. And Jesus said to them, "Follow me and I will make you into fishers of men." And at once they left their nets and followed him.

Going on a little further, he saw James son of Zebedee and his brother John; they too were in their boat, mending their nets. He called them at once and, leaving their father Zebedee in the boat with the men he employed, they went after him.

Prayer over the Gifts

Lord,
receive our gifts.
Let our offerings make us holy
and bring us salvation.

Preface of Sundays I-VIII, pages 562-565.

Communion Antiphon   Look up at the Lord with gladness and smile; your face will never be ashamed. Psalm 33:6.

or

I am the light of the world, says the Lord; the man who follows me will have the light of life. John 8:12.

Prayer after Communion

God, all-powerful Father,
may the new life you give us increase our love
and keep us in the joy of your kingdom.

4th SUNDAY IN ORDINARY TIME/B

*Christ taught with authority.
Christ is the great prophet for all times.
He speaks to us today with the same authority
as he did in his own native village at
Capernaum. When we free ourselves from
worrying about the wrong things we become
freer to serve the Lord who will himself put
his words in our mouths. In this way we
become his prophets.*

Entrance Antiphon Save us, Lord our God, and gather us together from the nations, that we may proclaim your holy name and glory in your praise. Psalm 105:47

Opening Prayer

Let us pray
  [for a greater love of God
  and of our fellow men]

Lord our God,
help us to love you with all our hearts
and to love all men as you love them.

or

FOURTH SUNDAY IN ORDINARY TIME/B

Let us pray
   [joining in the praise of the living God
   for we are his people]

Father in heaven,
from the days of Abraham and Moses
until this gathering of your Church in prayer,
you have formed a people in the image of your Son.

Bless this people with the gift of your kingdom.
May we serve you with our every desire
and show love for one another
even as you have loved us.

First Reading   Deuteronomy 18:15-20.
I will raise up a prophet and I will put my words into his mouth.

Moses said to the people: "Your God will raise up for you a prophet like myself, from among yourselves, from your own brothers; to him you must listen. This is what you yourselves asked of the Lord your God at Horeb on the day of the Assembly. 'Do not let me hear again' you said 'the voice of the Lord my God, nor look any longer on this great fire, or I shall die'; and the Lord said to me, 'All they have spoken is well said. I will raise up a prophet like yourself for them from their own brothers; I will put my words into his mouth and he shall tell them all I command him. The man who does not listen to my words that he speaks in my name, shall be held answerable to me for it. But the prophet who presumes to say in my name a thing I have not commanded him to say, or who speaks in the name of other gods, that prophet shall die.'"

Responsorial Psalm   Psalm 94.

R/ **O that today you would listen to his voice!
Harden not your hearts.**

1. Come, ring out our joy to the Lord;
   hail the rock who saves us.
   Let us come before him, giving thanks,
   with songs let us hail the Lord. R/

2. Come in; let us kneel and bend low;
   let us kneel before the God who made us
   for he is our God and we

FOURTH SUNDAY IN ORDINARY TIME/B

    the people who belong to his pasture,
    the flock that is led by his hand. R/

3. O that today you would listen to his voice!
    "Harden not your hearts as at Meribah,
    as on that day as Massah in the desert
    when your fathers put me to the test;
    when they tried me, though they saw my work." R/

Second Reading   1 Corinthians 7:32-35.

An unmarried woman can devote herself to the Lord's affairs; all she need worry about is being holy.

I would like to see you free from all worry. An unmarried man can devote himself to the Lord's affairs, all he need worry about is pleasing the Lord; but a married man has to bother about the world's affairs and devote himself to pleasing his wife: he is torn two ways. In the same way an unmarried woman, like a young girl, can devote herself to the Lord's affairs; all she need worry about is being holy in body and spirit. The married woman, on the other hand, has to worry about the world's affairs and devote herself to pleasing her husband. I say this only to help you, not to put a halter round your necks, but simply to make sure that everything is as it should be, and that you give your undivided attention to the Lord.

Alleluia   Alleluia, alleluia! Blessed are you, Father, Lord of heaven and earth, for revealing the mysteries of the kingdom to mere children. Alleluia! Matthew 11:25.

    or   Alleluia, alleluia! The people that lived in darkness has seen a great light; on those who dwell in the land and shadow of death a light has dawned. Alleluia!
                 Matthew 4:16

Gospel   Mark 1:21-28.

He taught them with authority.

Jesus and his followers went as far as Capernaum, and as soon as the sabbath came Jesus went to the synagogue and begun to teach. And his teaching made a deep impression on them because, unlike the scribes, he taught them with authority.

    In their synagogue just then there was a man possessed by an unclean spirit, and it shouted, "What do you want with us, Jesus of Nazareth? Have you come to destroy us? I know who you are:

FOURTH SUNDAY IN ORDINARY TIME/B

the Holy One of God." But Jesus said sharply, "Be quiet! Come out of him!" And the unclean spirit threw the man into convulsions and with a loud cry went out of him. The people were so astonished that they started asking each other what it all meant. "Here is a teaching that is new" they said "and with authority behind it: he gives orders even to unclean spirits and they obey him." And his reputation rapidly spread everywhere, through all the surrounding Galilean countryside.

Prayer over the Gifts

Lord,
be pleased with the gifts we bring to your altar,
and make them the sacrament of our salvation.

Preface of Sundays I-VIII, pages 562-565.

Communion Antiphon

Let your face shine on your servant, and save me by your love. Lord, keep me from shame, for I have called to you. Psalm 30:17-18.

or

Happy are the poor in spirit; the kingdom of heaven is theirs! Happy are the lowly; they shall inherit the land. Matthew 5:3-4.

Prayer after Communion

Lord,
you invigorate us with this help to our salvation.
By this eucharist give the true faith continued growth throughout the world.

5th SUNDAY IN ORDINARY TIME/B

> Everybody is looking for Christ.
> Christ gives meaning to our lives.
> Without him life would be no better than
> hired drudgery, but with his spirit in us all
> our service of others is done for love of him.
> It is a service which brings us perfect
> freedom. The world needs Christ and it is our
> duty to bring him to everyone.

Entrance Antiphon Come, let us worship the Lord. Let us bow down in the presence of our maker, for he is the Lord our God. Psalm 94:6-7.

Opening Prayer

Let us pray
  [that God will watch over us and protect us]

Father,
watch over your family
and keep us safe in your care,
for all our hope is in you.

or

Let us pray
  [with reverence in the presence of the living God]

In faith and love we ask you, Father,
to watch over your family gathered here.
In your mercy and loving kindness
no thought of ours is left unguarded,
no tear unheeded, no joy unnoticed.

Through the prayer of Jesus
may the blessings promised to the poor in spirit
lead us to the treasures of your heavenly kingdom.

FIFTH SUNDAY IN ORDINARY TIME/B

First Reading   Job 7:1-4.6-7.
Restlessly I fret till twilight falls.

Job began to speak:
Is not man's life on earth nothing more than pressed service,
his time no better than hired drudgery?
Like the slave, sighing for the shade,
or the workman with no thought but his wages,
months of delusion I have assigned to me,
nothing for my own but nights of grief.
Lying in bed I wonder, "When will it be day?"
Risen I think, "How slowly evening comes!"
Restlessly I fret till twilight falls.
Swifter than a weaver's shuttle my days have passed,
and vanished, leaving no hope behind.
Remember that my life is but a breath,
and that my eyes will never again see joy.

Responsorial Psalm   Psalm 146

℟ **Praise the Lord who heals the broken-hearted.**
or ℟ **Alleluia!**

1. Alleluia! Praise the Lord for he is good;
   sing to our God for he is loving:
   to him our praise is due. ℟

2. The Lord builds up Jerusalem
   and brings back Israel's exiles,
   he heals the broken-hearted,
   he binds up all their wounds.
   He fixes the number of the stars;
   he calls each one by its name. ℟

3. Our Lord is great and almighty;
   his wisdom can never be measured.
   The Lord raises the lowly;
   he humbles the wicked to the dust. ℟

Second Reading   1 Corinthians 9:16-19.22-23.
I should be punished if I did not preach the Gospel.

I do not boast of preaching the gospel, since it is a duty which has been laid on me; I should be punished if I did not preach it! If I had chosen this work myself, I might have been paid for it, but as

FIFTH SUNDAY IN ORDINARY TIME/B

I have not, it is a responsibility which has been put into my hands. Do you know what my reward is? It is this: in my preaching, to be able to offer the Good News free, and not insist on the rights which the gospel gives me.

So though I am not a slave of any man I have made myself the slave of everyone so as to win as many as I could. For the weak I made myself weak. I made myself all things to all men in order to save some at any cost; and I still do this, for the sake of the gospel, to have a share in its blessings.

Alleluia	Alleluia, alleluia! I am the light of the world, says the Lord, anyone who follows me will have the light of life. Alleluia! John 8:12.
or	Alleluia, alleluia! He took our sicknesses away, and carried our diseases for us. Alleluia! Matthew 8:17

Gospel   Mark 1:29-39.

He cured many who were suffering from diseases of one kind or another.

On leaving the synagogue, Jesus went with James and John straight to the house of Simon and Andrew. Now Simon's mother-in-law had gone to bed with fever, and they told him about her straight-away. He went to her, took her by the hand and helped her up. And the fever left her and she began to wait on them.

That evening, after sunset, they brought to him all who were sick and those who were possessed by devils. The whole town came crowding round the door, and he cured many who were suffering from diseases of one kind or another; he also cast out many devils, but he would not allow them to speak, because they knew who he was.

In the morning, long before dawn, he got up and left the house, and went off to a lonely place and prayed there. Simon and his companions set out in search of him, and when they found him they said, "Everybody is looking for you." He answered, "Let us go elsewhere, to the neighbouring country towns, so that I can preach there too, because that is why I came." And he went all through Galilee, preaching in their synagogues and casting out devils.

FIFTH SUNDAY IN ORDINARY TIME/B

Prayer over the Gifts

Lord our God,
may the bread and wine
you give us for our nourishment on earth
become the sacrament of our eternal life.

Preface of Sundays I-VIII, pages 562-565.

Communion Antiphon

Give praise to the Lord for his kindness, for his wonderful deeds towards men. He has filled the hungry with good things, he has satisfied the thirsty. Psalm 106:8-9.

or

Happy are the sorrowing; they shall be consoled. Happy those who hunger and thirst for what is right; they shall be satisfied. Matthew 5:5-6.

Prayer after Communion

God our Father,
you give us a share in the one bread and the one cup
and make us one in Christ.
Help us to bring your salvation and joy
to all the world.

6th SUNDAY IN ORDINARY TIME/B

> Be cured!
> We are like lepers who cry out to Christ
> who alone can cure us. He feels sorry for us
> and touches us with his grace telling us to
> be cured. We belong through him to the
> company of the saints and are now called
> to do everything for the glory of God. We are
> a people then of joy because we know that
> Christ delivers us from our sins.

Entrance Antiphon   Lord, be my rock of safety, the stronghold that saves me. For the honour of your name, lead me and guide me.
Psalm 30:3-4

Opening Prayer

Let us pray
   [that everything we do
   will be guided by God's law of love]

God our Father,
you have promised to remain for ever
with those who do what is just and right.
Help us to live in your presence.

or

Let us pray
   [for the wisdom that is greater than human words]

Father in heaven,
the loving plan of your wisdom took flesh in Jesus Christ,
and changed mankind's history
by his command of perfect love.

May our fulfilment of his command reflect your wisdom
and bring your salvation to the ends of the earth.

SIXTH SUNDAY IN ORDINARY TIME/B

First Reading Leviticus 13:1-2.44-46.

The leper must live apart: he must live outside the camp.

The Lord said to Moses and Aaron, "If a swelling or scab or shiny spot appears on a man's skin, a case of leprosy of the skin is to be suspected. The man must be taken to Aaron, the priest, or to one of the priests who are his sons.

"The man is leprous: he is unclean. The priest must declare him unclean; he is suffering from leprosy of the head. A man infected with leprosy must wear his clothing torn and his hair disordered; he must shield his upper lip and cry, 'Unclean, unclean'. As long as the disease lasts he must be unclean; and therefore he must live apart: he must live outside the camp."

Responsorial Psalm Psalm 31

℟ **You are my refuge, O Lord;
you fill me with the joy of salvation.**

1. Happy the man whose offence is forgiven,
   whose sin is remitted.
   O happy the man to whom the Lord
   imputes no guilt,
   in whose spirit is no guile. ℟

2. But now I have acknowledged my sins;
   my guilt I did not hide.
   I said: "I will confess
   my offence to the Lord."
   And you, Lord, have forgiven
   the guilt of my sin. ℟

3. Rejoice, rejoice in the Lord,
   exult, you just!
   O come, ring out your joy,
   all you upright of heart. ℟

Second Reading 1 Corinthians 10:31-11:1.

Take me for your model, as I take Christ.

Whatever you eat, whatever you drink, whatever you do at all, do it for the glory of God. Never do anything offensive to anyone — to Jews or Greeks or to the Church of God; just as I try to be helpful to everyone at all times, not anxious for my own advantage but for the advantage of everybody else, so that they may be saved.

Take me for your model, as I take Christ.

SIXTH SUNDAY IN ORDINARY TIME/B

Alleluia — Alleluia, alleluia! May the Father of our Lord Jesus Christ enlighten the eyes of our mind, so that we can see what hope his call holds for us. Alleluia!

Ephesians 1:17.18

or — Alleluia, alleluia! A great prophet has appeared among us; God has visited his people. Alleluia!

Luke 7:16.

Gospel Mark 1:40-45.

The leprosy left him at once and he was cured.

A leper came to Jesus and pleaded on his knees: "If you want to" he said "you can cure me." Feeling sorry for him, Jesus stretched out his hand and touched him. "Of course I want to!" he said. "Be cured!" And the leprosy left him at once and he was cured. Jesus immediately sent him away and sternly ordered him, "Mind you say nothing to anyone, but go and show yourself to the priest, and make the offering for your healing prescribed by Moses as evidence of your recovery." The man went away, but then started talking about it freely and telling the story everywhere, so that Jesus could no longer go openly into any town, but had to stay outside in places where nobody lived. Even so, people from all around would come to him.

Prayer over the Gifts

Lord,
we make this offering in obedience to your word.
May it cleanse and renew us,
and lead us to our eternal reward.

Preface of Sundays I-VIII, pages 562-565.

Communion Antiphon — They ate and were filled; the Lord gave them what they wanted: they were not deprived of their desire.

Psalm 77:29-30

or

God loved the world so much, he gave his only Son, that all who believe in him might not perish, but might have eternal life. *John 3:16.*

SEVENTH SUNDAY IN ORDINARY TIME/B

Prayer after Communion

Lord,
you give us food from heaven.
May we always hunger
for the bread of life.

7th SUNDAY IN ORDINARY TIME/B

> Your sins are forgiven.
> Christ came on earth to forgive sinners.
> His greatest miracles were a healing of the soul
> rather than the body. There is no need for us
> to worry about the past. Confide everything
> to the Lord as it is he alone
> who blots out our sins.

Entrance Antiphon

Lord, your mercy is my hope, my heart rejoices in your saving power. I will sing to the Lord for his goodness to me.

Psalm 12:6

Opening Prayer

Let us pray
  [that God will make us more like Christ, his Son]

Father,
keep before us the wisdom and love
you have revealed in your Son.
Help us to be like him
in word and deed,
for he lives and reigns with you and the Holy Spirit,
one God, for ever and ever.

SEVENTH SUNDAY IN ORDINARY TIME/B

or

Let us pray
  [to the God of power and might,
  for his mercy is our hope]

**Almighty God,
Father of our Lord Jesus Christ,
faith in your word is the way to wisdom,
and to ponder your divine plan is to grow in the truth.**

**Open our eyes to your deeds,
our ears to the sound of your call,
so that our every act may increase our sharing
in the life you have offered us.**

First Reading   Isaiah 43:18-19.21-22.24-25.

I it is who must blot out everything.

Thus says the Lord:
No need to recall the past,
no need to think about what was done before.
See, I am doing a new deed,
even now it comes to light; can you not see it?
Yes, I am making a road in the wilderness,
paths in the wilds.
The people I have formed for myself
will sing my praises.

Jacob, you have not invoked me,
you have not troubled yourself, Israel, on my behalf.
Instead you have burdened me with your sins,
troubled me with your iniquities.
I it is, I it is, who must blot out everything
and not remem*ber yo*ur sins.

Responsorial Psalm   Psalm 40.

R/ Heal my soul for I have sinned against you.

1. Happy the man who considers the poor and the weak.
   The Lord will save him in the day of evil,
   will guard him, give him life, make him happy in the land
   and will not give him up to the will of his foes. **R/**

SEVENTH SUNDAY IN ORDINARY TIME/B

2. The Lord will help him on his bed of pain,
   he will bring him back from sickness to health.
   As for me, I said: "Lord, have mercy on me,
   heal my soul for I have sinned against you." R/

3. If you uphold me I shall be unharmed
   and set in your presence for evermore.
   Blessed be the Lord, the God of Israel
   from age to age. Amen. Amen. R/

Second Reading   2 Corinthians 1:18-22.

Jesus was never Yes and No: with him it was always Yes.

I swear by God's truth, there is no Yes and No about what we say to you. The Son of God, the Christ Jesus that we proclaimed among you — I mean Silvanus and Timothy and I — was never Yes and No: with him it was always Yes, and however many the promises God made, the Yes to them all is in him. That is why it is "through him" that we answer Amen to the praise of God. Remember it is God himself who assures us all, and you, of our standing in Christ, and has anointed us, marking us with his seal and giving us the pledge, the Spirit, that we carry in our hearts.

Alleluia   Alleluia, alleluia! The Word was made flesh and lived among us; to all who did accept him he gave power to become children of God. Alleluia!
                                                   John 1:12.14

   or

Alleluia, alleluia! The Lord has sent me to bring the good news to the poor, to proclaim liberty to captives. Alleluia!   Luke 4:18.

Gospel   Mark 2:1-12.

The Son of Man has authority on earth to forgive sins.

When Jesus returned to Capernaum, word went round that he was back; and so many people collected that there was no room left, even in front of the door. He was preaching the word to them when some people came bringing him a paralytic carried by four men, but as the crowd made it impossible to get the man to him, they stripped the roof over the place where Jesus was; and when they had made an opening, they lowered the stretcher on which the paralytic lay. Seeing their faith, Jesus said to the

SEVENTH SUNDAY IN ORDINARY TIME/B

paralytic, "My child, your sins are forgiven." Now some scribes were sitting there, and they thought to themselves, "How can this man talk like that? He is blaspheming. Who can forgive sins but God?" Jesus, inwardly aware that this was what they were thinking, said to them, "Why do you have these thoughts in your hearts? Which of these is easier: to say to the paralytic, 'Your sins are forgiven' or to say, 'Get up, pick up your stretcher and walk'? But to prove to you that the Son of Man has authority on earth to forgive sins," — he said to the paralytic — "I order you: get up, pick up your stretcher, and go off home." And the man got up, picked up his stretcher at once and walked out in front of everyone, so that they were all astounded and praised God saying, "We have never seen anything like this."

Prayer over the Gifts

Lord,
as we make this offering,
may our worship in Spirit and truth
bring us salvation.

Preface of Sundays I-VIII, pages 562-565.

Communion Antiphon

I will tell all your marvellous works. I will rejoice and be glad in you, and sing to your name, Most High.

Psalm 9:2-3

or

Lord, I believe that you are the Christ, the Son of God, who was to come into this world. John 11:27.

Prayer after Communion

Almighty God,
help us to live the example of love
we celebrate in this eucharist,
that we may come to its fulfilment in your presence.

8th SUNDAY IN ORDINARY TIME/B

Christ, our bridegroom.
God is compassion and love. He gives us
Christ as a permanent sign of love.
We love God with the tender love of a young
bridegroom and it is the Spirit which writes
that love in our hearts. By the manner
in which we live as christians we become an
open letter of invitation to others to see what
true love really means. God wants us to
love him with Christ's love which brings life
not death.

Entrance Antiphon   The Lord has been my strength; he has led me into freedom. He saved me because he loves me. Psalm 17:19-20.

Opening Prayer

Let us pray
   [that God will bring peace to the world
   and freedom to his Church]

Lord,
guide the course of world events
and give your Church the joy and peace
of serving you in freedom.

or

Let us pray
   [that the peace of Christ
   may find welcome in the world]

Father in heaven,
form in us the likeness of your Son
and deepen his life within us.
Send us as witnesses of gospel joy
into a word of fragile peace and broken promises.
Touch the hearts of all men with your love
that they in turn may love one another.

EIGHTH SUNDAY IN ORDINARY TIME/B

First Reading   Hosea 2:16-17.21-22.

I will betroth you to myself for ever.

Thus says the Lord:
I am going to lure her
and lead her out into the wilderness
and speak to her heart.
There she will respond to me as she did when she was young,
as she did when she came out of the land of Egypt.
I will betroth you to myself for ever,
betroth you with integrity and justice,
with tenderness and love;
I will betroth you to myself with faithfulness,
and you will come to know the Lord.

Responsorial Psalm   Psalm 102.

℟ **The Lord is compassion and love.**

1. My soul, give thanks to the Lord,
all my being, bless his holy name.
My soul, give thanks to the Lord
and never forget all his blessings. ℟

2. It is he who forgives all your guilt,
who heals every one of your ills,
who redeems your life from the grave,
who crowns you with love and compassion. ℟

3. The Lord is compassion and love,
slow to anger and rich in mercy,
He does not treat us according to our sins
nor repay us according to our faults. ℟

4. As far as the east is from the west
so far does he remove our sins.
As a father has compassion on his sons
the Lord has pity on those who fear him. ℟

Second Reading   2 Corinthians 3:1-6.

You are a letter from Christ drawn up by us.

Unlike other people, we need no letters of recommendation either to you or from you, because you are yourselves our letter, written in our hearts, that anybody can see and read, and it is plain that you are a letter from Christ, drawn up by us, and

EIGHTH SUNDAY IN ORDINARY TIME/B

written not with ink but with the Spirit of the living God, not on stone tablets but on the tablets of your living hearts.

Before God, we are confident of this through Christ: not that we are qualified in ourselves to claim anything as our own work: all our qualifications come from God. He is the one who has given us the qualifications to be the administrators of this new covenant, which is not a covenant of written letters but of the Spirit: the written letters bring death, but the Spirit gives life.

Alleluia   Alleluia, alleluia! The sheep that belong to me listen to my voice, says the Lord, I know them and they follow me. Alleluia! John 10:27.

or   Alleluia, alleluia! By his own choice the Father made us his children by the message of his truth, so that we should be a sort of first-fruits of all that he created. Alleluia! James 1:18.

Gospel   Mark 2:18-22.

The bridegroom is with them.

One day when John's disciples and the Pharisees were fasting, some people came and said to Jesus, "Why is it that John's disciples and the disciples of the Pharisees fast, but your disciples do not?" Jesus replied, "Surely the bridegroom's attendants would never think of fasting while the bridegroom is still with them? As long as they have the bridegroom with them, they could not think of fasting. But the time will come for the bridegroom to be taken away from them, and then, on that day, they will fast. No one sews a piece of unshrunken cloth on an old cloak; if he does, the patch pulls away from it, the new from the old, and the tear gets worse. And nobody puts new wine into old wineskins; if he does, the wine will burst the skins, and the wine is lost and the skins too. No! New wine, fresh skins!"

Prayer over the Gifts

God our Creator,
may this bread and wine we offer
as a sign of our love and worship
lead us to salvation.

Preface of Sundays I-VIII, pages 562-565.

Communion Antiphon   I will sing to the Lord for his goodness to me, I will sing the name of the Lord, Most High. Psalm 12:6.

or I, the Lord, am with you always, until
the end of the world. Matthew 28:20.

Prayer after Communion

God of salvation,
may this sacrament which strengthens us here on earth
bring us to eternal life.

9th SUNDAY IN ORDINARY TIME/B

Christ is master of the Sabbath. We worship God through Christ on the sabbath day, the special day to be kept holy. We do this in joy realising however that we are fragile, earthenware jars which hold the precious treasure. It is this awareness that God is on our side through his power that helps us to keep going in the face of great difficulties on all sides. Christ has the message of eternal life.

Entrance Antiphon O look at me and be merciful, for I am wretched and alone. See my hardship and my poverty, and pardon all my sins.
Psalm 24:16.18

Opening Prayer

Let us pray
 [for God's care and protection]

Father,
your love never fails.
Hear our call.
Keep us from danger
and provide for all our needs.

NINTH SUNDAY IN ORDINARY TIME/B

or

Let us pray
  [for the confidence born of faith]
God our Father,
teach us to cherish the gifts that surround us.
Increase our faith in you
and bring our trust to its promised fulfilment
in the joy of your kingdom.

First Reading   Deuteronomy 5:12-15.

Remember that you were a servant in the land of Egypt.

The Lord says this: "Observe the sabbath day and keep it holy, as the Lord your God has commanded you. For six days you shall labour and do all your work, but the seventh day is a sabbath for the Lord your God. You shall do no work that day, neither you nor your son nor your daughter nor your servants, men or women, nor your ox nor your donkey nor any of your animals, nor the stranger who lives with you. Thus your servant, man or woman, shall rest as you do. Remember that you were a servant in the land of Egypt, and that the Lord your God brought you out from there with mighty hand and outstretched arm; because of this, the Lord your God has commanded you to keep the sabbath day."

Responsorial Psalm   Psalm 80.

R/ **Ring out your joy to God our strength.**

1. Raise a song and sound the timbrel,
   The sweet-sounding harp and the lute,
   blow the trumpet at the new moon,
   when the moon is full, on our feast. R/

2. For this is Israel's law,
   a command of the God of Jacob.
   He imposed it as a rule on Joseph,
   when he went out against the land of Egypt. R/

3. A voice I did not know said to me:
   "I freed your shoulder from the burden;
   your hands were freed from the load.
   You called in distress and I saved you. R/

NINTH SUNDAY IN ORDINARY TIME/B

4. "Let there be no foreign god among you,
no worship of an alien god.
I am the Lord your God,
who brought you from the land of Egypt." R/

Second Reading   2 Corinthians 4:6-11.

In our mortal flesh the life of Jesus is openly shown.

It is the same God that said, "Let there be light shining out of darkness," who has shone in our minds to radiate the light of the knowledge of God's glory, the glory on the face of Christ.

We are only the earthenware jars that hold this treasure, to make it clear that such an overwhelming power comes from God and not from us. We are in difficulties on all sides, but never cornered; we see no answer to our problems, but never despair; we have been persecuted, but never deserted; knocked down, but never killed; always, wherever we may be, we carry with us in our body the death of Jesus, so that the life of Jesus, too, may always be seen in our body. Indeed, while we are still alive, we are consigned to our death every day, for the sake of Jesus, so that in our mortal flesh the life of Jesus, too, may be openly shown.

Alleluia   Alleluia, alleluia! Your words are spirit, Lord, and they are life: you have the message of eternal life. Alleluia! John 6:63.68.

or

Alleluia, alleluia! Your word is truth, O Lord, consecrate us in the truth. Alleluia! John 17:17

Gospel   Mark 2:23-3:6.

The Son of Man is master even of the Sabbath.

One sabbath day Jesus happened to be taking a walk through the cornfields, and his disciples began to pick ears of corn as they went along. And the Pharisees said to him, "Look, why are they doing something on the sabbath day that is forbidden?" And he replied, "Did you ever read what David did in his time of need when he and his followers were hungry — how he went into the house of God when Abiathar was high priest, and ate the loaves of offering which only the priests are allowed to eat, and how he also gave some to the men with him?"

NINTH SUNDAY IN ORDINARY TIME/B

And he said to them, "The sabbath was made for man, not man for the sabbath; so the Son of Man is master even of the sabbath."

He went again into a synagogue, and there was a man there who had a withered hand. And they were watching him to see if he would cure him on the sabbath day, hoping for something to use against him. He said to the man with the withered hand, "Stand up out in the middle!" Then he said to them, "Is it against the law on the sabbath day to do good, or to do evil; to save life, or to kill?" But they said nothing. Then, grieved to find them so obstinate, he looked angrily round at them, and said to the man, "Stretch out your hand." He stretched it out and his hand was better. The Pharisees went out and at once began to plot with the Herodians against him, discussing how to destroy him.

Prayer over the Gifts

Lord,
as we gather to offer our gifts
confident in your love,
make us holy by sharing your life with us
and by this eucharist forgive our sins.

Preface of Sundays I-VIII, pages 562-565.

Communion Antiphon

I call upon you, God, for you will answer me; bend your ear and hear my prayer. Psalm 16:6.

or

I tell you solemnly, whatever you ask for in prayer, believe that you have received it, and it will be yours, says the Lord. Mark 11:23,24.

Prayer after Communion

Lord,
as you give us the body and blood of your Son,
guide us with your Spirit
that we may honour you
not only with our lips,
but also with the lives we lead,
and so enter your kingdom.

10th SUNDAY IN ORDINARY TIME/B

*Our Lady, help of christians.
We are constantly being tempted to put
people and things before God. Our Lady
reverses all that. She is not only the physical
mother of Christ but is also his mother
because she hears the will of God and keeps it.
There must be no weakening on our part
as we remember that we live in spiritual tents.
The glory to come that will be revealed
in us far outweighs all the difficulties
we encounter.*

Entrance Antiphon   The Lord is my light and my salvation. Who shall frighten me? The Lord is the defender of my life. Who shall make me tremble? Psalm 26:1-2.

Opening Prayer

Let us pray
 [for the guidance of the Holy Spirit]

God of wisdom and love,
source of all good,
send your Spirit to teach us your truth
and guide our actions
in your way of peace.

or

Let us pray
 [to our Father
 who calls us to freedom in Jesus his Son]

Father in heaven,
words cannot measure the boundaries of love
for those born to new life in Christ Jesus.
Raise us beyond the limits this world imposes,
so that we may be free to love as Christ teaches
and find our joy in your glory.

TENTH SUNDAY IN ORDINARY TIME/B

First Reading   Genesis 3:9-15.
I will make you enemies of each other: you and the woman, your offspring and her offspring.

The Lord God called to the man after he had eaten of the tree. "Where are you?" he asked. "I heard the sound of you in the garden," he replied "I was afraid because I was naked so I hid." Who told you that you were naked?" he asked "Have you been eating of the tree I forbade you to eat?" The man replied, "It was the woman you put with me; she gave me the fruit, and I ate it." Then the Lord God asked the woman, "What is this you have done?" The woman replied, "The serpent tempted me and I ate."

Then the Lord God said to the serpent, "Because you have done this,
"Be accursed beyond all cattle,
all wild beasts.
You shall crawl on your belly and eat dust
every day of your life.
I will make you enemies of each other:
you and the woman,
your offspring and her offspring.
It will crush your head and you will strike its heel."

Responsorial Psalm   Psalm 129

℟ **With the Lord there is mercy
and fullness of redemption.**

1. Out of the depths I cry to you, O Lord,
   Lord, hear my voice!
   O let your ears be attentive
   to the voice of my pleading. ℟

2. If you, O Lord, should mark our guilt,
   Lord, who would survive?
   But with you is found forgiveness:
   for this we revere you. ℟

3. My soul is waiting for the Lord,
   I count on his word.
   My soul is longing for the Lord
   more than watchman for daybreak. ℟

4. Because with the Lord there is mercy
   and fullness of redemption,
   Israel indeed he will redeem
   from all its iniquity. ℟

11th SUNDAY IN ORDINARY TIME/B

The kingdom and the mustard seed.
The mustard seed is very tiny yet when it is
sown in good soil it becomes a very large
shrub in which all types of little birds can
find shelter to build their nests.
The kingdom of God is within us and if we
allow it to grow then people will come to
us because they see that we are truly
witnesses to Christ. Waking or sleeping,
the kingdom is growing within us if we do
things pleasing to God. We may seem
insignificant in the world's eyes but we are
confident that it is God who gives the
increase and for this we thank him.

Entrance Antiphon Lord, hear my voice when I call to you.
You are my help; do not cast me off, do
not desert me, my Saviour God.

Psalm 26:7.9.

Opening Prayer

Let us pray
   [for the grace to follow Christ more closely]

Almighty God,
our hope and our strength,
without *you we* falter.
Help us to follow Christ
and to live according to your will.

or

Let us pray
   [to the Father
   whose love gives us strength to follow his Son]

God our Father,
we rejoice in the faith that draws us together,

ELEVENTH SUNDAY IN ORDINARY TIME/B

aware that selfishness can drive us apart.
Let your encouragement be our constant strength.
Keep us one in the love that has sealed our lives,
help us to live as one family
the gospel we profess.

First Reading   Ezekiel 17:22-24.
I make low trees grow.

The Lord says this:
"From the top of the cedar,
from the highest branch I will take a shoot
and plant it myself on a very high mountain.
I will plant it on the high mountain of Israel.
It will sprout branches and bear fruit,
and become a noble cedar.
Every kind of bird will live beneath it,
every winged creature rest in the shade of its branches.
And every tree of the field will learn that I, the Lord, am the one
who stunts tall trees and makes the low ones grow,
who withers green trees and makes the withered green.
I, the Lord, have spoken, and I will do it."

Responsorial Psalm   Psalm 91.

℟ **It is good to give you thanks, O Lord.**

1. It is good to give thanks to the Lord
   to make music to your name, O Most High,
   to proclaim your love in the morning
   and your truth in the watches of the night. ℟

2. The just will flourish like the palm-tree
   and grow like a Lebanon cedar. ℟

3. Planted in the house of the Lord
   they will flourish in the courts of our God,
   still bearing fruit when they are old,
   still full of sap, still green,
   to proclaim that the Lord is just.
   In him, my rock, there is no wrong. ℟

ELEVENTH SUNDAY IN ORDINARY TIME/B

Second Reading   2 Corinthians 5:6-10.

Whether we are living in the body or exiled from it, we are intent on pleasing the Lord.

We are always full of confidence when we remember that to live in the body means to be exiled from the Lord, going as we do by faith and not by sight — we are full of confidence, I say, and actually want to be exiled from the body and make our home with the Lord. Whether we are living in the body or exiled from it, we are intent on pleasing him. For all the truth about us will be brought out in the law court of Christ, and each of us will get what he deserves for the things he did in the body, good or bad.

Alleluia	Alleluia, alleluia! I call you friends, says the Lord, because I have made known to you everything I have learnt from my Father. Alleluia! John 15:15.
or	Alleluia, alleluia! The seed is the word of God, Christ the sower; whoever finds this seed will remain for ever. Alleluia!

Gospel   Mark 4:26-34.

It is the smallest of all the seeds; yet it grows into the biggest shrub of them all.

Jesus said, "This is what the kingdom of God is like. A man throws seed on the land. Night and day, while he sleeps, when he is awake, the seed is sprouting and growing; how, he does not know. Of its own accord the land produces first the shoot, then the ear, then the full grain in the ear. And when the crop is ready, he loses no time: he starts to reap because the harvest has come."

He also said, "What can we say the kingdom of God is like? What parable can we find for it? It is like a mustard seed which at the time of its sowing in the soil is the smallest of all the seeds on earth; yet once it is sown it grows into the biggest shrub of them all and puts out big branches so that the birds of the air can shelter in its shade."

Using many parables like these, he spoke the word to them, so far as they were capable of understanding it. He would not speak to them except in parables, but he explained everything to his disciples when they were alone.

ELEVENTH SUNDAY IN ORDINARY TIME/B

Prayer over the Gifts

Lord God,
in this bread and wine
you give us food for body and spirit.
May the eucharist renew our strength
and bring us health of mind and body.

Preface of Sundays I-VIII, pages 562-565.

Communion Antiphon

One thing I seek: to dwell in the house of the Lord all the days of my life. **Psalm 26:4.**

or

Father, keep in your name those you have given me, that they may be one as we are one, says the Lord.
John 17:11.

Prayer after Communion

Lord,
may this eucharist
accomplish in your Church
the unity and peace it signifies.

12th SUNDAY IN ORDINARY TIME/B

> Why are you so frightened?
> Fear plays far too large a part in our lives.
> Love casts out fear and God's love endures
> forever. Fear is due to our lack of faith
> that God really cares for us. Christ may
> seem to be asleep but he is there always as
> the son of the Father who has the power to
> calm the stormiest troubles of our lives and
> he tells us: "Quiet now! Be calm!"

Entrance Antiphon God is the strength of his people. In him, we his chosen live in safety. Save us, Lord, who share in your life, and give us your blessing; be our shepherd for ever.

Psalm 27:8-9

Opening Prayer

Let us pray
  [that we may grow in the love of God]

Father,
guide and protector of your people,
grant us an unfailing respect for your name,
and keep us always in your love.

or

Let us pray
  [to God whose fatherly love keeps us safe]

God of the universe,
we worship you as Lord.
God, ever close to us,
we rejoice to call you Father.
From this world's uncertainty we look to your covenant.
Keep us one in your peace, secure in your love.

TWELFTH SUNDAY IN ORDINARY TIME/B

First Reading   Job 38:1. 8-11.

Here your proud waves shall break.

Then from the heart of the tempest the Lord gave Job his answer. He said:
Who pent up the sea behind closed doors
when it leapt tumultuous out of the womb,
when I wrapped it in a robe of mist
and made black clouds its swaddling bands;
when I marked the bounds it was not to cross
and made it fast with a bolted gate?
Come thus far, I said, and no farther:
here your proud waves shall break.

Responsorial Psalm   Psalm 106

R/ **O give thanks to the Lord,
   for his love endures for ever.**

or R/ **Alleluia!**

1. Some sailed to the sea in ships
   to trade on the mighty waters.
   These men have seen the Lord's deeds,
   the wonders he does in the deep. R/

2. For he spoke; he summoned the gale.
   tossing the waves of the sea
   up to heaven and back into the deep;
   their soul melted away in their distress. R/

3. Then they cried to the Lord in their need
   and he rescued them from their distress.
   He stilled the storm to a whisper:
   all the waves of the sea were hushed. R/

4. They rejoiced because of the calm
   and he led them to the haven they desired.
   Let them thank the Lord for his love,
   the wonders he does for men. R/

Second Reading   2 Corinthians 5:14-17.

Now the new creation is here.

The love of Christ overwhelms us when we reflect that if one man has died for all, then all men should be dead; and the reason

TWELFTH SUNDAY IN ORDINARY TIME/B

he died for all was so that living men should live no longer for themselves, but for him who died and was raised to life for them.

From now onwards, therefore, we do not judge anyone by the standards of the flesh. Even if we did once know Christ in the flesh, that is not how we know him now. And for anyone who is in Christ, there is a new creation; the old creation has gone, and now the new one is here.

Alleluia   Alleluia, alleluia! May the Father of our Lord Jesus Christ enlighten the eyes of our mind, so that we can see what hope his call holds for us. Alleluia!

Ephesians 1:17.18.

or   Alleluia, alleluia! A great prophet has appeared among us; God has visited his people. Alleluia!

Luke 7:16.

Gospel   Mark 4:35-41.

Who can this be? Even the wind and the sea obey him.

With the coming of evening, Jesus said to his disciples, "Let us cross over to the other side." And leaving the crowd behind they took him, just as he was, in the boat; and there were other boats with him. Then it began to blow a gale and the waves were breaking into the boat so that it was almost swamped. But he was in the stern, his head on the cushion, asleep. They woke him and said to him, "Master, do you not care? We are going down!" And he woke up and rebuked the wind and said to the sea, "Quiet now! Be calm!" And the wind dropped, and all was calm again. Then he said to them, "Why are you so frightened? How is it that you have no faith?" They were filled with awe and said to one another, "Who can this be? Even the wind and the sea obey him."

Prayer over the Gifts

Lord,
receive our offering,
and may this sacrifice of praise
purify us in mind and heart
and make us always eager to serve you.

Preface of Sundays I-VIII, pages 562-565.

Communion Antiphon   The eyes of all look to you, O Lord, and you give them food in due season. *Psalm 144:15.*

THIRTEENTH SUNDAY IN ORDINARY TIME/B

or   I am the Good Shepherd; I give my
life for my sheep, says the Lord.
John 10:11.15

Prayer after Communion

Lord,
you give us the body and blood of your Son
to renew your life within us.
In your mercy, assure our redemption
and bring us to the eternal life
we celebrate in this eucharist.

13th SUNDAY IN ORDINARY TIME/B

Christ, Giver of life.
Christ came that we might have life and have it to the full. Death comes through the devil and it is to rescue us from his power that Christ came on earth to give his life for us. He tells us to wake from our sleep and come to him so that we might find life. If we have faith then it is life and not death which will conquer.

Entrance Antiphon All nations clap your hands. Shout with a voice of joy to God. Psalm 46:2.

Opening Prayer

Let us pray
  [that Christ may be our light]
Father,
you call your children

THIRTEENTH SUNDAY IN ORDINARY TIME/B

to walk in the light of Christ.
Free us from darkness
and keep us in the radiance of your truth.

or
Let us pray
[for the strength to reject the darkness of sin]

Father in heaven,
the light of Jesus
has scattered the darkness of hatred and sin.
Called to that light
we ask for your guidance.
Form our lives in your truth, our hearts in your love.

First Reading   Wisdom 1:13-15; 2:23-24.

It was the devil's envy that brought death into the world.

Death was not God's doing,
he takes no pleasure in the extinction of the living.
To be — for this he created all;
the world's created things have health in them,
in them no fatal poison can be found,
and Hades holds no power on earth;
for virtue is undying.
Yet God did make man imperishable,
he made him in the image of his own nature;
it was the devil's envy that brought death into the world,
as those who are his partners will discover.

Responsorial Psalm   Psalm 29

℟ **I will praise you, Lord, you have rescued me.**

1. I will praise you, Lord, you have rescued me
   and have not let my enemies rejoice over me.
   O Lord, you have raised my soul from the dead,
   restored me to life from those who sink into the grave. ℟

2. Sing psalms to the Lord, you who love him,
   give thanks to his holy name.
   His anger lasts but a moment; his favour through life.
   At night there are tears, but joy comes with dawn. ℟

3. The Lord listened and had pity.
   The Lord came to my help.
   For me you have changed my mourning into dancing,
   O Lord my God, I will thank you for ever. ℟

THIRTEENTH SUNDAY IN ORDINARY TIME/B

Second Reading 2 Corinthians 8:7. 9. 13-15.

In giving relief to others, balance what happens to be your surplus now against their present need.

You always have the most of everything — of faith, of eloquence, of understanding, of keenness for any cause, and the biggest share of our affection — so we expect you to put the most into this work of mercy too. Remember how generous the Lord Jesus was: he was rich, but he became poor for your sake, to make you rich out of his poverty. This does not mean that to give relief to others you ought to make things difficult for yourselves: it is a question of balancing what happens to be your surplus now against their present need, and one day they may have something to spare that will supply your own need. That is how we strike a balance: as scripture says: The man who gathered much had none too much, the man who gathered little did not go short.

Alleluia Alleluia, alleluia! Your words are spirit, Lord, and they are life: you have the message of eternal life. Alleluia! John 6:63.68.

or

Alleluia, alleluia! Our Saviour Christ Jesus abolished death, and he has proclaimed life through the Good News. Alleluia! 2 Timothy 1:10.

Gospel Mark 5:21-43.

Little girl, I tell you to get up.

When Jesus had crossed in the boat to the other side, a large crowd gathered round him and he stayed by the lakeside. Then one of the synagogue officials came up, Jairus by name, and seeing him, fell at his feet and pleaded with him earnestly, saying, "My little daughter is desperately sick. Do come and lay your hands on her to make her better and save her life." Jesus went with him and a large crowd followed him: they were pressing all round him.

Now there was a woman who had suffered from a haemorrhage for twelve years; after long and painful treatment under various doctors, she had spent all she had without being any the better for it, in fact, she was getting worse. She had heard about Jesus, and she came up behind him through the crowd and touched his

THIRTEENTH SUNDAY IN ORDINARY TIME/B

cloak. "If I can touch even his clothes," she had told herself, "I shall be well again." And the source of the bleeding dried up instantly, and she felt in herself that she was cured of her complaint. Immediately aware that power had gone out from him, Jesus turned round in the crowd and said, "Who touched my clothes?" His disciples said to him, "You see how the crowd is pressing round you and yet you say, 'Who touched me?'" But he continued to look all round to see who had done it. Then the woman came forward, frightened and trembling because she knew what had happened to her, and she fell at his feet and told him the whole truth. "My daughter" he said, "your faith has restored you to health; go in peace and be free from your complaint."

Some people arrived from the house of the synagogue official to say, "Your daughter is dead: why put the Master to any further trouble?" But Jesus had overheard this remark of theirs and he said to the official, "Do not be afraid; only have faith." And he allowed no one to go with him except Peter and James and John the brother of James. So they came to the official's house and Jesus noticed all the commotion, with people weeping and wailing unrestrainedly. He went in and said to them, "Why all this commotion and crying? The child is not dead, but asleep." But they laughed at him. So he turned them all out and, taking with him the child's father and mother and his own companions, he went into the place where the child lay. And taking the child by the hand he said to her, "Talitha, kum!" which means, "Little girl, I tell you to get up." The little girl got up at once and began to walk about, for she was twelve years old. At this they were overcome with astonishment, and he ordered them strictly not to let anyone know about it, and told them to give her something to eat.

Prayer over the Gifts
Lord God,
through your sacraments
you give us the power of your grace.
May this eucharist
help us to serve you faithfully.

Preface of Sundays I-VIII, pages 562-565.

FOURTEENTH SUNDAY IN ORDINARY TIME/B

Communion Antiphon O, bless the Lord, my soul, and all that is within me bless his holy name. **Psalm 102:1.**

or

Father, I pray for them: may they be one in us, so that the world may believe it was you who sent me. **John 17:20-21.**

Prayer after Communion
Lord,
may this sacrifice and communion
give us a share in your life
and help us bring your love to the world.

14th SUNDAY IN ORDINARY TIME/B

God's grace is enough for you. We must stand up and proclaim the kingdom of God to all men in every situation in which we find ourselves. Whether people listen or not we must still live out our lives to the full in witness to God's Spirit which has come upon us. Christ himself was rejected by his own people in his home town so we too must expect rejection because of his message. God's power is at its best in our weakness.

Entrance Antiphon Within your temple, we ponder your loving kindness, O God. As your name, so also your praise reaches to the ends of the earth; your right hand is filled with justice. **Psalm 47:10-11.**

FOURTEENTH SUNDAY IN ORDINARY TIME/B

Opening Prayer

Let us pray
   [for forgiveness through the grace of Jesus Christ]

Father,
through the obedience of Jesus,
your servant and your Son,
you raised a fallen world.
Free us from sin
and bring us the joy that lasts for ever.

or

Let us pray
   [for greater willingness
   to serve God and our fellow man]

Father,
in the rising of your Son
death gives birth to new life.
The sufferings he endured restored hope to a fallen world.
Let sin never ensnare us
with empty promises of passing joy.
Make us one with you always,
so that our joy may be holy,
and our love may give life.

First Reading   Ezekiel 2:2-5.

The sons are defiant and obstinate and they shall know that there is a prophet among them.

The spirit came into me and made me stand up, and I heard the Lord speaking to me. He said, "Son of man, I am sending you to the Israelites, to the rebels who have turned against me. Till now they and their ancestors have been in revolt against me. The sons are defiant and obstinate; I am sending you to them, to say, 'The Lord says this.' Whether they listen or not, this set of rebels shall know there is a prophet among them."

Responsional Psalm   Psalm 122

℟ **Our eyes are on the Lord
till he show us his mercy.**

1. To you have I lifted up my eyes,
   you who dwell in the heavens:

FOURTEENTH SUNDAY IN ORDINARY TIME/B

my eyes, like the eyes of slaves
on the hand of their lords. ℟

2. Like the eyes of a servant
on the hand of her mistress,
so our eyes are on the Lord our God
till he show us his mercy. ℟

3. Have mercy on us, Lord, have mercy.
We are filled with contempt.
Indeed all too full is our soul
with the scorn of the rich,
with the proud man's disdain. ℟

Second Reading   2 Corinthians 12:7-10.

I shall be very happy to make my weaknesses my special boast so that the power of Christ may stay over me.

In view of the extraordinary nature of these revelations, to stop me from getting too proud I was given a thorn in the flesh, an angel of Satan to beat me and stop me from getting too proud! About this thing, I have pleaded with the Lord three times for it to leave me, but he has said, "My grace is enough for you: my power is at its best in weakness." So I shall be very happy to make my weaknesses my special boast so that the power of Christ may stay over me, and that is why I am quite content with my weaknesses, and with insults, hardships, persecutions, and the agonies I go through for Christ's sake. For it is when I am weak that I am strong.

Alleluia   Alleluia, alleluia! The Word was made flesh and lived among us; to all who did accept him he gave power to become children of God. Alleluia!

John 1:12.14.

or

Alleluia, alleluia! The Lord has sent me to bring the good news to the poor, to proclaim liberty to captives. Alleluia! *Luke 4:18.*

Gospel   Mark 6:1-6.

A prophet is only despised in his own country.

Jesus went to his home town and his disciples accompanied him. With the coming of the sabbath he began teaching in the

FOURTEENTH SUNDAY IN ORDINARY TIME/B

synagogue and most of them were astonished when they heard him. They said, "Where did the man get all this? What is this wisdom that has been granted him, and these miracles that are worked through him? This is the carpenter, surely, the son of Mary, the brother of James and Joset and Jude and Simon? His sisters, too, are they not here with us?" And they would not accept him. And Jesus said to them, "A prophet is only despised in his own country, among his own relations and in his own house"; and he could work no miracle there, though he cured a few sick people by laying his hands on them. He was amazed at their lack of faith.

Prayer over the Gifts

Lord,
let this offering to the glory of your name
purify us and bring us closer to eternal life.

Preface of Sundays I-VIII, pages 562-565.

Communion Antiphon

Taste and see the goodness of the Lord; blessed is he who hopes in God. Psalm 33:9.

or

Come to me, all you that labour and are burdened, and I will give you rest, says the Lord. Matthew 11:28.

Prayer after Communion

Lord,
may we never fail to praise you
for the fullness of life and salvation
you give us in this eucharist.

15th SUNDAY IN ORDINARY TIME/B

God chose us in Christ as his missioners.
Before the world was made God chose us
in Christ to make us praise the glory of his
grace, his free gift to us in the beloved.
We are not to worry about material goods
because our authority comes from above.
Like Amos we are to prophesy to all
people because God sends us in the name
of Christ. The Lord is always near
with his saving help.

Entrance Antiphon   In my justice I shall see your face, O Lord; when your glory appears, my joy will be full. Psalm 16:15.

Opening Prayer

Let us pray
   [that the gospel may be our rule of life]

God our Father,
your light of truth
guides us to the way of Christ.
May all who follow him
reject what is contrary to the gospel.

or

Let us pray
   [to be faithful to the light we have received,
   to the name we bear]

Father,
let the light of your truth
guide us to your kingdom
through a world filled with lights contrary to your own.
Christian is the name and the gospel we glory in.
May your love make us what you have called us to be.

FIFTEENTH SUNDAY IN ORDINARY TIME/B

First Reading   Amos 7:12-15.

Go, prophesy to my people.

Amaziah, the priest of Bethel, said to Amos, "Go away, seer; get back to the land of Judah; earn your bread there, do your prophesying there. We want no more prophesying in Bethel; this is the royal sanctuary, the national temple." "I was no prophet, neither did I belong to any of the brotherhoods of prophets," Amos replied to Amaziah, "I was a shepherd, and looked after sycamores: but it was the Lord who took me from herding the flock, and the Lord who said, 'Go, prophesy to my people Israel.'"

Responsorial Psalm   Psalm 84

**R/ Let us see, O Lord, your mercy
and give us your saving help.**

1. I will hear what the Lord God has to say,
a voice that speaks of peace,
peace for his people.
His help is near for those who fear him
and his glory will dwell in our land. R/

2. Mercy and faithfulness have met;
justice and peace have embraced.
Faithfulness shall spring from the earth
and justice look down from heaven. R/

3. The Lord will make us prosper
and our earth shall yield its fruit.
Justice shall march before him
and peace shall follow his steps. R/

Second Reading   Ephesians 1:3-14.

Before the world was made, God chose us.

Blessed be God the Father of our Lord Jesus Christ,
who has blessed us with all the spiritual blessings of heaven in
    Christ.
Before the world was made, he chose us, chose us in Christ,
to be holy and spotless, and to live through love in his presence,
determining that we should become his adopted sons, through
    Jesus Christ
for his own kind purposes,
to make us praise the glory of his grace,

FIFTEENTH SUNDAY IN ORDINARY TIME/B

> his free gift to us in the Beloved,
> in whom, through his blood, we gain our freedom, the forgiveness of our sins.
> Such is the richness of the grace
> which he has showered on us
> in all wisdom and insight.
> He has let us know the mystery of his purpose,
> the hidden plan he so kindly made in Christ from the beginning
> to act upon when the times had run their course to the end:
> that he would bring everything together under Christ, as head, everything in the heavens and everything on earth.

And it is in him that we are claimed as God's own,
chosen from the beginning,
under the predetermined plan of the one who guides all things
as he decides by his own will;
chosen to be,
for his greater glory,
the people who would put their hopes in Christ before he came.
Now you too, in him,
have heard the message of the truth and the good news of your salvation,
and have believed it:
and you too have been stamped with the seal of the Holy Spirit of the Promise,
the pledge of our inheritance
which brings freedom for those whom God has taken for his own,
to make his glory praised.

Alleluia   Alleluia, alleluia! Your words are spirit, Lord, and they are life: you have the message of eternal life. Alleluia! John 6:63.68.

            or

Alleluia, alleluia! May the Father of our Lord Jesus Christ enlighten the eyes of our mind, so that we can see what hope his call holds for us. Alleluia!
Ephesians 1:17-18.

FIFTEENTH SUNDAY IN ORDINARY TIME — /B

Gospel Mark 6:7-13.
He began to send them out.

Jesus summoned the Twelve and began to send them out in pairs giving them authority over the unclean spirits. And he instructed them to take nothing for the journey except a staff — no bread, no haversack, no coppers for their purses. They were to wear sandals but, he added, "Do not take a spare tunic." And he said to them, "If you enter a house anywhere, stay there until you leave the district. And if any place does not welcome you and people refuse to listen to you, as you walk away shake off the dust from under your feet as a sign to them." So they set off to preach repentance; and they cast out many devils, and anointed many sick people with oil and cured them.

Prayer over the Gifts

Prepare the gifts of your Church.
May this eucharist
help us grow in holiness and faith.

Preface of Sundays I-VIII pages 562-565.

Communion Antiphon The sparrow even finds a home, the swallow finds a nest wherein her young, near to your altars, Lord of hosts, my King, my God! How happy they who dwell in your house! Forever they are praising you. Psalm 83:4-5.

or

Whoever eats my flesh and drinks my blood will live in me and I in him, says the Lord. John 6:57.

Prayer after Communion

Lord,
by our sharing in the mystery of this eucharist,
let your saving love grow within us.

16th SUNDAY IN ORDINARY TIME/B

Entrance Antiphon

Christ, shepherd of the people,
on them he came to save all men and the people.
sheep without pity because he looks
have the Good News, shepherd they
been dispersed people aches
be brought back to keep see
vocation to remain but Christ
through his blood, peace were

Opening Prayer

Let us pray
[to be kept faithful in the service of God]

Lord,
be merciful to your people.
Fill us with your gifts
and make us always eager to serve you
in faith, hope and love.

or

Let us pray
[that God will continue to bless us
with his compassion and love]

Father,
let the gift of your life
continue to grow in us,
drawing us from death to faith, hope, and love.
Keep us alive in Christ Jesus.

SIXTEENTH SUNDAY IN ORDINARY TIME/B

be by themselves. But people saw them going, and many could guess where; and from every town they all hurried to the place on foot and reached it before them. So as he stepped ashore he saw a large crowd; and he took pity on them because they were like sheep without a shepherd, and he set himself to teach them at some length.

Prayer over the Gifts

Lord,
bring us closer to salvation
through these gifts which we bring in your honour.
Accept the perfect sacrifice you have given us,
bless it as you blessed the gifts of Abel.

Preface of Sundays I-VIII, pages 562-565.

Communion Antiphon The Lord keeps in our minds the wonderful things he has done. He is compassion and love; he always provides for his faithful. Psalm 110:4-5.

or

I stand at the door and knock, says the Lord. If anyone hears my voice and opens the door, I will come in and sit down to supper with him, and he with me. Revelation 3:20.

Prayer after Communion

Merciful Father,
may these mysteries
give us new purpose
and bring us to a new life in you.

17th SUNDAY IN ORDINARY TIME/B

Christ feeds us.
Christ, through the miraculous multiplication of the loaves and the fishes feeds the hungry people just as he feeds us daily with his Gospel and the eucharist. There was plenty left over when everyone had eaten enough. We too have so much to give to others because of the superabundance of Christ's generosity to us. We must give generously and so preserve the unity of spirit given to us as we are all children of the same Lord and Father.

Entrance Antiphon God is in his holy dwelling; he will give a home to the lonely, he gives power and strength to his people. Psalm 67:6-7. 36.

Opening Prayer

Let us pray
  [that we will make good use of the gifts
  that God has given us]

God our Father and protector,
without you nothing is holy,
nothing has value.
Guide us to everlasting life
by helping us to use wisely
the blessings you have given to the world.

or

Let us pray
  [for the faith to recognize God's presence
  in our world]

God our Father,
open our eyes to see your hand at work
in the splendour of creation,
in the beauty of human life.

SEVENTEENTH SUNDAY IN ORDINARY TIME/B

Touched by your hand our world is holy.
Help us to cherish the gifts that surround us,
to share your blessings with our brothers and sisters,
and to experience the joy of life in your presence.

First Reading   2 Kings 4:42-44.
They will eat and have some left over.

A man came from Baal-shalishah, bringing Elisha, the man of God, bread from the first-fruits, twenty barley loaves and fresh grain in the ear. "Give it to the people to eat," Elisha said. But his servant replied, "How can I serve this to a hundred men?" "Give it to the people to eat," he insisted, "for the Lord says this, 'They will eat and have some left over.'" He served them; they ate and had some over, as the Lord had said.

Responsorial Psalm   Psalm 144

R/ **You open wide your hand, O Lord,
and grant our desires.**

1. All your creatures shall thank you, O Lord,
and your friends shall repeat their blessing.
They shall speak of the glory of your reign
and declare your might, O God. R/

2. The eyes of all creatures look to you
and you give them their food in due time.
You open wide your hand,
grant the desires of all who live. R/

3. The Lord is just in all his ways
and loving in all his deeds.
He is close to all who call him,
who call on him from their hearts. R/

Second Reading   Ephesians 4:1-6.
One Body, one Lord, one faith, one baptism.

I, the prisoner in the Lord, implore you to lead a life worthy of your vocation. Bear with one another charitably, in complete selflessness, gentleness and patience. Do all you can to preserve the unity of the Spirit by the peace that binds you together. There is one Body, one Spirit, just as you were all called into one

SEVENTEENTH SUNDAY IN ORDINARY TIME/B

and the same hope when you were called. There is one Lord, one faith, one baptism, and one God who is Father of all, through all and within all.

Alleluia	Alleluia, alleluia! Your words are spirit, Lord, and they are life: you have the message of eternal life. Alleluia! John 6:63. 68.
	or
	Alleluia, alleluia! A great prophet has appeared among us; God has visited his people. Alleluia! Luke 7:16.

Gospel   John 6:1-15.

Jesus gave out as much as was wanted to all who were sitting ready.

Jesus went off to the other side of the Sea of Galilee — or of Tiberias — and a large crowd followed him, impressed by the signs he gave by curing the sick. Jesus climbed the hillside, and sat down there with his disciples. It was shortly before the Jewish feast of Passover.

Looking up, Jesus saw the crowds approaching and said to Philip, "Where can we buy some bread for these people to eat?" He only said this to test Philip; he himself knew exactly what he was going to do. Philip answered, "Two hundred denarii would only buy enough to give them a small piece each." One of his disciples, Andrew, Simon Peter's brother, said, "There is a small boy here with five barley loaves and two fish; but what is that between so many?" Jesus said to them, "Make the people sit down." There was plenty of grass there, and as many as five thousand men sat down. Then Jesus took the loaves, gave thanks, and gave them out to all who were sitting ready; he then did the same with the fish, giving out as much as was wanted. When they had eaten enough he said to the disciples, "Pick up the pieces left over, so that nothing gets wasted." So they picked them up, and filled twelve hampers with scraps left over from the meal of five barley loaves. The people, seeing this sign that he had given, said, "This really is the prophet who is to come into the world." Jesus, who could see they were about to come and take him by force and make him king, escaped back to the hills by himself.

EIGHTEENTH SUNDAY IN ORDINARY TIME/B

for only your love makes us whole.
Keep us strong in your love.

First Reading   Exodus 16:2-4. 12-15.
I will rain down bread for you from the heavens.

The whole community of the sons of Israel began to complain against Moses and Aaron in the wilderness and said to them, "Why did we not die at the Lord's hand in the land of Egypt, when we were able to sit down to pans of meat and could eat bread to our heart's content! As it is, you have brought us to this wilderness to starve this whole company to death!"

Then the Lord said to Moses, "Now I will rain down bread for you from the heavens. Each day the people are to go out and gather the day's portion; I propose to test them in this way to see whether they will follow my law or not."

"I have heard the complaints of the sons of Israel. Say this to them, 'Between the two evenings you shall eat meat, and in the morning you shall have bread to your heart's content. Then you will learn that I, the Lord, am your God.'" And so it came about: quails flew up in the evening, and they covered the camp; in the morning there was a coating of dew all round the camp. When the coating of dew lifted, there on the surface of the desert was a thing delicate, powdery, as fine as hoarfrost on the ground. When they saw this, the sons of Israel said to one another, "What is that?" not knowing what it was. "That" said Moses to them "is the bread the Lord gives you to eat."

Responsorial Psalm   Psalm 77

℟ **The Lord gave them bread from heaven.**

1. The things we have heard and understood,
   the things our fathers have told us,
   we will tell to the next generation:
   the glories of the Lord and his might. ℟

2. He commanded the clouds above
   and opened the gates of heaven.
   He rained down manna for their food,
   and gave them bread from heaven. ℟

EIGHTEENTH SUNDAY IN ORDINARY TIME/B

3. Mere men ate the bread of angels.
   He sent them abundance of food.
   He brought them to his holy land,
   to the mountain which his right hand had won. ℟

Second Reading   Ephesians 4:17. 20-24.

Put on the new self that has been created in God's way.

I want to urge you in the name of the Lord, not to go on living the aimless kind of life that pagans live. Now that is hardly the way you have learnt from Christ, unless you failed to hear him properly when you were taught what the truth is in Jesus. You must give up your old way of life; you must put aside your old self, which gets corrupted by following illusory desires. Your mind must be renewed by a spiritual revolution so that you can put on the new self that has been created in God's way, in the goodness and holiness of the truth.

Alleluia   Alleluia, alleluia! I am the Way, the Truth and the Life, says the Lord; no one can come to the Father except through me. Alleluia! John 14:5.

or

Alleluia, alleluia! Man does not live on bread alone, but on every word that comes from the mouth of God. Alleluia! Matthew 4:4.

Gospel   John 6:24-35.

He who comes to me will never be hungry; he who believes in me will never thirst.

When the people saw that neither Jesus nor his disciples were there, they got into boats and crossed to Capernaum to look for Jesus. When they found him on the other side, they said to him, "Rabbi, when did you come here?" Jesus answered:
"I tell you most solemnly,
you are not looking for me
because you have seen the signs
but because you had all the bread you wanted to eat.
Do not work for food that cannot last,
but work for food that endures to eternal life,
the kind of food the Son of Man is offering you,
for on him the Father, God himself, has set his seal."

EIGHTEENTH SUNDAY IN ORDINARY TIME/B

Then they said to him, "What must we do if we are to do the works that God wants?" Jesus gave them this answer, "This is working for God: you must believe in the one he has sent." So they said, "What sign will you give to show us that we should believe in you? What work will you do? Our fathers had manna to eat in the desert; as scripture says: He gave them bread from heaven to eat."

Jesus answered:
"I tell you most solemnly,
it was not Moses who gave you bread from heaven,
it is my Father who gives you the bread from heaven,
the true bread;
for the bread of God
is that which comes down from heaven
and gives life to the world."

"Sir," they said "give us that bread always." Jesus answered:
"I am the bread of life.
He who comes to me will never be hungry;
he who believes in me will never thirst."

Prayer over the Gifts

Merciful Lord,
make holy these gifts,
and let our spiritual sacrifice
make us an everlasting gift to you.

Preface of Sundays I-VIII, pages 562-565.

Communion Antiphon

You gave us bread from heaven, Lord: a sweet-tasting bread that was very good to eat. Wisdom 16:20.

or

The Lord says: I am the bread of life. A man who comes to me will not go away hungry, and no one who believes in me will thirst. John 6:35.

Prayer after Communion

Lord,
you give us the strength of new life
by the gift of the eucharist.
Protect us with your love
and prepare us for eternal redemption.

19th SUNDAY IN ORDINARY TIME/B

The bread is my flesh for the life of the world. Christ is the living bread come down from heaven and anyone who eats this bread will live forever. Just as Elijah the prophet was strengthened by the food given to him by God so we too are helped by the eucharist to continue in our pilgrimage back to our Father. Through this eucharist we are reminded that if we are to follow Christ we must love as he loved us.

Entrance Antiphon   Lord, be true to your covenant, forget not the life of your poor ones for ever. Rise up, O God, and defend your cause; do not ignore the shouts of your enemies.

Psalm 73:20.19.22.23

Opening Prayer

Let us pray
  [in the Spirit
  that we may grow in the love of God]

Almighty and ever-living God,
your Spirit made us your children,
confident to call you Father.
Increase your Spirit within us
and bring us to our promised inheritance.

or

Let us pray
  [that through us
  others may find the way to life in Christ]

Father,
we come, reborn in the Spirit,
to celebrate our sonship in the Lord Jesus Christ.

NINETEENTH SUNDAY IN ORDINARY TIME/B

Touch our hearts,
help them grow towards the life you have promised.
Touch our lives,
make them signs of your love for all men.

First Reading   1 Kings 19:4-8.
Strengthened by the food he walked until he reached the mountain of God.

Elijah went into the wilderness, a day's journey, and sitting under a furze bush wished he were dead. "Lord," he said "I have had enough. Take my life; I am no better than my ancestors." Then he lay down and went to sleep. But an angel touched him and said, "Get up and eat." He looked round, and there at his head was a scone baked on hot stones, and a jar of water. He ate and drank and then lay down again. But the angel of the Lord came back a second time and touched him and said, "Get up and eat, or the journey will be too long for you." So he got up and ate and drank, and strengthened by that food he walked for forty days and forty nights until he reached Horeb, the mountain of God.

Responsorial Psalm   Psalm 33

℟ **Taste and see that the Lord is good.**

1. I will bless the Lord at all times,
   his praise always on my lips;
   in the Lord my soul shall make its boast.
   The humble shall hear and be glad. ℟

2. Glorify the Lord with me.
   Together let us praise his name.
   I sought the Lord and he answered me;
   from all my terrors he set me free. ℟

3. Look towards him and be radiant;
   let your faces not be abashed.
   This poor man called; the Lord heard him
   and rescued him from all his distress. ℟

4. The angel of the Lord is encamped
   around those who revere him, to rescue them.
   Taste and see that the Lord is good.
   He is happy who seeks refuge in him. ℟

NINETEENTH SUNDAY IN ORDINARY TIME/B

Second Reading Ephesians 4:30 - 5:2.
Follow Christ by loving as he loved you.

Do not grieve the Holy Spirit of God who has marked you with his seal for you to be set free when the day comes. Never have grudges against others, or lose your temper, or raise your voice to anybody, or call each other names, or allow any sort of spitefulness. Be friends with one another, and kind, forgiving each other as readily as God forgave you in Christ.

Try, then, to imitate God, as children of his that he loves, and follow Christ by loving as he loved you, giving himself up in our place as a fragrant offering and a sacrifice to God.

Alleluia Alleluia, alleluia! If anyone loves me he will keep my word, and my Father will love him, and we shall come to him. Alleluia! John 14:23.

or

Alleluia, alleluia! I am the living bread which has come down from heaven, says the Lord. Anyone who eats this bread will live for ever. Alleluia! John 6:51.

Gospel John 6:41-51.
I am the living bread which has come down from heaven.

The Jews were complaining to each other about Jesus, because he had said, "I am the bread that came down from heaven." "Surely this is Jesus son of Joseph" they said. "We know his father and mother. How can he now say, 'I have come down from heaven'?" Jesus said in reply, "Stop complaining to each other.
"No one can come to me
unless he is drawn by the Father who sent me,
and I will raise him up at the last day.
It is written in the prophets:
They will all be taught by God,
and to hear the teaching of the Father,
and learn from it,
is to come to me.
Not that anybody has seen the Father,
except the one who comes from God:
he has seen the Father.
I tell you most solemnly,

NINETEENTH SUNDAY IN ORDINARY TIME/B

everybody who believes has eternal life.
I am the bread of life.
Your fathers ate the manna in the desert
and they are dead;
but this is the bread that comes down from heaven,
so that a man may eat it and not die.
I am the living bread which has come down from heaven.
Anyone who eats this bread will live for ever;
and the bread that I shall give
is my flesh, for the life of the world."

Prayer over the Gifts

God of power,
giver of the gifts we bring,
accept the offering of your Church
and make it the sacrament of our salvation.

Preface of Sundays I-VIII, pages 562-565.

Communion Antiphon	Praise the Lord, Jerusalem; he feeds you with the finest wheat.
	Psalm 147:12.14
	or
	The bread I shall give is my flesh for the life of the world, says the Lord.
	John 6:52

Prayer after Communion

Lord,
may the eucharist you give us
bring us to salvation
and keep us faithful to the light of your truth.

20th SUNDAY IN ORDINARY TIME/B

Christ's blood is real drink.
Christ gave his life for us on the cross.
Blood is a sign of life and Christ shed it to the
last drop. In the eucharist we receive his
life-giving blood. We too must give our lives to
transform the world around us. Even though
this may be a wicked age our lives should
redeem it.

Entrance Antiphon God, our protector, keep us in mind; always give strength to your people. For if we can be with you even one day, it is better than a thousand without you.

Psalm 83:10-11

Opening Prayer
Let us pray
 [that the love of God
 may raise us beyond what we see
 to the unseen glory of his kingdom]

God our Father,
may we love you in all things and above all things
and reach the joy you have prepared for us
beyond all our imagining.

or

Let us pray
 [with humility and persistence]

Almighty God, ever-loving Father,
your care extends beyond the boundaries of race and nation
to the hearts of all who live.

May the walls, which prejudice raises between us,
crumble beneath the shadow of your outstretched arm.

TWENTIETH SUNDAY IN ORDINARY TIME/B

First Reading   Proverbs 9:1-6.

Eat my bread, drink the wine I have prepared for you.

Wisdom has built herself a house,
she has erected her seven pillars,
she has slaughtered her beasts, prepared her wine,
she has laid her table.
She has despatched her maidservants
and proclaimed from the city's heights:
"Who is ignorant? Let him step this way."
To the fool she says,
"Come and eat my bread,
drink the wine I have prepared!
Leave your folly and you will live,
walk in the ways of perception."

Responsorial Psalm   Psalm 33.

R/ Taste and see that the Lord is good.

1. I will bless the Lord at all times,
   his praise always on my lips;
   in the Lord my soul shall make its boast.
   The humble shall hear and be glad. R/

2. Revere the Lord, you his saints.
   They lack nothing, those who revere him.
   Strong lions suffer want and go hungry
   but those who seek the Lord lack no blessing. R/

3. Come, children, and hear me
   that I may teach you the fear of the Lord.
   Who is he who longs for life
   and many days, to enjoy his prosperity? R/

4. Then keep your tongue from evil
   and your lips from speaking deceit.
   Turn aside from evil and do good;
   seek and strive after peace. R/

Second Reading   Ephesians 5:15-20.

Recognise what is the will of God.

Be very careful about the sort of lives you lead, like intelligent and not like senseless people. This may be a wicked age, but your lives should redeem it. And do not be thoughtless but recognise

TWENTIETH SUNDAY IN ORDINARY TIME/B

what is the will of the Lord. Do not drug yourselves with wine, this is simply dissipation; be filled with the Spirit. Sing the words and tunes of the psalms and hymns when you are together, and go on singing and chanting to the Lord in your hearts, so that always and everywhere you are giving thanks to God who is our Father in the name of our Lord Jesus Christ.

Alleluia   Alleluia, alleluia! The Word was made flesh and lived among us; to all who did accept him he gave power to become children of God. Alleluia! **John 1:12.14.**

or

Alleluia, alleluia! He who eats my flesh and drinks my blood lives in me, and I live in him, says the Lord. Alleluia! **John 6:56.**

Gospel **John 6:51-58.**
My flesh is real food and my blood is real drink.
Jesus said to the crowd:
"I am the living bread which has come down from heaven.
Anyone who eats this bread will live for ever;
and the bread that I shall give
is my flesh, for the life of the world."
   Then the Jews started arguing with one another: "How can this man give us his flesh to eat?" they said. Jesus replied:
"I tell you most solemnly,
if you do not eat the flesh of the Son of Man
and drink his blood,
you will not have life in you.
Anyone who does eat my flesh and drink my blood
has eternal life,
and I shall raise him up on the last day.
For my flesh is real food
and my blood is real drink.
He who eats my flesh and drinks my blood
lives in me
and I live in him.
As I, who am sent by the living Father,
myself draw life from the Father,
so whoever eats me will draw life from me.
This is the bread come down from heaven;

not like the bread our ancestors ate:
they are dead,
but anyone who eats this bread will live for ever."

Prayer over the Gifts

Lord,
accept our sacrifice
as a holy exchange of gifts.
By offering what you have given us
may we receive the gift of yourself.

Preface of Sundays I-VIII, pages 562-565.

Communion Antiphon

With the Lord there is mercy, and fullness of redemption. **Psalm 129:7.**

or

I am the living bread from heaven, says the Lord; if anyone eats this bread he will live for ever.
John 6:51-52

Prayer after Communion

God of mercy,
by this sacrament you make us one with Christ.
By becoming more like him on earth,
may we come to share his glory in heaven,
where he lives and reigns for ever and ever.

21st SUNDAY IN ORDINARY TIME/B

Christ has the words of eternal life.
Christ lives in his Church and in loving it
we love him. Our faith deals with the
person of Christ. He has the words of eternal
life and there is no one else to whom we want
to go. We show our love for him in our service
of loyalty to the Church.

Entrance Antiphon Listen, Lord, and answer me. Save your servant who trusts in you. I call to you all day long, have mercy on me, O Lord.
Psalm 85:1-3

Opening Prayer

Let us pray
 [that God will make us one in mind and heart]

Father,
help us to seek the values
that will bring us lasting joy in this changing world.
In our desire for what you promise
make us one in mind and heart.

or

Let us pray
 [with minds fixed on eternal truth]

Lord our God,
all truth is from you,
and you alone bring oneness of heart.
Give your people the joy
of hearing your word in every sound

TWENTY-FIRST SUNDAY IN ORDINARY TIME/B

and of longing for your presence more than for life itself.
May all the attractions of a changing world
serve only to bring us
the peace of your kingdom which this world does not give.

First Reading   Joshua 24:1-2. 15-18.
We will serve the Lord, for he is our God.

Joshua gathered all the tribes of Israel together at Shechem; then he called the elders, leaders, judges and scribes of Israel, and they presented themselves before God. Then Joshua said to all the people: "If you will not serve the Lord, choose today whom you wish to serve, whether the gods that your ancestors served beyond the River, or the gods of the Amorites in whose land you are now living. As for me and my House, we will serve the Lord."

The people answered, "We have no intention of deserting the Lord and serving other gods! Was it not the Lord our God who brought us and our ancestors out of the land of Egypt, the house of slavery, who worked those great wonders before our eyes and preserved us all along the way we travelled and among all the peoples through whom we journeyed? We too will serve the Lord, for he is our God."

Responsorial Psalm   Psalm 33.

℟ **Taste and see that the Lord is good.**

1. I will bless the Lord at all times,
   his praise always on my lips;
   in the Lord my soul shall make its boast.
   The humble shall hear and be glad. ℟

2. The Lord turns his face against the wicked
   to destroy their remembrance from the earth.
   The Lord turns his eyes to the just
   and his ears to their appeal. ℟

3. They call and the Lord hears
   and rescues them in all their distress.
   The Lord is close to the broken-hearted;
   those whose spirit is crushed he will save. ℟

4. Many are the trials of the just man
   but from them all the Lord will rescue him.
   He will keep guard over all his bones,
   not one of his bones shall be broken. ℟

(continued)

TWENTY-FIRST SUNDAY IN ORDINARY TIME/B

5.Evil brings death to the wicked;
 those who hate the good are doomed.
 The Lord ransoms the souls of his servants.
 Those who hide in him shall not be condemned. R/

Second Reading   Ephesians 5:21-32.

This mystery has many implications for Christ and his Church.

Give way to one another in obedience to Christ. Wives should regard their husbands as they regard the Lord, since as Christ is head of the Church and saves the whole body, so is a husband the head of his wife; and as the Church submits to Christ, so should wives to their husbands, in everything. Husbands should love their wives just as Christ loved the Church and sacrificed himself for her to make her holy. He made her clean by washing her in water with a form of words, so that when he took her to himself she would be glorious, with no speck or wrinkle or anything like that, but holy and faultless. In the same way, husbands must love their wives as they love their own bodies; for a man to love his wife is for him to love himself. A man never hates his own body, but he feeds it and looks after it; and that is the way Christ treats the Church, because it is his body — and we are its living parts. For this reason, a man must leave his father and mother and be joined to his wife, and the two will become one body. This mystery has many implications; but I am saying it applies to Christ and the Church.

Alleluia   Alleluia, alleluia! Your words are spirit, Lord, and they are life: you have the message of eternal life. Alleluia! John 6:63.68.

Alternative Alleluias, pages 1004-1006.

Gospel   John 6:60-69.

Who shall we go to? You have the message of eternal life.

After hearing his doctrine many of the followers of Jesus said, "This is intolerable language. How could anyone accept it?" Jesus was aware that his followers were complaining about it and said, "Does this upset you? What if you should see the Son of Man ascend to where he was before?
"It is the spirit that gives life,
the flesh has nothing to offer.

TWENTY-FIRST SUNDAY IN ORDINARY TIME/B

The words I have spoken to you are spirit
and they are life.
"But there are some of you who do not believe." For Jesus knew from the outset those who did not believe, and who it was that would betray him. He went on, "This is why I told you that no one could come to me unless the Father allows him." After this, many of his disciples left him and stopped going with him.

Then Jesus said to the Twelve, "What about you, do you want to go away too?" Simon Peter answered, "Lord, who shall we go to? You have the message of eternal life, and we believe; we know that you are the Holy One of God."

Prayer over the Gifts

Merciful God,
the perfect sacrifice of Jesus Christ
made us your people.
In your love,
grant peace and unity to your Church.

Preface of Sundays I-VIII, pages 562-565.

Communion Antiphon

Lord, the earth is filled with your gift from heaven; man grows bread from earth, and wine to cheer his heart. Psalm 103:13-15

or

The Lord says: The man who eats my flesh and drinks my blood will live for ever; I shall raise him to life on the last day. John 6:55.

Prayer after Communion

Lord,
may this eucharist increase within us
the healing power of your love.
May it guide and direct our efforts
to please you in all things.

22nd SUNDAY IN ORDINARY TIME/B

Obey the commandments of God.
Christ did not come to set aside the
commandments but to fulfil them. In his
life-style he shows us how we are to act in
order to witness to the power of God's word
within us. Faith without good works is dead
and we show we are God's people by our care
of those in need. In this way we place
our trust in God.

Entrance Antiphon   I call to you all day long, have mercy on me, O Lord. You are good and forgiving, full of love for all who call to you.

Psalm 85:3.5

Opening Prayer

Let us pray
  [that God will increase our faith
  and bring to perfection the gifts he has given us]

Almighty God,
every good thing comes from you.
Fill our hearts with love for you,
increase our faith,
and by your constant care
protect the good you have given us.

  or

Let us pray
  [to God who forgives all who call upon him]

Lord God of power and might,
nothing is good which is against your will,
and all is of value which comes from your hand.
Place in our hearts a desire to please you

TWENTY-SECOND SUNDAY IN ORDINARY TIME/B

and fill our minds with insight into love,
so that every thought may grow in wisdom
and all our efforts may be filled with your peace.

First Reading   Deuteronomy 4:1-2.6-8.

Add nothing to what I command you, keep the commandments of the Lord.

Moses said to the people: "Now, Israel, take notice of the laws and customs that I teach you today, and observe them, that you may have life and may enter and take possession of the land that the Lord the God of your fathers is giving you. You must add nothing to what I command you, and take nothing from it, but keep the commandments of the Lord your God just as I lay them down for you. Keep them, observe them, and they will demonstrate to the peoples your wisdom and understanding. When they come to know of all these laws they will exclaim, 'No other people is as wise and prudent as this great nation.' And indeed, what great nation is there that has its gods so near as the Lord our God is to us whenever we call to him? And what great nation is there that has laws and customs to match this whole Law that I put before you today?"

Responsorial Psalm   Psalm 14.

℟ **The just will live in the presence of the Lord.**

1. Lord, who shall dwell on your holy mountain?
   He who walks without fault;
   he who acts with justice
   and speaks the truth from his heart.   ℟

2. He who does no wrong to his brother,
   who casts no slur on his neighbour,
   who holds the godless in disdain,
   but honours those who fear the Lord.   ℟

3. He who keeps his pledge, come what may;
   who takes no interest on a loan
   and accepts no bribes against the innocent.
   Such a man will stand firm for ever.   ℟

TWENTY-SECOND SUNDAY IN ORDINARY TIME/B

Second Reading James 1:17-18.21-22.27.
You must do what the word tells you.

It is all that is good, everything that is perfect, which is given us from above; it comes down from the Father of all light; with him there is no such thing as alteration, no shadow of a change. By his own choice he made us his children by the message of the truth so that we should be a sort of first-fruits of all that he had created.

Accept and submit to the word which has been planted in you and can save your souls. But you must do what the word tells you, and not just listen to it and deceive yourselves.

Pure, unspoilt religion, in the eyes of God our Father is this: coming to the help of orphans and widows when they need it, and keeping oneself uncontaminated by the world.

Alleluia Alleluia, alleluia! Your words are spirit, Lord, and they are life: you have the message of eternal life. Alleluia! John 6:63.68.

or

Alleluia, alleluia! By his own choice the Father made us his children by the message of his truth, so that we should be a sort of first-fruits of all that he created. Alleluia! James 1:18.

Gospel Mark 7:1-8.14-15.21-23.
You put aside the commandment of God to cling to human traditions.

The Pharisees and some of the scribes who had come from Jerusalem gathered round Jesus, and they noticed that some of his disciples were eating with unclean hands, that is, without washing them. For the Pharisees, and the Jews in general, follow the tradition of the elders and never eat without washing their arms as far as the elbow; and on returning from the market place they never eat without first sprinkling themselves. There are also many other observances which have been handed down to them concerning the washing of cups and pots and bronze dishes. So these Pharisees and scribes asked him, "Why do your disciples not respect the tradition of the elders but eat their food with unclean hands?" He answered, "It was of you hypocrites that Isaiah so rightly prophesied in this passage of scripture:

This people honours me only with lip-service,
while their hearts are far from me.
The worship they offer me is worthless,
the doctrines they teach are only human regulations.
You put aside the commandment of God to cling to human traditions."

He called the people to him again and said, "Listen to me, all of you, and understand. Nothing that goes into a man from outside can make him unclean; it is the things that come out of a man that make him unclean. For it is from within, from men's hearts, that evil intentions emerge: fornication, theft, murder, adultery, avarice, malice, deceit, indecency, envy, slander, pride, folly. All these evil things come from within and make a man unclean."

Prayer over the Gifts

Lord,
may this holy offering
bring us your blessing
and accomplish within us
its promise of salvation.

Preface of Sundays I-VIII, pages 562-565.

Communion Antiphon — O Lord, how great is the depth of the kindness which you have shown to those who love you. Psalm 30:20.

or

Happy are the peacemakers; they shall be called sons of God. Happy are they who suffer persecution for justice's sake; the kingdom of heaven is theirs. Matthew 5:9-10.

Prayer after Communion

Lord,
you renew us at your table with the bread of life.
May this food strengthen us in love
and help us to serve you in each other.

23rd SUNDAY IN ORDINARY TIME/B

Christ makes the deaf hear
and the dumb speak.
The power of Christ helps us to understand
the Gospel and to speak its message to other
people. Even though in the world's eyes we
are poor nevertheless it is God who chooses
people like us to be heirs to his kingdom.
When we are downhearted we must learn not
to be afraid. Our God is faithful
to his promises.

Entrance Antiphon   Lord, you are just, and the judgements you make are right. Show mercy when you judge me, your servant.

Psalm 118:137.124

Opening Prayer

Let us pray
 [that we may realise the freedom God has given us
 in making us his sons and daughters]

God our Father,
you redeem us
and make us your children in Christ.
Look upon us,
give us true freedom
and bring us to the inheritance you promised.

or

Let us pray
 [to our just and merciful God]

Lord our God,
in you justice and mercy meet.
With unparalleled love you have saved us from death
and drawn us into the circle of your life.

TWENTY-THIRD SUNDAY IN ORDINARY TIME/B

Open our eyes to the wonders this life sets before us,
that we may serve you free from fear
and address you as God our Father.

First Reading   Isaiah 35:4-7.
The ears of the deaf shall be unsealed and the tongues of the dumb shall be loosed.

Say to all faint hearts,
"Courage! Do not be afraid.

"Look, your God is coming,
vengeance is coming,
the retribution of God;
he is coming to save you."

Then the eyes of the blind shall be opened,
the ears of the deaf unsealed,
then the lame shall leap like a deer
and the tongues of the dumb sing for joy;

for water gushes in the desert,
streams in the wasteland,
the scorched earth becomes a lake,
the parched land springs of water.

Responsorial Psalm   Psalm 145.

℟ **My soul, give praise to the Lord.**

1. It is the Lord who keeps faith for ever,
   who is just to those who are oppressed.
   It is he who gives bread to the hungry,
   the Lord, who sets prisoners free. ℟

2. It is the Lord who gives sight to the blind,
   who raises up those who are bowed down,
   the Lord who loves the just,
   the Lord, who protects the stranger. ℟

3. The Lord upholds the widow and orphan,
   but thwarts the path of the wicked.
   The Lord will reign for ever,
   Zion's God, from age to age. Alleluia! ℟

TWENTY-THIRD SUNDAY IN ORDINARY TIME/B

Second Reading   James 2:1-5.

God chose the poor to be the heirs to the kingdom.

My brothers, do not try to combine faith in Jesus Christ, our glorified Lord, with the making of distinctions between classes of people. Now suppose a man comes into your synagogue, beautifully dressed and with a gold ring on, and at the same time a poor man comes in, in shabby clothes, and you take notice of the well-dressed man, and say, "Come this way to the best seats"; then you tell the poor man, "Stand over there" or "You can sit on the floor by my foot-rest." Can't you see that you have used two different standards in your mind and turned yourselves into judges, and corrupt judges at that?

Listen, my dear brothers: it was those who are poor according to the world that God chose, to be rich in faith and to be the heirs to the kingdom which he promised to those who love him.

Alleluia   Alleluia! Speak, Lord, your servant is listening: you have the message of eternal life. Alleluia!
                                                          1 Samuel 3:9; John 6:68

or

Alleluia, alleluia! Jesus proclaimed the Good News of the kingdom, and cured all kinds of sickness among the people. Alleluia!   Matthew 4:23.

Gospel   Mark 7:31-37.

He makes the deaf hear and the dumb speak.

Returning from the district of Tyre, Jesus went by way of Sidon towards the Sea of Galilee, right through the Decapolis region. And they brought him a deaf man who had an impediment in his speech; and they asked him to lay his hand on him. He took him aside in private, away from the crowd, put his fingers into the man's ears and touched his tongue with spittle. Then looking up to heaven he sighed; and he said to him, "Ephphatha", that is, "Be opened." And his ears were opened, and the ligament of his tongue was loosened and he spoke clearly. And Jesus ordered them to tell no one about it, but the more he insisted, the more widely they published it. Their admiration was unbounded. "He has done all things well," they said "he makes the deaf hear and the dumb speak."

TWENTY-THIRD SUNDAY IN ORDINARY TIME/B

Prayer over the Gifts

God of peace and love,
may our offering bring you true worship
and make us one with you.

Preface of Sundays I-VIII, pages 562-565.

Communion Antiphon

Like a deer that longs for running streams, my soul longs for you, my God. My soul is thirsting for the living God. Psalm 41:2-3.

or

I am the light of the world, says the Lord; the man who follows me will have the light of life. John 8:12.

Prayer after Communion

Lord,
your word and your sacrament
give us food and life.
May this gift of your Son
lead us to share his life for ever.

24th SUNDAY IN ORDINARY TIME/B

You are the Christ.
We believe that Jesus is the Christ
the Son of God.
In order to show his love for us he suffered
grievously and died for us upon a cross. If we
want to find life we must be prepared
apparently to lose it because it is in the
manner which we accept suffering that we
show our love for God.

Entrance Antiphon Give peace, Lord, to those who are faithful to you, and your prophets will proclaim you as you deserve. Hear the prayers of your servant and of your people Israel. cf. Ecclesiasticus 36:18.

Opening Prayer

Let us pray
  [that God will keep us faithful in his service]

Almighty God,
our creator and guide,
may we serve you with all our heart
and know your forgiveness in our lives.

or

Let us pray
  [for the peace which is born of faith and hope]

Father in heaven, Creator of all,
look down upon your people in their moments of need,
for you alone are the source of our peace.
Bring us to the dignity which distinguishes the poor in spirit
and show us how great is the call to serve,
that we may share in the peace of Christ
who offered his life in the service of all.

TWENTY-FOURTH SUNDAY IN ORDINARY TIME/B

First Reading Isaiah 50:5-9.

I offered my back to those who struck me.

The Lord has opened my ear.
For my part, I made no resistance,
neither did I turn away.
I offered my back to those who struck me,
my cheeks to those who tore at my beard;
I did not cover my face
against insult and spittle.
The Lord comes to my help,
so that I am untouched by the insults.
So, too, I set my face like flint;
I know I shall not be shamed.
My vindicator is here at hand. Does anyone start proceedings
  against me?
Then let us go to court together.
Who thinks he has a case against me?
Let him approach me.
The Lord is coming to my help,
who dare condemn me?

Responsorial Psalm Psalm 114.

℟ **I will walk in the presence of the Lord
in the land of the living.**

or ℟ **Alleluia!**

1. I love the Lord for he has heard
   the cry of my appeal;
   for he turned his ear to me
   in the day when I called him. ℟

2. They surrounded me, the snares of death,
   with the anguish of the tomb;
   they caught me, sorrow and distress.
   I called on the Lord's name.
   O Lord my God, deliver me! ℟

3. How gracious is the Lord, and just;
   our God has compassion.
   The Lord protects the simple hearts;
   I was helpless so he saved me. ℟

(continued)

TWENTY-FOURTH SUNDAY IN ORDINARY TIME/B

4. He has kept my soul from death,
   my eyes from tears
   and my feet from stumbling.
   I will walk in the presence of the Lord
   in the land of the living. ℟

Second Reading   James 2:14-18.
If good works do not go with faith, it is quite dead.

Take the case, my brothers, of someone who has never done a single good act but claims that he has faith. Will that faith save him? If one of the brothers or one of the sisters is in need of clothes and has not enough food to live on, and one of you says to them, "I wish you well; keep yourself warm and eat plenty", without giving them these bare necessities of life, then what good is that? Faith is like that: if good works do not go with it, it is quite dead.

This is the way to talk to people of that kind: "You say you have faith and I have good deeds; I will prove to you that I have faith by showing you my good deeds — now you prove to me that you have faith without any good deeds to show."

Alleluia

Alleluia, alleluia! I am the Way, the Truth and the Life, says the Lord; no one can come to the Father except through me. Alleluia! John 14:5.

or

Alleluia, alleluia! The only thing I can boast about is the cross of our Lord, through whom the world is crucified to me, and I to the world. Alleluia!

Galatians 6:14.

Gospel   Mark 8:27-35.
You are the Christ. The Son of Man is destined to suffer grievously.

Jesus and his disciples left for the villages round Caesarea Philippi. On the way he put this question to his disciples, "Who do people say I am?" And they told him. "John the Baptist," they said, "others Elijah; others again, one of the prophets." "But you," he asked, "who do you say I am?" Peter spoke up and said to him, "You are the Christ." And he gave them strict orders not to tell anyone about him.

And he began to teach them that the Son of Man was destined to suffer grievously, to be rejected by the elders and the chief priests and the scribes, and to be put to death, and after three days to rise again; and he said all this quite openly. Then, taking him aside, Peter started to remonstrate with him. But, turning and seeing his disciples, he rebuked Peter and said to him, "Get behind me, Satan! Because the way you think is not God's way but man's."

He called the people and his disciples to him and said, "If anyone wants to be a follower of mine, let him renounce himself and take up his cross and follow me. For anyone who wants to save his life will lose it; but anyone who loses his life for my sake, and for the sake of the gospel, will save it."

Prayer over the Gifts

Lord,
hear the prayers of your people
and receive our gifts.
May the worship of each one here
bring salvation to all.

Preface of Sundays I-VIII, pages 562-565.

Communion Antiphon

O God, how much we value your mercy! All mankind can gather under your protection. Psalm 35:8.

or

The cup that we bless is a communion with the blood of Christ; and the bread that we break is a communion with the body of the Lord.

cf. 1 Corinthians 10:16

Prayer after Communion

Lord,
may the eucharist you have given us
influence our thoughts and actions.
May your Spirit guide and direct us in your way.

25th SUNDAY IN ORDINARY TIME/B

Christ must die a shameful death.
When Christ explained to his followers that he must die a shameful death they did not understand him. We too do not understand suffering even though we are surrounded by it on all sides. When we carry our cross with resignation we discover a peace that the world cannot give.

Entrance Antiphon

I am the Saviour of all people, says the Lord. Whatever their troubles, I will answer their cry, and I will always be their Lord.

Opening Prayer

Let us pray
 [that we will grow in the love of God
 and of one another]

Father,
guide us, as you guide creation
according to your law of love.
May we love one another
and come to perfection
in the eternal life prepared for us.

or

Let us pray
 [to the Lord who is a God of love to all peoples]

Father in heaven,
the perfection of justice is found in your love
and all mankind is in need of your law.

TWENTY-FIFTH SUNDAY IN ORDINARY TIME/B

Help us to find this love in each other
that justice may be attained
through obedience to your law.

First Reading   Wisdom 2:12.17-20.
Let us condemn him to a shameful death.

The godless say to themselves,
"Let us lie in wait for the virtuous man, since he annoys us
and opposes our way of life,
reproaches us for our breaches of the law
and accuses us of playing false to our upbringing.
Let us see if what he says is true,
let us observe what kind of end he himself will have.
If the virtuous man is God's son, God will take his part
and rescue him from the clutches of his enemies.
Let us test him with cruelty and with torture,
and thus explore this gentleness of his
and put his endurance to the proof.
Let us condemn him to a shameful death
since he will be looked after — we have his word for it."

Responsorial Psalm   Psalm 53.

℟ **The Lord upholds my life.**

1. O God, save me by your name;
   by your power, uphold my cause.
   O God, hear my prayer;
   listen to the words of my mouth. ℟

2. For proud men have risen against me,
   ruthless men seek my life.
   They have no regard for God. ℟

3. But I have God for my help.
   The Lord upholds my life.
   I will sacrifice to you with willing heart
   and praise your name for it is good. ℟

TWENTY-FIFTH SUNDAY IN ORDINARY TIME/B

Second Reading James 3:16 - 4:3.

Peacemakers, when they work for peace, sow the seeds which will bear fruit in holiness.

Wherever you find jealousy and ambition, you find disharmony, and wicked things of every kind being done; whereas the wisdom that comes down from above is essentially something pure; it also makes for peace, and is kindly and considerate; it is full of compassion and shows itself by doing good; nor is there any trace of partiality or hypocrisy in it. Peacemakers, when they work for peace, sow the seeds which will bear fruit in holiness.

Where do these wars and battles between yourselves first start? Isn't it precisely in the desires fighting inside your own selves? You want something and you haven't got it; so you are prepared to kill. You have an ambition that you cannot satisfy; so you fight to get your way by force. Why you don't have what you want is because you don't pray for it; when you do pray and don't get it, it is because you have not prayed properly, you have prayed for something to indulge your own desires.

Alleluia Alleluia, alleluia! I am the light of the world, says the Lord, anyone who follows me will have the light of life. Alleluia! John 8:12.

or

Alleluia, alleluia! Through the Good News God called us to share the glory of our Lord Jesus Christ. Alleluia! 2 Thessalonians 2:14.

Gospel Mark 9:30-37.

The Son of Man will be delivered. If anyone wants to be first, he must make himself servant of all.

After leaving the mountain Jesus and his disciples made their way through Galilee; and he did not want anyone to know, because he was instructing his disciples; he was telling them, "The Son of Man will be delivered into the hands of men; they will put him to death; and three days after he has been put to death he will rise again." But they did not understand what he said and were afraid to ask him.

They came to Capernaum, and when he was in the house he asked them, "What were you arguing about on the road?" They said nothing because they had been arguing which of them was

TWENTY-FIFTH SUNDAY IN ORDINARY TIME/B

the greatest. So he sat down, called the Twelve to him and said, "If anyone wants to be first, he must make himself last of all and servant of all." He then took a little child, set him in front of them, put his arms round him, and said to them, "Anyone who welcomes one of these little children in my name, welcomes me; and anyone who welcomes me welcomes not me but the one who sent me."

Prayer over the Gifts

Lord,
may these gifts which we now offer
to show our belief and our love
be pleasing to you.
May they become for us
the eucharist of Jesus Christ your Son,
who is Lord for ever and ever.

Preface of Sundays I-VIII, pages 562-565.

Communion Antiphon

You have laid down your precepts to be faithfully kept. May my footsteps be firm in keeping your commands. Psalm 118:4-5.

or

I am the Good Shepherd, says the Lord; I know my sheep, and mine know me. John 10:14.

Prayer after Communion

Lord,
help us with your kindness.
Make us strong through the eucharist.
May we put into action
the saving mystery we celebrate.

26th SUNDAY IN ORDINARY TIME/B

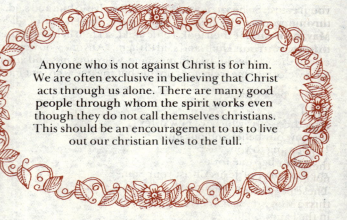

Anyone who is not against Christ is for him. We are often exclusive in believing that Christ acts through us alone. There are many good people through whom the spirit works even though they do not call themselves christians. This should be an encouragement to us to live out our christian lives to the full.

Entrance Antiphon O Lord, you had just cause to judge men as you did: because we sinned against you and disobeyed your will. But now show us your greatness of heart, and treat us with your unbounded kindness.

Daniel 3:31.29.30.43.42.

Opening Prayer

Let us pray
 [for God's forgiveness
 and for the happiness it brings]

Father,
you show your almighty power
in your mercy and forgiveness.
Continue to fill us with your gifts of love.
Help us to hurry toward the eternal life you promise
and come to share in the joys of your kingdom.

or

Let us pray
 [for the peace of the kingdom
 which we have been promised]

Father of our Lord Jesus Christ,
in your unbounded mercy

TWENTY-SIXTH SUNDAY IN ORDINARY TIME/B

you have revealed the beauty of your power
through your constant forgiveness of our sins.
May the power of this love be in our hearts
to bring your pardon and your kingdom to all we meet.

First Reading   Numbers 11:25-29.

Are you jealous on my account? If only the whole people of the Lord were prophets!

The Lord came down in the Cloud. He spoke with Moses, but took some of the spirit that was on him and put it on the seventy elders. When the spirit came on them they prophesied, but not again.

Two men had stayed back in the camp; one was called Eldad and the other Medad. The spirit came down on them; though they had not gone to the Tent, their names were enrolled among the rest. These began to prophesy in the camp. The young man ran to tell this to Moses, "Look," he said "Eldad and Medad are prophesying in the camp." Then said Joshua the son of Nun, who had served Moses from his youth, "My Lord Moses, stop them!" Moses answered him, "Are you jealous on my account? If only the whole people of the Lord were prophets, and the Lord gave his Spirit to them all!"

Responsorial Psalm   Psalm 18.

℟ **The precepts of the Lord gladden the heart.**

1. The law of the Lord is perfect,
   it revives the soul.
   The rule of the Lord is to be trusted,
   it gives wisdom to the simple. ℟

2. The fear of the Lord is holy,
   abiding for ever.
   The decrees of the Lord are truth
   and all of them just. ℟

3. So in them your servant finds instruction;
   great reward is in their keeping.
   But who can detect all his errors?
   From hidden faults acquit me. ℟

4. From presumption restrain your servant
   and let it not rule me.
   Then shall I be blameless,
   clean from grave sin. ℟

TWENTY-SIXTH SUNDAY IN ORDINARY TIME/B

Second Reading   James 5:1-6.
Your wealth is all rotting.

An answer for the rich. Start crying, weep for the miseries that are coming to you. Your wealth is all rotting, your clothes are all eaten up by moths. All your gold and your silver are corroding away, and the same corrosion will be your own sentence, and eat into your body. It was a burning fire that you stored up as your treasure for the last days. Labourers mowed your fields, and you cheated them — listen to the wages that you kept back, calling out; realise that the cries of the reapers have reached the ears of the Lord of hosts. On earth you have had a life of comfort and luxury; in the time of slaughter you went on eating to your heart's content. It was you who condemned the innocent and killed them; they offered you no resistance.

Alleluia   Alleluia, alleluia! Your word is truth, O Lord, consecrate us in the truth. Alleluia! John 17:17.
Alternative Alleluias, pages 1004-1006.

Gospel   Mark 9:38-43.45.47-48.
Anyone who is not against us is for us. If your hand should cause you to sin, cut it off.

John said to Jesus, "Master, we saw a man who is not one of us casting out devils in your name; and because he was not one of us we tried to stop him." But Jesus said, "You must not stop him: no one who works a miracle in my name is likely to speak evil of me. Anyone who is not against us is for us.

"If anyone gives you a cup of water to drink just because you belong to Christ, then I tell you solemnly, he will most certainly not lose his reward.

"But anyone who is an obstacle to bring down one of these little ones who have faith, would be better thrown into the sea with a great millstone round his neck. And if your hand should cause you to sin, cut it off; it is better for you to enter into life crippled, than to have two hands and go to hell, into the fire that cannot be put out. And if your foot should cause you to sin, cut it off; it is better for you to enter into life lame, than to have two feet and be thrown into hell. And if your eye should cause you to sin, tear it out; it is better for you to enter into the kingdom of God with one

TWENTY-SIXTH SUNDAY IN ORDINARY TIME/B

eye, than to have two eyes and be thrown into hell where their worm does not die nor their fire go out."

Prayer over the Gifts

God of mercy,
accept our offering
and make it a source of blessing for us.

Preface of Sundays I-VIII, pages 562-565.

Communion Antiphon

O Lord, remember the words you spoke to me, your servant, which made me live in hope and consoled me when I was downcast.
Psalm 118:49-50

or

This is how we know what love is: Christ gave up his life for us; and we too must give up our lives for our brothers. 1 John 3:16.

Prayer after Communion

Lord,
may this eucharist
in which we proclaim the death of Christ
bring us salvation
and make us one with him in glory,
for he is Lord for ever and ever.

27th SUNDAY IN ORDINARY TIME/B

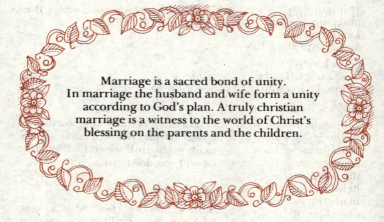

Marriage is a sacred bond of unity.
In marriage the husband and wife form a unity
according to God's plan. A truly christian
marriage is a witness to the world of Christ's
blessing on the parents and the children.

Entrance Antiphon

O Lord, you have given everything its place in the world, and no one can make it otherwise. For it is your creation, the heavens and the earth and the stars: you are the Lord of all. Esther 13:9.10-11.

Opening Prayer

Let us pray
  [that God will forgive our failings
  and bring us peace]

Father,
your love for us
surpasses all our hopes and desires.
Forgive our failings,
keep us in your peace
and lead us in the way of salvation.

or

Let us pray
  [before the face of God,
  in trusting faith]

Almighty and eternal God,
Father of the world to come,

TWENTY-SEVENTH SUNDAY IN ORDINARY TIME/B

your goodness is beyond what our spirit can touch
and your strength is more than the mind can bear.
Lead us to seek beyond our reach
and give us the courage to stand before your truth.

First Reading   Genesis 2:18-24.

They become one body.

The Lord God said, "It is not good that the man should be alone. I will make him a helpmate." So from the soil the Lord God fashioned all the wild beasts and all the birds of heaven. These he brought to the man to see what he would call them; each one was to bear the name the man would give it. The man gave names to all the cattle, all the birds of heaven and all the wild beasts. But no helpmate suitable for man was found for him. So the Lord God made the man fall into a deep sleep. And while he slept, he took one of his ribs and enclosed it in flesh. The Lord God built the rib he had taken from the man into a woman, and brought her to the man. The man exclaimed:
"This at last is bone from my bones,
and flesh from my flesh!
This is to be called woman,
for this was taken from man."
This is why a man leaves his father and mother and joins himself to his wife, and they become one body.

Responsorial Psalm   Psalm 127.

**R/ May the Lord bless us
all the days of our life.**

1. O blessed are those who fear the Lord
   and walk in his ways!
   By the labour of your hands you shall eat.
   You will be happy and prosper.   R/

2. Your wife will be like a fruitful vine
   in the heart of your house;
   your children like shoots of the olive,
   around your table.   R/

3. Indeed thus shall be blessed
   the man who fears the Lord.
   May the Lord bless you from Zion

TWENTY-SEVENTH SUNDAY IN ORDINARY TIME/B

in a happy Jerusalem
all the days of your life!
May you see your children's children.
On Israel, peace! ℟

Second Reading   Hebrews 2:9-11.

The one who sanctifies, and the ones who are sanctified, are of the same stock.

We see in Jesus one who was for a short while made lower than the angels and is now crowned with glory and splendour because he submitted to death; by God's grace he had to experience death for all mankind.

As it was his purpose to bring a great many of his sons into glory, it was appropriate that God, for whom everything exists and through whom everything exists, should make perfect, through suffering, the leader who would take them to their salvation. For the one who sanctifies, and the ones who are sanctified, are of the same stock; that is why he openly calls them brothers.

Alleluia

Alleluia, alleluia! Your word is truth, O Lord, consecrate us in the truth. Alleluia! John 17:17.

or

Alleluia, alleluia! As long as we love one another God will live in us and his love will be complete in us. Alleluia! 1 John 4:12

Gospel   Mark 10:2-16.

What God has united, man must not divide.

Some Pharisees approached Jesus and asked, "Is it against the law for a man to divorce his wife?" They were testing him. He answered them, "What did Moses command you?" "Moses allowed us" they said "to draw up a writ of dismissal and so to divorce." Then Jesus said to them, "It was because you were so unteachable that he wrote this commandment for you. But from the beginning of creation God made them male and female. This is why a man must leave father and mother, and the two become one body. They are no longer two, therefore, but one body. So then, what God has united, man must not divide." Back in the house the disciples questioned him again

TWENTY-SEVENTH SUNDAY IN ORDINARY TIME/B

about this, and he said to them, "The man who divorces his wife and marries another is guilty of adultery against her. And if a woman divorces her husband and marries another she is guilty of adultery too."

People were bringing little children to him, for him to touch them. The disciples turned them away, but when Jesus saw this he was indignant and said to them, "Let the little children come to me; do not stop them; for it is to such as these that the kingdom of God belongs. I tell you solemnly, anyone who does not welcome the kingdom of God like a little child will never enter it." Then he put his arms round them, laid his hands on them and gave them his blessing.

Prayer over the Gifts

Father,
receive these gifts
which our Lord Jesus Christ
has asked us to offer in his memory.
May our obedient service
bring us to the fullness of your redemption.

Preface of Sundays I-VIII, pages 562-565.

Communion Antiphon

The Lord is good to those who hope in him, to those who are searching for his love. Lamentations 3:25.

or

Because there is one bread, we, though many, are one body, for we all share in the one loaf and in the one cup. cf. 1 Corinthians 10:17

Prayer after Communion

Almighty God,
let the eucharist we share
fill us with your life.
May the love of Christ
which we celebrate here
touch our lives and lead us to you.

28th SUNDAY IN ORDINARY TIME/B

The poverty of riches.
Rich people are often too pre-occupied with
their worldly possessions to follow Christ.
He tells us that those with riches find it hard to
enter the kingdom of God but the most
important thing in the world is to be wise
through God's word and see wealth in its
proper perspective. We will then appreciate
the richness of poverty for Christ's sake.

Entrance Antiphon If you, O Lord, laid bare our guilt, who could endure it? But you are forgiving, God of Israel. Psalm 129:3-4.

Opening Prayer

Let us pray
   [that God will help us to love one another]

Lord,
our help and guide,
make your love the foundation of our lives.
May our love for you express itself
in our eagerness to do good for others.

or

Let us pray
   [in quiet for the grace of sincerity]

Father in heaven,
the hand of your loving kindness
powerfully yet gently guides all the moments of our day.

Go before us in our pilgrmage of life,
anticipate our needs and prevent our falling.
Send your Spirit to unite us in faith,
that sharing in your service,
we may rejoice in your presence.

TWENTY-EIGHTH SUNDAY IN ORDINARY TIME/B

First Reading   Wisdom 7:7-11.

Compared with wisdom, I held riches as nothing.

I prayed, and understanding was given me;
I entreated, and the spirit of Wisdom came to me.
I esteemed her more than sceptres and thrones;
compared with her, I held riches as nothing.
I reckoned no priceless stone to be her peer,
for compared with her, all gold is a pinch of sand,
and beside her silver ranks as mud.
I loved her more than health or beauty,
preferred her to the light,
since her radiance never sleeps.
In her company all good things came to me,
at her hands riches not to be numbered.

Responsorial Psalm   Psalm 89.

℟ **Fill us with your love that we may rejoice.**

1. Make us know the shortness of our life
   that we may gain wisdom of heart.
   Lord, relent! Is your anger for ever?
   Show pity to your servants.   ℟

2. In the morning, fill us with your love;
   we shall exult and rejoice all our days.
   Give us joy to balance our affliction
   for the years when we knew misfortune.   ℟

3. Show forth your work to your servants;
   let your glory shine on their children.
   Let the favour of the Lord be upon us:
   give success to the work of our hands.   ℟

Second Reading   Hebrews 4:12-13.

The word of God can judge secret emotions and thoughts.

The word of God is something alive and active: it cuts like any double-edged sword but more finely: it can slip through the place where the soul is divided from the spirit, or joints from the marrow; it can judge the secret emotions and thoughts. No created thing can hide from him; everything is uncovered and open to the eyes of the one to whom we must give account of ourselves.

TWENTY-EIGHTH SUNDAY IN ORDINARY TIME/B

Alleluia　Alleluia, alleluia! Blessed are you, Father, Lord of heaven and earth, for revealing the mysteries of the kingdom to mere children. Alleluia! Matthew 11:25.

or

Alleluia, alleluia! How happy are the poor in spirit; theirs is the kingdom of heaven. Alleluia!
Matthew 5:3.

Gospel　Mark 10:17-30.

Go and sell everything you own and follow me.

> Jesus was setting out on a journey when a man ran up, knelt before him and put this question to him, "Good master, what must I do to inherit eternal life?" Jesus said to him, "Why do you call me good? No one is good but God alone. You know the commandments: You must not kill; You must not commit adultery; You must not steal; You must not bring false witness; You must not defraud; Honour your father and mother." And he said to him, "Master, I have kept all these from my earliest days." Jesus looked steadily at him and loved him, and he said, "There is one thing you lack. Go and sell everything you own and give the money to the poor, and you will have treasure in heaven; then come, follow me." But his face fell at these words and he went away sad, for he was a man of great wealth.
>
> Jesus looked round and said to his disciples, "How hard it is for those who have riches to enter the kingdom of God!" The disciples were astounded by these words, but Jesus insisted, "My children," he said to them "how hard it is to enter the kingdom of God! It is easier for a camel to pass through the eye of a needle than for a rich man to enter the kingdom of God." They were more astonished than ever. "In that case" they said to one another "who can be saved?" Jesus gazed at them. "For men" he said "it is impossible, but not for God: because everything is possible for God."

Peter took this up. "What about us?" he asked him. "We have left *everything* and followed you." Jesus said, "I tell you solemnly, there is no one who has left house, brothers, sisters, father, children or land for my sake and for the sake of the gospel who will not be repaid a hundred times over, houses, brothers, sisters, mothers, children and land — not without persecutions — now in this present time and, in the world to come, eternal life."

TWENTY-EIGHTH SUNDAY IN ORDINARY TIME/B

Prayer over the Gifts

Lord,
accept the prayers and gifts
we offer in faith and love.
May this eucharist bring us to your glory.

Preface of Sundays I-VIII, pages 562-565

Communion Antiphon

The rich suffer want and go hungry, but nothing shall be lacking to those who fear the Lord. Psalm 33:11.

or

When the Lord is revealed we shall be like him, for we shall see him as he is.

1 John 3:2

Prayer after Communion

Almighty Father,
may the body and blood of your Son
give us a share in his life,
for he is Lord for ever and ever.

29th SUNDAY IN ORDINARY TIME/B

*Christ's death is our ransom.
God showed his love for us by sending his Son
to be our brother. Christ shows our love for
the Father by giving his life in atonement for
our sins. He is our high priest gone to the
highest heavens but not before experiencing
the depth of human suffering.*

Entrance Antiphon I call upon you, God, for you will answer me; bend your ear and hear my prayer. Guard me as the pupil of your eye; hide me in the shade of your wings. Psalm 16:6.8.

Opening Prayer

Let us pray
  [for the gift of simplicity and joy
  in our service of God and man]

Almighty and ever-living God,
our source of power and inspiration,
give us strength and joy
in serving you as followers of Christ,
who lives and reigns with you and the Holy Spirit,
one God, for ever and ever.

or

Let us pray
  [to the Lord who bends close to hear our prayer]

Lord our God, Father of all,
you guard us under the shadow of your wings
and search into the depths of our hearts.

TWENTY-NINTH SUNDAY IN ORDINARY TIME/B

Remove the blindness that cannot know you
and relieve the fear that would hide us from your sight.

First Reading   Isaiah 53:10-11.

If he offers his life in atonement, he shall see his heirs, he shall have a long life.

The Lord has been pleased to crush him with suffering.
If he offers his life in atonement,
he shall see his heirs, he shall have a long life
and through him what the Lord wishes will be done.
His soul's anguish over
he shall see the light and be content.
By his sufferings shall my servant justify many,
taking their faults on himself.

Responsorial Psalm   Psalm 32.

**R/ May your love be upon us, O Lord,
as we place all our hope in you.**

1. The word of the Lord is faithful
   and all his works to be trusted.
   The Lord loves justice and right
   and fills the earth with his love. R/

2. The Lord looks on those who revere him,
   on those who hope in his love,
   to rescue their souls from death,
   to keep them alive in famine. R/

3. Our soul is waiting for the Lord.
   The Lord is our help and our shield.
   May your love be upon us, O Lord,
   as we place all our hope in you. R/

Second Reading   Hebrews 4:14-16.

Let us be confident in approaching the throne of grace.

Since in Jesus, the Son of God, we have the supreme high priest who has gone through to the highest heaven, we must never let go of the faith that we have professed. For it is not as if we had a high priest who was incapable of feeling our weaknesses with us; but we have one who has been tempted in every way that we are, though he is without sin. Let us be confident, then, in aproaching the

TWENTY-NINTH SUNDAY IN ORDINARY TIME/B

throne of grace, that we shall have mercy from him and find grace when we are in need of help.

Alleluia Alleluia, alleluia! I am the Way, the Truth and the Life, says the Lord; no one can come to the Father except through me. Alleluia! John 14:5.

or Alleluia, alleluia! The Son of man came to serve, and to give his life as a ransom for many. Alleluia!
Mark 10:45.

Gospel Mark 10:35-45.
The Son of Man came to give his life as a ransom for many.

James and John, the sons of Zebedee, approached Jesus. "Master," they said to him "we want you to do us a favour." He said to them, "What is it you want me to do for you? They said to him, "Allow us to sit one at your right hand and the other at your left in your glory." "You do not know what you are asking" Jesus said to them. "Can you drink the cup that I must drink, or be baptised with the baptism with which I must be baptised?" They replied, "We can." Jesus said to them, "The cup that I must drink you shall drink, and with the baptism with which I must be baptised you shall be baptised, but as for seats at my right hand or my left, these are not mine to grant: they belong to those to whom they have been allotted."

When the other ten heard this they began to feel indignant with James and John, so
> Jesus called them to him and said to them, "You know that among the pagans their so-called rulers lord it over them, and their great men make their authority felt. This is not to happen among you. No; anyone who wants to become great among you must be your servant, and anyone who wants to be first among you must be slave to all. For the Son of Man himself did not come to be served but to serve, and to give his life as a ransom for many."

Prayer over the Gifts

Lord God,
may the gifts we offer
bring us your love and forgiveness
and give us freedom to serve you with our lives.

Preface of Sundays I-VIII, pages 562-565.

Communion Antiphon See how the eyes of the Lord are on those who fear him, on those who hope in his love; that he may rescue them from death and feed them in time of famine. Psalm 32:18-19.

or

The Son of Man came to give his life as a ransom for many. Mark 10:45.

Prayer after Communion

Lord,
may this eucharist help us to remain faithful.
May it teach us the way to eternal life.

30th SUNDAY IN ORDINARY TIME/B

Master let me see again.
God's gift of faith to us helps us to see the world with a new vision. Christ renews our faith so that we may see more clearly the world in which we live. We are God's children and share in Christ's priesthood and must never lose sight of this great privilege which has been given to us.

Entrance Antiphon Let hearts rejoice who search for the Lord. Seek the Lord and his strength, seek always the face of the Lord. Psalm 104:3-4.

THIRTIETH SUNDAY IN ORDINARY TIME/B

Opening Prayer

Let us pray
  [for the strength to do God's will]

Almighty and ever-living God,
strengthen our faith, hope, and love.
May we do with loving hearts
what you ask of us
and come to share the life you promise.

or

Let us pray
  [in humble hope for salvation]

Praised be you, God and Father of our Lord Jesus Christ.
There is no power for good
which does not come from your covenant,
and no promise to hope in
that your love has not offered.
Strengthen our faith to accept your covenant
and give us the love to carry out your command.

First Reading   Jeremiah 31:7-9.

I will comfort the blind and the lame as I lead them back.

The Lord says this:
Shout with joy for Jacob!
Hail the chief of nations!
Proclaim! Praise! Shout:
"The Lord has saved his people,
the remnant of Israel!"
See, I will bring them back
from the land of the North
and gather them from the far ends of earth;
all of them: the blind and the lame,
women with child, women in labour:
a great company returning here.
They had left in tears,
I will comfort them as I lead them back;
I will guide them to streams of water,
by a smooth path where they will not stumble.
For I am a father to Israel,
and Ephraim is my first-born son.

THIRTIETH SUNDAY IN ORDINARY TIME/B

Responsorial Psalm Psalm 125.

℟ **What marvels the Lord worked for us!**
 Indeed we were glad.

1. When the Lord delivered Zion from bondage,
   it seemed like a dream.
   Then was our mouth filled with laughter,
   on our lips there were songs. ℟

2. The heathens themselves said: "What marvels
   the Lord worked for them!"
   What marvels the Lord worked for us!
   Indeed we were glad. ℟

3. Deliver us, O Lord, from our bondage
   as streams in dry land.
   Those who are sowing in tears
   will sing when they reap. ℟

4. They go out, they go out, full of tears,
   carrying seed for the sowing:
   they come back, they come back, full of song,
   carrying their sheaves. ℟

Second Reading Hebrews 5:1-6.

You are a priest of the order of Melchizedek, and for ever.

Every high priest has been taken out of mankind and is appointed to act for men in their relations with God, to offer gifts and sacrifices for sins; and so he can sympathise with those who are ignorant or uncertain because he too lives in the limitations of weakness. That is why he has to make sin offerings for himself as well as for the people. No one takes this honour on himself, but each one is called by God, as Aaron was. Nor did Christ give himself the glory of becoming high priest, but he had it from the one who said to him: You are my son, today I have become your father, and in another text: You are a priest of the order of Melchizedek, and for ever.

Alleluia   Alleluia, alleluia! I am the light of the world, says the Lord, anyone who follows me will have the light of life. Alleluia! John 8:12.

THIRTIETH SUNDAY IN ORDINARY TIME/B

or

Alleluia, alleluia! Our Saviour Christ Jesus has abolished death, and he has proclaimed life through the Good News. Alleluia! 2 Timothy 1:10.

Gospel   Mark 10:46-52.

Master, let me see again.

As Jesus left Jericho with his disciples and a large crowd, Bartimaeus (that is, the son of Timaeus), a blind beggar, was sitting at the side of the road. When he heard that it was Jesus of Nazareth, he began to shout and to say, "Son of David, Jesus, have pity on me." And many of them scolded him and told him to keep quiet, but he only shouted all the louder, "Son of David, have pity on me." Jesus stopped and said, "Call him here." So they called the blind man. "Courage," they said "get up; he is calling you." So throwing off his cloak, he jumped up and went to Jesus. Then Jesus spoke, "What do you want me to do for you?" "Rabbuni," the blind man said to him "Master, let me see again." Jesus said to him, "Go; your faith has saved you." And immediately his sight returned and he followed him along the road.

Prayer over the Gifts

Lord God of power and might,
receive the gifts we offer
and let our service give you glory.

Preface of Sundays I-VIII, pages 562-565.

Communion Antiphon   We will rejoice at the victory of God and make our boast in his great name.
Psalm 19:6

or

Christ loved us and gave himself up for us as a fragrant offering to God.
Ephesians 5:2

Prayer after Communion

Lord,
bring to perfection within us
the communion we share in this sacrament.
May our celebration have an effect in our lives.

31st SUNDAY IN ORDINARY TIME/B

Love God and love your neighbour as yourself. Christ calls us to love God with all our hearts and our neighbour as ourselves. Love is of the essence of christian faith. This love demands nothing less than everything and that is why it is the greatest commandment of all.

Entrance Antiphon   Do not abandon me, Lord. My God, do not go away from me! Hurry to help me, Lord, my Saviour. Psalm 37:22-23.

Opening Prayer

Let us pray
 [that our lives will reflect our faith]

God of power and mercy,
only with your help
can we offer you fitting service and praise.
May we live the faith we profess
and trust your promise of eternal life.

or

Let us pray
 [in the presence of God, the source of every good]

Father in heaven, God of power and Lord of mercy,
from whose fullness we have received,
direct our steps in our everyday efforts.
May the changing moods of the human heart
and the limits which our failings impose on hope
never blind us to you, source of every good.

Faith gives us the promise of peace

THIRTY-FIRST SUNDAY IN ORDINARY TIME/B

and makes known the demands of love.
Remove the selfishness that blurs the vision of faith.

First Reading   Deuteronomy 6:2-6.

Listen, Israel: You shall love the Lord your God with all your heart.

Moses said to the people: "If you fear the Lord your God all the days of your life and if you keep all his laws and commandments which I lay on you, you will have a long life, you and your son and your grandson. Listen then, Israel, keep and observe what will make you prosper and give you great increase, as the Lord God of your fathers has promised you, giving you a land where milk and honey flow.

"Listen, Israel: The Lord our God is the one Lord. You shall love the Lord your God with all your heart, with all your soul, with all your strength. Let these words I urge on you today be written on your heart."

Responsorial Psalm   Psalm 17

℟ **I love you, Lord, my strength.**

1. I love you, Lord, my strength,
my rock, my fortress, my saviour.
My God is the rock where I take refuge;
my shield, my mighty help, my stronghold.
The Lord is worthy of all praise:
when I call I am saved from my foes. ℟

2. Long life to the Lord, my rock!
Praised be the God who saves me.
He has given great victories to his king
and shown his love for his anointed. ℟

Second Reading   Hebrews 7:23-28.

Because he remains for ever, Christ can never lose his priesthood.
There used to be a great number of priests under the former covenant, because death put an end to each one of them; but this one, Christ, because he remains for ever, can never lose his priesthood. It follows, then, that his power to save is utterly certain, since he is living for ever to intercede for all who come to God through him.

To suit us, the ideal priest would have to be holy, innocent and uncontaminated, beyond the influence of sinners, and raised up

THIRTY-FIRST SUNDAY IN ORDINARY TIME/B

above the heavens; one who would not need to offer sacrifices every day, as the other high priests do for their own sins and then for those of the people, because he has done this once and for all by offering himself. The Law appoints high priests who are men subject to weakness; but the promise on oath, which came after the Law, appointed the Son who is made perfect for ever.

Alleluia Alleluia, alleluia! Your words are spirit, Lord, and they are life: you have the message of eternal life. Alleluia! John 6:63. 68.

or Alleluia, alleluia! If anyone loves me he will keep my word, and my Father will love him, and we shall come to him. Alleluia! John 14:23.

Gospel Mark 12:28-34.

This is the first commandment. The second is like it.

One of the scribes came up and put a question to him, "Which is the first of all the commandments?" Jesus replied, "This is the first: Listen, Israel, the Lord our God is the one Lord, and you must love the Lord your God with all your heart, with all your soul, with all your mind and with all your strength. The second is this: You must love your neighbour as yourself. There is no commandment greater than these." The scribe said to him, "Well spoken, Master; what you have said is true: that he is one and there is no other. To love him with all your heart, with all your understanding and strength and to love your neighbour as yourself, this is far more important than any holocaust or sacrifice." Jesus, seeing how wisely he had spoken, said, "You are not far from the kingdom of God." And after that no one dared to question him any more.

Prayer over the Gifts

God of mercy,
may we offer a pure sacrifice
for the forgiveness of our sins.

Preface of Sundays I-VIII, pages 562-565.

Communion Antiphon Lord, you will show me the path of life and fill me with joy in your presence. Psalm 15:11.

THIRTY-SECOND SUNDAY IN ORDINARY TIME/B

or

As the living Father sent me, and I live because of the Father, so he who eats my flesh and drinks my blood will live because of me. John 6:58.

Prayer after Communion

Lord,
you give us new hope in this eucharist.
May the power of your love
continue its saving work among us
and bring us to the joy you promise.

32nd SUNDAY IN ORDINARY TIME/B

The widow's penny.
The widow's offering of a penny is made out of love and of the little on which she had to live. We must never be afraid to give generously to God who will always provide for the future. All our gifts must be given lovingly and generously.

Entrance Antiphon

Let my prayer come before you, Lord; listen, and answer me. Psalm 87:3.

Opening Prayer

Let us pray
 [for health of mind and body]
God of power and mercy,

THIRTY-SECOND SUNDAY IN ORDINARY TIME/B

protect us from all harm.
Give us freedom of spirit
and health in mind and body
to do your work on earth.

or

Let us pray
  [that our prayer rise like incense
  in the presence of the Lord]

Almighty Father,
strong is your justice and great is your mercy.
Protect us in the burdens and challenges of life.
Shield our minds from the distortion of pride
and enfold our desire with the beauty of truth.

Help us to become more aware of your loving design
so that we may more willingly give our lives in service to all.

First Reading   1 Kings 17:10-16.

The widow made a little scone from her meal and brought it to Elijah.

Elijah the prophet went off to Sidon. And when he reached the city gate, there was a widow gathering sticks; addressing her he said, "Please bring a little water in a vessel for me to drink." She was setting off to bring it when he called after her. "Please" he said "bring me a scrap of bread in your hand." "As the Lord your God lives," she replied "I have no baked bread, but only a handful of meal in a jar and little oil in a jug; I am just gathering a stick or two to go and prepare this for myself and my son to eat, and then we shall die." But Elijah said to her, "Do not be afraid, go and do as you have said; but first make a little scone of it for me and bring it to me, and then make some for yourself and for your son. For thus the Lord speaks, the God of Israel:

'Jar of meal shall not be spent,
jug of oil shall not be emptied,
before the day when the Lord sends
rain on the face of the earth.' "

The woman went and did as Elijah told her and they ate the food, she, himself and her son. The jar of meal was not spent nor the jug of oil emptied, just as the Lord had foretold through Elijah.

THIRTY-SECOND SUNDAY IN ORDINARY TIME/B

Responsorial Psalm   Psalm 145.

℟ **My soul, give praise to the Lord.**

or ℟ **Alleluia!**

1. It is the Lord who keeps faith for ever,
   who is just to those who are oppressed.
   It is he who gives bread to the hungry,
   the Lord, who sets prisoners free. ℟

2. It is the Lord who gives sight to the blind,
   who raises up those who are bowed down.
   It is the Lord who loves the just,
   the Lord, who protects the stranger. ℟

3. He upholds the widow and orphan
   but thwarts the path of the wicked.
   The Lord will reign for ever,
   Zion's God, from age to age. ℟

Second Reading   Hebrews 9:24-28.

Christ offers himself only once to take the faults of many on himself.

It is not as though Christ had entered a man-made sanctuary which was only modelled on the real one; but it was heaven itself, so that he could appear in the actual presence of God on our behalf. And he does not have to offer himself again and again, like the high priest going into the sanctuary year after year with the blood that is not his own, or else he would have had to suffer over and over again since the world began. Instead of that, he has made his appearance once and for all, now at the end of the last age, to do away with sin by sacrificing himself. Since men only die once, and after that comes judgement, so Christ, too, offers himself only once to take the faults of many on himself, and when he appears a second time, it will not be to deal with sin but to reward with salvation those who are waiting for him.

Alleluia   Alleluia, alleluia! Even if you have to die, says the Lord, keep faithful, and I will give you the crown of life. Alleluia! **Revelation 2:10.**

or

Alleluia, alleluia! How happy are the poor in spirit; theirs is the kingdom of heaven. Alleluia!

Matthew 5:3.

THIRTY-SECOND SUNDAY IN ORDINARY TIME/B

Gospel Mark 12:38-44.

This poor widow has put in more than all.

In his teaching Jesus said, "Beware of the scribes who like to walk about in long robes, to be greeted obsequiously in the market squares, to take the front seats in the synagogues and the places of honour at banquets; these are the men who swallow the property of widows, while making a show of lengthy prayers. The more severe will be the sentence they receive."

> He (Jesus) sat down opposite the treasury and watched the people putting money into the treasury, and many of the rich put in a great deal. A poor widow came and put in two small coins, the equivalent of a penny. Then he called his disciples and said to them, "I tell you solemnly, this poor widow has put more in than all who have contributed to the treasury; for they have all put in money they had over, but she from the little she had has put in everything she possessed, all she had to live on."

Prayer over the Gifts

God of mercy,
in this eucharist we proclaim the death of the Lord.
Accept the gifts we present
and help us follow him with love,
for he is Lord for ever and ever.

Preface of Sundays I-VIII, pages 562-565.

Communion Antiphon The Lord is my shepherd; there is nothing I shall want. In green pastures he gives me rest, he leads me beside the waters of peace.

Psalm 22:1-2

or The disciples recognized the Lord Jesus in the breaking of the bread.

Luke 24:35.

Prayer after Communion

Lord,
we thank you for the nourishment you give us
through your holy gift.
Pour out your Spirit upon us
and in the strength of this food from heaven
keep us single-minded in your service.

33rd SUNDAY IN ORDINARY TIME/B

The Son of man is coming
in power and glory.
Christ has died once and for all.
We await the second coming when he will
gather together his chosen ones from the
four corners of the earth. On that day we
will understand God's plan for our
salvation and we will praise him for
his compassion and mercy to us.

Entrance Antiphon   The Lord says: my plans for you are peace and not disaster; when you call to me, I will listen to you, and I will bring you back to the place from which I exiled you.

Jeremiah 29:11.12.14.

Opening Prayer
Let us pray
  [that God will help us to be faithful]

Father of all that is good,
keep us faithful in serving you,
for to serve you is our lasting joy.

or

Let us pray
  [with hearts that long for peace].

Father in heaven,
ever-living source of all that is good,
from the beginning of time you promised man salvation
through the future coming of your Son, our Lord Jesus Christ.

Help us to drink of his truth
and expand our hearts with the joy of his promises,
so that we may serve you in faith and in love
and know for ever the joy of your presence.

THIRTY-THIRD SUNDAY IN ORDINARY TIME/B

First Reading   Daniel 12:1-13.

When that time comes, your own people will be spared.

"At that time Michael will stand up, the great prince who mounts guard over your people. There is going to be a time of great distress, unparalleled since nations first came into existence. When that time comes, your own people will be spared, all those whose names are found written in the Book. Of those who lie sleeping in the dust of the earth many will awake, some to everlasting life, some to shame and everlasting disgrace. The learned will shine as brightly as the vault of heaven, and those who have instructed many in virtue, as bright as stars for all eternity."

Responsorial Psalm   Psalm 15

℟ **Preserve me, God, I take refuge in you.**

1. O Lord, it is you who are my portion and cup;
   it is you yourself who are my prize.
   I keep the Lord ever in my sight:
   since he is at my right hand, I shall stand firm. ℟

2. And so my heart rejoices, my soul is glad;
   even my body shall rest in safety.
   For you will not leave my soul among the dead,
   nor let your beloved know decay. ℟

3. You will show me the path of life,
   the fullness of joy in your presence,
   at your right hand happiness for ever. ℟

Second Reading   Hebrews 10:11-14. 18

By virtue of one single offering, he has achieved the eternal perfection of all whom he is sanctifying.

All the priests stand at their duties every day, offering over and over again the same sacrifices which are quite incapable of taking sins away. Christ, on the other hand, has offered one single sacrifice for sins, and then taken his place for ever, at the right hand of God, where he is now waiting until his enemies are made into a footstool for him. By virtue of that one single offering, he has achieved the eternal perfection of all whom he is sanctifying. When all sins have been forgiven, there can be no more sin offerings.

THIRTY-THIRD SUNDAY IN ORDINARY TIME/B

Alleluia   Alleluia, alleluia! Stay awake and stand ready, because you do not know the hour when the Son of Man is coming. Alleluia! Luke 21:36.

or   Alleluia, alleluia! Stay awake, praying at all times for the strength to stand with confidence before the Son of Man. Alleluia! Luke 21:36.

Gospel   Mark 13:24-32.

He will gather his chosen from the four winds.

Jesus said to his disciples: "In those days, after the time of distress, the sun will be darkened, the moon will lose its brightness, the stars will come falling from heaven and the powers in the heavens will be shaken. And then they will see the Son of Man coming in the clouds with great power and glory; then too he will send the angels to gather his chosen from the four winds, from the ends of the world to the ends of heaven.

"Take the fig tree as a parable: as soon as its twigs grow supple and its leaves come out, you know that summer is near. So with you when you see these things happening: know that he is near, at the very gates. I tell you solemnly, before this generation has passed away all these things will have taken place. Heaven and earth will pass away, but my words will not pass away.

"But as for that day or hour, nobody knows it, neither the angels of heaven, nor the Son; no one but the Father."

Prayer over the Gifts

Lord God,
may the gifts we offer
increase our love for you
and bring us to eternal life.

Preface of Sundays I-VIII, pages 562-565.

Communion Antiphon   It is good for me to be with the Lord and to put my hope in him.
Psalm 72:28.

or

I tell you solemnly, whatever you ask for in prayer, believe that you have received it, and it will be yours, says the Lord. Mark 11:23.24.

Prayer after Communion

Father,
may we grow in love
by the eucharist we have celebrated
in memory of the Lord Jesus,
who is Lord for ever and ever.

LAST SUNDAY IN ORDINARY TIME
OUR LORD JESUS CHRIST, UNIVERSAL KING/B

> Christ's kingdom is not of this world.
> It is difficult for us to understand the
> manner in which Christ is a king.
> His sovereignty will never pass away nor
> will his empire ever be destroyed, since his
> power comes from God and not from men.
> He has made us a line of kings to serve God
> until the end of time.

Entrance Antiphon The Lamb who was slain is worthy to receive strength and divinity, wisdom and power and honour: to him be glory and power for ever. Revelation 5:12; 1:6.

Opening Prayer

Let us pray
  [that all men will acclaim Jesus as Lord]

Almighty and merciful God,
you break the power of evil
and make all things new

OUR LORD JESUS CHRIST, UNIVERSAL KING/B

in your Son Jesus Christ, the King of the universe.
May all in heaven and earth acclaim your glory
and never cease to praise you.

or

Let us pray
   [that the kingdom of Christ
   may live in our hearts and come to our world]

Father all-powerful, God of love,
you have raised our Lord Jesus Christ from death to life,
resplendent in glory as King of creation.
Open our hearts,
free all the world to rejoice in his peace,
to glory in his justice, to live in his love.
Bring all mankind together in Jesus Christ your Son,
whose kingdom is with you and the Holy Spirit,
one God, for ever and ever.

First Reading   Daniel 7:13-14.

His sovereignty is an eternal sovereignty.

I gazed into the visions of the night.
And I saw, coming on the clouds of heaven,
one like a son of man.
He came to the one of great age
and was led into his presence.
On him was conferred sovereignty,
glory and kingship,
and men of all peoples, nations and languages became his
   servants.
His sovereignty is an eternal sovereignty
which shall never pass away,
nor will his empire ever be destroyed.

Responsorial Psalm   Psalm 92

℟ **The Lord is king, with majesty enrobed.**

1. The Lord is king, with majesty enrobed;
   the Lord has robed himself with might,
   he has girded himself with power.   ℟

OUR LORD JESUS CHRIST, UNIVERSAL KING/B

2. The world you made firm, not to be moved;
   your throne has stood firm from of old.
   From all eternity, O Lord, you are. ℟

3. Truly your decrees are to be trusted.
   Holiness is fitting to your house,
   O Lord, until the end of time. ℟

Second Reading   Apocalypse 1:5-8.

Ruler of the kings of the earth ... he made us a line of kings, priests to serve his God.

Jesus Christ is the faithful witness, the First-born from the dead, the Ruler of the kings of the earth. He loves us and has washed away our sins with his blood, and made us a line of kings, priests to serve his God and Father; to him, then, be glory and power for ever and ever. Amen. It is he who is coming on the clouds; everyone will see him, even those who pierced him, and all the races of the earth will mourn over him. This is the truth. Amen. "I am the Alpha and the Omega" says the Lord God, who is, who was, and who is to come, the Almighty.

Alleluia   Alleluia, alleluia! Blessings on him who comes in the name of the Lord! Blessings on the coming kingdom of our father David! Alleluia!   Mark 11:9,10.

Gospel   John 18:33-37.

It is you who say that I am a king.

"Are you the king of the Jews?" Pilate asked. Jesus replied, "Do you ask this of your own accord, or have others spoken to you about me?" Pilate answered, "Am I a Jew? It is your own people and the chief priests who have handed you over to me: what have you done?" Jesus replied, "Mine is not a kingdom of this world; if my kingdom were of this world, my men would have fought to prevent my being surrendered to the Jews. But my kingdom is not of this kind." "So you are a king then?" said Pilate. "It is you who say it" answered Jesus. "Yes, I am a king. I was born for this, I came into the world for this: to bear witness to the truth; and all who are on the side of truth listen to my voice."

OUR LORD JESUS CHRIST, UNIVERSAL KING/B

Prayer over the Gifts

Lord,
we offer you the sacrifice
by which your Son reconciles mankind.
May it bring unity and peace to the world.

Preface

Father, all-powerful and ever-living God,
we do well always and everywhere to give you thanks.

You anointed Jesus Christ, your only Son, with the oil of gladness,
as the eternal priest and universal king.

As priest he offered his life on the altar of the cross
and redeemed the human race
by this one perfect sacrifice of peace.

As king he claims dominion over all creation,
that he may present to you, his almighty Father,
an eternal and universal kingdom:
a kingdom of truth and life,
a kingdom of holiness and grace,
a kingdom of justice, love, and peace.

And so, with all the choirs of angels in heaven
we proclaim your glory
and join in their unending hymn of praise:

Holy, holy, holy ...

Communion Antiphon

The Lord will reign for ever and will give his people the gift of peace.

Psalm 28:10-11.

Prayer after Communion

Lord,
you give us Christ, the King of all creation.
as food for everlasting life.
Help us to live by his gospel
and bring us to the joy of his kingdom,
where he lives and reigns for ever and ever.

Sundays in Ordinary Time/C

Year C: The Year of Luke

THE whole emphasis in Luke's Gospel is to remind us that *Jesus Christ is the Saviour of the World.* Luke's version of the teaching of Jesus is of a Gospel destined for everyone no matter how poor, underprivileged or ill-equipped they might be. Jesus fulfils the words of the prophet Isaiah;

> The spirit of the Lord has been given to me,
> for he has anointed me.
> He has sent me to bring the good news to the poor,
> to proclaim liberty to captives
> and to the blind new sight,
> to set the downtrodden free,
> to proclaim the Lord's year of favour.
>
> Luke 4:18-19.

Luke is often given the title 'scribe of the gentleness of Christ' in so far as his portrait of Jesus is of an immensely compassionate and caring person. He balances this image with an insight into the character of Jesus whose mission is urgent and whose time is short. He expresses this in the total demand which Jesus makes of those who follow him. Luke offers us a catechism of discipleship with all its privileges and hardships. These are two sides of the same coin — compassion and discipline.

After the infancy narrative, Luke's description of the Galilean ministry is basically the same as that of Matthew and Mark. The whole of the central section describes the journey of Jesus to Jerusalem, to death and resurrection. In this 'Travel narrative' we find the episodes and parables, the controversies and miracles of which Luke tells us and nobody else. Luke's vision of the journey is neither geographical nor chronological since his main intention is that the journey of Jesus Christ should be seen as a journey for the Church and for the individual christian. Luke's Gospel is very much suited to express the mood of the Second Vatican Council which saw us all as members of a 'Pilgrim Church'. The special emphasis of his theology is to be found above all in 'the journey' and 19 of the 33 passages used in Year C come from this section. We are reminded that the journey to Jerusalem is the way to glorification and suffering, but Jesus is

YEAR C: YEAR OF LUKE

not alone. His disciples accompany him on the journey, and are drawn by him into a community.

Stage Four of Luke's Gospel is an instruction on the positive qualities required of the followers of Jesus Christ — dedication, charity, the spirit of prayer together with vigilance and humility. Stage Five, which is the 'Gospel within the Gospel' gives us the three parables of God's fatherhood and mercy which is the Gospel of reconciliation. Stage Six continues the theme of discipleship and lays emphasis on the temptations, difficulties and obstacles confronting the followers of Jesus.

Luke's character comes out clearly in his writings when we remember that he wrote the Acts of the Apostles as well as his Gospel. He came from a background and environment very different from the Judaism out of which christianity grew. This more than anything else makes his Gospel more accessible and relevant to us. Luke's thinking is very close to our own.

STAGE ONE:
THE FIGURE OF JESUS THE MESSIAH — SUNDAYS 1-2
1. The baptism of Jesus — Luke 3:15-16.21-22
2. The marriage feast at Cana — John 2:1-12

STAGE TWO:
LUKE'S PROGRAMME FOR JESUS' MINISTRY — SUNDAYS 3-4
3. The visit to Nazareth (1) — Luke 1:1-4,4:14-21
4. The visit to Nazareth (1) — 4:21-30

STAGE THREE:
THE GALILEAN MINISTRY — SUNDAYS 5-12
5. The call of the first Apostles* — Luke 5:1-11
6. The sermon on the plain (1) — 6:17,20-26
7. The sermon on the plain (2) — 6:27-38
8. The sermon on the plain (3) — 6:29-45
9. The cure of the centurion's servant — 7:1-10
10. The widow of Naim* — 7:11-17
11. Jesus' feet anointed: the sinful woman* — 7:36-8:3
12. Peter's confession of faith — 9:18-24

2nd SUNDAY IN ORDINARY TIME/C

> Christ is the bridegroom of the Church. Just as the bridegroom rejoices in his bride so Christ rejoices in his Church. Each day in the eucharist by the power of his Spirit he transforms bread and wine into his body and blood to be our daily food and drink. The Holy Spirit gives us a variety of gifts which we are to use for the mission of the Church.

Entrance Antiphon May all the earth give you worship and praise, and break into song to your name, O God, Most High. Psalm 65:4.

Opening Prayer

Let us pray
 [to our Father for the gift of peace]

Father of heaven and earth,
hear our prayers,
and show us the way to peace in the world.

or

Let us pray
 [for the gift of peace]

Almighty and ever-present Father,
your watchful care reaches from end to end
and orders all things in such power
that even the tensions and the tragedies of sin
cannot frustrate your loving plans.

Help us to embrace your will,
give us the strength to follow your call,
so that your truth may live in our hearts
and reflect peace to those who believe in your love.

SECOND SUNDAY IN ORDINARY TIME/C

First Reading   Isaiah 62:1-5.
The bridegroom rejoices in his bride.

About Zion I will not be silent,
about Jerusalem I will not grow weary,
until her integrity shines out like the dawn
and her salvation flames like a torch.

The nations then will see your integrity,
all the kings your glory,
and you will be called by a new name,
one which the mouth of the Lord will confer.
You are to be a crown of splendour in the hand of the Lord,
a princely diadem in the hand of your God;
no longer are you to be named "Forsaken",
nor your land "Abandoned",
but you shall be called "My Delight"
and your land "The Wedded";
for the Lord takes delight in you
and your land will have its wedding.
Like a young man marrying a virgin,
so will the one who built you wed you,
and as the bridegroom rejoices in his bride,
so will your God rejoice in you.

Responsorial Psalm   Psalm 95.

R/ **Proclaim the wonders of the Lord
among all the peoples.**

1. O sing a new song to the Lord,
   sing to the Lord all the earth.
   O sing to the Lord, bless his name.   R/

2. Proclaim his help day by day,
   tell among the nations his glory
   and his wonders among all the peoples.   R/

3. Give the Lord, you families of peoples,
   give the Lord glory and power,
   give the Lord the glory of his name.   R/

4. Worship the Lord in his temple.
   O earth, tremble before him.
   Proclaim to the nations: "God is king."
   He will judge the peoples in fairness.   R/

SECOND SUNDAY IN ORDINARY TIME/C

Second Reading 1 Corinthians 12:4-11.

One and the same Spirit, who distributes gifts to different people just as he chooses.

There is a variety of gifts but always the same Spirit; there are all sorts of service to be done, but always to the same Lord; working in all sorts of different ways in different people, it is the same God who is working in all of them. The particular way in which the Spirit is given to each person is for a good purpose. One may have the gift of preaching with wisdom given him by the Spirit; another may have the gift of preaching instruction given him by the same Spirit; and another the gift of faith given by the same Spirit; another again the gift of healing, through this one Spirit; one, the power of miracles; another, prophecy; another the gift of recognising spirits; another the gift of tongues and another the ability to interpret them. All these are the work of one and the same Spirit, who distributes different gifts to different people just as he chooses.

Alleluia   Alleluia, alleluia! Your words are spirit, Lord, and they are life: you have the message of eternal life. Alleluia! John 6:63.68.

or

Alleluia, alleluia! Through the Good News God called us to share the glory of our Lord Jesus Christ. Alleluia!
2 Thessalonians 2:14.

Gospel John 2:1-11.

This was the first of the signs given by Jesus: it was given at Cana in Galilee.

There was a wedding at Cana in Galilee. The mother of Jesus was there, and Jesus and his disciples had also been invited. When they ran out of wine, since the wine provided for the wedding was all finished, the mother of Jesus said to him, "They have no wine." Jesus said, "Woman, why turn to me? My hour has not come yet." His mother said to the servants, "Do whatever he tells you." There were six stone water jars standing there, meant for the ablutions that are customary among the Jews: each could hold twenty or thirty gallons. Jesus said to the servants, "Fill the jars with water," and they filled them to the brim. "Draw some out now" he told them "and take it to the steward." They did this; the steward tasted

SECOND SUNDAY IN ORDINARY TIME/C

the water, and it had turned into wine. Having no idea where it came from — only the servants who had drawn the water knew — the steward called the bridegroom and said, "People generally serve the best wine first, and keep the cheaper sort till the guests have had plenty to drink; but you have kept the best wine till now."

This was the first of the signs given by Jesus: it was given at Cana in Galilee. He let his glory be seen, and his disciples believed in him.

Prayer over the Gifts

Father,
may we celebrate the eucharist
with reverence and love,
for when we proclaim the death of the Lord
you continue the work of his redemption,
who is Lord for ever and ever.

Preface of Sundays I-VIII, pages 562-565.

Communion Antiphon

The Lord has prepared a feast for me: given wine in plenty for me to drink. Psalm 22:5

or

We know and believe in God's love for us. 1 John 4:16.

Prayer after Communion

Lord,
you have nourished us with bread from heaven.
Fill us with your Spirit,
and make us one in peace and love.

3rd SUNDAY IN ORDINARY TIME/C

> You together are Christ's body.
> We all belong to the Church of which the head
> is Christ. Just as the human body is made up of
> many parts all of which are interdependent, so
> we too are dependent on each other and
> ultimately on Christ. The Holy Spirit is given
> to us so that we may bring the Good News to
> the poor. In our lives we witness to the
> fulfilling of God's promises in the
> Holy Scripture.

Entrance Antiphon Sing a new song to the Lord! Sing to the Lord, all the earth. Truth and beauty surround him, he lives in holiness and glory. Psalm 95:1.6.

Opening Prayer

Let us pray
   [for unity and peace]

All-powerful and ever-living God,
direct your love that is within us,
that our efforts in the name of your Son
may bring mankind to unity and peace.

or

Let us pray
   [pleading that our vision
   may overcome our weakness]

Almighty Father,
the love you offer
always exceeds the furthest expression of our human longing,
for you are greater than the human heart.

Direct each thought, each effort of our life,
so that the limits of our faults and weaknesses

THIRD SUNDAY IN ORDINARY TIME/C

may not obscure the vision of your glory
or keep us from the peace you have promised.

First Reading   Nehemiah 8:2-6.8-10.

Ezra read from the law of God and the people understood what was read.

Ezra the priest brought the Law before the assembly, consisting of men, women, and children old enough to understand. This was the first day of the seventh month. On the square before the Water Gate, in the presence of the men and women, and children old enough to understand, he read from the book from early morning till noon; all the people listened attentively to the Book of the Law.

Ezra the scribe stood on a wooden dais erected for the purpose. In full view of all the people — since he stood higher than all the people — Ezra opened the book; and when he opened it all the people stood up. Then Ezra blessed the Lord, the great God, and all the people raised their hands and answered, "Amen! Amen!"; then they bowed down and, face to the ground, prostrated themselves before the Lord. And Ezra read from the Law of God, translating and giving the sense, so that the people understood what was read.

Then (Nehemiah — His Excellency — and) Ezra, priest and scribe (and the Levites who were instructing the people) said to all the people, "This day is sacred to the Lord your God. Do not be mournful, do not weep." For the people were all in tears as they listened to the words of the Law.

He then said, "Go, eat the fat, drink the sweet wine, and send a portion to the man who has nothing prepared ready. For this day is sacred to our Lord. Do not be sad: the joy of the Lord is your stronghold."

Responsional Psalm   Psalm 18.

℟ **Your words are spirit, Lord,
  and they are life.**

1. The law of the Lord is perfect,
   it revives the soul.
   The rule of the Lord is to be trusted,
   it gives wisdom to the simple. ℟

THIRD SUNDAY IN ORDINARY TIME/C

2. The precepts of the Lord are right,
   they gladden the heart.
   The command of the Lord is clear,
   it gives light to the eyes. ℟

3. The fear of the Lord is holy,
   abiding for ever.
   The decrees of the Lord are truth
   and all of them just. ℟

4. May the spoken words of my mouth,
   the thoughts of my heart,
   win favour in your sight, O Lord,
   my rescuer, my rock! ℟

Second Reading 1 Corinthians 12:12-30.

You together are Christ's body; but each of you is a different part of it.

Just as a human body, though it is made up of many parts, is a single unit because all these parts, though many, make one body, so it is with Christ. In the one Spirit we were all baptised, Jews as well as Greeks, slaves as well as citizens, and one Spirit was given to us all to drink.

Nor is the body to be identified with any one of its many parts. If the foot were to say, "I am not a hand and so I do not belong to the body", would that mean that it stopped being part of the body? If the ear were to say, "I am not an eye, and so I do not belong to the body," would that mean it was not part of the body? If your whole body was just one eye, how would you hear anything? If it was just one ear, how would you smell anything?

Instead of that, God put all the separate parts into the body on purpose. If all the parts were the same, how could it be a body? As it is, the parts are many but the body is one. The eye cannot say to the hand, "I do not need you," nor can the head say to the feet, "I do not need you."

What is more, it is precisely the parts of the body that seem to be the weakest which are the indispensable ones; and it is the least honourable parts of the body that we clothe with the greatest care. So our more improper parts get decorated in a way that our more proper parts do not need. God has arranged the body so that more dignity is given to the parts which are without it, and so that there may not be disagreements inside the body, but that each part may

THIRD SUNDAY IN ORDINARY TIME/C

be equally concerned for all the others. If one part is hurt, all parts are hurt with it. If one part is given special honour, all parts enjoy it.

Now you together are Christ's body; but each of you is a different part of it.

In the Church, God has given the first place to apostles, the second to prophets, the third to teachers; after them, miracles, and after them the gift of healing; helpers, good leaders, those with many languages. Are all of them apostles, or all of them prophets, or all of them teachers? Do they all have the gift of miracles, or all have the gift of healing? Do all speak strange languages, and all interpret them?

Alleluia   Alleluia, alleluia! The Lord has sent me to bring the Good News to the poor, to proclaim liberty to the captives. Alleluia! Luke 4:18-19.

Gospel   Luke 1:1-4;4:14-21.
This text is being fulfilled today.

Seeing that many others have undertaken to draw up accounts of the events that have taken place among us, exactly as these were handed down to us by those who from the outset were eye-witnesses and ministers of the word, I in my turn, after carefully going over the whole story from the beginning, have decided to write an ordered account for you, Theophilus, so that your Excellency may learn how well founded the teaching is that you have received.

Jesus, with the power of the Spirit in him, returned to Galilee; and his reputation spread throughout the countryside. He taught in their synagogues and everyone praised him.

He came to Nazara, where he had been brought up, and went into the synagogue on the sabbath day as he usually did. He stood up to read, and they handed him the scroll of the prophet Isaiah. Unrolling the scroll he found the place where it is written:
The spirit of the Lord has been given to me,
for he has anointed me.
He has sent me to bring the good news to the poor,
to proclaim liberty to captives
and to the blind new sight,
to set the downtrodden free,
to proclaim the Lord's year of favour.

THIRD SUNDAY IN ORDINARY TIME/C

He then rolled up the scroll, gave it back to the assistant and sat down. And all eyes in the synagogue were fixed on him. Then he began to speak to them, "This text is being fulfilled today even as you listen."

Prayer over the Gifts
Lord,
receive our gifts.
Let our offerings make us holy
and bring us salvation.

Preface of Sundays I-VIII, pages 562-565.

Communion Antiphon
Look up at the Lord with gladness and smile; your face will never be ashamed. Psalm 33:6.

or

I am the light of the world, says the Lord; the man who follows me will have the light of life. John 8:12.

Prayer after Communion
God, all-powerful Father,
may the new life you give us increase our love
and keep us in the joy of your kingdom.

4th SUNDAY IN ORDINARY TIME/C

The greatest gift is love. We are a people not only of faith and hope but especially of love. Love is the greatest gift which the spirit of Christ gives to the members of his Church. This gift is also given to those outside the Church and for this we should thank God. Love breaks down human barriers and divisions. Love will bring about christian unity and greater christian witness if we are open to the spirit.

Entrance Antiphon Save us, Lord our God, and gather us together from the nations, that we may proclaim your holy name and glory in your praise. Psalm 105:47.

Opening Prayer

Let us pray
  [for a greater love of God
  and of our fellow men]

Lord our God,
help us to love you with all our hearts
and to love all men as you love them.

or

Let us pray
  [joining in the praise of the living God
  for we are his people]

Father in heaven,
from the days of Abraham and Moses
until this gathering of your Church in prayer,
you have formed a people in the image of your Son.

Bless this people with the gift of your kingdom.
May we serve you with our every desire

FOURTH SUNDAY IN ORDINARY TIME/C

and show love for one another
even as you have loved us.

First Reading   Jeremiah 1:4-5.17-19.
I have appointed you as prophet to the nations.

The word of the Lord was addressed to me, saying,
"Before I formed you in the womb I knew you;
before you came to birth I consecrated you;
I have appointed you as prophet to the nations.
So now brace yourself for action.
Stand up and tell them
all I command you.
Do not be dismayed at their presence,
or in their presence I will make you dismayed.
I, for my part, today will make you
into a fortified city,
a pillar of iron,
and a wall of bronze
to confront all this land:
the kings of Judah, its princes,
its priests and the country people.
They will fight against you
but shall not overcome you,
for I am with you to deliver you —
it is the Lord who speaks."

Responsorial Psalm   Psalm 70.

R/ **My lips will tell of your help.**

1. In you, O Lord, I take refuge;
   let me never be put to shame.
   In your justice rescue me, free me:
   pay heed to me and save me.   R/

2. Be a rock where I can take refuge,
   a mighty stronghold to save me;
   for you are my rock, my stronghold.
   Free me from the hand of the wicked.   R/

3. It is you, O Lord, who are my hope,
   my trust, O Lord, since my youth.
   On you I have leaned from my birth,
   from my mother's womb you have been my help.   R/

FOURTH SUNDAY IN ORDINARY TIME/C

4. My lips will tell of your justice
   and day by day of your help.
   O God, you have taught me from my youth
   and I proclaim your wonders still. ℟

Second Reading   1 Corinthians 12:31 - 13:13.

There are three things that last: faith, hope and love; and the greatest of these is love.

Be ambitious for the higher gifts. And I am going to show you a way that is better than any of them.

If I have all the eloquence of men or of angels, but speak without love, I am simply a gong booming or a cymbal clashing. If I have the gift of prophecy, understanding all the mysteries there are, and knowing everything, and if I have faith in all its fullness, to move mountains, but without love, then I am nothing at all. If I give away all that I possess, piece by piece, and if I even let them take my body to burn it, but am without love, it will do me no good whatever.

Love is always patient and kind; it is never jealous; love is never boastful or conceited; it is never rude or selfish; it does not take offence, and is not resentful. Love takes no pleasure in other people's sins but delights in the truth; it is always ready to excuse, to trust, to hope, and to endure whatever comes.

Love does not come to an end. But if there are gifts of prophecy, the time will come when they must fail; or the gift of languages, it will not continue for ever; and knowledge — for this, too, the time will come when it must fail. For our knowledge is imperfect and our prophesying is imperfect; but once perfection comes, all imperfect things will disappear. When I was a child, I used to talk like a child, and think like a child, and argue like a child, but now I am a man, all childish ways are put behind me. Now we are seeing a dim reflection in a mirror; but then we shall be seeing face to face. The knowledge that I have now is imperfect; but then I shall know as fully as I am known.

In short, there are three things that last: faith, hope and love; and the greatest of these is love.

Alleluia   Alleluia, alleluia! I am the Way, the Truth and the Life, says the Lord; no one can come to the Father except through me. Alleluia! John 14:5.

or

FOURTH SUNDAY IN ORDINARY TIME/C

Alleluia, alleluia! A great prophet has appeared among us; God has visited his people. Alleluia!
Luke 7:16.

Gospel   Luke 4:21-30.

Like Elijah and Elisha, Jesus is not sent to the Jews only.

Jesus began to speak to them in the synagogue, "This text is being fulfilled today even as you listen." And he won the approval of all, and they were astonished by the gracious words that came from his lips.

They said, "This is Joseph's son, surely?" But he replied, "No doubt you will quote me the saying, 'Physician, heal yourself' and tell me, 'We have heard all that happened in Capernaum, do the same here in your own countryside.'" And he went on, "I tell you solemnly, no prophet is ever accepted in his own country.

"There were many widows in Israel, I can assure you, in Elijah's day, when heaven remained shut for three years and six months and a great famine raged throughout the land, but Elijah was not sent to any one of these: he was sent to a widow at Zarephath, a Sidonian town. And in the prophet Elisha's time there were many lepers in Israel, but none of these was cured, except the Syrian, Naaman."

When they heard this everyone in the synagogue was enraged. They sprang to their feet and hustled him out of the town; and they took him up to the brow of the hill their town was built on, intending to throw him down the cliff, but he slipped through the crowd and walked away.

Prayer over the Gifts

Lord,
be pleased with the gifts we bring to your altar,
and make them the sacrament of our salvation.

Preface of Sundays I-VIII, pages 562-565.

Communion Antiphon   Let your face shine on your servant, and save me by your love. Lord, keep me from shame, for I have called to you. Psalm 30:17-18.

or   Happy are the poor in spirit; the kingdom of heaven is theirs! Happy are the lowly; they shall inherit the land. Matthew 5:3-4.

FIFTH SUNDAY IN ORDINARY TIME/C

Prayer after Communion

Lord,
you invigorate us with this help to our salvation.
By this eucharist give the true faith continued growth
throughout the world.

5th SUNDAY IN ORDINARY TIME/C

> Here I am — send me.
> Christ calls his apostles. He transforms them
> from fishermen into fishers of men. We are all
> apostles and prophets to proclaim the saving
> power of God. Like Isaiah we are touched with
> the burning coal of the spirit. When the Lord
> wonders who will be his messenger we reply:
> "Here I am, Lord, send me".

Entrance Antiphon

Come, let us worship the Lord. Let us bow down in the presence of our maker, for he is the Lord our God. **Psalm 94:6-7.**

Opening Prayer

Let us pray
 [that God will watch over us and protect us]

Father,
watch over your family
and keep us safe in your care,
for all our hope is in you.

or

FIFTH SUNDAY IN ORDINARY TIME/C

Let us pray
  [with reverence in the presence of the living God]

In faith and love we ask you, Father,
to watch over your family gathered here.
In your mercy and loving kindness
no thought of ours is left unguarded,
no tear unheeded, no joy unnoticed.

Through the prayer of Jesus
may the blessings promised to the poor in spirit
lead us to the treasures of your heavenly kingdom.

First Reading   Isaiah 6:1-8.
Here I am, send me.

In the year of King Uzziah's death I saw the Lord seated on a high throne; his train filled the sanctuary; above him stood seraphs, each one with six wings.
And they cried out one to another in this way,
"Holy, holy, holy is the Lord of hosts.
His glory fills the whole earth."
  The foundations of the threshold shook with the voice of the one who cried out, and the Temple was filled with smoke. I said:
"What a wretched state I am in! I am lost,
for I am a man of unclean lips
and I live among a people of unclean lips,
and my eyes have looked at the King, the Lord of hosts."
  Then one of the seraphs flew to me, holding in his hand a live coal which he had taken from the altar with a pair of tongs. With this he touched my mouth and said:
"See now, this has touched your lips,
your sin is taken away,
your iniquity is purged."
Then I heard the voice of the Lord saying:
"Whom shall I send? Who will be our messenger?"
I answered, "Here I am, send me."

Responsorial Psalm   Psalm 137.
R/ **Before the angels I will bless you, O Lord.**
1. I thank you, Lord, with all my heart,
   you have heard the words of my mouth.

FIFTH SUNDAY IN ORDINARY TIME/C

Before the angels I will bless you.
I will adore before your holy temple. ℟

2. I thank you for your faithfulness and love
which excel all we ever knew of you.
On the day I called, you answered;
you increased the strength of my soul. ℟

3. All earth's kings shall thank you
when they hear the words of your mouth.
They shall sing of the Lord's ways:
"How great is the glory of the Lord!" ℟

4. You stretch out your hand and save me,
your hand will do all things for me.
Your love, O Lord, is eternal,
discard not the work of your hands. ℟

Second Reading   1 Corinthians 15:1-11.

I preach what they preach, and this is what you all believed.

Brothers, I want to remind you of the gospel I preached to you, the gospel that you received and in which you are firmly established; because the gospel will save you only if you keep believing exactly what I preached to you — believing anything else will not lead to anything.

Well then

> in the first place, I taught you what I had been taught myself, namely that Christ died for our sins, in accordance with the scriptures; that he was buried; and that he was raised to life on the third day, in accordance with the scriptures; that he appeared first to Cephas and secondly to the Twelve. Next he appeared to more than five hundred of the brothers at the same time, most of whom are still alive, though some have died; then he appeared to James, and then to all the apostles; and last of all he appeared to me too; it was as though I was born when no one expected it.

I am the least of the apostles; in fact, since I persecuted the Church of God, I hardly deserve the name apostle; but by God's grace that is what I am, and the grace that he gave me has not been fruitless. On the contrary, I, or rather the grace of God that is with me, have worked harder than any of the others;

> but what matters is that I preach what they preach, and this is what you all believed.

FIFTH SUNDAY IN ORDINARY TIME/C

Alleluia   Alleluia, alleluia! I call you friends, says the Lord, because I have made known to you everything I have learnt from my Father. Alleluia! John 15:15.

or   Alleluia, alleluia! Follow me, says the Lord, and I will make you fishers of men. Alleluia! Matthew 4:19.

Gospel   Luke 5:1-11.
They left everything and followed him.

Jesus was standing one day by the lake of Gennesaret, with the crowd pressing round him listening to the word of God, when he caught sight of two boats close to the bank. The fishermen had gone out of them and were washing their nets. He got into one of the boats — it was Simon's — and asked him to put out a little from the shore. Then he sat down and taught the crowds from the boat.

When he had finished speaking he said to Simon, "Put out into deep water and pay out your nets for a catch." "Master," Simon replied "we worked hard all night long and caught nothing, but if you say so, I will pay out the nets." And when they had done this they netted such a huge number of fish that their nets began to tear, so they signalled to their companions in the other boat to come and help them; when these came, they filled the two boats to sinking point.

When Simon Peter saw this he fell at the knees of Jesus saying, "Leave me, Lord; I am a sinful man." For he and all his companions were completely overcome by the catch they had made; so also were James and John, sons of Zebedee, who were Simon's partners. But Jesus said to Simon, "Do not be afraid; from now on it is men you will catch." Then, bringing their boats back to land, they left everything and followed him.

Prayer over the Gifts

Lord our God,
may the bread and wine
you give us for our nourishment on earth
become the sacrament of our eternal life.

Preface of Sundays I-VIII, pages 562-565.

Communion Antiphon   Give praise to the Lord for his kindness, for his wonderful deeds towards men. He has filled the hungry with good things, he has satisfied the thirsty. Psalm 106:8-9.

SIXTH SUNDAY IN ORDINARY TIME/C

or

Happy are the sorrowing; they shall be consoled. Happy those who hunger and thirst for what is right; they shall be satisfied. Matthew 5:5-6.

Prayer after Communion

God our Father,
you give us a share in the one bread and the one cup
and make us one in Christ.
Help us to bring your salvation and joy
to all the world.

6th SUNDAY IN ORDINARY TIME/C

Happy are those who trust in the Lord. We place all our trust in the resurrection of Christ. If our hope in him had been for this life only then we are the most unfortunate of all people. Christ is risen from the dead and this is the source of our happiness. In him we put our trust and ask for nothing more.

Entrance Antiphon

Lord, be my rock of safety, the stronghold that saves me. For the honour of your name, lead me and guide me.

Psalm 30:3-4

SIXTH SUNDAY IN ORDINARY TIME/C

Opening Prayer

Let us pray
  [that everything we do
  will be guided by God's law of love]

God our Father,
you have promised to remain for ever
with those who do what is just and right.
Help us to live in your presence.

or

Let us pray
  [for the wisdom that is greater than human words]

Father in heaven,
the loving plan of your wisdom took flesh in Jesus Christ,
and changed mankind's history
by his command of perfect love.

May our fulfilment of his command reflect your wisdom
and bring your salvation to the ends of the earth.

First Reading   Jeremiah 17:5-8.

A curse on the man who puts his trust in man, a blessing on the man who puts his trust in the Lord.

The Lord says this:
"A curse on the man who puts his trust in man,
who relies on things of flesh,
whose heart turns from the Lord.
He is like dry scrub in the wastelands:
if good comes, he has no eyes for it,
he settles in the parched places of the wilderness,
a salt land, uninhabited.

"A blessing on the man who puts his trust in the Lord,
with the Lord for his hope.
He is like a tree by the waterside
that thrusts its roots to the stream:
when the heat comes it feels no alarm,
its foliage stays green;
it has no worries in a year of drought,
and never ceases to bear fruit."

SIXTH SUNDAY IN ORDINARY TIME/C

Responsional Psalm   Psalm 1.

℟ **Happy the man who has placed his trust in the Lord.**

1. Happy indeed is the man
   who follows not the counsel of the wicked;
   nor lingers in the way of sinners
   nor sits in the company of scorners,
   but whose delight is the law of the Lord
   and who ponders his law day and night.   ℟

2. He is like a tree that is planted
   beside the flowing waters,
   that yields its fruit in due season
   and whose leaves shall never fade;
   and all that he does shall prosper.   ℟

3. Not so are the wicked, not so!
   For they like winnowed chaff
   shall be driven away by the wind.
   For the Lord guards the way of the just
   but the way of the wicked leads to doom.   ℟

Second Reading   1 Corinthians 15:12.16-20.

If Christ has not been raised, your believing is useless.

If Christ raised from the dead is what has been preached, how can some of you be saying that there is no resurrection of the dead? For if the dead are not raised, Christ has not been raised, and if Christ has not been raised, you are still in your sins. And what is more serious, all who have died in Christ have perished. If our hope in Christ has been for this life only, we are the most unfortunate of all people.

But Christ has in fact been raised from the dead, the first-fruits of all who have fallen asleep.

Alleluia   Alleluia, alleluia! Blessed are you, Father, Lord of heaven and earth, for revealing the mysteries of the kingdom to mere children. Alleluia!   Matthew 11:25.

or

Alleluia, alleluia! Rejoice and be glad: your reward will be great in heaven. Alleluia!   Luke 6:23.

SIXTH SUNDAY IN ORDINARY TIME/C

Gospel Luke 6:17.20-26.

How happy are you who are poor. Alas for you who are rich.

Jesus came down with the Twelve and stopped at a piece of level ground where there was a large gathering of his disciples with a great crowd of people from all parts of Judaea and from Jerusalem and from the coastal region of Tyre and Sidon who had come to hear him and to be cured of their diseases.

Then fixing his eyes on his disciples he said:
"How happy are you who are poor: yours is the kingdom of God.
Happy you who are hungry now: you shall be satisfied.
Happy you who weep now: you shall laugh.

"Happy are you when people hate you, drive you out, abuse you, denounce your name as criminal, on account of the Son of Man. Rejoice when that day comes and dance for joy, for then your reward will be great in heaven. This was the way their ancestors treated the prophets.

"But alas for you who are rich: you are having your consolation now.
Alas for you who have your fill now: you shall go hungry.
Alas for you who laugh now: you shall mourn and weep.

"Alas for you when the world speaks well of you! This was the way their ancestors treated the false prophets."

Prayer over the Gifts

Lord,
we make this offering in obedience to your word.
May it cleanse and renew us,
and lead us to our eternal reward.

Preface of Sundays I-VIII, pages 562-565.

Communion Antiphon They ate and were filled; the Lord gave them what they wanted: they were not deprived of their desire.

Psalm 77:29-30

or

God loved the world so much, he gave his only Son, that all who believe in him might not perish, but might have eternal life. *John 3:16.*

SEVENTH SUNDAY IN ORDINARY TIME/C

Prayer after Communion
Lord,
you give us food from heaven.
May we always hunger
for the bread of life.

7th SUNDAY IN ORDINARY TIME/C

Be compassionate as your Father is compassionate.
Our hope of salvation lies in God's mercy. We must learn to be compassionate as our heavenly Father is compassionate. If we learn to love our enemies then we will be modelling ourselves on Christ the new Adam, who will teach us how to lead the life of the spirit.

Entrance Antiphon Lord, your mercy is my hope, my heart rejoices in your saving power. I will sing to the Lord, for his goodness to me.

Psalm 12:6

Opening Prayer
Let us pray
   [that God will make us more like Christ, his Son]

Father,
keep before us the wisdom and love
you have revealed in your Son.
Help us to be like him

SEVENTH SUNDAY IN ORDINARY TIME/C

in word and deed,
for he lives and reigns with you and the Holy Spirit,
one God, for ever and ever.

or

Let us pray
  [to the God of power and might
  for his mercy is our hope]

Almighty God,
Father of our Lord Jesus Christ,
faith in your word is the way to wisdom,
and to ponder your divine plan is to grow in the truth.

Open our eyes to your deeds,
our ears to the sound of your call,
so that our every act may increase our sharing
in the life you have offered us.

First Reading   1 Samuel 26:2.7-9.12-13.22-23.

The Lord put you in my power, but I would not raise my hand.

Saul set off and went down to the wilderness of Ziph, accompanied by three thousand men chosen from Israel to search for David in the wilderness of Ziph.

So in the dark David and Abishai made their way towards the force, where they found Saul asleep inside the camp, his spear stuck in the ground beside his head, with Abner and the troops lying round him.

Then Abishai said to David, "Today God has put your enemy in your power; so now let me pin him to the ground with his own spear. Just one stroke! I will not need to strike him twice." David answered Abishai, "Do not kill him, for who can lift his hand against the Lord's anointed and be without guilt?" David took the spear and the pitcher of water from beside Saul's head, and they made off. No one saw, no one knew, no one woke up; they were all asleep, for a deep sleep from the Lord had fallen on them.

David crossed to the other side and halted on the top of the mountain a long way off; there was a wide space between them. David then called out, "Here is the king's spear. Let one of the soldiers come across and take it. The Lord repays everyone for his uprightness and loyalty. Today the Lord put you in my power, but I would not raise my hand against the Lord's anointed."

SEVENTH SUNDAY IN ORDINARY TIME/C

Responsorial Psalm   Psalm 102.

℟ **The Lord is compassion and love.**

1. My soul, give thanks to the Lord,
   all my being, bless his holy name.
   My soul, give thanks to the Lord
   and never forget all his blessings. ℟

2. It is he who forgives all your guilt,
   who heals every one of your ills,
   who redeems your life from the grave,
   who crowns you with love and compassion. ℟

3. The Lord is compassion and love,
   slow to anger and rich in mercy.
   He does not treat us according to our sins
   nor repay us according to our faults. ℟

4. As far as the east is from the west
   so far does he remove our sins.
   As a father has compassion on his sons,
   the Lord has pity on those who fear him. ℟

Second Reading   1 Corinthians 15:45-49.

We who have been modelled on the earthly man will be modelled on the heavenly man.

The first man, Adam, as scripture says, became a living soul; but the last Adam has become a life-giving spirit. That is, first the one with the soul, not the spirit, and after that, the one with the spirit. The first man, being from the earth, is earthly by nature; the second man is from heaven. As this earthly man was, so are we on earth; and as the heavenly man is, so are we in heaven. And we, who have been modelled on the earthly man, will be modelled on the heavenly man.

Alleluia

Alleluia, alleluia! Open our heart, O Lord, to accept the words of your Son. Alleluia! Acts 16:4.

or

Alleluia, alleluia! I give you a new commandment: love one another, just as I have loved you, says the Lord. Alleluia! John 13:34.

SEVENTH SUNDAY IN ORDINARY TIME/C

Gospel Luke 6:27-38.

Be compassionate as your Father is compassionate.

Jesus said to his disciples: "But I say this to you who are listening: Love your enemies, do good to those who hate you, bless those who curse you, pray for those who treat you badly. To the man who slaps you on one cheek, present the other cheek too; to the man who takes your cloak from you, do not refuse your tunic. Give to everyone who asks you, and do not ask for your property back from the man who robs you. Treat others as you would like them to treat you. If you love those who love you, what thanks can you expect? Even sinners love those who love them. And if you do good to those who do good to you, what thanks can you expect? For even sinners do that much. And if you lend to those from whom you hope to receive, what thanks can you expect? Even sinners lend to sinners to get back the same amount. Instead, love your enemies and do good, and lend without any hope of return. You will have a great reward, and you will be sons of the Most High, for he himself is kind to the ungrateful and the wicked.

"Be compassionate as your Father is compassionate. Do not judge, and you will not be judged yourselves; do not condemn, and you will not be condemned yourselves; grant pardon, and you will be pardoned. Give, and there will be gifts for you: a full measure, pressed down, shaken together, and running over, will be poured into your lap; because the amount you measure out is the amount you will be given back."

Prayer over the Gifts

Lord,
as we make this offering,
may our worship in Spirit and truth
bring us salvation.

Preface of Sundays I-VIII, pages 562-565.

Communion Antiphon	I will tell all your marvellous works. I will rejoice and be glad in you, and sing to your name, Most High.
	Psalm 9:2-3
or	Lord, I believe that you are the Christ, the Son of God, who was to come into this world. John 11:27.

EIGHTH SUNDAY IN ORDINARY TIME/C

Prayer after Communion

Almighty God,
help us to live the example of love
we celebrate in this eucharist,
that we may come to its fulfillment in your presence.

8th SUNDAY IN ORDINARY TIME/C

> The test of a man is in his conversation.
> Our words flow from what is in our heart. If we
> are filled with the love of God then we will
> judge mercifully. Too often we are negative in
> our criticisms of the petty faults of others
> forgetting that we too are imperfect. We need
> to turn to Christ in our weakness, never
> admitting defeat, knowing that in the Lord we
> can never labour in vain.

Entrance Antiphon

The Lord has been my strength; he has led me into freedom. He saved me because he loves me. Psalm 17:19-20.

Opening Prayer

Let us pray
  [that God will bring peace to the world
  and freedom to this Church]

Lord,
guide the course of world events
and give your Church the joy and peace
of serving you in freedom.

EIGHTH SUNDAY IN ORDINARY TIME/C

or

Let us pray
   [that the peace of Christ
   may find welcome in the world]

Father in heaven,
form in us the likeness of your Son
and deepen his life within us.
Send us as witnesses of gospel joy
into a world of fragile peace and broken promises.
Touch the hearts of all men with your love
that they in turn may love one another.

First Reading   Ecclesiasticus 27:4-7.

Do not praise a man before he has spoken.

In a shaken sieve the rubbish is left behind,
so too the defects of a man appear in his talk.
The kiln tests the work of the potter,
the test of a man is in his conversation.
The orchard where the tree grows is judged on the quality of its fruit,
similarly a man's words betray what he feels.
Do not praise a man before he has spoken,
since this is the test of men.

Responsorial Psalm   Psalm 91.

℟ **It is good to give you thanks, O Lord.**

1. It is good to give thanks to the Lord
   to make music to your name, O Most High,
   to proclaim your love in the morning
   and your truth in the watches of the night. ℟

2. The just will flourish like the palm-tree
   and grow like a Lebanon cedar. ℟

3. Planted in the house of the Lord
   they will flourish in the courts of our God,
   still bearing fruit when they are old,
   still full of sap, still green.
   In him, my rock, there is no wrong. ℟

Second Reading   1 Corinthians 15:54-58.

He has given us the victory through our Lord Jesus Christ.

EIGHTH SUNDAY IN ORDINARY TIME/C

When this perishable nature has put on imperishability, and when this mortal nature has put on immortality, then the words of scripture will come true: Death is swallowed up in victory. Death, where is your victory? Death, where is your sting? Now the sting of death is sin, and sin gets its power from the Law. So let us thank God for giving us the victory through our Lord Jesus Christ.

Never give in then, my dear brothers, never admit defeat; keep on working at the Lord's work always, knowing that, in the Lord, you cannot be labouring in vain.

Alleluia   Alleluia, alleluia! Open our heart, O Lord, to accept the words of your Son. Alleluia! Acts 16:4.

or   Alleluia, alleluia! You will shine in the world like bright stars because you are offering it the word of life. Alleluia! Philippians 2:15-16.

Gospel Luke 6:39-45.

A man's words flow out of what fills his heart.

Jesus told a parable to them, "Can one blind man guide another? Surely both will fall into a pit? The disciple is not superior to his teacher; the fully trained disciple will always be like his teacher. Why do you observe the splinter in your brother's eye and never notice the plank in your own? How can you say to your brother, 'Brother let me take out the splinter that is in your eye,' when you cannot see the plank in your own? Hypocrite! Take the plank out of your own eye first, and then you will see clearly enough to take out the splinter that is in your brother's eye.

"There is no sound tree that produces rotten fruit, nor again a rotten tree that produces sound fruit. For every tree can be told by its own fruit: people do not pick figs from thorns, nor gather grapes from brambles. A good man draws what is good from the store of goodness in his heart; a bad man draws what is bad from the store of badness. For a man's words flow out of what fills his heart."

Prayer over the Gifts

God our Creator,
may this bread and wine we offer
as a sign of our love and worship
lead us to salvation.

Preface of Sundays I-VIII, pages 562-565.

NINTH SUNDAY IN ORDINARY TIME/C

Communion Antiphon I will sing to the Lord for his goodness to me, I will sing the name of the Lord, Most High. Psalm 12:6.

or

I, the Lord, am with you always, until the end of the world. Matthew 28:20.

Prayer after Communion
God of salvation,
may this sacrament which strengthens us here on earth
bring us to eternal life.

9th SUNDAY IN ORDINARY TIME/C

God has no favourites. The Holy Spirit pours his graces not only upon christians but also on people outside the Church. God loves everyone and wants them to be saved. Today's Gospel reminds us that just as Christ did not find faith among the Jews of such quality and depth as that of the centurion so also we acknowledge that we too find christian virtues outside the fold of the Church. For this we praise God in his goodness to all people.

Entrance Antiphon O look at me and be merciful, for I am wretched and alone. See my hardship and my poverty, and pardon all my sins.

Psalm 24:16.18

Opening Prayer
Let us pray
   [for God's care and protection]

NINTH SUNDAY IN ORDINARY TIME/C

Father,
your love never fails.
Hear our call.
Keep us from danger
and provide for all our needs.

or

Let us pray
  [for the confidence born of faith]
God our Father,
teach us to cherish the gifts that surround us.
Increase our faith in you
and bring our trust to its promised fulfilment
in the joy of your kingdom.

First Reading   1 Kings 8:41-43.

If a foreigner comes, grant all he asks.

Solomon stood before the altar of the Lord and, stretching out his hands towards heaven, said:

"And the foreigner too, not belonging to your people Israel, if he comes from a distant country for the sake of your name — for men will hear of your name, of your mighty hand and outstretched arm — if he comes and prays in this Temple, hear from heaven where your home is, and grant all the foreigner asks, so that all the peoples of the earth may come to know your name and, like your people Israel, revere you, and know that your name is given to the Temple I have built."

Responsorial Psalm   Psalm 116.

R/ **Go out to the whole world
and proclaim the Good News.**

or R/ **Alleluia!**

1. O praise the Lord, all you nations,
   acclaim him all you peoples!
2. Strong is his love for us;
   he is faithful for ever. R/

NINTH SUNDAY IN ORDINARY TIME/C

Second Reading   Galatians 1:1-2.6-10.

If I still wanted men's approval, I should not be a servant of Christ.

From Paul to the churches of Galatia, and from all the brothers who are here with me, an apostle who does not owe his authority to men or his appointment to any human being but who has been appointed by Jesus Christ and by God the Father who raised Jesus from the dead.

    I am astonished at the promptness with which you have turned away from the one who called you and have decided to follow a different version of the Good News. Not that there can be more than one Good News; it is merely that some troublemakers among you want to change the Good News of Christ; and let me warn you that if anyone preaches a version of the Good News different from the one we have already preached to you, whether it be ourselves or an angel from heaven, he is to be condemned. I am only repeating what we told you before: if anyone preaches a version of the Good News different from the one you have already heard, he is to be condemned. So now whom am I trying to please — man, or God? Would you say it is men's approval I am looking for? If I still wanted that, I should not be what I am — a servant of Christ.

Alleluia   Alleluia, alleluia! The Word was made flesh and lived among us; to all who did accept him he gave power to become children of God. Alleluia! John 1:12.14.

    or

    Alleluia, alleluia! God loved the world so much that he gave his only Son so that anyone who believes in him may have eternal life. Alleluia! John 3:16.

Gospel   Luke 7;1-10.

Not even in Israel have I found faith like this.

When Jesus had come to the end of all he wanted the people to hear, he went into Capernaum. A centurion there had a servant, a favourite of his, who was sick and near death. Having heard about Jesus he sent some Jewish elders to him to ask him to come and heal his servant. When they came to Jesus they pleaded earnestly with him. "He deserves this of you," they said "because he is friendly towards our people; in fact, he is the one who built the synagogue." So Jesus went with them, and was not very far from

NINTH SUNDAY IN ORDINARY TIME/C

the house when the centurion sent word to him by some friends: "Sir," he said "do not put yourself to trouble; because I am not worthy to have you under my roof; and for this same reason I did not presume to come to you myself; but give the word and let my servant be cured. For I am under authority myself, and have soldiers under me; and I say to one man: Go, and he goes: to another: Come here, and he comes; to my servant: Do this, and he does it." When Jesus heard these words he was astonished at him and, turning round, said to the crowd following him, "I tell you, not even in Israel have I found faith like this." And when the messengers got back to the house they found the servant in perfect health.

Prayer over the Gifts

Lord,
as we gather to offer our gifts
confident in your love,
make us holy by sharing your life with us
and by this eucharist forgive our sins.

Preface of Sundays I-VIII, pages 562-565.

Communion Antiphon

I call upon you, God, for you will answer me; bend your ear and hear my prayer. Psalm 16:6.

or

I tell you solemnly, whatever you ask for in prayer, believe that you have received it, and it will be yours, says the Lord. Mark 11:23,24.

Prayer after Communion

Lord,
as you give us the body and blood of your Son,
guide us with your Spirit
that we may honour you
not only with our lips,
but also with the lives we lead,
and so enter your kingdom.

10th SUNDAY IN ORDINARY TIME/C

Christ restorer of life.
Christ restores us to life through his own death and resurrection. He has pity on our human nature weakened through sin, and, obeying his words, like the dead young man in today's Gospel story, we get up to live the new life of grace. God's kindness to us is what we preach to those who do not believe in him and so we praise the Lord who has rescued us from sin and death.

Entrance Antiphon The Lord is my light and my salvation. Who shall frighten me? The Lord is the defender of my life. Who shall make me tremble? Psalm 26:1-2.

Opening Prayer
Let us pray
 [for the guidance of the Holy Spirit]

God of wisdom and love,
source of all good,
send your Spirit to teach us your truth
and guide our actions
in your way of peace.

or
Let us pray
 [to our Father
 who calls us to freedom in Jesus his Son]

Father in heaven,
words cannot measure the boundaries of love
for those born to new life in Christ Jesus.
Raise us beyond the limits this world imposes,

TENTH SUNDAY IN ORDINARY TIME/C

so that we may be free to love as Christ teaches
and find our joy in your glory.

First Reading   1 Kings 17:17-24.
Look, your son is alive.

The son of the mistress of the house fell sick; his illness was so severe that in the end he had no breath left in him. And the woman said to Elijah, "What quarrel have you with me, man of God? Have you come here to bring my sins home to me and to kill my son?" "Give me your son," he said, and taking him from her lap, carried him to the upper room where he was staying and laid him on his own bed. He cried out to the Lord, "Lord my God, do you mean to bring grief to the widow who is looking after me by killing her son?" He stretched himself on the child three times and cried out to the Lord, "Lord my God, may the soul of this child, I beg you, come into him again!" The Lord heard the prayer of Elijah and the soul of the child returned to him again and he revived. Elijah took the child, brought him down from the upper room into the house, and gave him to his mother. "Look," Elijah said "your son is alive." And the woman "Now I know you are a man of God and the word of the Lord in your mouth is truth itself."

Responsorial Psalm   Psalm 29.

R/ **I will praise you, Lord, you have rescued me.**

1. I will praise you, Lord, you have rescued me
   and have not let my enemies rejoice over me.
   O Lord, you have raised my soul from the dead,
   restored me to life from those who sink into the grave. R/

2. Sing psalms to the Lord, you who love him,
   give thanks to his holy name.
   His anger lasts a moment; his favour all through life.
   At night there are tears, but joy comes with dawn. R/

3. The Lord listened and had pity.
   The Lord came to my help.
   For me you have changed my mourning into dancing;
   O Lord my God, I will thank you for ever. R/

Second Reading   Galatians 1:11-19.

God revealed his Son to me, so that I might preach the Good News about him to the pagans.

TENTH SUNDAY IN ORDINARY TIME/C

The Good News I preached is not a human message that I was given by men, it is something I learnt only through a revelation of Jesus Christ. You must have heard of my career as a practising Jew, how merciless I was in persecuting the Church of God, how much damage I did to it, how I stood out among other Jews of my generation, and how enthusiastic I was for the traditions of my ancestors.

Then God, who had specially chosen me while I was still in my mother's womb, called me through his grace and chose to reveal his Son in me, so that I might preach the Good News about him to the pagans. I did not stop to discuss this with any human being, nor did I go up to Jerusalem to see those who were already apostles before me, but I went off to Arabia at once and later went straight back from there to Damascus. Even when after three years I went up to Jerusalem to visit Cephas and stayed with him for fifteen days, I did not see any of the other apostles; I only saw James, the brother of the Lord.

Alleluia Alleluia, alleluia! May the Father of our Lord Jesus Christ enlighten the eyes of our mind, so that we can see what hope his call holds for us. Alleluia!

Ephesians 1:17.18.

or

Alleluia, alleluia! A great prophet has appeared among us: God has visited his people. Alleluia!

Luke 7:16.

Gospel Luke 7:11-17.
Young man, I tell you to get up.

Jesus went to a town called Nain, accompanied by his disciples and a great number of people. When he was near the gate of the town it happened that a dead man was being carried out for burial, the only son of his mother, and she was a widow. And a considerable number of the townspeople were with her. When the Lord saw her he felt sorry for her. "Do not cry" he said. Then he went up and put his hand on the bier and the bearers stood still, and he said, "Young man, I tell you to get up." And the dead man sat up and began to talk, and Jesus gave him to his mother. Everyone was filled with awe and praised God saying, "A great prophet has appeared among us; God has visited his people." And this opinion of him spread throughout Judaea and all over the countryside.

TENTH SUNDAY IN ORDINARY TIME/C

Prayer over the Gifts

Lord,
look with love on our service.
Accept the gifts we bring
and help us grow in Christian love.

Preface of Sundays I-VIII, pages 562-565.

Communion Antiphon

I can rely on the Lord; I can always turn to him for shelter. It was he who gave me my freedom. My God, you are always there to help me! Psalm 17:3.

or

God is love, and he who lives in love, lives in God, and God in him.

I John 4:16.

Prayer after Communion

Lord,
may your healing love
turn us from sin
and keep us on the way that leads to you.

11th SUNDAY IN ORDINARY TIME/C

> Christ, the forgiver of sins.
> We are all sinners and come to Christ for forgiveness. It is our faith in Christ's saving power rather than in any observance of the law which brings us pardon for our sins. Forgiveness is given to those who love and if we love Christ then we live a life of peace with God. It is Christ who lives in us once we die to sin.

Entrance Antiphon Lord, hear my voice when I call to you. You are my help; do not cast me off, do not desert me, my Saviour God. Psalm 26:7.9.

Opening Prayer

Let us pray
 [for the grace to follow Christ more closely]

Almighty God,
our hope and our strength,
without you we falter.
Help us to follow Christ
and to live according to your will.

or

Let us pray
 [to the Father
 whose love gives us strength to follow his Son]

God our Father,
we rejoice in the faith that draws us together,
aware that selfishness can drive us apart.
Let your encouragement be our constant strength.
Keep us one in the love that has sealed our lives,
help us to live as one family
the gospel we profess.

ELEVENTH SUNDAY IN ORDINARY TIME/C

First Reading   2 Samuel 12:7-10.13.
The Lord forgives your sin: you are not to die.

Nathan said to David, "The Lord the God of Israel says this, 'I anointed you king over Israel; I delivered you from the hands of Saul; I gave your master's house to you, his wives into your arms; I gave you the House of Israel and of Judah; and if this were not enough, I would add as much again for you. Why have you shown contempt for the Lord, doing what displeases him? You have struck down Uriah the Hittite with the sword, taken his wife for your own, and killed him with the sword of the Ammonites. So now the sword will never be far from your House, since you have shown contempt for me and taken the wife of Uriah the Hittite to be your wife.' "

David said to Nathan, "I have sinned against the Lord." Then Nathan said to David, "The Lord, for his part, forgives your sin; you are not to die."

Responsorial Psalm   Psalm 31

℟ **Forgive, Lord, the guilt of my sin.**

1. Happy the man whose offence is forgiven,
   whose sin is remitted.
   O happy the man to whom the Lord
   imputes no guilt,
   in whose spirit is no guile. ℟

2. But now I have acknowledged my sins;
   my guilt I did not hide.
   I said: "I will confess
   my offence to the Lord."
   And you, Lord, have forgiven
   the guilt of my sin. ℟

3. You are my hiding place, O Lord;
   you save me from distress.
   You surround me with cries of deliverance. ℟

4. Rejoice, rejoice in the Lord,
   exult, you just!
   O come, sing out your joy,
   all you upright of heart. ℟

ELEVENTH SUNDAY IN ORDINARY TIME/C

Second Reading Galatians 2:16.19-21.

I live now not with my own life but with the life of Christ who lives in me.

We acknowledge that what makes a man righteous is not obedience to the Law, but faith in Jesus Christ. We had to become believers in Christ Jesus no less than you had, and now we hold that faith in Christ rather than fidelity to the Law is what justifies us, and that no one can be justified by keeping the Law. In other words, through the Law I am dead to the Law, so that now I can live for God. I have been crucified with Christ, and I live now not with my own life but with the life of Christ who lives in me. The life I now live in this body I live in faith: faith in the Son of God who loved me and who sacrificed himself for my sake. I cannot bring myself to give up God's gift: if the Law can justify us, there is no point in the death of Christ."

Alleluia   Alleluia, alleluia! I am the Way, the Truth and the Life, says the Lord; no one can come to the Father except through me. Alleluia! John 14:5.

or   Alleluia, alleluia! God so loved us when he sent his Son to be the sacrifice that takes our sins away. Alleluia! 1 John 4:10.

Gospel Luke 7:36-8:3.

Her many sins have been forgiven, or she would not have shown such great love.

One of the Pharisees invited Jesus to a meal. When he arrived at the Pharisee's house and took his place at table, a woman came in, who had a bad name in the town. She had heard he was dining with the Pharisee and had brought with her an alabaster jar of ointment. She waited behind him at his feet, weeping, and her tears fell on his feet, and she wiped them away with her hair; then she covered his feet with kisses and anointed them with the ointment.

When the Pharisee who had invited him saw this, he said to himself, "If this man were a prophet, he would know who this woman is that is touching him and what a bad name she has." Then Jesus took him up and said, "Simon, I have something to say to you." "Speak, Master" was the reply. "There was once a creditor who had two men in his debt; one owed him five

ELEVENTH SUNDAY IN ORDINARY TIME/C

hundred denarii, the other fifty. They were unable to pay, so he pardoned them both. Which of them will love him more? The one who was pardoned more, I suppose" answered Simon. Jesus said, "You are right."

Then he turned to the woman. "Simon", he said, "you see this woman? I came into your house, and you poured no water over my feet, but she has poured out her tears over my feet and wiped them away with her hair. You gave me no kiss, but she has been covering my feet with kisses ever since I came in. You did not anoint my head with oil, but she has anointed my feet with ointment. For this reason I tell you that her sins, her many sins, must have been forgiven her, or she would not have shown such great love. It is the man who is forgiven little who shows little love." Then he said to her, "Your sins are forgiven." Those who were with him at table began to say to themselves, "Who is this man, that he even forgives sins?" But he said to the woman "Your faith has saved you; go in peace."

Now after this he made his way through towns and villages, preaching and proclaiming the Good News of the kingdom of God. With him went the Twelve, as well as certain women who had been cured of evil spirits and ailments: Mary surnamed the Magdalene, from whom seven demons had gone out, Joanna the wife of Herod's steward Chuza, Susanna, and several others who provided for them out of their own resources.

Prayer over the Gifts

Lord God,
in this bread and wine
you give us food for body and spirit.
May the eucharist renew our strength
and bring us health of mind and body.

Preface of Sundays I-VIII, pages 562-565.

Communion Antiphon

One thing I seek: to dwell in the house of the Lord all the days of my life.

Psalm 26:4.

or

Father, keep in your name those you have given me, that they may be one as we are one, says the Lord. *John 17:11.*

Prayer after Communion
Lord,
may this eucharist
accomplish in your Church
the unity and peace it signifies.

12th SUNDAY IN ORDINARY TIME/C

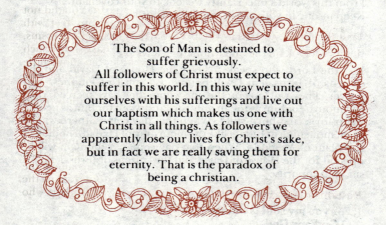

The Son of Man is destined to suffer grievously. All followers of Christ must expect to suffer in this world. In this way we unite ourselves with his sufferings and live out our baptism which makes us one with Christ in all things. As followers we apparently lose our lives for Christ's sake, but in fact we are really saving them for eternity. That is the paradox of being a christian.

Entrance Antiphon God is the strength of his people. In him, we his chosen live in safety. Save us, Lord, who share in your life, and give us your blessing; be our shepherd for ever.

Psalm 27:8-9.

Opening Prayer
Let us pray
  [that we may grow in the love of God]

Father,
guide and protector of your people,
grant us an unfailing respect for your name,
and keep us always in your love.

TWELFTH SUNDAY IN ORDINARY TIME/C

or

Let us pray
  [to God whose fatherly love keeps us safe]

God of the universe,
we worship you as Lord.
God, ever close to us,
we rejoice to call you Father.
From this world's uncertainty we look to your covenant.
Keep us one in your peace, secure in your love.

First Reading   Zechariah 12:10-11; 13:1.
They will look on the one whom they have pierced.

It is the Lord who speaks: "Over the House of David and the citizens of Jerusalem I will pour out a spirit of kindness and prayer. They will look on the one whom they have pierced; they will mourn for him as for an only son, and weep for him as people weep for a first-born child. When that day comes, there will be great mourning in Judah, like the mourning of Hadad-rimmon in the plain of Megiddo. When that day comes, a fountain will be opened for the House of David and the citizens of Jerusalem, for sin and impurity."

Responsorial Psalm   Psalm 62

R/ **For you my soul is thirsting,**
   O God, my God.

1. O God, you are my God, for you I long;
   for you my soul is thirsting.
   My body pines for you
   like a dry, weary land without water.   R/

2. So I gaze on you in the sanctuary
   to see your strength and your glory.
   For your love is better than life,
   my lips will speak your praise.   R/

3. So I will bless you all my life,
   in your name I will lift up my hands.
   My soul shall be filled as with a banquet,
   my mouth shall praise you with joy.   R/

4. For you have been my help;
   in the shadow of your wings I rejoice.

TWELFTH SUNDAY IN ORDINARY TIME/C

My soul clings to you;
your right hand holds me fast. ℟

Second Reading Galatians 3:26-29.

All baptised in Christ, you have all clothed yourselves in Christ.

You are, all of you, sons of God through faith in Christ Jesus. All baptised in Christ, you have all clothed yourselves in Christ, and there are no more distinctions between Jew and Greek, slave and free, male and female, but all of you are one in Christ Jesus. Merely by belonging to Christ you are the posterity of Abraham, the heirs he was promised.

Alleluia Alleluia, alleluia! I am the light of the world, says the Lord, anyone who follows me will have the light of life. Alleluia! John 8:12.

or

Alleluia, alleluia! The sheep that belong to me listen to my voice, says the Lord, I know them and they follow me. Alleluia. John 10:27.

Gospel Luke 9:18-24.

You are the Christ of God. The Son of Man is destined to suffer grievously.

One day when Jesus was praying alone in the presence of his disciples he put this question to them, "Who do the crowds say I am?" And they answered, "John the Baptist; others Elijah; and others say one of the ancient prophets come back to life." "But you", he said, "who do you say I am?" It was Peter who spoke up. "The Christ of God" he said. But he gave them strict orders not to tell anyone anything about this.

"The Son of Man" he said "is destined to suffer grievously, to be rejected by the elders and chief priests and scribes and to be put to death, and to be raised up on the third day."

Then to all he said, "If anyone wants to be a follower of mine, let him renounce himself and take up his cross every day and follow me. For anyone who wants to save his life will lose it; but anyone who loses his life for my sake, that man will save it."

Prayer over the Gifts

Lord,
receive our offering,

THIRTEENTH SUNDAY IN ORDINARY TIME/C

and may this sacrifice of praise
purify us in mind and heart
and make us always eager to serve you.

Preface of Sundays I-VIII, pages 562-565.

Communion Antiphon

The eyes of all look to you, O Lord, and you give them food in due season.
Psalm 144:15.

or

I am the Good Shepherd; I give my life for my sheep, says the Lord.
John 10:11.15.

Prayer after Communion

Lord,
you give us the body and blood of your Son
to renew your life within us.
In your mercy, assure our redemption
and bring us to the eternal life
we celebrate in this eucharist.

13th SUNDAY IN ORDINARY TIME/C

> I will follow you wherever you go. When Christ calls us to follow him we must make no excuses but follow him immediately. His service is perfect freedom and it is in this service of each other through the love of Christ that we discover the true meaning of liberty. God's spirit will keep us close to Christ and we have nothing to fear since love casts out fear.

Entrance Antiphon

All nations, clap your hands. Shout with a voice of joy to God. Psalm 46:2.

THIRTEENTH SUNDAY IN ORDINARY TIME/C

Opening Prayer

Let us pray
  [that Christ may be our light]

Father,
you call your children
to walk in the light of Christ.
Free us from darkness
and keep us in the radiance of your truth.

or

Let us pray
  [for the strength to reject the darkness of sin]

Father in heaven,
the light of Jesus
has scattered the darkness of hatred and sin.
Called to that light
we ask for your guidance.
Form our lives in your truth, our hearts in your love.

First Reading   1 Kings 19:16.19-21.
Elisha rose and followed Elijah.

The Lord said to Elijah: "Go, you are to anoint Elisha son of Shaphat, of Abel Meholah, as prophet to succeed you."

  Leaving there, Elijah came on Elisha son of Shaphat as he was ploughing behind twelve yoke of oxen, he himself being with the twelfth. Elijah passed near to him and threw his cloak over him. Elisha left his oxen and ran after Elijah. "Let me kiss my father and mother, then I will follow you" he said. Elijah answered, "Go, go back; for have I done anything to you?" Elisha turned away, took the pair of oxen and slaughtered them. He used the plough for cooking the oxen, then gave to his men, who ate. He then rose, and followed Elijah and became his servant.

Responsorial Psalm   Psalm 15

R/ **O Lord, it is you who are my portion.**

1. Preserve me, God, I take refuge in you.
   I say to the Lord: "You are my God."
   O Lord, it is you who are my portion and cup;
   it is you yourself who are my prize. R/

THIRTEENTH SUNDAY IN ORDINARY TIME/C

2. I will bless the Lord who gives me counsel,
   who even at night directs my heart.
   I keep the Lord ever in my sight:
   since he is at my right hand, I shall stand firm. ℟

3. And so my heart rejoices, my soul is glad;
   even my body shall rest in safety.
   For you will not leave my soul among the dead,
   nor let your beloved know decay. ℟

4. You will show me the path of life,
   the fullness of joy in your presence,
   at your right hand happiness for ever. ℟

Second Reading   Galatians 5:1.13-18.

You were called to liberty.

When Christ freed us, he meant us to remain free. Stand firm, therefore, and do not submit again to the yoke of slavery.

My brothers, you were called, as you know, to liberty; but be careful, or this liberty will provide an opening for self-indulgence. Serve one another, rather, in works of love, since the whole of the Law is summarised in a single command: Love your neighbour as yourself. If you go snapping at each other and tearing each other to pieces, you had better watch or you will destroy the whole community.

Let me put it like this: if you are guided by the Spirit you will be in no danger of yielding to self-indulgence, since self-indulgence is the opposite of the Spirit, the Spirit is totally against such a thing, and it is precisely because the two are so opposed that you do not always carry out your good intentions. If you are led by the Spirit, no law can touch you.

Alleluia   Alleluia, alleluia! Speak, Lord, your servant is listening: you have the message of eternal life. Alleluia! **Samuel 3:9; John 6:68.**

Alternative Alleluias, pages 1004-1006.

Gospel   Luke 9:51-62.

Jesus resolutely took the road for Jerusalem. I will follow you wherever you go.

As the time drew near for him to be taken up to heaven, Jesus resolutely took the road for Jerusalem and sent messengers ahead

THIRTEENTH SUNDAY IN ORDINARY TIME/C

of him. These set out, and they went into a Samaritan village to make preparations for him, but the people would not receive him because he was making for Jerusalem. Seeing this, the disciples James and John said, "Lord, do you want us to call down fire from heaven to burn them up?" But he turned and rebuked them, and they went off to another village.

As they travelled along they met a man on the road who said to him, "I will follow you wherever you go." Jesus answered, "Foxes have holes and the birds of the air have nests, but the Son of Man has nowhere to lay his head."

Another to whom he said, "Follow me," replied, "Let me go and bury my father first." But he answered, "Leave the dead to bury their dead; your duty is to go and spread the news of the kingdom of God."

Another said, "I will follow you, sir, but first let me go and say good-bye to my people at home." Jesus said to him, "Once the hand is laid on the plough, no one who looks back is fit for the kingdom of God."

Prayer over the Gifts

Lord God,
through your sacraments
you give us the power of your grace.
May this eucharist
help us to serve you faithfully.

Preface of Sundays I-VIII pages 562-565.

Communion Antiphon

O, bless the Lord, my soul, and all that is within me bless his holy name.
Psalm 102:1.

or

Father, I pray for them: may they be one in us, so that the world may believe it was you who sent me. John 17:20-21.

Prayer after Communion

Lord,
may this sacrifice and communion
give us a share in your life
and help us bring your love to the world.

14th SUNDAY IN ORDINARY TIME/C

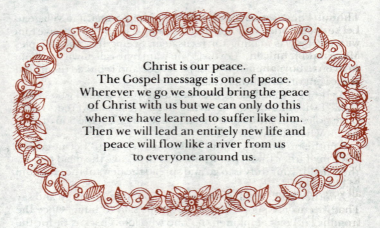

Christ is our peace.
The Gospel message is one of peace.
Wherever we go we should bring the peace
of Christ with us but we can only do this
when we have learned to suffer like him.
Then we will lead an entirely new life and
peace will flow like a river from us
to everyone around us.

Entrance Antiphon   Within your temple, we ponder your loving kindness, O God. As your name, so also your praise reaches to the ends of the earth; your right hand is filled with justice.
                                                 Psalm 47:10-11.

Opening Prayer

Let us pray
   [for forgiveness through the grace of Jesus Christ]

Father,
through the obedience of Jesus,
your servant and your Son,
you raised a fallen world.
Free us from sin
and bring us the joy that lasts for ever.

or

Let us pray
   [for greater willingness
   to serve God and our fellow man]

Father,
in the rising of your Son
death gives birth to new life.

FOURTEENTH SUNDAY OF ORDINARY TIME/C

lambs among wolves. Carry no purse, no haversack, no sandals. Salute no one on the road. Whatever house you go into, let your first words be, 'Peace to this house!' And if a man of peace lives there, your peace will go and rest on him; if not, it will come back to you. Stay in the same house, taking what food and drink they have to offer, for the labourer deserves his wages; do not move from house to house. Whenever you go into a town where they make you welcome, eat what is set before you. Cure those in it who are sick, and say, 'The kingdom of God is very near you.'

But whenever you enter a town and they do not make you welcome, go out into its streets and say, 'We wipe off the very dust of your town that clings to our feet, and leave it with you. Yet be sure of this: the kingdom of God is very near.' I tell you, on that day it will not go as hard with Sodom as with that town."

The seventy-two came back rejoicing. "Lord", they said "even the devils submit to us when we use your name." He said to them, "I watched Satan fall like lightning from heaven. Yes, I have given you power to tread underfoot serpents and scorpions and the whole strength of the enemy; nothing shall ever hurt you. Yet do not rejoice that the spirits submit to you; rejoice rather that your names are written in heaven."

Prayer over the Gifts

Lord,
let this offering to the glory of your name
purify us and bring us closer to eternal life.

Preface of Sundays I-VIII, pages 562-565.

Communion Antiphon Taste and see the goodness of the Lord; blessed is he who hopes in God. Psalm 33:9.

or

Come to me, all you that labour and are burdened, and I will give you rest, says the Lord. Matthew 11:28.

Prayer after Communion

Lord,
may we never fail to praise you
for the fullness of life and salvation
you give us in this eucharist.

15th SUNDAY IN ORDINARY TIME/C

> Love your neighbour as yourself.
> God is as near to us as our own hearts.
> If we wish to become like Christ then we
> will serve all men without distinction of race,
> colour or creed. We will become reconcilers
> and so love God with all our hearts.
> In this way we become the Good
> Samaritans of a wounded world.

Entrance Antiphon In my justice I shall see your face, O Lord; when your glory appears, my joy will be full. Psalm 16:15.

Opening Prayer

Let us pray
 [that the gospel may be our rule of life]

God our Father,
your light of truth
guides us to the way of Christ.
May all who follow him
reject what is contrary to the gospel.

or

Let us pray
 [to be faithful to the light we have received,
  to the name we bear]

Father,
let the light of your truth
guide us to your kingdom
through a world filled with lights contrary to your own.
Christian is the name and the gospel we glory in.
May your love make us what you have called us to be.

FIFTEENTH SUNDAY IN ORDINARY TIME/C

First Reading   Deuteronomy 30:10-14.
The Word is very near to you for your observance.

Moses said to the people: "Obey the voice of the Lord your God, keeping those commandments and laws of his that are written in the Book of this Law, and you shall return to the Lord your God with all your heart and soul.

"For this Law that I enjoin on you today is not beyond your strength or beyond your reach. It is not in heaven, so that you need to wonder, 'Who will go up to heaven for us and bring it down to us, so that we may hear it and keep it?' Nor is it beyond the seas, so that you need to wonder, 'Who will cross the seas for us and bring it back to us, so that we may hear it and keep it?' No, the Word is very near to you, it is in your mouth and in your heart for your observance."

Responsorial Psalm   Psalm 68

℟ **Seek the Lord, you who are poor,**
   and your hearts will revive.

1. This is my prayer to you,
   my prayer for your favour.
   In your great love, answer me, O God,
   with your help that never fails:
   Lord, answer, for your love is kind;
   in your compassion, turn towards me. ℟

2. As for me in my poverty and pain
   let your help, O God, lift me up.
   I will praise God's name with a song;
   I will glorify him with thanksgiving. ℟

3. The poor when they see it will be glad
   and God-seeking hearts will revive;
   for the Lord listens to the needy
   and does not spurn his servants in their chains. ℟

4. For God will bring help to Zion
   and rebuild the cities of Judah.
   The sons of his servants shall inherit it;
   those who love his name shall dwell there. ℟

or Psalm 18
℟ **The precepts of the Lord gladden the heart.**
Psalm as on page 355.

FIFTEENTH SUNDAY IN ORDINARY TIME/C

Second Reading Colossians 1:15-20.

All things were created through Christ and for him.

Christ Jesus is the image of the unseen God
and the first-born of all creation,
for in him were created
all things in heaven and on earth:
everything visible and everything invisible,
Thrones, Dominations, Sovereignties, Powers —
Before anything was created, he existed,
and he holds all things in unity.
Now the Church is his body,
he is its head.
As he is the Beginning,
he was first to be born from the dead,
so that he should be first in every way;
because God wanted all perfection
to be found in him
and all things to be reconciled through him and for him,
everything in heaven and everything on earth,
when he made peace
by his death on the cross.

Alleluia	Alleluia, alleluia! The sheep that belong to me listen to my voice, says the Lord, I know them and they follow me. Alleluia! John 10:27.
or	Alleluia, alleluia! Your words are spirit, Lord, and they are life: you have the message of eternal life. Alleluia! John 6:63.68.

Gospel Luke 10:25-37.

Who is my neighbour?

There was a lawyer who, to disconcert Jesus, stood up and said to him, "Master, what must I do to inherit eternal life?" He said to him, "What is written in the Law? What do you read there?" He *replied*, "*You must love the Lord your God with all your heart, with all your soul, with all your strength, and with all your mind, and your neighbour as yourself.*" "You have answered right," said Jesus. "Do this and life is yours."

But the man was anxious to justify himself and said to Jesus, "And who is my neighbour?" Jesus replied, "A man was once on his way down from Jerusalem to Jericho and fell into the hands of brigands; they took all he had, beat him and then made off, leaving him half dead. Now a priest happened to be travelling down the same road, but when he saw the man, he passed by on the other side. In the same way a Levite who came to the place saw him, and passed by on the other side. But a Samaritan traveller who came upon him was moved with compassion when he saw him. He went up and bandaged his wounds, pouring oil and wine on them. He then lifted him on to his own mount, carried him to the inn and looked after him. Next day, he took out two denarii and handed them to the innkeeper. 'Look after him,' he said, 'and on my way back I will make good any extra expense you have.' Which of these three, do you think, proved himself a neighbour to the man who fell into the brigands' hands?" "The one who took pity on him," he replied. Jesus said to him, "Go, and do the same yourself."

Prayer over the Gifts

Lord,
accept the gifts of your Church.
May this eucharist
help us grow in holiness and faith.

Preface of Sundays I-VIII, pages 562-565.

Communion Antiphon

The sparrow even finds a home, the swallow finds a nest wherein to place her young, near to your altars, Lord of hosts, my King, my God! How happy they who dwell in your house! For ever they are praising you.

Psalm 83:4-5.

or

Whoever eats my flesh and drinks my blood will live in me and I in him, says the Lord. John 6:57.

Prayer after Communion

Lord,
by our sharing in the mystery of this eucharist,
let your saving love grow within us.

16th SUNDAY IN ORDINARY TIME/C

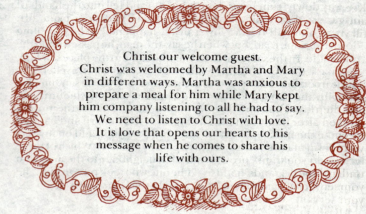

Christ our welcome guest.
Christ was welcomed by Martha and Mary
in different ways. Martha was anxious to
prepare a meal for him while Mary kept
him company listening to all he had to say.
We need to listen to Christ with love.
It is love that opens our hearts to his
message when he comes to share his
life with ours.

Entrance Antiphon God himself is my help. The Lord upholds my life. I will offer you a willing sacrifice; I will praise your name, O Lord, for its goodness. Psalm 53:6.8.

Opening Prayer

Let us pray
   [to be kept faithful in the service of God]

Lord,
be merciful to your people.
Fill us with your gifts
and make us always eager to serve you
in faith, hope, and love.

or

Let us pray
   [that God will continue to bless us
   with his compassion and love]

Father,
let the gift of your life
continue to grow in us,
drawing us from death to faith, hope, and love.
Keep us alive in Christ Jesus.

SIXTEENTH SUNDAY IN ORDINARY TIME/C

Keep us watchful in prayer
and true to his teaching
till your glory is revealed in us.

First Reading   Genesis 18:1-10.
Lord, do not pass your servant by.

The Lord appeared to Abraham at the Oak of Mamre while he was sitting by the entrance of the tent during the hottest part of the day. He looked up, and there he saw three men standing near him. As soon as he saw them he ran from the entrance of the tent to meet them, and bowed to the ground. "My lord," he said, "I beg you, if I find favour with you, kindly do not pass your servant by. A little water shall be brought; you shall wash your feet and lie down under the tree. Let me fetch a little bread and you shall refresh yourselves before going further. That is why you have come in your servant's direction." They replied, "Do as you say."

Abraham hastened to the tent to find Sarah. "Hurry," he said "knead three bushels of flour and make loaves." Then running to the cattle Abraham took a fine and tender calf and gave it to the servant, who hurried to prepare it. Then taking cream, milk and the calf he had prepared, he laid all before them, and they ate while he remained standing near them under the tree.

"Where is your wife Sarah?" they asked him. "She is in the tent" he replied. Then his guest said, "I shall visit you again next year without fail, and your wife will then have a son."

Responsorial Psalm   Psalm 14

℟ **The just will live in the presence of the Lord.**

1. Lord, who shall dwell on your holy mountain?
   He who walks without fault;
   he who acts with justice
   and speaks the truth from his heart;
   he who does not slander with his tongue. ℟

2. He who does no wrong to his brother,
   who casts no slur on his neighbour,
   who holds the godless in disdain,
   but honours those who fear the Lord. ℟

3. He who keeps his pledge, come what may;
   who takes no interest on a loan
   and accepts no bribes against the innocent.
   Such a man will stand firm for ever. ℟

SIXTEENTH SUNDAY IN ORDINARY TIME/C

Second Reading Colossians 1:24-28.

A mystery hidden for centuries has now been revealed to God's saints.

It makes me happy to suffer for you, as I am suffering now, and in my own body to do what I can to make up all that has still to be undergone by Christ for the sake of his body, the Church. I became the servant of the Church when God made me responsible for delivering God's message to you, the message which was a mystery hidden for generations and centuries and has now been revealed to his saints. It was God's purpose to reveal it to them and to show all the rich glory of this mystery to pagans. The mystery is Christ among you, your hope of glory: this is the Christ we proclaim, this is the wisdom in which we thoroughly train everyone and instruct everyone, to make them all perfect in Christ.

Alleluia Alleluia, alleluia! Open our heart, O Lord, to accept the words of your Son. Alleluia! Acts 16:14.

or

Alleluia, alleluia! Blessed are those who, with a noble and generous heart, take the word of God to themselves and yield a harvest through their perseverance. Alleluia! Luke 8:15.

Gospel Luke 10:38-42.

Martha welcomed Jesus into her house. Mary has chosen the better part.

Jesus came to a village, and a woman named Martha welcomed him into her house. She had a sister called Mary, who sat down at the Lord's feet and listened to him speaking. Now Martha who was distracted with all the serving said, "Lord, do you not care that my sister is leaving me to do the serving all by myself? Please tell her to help me." But the Lord answered: "Martha, Martha," he said, "you worry and fret about so many things, and yet few are needed, indeed only one. It is Mary who has chosen the better part; it is not to be taken from her."

SIXTEENTH SUNDAY IN ORDINARY TIME/C

Prayer over the Gifts

Lord,
bring us closer to salvation
through these gifts which we bring in your honour.
Accept the perfect sacrifice you have given us,
bless it as you blessed the gifts of Abel.

Preface of Sundays I-VIII, pages 562-565.

Communion Antiphon	The Lord keeps in our minds the wonderful things he has done. He is compassion and love; he always provides for his faithful. Psalm 110:4-5.
	or
	I stand at the door and knock, says the Lord. If anyone hears my voice and opens the door, I will come in and sit down to supper with him, and he with me. Revelation 3:20.

Prayer after Communion

Merciful Father,
may these mysteries
give us new purpose
and bring us to a new life in you.

17th SUNDAY IN ORDINARY TIME/C

God is our Father.
When we pray Christ tells us that we are to
call God our "Father". Through Baptism
we share with Christ in the sonship of God.
We are to persist in our prayers to God
and he will answer us just because he
is our Father. We must ask until we
receive and seek until we find.

Entrance Antiphon God is in his holy dwelling; he will give a home to the lonely, he gives power and strength to his people. Psalm 67:6-7.36.

Opening Prayer

Let us pray
 [that we will make good use of the gifts
 that God has given us]

God our Father and protector,
without you nothing is holy,
nothing has value.
Guide us to everlasting life
by helping us to use wisely
the blessings you have given to the world.

or

Let us pray
 [for the faith to recognize God's presence
 in our world]

God our Father,
open our eyes to see your hand at work
in the splendour of creation,
in the beauty of human life.

SEVENTEENTH SUNDAY IN ORDINARY TIME/C

Touched by your hand our world is holy.
Help us to cherish the gifts that surround us,
to share your blessings with our brothers and sisters,
and to experience the joy of life in your presence.

First Reading   Genesis 18:20-32.
I trust my Lord will not be angry, but give me leave to speak.

The Lord said, "How great an outcry there is against Sodom and Gomorrah! How grievous is their sin! I propose to go down and see whether or not they have done all that is alleged in the outcry against them that has come up to me, I am determined to know."

The men left there and went to Sodom while Abraham remained standing before the Lord. Approaching him he said, "Are you really going to destroy the just man with the sinner? Perhaps there are fifty just men in the town. Will you really overwhelm them, will you not spare the place for the fifty just men in it? Do not think of doing such a thing: to kill the just man with the sinner, treating just and sinner alike! Do not think of it! Will the judge of the whole earth not administer justice?" The Lord replied, "If at Sodom I find fifty just men in the town, I will spare the whole place because of them."

Abraham replied, "I am bold indeed to speak like this to my Lord, I who am dust and ashes. But perhaps the fifty just men lack five: will you destroy the whole city for five?" "No," he replied. "I will not destroy it if I find forty-five just men there." Again Abraham said to him, "Perhaps there will only be forty there." "I will not do it," he replied, "for the sake of the forty."

Abraham said, "I trust my Lord will not be angry, but give me leave to speak: perhaps there will only be thirty there." "I will not do it," he replied, "if I find thirty there." He said, "I am bold indeed to speak like this, but perhaps there will only be twenty there." "I will not destroy it," he replied, "for the sake of the twenty." He said, "I trust my Lord will not be angry if I speak once more: perhaps there will only be ten." "I will not destroy it," he replied, "for the sake of the ten."

Responsorial Psalm   Psalm 137

R/ **On the day I called,
you answered me, O Lord.**

1. I thank you, Lord, with all my heart,
you have heard the words of my mouth.

SEVENTEENTH SUNDAY IN ORDINARY TIME/C

   Before the angels I will bless you.
   I will adore before your holy temple. R/

2. I thank you for your faithfulness and love
   which excel all we ever knew of you.
   On the day I called, you answered;
   you increased the strength of my soul. R/

3. The Lord is high yet he looks on the lowly
   and the haughty he knows from afar.
   Though I walk in the midst of affliction
   you give me life and frustrate my foes. R/

4. You stretch out your hand and save me,
   your hand will do all things for me.
   Your love, O Lord, is eternal,
   discard not the work of your hands. R/

Second Reading   Colossians 2:12-24.

He has brought you to life with him, he has forgiven us all our sins.

You have been buried with Christ, when you were baptised; and by baptism, too, you have been raised up with him through your belief in the power of God who raised him from the dead. You were dead, because you were sinners and had not been circumcised: he has brought you to life with him, he has forgiven us all our sins.

He has overriden the Law, and cancelled every record of the debt that we had to pay; he has done away with it by nailing it to the cross.

Alleluia	Alleluia, alleluia! The Word was made flesh and lived among us; to all who did accept him he gave power to become children of God. Alleluia! John 1:12.14.
or	Alleluia, alleluia! The spirit you received is the spirit of sons, and it makes us cry out, "Abba, Father!" Alleluia! Romans 8:15.

Gospel   Luke 11:1-13.

Ask, and it will be given to you.

Once Jesus was in a certain place praying, and when he had finished, one of his disciples said, "Lord, teach us to pray, just as John taught his disciples," He said to them, "Say this when you pray:

SEVENTEENTH SUNDAY IN ORDINARY TIME/C

'Father, may your name be held holy,
your kingdom come;
give us each day our daily bread,
and forgive us our sins,
for we ourselves forgive each one who is in debt to us.
And do not put us to the test.'"

He also said to them, "Suppose one of you has a friend and goes to him in the middle of the night to say, 'My friend, lend me three loaves, because a friend of mine on his travels has just arrived at my house and I have nothing to offer him'; and the man answers from inside the house, 'Do not bother me. The door is bolted now, and my children and I are in bed; I cannot get up to give it to you.' I tell you, if the man does not get up and give it him for friendship's sake, persistence will be enough to make him get up and give his friend all he wants.

"So I say to you: Ask, and it will be given to you; search, and you will find; knock, and the door will be opened to you. For the one who asks always receives; the one who searches always finds; the one who knocks will always have the door opened to him. What father among you would hand his son a stone when he asked for bread? Or hand him a snake instead of a fish? Or hand him a scorpion if he asked for an egg? If you then, who are evil, know how to give your children what is good, how much more will the heavenly Father give the Holy Spirit to those who ask him!"

Prayer over the Gifts

Lord,
receive these offerings
chosen from your many gifts.
May these mysteries make us holy
and lead us to eternal joy.

Preface of Sundays I-VIII, pages 562-565.

Communion Antiphon

O, bless the Lord, my soul, and remember all his kindness.

Psalm 102:2

or

Happy are those who show mercy; mercy shall be theirs. Happy are the pure of heart, for they shall see God.

Matthew 5:7-8.

EIGHTEENTH SUNDAY IN ORDINARY TIME/C

Prayer after Communion

Lord,
we receive the sacrament
which celebrates the memory
of the death and resurrection of Christ your Son.
May this gift bring us closer to our eternal salvation.

18th SUNDAY IN ORDINARY TIME/C

> There is more to life than wealth and riches. We tend to look for material security in this world until it becomes an obsession with us. Yet we cannot take our riches with us when we die. We need to live the life of grace as people who have died to the things of this world in order to live for the spiritual riches of a life given to Christ. In this way we will get our priorities right and our lives will be full of true happiness and meaning.

Entrance Antiphon God, come to my help. Lord, quickly give me assistance. You are the one who helps me and sets me free: Lord, do not be long in coming. Psalm 69:2.6.

Opening Prayer

Let us pray
   [for the gift of God's forgiveness and love]

*Father of everlasting goodness,
our origin and guide,
be close to us
and hear the prayers of all who praise you.
Forgive our sins and restore us to life.
Keep us safe in your love.*

and hear the prayers of all who praise you.
Forgive our sins and restore us to life.
Keep us safe in your love.

or

Let us pray
  [to the Father whose kindness never fails]

God our Father,
gifts without measure flow from your goodness
to bring us your peace.
Our life is your gift.
Guide our life's journey,
for only your love makes us whole.
Keep us strong in your love.

First Reading   Ecclesiastes 1:2; 2:21-23.

What does a man gain for all his toil?

Vanity of vanities, the Preacher says. Vanity of vanities. All is vanity!

For so it is that a man who has laboured wisely, skilfully and successfully must leave what is his own to someone who has not toiled for it at all. This, too, is vanity and great injustice; for what does he gain for all the toil and strain that he has undergone under the sun? What of all his laborious days, his cares of office, his restless nights? This, too, is vanity.

Responsorial Psalm   Psalm 89

R' **O Lord, you have been our refuge
from one generation to the next.**

1. You turn men back into dust
   and say: "Go back, sons of men."
   To your eyes a thousand years
   are like yesterday, come and gone,
   no more than a watch in the night. R'

2. You sweep men away like a dream,
   like grass which springs up in the morning.
   In the morning it springs up and flowers:
   by evening it withers and fades. R'

3. Make us know the shortness of our life
   that we may gain wisdom of heart.
   Lord, relent! Is your anger for ever?
   Show pity to your servants. R'

EIGHTEENTH SUNDAY IN ORDINARY TIME/C

4. In the morning, fill us with your love;
we shall exult and rejoice all our days.
Let the favour of the Lord be upon us:
give success to the work of our hands. R'

or Psalm 94

R' **O that today you would listen to his voice!
Harden not your hearts.**

Psalm verses as on pages 974-975.

Second Reading Colossians 3:1-5. 9-11.

You must look for the things that are in heaven, where Christ is.

Since you have been brought back to true life with Christ, you must look for the things that are in heaven, where Christ is, sitting at God's right hand. Let your thoughts be on heavenly things, not on the things that are on the earth, because you have died, and now the life you have is hidden with Christ in God. But when Christ is revealed — and he is your life — you too will be revealed in all your glory with him.

That is why you must kill everything in you that belongs only to the earthly life: fornication, impurity, guilty passion, evil desires and especially greed, which is the same thing as worshipping a false god; and never tell each other lies. You have stripped off your old behaviour with your old self, and you have put on a new self which will progress towards true knowledge the more it is renewed in the image of its creator; and in that image there is no room for distinction between Greek and Jew, between the circumcised or the uncircumcised, or between barbarian and Scythian, slave and free man. There is only Christ: he is everything and he is in everything.

Alleluia Alleluia, alleluia! Your word is truth, O Lord, consecrate us in the truth. Alleluia! John 17:17.

or Alleluia, alleluia! How happy are the poor in spirit; theirs is the kingdom of heaven. Alleluia!

Matthew 5:3.

Gospel Luke 12:13-21.

This hoard of yours, whose will it be?

A man in the crowd said to Jesus, "Master, tell my brother to give me a share of our inheritance." "My friend," he replied "who

EIGHTEENTH SUNDAY IN ORDINARY TIME, C

appointed me your judge, or the arbitrator of your claims?" Then he said to them, "Watch, and be on your guard against avarice of any kind, for a man's life is not made secure by what he owns, even when he has more than he needs."

Then he told them a parable: "There was once a rich man who, having had a good harvest from his land, thought to himself, 'What am I to do? I have not enough room to store my crops.' Then he said, 'This is what I will do: I will pull down my barns and build bigger ones, and store all my grain and my goods in them, and I will say to my soul: My soul, you have plenty of good things laid by for many years to come; take things easy, eat, drink, have a good time.' But God said to him, 'Fool! This very night the demand will be made for your soul; and this hoard of yours, whose will it be then?' So it is when a man stores up treasure for himself in place of making himself rich in the sight of God."

Prayer over the Gifts

Merciful Lord,
make holy these gifts,
and let our spiritual sacrifice
make us an everlasting gift to you.

Preface of Sundays, I-VIII, pages 562-565.

Communion Antiphon You gave us bread from heaven, Lord: a sweet-tasting bread that was very good to eat. Wisdom 16:20.

or

The Lord says: I am the bread of life. A man who comes to me will not go away hungry, and no one who believes in me will thirst. John 6:35.

Prayer after Communion

Lord,
you give us the strength of new life
by the gift of the eucharist.
Protect us with your love
and prepare us for eternal redemption.

19th SUNDAY IN ORDINARY TIME/C

*You must stand ready.
We have to be ready when the Lord comes
to call us to our heavenly home. A good life
is the best preparation we can make.
We will enter into a kingdom promised to us
by our heavenly Father who through his
own kindness and generosity has chosen
us as his own.*

Entrance Antiphon Lord, be true to your covenant, forget not the life of your poor ones for ever. Rise up, O God, and defend your cause; do not ignore the shouts of your enemies.

Psalm 73:20.19.22.23.

Opening Prayer

Let us pray
   [in the Spirit
   that we may grow in the love of God]

Almighty and ever-living God,
your Spirit made us your children,
confident to call you Father.
Increase your Spirit within us
and bring us to our promised inheritance.

or

Let us pray
   [that through us
   others may find the way to life in Christ]

Father,
we come, reborn in the Spirit,
to celebrate our sonship in the Lord Jesus Christ.
Touch our hearts,

NINETEENTH SUNDAY IN ORDINARY TIME/C

help them grow towards the life you have promised.
Touch our lives,
make them signs of your love for all men.

First Reading   Wisdom 18:6-9.

By the same act with which you took vengeance on our foes you made us glorious by calling us to you.

That night had been foretold to our ancestors,
so that, once they saw what kind of oaths they had put their
   trust in, they would joyfully take courage.
This was the expectation of your people,
the saving of the virtuous and the ruin of their enemies;
for by the same act with which you took vengeance on our foes
you made us glorious by calling us to you.
The devout children of worthy men offered sacrifice in secret
and this divine pact they struck with one accord:
that the saints would share the same blessings and dangers
   alike;
and forthwith they had begun to chant the hymn of the fathers.

Responsorial Psalm   Psalm 32.

℟ **Happy are the people the Lord has chosen as his own.**

1. Ring out your joy to the Lord, O you just;
   for praise is fitting for loyal hearts.
   They are happy, whose God is the Lord,
   the people he has chosen as his own. ℟

2. The Lord looks on those who revere him,
   on those who hope in his love,
   to rescue their souls from death,
   to keep them alive in famine. ℟

3. Our soul is waiting for the Lord.
   The Lord is our help and our shield.
   May your love be upon us, O Lord,
   as we place all our hope in you. ℟

NINETEENTH SUNDAY IN ORDINARY TIME/C

Second Reading   Hebrews 11:1-2.8-19.
Abraham looked forward to a city founded, designed and built by God.

Only faith can guarantee the blessings that we hope for, or prove the existence of the realities that at present remain unseen. It was for faith that our ancestors were commended.

It was by faith that Abraham obeyed the call to set out for a country that was the inheritance given to him and his descendants, and that he set out without knowing where he was going. By faith he arrived, as a foreigner, in the Promised Land, and lived there as if in a strange country, with Isaac and Jacob, who were heirs with him of the same promise. They lived there in tents while he looked forward to a city founded, designed and built by God.

It was equally by faith that Sarah, in spite of being past the age, was made able to conceive, because she believed that he who had made the promise would be faithful to it. Because of this, there came from one man, and one who was already as good as dead himself, more descendants than could be counted, as many as the stars of heaven or the grains of sand on the seashore.

All these died in faith, before receiving any of the things that had been promised, but they saw them in the far distance and welcomed them, recognising that they were only strangers and nomads on earth. People who use such terms about themselves make it quite plain that they are in search of their real homeland. They can hardly have meant the country they came from, since they had the opportunity to go back to it; but in fact they were longing for a better homeland, their heavenly homeland. That is why God is not ashamed to be called their God, since he has founded the city for them.

It was by faith that Abraham, when put to the test, offered up Isaac. He offered to sacrifice his only son even though the promises had been made to him and he had been told: It is through Isaac that your name will be carried on. He was confident that God had the power even to raise the dead; and so, figuratively speaking, he was given back Isaac from the dead.

20th SUNDAY IN ORDINARY TIME/C

Do not lose sight of Jesus.
The path to heaven is like a race and we must keep our eyes on Jesus our leader. The saints too are praying for us so that we will win. With so many cheering us on to the finish how can we lose? We must never give up even when the going is hardest. We are bound to suffer for our faith just as Jeremiah the prophet did but the Lord will deliver us.

Entrance Antiphon   God, our protector, keep us in mind; always give strength to your people. For if we can be with you even one day, it is better than a thousand without you.

Psalm 83:10-11

Opening Prayer

Let us pray
  [that the love of God
  may raise us beyond what we see
  to the unseen glory of his kingdom]

God our Father,
may we love you in all things and above all things
and reach the joy you have prepared for us
beyond all our imagining.

or

Let us pray
  [with humility and persistence]

Almighty God, ever-loving Father,
your care extends beyond the boundaries of race and nation
to the hearts of all who live.

May the walls, which prejudice raises between us,
crumble beneath the shadow of your outstretched arm.

TWENTIETH SUNDAY IN ORDINARY TIME/C

First Reading   Jeremiah 38:4-6.8-10.
You have borne me to be a man of dissension for all the land.

The king's leading men spoke to the king. "Let Jeremiah be put to death: he is unquestionably disheartening the remaining soldiers in the city, and all the people too, by talking like this. The fellow does not have the welfare of this people at heart so much as its ruin." "He is in your hands as you know," King Zedekiah answered, "for the king is powerless against you." So they took Jeremiah and threw him into the well of Prince Malchiah in the Court of the Guard, letting him down with ropes. There was no water in the well, only mud, and into the mud Jeremiah sank.

Ebed-melech came out from the palace and spoke to the king, "My lord king," he said "these men have done a wicked thing by treating the prophet Jeremiah like this; they have thrown him into the well where he will die." At this the king gave Ebed-melech the Cushite the following order: "Take three men with you from here and pull the prophet Jeremiah out of the well before he dies."

Responsorial Psalm   Psalm 39.

R/ **Lord, come to my aid.**

1. I waited, I waited for the Lord
   and he stooped down to me;
   he heard my cry. R/

2. He drew me from the deadly pit,
   from the miry clay.
   He set my feet upon a rock
   and made my footsteps firm. R/

3. He put a new song into my mouth,
   praise of our God.
   Many shall see and fear
   and shall trust in the Lord. R/

4. As for me, wretched and poor,
   the Lord thinks of me.
   You are my rescuer, my help,
   O God, do not delay. R/

Second Reading   Hebrews 12:1-4.
We shall keep running steadily in the race we have started.

TWENTIETH SUNDAY IN ORDINARY TIME/C

With so many witnesses in a great cloud on every side of us, we too, then, should throw off everything that hinders us, especially the sin that clings so easily, and keep running steadily in the race we have started. Let us not lose sight of Jesus, who leads us in our faith and brings it to perfection: for the sake of the joy which was still in the future, he endured the cross, disregarding the shamefulness of it, and from now on has taken his place at the right of God's throne. Think of the way he stood such opposition from sinners and then you will not give up for want of courage. In the fight against sin, you have not yet had to keep fighting to the point of death.

Alleluia Alleluia, alleluia! Open our heart, O Lord, to accept the words of your Son. Alleluia! Acts 16:14.

or Alleluia, alleluia! The sheep that belong to me listen to my voice, says the Lord, I know them and they follow me. Alleluia! John 10:27.

Gospel Luke 12:49-53.

I am not here to bring peace, but rather division.

Jesus said to his disciples: "I have come to bring fire to the earth, and how I wish it were blazing already! There is a baptism I must still receive, and how great is my distress till it is over!

"Do you suppose that I am here to bring peace on earth? No, I tell you, but rather division. For from now on a household of five will be divided: three against two and two against three; the father divided against the son, son against father, mother against daughter, daughter against mother, mother-in-law against daughter-in-law, daughter-in-law against mother-in-law."

Prayer over the Gifts

Lord,
accept our sacrifice
as a holy exchange of gifts.
By offering what you have given us
may we receive the gift of yourself.

Preface of Sundays I-VIII, pages 562-565.

Communion Antiphon With the Lord there is mercy, and fullness of redemption. Psalm 129:7.

or

TWENTY-FIRST SUNDAY IN ORDINARY TIME/C

I am the living bread from heaven, says the Lord; if anyone eats this bread he will live for ever. John 6:51-52.

Prayer after Communion
God of mercy,
by this sacrament you make us one with Christ.
By becoming more like him on earth,
may we come to share his glory in heaven,
where he lives and reigns for ever and ever.

21st SUNDAY IN ORDINARY TIME/C

The last shall be first.
We must not think of ourselves as better than others just because we are christians. In fact many people of other faiths from the East and the West will find their way into God's kingdom before us. We must set ourselves high standards and try our best to enter the kingdom by the narrow door.

Entrance Antiphon
Listen, Lord, and answer me. Save your servant who trusts in you. I call to you all day long, have mercy on me, O Lord.

Psalm 85:1-3

Opening Prayer
Let us pray
  [that God will make us one in mind and heart]

TWENTY-FIRST SUNDAY IN ORDINARY TIME/C

Father,
help us to seek the values
that will bring us lasting joy in this changing world.
In our desire for what you promise
make us one in mind and heart.

or

Let us pray
   [with minds fixed on eternal truth]

Lord our God,
all truth is from you,
and you alone bring oneness of heart.
Give your people the joy
of hearing your word in every sound
and of longing for your presence more than for life itself.
May all the attractions of a changing world
serve only to bring us
the peace of your kingdom which this world does not give.

First Reading   Isaiah 66:18-21.
They will bring all your brothers from all the nations.

The Lord says this: I am coming to gather the nations of every language. They shall come to witness my glory. I will give them a sign and send some of their survivors to the nations: to Tarshish, Put, Lud, Moshech, Rosh, Tubal, and Javan, to the distant islands that have never heard of me or seen my glory. They will proclaim my glory to the nations. As an offering to the Lord they will bring all your brothers, on horses, in chariots, in litters, on mules, on dromedaries, from all the nations to my holy mountain in Jerusalem, says the Lord, like Israelites bringing oblations in clean vessels to the Temple of the Lord. And of some of them I will make priests and Levites, says the Lord.

Responsorial Psalm   Psalm 116.

℟ **Go out to the whole world;
   proclaim the Good News.**
   or ℟ **Alleluia!**

1. O praise the Lord, all you nations,
   acclaim him all you peoples!   ℟

TWENTY-FIRST SUNDAY IN ORDINARY TIME/C

2. Strong is his love for us:
he is faithful for ever. ℟

Second Reading Hebrews 12:5-7.11-13.

The Lord trains the one that he loves.

Have you forgotten that encouraging text in which you are addressed as sons? My son, when the Lord corrects you, do not treat it lightly; but do not get discouraged when he reprimands you. For the Lord trains the ones that he loves and he punishes all those that he acknowledges as his sons. Suffering is part of your training; God is treating you as his sons. Has there ever been any son whose father did not train him? Of course, any punishment is most painful at the time, and far from pleasant; but later, in those on whom it has been used, it bears fruit in peace and goodness. So hold up your limp arms and steady your trembling knees and smooth out the path you tread; then the injured limb will not be wrenched, it will grow strong again.

Alleluia Alleluia, alleluia! If anyone loves me he will keep my word, and my Father will love him, and we shall come to him. Alleluia! John 14:23.

or

Alleluia, alleluia! I am the Way, the Truth and the Life, says the Lord; no one can come to the Father except through me. Alleluia! John 14:6.

Gospel Luke 13:22-30.

Men from east and west will come to take their places at the feast in the kingdom of God.

Through towns and villages Jesus went teaching, making his way to Jerusalem. Someone said to him, "Sir, will there be only a few saved?" He said to them, "Try your best to enter by the narrow door, because, I tell you, many will try to enter and will not succeed.

"Once the master of the house has got up and locked the door, you may find yourself knocking on the door, saying, 'Lord, open to us,' but he will answer, 'I do not know where you come from.' Then you will find yourself saying, 'We once ate and drank in your company; you taught in our streets,' but he will reply, 'I do not know where you come from. Away from me, all you wicked men!'

TWENTY-FIRST SUNDAY IN ORDINARY TIME/C

"Then there will be weeping and grinding of teeth, when you see Abraham and Isaac and Jacob and all the prophets in the kingdom of God, and yourselves turned outside. And men from east and west, from north and south, will come to take their places at the feast in the kingdom of God.

"Yes, there are those now last who will be first, and those now first who will be last."

Prayer over the Gifts

Merciful God,
the perfect sacrifice of Jesus Christ
made us your people.
In your love,
grant peace and unity to your Church.

Preface of Sundays I-VIII, pages 562-565.

Communion Antiphon

Lord, the earth is filled with your gift from heaven; man grows bread from earth, and wine to cheer his heart.
Psalm 103:13-15

or

The Lord says: The man who eats my flesh and drinks my blood will live for ever; I shall raise him to life on the last day. John 6:55.

Prayer after Communion

Lord,
may this eucharist increase within us
the healing power of your love.
May it guide and direct our efforts
to please you in all things.

22nd SUNDAY IN ORDINARY TIME/C

Behave humbly.
God's blessing comes to those who behave humbly. Jesus warns us against seeking honour from among men. We are to be humble like him if we are to find favour with God. Jesus our leader will bring us to the heavenly Jerusalem, the city of the living God, only if we follow him humbly.

Entrance Antiphon I call to you all day long, have mercy on me, O Lord. You are good and forgiving, full of love for all who call to you.
Psalm 85:3.5

Opening Prayer

Let us pray
  [that God will increase our faith
  and bring to perfection the gifts he has given us]

Almighty God,
every good thing comes from you.
Fill our hearts with love for you,
increase our faith,
and by your constant care
protect the good you have given us.

or

Let us pray
  [to God who forgives all who call upon him]

Lord God of power and might,
nothing is good which is against your will,
and all is of value which comes from your hand.
Place in our hearts a desire to please you
and fill our minds with insight into love,

TWENTY-SECOND SUNDAY IN ORDINARY TIME/C

so that every thought may grow in wisdom
and all our efforts may be filled with your peace.

First Reading   Ecclesiasticus 3:17-20.28-29.
Behave humbly, and then you will find favour with the Lord.

My son, be gentle in carrying out your business,
and you will be better loved than a lavish giver.
The greater you are, the more you should behave humbly,
and then you will find favour with the Lord;
for great though the power of the Lord is,
he accepts the homage of the humble.
There is no cure for the proud man's malady,
since an evil growth has taken root in him.
The heart of a sensible man will reflect on parables,
an attentive ear is the sage's dream.

Responsorial Psalm   Psalm 67.

R/ In your goodness, O God, you prepared a home for the poor.

1. The just shall rejoice at the presence of God,
   they shall exult and dance for joy.
   O sing to the Lord, make music to his name;
   rejoice in the Lord, exult at his presence. R/

2. Father of the orphan, defender of the widow,
   such is God in his holy place.
   God gives the lonely a home to live in;
   he leads the prisoners forth into freedom. R/

3. You poured down, O God, a generous rain:
   when your people were starved you gave them new life.
   It was there that your people found a home,
   prepared in your goodness, O God, for the poor. R/

Second Reading   Hebrews 12:18-19.22-24.
You have to come to Mount Zion and the city of the living God.

What you have come to is nothing known to the senses: not a
blazing fire, or a gloom turning to total darkness, or a storm; or
trumpeting thunder or the great voice speaking which made
everyone that heard it beg that no more should be said to them.
But what you have come to is Mount Zion and the city of the living
God, the heavenly Jerusalem where the millions of angels have

TWENTY-SECOND SUNDAY IN ORDINARY TIME/C

gathered for the festival, with the whole Church in which everyone is a "first-born son" and a citizen of heaven. You have come to God himself, the supreme Judge, and been placed with spirits of the saints who have been made perfect; and to Jesus, the mediator who brings a new covenant.

Alleluia   Alleluia, alleluia! If anyone loves me he will keep my word, and my Father will love him, and we shall come to him. Alleluia! John 14:23.

or

Alleluia, alleluia! Shoulder my yoke and learn from me, for I am gentle and humble in heart. Alleluia! Matthew 11:29.

Gospel   Luke 14:1.7-14.

Everyone who exalts himself will be humbled, and the man who humbles himself will be exalted.

On a sabbath day Jesus had gone for a meal to the house of one of the leading Pharisees; and they watched him closely. He then told the guests a parable, because he had noticed how they picked the places of honour. He said this, "When someone invites you to a wedding feast, do not take your seat in the place of honour. A more distinguished person than you may have been invited, and the person who invited you both may come and say, 'Give up your place to this man.' And then, to your embarrassment, you would have to go and take the lowest place. No; when you are a guest, make your way to the lowest place and sit there, so that, when your host comes, he may say, 'My friend, move up higher.' In that way, everyone with you at the table will see you honoured. For everyone who exalts himself will be humbled, and the man who humbles himself will be exalted."

Then he said to his host, "When you give a lunch or a dinner, do not ask your friends, brothers, relations or rich neighbours, for fear they repay your courtesy by inviting you in return. No; when you have a party, invite the poor, the crippled, the lame, the blind; that they cannot pay you back means that you are fortunate, because repayment will be made to you when the virtuous rise again."

TWENTY-SECOND SUNDAY IN ORDINARY TIME/C

Prayer over the Gifts

Lord,
may this holy offering
bring us your blessing
and accomplish within us
its promise of salvation.

Preface of Sundays I-VIII, pages 562-565.

Communion Antiphon

O Lord, how great is the depth of the kindness which you have shown to those who love you. Psalm 30:20.

or

Happy are the peacemakers; they shall be called sons of God. Happy are they, who suffer persecution for justice's sake; the kingdom of heaven is theirs. Matthew 5:9-10.

Prayer after Communion

Lord,
you renew us at your table with the bread of life.
May this food strengthen us in love
and help us to serve you in each other.

23rd SUNDAY IN ORDINARY TIME/C

The cost of being a christian.
God has created us free. Nothing must come
between him and us. Yet we sometimes have an
inordinate affection for worldly possessions.
Through the correct use of freedom we are
given the privilege of being sons of God and
escape remaining slaves of the world.

Entrance Antiphon   Lord, you are just, and the judgements you make are right. Show mercy when you judge me, your servant.

Psalm 118:137.124

Opening Prayer

Let us pray
  [that we may realise the freedom God has given us
in making us his sons and daughters]

God our Father,
you redeem us
and make us your children in Christ.
Look upon us,
give us true freedom
and bring us to the inheritance you promised.

or

Let us pray
  [to our just and merciful God]

Lord our God,
in you justice and mercy meet.
With unparalleled love you have saved us from death
and drawn us into the circle of your life.

TWENTY-THIRD SUNDAY IN ORDINARY TIME/C

Open our eyes to the wonders this life sets before us,
that we may serve you free from fear
and address you as God our Father.

First Reading   Wisdom 9:13-18.
Who can divine the will of the Lord?

"What man indeed can know the intentions of God?
Who can divine the will of the Lord?
The reasonings of mortals are unsure
and our intentions unstable;
for a perishable body presses down the soul,
and this tent of clay weighs down the teeming mind.
It is hard enough for us to work out what is on earth,
laborious to know what lies within our reach;
who, then, can discover what is in the heavens?
As for your intention, who could have learnt it, had you not
   granted Wisdom
and sent your holy spirit from above?
Thus have the paths of those on earth been straightened
and men been taught what pleases you,
and saved, by Wisdom."

Responsorial Psalm   Psalm 89.

**R/ O Lord, you have been our refuge
from one generation to the next.**

1. You turn men back into dust
   and say: "Go back, sons of men."
   To your eyes a thousand years
   are like yesterday, come and gone,
   no more than a watch in the night. R/

2. You sweep men away like a dream,
   like grass which springs up in the morning.
   In the morning it springs up and flowers:
   by evening it withers and fades. R/

3. Make us know the shortness of our life
   that we may gain wisdom of heart.
   Lord, relent! Is your anger for ever?
   Show pity to your servants. R/

(continued)

TWENTY-THIRD SUNDAY IN ORDINARY TIME/C

4. In the morning, fill us with your love;
   we shall exult and rejoice all our days.
   Let the favour of the Lord be upon us:
   give success to the work of our hands. R/

Second Reading Philemon 9-10.12-17.

Have him back, not as a slave any more, but as a dear brother.

This is Paul writing, an old man now and, what is more, still a prisoner of Christ Jesus. I am appealing to you for a child of mine, whose father I became while wearing these chains: I mean Onesimus. I am sending him back to you, and with him — I could say — a part of my own self. I should have liked to keep him with me; he could have been a substitute for you, to help me while I am in the chains that the Good News has brought me. However, I did not want to do anything without your consent; it would have been forcing your act of kindness, which should be spontaneous. I know you have been deprived of Onesimus for a time, but it was only so that you could have him back for ever, not as a slave any more, but something much better than a slave, a dear brother; especially dear to me, but how much more to you, as a blood-brother as well as a brother in the Lord. So if all that we have in common means anything to you, welcome him as you would me.

Alleluia Alleluia, alleluia! I call you friends, says the Lord, because I have made known to you everything I have learnt from my Father. Alleluia! John 15:15.

or Alleluia, alleluia! Let your face shine on your servant, and teach me your decrees. Alleluia! Psalm 118:135.

Gospel Luke 14:25-33.

None of you can be my disciple unless he gives up all his possessions.

Great crowds accompanied Jesus on his way and he turned and spoke to them. "If any man comes to me without hating his father, mother, wife, children, brother, sisters, yes and his own life too, he cannot be my disciple. Anyone who does not carry his cross and come after me cannot be my disciple.

"And indeed, which of you here, intending to build a tower, would not first sit down and work out the cost to see if he had enough to complete it? Otherwise, if he laid the foundation and

TWENTY-THIRD SUNDAY IN ORDINARY TIME/C

then found himself unable to finish the work, the onlookers would all start making fun of him and saying, 'Here is a man who started to build and was unable to finish .' Or again, what king marching to war against another king would not first sit down and consider whether with ten thousand men he could stand up to the other who advanced against him with twenty thousand? If not, then while the other king was still a long way off, he would send envoys to sue for peace. So in the same way, none of you can be my disciple unless he gives up all his possessions."

Prayer over the Gifts

God of peace and love,
may our offering bring you true worship
and make us one with you.

Preface of Sundays I-VIII, pages 562-565.

Communion Antiphon

Like a deer that longs for running streams, my soul longs for you, my God. My soul is thirsting for the living God. Psalm 41:2-3.

or

I am the light of the world, says the Lord; the man who follows me will have the light of life. John 8:12.

Prayer after Communion

Lord,
your word and your sacrament
give us food and life.
May this gift of your Son
lead us to share his life for ever.

24th SUNDAY IN ORDINARY TIME/C

Christ welcomes and forgives sinners. The story of the prodigal son is one of the most famous ever told by Jesus. The father in this story is merciful to his wayward son because he loves him and forgives him his past misdeeds. God is our Father who forgives us because he loves us. We should have no fear in returning to him no matter what we have done in the past. Our forgiveness is to be found in Christ who came into this world to forgive sinners.

Entrance Antiphon Give peace, Lord, to those who wait for you and your prophets will proclaim you as you deserve. Hear the prayers of your servant and of your people Israel.

cf. Ecclesiasticus 36:18

Opening Prayer

Let us pray
 [that God will keep us faithful in his service]

Almighty God,
our creator and guide,
may we serve you with all our heart
and know your forgiveness in our lives.

or

Let us pray
 [for the peace which is born of faith and hope]

Father in heaven, Creator of all,
look down upon your people in their moments of need,
for you alone are the source of our peace.
Bring us to the dignity which distinguishes the poor in spirit
and show us how great is the call to serve,
that we may share in the peace of Christ
who offered his life in the service of all.

TWENTY-FOURTH SUNDAY IN ORDINARY TIME/C

First Reading   Exodus 32:7-11.13-14.

The Lord relented and did not bring on his people the disaster he had threatened.

The Lord spoke to Moses, "Go down now, because your people whom you brought out of Egypt have apostasised. They have been quick to leave the way I marked out for them; they have made themselves a calf of molten metal and have worshipped it and offered it sacrifice. 'Here is your God, Israel,' they have cried, 'who brought you up from the land of Egypt!' " The Lord said to Moses, "I can see how headstrong these people are! Leave me, now, my wrath will blaze out against them and devour them; of you, however, I will make a great nation."

But Moses pleaded with the Lord his God. "Lord," he said, "why should your wrath blaze out against this people of yours whom you brought out of the land of Egypt with arm outstretched and mighty hand? Remember Abraham, Isaac and Jacob, your servants to whom by your own self you swore and made this promise: I will make your offspring as many as the stars of heaven, and all this land which I promised I will give to your descendants, and it shall be their heritage for ever." So the Lord relented and did not bring on his people the disaster he had threatened.

Responsorial Psalm   Psalm 50.

℟ **I will leave this place and go to my father.**

1. Have mercy on me, God, in your kindness.
   In your compassion blot out my offence.
   O wash me more and more from my guilt
   and cleanse me from my sin. ℟

2. A pure heart create for me, O God,
   put a steadfast spirit within me.
   Do not cast me away from your presence,
   nor deprive me of your holy spirit. ℟

3. O Lord, open my lips
   and my mouth shall declare your praise.
   My sacrifice is a contrite spirit;
   a humbled, contrite heart you will not spurn. ℟

TWENTY-FOURTH SUNDAY IN ORDINARY TIME/C

Second Reading   1 Timothy 1:12-17.

Christ Jesus came into the world to save sinners.

I thank Christ Jesus our Lord, who has given me strength, and who judged me faithful enough to call me into his service even though I used to be a blasphemer and did all I could to injure and discredit the faith. Mercy, however, was shown me, because until I became a believer I had been acting in ignorance; and the grace of our Lord filled me with faith and with the love that is in Christ Jesus. Here is a saying that you can rely on and nobody should doubt: that Christ Jesus came into the world to save sinners. I myself am the greatest of them; and if mercy has been shown to me, it is because Jesus Christ meant to make me the greatest evidence of his inexhaustible patience for all the other people who would later have to trust in him to come to eternal life. To the eternal King, the undying, invisible and only God be honour and glory for ever and ever. Amen.

Alleluia   Alleluia, alleluia! May the Father of our Lord Jesus Christ enlighten the eyes of our mind, so that we can see what hope his call holds for us. Alleluia!

Ephesians 1:17.18

or

Alleluia, alleluia! God in Christ was reconciling the world to himself, and he has entrusted to us the news that they are reconciled. Alleluia! *2 Corinthians 5:19.*

Gospel   Luke 15:1-32.

There will be rejoicing in heaven over one repentant sinner.

The tax collectors and the sinners were all seeking the company of Jesus to hear what he had to say, and the Pharisees and the scribes complained. "This man," they said, "welcomes sinners and eats with them." So he spoke this parable to them:

"What man among you with a hundred sheep, losing one, would not leave the ninety-nine in the wilderness and go after the missing one till he found it? And when he found it, would he not joyfully take it on his shoulders and then, when he got home, call together his friends and neighbours? 'Rejoice with me,' he would say, 'I have found my sheep that was lost.' In the same way, I tell you, there will be more rejoicing in heaven over one repentant sinner than over ninety-nine virtuous men who have no need of repentance.

"Or again, what woman with ten drachmas would not, if she lost one, light a lamp and sweep out the house and search thoroughly till she found it? And then, when she had found it, call together her friends and neighbours? "Rejoice with me.' she would say, 'I have found the drachma I lost.' In the same way, I tell you, there is rejoicing among the angels of God over one repentant sinner."

He also said, "A man had two sons. The younger said to his father, 'Father, let me have the share of the estate that would come to me.' So the father divided the property between them. A few days later, the younger son got together everything he had and left for a distant country where he squandered his money on a life of debauchery.

"When he had spent it all, that country experienced a severe famine, and now he began to feel the pinch, so he hired himself out to one of the local inhabitants who put him on his farm to feed the pigs. And he would willingly have filled his belly with the husks the pigs were eating but no one offered him anything. Then he came to his senses and said, 'How many of my father's paid servants have more food than they want, and here am I dying of hunger! I will leave this place and go to my father and say: Father, I have sinned against heaven and against you; I no longer deserve to be called your son; treat me as one of your paid servants.' So he left the place and went back to his father.

"While he was still a long way off, his father saw him and was moved with pity. He ran to the boy, clasped him in his arms and kissed him tenderly. Then his son said, 'Father, I have sinned against heaven and against you. I no longer deserve to be called your son.' But the father said to his servants, 'Quick! Bring out the best robe and put it on him; put a ring on his finger and sandals on his feet. Bring the calf we have been fattening, and kill it; we are going to have a feast, a celebration, because this son of mine was dead and has come back to life; he was lost and is found.' And they began to celebrate.

"Now the elder son was out in the fields, and on his way back, as he drew near the house, he could hear music and dancing. Calling one of the servants, he asked what it was all about. 'Your brother has come,' replied the servant, 'and your father has killed the calf we had fattened because he has got him back safe and sound.' He was angry then and refused to go in, and his father came out to plead with him; but he answered his father, 'Look, all these years I

TWENTY-FOURTH SUNDAY IN ORDINARY TIME/C

have slaved for you and never once disobeyed your orders, yet you never offered me so much as a kid for me to celebrate with my friends. But, for this son of yours, when he comes back after swallowing up your property — he and his women — you kill the calf we had been fattening.'

"The father said, 'My son, you are with me always and all I have is yours. But it was only right we should celebrate and rejoice, because your brother here was dead and has come to life; he was lost and is found.' "

Prayer over the Gifts

Lord,
hear the prayers of your people
and receive our gifts.
May the worship of each one here
bring salvation to all.

Preface of Sundays I-VIII, pages 562-565.

Communion Antiphon

O God, how much we value your mercy! All mankind can gather under your protection. Psalm 35:8.

or

The cup that we bless is a communion with the blood of Christ; and the bread that we break is a communion with the body of the Lord.
cf. 1 Corinthians 10:16

Prayer after Communion

Lord,
may the eucharist you have given us
influence our thoughts and actions.
May your Spirit guide and direct us in your way.

25th SUNDAY IN ORDINARY TIME/C

The call to social justice and peace.
The christian is called by Christ to be a person who is on the side of the oppressed. The poor must never be exploited by the rich for the sake of material gain. Money and power need to be put into proper perspective in our lives. We cannot serve God and money.

Entrance Antiphon I am the Saviour of all people, says the Lord. Whatever their troubles, I will answer their cry, and I will always be their Lord.

Opening Prayer

Let us pray
   [that we will grow in the love of God
   and of one another]

Father,
guide us, as you guide creation
according to your law of love.
May we love one another
and come to perfection
in the eternal life prepared for us.

or

Let us pray
   [to the Lord who is a God of love to all peoples]

Father in heaven,
the perfection of justice is found in your love
and all mankind is in need of your law.

TWENTY-FIFTH SUNDAY IN ORDINARY TIME/C

Help us to find this love in each other
that justice may be attained
through obedience to your law.

First Reading   Amos 8:4-7.

Against those who "buy up the poor for money".

"Listen to this, you who trample on the needy
and try to suppress the poor people of the country,
you who say, "When will New Moon be over
so that we can sell our corn,
and sabbath, so that we can market our wheat?
Then by lowering the bushel, raising the shekel,
by swindling and tampering with the scales,
we can buy up the poor for money,
and the needy for a pair of sandals,
and get a price even for the sweepings of the wheat."
The Lord swears it by the pride of Jacob,
"Never will I forget a single thing you have done."

Responsorial Psalm   Psalm 112.

℟ **Praise the Lord, who raises the poor.**
or ℟ **Alleluia!**

1. Praise, O servants of the Lord,
   praise the name of the Lord!
   May the name of the Lord be blessed
   both now and for evermore!   ℟

2. High above all nations is the Lord,
   above the heavens his glory.
   Who is like the Lord, our God,
   who has risen on high to his throne
   yet stoops from the heights to look down,
   to look down upon heaven and earth?   ℟

3. From the dust he lifts up the lowly,
   from the dungheap he raises the poor
   to set him in the company of princes,
   yes, with the princes of his people.   ℟

Second Reading   1 Timothy 2:1-8.

There should be prayers offered for everyone to God, who wants everyone to be saved.

TWENTY-FIFTH SUNDAY IN ORDINARY TIME/C

My advice is that, first of all, there should be prayers offered for everyone — petitions, intercessions and thanksgiving — and especially for kings and others in authority, so that we may be able to live religious and reverent lives in peace and quiet. To do this is right, and will please God our saviour: he wants everyone to be saved and reach full knowledge of the truth. For there is only one God, and there is only one mediator between God and mankind, himself a man, Christ Jesus, who sacrificed himself as a ransom for them all. He is the evidence of this, sent at the appointed time, and I have been named a herald and apostle of it and — I am telling the truth and no lie — a teacher of the faith and the truth to the pagans.

In every place, then, I want the men to lift their hands up reverently in prayer, with no anger or argument.

Alleluia   Alleluia, alleluia! Open our heart, O Lord, to accept the words of your Son, Alleluia! Acts 16:14.

    or   Alleluia, alleluia! Jesus Christ was rich, but he became poor for your sake, to make you rich out of his poverty. Alleluia! 2 Corinthians 8:9.

Gospel   Luke 16:1-13.

You cannot be the slave both of God and of money.

Jesus said to his disciples,
"There was a rich man and he had a steward who was denounced to him for being wasteful with his property. He called for the man and said, 'What is this I hear about you? Draw me up an account of your stewardship because you are not to be my steward any longer.' Then the steward said to himself, 'Now that my master is taking the stewardship from me, what am I to do? Dig? I am not strong enough. Go begging? I should be too ashamed. Ah, I know what I will do to make sure that when I am dismissed from office there will be some to welcome me into their homes.'

"Then he called his master's debtors one by one. To the first he said, 'How much do you owe my master?' 'One hundred measures of oil' was the reply. The steward said, 'Here, take your bond; sit down straight away and write fifty.' To another he said, 'And you, sir, how much do you owe?' 'One hundred measures of wheat' was the reply. The steward said, 'Here, take your bond and write eighty.'

"The master praised the dishonest steward for his astuteness.

TWENTY-FIFTH SUNDAY IN ORDINARY TIME/C

For the children of this world are more astute in dealing with their own kind than are the children of light.

"And so I tell you this: use money, tainted as it is, to win you friends, and thus make sure that when it fails you, they will welcome you into the tents of eternity.

The man who can be trusted in little things can be trusted in great; the man who is dishonest in little things will be dishonest in great. If then you cannot be trusted with money, that tainted thing, who will trust you with genuine riches? And if you cannot be trusted with what is not yours, who will give you what is your very own?

"No servant can be the slave of two masters: he will either hate the first and love the second, or treat the first with respect and the second with scorn. You cannot be the slave both of God and of money."

Prayer over the Gifts

Lord,
may these gifts which we now offer
to show our belief and our love
be pleasing to you.
May they become for us
the eucharist of Jesus Christ your Son,
who is Lord for ever and ever.

Preface of Sundays I-VIII, pages 562-565.

Communion Antiphon

You have laid down your precepts to be faithfully kept. May my footsteps be firm in keeping your commands.
Psalm 118:4-5

or

I am the Good Shepherd, says the Lord; I know my sheep, and mine know me. **John 10:14.**

Prayer after Communion

Lord,
help us with your kindness.
Make us strong through the eucharist.
May we put into action
the saving mystery we celebrate.

26th SUNDAY IN ORDINARY TIME/C

The rich and the poor.
Christ drives home the dangers of inequality in the distribution of wealth. The rich man will be punished in the next life because of his indifference to the poor man who lay hungry at the gate of his house. Luxury and holiness are very rarely found together. We must share our goods just as we are obliged to try to share our faith in Christ with others through the manner in which we live our lives.

Entrance Antiphon   O Lord, you had just cause to judge men as you did: because we sinned against you and disobeyed your will. But now show us your greatness of heart, and treat us with your unbounded kindness.

Daniel 3:31.29.30.43.42

Opening Prayer

Let us pray
  [for God's forgiveness
  and for the happiness it brings]

Father,
you show your almighty power
in your mercy and forgiveness.
Continue to fill us with your gifts of love.
Help us to hurry towards the eternal life you promise
and come to share in the joys of your kingdom.

or

Let us pray
  [for the peace of the kingdom
  which we have been promised]

Father of our Lord Jesus Christ,

TWENTY-SIXTH SUNDAY IN ORDINARY TIME/C

in your unbounded mercy
you have revealed the beauty of your power
through your constant forgiveness of our sins.
May the power of this love be in our hearts
to bring your pardon and your kingdom to all we meet.

First Reading   Amos 6:1.4-7.
Those who sprawl and those who bawl will be exiled.

The almighty Lord says this:
Woe to those ensconced so snugly in Zion
and to those who feel so safe on the mountain of Samaria.
Lying on ivory beds
and sprawling on their divans,
they dine on lambs from the flock,
and stall-fattened veal;
they bawl to the sound of the harp,
they invent new instruments of music like David,
they drink wine by the bowlful,
and use the finest oil for anointing themselves,
but about the ruin of Joseph they do not care at all.
That is why they will be the first to be exiled;
the sprawlers' revelry is over.

Responsorial Psalm   Psalm 145.

R/ **My soul, give praise to the Lord.**
or R' **Alleluia!**

1. It is the Lord who keeps faith for ever,
    who is just to those who are oppressed.
    It is he who gives bread to the hungry,
    the Lord, who sets prisoners free.   R/

2. It is the Lord who gives sight to the blind,
    who raises up those who are bowed down.
    It is the Lord who loves the just,
    the Lord, who protects the stranger.   R/

3. He upholds the widow and orphan
    but thwarts the path of the wicked.
    The Lord will reign for ever,
    Zion's God, from age to age.   R/

TWENTY-SIXTH SUNDAY IN ORDINARY TIME/C

Second Reading   1 Timothy 6:11-16.

Do all that you have been told until the Appearing of the Lord.

As a man dedicated to God, you must aim to be saintly and religious, filled with faith and love, patient and gentle. Fight the good fight of the faith and win for yourself the eternal life to which you were called when you made your profession and spoke up for the truth in front of many witnesses. Now, before God the source of all life and before Jesus Christ, who spoke up as a witness for the truth in front of Pontius Pilate, I put to you the duty of doing all that you have been told, with no faults or failures, until the Appearing of our Lord Jesus Christ,
who at the due time will be revealed
by God, the blessed and only Ruler of all,
the King of kings and the Lord of lords,
who alone is immortal,
whose home is in inaccessible light,
whom no man has seen and no man is able to see:
to him be honour and everlasting power. Amen.

Alleluia	Alleluia, alleluia! The sheep that belong to me listen to my voice, says the Lord, I know them and they follow me. Alleluia! John 10:27.
or	Alleluia, alleluia! Jesus Christ was rich, but he became poor for your sake, to make you rich out of his poverty. Alleluia! 2 Corinthians 8:9.

Gospel   Luke 16:19-31.

Good things come your way, just as bad things came the way of Lazarus. Now he is being comforted here while you are in agony.

Jesus said to the Pharisees: "There was a rich man who used to dress in purple and fine linen and feast magnificently every day. And at his gate there lay a poor man called Lazarus, covered with sores, who longed to fill himself with the scraps that fell from the rich man's table. Dogs even came and licked his sores. Now the poor man died and was carried away by the angels to the bosom of Abraham. The rich man also died and was buried.

"In his torment in Hades he looked up and saw Abraham a long way off with Lazarus in his bosom. So he cried out, 'Father Abraham, pity me and send Lazarus to dip the tip of his finger in water and cool my tongue, for I am in agony in these flames.' 'My

TWENTY-SIXTH SUNDAY IN ORDINARY TIME/C

son,' Abraham replied 'remember that during your life good things came your way, just as bad things came the way of Lazarus. Now he is being comforted here while you are in agony. But that is not all: between us and you a great gulf has been fixed, to stop anyone, if he wanted to, crossing from our side to yours, and to stop any crossing from your side to ours.'

"The rich man replied, 'Father, I beg you then to send Lazarus to my father's house, since I have five brothers, to give them warning so that they do not come to this place of torment too.' 'They have Moses and the prophets,' said Abraham, 'let them listen to them.' 'Ah no, father Abraham, said the rich man 'but if someone comes to them from the dead, they will repent.' Then Abraham said to him, 'If they will not listen either to Moses or to the prophets, they will not be convinced even if someone should rise from the dead.'"

Prayer over the Gifts

God of mercy,
accept our offering
and make it a source of blessing for us.

Preface of Sundays I-VIII, pages 562-565.

Communion Antiphon

O Lord, remember the words you spoke to me, your servant, which made me live in hope and consoled me when I was downcast.

Psalm 118:49-50

or

This is how we know what love is: Christ gave up his life for us; and we too must give up our lives for our brothers. 1 John 3:16.

Prayer after Communion

Lord,
may this eucharist
in which we proclaim the death of Christ
bring us salvation
and make us one with him in glory,
for he is Lord for ever and ever.

27th SUNDAY IN ORDINARY TIME/C

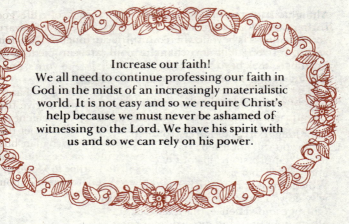

Increase our faith!
We all need to continue professing our faith in God in the midst of an increasingly materialistic world. It is not easy and so we require Christ's help because we must never be ashamed of witnessing to the Lord. We have his spirit with us and so we can rely on his power.

Entrance Antiphon O Lord, you have given everything its place in the world, and no one can make it otherwise. For it is your creation, the heavens and the earth and the stars: you are the Lord of all. Esther 13:9.10-11.

Opening Prayer

Let us pray
 [that God will forgive our failings
 and bring us peace]

Father,
your love for us
surpasses all our hopes and desires.
Forgive our failings,
keep us in your peace
and lead us in the way of salvation.

or

Let us pray
 [before the face of God
 in trusting faith]

TWENTY-SEVENTH SUNDAY IN ORDINARY TIME/C

Almighty and eternal God,
Father of the world to come,
your goodness is beyond what our spirit can touch
and your strength is more than the mind can bear.
Lead us to seek beyond our reach
and give us the courage to stand before your truth.

First Reading   Habakkuk 1:2-3;2:2-4.
The upright man will live by his faithfulness.

How long, Lord, am I to cry for help
while you will not listen;
to cry "Oppression!" in your ear
and you will not save?
Why do you set injustice before me,
why do you look on where there is tyranny?
Outrage and violence, this is all I see,
all is contention, and discord flourishes.
Then the Lord answered and said,
"Write the vision down,
inscribe it on tablets
to be easily read,
since this vision is for its own time only:
eager for its fulfilment, it does not deceive;
if it comes slowly, wait,
for come it will, without fail.
See how he flags, he whose soul is not at rights,
but the upright man will live by his faithfulness."

Responsorial Psalm   Psalm 94.

℟ **O that today you would listen to his voice!
Harden not your hearts.**

1. Come, ring out our joy to the Lord;
   hail the rock who saves us.
   Let us come before him, giving thanks,
   with songs let us hail the Lord. ℟

2. Come in; let us bow and bend low;
   let us kneel before the God who made us
   for he is our God and we
   the people who belong to his pasture,
   the flock that is led by his hand. ℟

TWENTY-SEVENTH SUNDAY IN ORDINARY TIME/C

3. O that today you would listen to his voice!
   "Harden not your hearts as at Meribah,
   as on that day at Massah in the desert
   when your fathers put me to the test;
   when they tried me, though they saw my work." ℟

Second Reading   2 Timothy 1:6-8.13-14.
Never be ashamed of witnessing the Lord.

I am reminding you to fan into a flame the gift that God gave you when I laid my hands on you. God's gift was not a spirit of timidity, but the Spirit of power, and love, and self-control. So you are never to be ashamed of witnessing to the Lord, or ashamed of me for being his prisoner; but with me, bear the hardships for the sake of the Good News, relying on the power of God.

Keep as your pattern the sound teaching you have heard from me, in the faith and love that are in Christ Jesus. You have been trusted to look after something precious; guard it with the help of the Holy Spirit who lives in us.

Alleluia   Alleluia, alleluia! Speak, Lord, your servant is listening: you have the message of eternal life. Alleluia! 1 Samuel 3:9; John 6:68.

or·   Alleluia, alleluia! The word of the Lord remains for ever: What is this word? It is the Good News that has been brought to you. Alleluia! 1 Peter 1:25.

Gospel   Luke 17:5-10.
If only you had faith!

The apostles said to the Lord, "Increase our faith." The Lord replied, "Were your faith the size of a mustard seed you could say to this mulberry tree, 'Be uprooted and planted in the sea', and it would obey you.

"Which of you, with a servant ploughing or minding sheep, would say to him when he returned from the fields, 'Come and have your meal immediately'? Would he not be more likely to say, 'Get my supper laid; make yourself tidy and wait on me while I eat and drink. You can eat and drink yourself afterwards'? Must he be grateful to the servant for doing what he was told? So with you: when you have done all you have been told to do, say, 'We are merely servants: we have done no more than our duty.'"

TWENTY-SEVENTH SUNDAY IN ORDINARY TIME/C

Prayer over the Gifts

Father,
receive these gifts
which our Lord Jesus Christ
has asked us to offer in his memory.
May our obedient service
bring us to the fullness of your redemption.

Preface of Sundays I-VIII, pages 562-565.

Communion Antiphon

The Lord is good to those who hope in him, to those who are searching for his love. Lamentations 3:25.

or

Because there is one bread, we, though many, are one body, for we all share in the one loaf and in the one cup. cf. 1 Corinthians 10:17.

Prayer after Communion

Almighty God,
let the eucharist we share
fill us with your life.
May the love of Christ
which we celebrate here
touch our lives and lead us to you.

TWENTY-EIGHTH SUNDAY IN ORDINARY TIME/C

Here is a saying that you can rely on:
If we have died with him, then we shall live with him.
If we hold firm, then we shall reign with him.
If we disown him, then he will disown us.
We may be unfaithful, but he is always faithful,
for he cannot disown his own self.

Alleluia — Alleluia, alleluia! Your words are spirit, Lord, and they are life: you have the message of eternal life. Alleluia! John 6:63.68.

or — Alleluia, alleluia! For all things give thanks, because this is what God expects you to do in Christ Jesus. Alleluia! 1 Thessalonians 5:18.

Gospel   Luke 17:11-19.

No one has come back to give praise to God, except this foreigner.

On the way to Jerusalem Jesus travelled along the border between Samaria and Galilee. As he entered one of the villages, ten lepers came out to meet him. They stood some way off and called to him, "Jesus! Master! Take pity on us." When he saw them he said, "Go and show yourselves to the priests." Now as they were going away they were cleansed. Finding himself cured, one of them turned back praising God at the top of his voice and threw himself at the feet of Jesus and thanked him. The man was a Samaritan. This made Jesus say, "Were not all ten made clean? The other nine, where are they? It seems that no one has come back to give praise to God, except this foreigner." And he said to the man, "Stand up and go on your way. Your faith has saved you."

Prayer over the Gifts

Lord,
accept the prayers and gifts
we offer in faith and love.
May this eucharist bring us to your glory.

Preface of Sundays I-VIII, pages 562-565.

Communion Antiphon — The rich suffer want and go hungry, but nothing shall be lacking to those who fear the Lord. Psalm 33:11.

or

TWENTY-NINTH SUNDAY IN ORDINARY TIME/C

> When the Lord is revealed we shall be like him, for we shall see him as he is.
>
> 1 John 3:2

Prayer after Communion

Almighty Father,
may the body and blood of your Son
give us a share in his life,
for he is Lord for ever and ever.

29th SUNDAY IN ORDINARY TIME/C

> Pray continually and never lose heart. When we pray we are inclined to give up if God does not seem to answer us immediately. We should persevere knowing that Christ is always interceding for us to his Father for our protection and welfare. As long as we pray in faith then we can never be beaten by our enemies.

Entrance Antiphon

I call upon you, God, for you will answer me; bend your ear and hear my prayer. Guard me as the pupil of your eye; hide me in the shade of your wings.

Psalm 16:6.8.

Opening Prayer

Let us pray
  [for the gift of simplicity and joy
  in our service of God and man]

TWENTY-NINTH SUNDAY IN ORDINARY TIME/C

Almighty and ever-living God,
our source of power and inspiration,
give us strength and joy
in serving you as followers of Christ,
who lives and reigns with you and the Holy Spirit,
one God, for ever and ever.

or

Let us pray
  [to the Lord who bends close to hear our prayer]

Lord our God, Father of all,
you guard us under the shadow of your wings
and search into the depths of our hearts.

Remove the blindness that cannot know you
and relieve the fear that would hide us from your sight.

First Reading   Exodus 17:8-13.

As long as Moses kept his arms raised, Israel had the advantage.

The Amalekites came and attacked Israel at Rephidim. Moses said to Joshua, "Pick out men for yourself, and tomorrow morning march out to engage Amalek. I, meanwhile, will stand on the hilltop, the staff of God in my hand." Joshua did as Moses told him and marched out to engage Amalek, while Moses and Aaron and Hur went up to the top of the hill. As long as Moses kept his arms raised, Israel had the advantage; when he let his arms fall, the advantage went to Amalek. But Moses' arms grew heavy, so they took a stone and put it under him and on this he sat, Aaron and Hur supporting his arms, one on one side, one on the other; and his arms remained firm till sunset. With the edge of the sword Joshua cut down Amalek and his people.

Responsorial Psalm   Psalm 120

℟ **Our help is in the name of the Lord
  who made heaven and earth.**

1. I lift up my eyes to the mountains:
   from where shall come my help?
   My help shall come from the Lord
   who made heaven and earth. ℟

TWENTY-NINTH SUNDAY IN ORDINARY TIME/C

2. May he never allow you to stumble!
   Let him sleep not, your guard.
   No, he sleeps not nor slumbers,
   Israel's guard. R/

3. The Lord is your guard and your shade;
   at your right side he stands.
   By day the sun shall not smite you
   nor the moon in the night. R/

4. The Lord will guard you from evil,
   he will guard your soul.
   The Lord will guard your going and coming
   both now and for ever. R/

Second Reading   2 Timothy 3:14-4:2.

The man who is dedicated to God becomes fully equipped and ready for any good work.

You must keep to what you have been taught and know to be true; remember who your teachers were, and how, ever since you were a child, you have known the holy scriptures — from these you can learn the wisdom that leads to salvation through faith in Christ Jesus. All scripture is inspired by God and can profitably be used for teaching, for refuting error, for guiding people's lives and teaching them to be holy. This is how the man who is dedicated to God becomes fully equipped and ready for any good work.

Before God and before Christ Jesus who is to be judge of the living and the dead, I put this duty to you, in the name of his Appearing and of his kingdom: proclaim the message and, welcome or unwelcome, insist on it. Refute falsehood, correct error, call to obedience — but do all with patience and with the intention of teaching.

Alleluia   Alleluia, alleluia! May the Father of our Lord Jesus Christ enlighten the eyes of our mind, so that we can see what hope his call holds for us. Alleluia!
                                                              Ephesians 1:17.18.

or

Alleluia, alleluia! The word of God is something alive and active; it can judge secret emotions and thoughts. Alleluia! Hebrews 4:12.

TWENTY-NINTH SUNDAY IN ORDINARY TIME/C

Gospel   Luke 18:1-8.
God will see justice done to his chosen who cry to him.

Jesus told his disciples a parable about the need to pray continually and never lose heart. "There was a judge in a certain town", he said "who had neither fear of God nor respect for man. In the same town there was a widow who kept on coming to him and saying, 'I want justice from you against my enemy!' For a long time he refused, but at last he said to himself, 'Maybe I have neither fear of God nor respect for man, but since she keeps pestering me I must give this widow her just rights, or she will persist in coming and worry me to death.' "

And the Lord said, "You notice what the unjust judge has to say? Now will not God see justice done to his chosen who cry to him day and night even when he delays to help them? I promise you, he will see justice done to them, and done speedily. But when the Son of Man comes, will he find any faith on earth?"

Prayer over the Gifts

Lord God,
may the gifts we offer
bring us your love and forgiveness
and give us freedom to serve you with our lives.

Preface of Sundays I-VIII, pages 562-565.

Communion Antiphon   See how the eyes of the Lord are on those who fear him, on those who hope in his love, that he may rescue them from death and feed them in time of famine. Psalm 32:18-19.

or

The Son of Man came to give his life as a ransom for many. Mark 10:45.

Prayer after Communion

Lord,
may this eucharist help us to remain faithful.
May it teach us the way to eternal life.

30th SUNDAY IN ORDINARY TIME/C

The prayer of the humble man. The self-righteous person has a closed mind and heart. Like the Pharisee he considers himself superior to others whereas the humble man recognises that he is a sinner before God. It is his prayer which will be answered. When we recognise that we need help we will receive it because we know that the answer to our prayer is due to God's mercy and not to our own goodness.

Entrance Antiphon   Let hearts rejoice who search for the Lord. Seek the Lord and his strength, seek always the face of the Lord.

Psalm 104:3-4.

Opening Prayer

Let us pray
  [for the strength to do God's will]

**Almighty and ever-living God,
strengthen our faith, hope, and love.
May we do with loving hearts
what you ask of us
and come to share the life you promise.**

or

Let us pray
  [in humble hope for salvation]

**Praised be you, God and Father of our Lord Jesus Christ.
There is no power for good
which does not come from your covenant,
and no promise to hope in
that your love has not offered.
Strengthen our faith to accept your covenant
and give us the love to carry out your command.**

THIRTIETH SUNDAY IN ORDINARY TIME/C

First Reading   Ecclesiasticus 35:12-14. 16-19.

The humble man's prayer pierces the clouds.

The Lord is a judge
who is no respecter of personages.
He shows no respect of personages to the detriment of a poor man,
he listens to the plea of the injured party.
He does not ignore the orphan's supplication,
nor the widow's as she pours out her story.

The man who with his whole heart serves God will be accepted,
his petitions will carry to the clouds.
The humble man's prayer pierces the clouds,
until it arrives he is inconsolable,
nor will he desist until the Most High takes notice of him,
acquits the virtuous and delivers judgement.
And the Lord will not be slow,
nor will he be dilatory on their behalf.

Responsorial Psalm   Psalm 33

℟ **This poor man called; the Lord heard him.**

1. I will bless the Lord at all times,
   his praise always on my lips;
   in the Lord my soul shall make its boast.
   The humble shall hear and be glad. ℟

2. The Lord turns his face against the wicked
   to destroy their remembrance from the earth.
   The just call and the Lord hears
   and rescues them in all their distress. ℟

3. The Lord is close to the broken-hearted;
   those whose spirit is crushed he will save.
   The Lord ransoms the souls of his servants.
   Those who hide in him shall not be condemned. ℟

THIRTIETH SUNDAY IN ORDINARY TIME/C

Second Reading 2 Timothy 4:6-8. 16-18.

All there is to come now is the crown of righteousness reserved for me.

My life is already being poured away as a libation, and the time has come for me to be gone. I have fought the good fight to the end; I have run the race to the finish; I have kept the faith; all there is to come now is the crown of righteousness reserved for me, which the Lord, the righteous judge, will give to me on that Day; and not only to me but to all those who have longed for his Appearing.

The first time I had to present my defence, there was not a single witness to support me. Every one of them deserted me — may they not be held accountable for it. But the Lord stood by me and gave me power, so that through me the whole message might be proclaimed for all the pagans to hear; and so I was rescued from the lion's mouth. The Lord will rescue me from all evil attempts on me, and bring me safely to his heavenly kingdom. To him be glory for ever and ever. Amen.

Alleluia

Alleluia, alleluia! Blessed are you, Father, Lord of heaven and earth, for revealing the mysteries of the kingdom to mere children. Alleluia! Matthew 11:25.

or

Alleluia, alleluia! God in Christ was reconciling the world to himself, and he has entrusted to us the news that they are reconciled. Alleluia! 2 Corinthians 5:19.

Gospel Luke 18:9-14.

The publican went home at rights with God; the Pharisee did not.

Jesus spoke the following parable to some people who prided themselves on being virtuous and despised everyone else, "Two men went up to the Temple to pray, one a Pharisee, the other a tax collector. The Pharisee stood there and said this prayer to himself, 'I thank you, God, that I am not grasping, unjust, adulterous like the rest of mankind, and particularly that I am not like this tax collector here. I fast twice a week; I pay tithes on all I get.' The tax collector stood some distance away, not daring even to raise his eyes to heaven; but he beat his breast and said,

THIRTIETH SUNDAY IN ORDINARY TIME/C

'God, be merciful to me, a sinner.' This man, I tell you, went home again at rights with God; the other did not. For everyone who exalts himself will be humbled, but the man who humbles himself will be exalted."

Prayer over the Gifts

Lord God of power and might,
receive the gifts we offer
and let our service give you glory.

Preface of Sundays I-VIII, pages 562-565.

Communion Antiphon We will rejoice at the victory of God and make our boast in his great name. **Psalm 19:6.**

or

Christ loved us and gave himself up for us as a fragrant offering to God.
Ephesians 5:2.

Prayer after Communion

Lord,
bring to perfection within us
the communion we share in this sacrament.
May our celebration have an effect in our lives.

31st SUNDAY IN ORDINARY TIME/C

Today salvation has come to this house. God is the lover of life and his imperishable spirit is in all things. He overlooks men's sins so that they can repent. His love reaches its fulfilment in Jesus who has come to save every person in the world if only like Zaccheus they wish to meet him and live better lives. Today salvation comes to us too if we are prepared to welcome Jesus into our hearts.

Entrance Antiphon Do not abandon me, Lord. My God, do not go away from me! Hurry to help me, Lord, my Saviour. Psalm 37:22-23.

Opening Prayer

Let us pray
   [that our lives will reflect our faith]

God of power and mercy,
only with your help
can we offer you fitting service and praise.
May we live the faith we profess
and trust your promise of eternal life.

or

Let us pray
   [in the presence of God, the source of every good]

Father in heaven, God of power and Lord of mercy,
from whose fullness we have received,
direct our steps in our everyday efforts.
May the changing moods of the human heart
and the limits which our failings impose on hope
never blind us to you, source of every good.

Faith gives us the promise of peace

THIRTY-FIRST SUNDAY IN ORDINARY TIME/C

and makes known the demands of love.
Remove the selfishness that blurs the vision of faith.

First Reading   Wisdom 11:22-12:2.

You are merciful to all because you love all that exists.

In your sight, Lord, the whole world is like a grain of dust that tips the scales,
like a drop of morning dew falling on the ground.
Yet you are merciful to all, because you can do all things
and overlook men's sins so that they can repent.
Yes, you love all that exists, you hold nothing of what you have made in abhorrence,
for had you hated anything, you would not have formed it.
And how, had you not willed it, could a thing persist,
how be conserved if not called forth by you?
You spare all things because all things are yours, Lord, lover of life,
you whose imperishable spirit is in all.
Little by little, therefore, you correct those who offend,
you admonish and remind them of how they have sinned,
so that they may abstain from evil and trust in you, Lord.

Responsorial Psalm   Psalm 144

℟ **I will bless your name for ever,
O God my King.**

1. I will give you glory, O God my King,
   I will bless your name for ever.
   I will bless you day after day
   and praise your name for ever. ℟

2. The Lord is kind and full of compassion,
   slow to anger, abounding in love.
   How good is the Lord to all,
   compassionate to all his creatures. ℟

3. All your creatures shall thank you, O Lord,
   and your friends shall repeat their blessing.
   They shall speak of the glory of your reign
   and declare your might, O God. ℟

(continued)

THIRTY-FIRST SUNDAY IN ORDINARY TIME/C

4. The Lord is faithful in all his words
   and loving in all his deeds.
   The Lord supports all who fall
   and raises all who are bowed down. R/

Second Reading   Thessalonians 1:11-2:2.

The name of Christ will be glorified in you and you in him.

We pray continually that our God will make you worthy of his call and by his power fulfil all your desires for goodness and complete all that you have been doing through faith; because in this way the name of our Lord Jesus Christ will be glorified in you and you in him, by the grace of our God and the Lord Jesus Christ.

To turn now, brothers, to the coming of our Lord Jesus Christ and how we shall all be gathered round him: please do not get excited too soon or alarmed by any prediction or rumour or any letter claiming to come from us, implying that the Day of the Lord has already arrived.

Alleluia   Alleluia, alleluia! Blessings on the King who comes, in the name of the Lord! Peace in heaven and glory in the highest heavens! Alleluia! Luke 19:38.

   or   Alleluia, alleluia! God loved the world so much that he gave his only Son so that anyone who believes in him may have eternal life. Alleluia! John 3:16.

Gospel   Luke 19:1-10.

The Son of Man has come to seek out and save what was lost.

Jesus entered Jericho and was going through the town when a man whose name was Zacchaeus made his appearance; he was one of the senior tax collectors and a wealthy man. He was anxious to see what kind of man Jesus was, but he was too short and could not see him for the crowd; so he ran ahead and climbed a sycamore tree to catch a glimpse of Jesus who was to pass that way. When Jesus reached the spot he looked up and spoke to him: "Zacchaeus, come down. Hurry, because I must stay at your house today." And he hurried down and welcomed him joyfully. They all complained when they saw what was happening. "He has gone to stay at a sinner's house" they said. But Zacchaeus stood his ground and said to the Lord, "Look, sir, I am going to give half my property to the poor, and if I have

THIRTY-FIRST SUNDAY IN ORDINARY TIME/C

cheated anybody I will pay him back four times the amount." And Jesus said to him, "Today salvation has come to this house, because this man too is a son of Abraham; for the Son of Man has come to seek out and save what was lost."

Prayer over the Gifts

God of mercy,
may we offer a pure sacrifice
for the forgiveness of our sins.

Preface of Sundays I-VIII, pages 562-565.

Communion Antiphon

Lord, you will show me the path of life and fill me with joy in your presence. **Psalm 15:11.**

or

As the living Father sent me, and I live because of the Father, so he who eats my flesh and drinks my blood will live because of me. **John 6:58.**

Prayer after Communion

Lord,
you give us new hope in this eucharist.
May the power of your love
continue its saving work among us
and bring us to the joy you promise.

32nd SUNDAY IN ORDINARY TIME/C

Our God is of the living.
In the midst of all the trials of this life God
is at our side constantly strengthening us
through Jesus Christ. We believe in the
resurrection from the dead and so are
called as sons of God to this great hope of
life without end. Our God is not of the dead
but of the living.

Entrance Antiphon   Let my prayer come before you, Lord; listen and answer me. Psalm 87:3.

Opening Prayer

Let us pray
  [for health of mind and body]

God of power and mercy,
protect us from all harm.
Give us freedom of spirit
and health in mind and body
to do your work on earth.

or

Let us pray
  [that our prayer rise like incense
  in the presence of the Lord]

Almighty Father,
strong is your justice and great is your mercy.
Protect us in the burdens and challenges of life.
Shield our minds from the distortion of pride
and enfold our desire with the beauty of truth.

Help us to become more aware of your loving design
so that we may more willingly give our lives in service to all.

THIRTY-SECOND SUNDAY IN ORDINARY TIME/C

First Reading   Maccabees 7:1-2. 9-14.
The King of the world will raise us up to live again for ever.

There were seven brothers who were arrested with their mother. The king tried to force them to taste pig's flesh, which the Law forbids, by torturing them with whips and scourges. One of them acting as spokesman for the others, said, "What are you trying to find out from us? We are prepared to die rather than break the Law of our ancestors."

With his last breath the second brother exclaimed, "Inhuman fiend, you may discharge us from this present life, but the King of the world will raise us up, since it is for his laws that we die, to live again for ever."

After him, they amused themselves with the third, who on being asked for his tongue promptly thrust it out and boldly held out his hands, with these honourable words, "It was heaven that gave me these limbs; for the sake of his laws I disdain them; from him I hope to receive them again." The king and his attendants were astounded at the young man's courage and his utter indifference to suffering.

When this one was dead they subjected the fourth to the same savage torture. When he neared his end he cried, "Ours is the better choice, to meet death at men's hands, yet relying on God's promise that we shall be raised up by him; whereas for you there can be no resurrection, no new life."

Responsorial Psalm   Psalm 16

℟ **I shall be filled, when I awake,**
   with the sight of your glory, O Lord.

1. Lord, hear a cause that is just,
   pay heed to my cry.
   Turn your ear to my prayer:
   no deceit is on my lips. ℟

2. I kept my feet firmly in your paths;
   there was no faltering in my steps.
   I am here and I call, you will hear me, O God.
   Turn your ear to me; hear my words. ℟

3. Guard me as the apple of your eye.
   Hide me in the shadow of your wings.
   As for me, in my justice I shall see your face
   and be filled, when I awake, with the sight of your glory. ℟

THIRTY-SECOND SUNDAY IN ORDINARY TIME/C

Second Reading   2 Thessalonians 2:16-3:5.

May the Lord strengthen you in everything good that you do or say.

May our Lord Jesus Christ himself, and God our Father who has given us his love and, through his grace, such inexhaustible comfort and such sure hope, comfort you and strengthen you in everything good that you do or say.

Finally, brothers, pray for us; pray that the Lord's message may spread quickly, and be received with honour as it was among you; and pray that we may be preserved from the interference of bigoted and evil people, for faith is not given to everyone. But the Lord is faithful, and he will give you strength and guard you from the evil one, and we, in the Lord, have every confidence that you are doing and will go on doing all that we tell you. May the Lord turn your hearts towards the love of God and the fortitude of Christ.

Alleluia   Alleluia, alleluia! Stay awake, praying at all times for the strength to stand with confidence before the Son of Man. Alleluia! Matthew 24:42.44

or

Alleluia, alleluia! Jesus Christ is the First-born from the dead; to him be glory and power for ever and ever. Alleluia! Apocalypse 1:5.6.

Gospel   Luke 20:27-38.

He is God, not of the dead, but of the living.

Some Sadducees — those who say that there is no resurrection — approached Jesus and they put a question to him.
Master, we have it from Moses in writing, that if a man's married brother dies childless, the man must marry the widow to raise up children for his brother. Well, then, there were seven brothers. The first, having married a wife, died childless. The second and then the third married the widow. And the same with all seven, they died leaving no children. Finally the woman herself died. Now, at the resurrection, to which of them will she be wife since she had been married to all seven?"

Jesus replied, "The children of this world take wives and husbands, but those who are judged worthy of a place in the other world and in the resurrection from the dead do not

THIRTY-SECOND SUNDAY IN ORDINARY TIME/C

marry because they can no longer die, for they are the same as the angels, and being children of the resurrection they are sons of God. And Moses himself implies that the dead rise again, in the passage about the bush where he calls the Lord the God of Abraham, the God of Isaac and the God of Jacob. Now he is God, not of the dead, but of the living; for to him all men are in fact alive."

Prayer over the Gifts

God of mercy,
in this eucharist we proclaim the death of the Lord.
Accept the gifts we present
and help us follow him with love,
for he is Lord for ever and ever.

Preface of Sundays I-VIII, pages 562-565.

Communion Antiphon

The Lord is my shepherd; there is nothing I shall want. In green pastures he gives me rest, he leads me beside the waters of peace.

Psalm 22:1-2.

or

The disciples recognised the Lord Jesus in the breaking of bread.

Luke 24:35.

Prayer after Communion

Lord,
we thank you for the nourishment you give us
through your holy gift.
Pour out your Spirit upon us
and in the strength of this food from heaven
keep us single-minded in your service.

33rd SUNDAY IN ORDINARY TIME/C

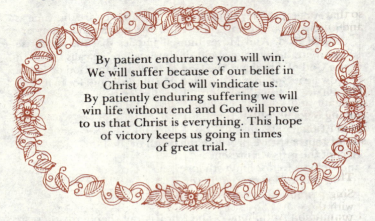

By patient endurance you will win.
We will suffer because of our belief in
Christ but God will vindicate us.
By patiently enduring suffering we will
win life without end and God will prove
to us that Christ is everything. This hope
of victory keeps us going in times
of great trial.

Entrance Antiphon   The Lord says: my plans for you are peace and not disaster; when you call to me, I will listen to you, and I will bring you back to the place from which I exiled you. Jeremiah 29:11.12.14.

Opening Prayer

Let us pray
   [that God will help us to be faithful]

Father of all that is good,
keep us faithful in serving you,
for to serve you is our lasting joy.

or

Let us pray
   [with hearts that long for peace]

Father in heaven,
ever-living source of all that is good,
from the beginning of time you promised man salvation
through the future coming of your Son, our Lord Jesus Christ.

Help us to drink of his truth
and expand our hearts with the joy of his promises,

so that we may serve you in faith and in love
and know for ever the joy of your presence.

First Reading Malachi 3:19-20.
For you the sun of righteousness will shine out.

The day is coming now, burning like a furnace; and all the arrogant and evil-doers will be like stubble. The day that is coming is going to burn them up, says the Lord of hosts, leaving them neither root nor stalk. But for you who fear my name, the sun of righteousness will shine out with healing in its rays.

Responsorial Psalm Psalm 97

℟ The Lord comes to rule the peoples with fairness.

1. Sing psalms to the Lord with the harp
   with the sound of music.
   With trumpets and the sound of the horn
   acclaim the King, the Lord. ℟

2. Let the sea and all within it, thunder;
   the world, and all its peoples.
   Let the rivers clap their hands
   and the hills ring out their joy
   at the presence of the Lord. ℟

3. For the Lord comes, comes to rule the earth.
   He will rule the world with justice
   and the peoples with fairness. ℟

Second Reading 2 Thessalonians 3:7-12.
Do not let anyone have food if he refuses to work.

You know how you are supposed to imitate us: now we were not idle when we were with you, nor did we ever have our meals at anyone's table without paying for them; no, we worked night and day, slaving and straining, so as not to be a burden on any of you. This was not because we had no right to be, but in order to make ourselves an example for you to follow.

We gave you a rule when we were with you: not to let anyone have any food if he refused to do any work. Now we hear that there are some of you who are living in idleness, doing no work themselves but interfering with everyone else's. In the Lord

THIRTY-THIRD SUNDAY IN ORDINARY TIME/C

Jesus Christ, we order and call on people of this kind to go on quietly working and earning the food that they eat.

Alleluia Alleluia, alleluia! Stay awake, praying at all times for the strength to stand with confidence before the Son of Man. Matthew 24:42.44.

or

Alleluia, alleluia! Stand erect, hold your heads high, because your liberation is near at hand. Alleluia!
                                                             Luke 21:28.

Gospel Luke 21:5-19.

Your endurance will win you your lives.

When some were talking about the Temple, remarking how it was adorned with fine stonework and votive offerings, Jesus said, "All these things you are staring at now — the time will come when not a single stone will be left on another: everything will be destroyed." And they put to him this question: "Master," they said "when will this happen, then, and what sign will there be that this is about to take place?"

"Take care not to be deceived," he said "because many will come using my name and saying, 'I am he' and, 'The time is near at hand.' Refuse to join them. And when you hear of wars and revolutions, do not be frightened, for this is something that must happen but the end is not so soon." Then he said to them, "Nation will fight against nation, and kingdom against kingdom. There will be great earthquakes and plagues and famines here and there; there will be fearful sights and great signs from heaven.

"But before all this happens, men will seize you and persecute you; they will hand you over to the synagogues and to imprisonment, and bring you before kings and governors because of my name — and that will be your opportunity to bear witness. Keep this carefully in mind: you are not to prepare your defence, because I myself shall give you an eloquence and a wisdom that none of your opponents will be able to resist or contradict. You will be betrayed even by parents and brothers, relations and friends; and some of you will be put to death. You will be hated by all men on account of my name, but not a hair of your head will be lost. Your endurance will win you your lives."

THIRTY-THIRD SUNDAY IN ORDINARY TIME/C

Prayer over the Gifts

Lord God,
may the gifts we offer
increase our love for you
and bring us to eternal life.

Preface of Sundays I-VIII, pages 562-565.

Communion Antiphon

It is good for me to be with the Lord
and to put my hope in him.
Psalm 72:28.

or

I tell you solemnly, whatever you ask for in prayer, believe that you have received it, and it will be yours, says the Lord. Mark 11:23.24.

Prayer after Communion

Father,
may we grow in love
by the eucharist we have celebrated
in memory of the Lord Jesus,
who is Lord for ever and ever.

LAST SUNDAY IN ORDINARY TIME
OUR LORD JESUS CHRIST, UNIVERSAL KING/C

The King who promises us his kingdom! Christ on the cross promises his kingdom to a penitent thief. We, like the criminal, receive redemption and forgiveness of our sins through Christ who through his glorious power gives us the strength to bear everything joyfully. If we suffer with him we will reign with him. He is the first-born from the dead never to die again.

Entrance Antiphon

The Lamb who was slain is worthy to receive strength and divinity, wisdom and power and honour: to him be glory and power for ever. Revelation 5:12; 1:6.

Opening Prayer

Let us pray
 [that all men will acclaim Jesus as Lord]

Almighty and merciful God,
you break the power of evil
and make all things new
in your Son Jesus Christ, the King of the universe.
May all in heaven and earth acclaim your glory
and never cease to praise you.

or

Let us pray
 [that the kingdom of Christ
 may live in our hearts and come to our world]

Father all-powerful, God of love,
you have raised our Lord Jesus Christ from death to life,

OUR LORD JESUS CHRIST, UNIVERSAL KING/C

resplendent in glory as King of creation.
Open our hearts,
free all the world to rejoice in his peace,
to glory in his justice, to live in his love.
Bring all mankind together in Jesus Christ your Son,
whose kingdom is with you and the Holy Spirit,
one God, for ever and ever.

First Reading   2 Samuel 5:1-3.
They anointed David king of Israel.

All the tribes of Israel came to David at Hebron. "Look" they said "we are your own flesh and blood. In days past when Saul was our king, it was you who led Israel in all their exploits; and the Lord said to you, 'You are the man who shall be shepherd of my people Israel, you shall be the leader of Israel.'" So all the elders of Israel came to the king at Hebron, and King David made a pact with them at Hebron in the presence of the Lord, and they anointed David king of Israel.

Responsorial Psalm   Psalm 121

R/ **I rejoiced when I heard them say:
"Let us go to God's house."**

1. I rejoiced when I heard them say:
   "Let us go to God's house."
   And now our feet are standing
   within your gates, O Jerusalem.   R/

2. Jerusalem is built as a city
   strongly compact.
   It is there that the tribes go up,
   the tribes of the Lord.   R/

3. For Israel's law it is,
   there to praise the Lord's name.
   There were set the thrones of judgement
   of the house of David.   R/

OUR LORD JESUS CHRIST, UNIVERSAL KING/C

Second reading   Colossians 1:12-20.

He has created a place for us in the kingdom of the Son that he loves.

We give thanks to the Father who has made it possible for you to join the saints and with them inherit the light.

Because that is what he has done: he has taken us out of the power of darkness and created a place for us in the kingdom of the Son that he loves, and in him, we gain our freedom, the forgiveness of our sins.
He is the image of the unseen God
and the first-born of all creation
for in him were created
all things in heaven and on earth:
everything visible and everything invisible,
Thrones, Dominations, Sovereignties, Powers —
all things were created through him and for him.
Before anything was created, he existed,
and he holds all things in unity.
Now the Church is his body,
he is its head.
As he is the Beginning,
he was first to be born from the dead,
so that he should be first in every way;
because God wanted all perfection
to be found in him
and all things to be reconciled through him and for him,
everything in heaven and everything on earth,
when he made peace
by his death on the cross.

Alleluia   Alleluia, alleluia! Blessings on him who comes in the name of the Lord! Blessings on the coming kingdom of our father David! Alleluia! Mark 11:10.

Gospel   Luke 23:35-43.

Lord, remember me when you come into your kingdom.

The people stayed there watching Jesus. As for the leaders, they jeered at him. "He saved others," they said "let him save himself if he is the Christ of God, the Chosen One." The soldiers mocked him too, and when they approached to offer him vinegar they said, "If you are the king of the Jews, save yourself." Above him there was an inscription: "This is the King of the Jews."

One of the criminals hanging there abused him. "Are you not the Christ?" he said. "Save yourself and us as well." But the other spoke up and rebuked him. "Have you no fear of God at all?" he said. "You got the same sentence as he did, but in our case we deserved it: we are paying for what we did. But this man has done nothing wrong. Jesus," he said "remember me when you come into your kingdom." "Indeed, I promise you," he replied "today you will be with me in paradise."

Prayer over the Gifts

Lord,
we offer you the sacrifice
by which your Son reconciles mankind.
May it bring unity and peace to the world.

Preface of Christ the King, page 735.

Communion Antiphon

The Lord will reign for ever and will give his people the gift of peace.
Psalm 28:10-11.

Prayer after Communion

Lord,
you give us Christ, the King of all creation,
as food for everlasting life.
Help us to live by his gospel
and bring us to the joy of his kingdom,
where he lives and reigns for ever and ever.

Alleluia

FOR THE SUNDAYS OF THE YEAR

The following Alleluia verses may be used instead of that printed for each Sunday.

1. Alleluia, alleluia!
   Speak, Lord, your servant is listening:
   you have the message of eternal life.
   Alleluia! 1 Samuel 3:9; John 6:68

2. Alleluia, alleluia!
   Blessed are you, Father,
   Lord of heaven and earth,
   for revealing the mysteries of the kingdom
   to mere children.
   Alleluia! Matthew 11:25

3. Alleluia, alleluia!
   Blessings on the King who comes,
   in the name of the Lord!
   Peace in heaven
   and glory in the highest heavens!
   Alleluia! Luke 19:38

4. Alleluia, alleluia!
   The Word was made flesh and lived among us;
   to all who did accept him
   he gave power to become children of God.
   Alleluia! John 1:14.12

5. Alleluia, alleluia!
   Your words are spirit, Lord,
   and they are life:
   you have the message of eternal life.
   Alleluia! John 6:63.68

6. Alleluia, alleluia!
   I am the light of the world, says the Lord,
   anyone who follows me
   will have the light of life. Alleluia! John 8:12

ALTERNATIVE ALLELUIAS

7. Alleluia, alleluia!
   The sheep that belong to me listen to my voice,
   says the Lord,
   I know them and they follow me.
   Alleluia! John 10:27

8. Alleluia, alleluia!
   I am the Way, the Truth and the Life, says the Lord;
   no one can come to the Father except through me.
   Alleluia! John 14:6

9. Alleluia, alleluia!
   If anyone loves me he will keep my word,
   and my Father will love him,
   and we shall come to him.
   Alleluia! John 14:23

10. Alleluia, alleluia!
    I call you friends, says the Lord,
    because I have made known to you
    everything I have learnt from my Father.
    Alleluia! John 15:15

11. Alleluia, alleluia!
    Your word is truth, O Lord,
    consecrate us in the truth.
    Alleluia! John 17:17

12. Alleluia, alleluia!
    Open our heart, O Lord,
    to accept the words of your Son.
    Alleluia! Acts 16:14

13. Alleluia, alleluia!
    May the Father of our Lord Jesus Christ
    enlighten the eyes of our mind,
    so that we can see what hope his call holds for us.
    Alleluia! Ephesians 1:17.18

For the last Sundays of the Year

14. Alleluia, alleluia!
    Stay awake and stand ready,
    because you do not know the hour
    when the Son of Man is coming.
    Alleluia! Matthew 24:42.44

ALTERNATIVE ALLELUIAS

15. Alleluia, alleluia!
    Stay awake, praying at all times
    for the strength to stand with confidence
    before the Son of Man.
    Alleluia! Luke 21:36

16. Alleluia, alleluia!
    Even if you have to die, says the Lord,
    keep faithful, and I will give you
    the crown of life.
    Alleluia! Revelation 2:10

Solemnities and Feasts

FEBRUARY 2
THE PRESENTATION OF THE LORD
Feast

> Christ the light of the nations.
> Christ brings God's light into a world darkened by sin. We are to bring this light into our world since we share in Christ's mission and life. He accomplished this for us through his death by which he took away the power of evil. He became one of us through the incarnation and because he has himself been through temptation he is able to help others who are tempted.

BLESSINGS OF CANDLES AND PROCESSION

First Form: Procession

The people gather in a chapel or other suitable place outside the church where the Mass will be celebrated. They carry unlighted candles. While the candles are being lighted, this canticle or another hymn is sung:

The Lord will come with mighty power,
and give light to the eyes of all who serve him, alleluia.

The priest greets the people in these or similar words:

Forty days ago we celebrated the joyful feast of the birth of our Lord Jesus Christ. Today we recall the holy day on which he was presented in the temple, fulfilling the law of Moses and at the same time going to meet his faithful people. Led by the Spirit, Simeon and Anna came to the temple, recognised Christ as their Lord, and proclaimed him with joy.

United by the Spirit, may we now go to the house of God to welcome Christ the Lord. There we shall recognise him in the breaking of bread until he comes again in glory.

THE PRESENTATION OF THE LORD

The priest blesses the candles:

Let us pray.
God our Father, source of all light,
today you revealed to Simeon
your Light of revelation to the nations.
Bless ✠ these candles and make them holy.
May we who carry them to praise your glory
walk in the path of goodness
and come to the light that shines for ever.

or

God our Father, source of eternal light,
fill the hearts of all believers
with the light of faith.
May we who carry these candles in your church
come with joy to the light of glory.

The priest then takes the candle prepared for him, and the procession begins with the acclamation:

Let us go in peace to meet the Lord.

During the procession, the canticle of Simeon, or another hymn, is sung:

Antiphon   Christ is the light of the nations
and the glory of Israel his people.

Now, Lord, you have kept your word:
let your servant go in peace. ℟

With my own eyes I have seen the salvation
which you have prepared in the sight of every
    people. ℟

A light to reveal you to the nations
and the glory of your people Israel. ℟

As the procession enters the church, the entrance chant of the Mass is sung. The Mass continues as usual.

Second Form: Solemn Entrance

The people, carrying unlighted candles, assemble in the church. The priest, accompanied by his ministers and by a representative

THE PRESENTATION OF THE LORD

group of the faithful, goes to a suitable place where most of the congregation can easily take part.

The candles are lighted while the antiphon, Christ is the Light, (see above) or another hymn is sung.

After the greeting and introduction, the priest blesses the candles, as above, and goes in procession to the altar, while all are singing. The Mass continues as usual.

THE MASS

Entrance Antiphon Within your temple, we ponder your loving kindness, O God. As your name, so also your praise reaches to the ends of the earth; your right hand is filled with justice.
Psalm 47:10-11

Opening Prayer

All-powerful Father,
Christ your Son became man for us
and was presented in the temple.
May he free our hearts from sin
and bring us into your presence.

First Reading   Malachi 3:1-4.

The Lord you are seeking will suddenly enter his Temple.

The Lord God says this: Look, I am going to send my messenger to prepare a way before me. And the Lord you are seeking will suddenly enter his Temple; and the angel of the covenant whom you are longing for, yes, he is coming, says the Lord of hosts. Who will be able to resist the day of his coming? Who will remain standing when he appears? For he is like the refiner's fire and the fullers' alkali. He will take his seat as refiner and purifier; he will purify the sons of Levi and refine them like gold and silver, and then they will make the offering to the Lord as it should be made. The offering of Judah and Jerusalem will then be welcomed by the Lord as in former days, as in the years of old.

THE PRESENTATION OF THE LORD

Responsorial Psalm   Psalm 23.

℟ **Who is the king of glory?
It is the Lord.**

1. O gates, lift up your heads;
   grow higher, ancient doors.
   Let him enter, the king of glory! ℟

2. Who is the king of glory?
   The Lord, the mighty, the valiant,
   the Lord, the valiant in war. ℟

3. O gates, lift high your heads;
   grow higher, ancient doors.
   Let him enter, the king of glory! ℟

4. Who is he, the king of glory?
   He, the Lord of armies,
   he is the king of glory. ℟

Second Reading   Hebrews 2:14-18.

It was essential that he should in this way become completely like his brothers.

Since all the children share the same blood and flesh, he too shared equally in it, so that by his death he could take away all the power of the devil, who had power over death, and set free all those who had been held in slavery all their lives by the fear of death. For it was not the angels that he took to himself; he took to himself descent from Abraham. It was essential that he should in this way become completely like his brothers so that he could be a compassionate and trustworthy high priest of God's religion, able to atone for human sins. That is, because he has himself been through temptation he is able to help others who are tempted.

Alleluia   Alleluia, alleluia! The light to enlighten the Gentiles and give glory to Israel, your people. Alleluia!

Luke 2:32

Gospel   Luke 2:22-40.

My eyes have seen your salvation.

When the day came for them to be purified as laid down by the Law of Moses, the parents of Jesus took him up to Jerusalem to present him to the Lord — observing what stands written in the

THE PRESENTATION OF THE LORD

Law of the Lord: Every first-born male must be consecrated to the Lord — and also to offer in sacrifice, in accordance with what is said in the Law of the Lord, a pair of turtle-doves or two young pigeons. Now in Jerusalem there was a man named Simeon. He was an upright and devout man; he looked forward to Israel's comforting and the Holy Spirit rested on him. It had been revealed to him by the Holy Spirit that he would not see death until he had set eyes on the Christ of the Lord. Prompted by the Spirit he came to the Temple; and when the parents brought in the child Jesus to do for him what the Law required, he took him into his arms and blessed God; and he said:

"Now, Master, you can let your servant go in peace,
just as you promised;
because my eyes have seen the salvation
which you have prepared for all the nations to see,
a light to enlighten the pagans
and the glory of your people Israel."

As the child's father and mother stood there wondering at the things that were being said about him, Simeon blessed them and said to Mary his mother, "You see this child: he is destined for the fall and for the rising of many in Israel, destined to be a sign that is rejected — and a sword will pierce your own soul too — so that the secret thoughts of many may be laid bare."

There was a prophetess also, Anna the daughter of Phanuel, of the tribe of Asher. She was well on in years. Her days of girlhood over, she had been married for seven years before becoming a widow. She was now eighty-four years old and never left the Temple, serving God night and day with fasting and prayer. She came by just at that moment and began to praise God; and she spoke of the child to all who looked forward to the deliverance of Jerusalem.

When they had done everything the Law of the Lord required, they went back to Galilee, to their own town of Nazareth. Meanwhile the child grew to maturity, and he was filled with wisdom; and God's favour was with him.

Prayer over the Gifts

Lord,
accept the gifts your Church offers you with joy,
since in fulfillment of your will

THE PRESENTATION OF THE LORD

your Son offered himself as a lamb without blemish
for the life of the world.

Preface

Father, all-powerful and ever-living God,
we do well always and everywhere to give you thanks
through Jesus Christ our Lord.

Today your Son,
who shares your eternal splendour,
was presented in the temple,
and revealed by the Spirit
as the glory of Israel
and the light of all peoples.

Our hearts are joyful,
for we have seen your salvation,
and now with the angels and saints
we praise you for ever:

Holy, holy, holy ...

Communion Antiphon

With my own eyes I have seen the salvation which you have prepared in the sight of all the nations.

Luke 2:30-31

Prayer after Communion

Lord,
you fulfilled the hope of Simeon,
who did not die
until he had been privileged to welcome the Messiah.
May this communion perfect your grace in us
and prepare us to meet Christ
when he comes to bring us into everlasting life,
for he is Lord for ever and ever.

MARCH 1
ST DAVID, BISHOP
PATRON OF WALES
In Wales: Solemnity
In England: Feast

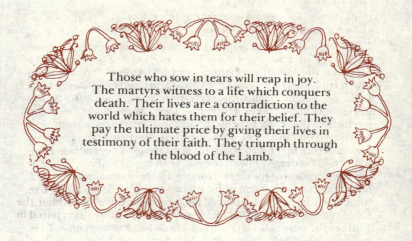

Those who sow in tears will reap in joy. The martyrs witness to a life which conquers death. Their lives are a contradiction to the world which hates them for their belief. They pay the ultimate price by giving their lives in testimony of their faith. They triumph through the blood of the Lamb.

Entrance Antiphon

My teaching, which I have put in your mouth, will never fail, says the Lord; the gifts which you offered on my altar will be accepted. Isaiah 59:21;56:7.

or

You, Lord, are my portion and cup, you restore my inheritance to me; the way of life you marked out for me has made my heritage glorious. Psalm 15:5-6.

Opening Prayer

God our Father,
you gave the bishop David to the Welsh Church
to uphold the faith
and to be an example of Christian perfection.
In this changing world

SAINT DAVID

may he help us to hold fast to the values
which bring eternal life.

Other readings may be used instead of those given here.

First Reading   Philippians 3:8-14.

I am racing for the finish, for the prize to which God calls us upwards to receive in Christ Jesus.

I believe nothing can happen that will outweigh the supreme advantage of knowing Christ Jesus my Lord. For him I have accepted the loss of everything, and I look on everything as so much rubbish if only I can have Christ and be given a place in him. I am no longer trying for perfection by my own efforts, the perfection that comes from the Law, but I want only the perfection that comes through faith in Christ, and is from God and based on faith. All I want is to know Christ and the power of his resurrection and to share his sufferings by reproducing the pattern of his death. That is the way I can hope to take my place in the resurrection of the dead. Not that I have become perfect yet: I have not yet won, but I am still running, trying to capture the prize for which Christ Jesus captured me. I can assure you my brothers, I am far from thinking that I have already won. All I can say is that I forget the past and I strain ahead for what is still to come; I am racing for the finish, for the prize to which God calls us upwards to receive in Christ Jesus.

Responsorial Psalm   Psalm 1.

**℟ Happy the man who has placed
his trust in the Lord.**

1. Happy indeed is the man
   who follows not the counsel of the wicked;
   nor lingers in the way of sinners
   nor sits in the company of scorners,
   but whose delight is the law of the Lord
   and who ponders his law day and night. ℟

2. *He is like a tree that is planted
   beside the flowing waters,
   that yields its fruit in due season
   and whose leaves shall never fade;
   and all that he does shall prosper.* ℟

SAINT DAVID

3. Not so are the wicked, not so!
   For they like winnowed chaff
   shall be driven away by the wind;
   for the Lord guards the way of the just
   but the way of the wicked leads to doom. ℟

Alleluia   Alleluia, alleluia! If you make my word your home you will indeed be my disciples, and you will learn the truth, says the Lord. Alleluia! John 8:31-32.

Gospel   Matthew 5:13-16.

You are the light of the world.

Jesus said to his disciples, "You are the salt of the earth. But if salt becomes tasteless, what can make it salty again? It is good for nothing, and can only be thrown out to be trampled underfoot by men.

"You are the light of the world. A city built on a hill-top cannot be hidden. No one lights a lamp to put it under a tub; they put it on the lamp-stand where it shines for everyone in the house. In the same way your light must shine in the sight of men, so that, seeing your good works, they may give the praise to your Father in heaven."

Prayer over the Gifts

Lord, accept the gifts we bring
on the feast of Saint David.
We offer them to win your forgiveness
and to give honour to your name.

Preface

Father, all-powerful and ever-living God,
we do well always and everywhere to give you thanks.

You are glorified in your saints,
for their glory is the crowning of your gifts.
In their lives on earth
you give us an example.
In our communion with them
you give us their friendship.
In their prayer for the Church
you give us strength and protection.
This great company of witnesses spurs us on to victory,

SAINT DAVID

to share their prize of everlasting glory,
through Jesus Christ our Lord.

With angels and archangels
and the whole company of saints
we sing our unending hymn of praise:

Holy, holy, holy ...

Communion Antiphon   The Son of Man came to give his life as a ransom for all. Mark 10:45.

or

I assure you who left all and followed me; you will receive a hundredfold in return and inherit eternal life.
cf. Matthew 19:27-29

Prayer after Communion

All-powerful God,
you have strengthened us with this sacrament.
May we learn from Saint David's example
to seek you above all things,
and to live always as new men in Christ,
who lives and reigns for ever and ever.

MARCH 17
ST PATRICK, BISHOP
PATRON OF IRELAND
In Ireland and Australia: Solemnity
In England, Wales and Scotland: Feast

> I have appointed you as prophet to the nations. Throughout the ages God calls people to witness to the power of his name. They are his witnesses and missionaries. Just as Christ sent his seventy two disciples to preach the Good News, so too we are sent to be a light to those around us so that God's salvation may reach the ends of the earth.

Entrance Antiphon Go from your country and your kindred and your Father's house to the land that I will show you; and I will make you the father of a great people. Genesis 12:1-2.

Opening Prayer
Let us pray
   [that like Saint Patrick the missionary
   we will be fearless witnesses
   to the gospel of Jesus Christ]

God our Father,
you sent St Patrick
to preach your glory to the people of Ireland.
By the help of his prayers,
may all Christians proclaim your love to all men.

or

Father in heaven,

SAINT PATRICK

you sent the great bishop Patrick
to the people of Ireland to share his faith
and to spend his life in loving service.

May our lives bear witness
to the faith we profess,
and our love bring others
to the peace and joy of your gospel.

Other readings may be used instead of those given here.

First Reading   Jeremiah 1:4-9.
Go now to those to whom I send you.

The word of the Lord was addressed to me, saying,
"Before I formed you in the womb I knew you;
before you came to birth I consecrated you;
I have appointed you as prophet to the nations."
I said, "Ah, Lord; look, I do not know how to speak: I am a child."
But the Lord replied,
"Do not say, 'I am a child.'
Go now to those to whom I send you
and say whatever I command you.
Do not be afraid of them,
for I am with you to protect you —
it is the Lord who speaks!"
Then the Lord put out his hand and touched my mouth and said to me:
"There! I am putting my words into your mouth."

Responsorial Psalm   Psalm 116.

R/ **Go out to the world
and proclaim the Good News.**

1. Alleluia!
   O praise the Lord, all you nations,
   acclaim him all you peoples!   R/

2. Strong is his love for us;
   he is faithful for ever.   R/

SAINT PATRICK

Second Reading   Acts 13:46-49.
We must turn to the pagans.

Paul and Barnabas spoke out boldly to the Jews, "We had to proclaim the word of God to you first, but since you have rejected it, since you do not think yourselves worthy of eternal life, we must turn to the pagans. For this is what the Lord commanded us to do when he said:
'I have made you a light for the nations,
so that my salvation may reach the ends of the earth.' "

It made the pagans very happy to hear this and they thanked the Lord for his message; all who were destined for eternal life became believers. Thus the word of the Lord spread through the whole countryside.

Acclamation or Alleluia   [Alleluia, alleluia!] The Lord has sent me to bring the good news to the poor, to proclaim liberty to captives. [alleluia!] Luke 4:18-19.

Gospel   Luke 10:1-12.17-20.
Your peace will rest on that man.

The Lord appointed seventy-two others and sent them out ahead of him, in pairs, to all the towns and places he himself was to visit. He said to them, "The harvest is rich but the labourers are few, so ask the Lord of the harvest to send labourers to his harvest. Start off now, but remember, I am sending you out like lambs among wolves. Carry no purse, no haversack, no sandals. Salute no one on the road. Whatever house you go into, let your first words be, 'Peace to this house!' And if a man of peace lives there, your peace will go and rest on him; if not, it will come back to you. Stay in the same house, taking what food and drink they have to offer, for the labourer deserves his wages; do not move from house to house. Whenever you go into a town where they make you welcome, eat what is set before you. Cure those in it who are sick, and say, 'The kingdom of God is very near you.' But whenever you enter a town and they do not make you welcome, go out into its streets and say, 'We wipe off the very dust of your town that clings to our feet, and leave it with you. Yet be sure of this, the kingdom of God is very near.' I tell you, on that day it will not go as hard with Sodom as with that town."

The seventy-two came back rejoicing. "Lord," they said, "even

SAINT PATRICK

the devils submit to us when we use your name." He said to them, "I watched Satan fall like lightning from heaven. Yes, I have given you power to tread underfoot serpents and scorpions and the whole strength of the enemy; nothing shall ever hurt you. Yet do not rejoice that the spirits submit to you; rejoice rather that your names are written in heaven."

The Creed is said in Ireland and Australia.

Prayer over the Gifts

Lord our God,
by the power of this sacrament
deepen our love and strengthen our faith:
as we celebrate the feast of Saint Patrick
bind us more and more to each other
in unity and peace.

Preface

Father, all-powerful and ever-living God,
we do well always and everywhere to give you thanks.

You are glorified in your saints,
for their glory is the crowning of your gifts.
In their lives on earth
you give us an example,
In our communion with them
you give us their friendship.
In their prayer for the Church
you give us strength and protection.
This great company of witnesses spurs us on to victory,
to share their prize of everlasting glory,
through Jesus Christ our Lord.

With angels and archangels
and the whole company of saints
we sing our unending hymn of praise:

Holy, holy, holy ...

Communion Antiphon

The Lord sent disciples to proclaim to the people: The kingdom of God is very near to you. cf. Luke 10:1-9.

or

SAINT PATRICK

The Lord sent me to bring the good news to the poor, to proclaim liberty to captives. Luke 4:18-19.

Prayer after Communion

Lord,
by the power of this sacrament
strengthen our faith:
may all we do or say
proclaim your truth
in imitation of Saint Patrick,
who did not spare himself
but gave his whole life
to the preaching of your Word.

MARCH 19
ST JOSEPH
HUSBAND OF THE BLESSED VIRGIN MARY
Solemnity

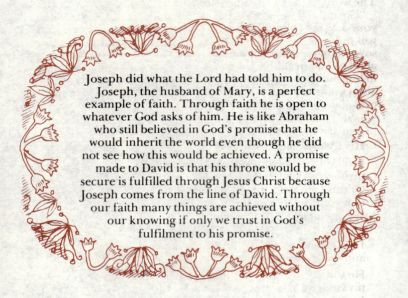

Joseph did what the Lord had told him to do. Joseph, the husband of Mary, is a perfect example of faith. Through faith he is open to whatever God asks of him. He is like Abraham who still believed in God's promise that he would inherit the world even though he did not see how this would be achieved. A promise made to David is that his throne would be secure is fulfilled through Jesus Christ because Joseph comes from the line of David. Through our faith many things are achieved without our knowing if only we trust in God's fulfilment to his promise.

Entrance Antiphon The Lord has put his faithful servant in charge of his household. Luke 12:42.

Opening Prayer

Let us pray
 [that the Church will continue
 the saving work of Christ]

Father,
you entrusted our Saviour to the care of Saint Joseph.
By the help of his prayers
may your Church continue to serve its Lord, Jesus Christ,
who lives and reigns with you and the Holy Spirit,
one God, for ever and ever.

SAINT JOSEPH

First Reading   2 Samuel 7:4-5.12-14.16.

The Lord will give him the throne of his ancestor David.

The word of the Lord came to Nathan:

"Go and tell my servant David, 'Thus the Lord speaks: When your days are ended and you are laid to rest with your ancestors, I will preserve the offspring of your body after you and make his sovereignty secure. (It is he who shall build a house for my name, and I will make his royal throne secure for ever.) I will be a father to him and he a son to me. Your House and your sovereignty will always stand secure before me and your throne be established for ever.'"

Responsorial Psalm   Psalm 88.

℟ **His dynasty shall last for ever.**

1. I will sing for ever of your love, O Lord;
   through all ages my mouth will proclaim your truth.
   Of this I am sure, that your love lasts for ever,
   that your truth is firmly established as the heavens.   ℟

2. "I have made a covenant with my chosen one;
   I have sworn to David my servant:
   I will establish your dynasty for ever
   and set up your throne through all ages."   ℟

3. He will say to me: "You are my father,
   my God, the rock who saves me."
   I will keep my love for him always;
   with him my covenant shall endure.   ℟

Second Reading   Romans 4:13.16-18.22.

Though it seemed Abraham's hope could not be fulfilled, he hoped and he believed.

The promise of inheriting the world was not made to Abraham and his descendants on account of any law but on account of the righteousness which consists in faith. That is why what fulfills the promise depends on faith, so that it may be a free gift and be available to all of Abraham's descendants, not only those who belong to the Law but also those who belong to the faith of Abraham who is the Father of all of us. As scripture says: I have made you the ancestor of many nations — Abraham is our father

SAINT JOSEPH

in the eyes of God, in whom he put his faith, and who brings the dead to life and calls into being what does not exist.

Though it seemed Abraham's hope could not be fulfilled, he hoped and he believed, and through doing so he did become the father of many nations exactly as he had been promised: Your descendants will be as many as the stars. This is the faith that was "considered as justifying him".

Acclamation Glory and praise to you, O Christ!
or Alleluia They are happy who dwell in your house, O Lord, for ever singing your praise.
Glory and praise to you, O Christ! Psalm 83:5.

Gospel Matthew 1:16.18-21.24.

Joseph did what the angel of the Lord had told him to do.

Jacob was the father of Joseph the husband of Mary; of her was born Jesus who is called Christ.

This is how Jesus Christ came to be born. His mother Mary was betrothed to Joseph; but before they came to live together she was found to be with child through the Holy Spirit. Her husband Joseph, being a man of honour and wanting to spare her publicity, decided to divorce her informally. He had made up his mind to do this when the angel of the Lord appeared to him in a dream and said, "Joseph son of David, do not be afraid to take Mary home as your wife, because she has conceived what is in her by the Holy Spirit. She will give birth to a son and you must name him Jesus, because he is the one who is to save his people from their sins." When Joseph woke up he did what the angel of the Lord had told him to do.

or

Gospel Luke 2:41-51.

See how worried your father and I have been, looking for you.

Every year the parents of Jesus used to go to Jerusalem for the feast of the Passover. When he was twelve years old, they went up for the feast as usual. When they were on their way home after the feast, the boy Jesus stayed behind in Jerusalem without his parents knowing it. they assumed he was with the caravan, and it was only after a day's journey that they went to look for him among their relations and acquaintances. When they failed to find him they went back to Jerusalem looking for him everywhere.

Three days later, they found him in the Temple, sitting among the doctors, listening to them, and asking them questions; and all those who heard him were astounded at his intelligence and his replies. They were overcome when they saw him, and his mother said to him, "My child, why have you done this to us? See how worried your father and I have been, looking for you." "Why were you looking for me?" he replied "Did you not know that I must be busy with my Father's affairs?" But they did not understand what he meant.

He then went down with them and came to Nazareth and lived under their authority.

The Creed is said.

Prayer over the Gifts

Father,
with unselfish love Saint Joseph cared for your Son,
born of the Virgin Mary.
May we also serve you at your altar with pure hearts.

Preface

Father, all-powerful and ever-living God,
we do well always and everywhere to give you thanks
as we honour Saint Joseph.

He is that just man,
that wise and loyal servant,
whom you placed at the head of your family.
With a husband's love he cherished Mary,
the virgin Mother of God.
With fatherly care he watched over Jesus Christ your Son,
conceived by the power of the Holy Spirit.

Through Christ the choirs of angels
and all the powers of heaven
praise and worship your glory.
May our voices blend with theirs
as we join in their unending hymn:
Holy, holy, holy ...

Communion Antiphon

Come, good and faithful servant!
Share the joy of your Lord!

Matthew 25:21

SAINT JOSEPH

Prayer after Communion

Lord,
today you nourish us at this altar
as we celebrate the feast of Saint Joseph.
Protect your Church always
and in your love watch over the gifts you have given us.

MARCH 25
THE ANNUNCIATION OF THE LORD
Solemnity

Let what you have said be done to me.
Mary said 'yes' to God and so became the
mother of our saviour. All things are possible
through the the power of God's spirit for those who
truly believe in Him. We too say to God in
faith, 'here I am coming to obey your will'. In
this way Christ, through faith, lives in us and
like our Lady we bring him into our world.

Entrance Antiphon As Christ came into the world, he said: Behold! I have come to do your will, O God. Hebrews 10:5.7.

Opening Prayer

Let us pray
  [that Christ, the Word-made flesh,
  will make us more like him]

God our Father,
your Word became man and was born of the Virgin Mary.
May we become more like Jesus Christ,
whom we acknowledge as our redeemer, God and man.

First Reading   Isaiah 7:10-14.
The maiden is with child.

The Lord spoke to Ahaz and said, "Ask the Lord your God for a sign for yourself coming either from the depths of Sheol or from the heights above." "No," Ahaz answered "I will not put the Lord to the test."

THE ANNUNCIATION OF THE LORD

   Then he said:
Listen now, House of David:
are you not satisfied with trying the patience of men
without trying the patience of my God, too?
The Lord himself, therefore,
will give you a sign.
It is this: the maiden is with child
and will soon give birth to a son
whom she will call Immanuel,
a name which means "God-is-with-us".

Responsional Psalm   Psalm 39.

℟ **Here I am, Lord! I come to do your will.**

1. You do not ask for sacrifice and offerings,
   but an open ear.
   You do not ask for holocaust and victim.
   Instead, here am I. ℟

2. In the scroll of the book it stands written
   that I should do your will.
   My God, I delight in your law
   in the depth of my heart. ℟

3. Your justice I have proclaimed
   in the great assembly.
   My lips I have not sealed;
   you know it, O Lord. ℟

4. I have not hidden your justice in my heart
   but declared your faithful help.
   I have not hidden your love and your truth
   from the great assembly. ℟

Second Reading   Hebrews 10:4-10.

I was commanded in the scroll of the book, "God, here I am! I am coming to obey your will."

Bulls' blood and goats' blood are useless for taking away sins, and this is what Christ said, on coming into the world:
You who wanted no sacrifice or oblation,
prepared a body for me.

THE ANNUNCIATION OF THE LORD

You took no pleasure in holocausts or sacrifices for sin;
then I said,
just as I was commanded in the scroll of the book,
"God, here I am! I am coming to obey your will."
Notice that he says first: You did not want what the Law lays down as the things to be offered, that is: the sacrifices, the oblations, the holocausts and the sacrifices for sin, and you took no pleasure in them; and then he says: Here I am! I am coming to obey your will. He is abolishing the first sort to replace it with the second. And this will was for us to be made holy by the offering of his body made once and for all by Jesus Christ.

Acclamation or Alleluia [Alleluia, alleluia!] The Word was made flesh, he lived among us, and we saw his glory. [Alleluia!]
John 1:14

Gospel   Luke 1:26-38.

Listen! You are to conceive and bear a son.

The angel Gabriel was sent by God to a town in Galilee called Nazareth, to a virgin betrothed to a man named Joseph, of the House of David; and the virgin's name was Mary. He went in and said to her, "Rejoice, so highly favoured! The Lord is with you." She was deeply disturbed by these words and asked herself what this greeting could mean, but the angel said to her, "Mary, do not be afraid; you have won God's favour. Listen! You are to conceive and bear a son, and you must name him Jesus. He will be great and will be called Son of the Most High. The Lord God will give him the throne of his ancestor David; he will rule over the House of Jacob for ever and his reign will have no end." Mary said to the angel, "But how can this come about, since I am a virgin?" "The Holy Spirit will come upon you" the angel answered "and the power of the Most High will cover you with its shadow. And so the child will be holy and will be called son of God. Know this too: your kinswoman Elizabeth has, in her old age, herself conceived a son, and she whom people called barren is now in her sixth month, for nothing is impossible to God." "I am the handmaid of the Lord" said Mary "let what you have said be done to me." And the angel left her.

In the Creed, all genuflect at the words, and became man.

THE ANNUNCIATION OF THE LORD

Prayer over the Gifts

Almighty Father,
as we recall the beginning of the Church
when your Son became man,
may we celebrate with joy today
this sacrament of your love.

Preface

Father, all-powerful and ever-living God,
we do well always and everywhere to give you thanks
through Jesus Christ our Lord.

He came to save mankind by becoming a man himself.
The Virgin Mary, receiving the angel's message in faith,
conceived by the power of the Spirit
and bore your Son in purest love.

In Christ, the eternal truth,
your promise to Israel came true.
In Christ, the hope of all peoples,
man's hope was realised beyond all expectation.

Through Christ the angels of heaven
offer their prayer of adoration
as they rejoice in your presence for ever.
May our voices be one with theirs
in their triumphant hymn of praise:

Holy, holy, holy ...

Communion Antiphon

The Virgin is with child and shall bear a son, and she will call him Emmanuel.

Isaiah 7:14

Prayer after Communion

Lord,
may the sacrament we share
strengthen our faith and hope in Jesus, born of a virgin
and truly God and Man.
By the power of his resurrection
may we come to eternal joy.

APRIL 23

ST GEORGE, MARTYR
PATRON OF ENGLAND
In England and Wales: Feast

You are the salt of the earth and the
light of the world.
Our lives must be based on Christ. This is the
true way of christian salvation. If we share his
sufferings and pattern of his death then we will
also be given a share in the power of his
resurrection.

Entrance Antiphon Light forever will shine on your saints, O Lord, alleluia. cf. 4 Ezra 2:35.

Opening Prayer

Lord,
hear the prayers of those who praise your mighty power.
As Saint George was ready to follow Christ in suffering and death,
so may he be ready to help us in our weakness.

Other readings may be used instead of those given here.

First Reading Revelation 12:10-12.
In the face of death they would not cling to life.

I, John, heard a voice shout from heaven, "Victory and power and empire for ever have been won by our God, and all authority for his Christ, now that the persecutor, who accused our brothers day and night before our God, has been brought down. They have triumphed over him by the blood of the Lamb and by the witness of their martyrdom, because even in the face of death they would not cling to life. Let the heavens rejoice and all who live there."

SAINT GEORGE

Responsional Psalm   Psalm 125.

℟ **Those who are sowing in tears
will sing when they reap.**

1. When the Lord delivered Zion from bondage,
   It seemed like a dream.
   Then was our mouth filled with laughter,
   on our lips there were songs. ℟

2. The heathens themselves said: 'What marvels
   the Lord worked for them!'
   What marvels the Lord worked for us!
   Indeed we were glad. ℟

3. Deliver us, O Lord, from our bondage
   as streams in dry land.
   Those who are sowing in tears
   will sing when they reap. ℟

4. They go out, they go out, full of tears,
   carrying seed for the sowing:
   they come back, they come back, full of song,
   carrying their sheaves. ℟

Alleluia   Alleluia, alleluia! Happy the man who stands firm for he has proved himself, and will win the crown of life. Alleluia! James 1:12.

Gospel   John 15:18-21

If they persecuted me, they will persecute you too.

Jesus said to his disciples:
"If the world hates you,
remember that it hated me before you.
If you belonged to the world,
the world would love you as its own;
but because you do not belong to the world,
because my choice withdrew you from the world,
therefore the world hates you.
Remember the words I said to you:
A servant is not greater than his master.
If they persecuted me,
they will persecute you too;
if they kept my word,

they will keep yours as well.
But it will be on my account that they will do all this,
because they do not know the one who sent me."

Prayer over the Gifts

Lord, bless our offerings and make them holy.
May these gifts fill our hearts
with the love which gave Saint George victory
over all his suffering.

Preface

Father, all-powerful and ever-living God,
we do well always and everywhere to give you thanks.

Your holy martyr George followed the example of Christ,
and gave his life for the glory of your name.
His death reveals your power
shining through our human weakness.
You choose the weak and make them strong
in bearing witness to you,
through Jesus Christ our Lord.

In our unending joy we echo on earth
the song of the angels in heaven
as they praise your glory for ever:

Holy, holy, holy ...

Communion Antiphon

I tell you solemnly: unless a grain of wheat falls on the ground and dies, it remains a single grain; but if it dies, it yields a rich harvest, alleluia.
John 12:24-25

Prayer after Communion

Lord, we receive your gifts from heaven
at this joyful feast.
May we who proclaim at this holy table
the death and resurrection of your Son
come to share his glory with Saint George
and all your holy martyrs.

JUNE 24
BIRTH OF ST JOHN THE BAPTIST
Solemnity

Prepare the Way of the Lord!
John the Baptist was called by God from his
birth to be the prophet specially chosen to
prepare the people for the birth of Christ. We,
too, are called from our re-birth in baptism to
prepare all people for the second coming of
Christ. We are through God's grace the light of
all the nations.

Entrance Antiphon   There was a man sent from God whose name was John. He came to bear witness to the light, to prepare an upright people for the Lord. John 1:6-7; Luke 1—17.

Let us pray
  [that God will give us joy and peace]

God our Father,
you raised up John the Baptist
to prepare a perfect people for Christ the Lord.
Give your Church joy in spirit
and guide those who believe in you
into the way of salvation and peace.

First Reading   Isaiah 49:1-6.
I will make you the light of the nations.

Islands, listen to me,
pay attention, remotest peoples.
The Lord called me before I was born,
from my mother's womb he pronounced my name.

BIRTH OF SAINT JOHN THE BAPTIST

He made my mouth a sharp sword,
and hid me in the shadow of his hand.
He made me into a sharpened arrow,
and concealed me in his quiver.

He said to me, "You are my servant (Israel)
in whom I shall be glorified";
while I was thinking, "I have toiled in vain,
I have exhausted myself for nothing";
and all the while my cause was with the Lord,
my reward with my God.
I was honoured in the eyes of the Lord,
my God was my strength.

And now the Lord has spoken,
he who formed me in the womb to be his servant,
to bring Jacob back to him,
to gather Israel to him:

"It is not enough for you to be my servant,
to restore the tribes of Jacob and bring back the survivors of
   Israel;
I will make you the light of the nations
so that my salvation may reach to the ends of the earth."

Responsorial Psalm   Psalm 138.

℟ **I thank you for the wonder of my being.**

1. O Lord, you search me and you know me,
   you know my resting and my rising,
   you discern my purpose from afar.
   You mark when I walk or lie down,
   all my ways lie open to you. ℟

2. For it was you who created my being,
   knit me together in my mother's womb.
   I thank you for the wonder of my being,
   for the wonders of all your creation. ℟

3. Already you knew my soul,
   my body held no secret from you
   when I was being fashioned in secret
   and moulded in the depths of the earth. ℟

BIRTH OF SAINT JOHN THE BAPTIST

Second Reading   Acts 13:22-26.

Jesus, whose coming was heralded by John.

Paul said: "God made David the king of our ancestors, of whom he approved in these words, 'I have selected David son of Jesse, a man after my own heart, who will carry out my whole purpose.' To keep his promise, God has raised up for Israel one of David's descendants, Jesus, as Saviour, whose coming was heralded by John when he proclaimed a baptism of repentance for the whole people of Israel. Before John ended his career he said, 'I am not the one you imagine me to be; that one is coming after me and I am not fit to undo his sandal.'

"My brothers, sons of Abraham's race, and all you who fear God, this message of salvation is meant for you."

Alleluia   Alleluia, alleluia! As for you, little child, you shall be called a prophet of God, the Most High. You shall go ahead of the Lord to prepare his ways before him. Alleluia! Luke 1:76.

Gospel   Luke 1:57-66. 80.

His name is John.

The time came for Elizabeth to have her child, and she gave birth to a son; and when her neighbours and relations heard that the Lord had shown her so great a kindness, they shared her joy.

Now on the eighth day they came to circumcise the child; they were going to call him Zechariah after his father, but his mother spoke up. "No," she said "he is to be called John." They said to her, "But no one in your family has that name", and made signs to his father to find out what he wanted him called. The father asked for a writing tablet and wrote, "His name is John." And they were all astonished. At that instant his power of speech returned and he spoke and praised God. All their neighbours were filled with awe and the whole affair was talked about throughout the hill country of Judaea. All those who heard of it treasured it in their hearts. "What will this child turn out to be?" they wondered. And indeed the hand of the Lord was with him. The child grew up and his spirit matured. And he lived out in the wilderness until the day he appeared openly to Israel.

BIRTH OF SAINT JOHN THE BAPTIST

The Creed is said.

Prayer over the Gifts
Father,
accept the gifts we bring to your altar
to celebrate the birth of John the Baptist,
who foretold the coming of our Saviour
and made him known when he came.

Preface

Father, all-powerful and ever-living God,
we do well always and everywhere to give you thanks
through Jesus Christ our Lord.

We praise your greatness
as we honour the prophet
who prepared the way before your Son.
You set John the Baptist apart from other men,
marking him out with special favour.
His birth brought great rejoicing:
even in the womb he leapt for joy,
so near was man's salvation.

You chose John the Baptist from all the prophets
to show the world its redeemer,
the lamb of sacrifice.
He baptised Christ, the giver of baptism,
in waters made holy by the one who was baptised.
You found John worthy of a martyr's death,
his last and greatest act of witness to your Son.

In our unending joy we echo on earth
the song of the angels in heaven
as they praise your glory for ever:

Holy, holy, holy ...

Communion Antiphon

Through the tender compassion of our God, the dawn from on high shall break upon us. Luke 1:78.

BIRTH OF SAINT JOHN THE BAPTIST

Prayer after Communion

Lord,
you have renewed us with this eucharist,
as we celebrate the feast of John the Baptist,
who foretold the coming of the Lamb of God.
May we welcome your Son as our Saviour,
for he gives us new life,
and is Lord for ever and ever.

JUNE 29
SS PETER AND PAUL, APOSTLES
Solemnity

The keys of the kingdom. Christ promised to remain forever with his Church through Peter the head of the apostles. The Lord rescued Peter from the hatred of Herod and always comes to the aid of his Church against which the forces of evil will never win. Paul is the apostle of the Gentiles so that the Good News is spread throughout the whole world. Christ is with us too as we witness to his power in our lives. In this way we pray that the world may learn to believe in Jesus Christ.

Entrance Antiphon These men, conquering all human frailty, shed their blood and helped the Church to grow. By sharing the cup of the Lord's suffering, they became the friends of God.

Opening Prayer

Let us pray
 [that we will remain true to the faith of the apostles]

God our Father,
today you give us the joy
of celebrating the feast of the apostles Peter and Paul.
Through them your Church first received the faith.
Keep us true to their teaching.

or

Let us pray
 [one with Peter and Paul in our faith in
 Christ the Son of the living God]

SAINT PETER AND SAINT PAUL

Praise to you, the God and Father of our Lord Jesus Christ,
who in your great mercy
have given us new birth and hope
through the power of Christ's resurrection.

Through the prayers of the apostles Peter and Paul
may we who received this faith through their preaching
share their joy in following the Lord
to the unfading inheritance
reserved for us in heaven.

First Reading   Acts 12:1-11.
Now I know the Lord really did save me from Herod.

King Herod started persecuting certain members of the Church. He beheaded James the brother of John, and when he saw that this pleased the Jews he decided to arrest Peter as well. This was during the days of Unleavened Bread, and he put Peter in prison, assigning four squads of four soldiers each to guard him in turns. Herod meant to try Peter in public after the end of Passover week. All the time Peter was under guard the Church prayed to God for him unremittingly.

On the night before Herod was to try him, Peter was sleeping between two soldiers, fastened with double chains, while guards kept watch at the main entrance to the prison. Then suddenly the angel of the Lord stood there, and the cell was filled with light. He tapped Peter on the side and woke him. "Get up!" he said "Hurry!" — and the chains fell from his hands. The angel then said, "Put on your belt and sandals." After he had done this, the angel next said, "Wrap your cloak round you and follow me." Peter followed him, but had no idea what the angel did was all happening in reality; he thought he was seeing a vision. They passed through two guard posts one after the other, and reached the iron gate leading to the city. This opened of its own accord; they went through it and had walked the whole length of one street when suddenly the angel left him. It was only then that Peter came to himself. "Now I know it is all true," he said. "The Lord really did send his angel and has saved me from Herod and from all that the Jewish people were so certain would happen to me."

SAINT PETER AND SAINT PAUL

Responsorial Psalm   Psalm 33.

℟ **The angel of the Lord rescues those who revere him.**

1. I will bless the Lord at all times.
   his praise always on my lips;
   in the Lord my soul shall make its boast.
   The humble shall hear and be glad. ℟

2. Glorify the Lord with me.
   Together let us praise his name.
   I sought the Lord and he answered me;
   from all my terrors he set me free. ℟

3. Look towards him and be radiant;
   let your faces not be abashed.
   This poor man called; the Lord heard him
   and rescued him from all his distress. ℟

4. The angel of the Lord is encamped
   around those who revere him, to rescue them.
   Taste and see that the Lord is good.
   He is happy who seeks refuge in him. ℟

Second Reading   2 Timothy 4:6-8.17-18.

All there is to come now is the crown of righteousness reserved for me.

As for me, my life is already being poured away as a libation, and the time has come for me to be gone. I have fought the good fight to the end; I have run the race to the finish; I have kept the faith; all there is to come now is the crown of righteousness reserved for me, which the Lord, the righteous judge, will give to me on that Day; and not only to me but to all those who have longed for his Appearing.

But the Lord stood by me and gave me power, so that through me the whole message might be proclaimed for all the pagans to hear; and so I was rescued from the lion's mouth. The Lord will rescue me from all evil attempts on me, and bring me safely to his heavenly kingdom. To him be glory for ever and ever. Amen.

Alleluia   Alleluia, alleluia! You are Peter and on this rock I will build my Church. And the gates of the underworld can never hold out against it. Alleluia! Matthew 16:18.

SAINT PETER AND SAINT PAUL

Gospel Matthew 16:13-19.

You are Peter, and I will give you the keys of the kingdom of heaven.

When Jesus came to the region of Caesarea Philippi he put this question to his disciples, "Who do people say the Son of Man is?" And they said, "Some say he is John the Baptist, some Elijah, and others Jeremiah or one of the prophets." "But you," he said, "who do you say I am?" Then Simon Peter spoke up. "You are the Christ," he said "the Son of the living God." Jesus replied, "Simon son of Jonah, you are a happy man! Because it was not flesh and blood that revealed this to you but my Father in heaven. So I now say to you: You are Peter and on this rock I will build my Church. And the gates of the underworld can never hold out against it. I will give you the keys of the kingdom of heaven: whatever you bind on earth shall be considered bound in heaven; whatever you loose on earth shall be considered loosed in heaven."

Prayer over the Gifts

Lord,
may your apostles join their prayers to our offering
and help us to celebrate this sacrifice in love and unity.

Preface

Father, all-powerful and ever-living God,
we do well always and everywhere to give you thanks.

You fill our hearts with joy
as we honour your great apostles:
Peter, our leader in the faith,
and Paul, its fearless preacher.

Peter raised up the Church
from the faithful flock of Israel.
Paul brought your call to the nations,
and became the teacher of the world.
Each in his chosen way gathered into unity
the one family of Christ.
Both shared a martyr's death
and are praised throughout the world.

SAINT PETER AND SAINT PAUL

Now, with the apostles and all the angels and saints,
we praise you for ever:

Holy, holy, holy ...

Communion Antiphon

Peter said: You are the Christ, the Son of the living God. Jesus answered: You are Peter, the rock on which I will build my Church.

Matthew 16:16,18

Prayer after Communion

Lord,
renew the life of your Church
with the power of this sacrament.
May the breaking of bread
and the teaching of the apostles
keep us united in your love.

Solemn Blessing

Bow your heads and pray for God's blessing.

The Lord has set you firm within his Church,
which he built upon the rock of Peter's faith.
May he bless you with a faith that never falters.
R/ **Amen.**

The Lord has given you knowledge of the faith
through the labours and preaching of Saint Paul.
May his example inspire you to lead others to Christ
by the manner of your life.
R/ **Amen.**

May the keys of Peter, and the words of Paul,
their undying witness and their prayers,
lead you to the joy of that eternal home
which Peter gained by his cross, and Paul by the sword.
R/ **Amen.**

May almighty God bless you,
the Father, and the Son, ✠ and the Holy Spirit.
R/ **Amen.**

AUGUST 6
THE TRANSFIGURATION OF THE LORD
Feast

Jesus in his glory.
Jesus is seen by Peter, James and John in his glory as Christ, Messiah, King of the universe. It was wonderful for them to be there and witness the power of their leader even though they were overcome by fear at what they saw. God reveals Christ to us too and we look forward in joy and hope to sharing fully in his glory. We have no need to fear. Christ is God's Son and our brother.

Entrance Antiphon In the shining cloud the Spirit is seen; from it the voice of the Father is heard: This is my Son, my beloved, in whom is all my delight. Listen to him.

cf. Matthew 17:5

Opening Prayer

Let us pray.
[that we may hear the Lord Jesus
and share his everlasting life]

God our Father,
in the transfigured glory of Christ your Son,
your strengthen our faith
by confirming the witness of your prophets,
and show us the splendour of your beloved sons and daughters.
As we listen to the voice of your Son,
help us to become heirs to eternal life with him
for he lives and reigns with you and the Holy Spirit,
one God, for ever and ever.

THE TRANSFIGURATION OF THE LORD

First Reading   Daniel 7:9-10.13-14.

His robe was white as snow.

As I watched:
Thrones were set in place
and one of great age took his seat.
His robe was white as snow,
the hair of his head as pure as wool.
His throne was a blaze of flames,
its wheels were a burning fire.
A stream of fire poured out,
issuing from his presence.
A thousand thousand waited on him,
ten thousand times ten thousand stood before him.
A court was held and the books were opened.
I gazed into the visions of the night.
And I saw, coming on the clouds of heaven,
one like a son of man.
He came to the one of great age
and was led into his presence.
On him was conferred sovereignty, glory and kingship,
and men of all peoples, nations and languages became his
  servants.
His sovereignty is an eternal sovereignty
which shall never pass away,
nor will his empire ever be destroyed.

Responsorial Psalm   Psalm 96.

℟ **The Lord is king, most high above all the earth**

1. The Lord is king, let earth rejoice,
   let all the coastlands be glad.
   Cloud and darkness are his raiment;
   his throne, justice and right. ℟

2. The mountains melt like wax
   before the Lord of all the earth.
   The skies proclaim his justice;
   all peoples see his glory. ℟

3. For you indeed are the Lord
   most high above all the earth
   exalted far above all spirits. ℟

THE TRANSFIGURATION OF THE LORD

Second Reading   2 Peter 1:16-19.

We heard this ourselves, spoken from heaven.

It was not any cleverly invented myths that we were repeating when we brought you the knowledge of the power and the coming of our Lord Jesus Christ; we had seen his majesty for ourselves. He was honoured and glorified by God the Father, when the Sublime Glory itself spoke to him and said, "This is my Son, the Beloved; he enjoys my favour." We heard this ourselves, spoken from heaven, when we were with him on the holy mountain.

So we have confirmation of what was said in prophecies; and you will be right to depend on prophecy and take it as a lamp for lighting a way through the dark until the dawn comes and the morning star rises in your minds.

Alleluia   Alleluia, alleluia! This is my Son, the Beloved, he enjoys my favour; listen to him. Alleluia!

Matthew 17:5

Gospel A, B or C is read according to the Cycle for the Year.

A
Gospel   Matthew 17:1-9.

His face shone like the sun.

Jesus took with him Peter and James and his brother John and led them up a high mountain where they could be alone. There in their presence he was transfigured: his face shone like the sun and his clothes became as white as the light. Suddenly Moses and Elijah appeared to them; they were talking with him. Then Peter spoke to Jesus. "Lord," he said "it is wonderful for us to be here; if you wish, I will make three tents here, one for you, one for Moses and one for Elijah." He was still speaking when suddenly a bright cloud covered them with shadow, and from the cloud there came a voice which said, "This is my Son, the Beloved; he enjoys my favour. Listen to him." When they heard this, the disciples fell on their faces, overcome with fear. But Jesus came up and touched them. "Stand up," he said "do not be afraid." And when they raised their eyes they saw no one but only Jesus.

THE TRANSFIGURATION OF THE LORD

As they came down from the mountain Jesus gave them this order. "Tell no one about the vision until the Son of Man has risen from the dead."

B
Gospel   Mark 9:2-10.
This is my Son the Beloved.

Jesus took with him Peter and James and John and led them up a high mountain where they could be alone by themselves. There in their presence he was transfigured; his clothes became dazzlingly white, whiter than any earthly bleacher could make them. Elijah appeared to them with Moses; and they were talking with Jesus. Then Peter spoke to Jesus: "Rabbi," he said "it is wonderful for us to be here; so let us make three tents, one for you, one for Moses and one for Elijah." He did not know what to say; they were so frightened. And a cloud came, covering them in shadow; and there came a voice from the cloud, "This is my Son, the Beloved. Listen to him." Then suddenly, when they looked round, they saw no one with them any more but only Jesus.

As they came down from the mountain he warned them to tell no one what they had seen, until after the Son of Man had risen from the dead. They observed the warning faithfully, though among themselves they discussed what "rising from the dead" could mean.

C
Gospel   Luke 9:28-36.
As he prayed the aspect of his face was changed.

Jesus took with him Peter and John and James and went up the mountain to pray. As he prayed, the aspect of his face was changed and his clothing became brilliant as lightning. Suddenly there were two men there talking to him; they were Moses and Elijah appearing in glory, and they were speaking of his passing which he was to accomplish in Jerusalem. Peter and his companions were heavy with sleep, but they kept awake and saw his glory and the two men standing with him. As these were leaving him, Peter said to Jesus, "Master, it is wonderful for us to be here; so let us make three tents, one for you, one for Moses and one for Elijah." — He did not know what he was saying. As

THE TRANSFIGURATION OF THE LORD

he spoke, a cloud came and covered them with shadow; and when they went into the cloud the disciples were afraid. And a voice came from the cloud, saying, "This is my Son, the Chosen One. Listen to him." And after the voice had spoken, Jesus was found alone. The disciples kept silence and, at that time, told no one what they had seen.

Prayer over the Gifts
Lord,
by the transfiguration of your Son
make our gifts holy,
and by his radiant glory free us from our sins.

Preface
Father, all-powerful and ever-living God,
we do well always and everywhere to give you thanks
through Jesus Christ our Lord.

He revealed his glory to the disciples
to strengthen them for the scandal of the cross.
His glory shone from a body like our own,
to show that the Church,
which is the body of Christ,
would one day share his glory.

In our unending joy we echo on earth
the song of the angels in heaven
as they praise your glory for ever:

Holy, holy, holy ...

Communion Antiphon
When Christ is revealed we shall be like him, for we shall see him as he is.

1 John 3:2

Prayer after Communion
Lord,
you revealed the true radiance of Christ
in the glory of his transfiguration.
May the food we receive from heaven
change us into his image.

AUGUST 15
THE ASSUMPTION OF THE BLESSED VIRGIN MARY

Solemnity

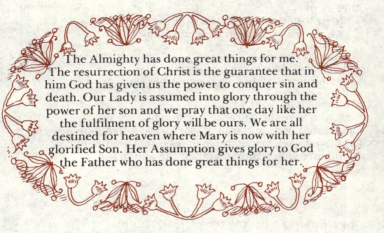

The Almighty has done great things for me. The resurrection of Christ is the guarantee that in him God has given us the power to conquer sin and death. Our Lady is assumed into glory through the power of her son and we pray that one day like her the fulfilment of glory will be ours. We are all destined for heaven where Mary is now with her glorified Son. Her Assumption gives glory to God the Father who has done great things for her.

Entrance Antiphon A great sign appeared in heaven: a woman clothed with the sun, the moon beneath her feet, and a crown of twelve stars on her head. **Revelation 12:1.**

or

Let us rejoice in the Lord and celebrate this feast in honour of the Virgin Mary, at whose assumption the angels rejoice, giving praise to the Son of God.

Opening Prayer

Let us pray
  [that we will join Mary, the mother of the Lord, in the glory of heaven]

All-powerful and ever-living God,
you raised the sinless Virgin Mary, mother of your Son,
body and soul to the glory of heaven.

THE ASSUMPTION

May we see heaven as our final goal
and come to share her glory.

or

Let us pray
   [that with the help of Mary's prayers
   we too may reach our heavenly home]

Father in heaven,
all creation rightly gives you praise,
for all life and all holiness come from you.

In the plan of your wisdom
she who bore the Christ in her womb
was raised body and soul in glory to be with him in heaven.
May we follow her example in reflecting your holiness
and join in her hymn of endless life and praise.

First Reading   Apocalypse 11:19;12:1-6.10.

A woman adorned with the sun standing on the moon.

The sanctuary of God in heaven opened, and the ark of the covenant could be seen inside it. Now a great sign appeared in heaven: a woman, adorned with the sun, standing on the moon, and with the twelve stars on her head for a crown. She was pregnant, and in labour, crying aloud in the pangs of childbirth. Then a second sign appeared in the sky, a huge red dragon which had seven heads and ten horns, and each of the seven heads crowned with a coronet. Its tail dragged a third of the stars from the sky and dropped them to the earth, and the dragon stopped in front of the woman as she was having the child, so that he could eat it as soon as it was born from its mother. The woman brought a male child into the world, the son who was to rule all the nations with an iron sceptre, and the child was taken straight up to God and to his throne, while the woman escaped into the desert, where God had made a place of safety ready. Then I heard a voice shout from heaven. "Victory and power and empire for ever have been won by our God, and all authority for his Christ."

THE ASSUMPTION

Responsorial Psalm: Psalm 44

℟ **On your right stands the queen, in gold of Ophir.**

1. The daughters of kings are among your loved ones.
   On your right stands the queen in gold of Ophir.
   Listen, O daughter, give ear to my words:
   forget your own people and your father's house. ℟

2. So will the king desire your beauty:
   He is your lord, pay homage to him.
   They are escorted amid gladness and joy;
   they pass within the palace of the king. ℟

Second Reading   1 Corinthians 15:20-26

Christ as the first-fruits and then those who belong to him.

Christ has been raised from the dead, the first-fruits of all who have fallen asleep. Death came through one man and in the same way the resurrection of the dead has come through one man. Just as all men die in Adam, so all men will be brought to life in Christ; but all of them in their proper order: Christ as the first-fruits and then, after the coming of Christ, those who belong to him. After that will come the end, when he hands over the kingdom to God the Father, having done away with every sovereignty, authority and power. For he must be king until he has put all his enemies under his feet and the last of the enemies to be destroyed is death, for everything is to be put under his feet.

Alleluia   Alleluia, alleluia! Mary has been taken up into heaven; all the choirs of angels are rejoicing. Alleluia!

Gospel   Luke 1:39-56.

The Almighty has done great things for me, he has exalted the lowly.

Mary set out and went as quickly as she could to a town in the hill country of Judah. She went into Zechariah's house and greeted Elizabeth. Now as soon as Elizabeth heard Mary's greeting, the child leapt in her womb and Elizabeth was filled with the Holy Spirit. She gave a loud cry and said, "Of all women you are the most blessed, and blessed is the fruit of your womb. Why should

THE ASSUMPTION

I be honoured with a visit from the mother of my Lord? For the moment your greeting reached my ears, the child in my womb leapt for joy. Yes, blessed is she who believed that the promise made her by the Lord would be fulfilled."
And Mary said:
"My soul proclaims the greatness of the Lord
and my spirit exults in God my saviour;
because he has looked upon his lowly handmaid.
Yes, from this day forward all generations will call be blessed,
for the Almighty has done great things for me.
Holy is his name,
and his mercy reaches from age to age for those who fear him.
He has shown the power of his arm,
he has routed the proud of heart.
He has pulled down princes from their thrones and exalted the lowly.
The hungry he has filled with good things, the rich sent empty away.
He has come to the help of Israel his servant, mindful of his mercy
— according to the promise he made to our ancestors —
of his mercy to Abraham and to his descendants for ever."
Mary stayed with Elizabeth about three months and then went back home.

Prayer over the Gifts

Lord,
receive this offering of our service.
You raised the Virgin Mary to the glory of heaven.
By her prayers, help us to seek you
and to live in your love.

Preface

Father, all-powerful and ever-living God,
we do well always and everywhere to give you thanks,
through Jesus Christ our Lord.

Today the virgin Mother of God was taken up into heaven
to be the beginning and the pattern of the Church in its perfection,
and a sign of hope and comfort for your people on their pilgrim way.

THE ASSUMPTION

You would not allow decay to touch her body,
for she had given birth to your Son, the Lord of all life,
in the glory of the incarnation.

In our joy we sing to your glory
with all the choirs of angels:

Holy, holy, holy ...

Communion Antiphon

All generations will call me blessed, for the Almighty has done great things for me. Luke 1:48-49.

Prayer after Communion

Lord,
may we who receive this sacrament of salvation
be led to the glory of heaven
by the prayers of the Virgin Mary.

SEPTEMBER 14

THE TRIUMPH OF THE CROSS
Feast

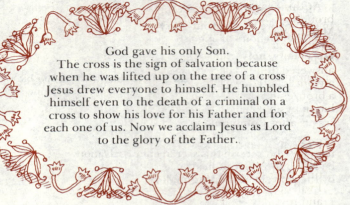

God gave his only Son.
The cross is the sign of salvation because when he was lifted up on the tree of a cross Jesus drew everyone to himself. He humbled himself even to the death of a criminal on a cross to show his love for his Father and for each one of us. Now we acclaim Jesus as Lord to the glory of the Father.

Entrance Antiphon We should glory in the cross of our Lord Jesus Christ, for he is our salvation, our life and our resurrection; through him we are saved and made free.

cf. Galatians 6:14

Opening Prayer

Let us pray
  [that the death of Christ on the cross
  will bring us to the glory of the resurrection]

God our Father,
in obedience to you
your only Son accepted death on the cross
for the salvation of mankind.
We acknowledge the mystery of the cross on earth.
May we receive the gift of redemption in heaven.

First Reading   Numbers 21:4-9.

If anyone was bitten by a serpent, he looked at the bronze serpent and lived.

On the way through the wilderness, the Israelites lost patience. They spoke against God and against Moses, "Why did you bring

THE TRIUMPH OF THE CROSS

us out of Egypt to die in this wilderness? For there is neither bread nor water here: we are sick of this unsatisfying food."

At this God sent fiery serpents among the people: their bite brought death to many in Israel. The people came and said to Moses, "We have sinned by speaking against the Lord and against you. Intercede for us with the Lord to save us from these serpents." Moses interceded for the people, and the Lord answered him, "Make a fiery serpent and put it on a standard. If anyone is bitten and looks at it, he shall live." So Moses fashioned a bronze serpent which he put on a standard, and if anyone was bitten by a serpent, he looked at the bronze serpent and lived.

Responsorial Psalm   Psalm 77.

℟ **Never forget the deeds of the Lord.**

1. Give heed, my people, to my teaching;
   turn your ear to the words of my mouth.
   I will open my mouth in a parable
   and reveal hidden lessons of the past. ℟

2. When he slew them then they would seek him.
   Return and seek him in earnest.
   They would remember that God was their rock,
   God the Most High their redeemer. ℟

3. But the words they spoke were mere flattery;
   they lied to him with their lips.
   For their hearts were not truly with him;
   they were not faithful to his covenant. ℟

4. Yet he who is full of compassion
   forgave their sin and spared them.
   So often he held back his anger
   when he might have stirred up his rage. ℟

Second Reading   Philippians 2:6-11.

He humbled himself, therefore God raised him high.

The state of Jesus Christ was divine,
yet he did not cling
to his equality with God
but emptied himself
to assume the condition of a slave,
and became as men are;

THE TRIUMPH OF THE CROSS

and being as all men are,
he was humbler yet,
even to accepting death,
death on a cross.
But God raised him high
and gave him the name
which is above all other names
so that all beings
in the heavens, on earth and in the underworld,
should bend the knee at the name of Jesus
and that every tongue should acclaim
Jesus Christ as Lord,
to the glory of God the Father.

Alleluia Alleluia, alleluia! We adore you, O Christ, and we bless you; because by your cross you have redeemed the world. Alleluia!

Gospel   John 3:13-17.
The Son of Man must be lifted up.

Jesus said to Nicodemus:
"No one has gone up to heaven
except the one who came down from heaven,
the Son of Man who is in heaven;
and the Son of Man must be lifted up
as Moses lifted up the serpent in the desert,
so that everyone who believes may have eternal life in him.
Yes, God loved the world so much
that he gave his only Son,
so that everyone who believes in him may not be lost
but may have eternal life.
For God sent his Son into the world
not to condemn the world,
but so that through him the world might be saved."

Prayer over the Gifts
Lord,
may this sacrifice once offered on the cross
to take away the sins of the world
now free us from our sins.

THE TRIUMPH OF THE CROSS

Preface

Father, all-powerful and ever-living God,
we do well always and everywhere to give you thanks.

You decreed that man should be saved through the wood of the cross.
The tree of man's defeat became his tree of victory;
where life was lost, there life has been restored
through Christ our Lord.

Through him the choirs of angels
and all the powers of heaven
praise and worship your glory.
May our voices blend with theirs
as we join in their unending hymn:

Holy, holy, holy ...

or

Preface of the Passion of the Lord, page 291.

Communion Antiphon — When I am lifted up from the earth, I will draw all men to myself, says the Lord. John 12:32.

Prayer after Communion

Lord Jesus Christ,
you are the holy bread of life.
Bring to the glory of the resurrection
the people you have redeemed by the wood of the cross.

OCTOBER 25
THE FORTY MARTYRS OF ENGLAND AND WALES
In England and Wales: Feast

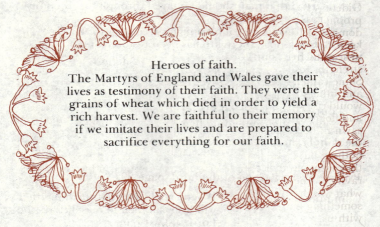

Heroes of faith.
The Martyrs of England and Wales gave their lives as testimony of their faith. They were the grains of wheat which died in order to yield a rich harvest. We are faithful to their memory if we imitate their lives and are prepared to sacrifice everything for our faith.

Entrance Antiphon The saints are happy in heaven because they followed Christ. They rejoice with him for ever because they shed their blood for love of him.

Opening Prayer

God our Father,
you raised up martyrs — saints among our countrymen
from every walk of life.
They vindicated the authority of your Church
in teaching and worship.
Through their prayers
may all our people be gathered once again
to celebrate the same sacraments
under one Shepherd, Jesus Christ, your Son,
who lives and reigns with you and the Holy Spirit,
one God, for ever and ever.

THE FORTY MARTYRS

First Reading   Hebrews 11:33-40.

Through faith they conquered kingdoms. God will make provision for us to have something better.

Gideon, Barak, Samson, Jephtah, David, Samuel and the prophets — these were men who through faith conquered kingdoms, did what is right and earned the promises. They could keep a lion's mouth shut, put out blazing fires and emerge unscathed from battle. They were weak people who were given strength, to be brave in war and drive back foreign invaders. Some came back to their wives from the dead, by resurrection; and others submitted to torture, refusing release so that they would rise again to a better life. Some had to bear being pilloried and flogged, or even chained up in prison. They were stoned, or sawn in half, or beheaded; they were homeless, and dressed in the skins of sheep and goats; they were penniless and were given nothing but ill-treatment. They were too good for the world and they went out to live in deserts and mountains and in caves and ravines. These are all heroes of faith, but they did not receive what was promised, since God had made provision for us to have something better, and they were not to reach perfection except with us.

Responsorial Psalm   Psalm 15.

℟ **You are my inheritance, O Lord.**

1. Preserve me, God, I take refuge in you.
   I say to the Lord: "You are my God."
   O Lord, it is you who are my portion and cup;
   it is you yourself who are my prize. ℟

2. I will bless the Lord who gives me counsel,
   who even at night directs my heart.
   I keep the Lord ever in my sight:
   since he is at my right hand, I shall stand firm. ℟

3. You will show me the path of life,
   the fullness of joy in your presence,
   at your right hand happiness for ever. ℟

Alleluia   Alleluia, alleluia! We praise you, O God, we acknowledge you to be the Lord; the noble army of martyrs praise you, O Lord. Alleluia!

THE FORTY MARTYRS

Gospel   John 12:24-26.
If a grain of wheat dies, it yields a rich harvest.

I tell you, most solemnly,
unless a wheat grain falls on the ground and dies,
it remains only a single grain;
but if it dies,
it yields a rich harvest.
Anyone who loves his life loses it;
anyone who hates his life in this world
will keep it for the eternal life.
If a man serves me, he must follow me,
wherever I am, my servant will be there too.
If anyone serves me, my Father will honour him.

Prayer over the Gifts

Lord, accept the gifts of your people,
who honour the suffering and death
of these forty martyrs.
As the eucharist gave the strength in persecution
may it keep us faithful in every difficulty.

Communion Antiphon

Neither death nor life, nor anything in all creation can come between us and Christ's love for us.
cf. Romans 8:38-39

Prayer after Communion

Lord,
we eat the bread from heaven
and become one body in Christ.
Never let us be separated from his love
and, through the example of your martyrs,
may all who glory in the name of Christian
come to serve you in the unity of faith.

NOVEMBER 1
ALL SAINTS
Solemnity

Your reward will be great in heaven. The saints forever praise God's glory in heaven. In their lives on earth they lived out the beatitudes preached by Jesus in his Sermon on the Mount and that is why they are so happy now. We too need to model our lives on them so that where they are we may one day be. We, like they, will see God face to face.

Entrance Antiphon Let us all rejoice in the Lord and keep a festival in honour of all the saints. Let us join with the angels in joyful praise to the Son of God.

Opening Prayer

Let us pray
 [that the prayers of all the saints
 will bring us forgiveness for our sins]

Father, all-powerful and ever-living God,
today we rejoice in the holy men and women
of every time and place.
May their prayers bring us your forgiveness and love.

or

Let us pray
 [as we rejoice and keep festival
 in honour of all the saints]

God our Father,
source of all holiness,
the work of your hands is manifest in your saints,
the beauty of your truth is reflected in their faith.

ALL SAINTS

May we who aspire to have part in their joy
be filled with the Spirit that blessed their lives,
so that having shared their faith on earth
we may also know their peace in your kingdom.

First Reading   Apocalypse 7:2-4.9-14.

I saw a huge number, impossible to count, of people from every nation, race, tribe and language.

I, John, saw another angel rising where the sun rises, carrying the seal of the living God; he called in a powerful voice to the four angels whose duty was to devastate land and sea, "Wait before you do any damage on land or at sea or to the trees, until we have put the seal on the foreheads of the servants of our God." Then I heard how many were sealed: a hundred and forty-four thousand, out of all the tribes of Israel.

After that I saw a huge number, impossible to count, of people from every nation, race, tribe and language; they were standing in front of the throne and in front of the Lamb, dressed in white robes and holding palms in their hands. They shouted aloud, "Victory to our God, who sits on the throne, and to the Lamb!" And all the angels who were standing in a circle round the throne, surrounding the elders and the four animals, prostrated themselves before the throne, and touched the ground with their foreheads, worshipping God with these words. "Amen. Praise and glory and wisdom and thanksgiving and honour and power and strength to our God for ever and ever. Amen."

One of the elders then spoke, and asked me, "Do you know who these people are, dressed in white robes, and where they have come from?" I answered him, "You can tell me, my lord." Then he said, "These are the people who have been through the great persecution, and they have washed their robes white again in the blood of the Lamb."

Responsorial Psalm   Psalm 23.

℟ **Such are the men who seek your face, O Lord.**

1. The Lord's is the earth and its fullness,
   the world and all its peoples.
   It is he who set it on the seas;
   on the waters he made it firm. ℟

ALL SAINTS

2. Who shall climb the mountain of the Lord?
   Who shall stand in his holy place?
   The man with clean hands and pure heart,
   who desires not worthless things. ℟

3. He shall receive blessings from the Lord
   and reward from the God who saves him.
   Such are the men who seek him,
   seek the face of the God of Jacob. ℟

Second Reading 1 John 3:1-3.
We shall see God as he really is.

Think of the love that the Father has lavished on us,
by letting us be called God's children;
and that is what we are.
Because the world refused to acknowledge him,
therefore it does not acknowledge us.
My dear people, we are already the children of God
but what we are to be in the future has not yet been revealed;
all we know is, that when it is revealed
we shall be like him
because we shall see him as he really is.
Surely everyone who entertains this hope
must purify himself, must try to be as pure as Christ.

Alleluia

Alleluia, alleluia! Come to me, all you who labour and are overburdened, and I will give you rest, says the Lord. Alleluia! Matthew 11:28.

Gospel Matthew 5:1-12.
Rejoice and be glad, for your reward will be great in heaven.

Seeing the crowds, Jesus went up the hill. There he sat down and was joined by his disciples. Then he began to speak. This is what he taught them:
"How happy are the poor in spirit;
theirs is the kingdom of heaven.
Happy the gentle:
they shall have the earth for their heritage.
Happy those who mourn:
they shall be comforted
Happy those who hunger and thirst for what is right:

ALL SAINTS

they shall be satisfied.
Happy the merciful:
they shall have mercy shown them.
Happy the pure in heart:
they shall see God.
Happy the peacemakers:
they shall be called sons of God.
Happy those who are persecuted in the cause of right:
theirs is the kingdom of heaven.
"Happy are you when people abuse you and persecute you and speak all kinds of calumny against you on my account. Rejoice and be glad, for your reward will be great in heaven."

Prayer over the Gifts

Lord,
receive our gifts in honour of the holy men and women
who live with you in glory.
May we always be aware
of their concern to help and save us.

Preface

Father, all-powerful and ever-living God,
we do well always and everywhere to give you thanks.

Today we keep the festival of your holy city,
the heavenly Jerusalem, our mother.
Around your throne
the saints, our brothers and sisters,
sing your praise for ever.
Their glory fills us with joy,
and their communion with us in your Church
gives us inspiration and strength
as we hasten on our pilgrimage of faith,
eager to meet them.

With their great company and all the angels
we praise your glory
as we cry out with one voice:

Holy, holy, holy ...

ALL SAINTS

Communion Antiphon   Happy are the pure of heart for they shall see God. Happy the peacemakers; they shall be called the sons of God. Happy are they who suffer persecution for justice' sake; the kingdom of heaven is theirs.

Matthew 5:8-10

Prayer after Communion

Father, holy one,
we praise your glory reflected in the saints.
May we who share at this table
be filled with your love
and prepared for the joy of your kingdom,
where Jesus is Lord for ever and ever.

NOVEMBER 2
ALL SOULS

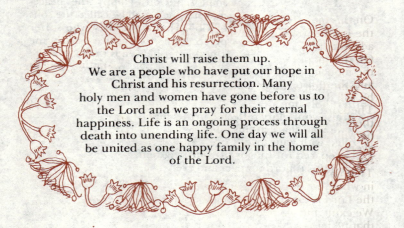

Christ will raise them up. We are a people who have put our hope in Christ and his resurrection. Many holy men and women have gone before us to the Lord and we pray for their eternal happiness. Life is an ongoing process through death into unending life. One day we will all be united as one happy family in the home of the Lord.

FIRST MASS

Entrance Antiphon Just as Jesus died and rose again, so will the Father bring with him those who have died in Jesus. Just as in Adam all men die, so in Christ all will be made alive.
1 Thessalonians 4:14; 1 Corinthians 15:22

Opening Prayer

Let us pray
  [for all our departed brothers and sisters]

Merciful Father,
hear our prayers and console us.
As we renew our faith in your Son,
whom you raised from the dead,
strengthen our hope that all our departed brothers and sisters
will share in his resurrection,
who lives and reigns with you and the Holy Spirit,
one God, for ever and ever.

ALL SOULS

First Reading   Isaiah 25:6-9.
The Lord will destroy death for ever.

On this mountain,
the Lord of hosts will prepare for all peoples
a banquet of rich food.
On this mountain he will remove
the mourning veil covering all peoples,
and the shroud enwrapping all nations,
he will destroy Death for ever.
The Lord will wipe away
the tears from every cheek;
he will take away his people's shame
everywhere on earth,
for the Lord has said so.
That day, it will be said: See, this is our God
in whom we hoped for salvation;
the Lord is the one in whom we hoped.
We exult and we rejoice
that he has saved us.

Responsorial Psalm   Psalm 22.

℟ **The Lord is my shepherd;**
there is nothing I shall want.

or ℟ **If I should walk in the valley of darkness**
no evil would I fear,
for you are there with me.

1. The Lord is my shepherd;
there is nothing I shall want.
Fresh and green are the pastures
where he gives me repose.
Near restful waters he leads me,
to revive my drooping spirit. ℟

2. He guides me along the right path;
he is true to his name.
If I should walk in the valley of darkness
no evil would I fear.
You are there with your crook and your staff;
with these you give me comfort. ℟

ALL SOULS

3. You have prepared a banquet for me
   in the sight of my foes.
   My head you have anointed with oil;
   my cup is overflowing. ℟

4. Surely goodness and kindness shall follow me
   all the days of my life.
   In the Lord's own house shall I dwell
   for ever and ever. ℟

Second Reading   Romans 5:5-11.
Having died to make us righteous, is it likely that he would now fail to save us from God's anger?

Hope is not deceptive, because the love of God has been poured into our hearts by the Holy Spirit which has been given us. We were still helpless when at his appointed moment Christ died for sinful men. It is not easy to die even for a good man — though of course for someone really worthy, a man might be prepared to die — but what proves that God loves us is that Christ died for us while we were still sinners. Having died to make us righteous, is it likely that he would now fail to save us from God's anger? When we were reconciled to God by the death of his Son, we were still enemies; now that we have been reconciled, surely we may count on being saved by the life of his Son? Not merely because we have been reconciled but because we are filled with joyful trust in God, through our Lord Jesus Christ, through whom we have already gained our reconciliation.

Alleluia   Alleluia, alleluia! It is my Father's will, says the Lord, that I should lose nothing of all that he has given to me, and that I should raise it up on the last day. Alleluia! John 6:39.

Gospel   John 6:37-40.
Whoever believes in the Son has eternal life, and I shall raise him up on the last day.

Jesus said to the crowd:
'All that the Father gives me will come to me,
and whoever comes to me
I shall not turn him away;
because I have come from heaven,

ALL SOULS

not to do my own will,
but to do the will of the one who sent me.
Now the will of him who sent me
is that I should lose nothing
of all that he has given to me,
and that I should raise it up on the last day.
Yes, it is my Father's will
that whoever sees the Son and believes in him
shall have eternal life,
and that I shall raise him up on the last day.'

Prayer over the Gifts

Lord,
we are united in this sacrament
by the love of Jesus Christ.
Accept these gifts
and receive our brothers and sisters
into the glory of your Son,
who is Lord for ever and ever.

Preface

Father, all-powerful and ever-living God,
we do well always and everywhere to give you thanks
through Jesus Christ our Lord.

In him, who rose from the dead,
our hope of resurrection dawned.
The sadness of death gives way
to the bright promise of immortality.

Lord, for your faithful people life is changed, not ended.
When the body of our earthly dwelling lies in death
we gain an everlasting dwelling place in heaven.

And so, with all the choirs of angels in heaven
we proclaim your glory
and join in their unending hymn of praise:

Holy, holy, holy ...
or
Another Preface of Christian Death may be said.

ALL SOULS

Communion Antiphon

I am the resurrection and the life, says the Lord. If anyone believes in me, even though he dies, he will live. Anyone who lives and believes in me, will not die. John 11:25-26.

Prayer after Communion

Lord God,
may the death and resurrection of Christ
which we celebrate in this eucharist
bring the departed faithful to the peace of your eternal home.

SECOND MASS

Entrance Antiphon

Give them eternal rest, O Lord, and may your light shine on them for ever.
cf. 4 Ezra 2:34-35

Opening Prayer

Let us pray
  [for all our departed brothers and sisters]

Lord God,
you are the glory of believers
and the life of the just.
Your Son redeemed us
by dying and rising to life again.
Since our departed brothers and sisters believed in the
  mystery of our resurrection,
let them share the joys and blessings of the life to come.

The Readings from the First Mass on pages 1069-1071 may be used, or others from the Lectionary.

Prayer over the Gifts

All-powerful Father,
may this sacrifice wash away
the sins of our departed brothers and sisters in the blood of Christ.
You cleansed them in the waters of baptism.
In your loving mercy grant them pardon and peace.

Preface as in First Mass, page 1071, or another of Christian Death.

ALL SOULS

Communion Antiphon May eternal light shine on them, O Lord, with all your saints for ever, for you are rich in mercy. Give them eternal rest, O Lord, and may perpetual light shine on them for ever, for you are rich in mercy.

cf. 4 Ezra 2:35.34

Prayer after Communion

Lord,
in this sacrament you give us your crucified and risen Son.
Bring to the glory of the resurrection our departed brothers and sisters
who have been purified by this holy mystery.

THIRD MASS

Entrance Antiphon God, who raised Jesus from the dead, will give new life to our own mortal bodies through his Spirit living in us.

cf. Romans 8:11

Opening Prayer

Let us pray
   [for all our departed brothers and sisters]

God our creator and redeemer,
by your power Christ conquered death
and returned to you in glory.
May all your people who have gone before us in faith
share his victory
and enjoy the vision of your glory for ever.

The Readings from the First Mass on pages 1069-1071 may be used, or others from the Lectionary.

Prayer over the Gifts

Lord,
in your kindness accept these gifts for our departed brothers and sisters
and for all who sleep in Christ.
May his perfect sacrifice

ALL SOULS

free them from the power of death
and give them eternal life.

Preface as in First Mass, page 1071, or another of Christian Death.

Communion Antiphon   We are waiting for our Saviour, the Lord Jesus Christ; he will transfigure our lowly bodies into copies of his own glorious body.

Philippians 3:20-21

Prayer after Communion
Lord,
may our sacrifice bring peace and forgiveness
to our brothers and sisters who have died.
Bring the new life given to them in baptism
to the fullness of eternal joy.

NOVEMBER 30
ST ANDREW, APOSTLE

PATRON OF SCOTLAND
In Scotland: Solemnity
Elsewhere: Feast

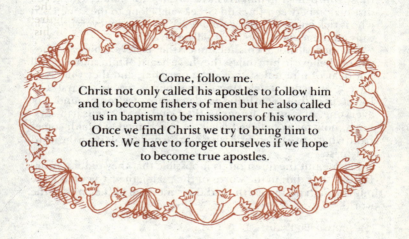

Come, follow me.
Christ not only called his apostles to follow him
and to become fishers of men but he also called
us in baptism to be missioners of his word.
Once we find Christ we try to bring him to
others. We have to forget ourselves if we hope
to become true apostles.

Entrance Antiphon By the Sea of Galilee the Lord saw two brothers, Peter and Andrew. He called them: come and follow me, and I will make you fishers of men. cf. Matthew 4:18-19.

Opening Prayer
Lord,
in your kindness hear our petitions.
You called Andrew the apostle
to preach the gospel and guide your Church in faith.
May he always be our friend in your presence
to help us with his prayers.

First Reading   Romans 10:9-18.

**Faith comes from what is preached,
and what is preached comes from the word of Christ.**

SAINT ANDREW

If your lips confess that Jesus is Lord and if you believe in your heart that God raised him from the dead, then you will be saved. By believing from the heart you are made righteous; by confessing with your lips you are saved. When scripture says: those who believe in him will have no cause for shame, it makes no distinction between Jew and Greek: all belong to the same Lord who is rich enough, however many ask his help, for everyone who calls on the name of the Lord will be saved.

But they will not ask his help unless they believe in him, and they will not believe in him unless they have heard of him, and they will not hear of him unless they get a preacher, and they will never have a preacher unless one is sent, but as scripture says: The footsteps of those who bring good news are a welcome sound. Not everyone, of course, listens to the Good News. As Isaiah says: Lord, how many believed what we proclaimed? So faith comes from what is preached, and what is preached comes from the word of Christ.

Let me put the question: is it possible that they did not hear? Indeed they did; in the words of the psalm, their voice has gone out through all the earth, and their message to the ends of the world.

Responsorial Psalm   Psalm 18.

℟ **Their span goes forth through all the earth.**

1. The heavens proclaim the glory of God
and the firmament shows forth the work of his hands.
Day unto day takes up the story
and night unto night makes known the message.   ℟

2. No speech, no word, no voice is heard
yet their span goes forth through all the earth,
their words to the utmost bounds of the world.   ℟

Alleluia
Alleluia, alleluia! Follow me, says the Lord, and I will make you fishers of men. Alleluia!   Matthew 4:19.

Gospel   Matthew 4:18-22.
And they left their nets at once and followed him.

As Jesus was walking by the Sea of Galilee he saw two brothers, Simon, who was called Peter, and his brother Andrew; they were making a cast in the lake with their net, for they were fishermen.

SAINT ANDREW

And he said to them, "Follow me and I will make you fishers of men." And they left their nets at once and followed him.

Going on from there he saw another pair of brothers, James son of Zebedee and his brother John; they were in their boat with their father Zebedee, mending their nets, and he called them. At once, leaving the boat and their father, they followed him.

Prayer over the Gifts

All-powerful God,
may these gifts we bring on the feast of Saint Andrew
be pleasing to you
and give life to all who receive them.

Preface

Father, all-powerful and ever-living God,
we do well always and everywhere to give you thanks.

You are the eternal Shepherd
who never leaves his flock untended.
Through the apostles
you watch over us and protect us always.
You made them shepherds of the flock
to share in the work of your Son,
and from their place in heaven they guide us still.

And so, with all the choirs of angels in heaven
we proclaim your glory
and join in their unending hymn of praise:

Holy, holy, holy . . .

Communion Antiphon

Andrew told his brother Simon: We have found the Messiah, the Christ; and he brought him to Jesus.

John 1:41-42

Prayer after Communion

Lord,
may the sacrament we have received give us courage
to follow the example of Andrew the apostle.
By sharing in Christ's suffering
may we live with him for ever in glory,
for he is Lord for ever and ever.

DECEMBER 8

THE IMMACULATE CONCEPTION OF THE BLESSED VIRGIN MARY

Hail, Mary, full of grace.
God chose Mary to be the mother of his Son.
From her conception, she who was to bear the sinless one, was herself free from sin. This showed God's special love for her who was indeed full of grace. We admire her for her promptness in doing God's will. We have to be prepared to do likewise.

Entrance Antiphon I exult for joy in the Lord, my soul rejoices in my God; for he has clothed me in the garment of salvation and robed me in the cloak of justice, like a bride adorned with her jewels. Isaiah 61:10.

Opening Prayer

Let us pray
  [that through the prayers of the sinless
  Virgin Mary, God will free us from our sins]

Father,
you prepared the Virgin Mary
to be the worthy mother of your Son.
You let her share beforehand
in the salvation Christ would bring by his death,
and kept her sinless from the first moment of her conception.
Help us by her prayers
to live in your presence without sin.

or

THE IMMACULATE CONCEPTION

Let us pray
   [on this feast of Mary
   who experienced the perfection of
   God's saving power]

Father,
the image of the Virgin is found in the Church.
Mary had a faith that your Spirit prepared
and a love that never knew sin,
for you kept her sinless from the first moment of her conception.

Trace in our actions the lines of her love,
in our hearts her readiness of faith.
Prepare once again a world for your Son
who lives and reigns with you and the Holy Spirit,
one God, for ever and ever.

First Reading   Genesis 3:9-15.20.

I will make you enemies of each other: your offspring and her offspring.

After Adam had eaten of the tree, the Lord God called to him. 'Where are you?' he asked. 'I heard the sound of you in the garden,' he replied. 'I was afraid because I was naked, so I hid.' 'Who told you that you were naked?' he asked. 'Have you been eating of the tree I forbade you to eat?' The man replied, 'It was the woman you put with me; she gave me the fruit, and I ate it.' Then the Lord God asked the woman, 'What is this you have done?' The woman replied, 'The serpent tempted me and I ate.'

    Then the Lord God said to the serpent, 'Because you have done this,

'Be accursed beyond all cattle,
all wild beasts.
You shall crawl on your belly and eat dust
every day of your life.
I will make you enemies of each other:
you and the woman,
your offspring and her offspring.
It will crush your head
and you will strike its heel'.

    The man named his wife 'Eve' because she was the mother of all those who live.

THE IMMACULATE CONCEPTION

Responsorial Psalm   Psalm 97.

℟ **Sing a new song to the Lord
for he has worked wonders.**

1. Sing a new song to the Lord
   for he has worked wonders.
   His right hand and his holy arm
   have brought salvation. ℟

2. The Lord has made known his salvation;
   has shown his justice to the nations.
   He has remembered his truth and love
   for the house of Israel. ℟

3. All the ends of the earth have seen
   the salvation of our God.
   Shout to the Lord all the earth,
   ring out your joy. ℟

Second Reading   Ephesians 1:3-6.11-12.
Before the world was made, God chose us in Christ.

Blessed be God the Father of our Lord Jesus Christ,
who has blessed us with all the spiritual blessings of heaven in
   Christ.
Before the world was made, he chose us, chose us in Christ,
to be holy and spotless, and to live through love in his presence,
determining that we should become his adopted sons, through
   Jesus Christ
for his own kind purposes,
to make us praise the glory of his grace,
his free gift to us in the Beloved.
And it is in him that we were claimed as God's own,
chosen from the beginning,
under the predetermined plan of the one who guides all things
as he decides by his own will;
chosen to be,
for his greater glory,
the people who would put their hopes in Christ before he came.

Alleluia   Alleluia, alleluia! Hail, Mary, full of grace; the Lord is with thee! Blessed art thou among women. Alleluia! Luke 1:28.

THE IMMACULATE CONCEPTION

Gospel   Luke 1:26-38.
You are to conceive and bear a son.

The angel Gabriel was sent by God to a town in Galilee called Nazareth, to a virgin betrothed to a man named Joseph, of the House of David; and the virgin's name was Mary. He went in and said to her, 'Rejoice, so highly favoured! The Lord is with you.' She was deeply disturbed by these words and asked herself what this greeting could mean, but the angel said to her, 'Mary, do not be afraid; you have won God's favour. Listen! You are to conceive and bear a son, and you must name him Jesus. He will be great and will be called Son of the Most High. The Lord God will give him the throne of his ancestor David; he will rule over the House of Jacob for ever and his reign will have no end.' Mary said to the angel, 'But how can this come about, since I am a virgin?' 'The Holy Spirit will come upon you' the angel answered 'and the power of the Most High will cover you with its shadow. And so the child will be holy and will be called Son of God. Know this too: your kinswoman Elizabeth has, in her old age, herself conceived a son, and she whom people called barren is now in her sixth month, for nothing is impossible to God.' 'I am the handmaid of the Lord,' said Mary 'let what you have said be done to me.' And the angel left her.

Prayer over the Gifts

Lord,
accept this sacrifice
on the feast of the sinless Virgin Mary.
You kept her free from sin
from the first moment of her life.
Help us by her prayers,
and free us from our sins.

Preface

Father, all-powerful and ever-living God,
we do well always and everywhere to give you thanks.

You allowed no stain of Adam's sin
to touch the Virgin Mary.
Full of grace, she was to be a worthy mother of your Son,
your sign of favour to the Church at its beginning,

THE IMMACULATE CONCEPTION

and the promise of its perfection as the bride of Christ, radiant in beauty.

Purest of virgins, she was to bring forth your Son,
the innocent lamb who takes away our sins.
You chose her from all women to be our advocate with you
and our pattern of holiness.

In our joy we sing to your glory
with all the choirs of angels:

Holy, holy, holy ...

Communion Antiphon

All honour to you, Mary! From you arose the sun of justice, Christ our God.

Prayer after Communion

Lord our God,
in your love, you chose the Virgin Mary
and kept her free from sin.
May this sacrament of your love
free us from our sins.

ANNIVERSARY OF THE DEDICATION OF A CHURCH

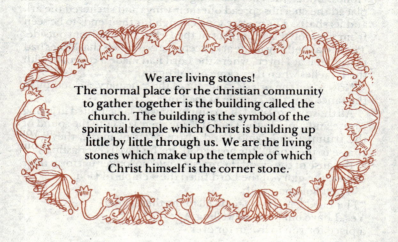

We are living stones!
The normal place for the christian community to gather together is the building called the church. The building is the symbol of the spiritual temple which Christ is building up little by little through us. We are the living stones which make up the temple of which Christ himself is the corner stone.

Entrance Antiphon Greatly to be feared is God in his sanctuary; he, the God of Israel, gives power and strength to his people. Blessed be God! Psalm 67:36.

Opening Prayer

Father,
each year we recall the dedication of this church to your service.
Let our worship always be sincere
and help us to find your saving love in this church.

Other readings may be used instead of those given here.

Outside the Easter Season

First Reading 2 Chronicles 5:6-11,13 - 6:2.

I have built you a dwelling, a place for you to live in for ever.

King Solomon, and all the community of Israel gathering with him in front of the ark, sacrificed sheep and oxen, countless, innumerable. The priests brought the ark of the covenant of the Lord to its place, in the Debir of the Temple, that is, in the Holy of

ANNIVERSARY OF THE DEDICATION OF A CHURCH

Holies, under the cherubs' wings. For there where the ark was placed the cherubs spread out their wings and sheltered the ark and its shafts. These were long enough for their ends to be seen from the Holy Place in front of the Debir, but not from outside. There was nothing in the ark except the two tablets that Moses had placed in it at Horeb, where the Lord had made a covenant with the Israelites when they came out of Egypt.

Now when the priests came out of the sanctuary, a cloud filled the sanctuary, the Temple of the Lord.

All those who played the trumpet, or who sang, united in giving praise and glory to the Lord. Lifting their voices to the sound of the trumpet and cymbal and instruments of music, they gave praise to the Lord, "for he is good, for his love is everlasting."

Because of the cloud the priests could no longer perform their duties: the glory of the Lord filled the Temple of God.

Then Solomon said:
"The Lord has chosen to dwell in the thick cloud.
Yes, I have built you a dwelling,
a place for you to live in for ever."

or In the Easter Season

First Reading   Acts 7:44-50.

The Most High does not live in a house that human hands have built.

Stephen said to the people, the elders and scribes, "While they were in the desert our ancestors possessed the Tent of Testimony that has been constructed according to the instructions God gave Moses, telling him to make an exact copy of the pattern he had been shown. It was handed down from one ancestor of ours to another until Joshua brought it into the country we had conquered from the nations which were driven out by God as we advanced. Here it stayed until the time of David. He won God's favour and asked permission to have a temple built for the House of Jacob, though it was Solomon who actually built God's house for him. Even so the Most High does not live in a house that human hands have built: for as the prophet says:
'With heaven my throne
and earth my footstool,
what house could you build me,
what place could you make for my rest?
Was not all this made by my hand?'"

ANNIVERSARY OF THE DEDICATION OF A CHURCH

Responsorial Psalm   Psalm 83.

℟ **How lovely is your dwelling place,
Lord, God of hosts.**

or **Here God lives among men.**

1. My soul is longing and yearning,
   is yearning for the courts of the Lord.
   My heart and my soul ring out their joy
   to God, the living God.

2. The sparrow herself finds a home
   and the swallow a nest for her brood;
   she lays her young by your altars,
   Lord of hosts, my king and my God.   ℟

3. They are happy, who dwell in your house,
   for ever singing your praise.
   Turn your eyes, O God our shield,
   look on the face of your anointed.

4. One day within your courts
   is better than a thousand elsewhere.
   The threshold of the house of God
   I prefer to the dwellings of the wicked.   ℟

Second Reading   1 Corinthians 3:9–11.16-17.

You are the temple of God.

You are God's building. By the grace God gave me, I succeeded as an architect and laid the foundations, on which someone else is doing the building. Everyone doing the building must work carefully. For the foundation, nobody can lay any other than the one which has already been laid, that is Jesus Christ.

Didn't you realise that you were God's temple and that the Spirit of God was living among you? If anybody should destroy the temple of God, God will destroy him, because the temple of God is sacred; and you are that temple.

ANNIVERSARY OF THE DEDICATION OF A CHURCH

Alleluia Alleluia, alleluia! I shall make my home among them, says the Lord; I will be their God, they shall be my people. Alleluia! Ezra 37:27.

Gospel John 4:19-24.

True worshippers will worship the Father in spirit and truth.

The Samaritan woman said to Jesus, "I see you are a prophet, sir. Our fathers worshipped on this mountain, while you say that Jerusalem is the place where one ought to worship." Jesus said:
"Believe me, woman, the hour is coming
when you will worship the Father
neither on this mountain nor in Jerusalem.
You worship what you do not know;
we worship what we do know;
for salvation comes from the Jews.
But the hour will come — in fact it is here already —
when true worshippers will worship the Father in spirit and
  truth:
that is the kind of worshipper
the Father wants.
God is spirit,
and those who worship
must worship in spirit and truth."

Prayer over the Gifts
Lord,
as we recall the day you filled this church
with your glory and holiness,
may our lives also become an acceptable offering to you.

Preface
Father, all-powerful and ever-living God,
we do well always and everywhere to give you thanks.

We thank you now for this house of prayer
in which you bless your family
as we come to you on pilgrimage.

Here you reveal your presence
by sacramental signs,
and make us one with you
through the unseen bond of grace.

ANNIVERSARY OF THE DEDICATION OF A CHURCH

Here you build your temple of living stones,
and bring the Church to its full stature
as the body of Christ throughout the world,
to reach its perfection at last
in the heavenly city of Jerusalem,
which is the vision of your peace.

In communion with all the angels and saints
we bless and praise your greatness
in the temple of your glory:

Holy, holy, holy . . .

Communion Antiphon   You are the temple of God, and God's Spirit dwells in you. The temple of God is holy; you are that temple.

1 Corinthians 3:16-17

Prayer after Communion

Lord,
we know the joy and power of your blessing in our lives.
As we celebrate the dedication of this church,
may we give ourselves once more to your service.

Prayer

Prayer

Personal Prayer

WE pray as individuals or in a group. In a later section on prayer groups we will reflect on community prayer since we are all called to be members of a community, Christ's church. Here we will deal with personal prayer only.

All prayer begins from the fact that God is more ready to listen to us than we are to speak to him and even more ready to give than we are to ask. We do not pray to a miserly and unloving God. 'Since God did not spare his own Son, but gave him up to benefit us all, we may be certain, after such a gift, that he will not refuse anything he can give'. Romans 8:32. We need to be honest in prayer so that we really mean what we say. There is little point in praying to be made into a certain kind of person when the last thing we in fact want is to be changed. God sees the secrets of our hearts.

We should remember too that we are intimately bound up with society and therefore our prayer must never be selfish. It is pointless to even start to pray if our life pattern is completely centred on our own self interests. God is our Father and he knows what is best and it is only the Holy Spirit who will renew us and put a new heart in us. Neither does God do for us what we are not prepared to do for ourselves. As soon as we have prayed we must set out in work to make that prayer come true. In this way we realise that prayer is the cooperation of our effort with the grace of God.

Prayer works within situations and brings us power and grace to meet and cope with every situation so we can always be sure that God's grace is sufficient for us. In the Garden of Gethsemane Jesus prayed, if it was God's will, to be released from the cross. He was not released from the cross but was given the power to endure it.

Different Forms of Prayer

Prayer is often divided up into categories but we should always remember that what we are doing is still prayer. We will automatically move from one type of prayer to another as the Spirit shows us, spending more time on one form and less on another, while reversing the process on another occasion. There are five great divisions of prayer: invocation, confession, thanksgiving, petition, intercession.

PERSONAL PRAYER

Invocation does not mean that we invite God to be present at our prayers since he is always present. He is closer to us than breathing and nearer than hands and feet. In invocation we remind ourselves that God is here and thus allows ourselves to be saturated by his presence.

Confession is the prayer in which we tell God of our sins and failings. We are a healed people who are still very much in need of healing and so we are completely honest in our self-examination remembering that 'if we say we have no sin in us, we are deceiving ourselves and refusing to admit the truth; but if we acknowledge our sins, then God who is faithful and just will forgive our sins and purify us from everything that is wrong. To say that we have never sinned is to call God a liar and to show that his word is not in us.' I John 1:8-10.

Thanksgiving is the outcome of the gratitude of our hearts for all that God has done for us in Christ Jesus, Our Lord. This form of prayer is the one that comes quickest to our lips whenever our prayer life tends to become dry.

Petition is when we pray to God for the things we need for our life. It is born out of our own insufficiency and reveals our dependence on a bountiful God who so respects our freedom that he waits for us to tell him our needs. We do not so much tell God what we want but rather we ask him to give what he wills.

Intercession is the prayer which takes the needs of the world and brings them to God. We know that all is safe in his keeping and we remember before him those in distress and difficulties for whom he will provide.

Prayer is a relationship

Prayer is, above all, a relationship between two people — God and myself. It is recognising that we are in the company of 'the other' whom we love and who loves us. There are two ways in which any personal relationship grows. There are times spent together *talking* about every conceivable subject under the sun so as to get to know each other's history and background. But there are also times spent in *silence* together quietly enjoying each other's company, secure in the knowledge that the other person is there and that is all that really matters.

PERSONAL PRAYER

It is this second aspect of 'being' to each other which is the more important in any form of deep prayer. We are frightened by silence if through it we are only conscious of being isolated individuals instead of being part of a family. Yet silence which is creative is one of the most powerful means of communication. In this silence we have not the same opportunity to cover up the frightening emptiness of our own egoism. In relaxed, creative silence there is a union of spirits in which we offer to God a pure heart undisturbed by the hustle and bustle of daily life. Silence is not just the absence of speech; it is the stillness of spirit in which the true self, made in God's image and likeness, is released from the shackles of fear which imprison it. We experience the beauty of the liberty of the sons of God.

The Problems

There are many problems confronting us, the main one being the priority that we should give to prayer in our lives. We are pressurised by an overactive society. Much of what has been written on prayer seems more applicable to members of religious communities or people in more relaxed circumstances than exist today. The busy person, however, cannot afford not to pray. It is a very foolish person indeed who says he is too busy to pray.

How can we pray without ceasing? Does this mean that we must set aside more time for prayer and get away from work in order to do it? How do I balance work and prayer so that my work is, in fact, the fruit of my time spent in prayer? These are problems we have to grapple with and for which a solution has to be found if we are to become true christians. The first risk in prayer is, of course, to pray; the second risk is to follow up the consequences of prayer. There is no such thing as unanswered prayer because we always get what we really need. To play with prayer is to play with fire.

Prayer brings us into direct contact with Jesus Christ who is the very life of God himself. We pray to the Father by the power of the Holy Spirit in Jesus Christ. This is the life into which we were initiated by baptism and are continually fed by the eucharist. We become aware that life is a pilgrimage and as we grow in prayer then our awareness of God becomes less verbalised and tends towards silence and wonder. The terms in which we first began to think of God now change under the influence of love. So we may be tempted to think we are losing God just at the very point

PERSONAL PRAYER

where we are both finding and being found by him. God is so beautiful we have no words to describe him.

Seeing God in our lives

God calls us by name. It is important that through prayer we recognise what God is asking each of us to do in our own particular set of circumstances. It is easy to excuse oneself on the ground that if things were different we would pray, would serve God better. But things are not different. God calls each person to serve him and love him in his own set of circumstances and not in those of someone else. Of course, there must be tension between involvement in the world and withdrawal from it; between personal effort and relaxing with God. The solution differs from person to person because prayer is basically a very personal thing. We need to remember that Christ 'stands at the door and knocks'. It is not sufficient to let him into the house of our being; we must let him into every room and allow him to explore every nook and cranny. It is only then that we will have a sense of the all-pervading presence of God.

Praying in the Spirit of Christ

Christ is the turning-point of human history. The Jesus of the New Testament is not only the Word made flesh but also a Person entering into personal relationships with other people. 'Christ took human flesh so that we might know him and the power of his resurrection and the fellowship of his suffering.' Philippians 3:10. The word 'know' for the Jews implied a personal relationship. Christ is our brother who enters into a relationship with us and God so that we can really pray the Our Father. Christ is a perfect reconciler between God and us. He is for ever reconciling the world to the Father and in our prayers and sufferings we enter into the self-same saving act of reconciliation.

God acting in Christ was subject to the limitations of a single historic person. He could preach to so few people that he said, referring to his death: "I have a baptism to be baptized with and I am limited until it be accomplished". He promised his followers that after his resurrection he would dwell in them in a new way. The Holy Spirit would be with them to enlighten, guide and strengthen their lives, but not limited as he had been by time and

PERSONAL PRAYER

space. It was this indwelling Spirit, who completed the relationship with the Father, which Christ had made possible for them. He was the 'Spirit of adoption whereby we cry "Abba — Father" '. Romans 8:15. The Spirit of the one who makes it possible for us to become God in a very special way: 'We know not how to pray as we ought, but the Spirit himself intercedes for us with sighs which we cannot articulate'. Romans 8:26-27.

Prayer is like paying attention to our breathing knowing that without breathing we would not be able to live. It is the God in us praying to the God beyond us. When effort fails and one does not know what to say or pray at all then in our stillness and nothingness we acknowledge that it is the Spirit alone who prays in us and for us.

Praying in the World

An exaggerated and therefore unhealthy fear of Pantheism has denied us for many years the unlimited avenues of praying to the Father in and through creation. We believe not only that God made the world but also that he keeps it in being. He is a loving Father who watches over every aspect of our lives. We recognise God in the material world which yet has something beyond it — the immanent and transcendent. God is in all things because he sustains all things.

> O Light Invisible, we praise Thee!
> Too bright for mortal vision.
> O Greater Light, we praise Thee for the less;
> The eastern light our spires touch at morning,
> The light that slants upon our western doors at evening,
> The twilight over stagnant pools at batflight,
> Moon light and star light, owl and moth light,
> Glow-worm glowlight on a grassblade.
> O Light Invisible we worship Thee!
> T. S. Eliot from 'The Rock'.

Prayer Groups

THROUGH the sacrament of baptism we are initiated into our life in the community. We nourish that life by prayer and the sacraments. We belong not only to our own natural family but also to the wider spiritual family of all baptized people. When we come together to pray we are doing what the Church has been doing from its foundation. 'These remained faithful to the teaching of the apostles, to the brotherhood, to the breaking of bread and to the prayers. They went as a body to the Temple every day but met in their houses for the breaking of bread; they shared their food gladly and generously; they praised God and were looked up to by everyone. Day by day the Lord added to their community those destined to be saved.' **Acts 2:42.46-47**.

We remember the Lord's words: "Where two or three meet in my name, I shall be there with them". **Matthew 18:20.** There has been an upsurge of interest and dedication to prayer in recent years with the consequent increase in the numbers of people who want to pray together. It is sometimes useful to use fixed structures for these prayer sessions such as vespers from the Prayer of the Church or the rosary, but more and more people prefer to wait on the Lord and see how the Spirit moves them.

Shared prayer itself

The major prayer is the praise of God so that when the prayer goes dead and the silence is not that of the awareness of God's presence, we should look to the lack of praise. We are 'a people set apart to sing the praises of God'. **Peter 2:9.** Hearing other people praise God in their own words strengthens our faith as well as teaching us how to praise God in prayer. There are many ways of praising God such as responding to the glories of creation and redemption and to God's power and presence.

The Christ-centredness or God-centredness of shared prayer is the measure of its depth. Shared prayer is difficult for many people because praying out loudly before others in our own words is something for which we have never been trained. The important thing to remember is that we are all praying together in Christ. When the group is composed of people who have a habit of prayer then the extended moments of shared, creative silence are frequent. In this silence we all share the presence of God.

PRAYER GROUPS

There is a great deal of spontaneity in shared prayer even though it should always be well prepared beforehand. The best preparation is the personal prayer and penance of each individual. As a rule, shared prayer is based on scripture from which a theme usually develops and on which the group should linger. We pay attention to what the Spirit is saying to us in the group and soon we become sensitive to the way he leads us. We should avoid dialogue with each other just as much as we should avoid using shared prayer for public confession or complaining about difficulties.

Shared prayer in its ultimate analysis leads us to deeper fuller personal prayer-life. The prayer itself is a blend of vocal praise, conversational prayer, scripture readings, shared silence, shared faith experience and shared prayers of petition. Shared prayer builds up the community and in a loving community we find that mutual forgiveness is an important element in our spiritual growth. "And when you stand in prayer, forgive whatever you have against anybody, so that your Father in heaven may forgive your failings too". Mark 11:25.

The Holy Spirit in Groups

The whole thrust of renewal in the Second Vatican Council was directed to making us all aware of the presence and power of the Holy Spirit at work in us. Those renewed in the Spirit feel themselves to be in the heart of the church. The Church is 'charismatic' in itself in so far as it is Christ's gift to us for the salvation of the world. The Holy Spirit changes our lives as we realise more profoundly our total dependence on Christ. Through the power of the Spirit the gospel message comes alive for us more and more and we become a source of renewal within the Church.

It is wrong to label some people as 'charismatic' because this implies that others are 'non-charismatic'. Every christian is charismatic in so far as he is baptized and has received the Spirit even though he may not necessarily be *conscious* of the workings of the Spirit within him, changing and guiding his life. Many charismatic people of deep prayer and spiritual commitment may never even have heard of Catholic charismatic renewal and that is why it is wrong to call some prayer groups 'charismatic' and others 'non-charismatic'. No group or any section of a group

PRAYER GROUPS

can claim to possess the Spirit alone. God is infinitely variable in the distribution and expression of his gifts. Prayer is always an ongoing process towards contemplation rather than something forced, noisy, tense and artificial.

Baptism of the Spirit

Nowadays people worry whether or not they were 'baptized in the Spirit'. The term 'release of the Spirit' is also often used. True there are some people who can recall specific moments in their lives when God spoke to them in an immediate, direct, personal way. They are very fortunate as indeed was St. Paul on the road to Damascus. This is not the usual way in which the Spirit acts. He gradually manifests himself in our daily living of our normal situations so that the process is a gradual awakening rather than a blinding flash of light. The one type of conversion is not greater or less than the other.

Not all christians respond to the Spirit and yet it is on this response that the whole value of christian life depends. People can go through the motions of prayer without actually praying. The baptism of the Spirit marks the beginning of learning to live with God at a *deeper* level of relationship. Humility is the cornerstone upon which the Holy Spirit builds. The perfect example of charismatic renewal is Our Lady. Bride of the Holy Spirit she gave the Saviour to the world. Her silence is the hymn of the Universe and the most powerful example of shared prayer which we can find is when Our Lady filled with the Holy Spirit together with Elizabeth uttered the praises of God.

Praying the Bible

THE bible is not just a book which relates past events. It speaks to us in our daily lives and challenges us with its message. We are not to meditate on the bible and leave it on the shelf with the intention to return later for further material for meditation. The bible invites us to change our life pattern and that of course means action. 'You must do what the word tells you, and not just listen to it and deceive yourselves. To listen to the word and not obey is like looking at your own features in a mirror and then, after a quick look, going off and immediately forgetting what you looked like. But the man who looks steadily at the perfect law of freedom and makes that his habit — not listening and then forgetting, but actively putting it into practice — will be happy in all that he does.'
James 1:22-25.

God speaks to us of his love in the written words of the bible. He sent his only-begotten Son to become one of the human family so that we through the Holy Spirit would become his sons. God always takes the initiative when he approaches us: that is *grace*. We refuse God's love: that is *sin*. The bible is the story of God's love and our sinfulness but finally God's love overcomes our sin through the passion and death of Jesus Christ.

The bible is an on-going story which begins with creation, flows into the life, death and resurrection of Christ and on into the ocean which is our world. We are a people whose lives are fashioned by the rule of life laid down in God's law and revealed in the fullness of love in the life of Christ. We are encouraged to build our prayer-life round the Prayer of the Church which will make us more and more a Gospel people. We can preach the Good News because we try to live it in the everyday situations in which we find ourselves. We live the Gospel in such a way that it becomes a prayer. We should let the Gospel happen to us since it has no other reason for being written.

In the Sunday eucharist there is a strong emphasis on the liturgy of the word as being essential to our lives as christians. We listen to God's word, remain silent so that we can appreciate it and then are exhorted by the president of the assembly to put it into practice. It is obvious that everyone should have a bible which should be the

PRAYING THE BIBLE

most used book in the home. From it we take our morning and evening prayers. We ask God our Father to open our minds and hearts to his word so that in it we may receive the precious things which he is waiting to give.

Prayers

The Lord's Prayer

Our Father, who art in heaven,
hallowed be thy name;
thy kingdom come;
thy will be done on earth as it is in heaven.
Give us this day our daily bread;
and forgive us our trespasses,
as we forgive those who trespass against us;
and lead us not into temptation, but deliver us from evil.
Amen.

The Hail, Mary

Hail, Mary, full of grace,
the Lord is with thee.
Blessed art thou among women,
and blessed is the fruit of thy womb, Jesus.
Holy Mary, Mother of God,
pray for us sinners, now,
and at the hour of our death.
Amen.

The Doxology

Glory be to the Father
and to the Son
and to the Holy Spirit
as it was in the beginning
is now and ever shall be
world without end.
Amen.

The Apostles' Creed

I believe in God, the Father almighty, creator of heaven and earth, and in Jesus Christ, his only Son, our Lord, who was conceived by the Holy Spirit, born of the Virgin Mary, suffered under Pontius

PRAYERS

Pilate, was crucified, died, and was buried. He descended into hell. The third day he rose again from the dead. He ascended into heaven, sitteth at the right hand of God the almighty Father. From thence he shall come to judge the living and the dead. I believe in the Holy Spirit, the holy Catholic Church, the Communion of Saints, the forgiveness of sins, the resurrection of the body, and life everlasting. Amen.

An Act of Faith

O God, I firmly believe all the truths that you have revealed and that you teach us through your Church, for you are Truth itself and can neither deceive nor be deceived.

An Act of Hope

O God, I hope with complete trust that you will give me, through the merits of Jesus Christ, all necessary grace in this world and everlasting life in the world to come, for this is what you have promised and you always keep your promises.

An Act of Charity

O God, I love you with my whole heart above all things, because you are infinitely good; and for your sake I love my neighbour as I love myself.

An Act of Contrition

O God, I am sorry with my whole heart for all my sins because you are Goodness itself and sin is an offence against you. Therefore I firmly resolve, with the help of your grace, not to sin again and to avoid the occasions of sin.

For self knowledge

I thank thee, Lord, for knowing me better than I know myself, and for letting me know myself better than others know me.
Make me, I pray, better than they suppose, and forgive me for what they do not know.

Abu Bekr

Psalm 139

Yahweh, you examine me and know me,
you know if I am standing or sitting,
you read my thoughts from far away,

whether I walk or lie down, you are watching,
you know every detail of my conduct.

The word is not even on my tongue
Yahweh, before you know all about it;
close behind and close in front you fence me round,
shielding me with your hand.
Such knowledge is beyond my understanding,
a height to which my mind cannot attain.

Where could I go to escape your spirit?
Where could I flee from your presence?
If I climb the heavens, you are there,
there too, if I lie in Sheol.

If I flew to the point of sunrise,
or westward across the sea.
Your hand would still be guiding me,
your right hand holding me.

If I asked darkness to cover me,
and light to become night around me,
that darkness would not be dark to you,
night would be as light as day.

It was you who created my inmost self,
and put me together in my mother's womb;
for all these mysteries I thank you:
for the wonder of myself, for the wonder of your works.

You know me through and through,
from having watched my bones take shape
when I was being formed in secret,
knitted together in the limbo of the womb.

You had scrutinised my every action,
all were recorded in your book,
my days listed and determined,
even before the first of them occurred.

God, how hard it is to grasp your thoughts!
How impossible to count them!
I could no more count them than I could the sand,
and suppose I could, you would still be with me.

God, examine me and know my heart,
probe me and know my thoughts;

PRAYERS

make sure I do not follow pernicious ways,
and guide me in the way that is everlasting.

For serenity

God grant me
the serenity to accept the things I cannot change,
the courage to change the things I can,
and the wisdom to distinguish the one from the other.

Reinhold Niebuhr

Prayer to the Holy Spirit

Come, Holy Spirit, fill the hearts of your faithful, and enkindle in them the fire of your love.
Send forth your Spirit and they shall be created.
And you shall renew the face of the earth.
Let us pray. O God, who has taught the hearts of the faithful by the light of the Holy Spirit, grant that by the gift of the same Spirit we may be always truly wise and ever rejoice in his consolation.

The Angelus

In this prayer we recall the great mystery of the incarnation by which God took human flesh and became one of us through the power of the Holy Spirit and the consent of our Blessed Lady. We commemorate the angel's announcement to Mary revealing to her the unique part which she was destined to play in the history of salvation. This prayer is said in the morning, at noon and in the evening.

℣ The angel of the Lord declared unto Mary.
℟ And she conceived of the Holy Spirit.
Hail Mary ...

℣ Behold the handmaid of the Lord.
℟ Be it done unto me according to thy word.
Hail Mary ...

℣ And the Word was made flesh,
℟ and dwelt among us.
Hail Mary ...

℣ Pray for us, O holy Mother of God.
℟ That we may be made worthy of the promises of Christ.

Let us pray. Pour forth, we beseech thee, O Lord, thy grace into our hearts, that we, to whom the incarnation of Christ thy Son was made known by the message of an angel, may be brought, by his passion and cross, to the glory of his resurrection. Through the same Christ our Lord. Amen.

Regina Coeli

This prayer is said instead of the Angelus from the Easter Vigil until the evening of Pentecost Sunday. In it we remember the joys of the Risen Lord in which with Our Lady we all share.

O Queen of heaven, rejoice, alleluia!
For he whom thou didst merit to bear, alleluia!
Has risen, as he said, alleluia!
Pray for us to God, alleluia!

℣ Rejoice and be glad, O Virgin Mary, alleluia!
℟ For the Lord has risen indeed, alleluia!

Let us pray. O God, who gavest joy to the world through the resurrection of thy Son our Lord Jesus Christ; grant that we may obtain, through his Virgin Mother, Mary, the joys of everlasting life. Through the same Christ our Lord. Amen.

Hail, Holy Queen

Hail, holy Queen, Mother of mercy! Hail, our life, our sweetness and our hope. To thee do we cry, poor banished children of Eve; to thee do we send up our sighs, mourning and weeping in this vale of tears.
Turn, then, most gracious advocate, thine eyes of mercy towards; and after this our exile, show unto us the blessed fruit of thy womb, Jesus. O clement, O loving, O sweet Virgin Mary.

℣ Pray for us, O holy Mother of God.
℟ That we may be made worthy of the promises of Christ.

Let us pray. Almighty, everlasting God, who, through the working of the Holy Spirit, didst prepare the body and soul of the glorious Virgin Mary to be a worthy dwelling for thy Son: grant that we who remember her with joy may be delivered by her prayers from the evils that beset us in this world and from everlasting death in the next. Through the same Christ our Lord. Amen.

PRAYERS

The Memorare
Remember, O most loving Virgin Mary, that never was it known that anyone who fled to your protection, implored your help, or sought your intercession was left unaided. Inspired by this confidence, we fly unto you, O Virgin of virgins, our Mother! To you we come, before you we stand, sinful and sorrowful. O Mother of the Word incarnate, despise not our petitions, but in your mercy hear and answer us. Amen.

Morning Offering
O Jesus, through the most pure heart of Mary, I offer you all the prayers, thoughts, works and sufferings of this day for all the intentions of thy Divine Heart.

or
Grant, O Lord, that none may love you less this day because of me;
that never word or act of mine may turn one soul from thee;
and ever daring, yet one other grace would I implore,
that many souls this day, because of me, may love thee more.

At daybreak
O Lord, when I awake and day begins
waken me to thy presence;
waken me to thy indwelling;
waken me to inward sight of thee,
and speech with thee
and strength from thee;
that all my earthly walk may waken into song
and my spirit leap up to thee all day,
all ways.

Eric Milner-White

The road ahead
My Lord God,
I have no idea where I am going.
I do not see the road ahead of me.
I cannot know for certain where it will end.
Nor do I really know myself,
and the fact that I think that I am following
 your will does not mean that I am
 actually doing so.

PRAYERS

But I believe that the desire to please you
   does in fact please you.
And I hope I have that desire in all that I am
   doing.
I hope that I will never do anything apart
   from that desire.
And I know that if I do this,
you will lead me by the right road though I
   may know nothing about it.
Therefore will I trust you always though I
   may seem lost and in the shadow
   of death.
I will not fear, for you are ever with me,
and you will never leave me to face my
   perils alone.

Thomas Merton

Prayer to our Guardian Angel
O angel of God, appointed by divine mercy to be my guardian, enlighten and protect, direct and govern me this day.

Prayer for generosity
Take, Lord, all my liberty. Receive my memory, my understanding, and my whole will. Whatever I have and possess, you have given me; to you I restore it wholly and to your will I utterly surrender it for my direction. Give me the love of you only, with your grace, and I am rich enough; nor do I ask anything beside.

St. Ignatius Loyola

For light and guidance
Be thou my vision, O Lord of my heart,
Be all else but naught to me, save that thou art;
Be thou my best thought in the day and the night,
Both waking and sleeping, thy presence my light.
Be thou my wisdom, be thou my true word,
Be thou ever with me, and I with thee Lord;
Be thou my great Father, and I thy true son;
Be thou in me dwelling, and I with thee one.
Be thou my breastplate, my sword for the fight;
Be thou my whole armour, be thou my true might;
Be thou my soul's shelter, be thou my strong tower;

PRAYERS

O raise thou me heavenward, great power of my power.
Riches I heed not, nor man's empty praise;
Be thou mine inheritance now and always;
Be thou and thou only the first in my heart:
O sovereign of heaven, my treasure thou art.
High king of heaven, thou heaven's bright sun
O grant me its joys after victory is won;
Great heart of my own heart, whatever befall,
Still be thou my vision, O ruler of all.

Irish Prayer

For perseverance

O Lord, support us all the day long until the shades lengthen and the evening comes, and the busy world is hushed, and the fever of life is over, and our work is done. Then, Lord, in thy mercy, grant us a safe lodging, a holy rest, and peace at the last.

John Henry Newman

For Courage

Give us courage, O Lord, to stand up and be counted,
to stand up for those who cannot stand up for themselves,
to stand up for ourselves when it is needful for us to do so.
Let us fear nothing more than we fear you. Let us love
nothing more than we love you, for thus we shall fear
nothing also.

Let us have no other god before you, whether nation
or party or state or church. Let us seek no other peace
but the peace which is yours, and make us its instruments,
opening our eyes and our ears and our hearts, so that we
should know always what work of peace we may do for
you.

Alan Paton

For Community Spirit

O God, teach us to live together in love and joy and peace, to check all bitterness, to disown discouragement, to practise thanksgiving, and to leap with joy to any task for others. Strengthen the good thing thus begun, that with gallant and high-hearted happiness we may look for your kingdom in the wills of men. Through Jesus Christ our Lord.

The prayer of Toc H

PRAYERS

Prayer of Dedication

O God, to whom all hearts are open, all desires known, and from whom no secrets are hidden, cleanse the thoughts of our hearts by the inpouring of your Holy Spirit, that every thought and word of ours may begin from you, and in you be perfectly completed, through Christ our Lord. Amen.

or

O Lord, grant that we may not be conformed to the world, but may love it and serve it. Grant that we may never shrink from being the instruments of your peace because of the judgment of the world. Grant that we may love you without fear of the world, grant that we may never believe that the inexpressible majesty of yourself may be found in any power of this earth. May we firstly love you and our neighbours as ourselves. May we remember the poor and the prisoner and the sick and the lonely, and the young searchers, and the tramps and vagabonds, and the lost and lonely, as we remember Christ, who is in them all. And may we this coming day be able to do some work of peace for you.

Alan Paton

Prayer of St. Francis of Assisi

Lord, make me an instrument of your peace:
    where there is hatred let me sow peace,
    where there is injury let me sow pardon,
    where there is doubt let me sow faith,
    where there is despair let me give hope,
    where there is darkness let me give light,
    where there is sadness let me give joy.
O Divine Master, grant that I may
    not try to be comforted but to comfort,
    not try to be understood but to understand,
    not try to be loved but to love.
Because it is in giving that we receive,
    it is in forgiving that we are forgiven,
    and it is in dying that we are born to eternal life.

Prayer of self-offering

Lord Jesus,
    I give you my hands to do your work.
    I give you my feet to go your way.

PRAYERS

I give you my eyes to see you as you do.
I give you my tongue to speak your words.
I give you my mind that you may think in me.
I give you my spirit that you may pray in me.
Above all
I give you my heart that you may love in me,
your Father, and all mankind.
I give you my whole self that you may grow in me,
so that it is you, Lord Jesus,
who live and work and pray in me.

or

I hand over to your care, Lord,
my soul and body,
my mind and thoughts,
my prayers and my hopes,
my health and my work,
my life and my death,
my parents and my family,
my friends and my neighbours,
my country and all men.
Today
and always.

Lancelot Andrews

God be in my head

God be in my head, and in my understanding,
God be in mine eyes, and in my looking,
God be in my mouth, and in my speaking,
God be in my heart, and in my thinking,
God be at my end, and at my departing.

Book of Hours (1514)

To grow nearer to God

Day by day,
O Lord,
three things I pray:
to see thee more clearly,
love thee more dearly,
follow thee more nearly,
day by day.

St. Richard of Chichester (d. 1283)

PRAYERS

Help me to be human

God, help me to be truly human.
Help me to be able to appreciate
   and bring out the best in everyone around me.
Help me to be able to give of the best in myself.
   Many people think that to be human is
to make mistakes, to hate, to be imperfect.
But this is not true.
When Jesus was on earth,
he showed us the way
in which we should live.
   Man is not like the animal.
He does not exist, he lives.
He does not feed, he eats.
He does not mate, he loves.
He does not breed, he co-creates.
   You have created man,
so that he is capable
to appreciate consciously
all the gifts
that you have given him.
Lord, help me to appreciate all
that you have given me.
Help me to be truly human.

Teenagers' prayers from Salisbury, Rhodesia

Prayer for sharing

Make us worthy, Lord, to serve our fellow men throughout the world who live and die in poverty and hunger. Give them through our hands this day their daily bread, and by our understanding love, give peace and joy.

Mother Teresa of Calcutta

For Christian witness

Guide me, teach me, strengthen me, till I become such a person as thou wouldst have me be, pure and gentle, truthful and high-minded, brave and able, courteous and generous, dutiful and useful.

Charles Kingsley (1819-1875)

PRAYERS

In time of famine

**All-powerful Father,
God of goodness,
you provide for all your creation.
Give us an effective love for our brothers and sisters
who suffer from lack of food.
Help us to do all we can to relieve their hunger,
that they may serve you with carefree hearts.**

For Refugees

**Lord,
no one is a stranger to you
and no one is ever far from your loving care.
In your kindness watch over refugees and exiles,
those separated from their loved ones,
young people who are lost,
and those who have left or run away from home.
Bring them back safely to the place where they belong to be
and help us always to show your kindness
to strangers and those in need.**

For those unjustly deprived of liberty

**Father,
your Son came among us as a slave
to free the human race from the bondage of sin.
Rescue those unjustly deprived of liberty
and restore them to the freedom you wish for all men as your sons.**

For persecuted Christians

**Father,
in your mysterious providence,
your Church must share in the sufferings of Christ your Son.
Give the spirit of patience and love
to those who are persecuted for their faith in you
that they may always be true and faithful witnesses
to your promise of eternal life.**

For Prisoners

**Father of mercy,
the secrets of all hearts are known to you alone.
You know who is just and you forgive the unjust.**

Hear our prayers for those in prison.
Give them patience and hope in their sufferings,
and bring them home again soon.

In time of war

God our Father,
maker and lover of peace,
to know you is to live,
and to serve you is to reign.
All our faith is in your saving help;
protect us from men of violence
and keep us safe from weapons of hate.

For Peace and Justice

God our Father,
you reveal that those who work for peace
will be called your sons.
Help us to work without ceasing
for that justice
which brings true and lasting peace.

or

O God, source of holy desires, right counsels and just actions,
grant to your servants that peace which the world cannot give, so
that our hearts may be wholly devoted to your service, and all
our days, freed from dread of our enemies, may be passed in
quietness under your protection.

or

Almighty and eternal God,
may your grace enkindle in all of us
a love for the many unfortunate people
whom poverty and misery reduce to a
  condition of life
  unworthy of human beings.
Arouse in the hearts of those who call you
  Father
a hunger and thirst for justice and peace,
and for fraternal charity in deeds and in
  truth.
Grant, O Lord, peace in our days,

peace to souls, peace to families, peace to
 our country,
and peace among nations. Amen.

God our Father,
by the labour of man you govern and guide to perfection
the work of creation.
Hear the prayers of your people
and give all men work that enhances their human dignity
and draws them closer to each other
in the service of their brothers.

Have mercy, O Lord our God, on those whom war or oppression
or famine have robbed of homes and friends, and aid all those who
try to help them. We commend also into thy care those whose
homes are broken by conflict and lack of love; grant that where the
love of man has failed, the divine compassion may heal; through
Jesus Christ our Lord.

O loving Father, we pray for all who are handicapped in the race
of life; the blind, the defective and the delicate, and all who are
permanently injured. We pray for those worn out with sickness
and those who are wasted with misery, for the dying and all
unhappy children. May they learn the mystery of the road of
suffering which Christ has trodden and the saints have followed,
and bring thee this gift that angels cannot bring, a heart that trusts
thee even in the dark; and this we ask in the name of him who
himself took our infirmities upon him, even the same Jesus Christ,
our Saviour.

Lord Jesus, when you were on earth, they brought the sick to you
and you healed them all. Today we ask you to bless all those in
sickness, in weakness and in pain;
 those who are blind and who cannot see the light of

the sun, the beauty of the world, or the faces of their
friends;
those who are deaf and cannot hear the voices which
speak to them;
those who are helpless and who must lie in bed while
others go out and in;
Bless all such.
those whose minds have lost their reason;
those who are so nervous that they cannot cope with
life;
those who worry about everything:
Bless all such.
those who must face life under some handicap;
those whose weakness means that they must always
be careful;
those who are lame and maimed and cannot enter
into any of the strenuous activities or pleasures of
life;
Bless all such.
Grant that we in our health and our strength may never find those
who are weak and handicapped a nuisance, but grant that we may
always do and give all that we can to help them and to make life
easier for them.

William Barclay

For the Church

God our Father,
by the promise you made
in the life, death, and resurrection of Christ your Son,
you bring together in your Spirit, from all the nations,
a people to be your own.
Keep the Church faithful to its mission:
may it be a leaven in the world
renewing us in Christ,
and transforming us into your family.

For the spread of the Gospel

God our Father,
you will all men to be saved

PRAYERS

and come to the knowledge of your truth.
Send workers into your great harvest
that the Gospel may be preached to every creature
and your people, gathered together by the word of life
and strengthened by the power of the sacraments,
may advance in the way of salvation and love.

For Christian Unity

Lord,
pour out upon us the fullness of your mercy
and by the power of your Spirit
remove divisions among Christians.
Let your Church rise more clearly as a sign for all the nations
that the world may be filled with the light of your Spirit
and believe in Jesus Christ whom you have sent.

or

Lord Jesus Christ, who said to your apostles: "Peace I leave with you, my peace I give to you", look not upon our sins but upon the faith of your Church and grant her that peace and unity which is according to your will.

For the Pope

Lord,
source of eternal life and truth,
give to your servant N.
a spirit of courage and right judgment,
a spirit of knowledge and love.
By governing with fidelity those entrusted to his care
may he, as successor to the apostle Peter and vicar of Christ,
build your Church into a sacrament of unity, love, and peace for
all the world.

For the Bishop

God our Father, our shepherd and guide,
look with love on N. your servant,
your appointed pastor of the Church.
May his word and example inspire and guide the Church;
may he, and all those in his care,
come to the joy of everlasting life.

PRAYERS

For Priests

Father,
you have appointed your Son Jesus Christ eternal High Priest.
Guide those he has chosen to be ministers of word and sacrament
and help them to be faithful
in fulfilling the ministry they have received.

For Priestly Vocations

Father,
in your plan for our salvation you provide shepherds for your people.
Fill your Church with the spirit of courage and love.
Raise up worthy ministers for your altars
and ardent but gentle servants of the Gospel.

or

Jesus, Good Shepherd, you have come to search out and to save what was lost. You have instituted the priesthood of the Church to continue your work for all time. We beseech you earnestly: send labourers into your vineyard. Raise up in your Church holy priests and religious brothers and sisters. Grant that all whom you have chosen from eternity for your service may follow your call, but that nobody may intrude into your sanctuary without being called.

Strengthen all priests in their difficult vocation and bless their efforts and labours. Let them be the salt of the earth that will preserve it from corruption, the light of the world that enlightens all the faithful through word and example. Give them wisdom, patience and strength so that they may promote your kingdom in the hearts of men and lead the souls entrusted to them to eternal life. Amen.

Mary, Queen of the Apostles, pray for us.

For Religious

Father,
you inspire and bring to fulfilment every good intention.
Guide your people in the way of salvation
and watch over those who have left all things
to give themselves entirely to you.
By following Christ and renouncing worldly power and profit,

PRAYERS

may they serve you and their brothers faithfully
in the spirit of poverty and humility.

For the Laity
God our Father,
you send the power of the Gospel into the world
as a life-giving leaven.
Fill with the Spirit of Christ
those whom you call to live in the midst of the world and its
　concerns;
help them by their work on earth
to build up your eternal kingdom.

For the Queen [King]
God, our Father,
all earthly powers must serve you.
Help your servant N. [our Queen/King]
to fulfil her/his responsibilities worthily and well.
By honouring and striving to please you at all times,
may she/he secure peace and freedom
for the people entrusted to her/him.

Prayer for Married People
God our Father,
you created man and woman
to love each other
in the bond of marriage.
Bless and strengthen N. and N.
May their marriage become an increasingly more perfect sign
　of the union between Christ and his Church.

Family and friends
Lord Jesus Christ,
I praise and thank you for my parents and
　my brothers and sisters
whom you have given me to cherish.
Surround them with your tender, loving care,
teach them to love and serve one another in true affection
and to look to you in all their needs
I place them all in your care,
knowing that your love for them is greater than my own.

Keep us close to one another in this life
and conduct us at the last to our true and heavenly home.
Blessed be God for ever.
Amen.

In time of illness

O God, our Father, bless and help us in the illness
   which has come upon us.
Give us courage and patience, endurance and cheerfulness
   to bear all weakness and all pain; and give us the mind
   at rest, which will make our recovery all the quicker.
Give to all doctors, surgeons and nurses who attend us
   skill in their hands, wisdom in their minds, and
   gentleness and sympathy in their hearts.
Help us not to worry too much, but to leave ourselves
   in the hands of wise and skilful people who have the
   gift of healing, and in thy hands.
Lord Jesus, come to us this day and at this time, and show
   us that thy healing touch has never lost its ancient
   power. This we ask for thy love's sake.

William Barclay

In any need

God our Father,
our strength in adversity,
our health in weakness,
our comfort in sorrow,
be merciful to your people.
As you have given us the punishment we deserve,
give us also new life and hope as we rest in your kindness.

When distracted

   When *the heart is* hard and parched up, come upon
me with a shower of mercy.
   When grace is lost from life, come with a burst of
song.
   When tumultuous work raises its din on all sides
shutting me out from beyond, come to me, my Lord of
silence, with thy peace and rest.
   When my beggarly heart sits crouched, shut up in a
corner, break open the door, my king, and come with
the ceremony of a king.

PRAYERS

When desire blinds the mind with delusion and dust, O thou holy one, thou wakeful, come with thy light and thy thunder.

Rabindranath Tagore

For the sick

Father,
your Son accepted our sufferings
to teach us the virtue of patience in human illness.
Hear the prayers we offer for our sick brothers and sisters.
May all who suffer pain, illness or disease
realize that they are chosen to be saints,
and know that they are joined to Christ
in his sufferings for the salvation of the world.

For a happy death

Father,
you made us in your own image
and your Son accepted death for our salvation.
Help us to keep watch in prayer at all times.
May we be free from sin when we leave this world
and rejoice in peace with you for ever.

or

Jesus, Mary and Joseph, I give you my heart and my soul.
Jesus, Mary and Joseph, assist me in my last agony.
Jesus, Mary and Joseph, may I breathe forth my soul in peace
   with you. Amen.

For the dying

God of power and mercy,
you have made death itself
the gateway to eternal life.
Look with love on our dying brother [sister],
and make him [her] one with your Son in his sufferings and death,
that sealed with the blood of Christ,
he [she] may come before you free from sin.

or

Go forth, O Christian soul, out of this world, in the name of God the Father almighty, who created you, in the name of Jesus Christ, the Son of the living God, who suffered for you, in the name of the Holy Spirit, who was given to you, in the name of the holy and glorious Mary, Virgin Mother of God, in the name of blessed Joseph, in the name of the angels, archangels and prophets, of the holy apostles and evangelists, of the holy martyrs, confessors, monks and hermits, of the holy virgins, and of all the saints of God, may peace be yours this day, and may your home be in heaven. Through the same Christ our Lord. Amen.

or

God of mercy, God of pity, again and again your mercy blots out the sins of penitent sinners, and wipes away the stain of their sin. Look kindly upon this servant of yours, and forgive the wrong he has done you, for with all his heart he admits that he has done it, and only asks for pardon. Human weakness and the devil's snares have done much evil in his soul. Undo this harm, and make him again a sound member of your Church. Hear his sorrowful prayers, O Lord, see his tears, and pity him. He has no other hope except your mercy. Show him your mercy, therefore, and take him back to you. Through Christ Jesus our Lord. Amen.

For the Dead

Out of the depths I have cried to you, O Lord.
Lord, hear my voice.
Let your ears be attentive
to the voice of my supplication.

If you, O Lord, shall observe iniquities,
Lord, who shall endure it?
For with you there is merciful forgiveness;
and by reason of your Law I have waited for you, O Lord.

My soul has relied on his word;
my soul has hoped in the Lord.
From the morning watch even until night
let Israel hope in the Lord.

Because with the Lord there is mercy,
and with him plentiful redemption.
And he shall redeem Israel
from all his iniquities.

PRAYERS

Eternal rest grant to them, O Lord.
And let perpetual light shine upon them.
May they rest in peace.
Amen.

Psalm 129

℣ O Lord hear my prayer.
℟ And let my cry come to you.

Let us pray. O God, the creator and redeemer of all the faithful, grant to the souls of your servants departed the remission of all their sins, that through our pious supplications they may obtain that pardon which they have always desired; who lives and reigns for ever and ever. Amen.

For the bereaved

We seem to give them back to thee, O God, who gavest them to us. Yet as thou didst not lose them in giving, so we do not lose them by their return. Not as the world giveth, givest thou, O lover of souls. What thou givest, thou takest not away, for what is thine is ours also if we are thine. And life is eternal and love is immortal, and death is only an horizon, and an horizon is nothing save the limit of our sight. Lift us up, strong Son of God, that we may see further; cleanse our eyes that we may see more clearly: draw us closer to thyself that we may know ourselves to be nearer to our loved ones who are with thee. And while thou dost prepare a place for us, prepare us also for that happy place, that where thou art we may be also for evermore. Amen.

Bede Jarrett, O.P.

or

O God, our Father, we know that you are afflicted in
   all our afflictions; and in our sorrow we come to you
   today that you may give us the comfort which you alone
   can give.
Make us to be sure that in perfect wisdom, perfect love, and
   perfect power you are working ever for the best.
Make us sure that a Father's hand will never cause His
   child a needless tear.
Make us so sure of your love that we will be able to
   accept even that which we cannot understand.
Help us today to be thinking not of the darkness of death,

but of the splendour of the life everlasting, for ever in your presence and for ever with you.

Help us still to face life with grace and gallantry; and help us to find courage to go on in the memory that the best tribute we can pay to our loved one is not the tribute of tears, but the constant memory that another has been added to the unseen cloud of witnesses who compass us about.

Comfort and uphold us, strengthen and support us, until we also come to the green pastures which are beside the still waters, and until we meet again those whom we have loved and lost awhile: through Jesus Christ our Lord. Amen.

William Barclay

Prayer before a Crucifix

Behold, O kind and most sweet Jesus, I cast myself on my knees in your sight, and with the most fervent desire of my soul, I pray and beseech you that you would impress upon my heart lively sentiments of faith, hope and charity, with a true repentance for my sins and a firm desire of amendment, while with deep affection and grief of soul I ponder within myself and mentally contemplate your five most precious wounds, having before my eyes that which David spoke in prophecy of you, O good Jesus: 'They have pierced my hands and my feet; they have numbered all my bones'.

Anima Christi

Soul of Christ, sanctify me.
Body of Christ, save me.
Blood of Christ, fill me.
Water from the side of Christ, wash me.
Passion of Christ, strengthen me.
O good Jesu, hear me.
Suffer me not to be separated from thee.
From the malicious enemy defend me.
In the hour of my death call me,
And bid me come unto thee.
That with thy saints I may praise thee.
For ever and ever.

PRAYERS

Prayer to St. Joseph

Unto you, O blessed Joseph, do we fly in our tribulation and, having implored the help of your holy spouse, we now also confidently seek your protection. By that affection which united you to the Immaculate Virgin Mother of God, and by your fatherly love for the Child Jesus, we humbly beg you to look down with compassion on the inheritance which Jesus Christ purchased with his blood, and in our need to help us by your powerful intercession.

Do you, O prudent guardian of the Holy Family, watch over the chosen people of Jesus Christ. Keep us, O loving father, safe from all error and corruption. O great protector, from your safe place in heaven, graciously help us in our contest against the powers of darkness. And as of old you did rescue the Child Jesus from the danger of death, so now defend God's holy Church from the snares of the enemy and from all adversity. Extend to each one of us your continual protection, that led on by your example and strengthened by your aid; we may live and die in holiness, and obtain everlasting happiness in heaven. Amen.

Grace before meals

Bless us, O Lord, and these your gifts which we are about to receive by your goodness, through Christ our Lord. Amen.

Grace after meals

We thank you, almighty God, for all that we have received, you who live and reign for ever and ever. Amen.

℣ Let us bless the Lord
℟ Thanks be to God.
℣ May the souls of the faithful departed through the mercy of God rest in peace. Amen.

Evening Prayer

Save us, O Lord, while waking, and guard us while sleeping, that when we wake, we may watch with Christ, and when we sleep, we may rest in peace. Amen.

Roman Breviary

The Jesus Prayer

ONE of the simplest, oldest and most used of our christian prayers is when we call in faith upon the Holy Name of Jesus. The common form of the full invocation is:

> Lord Jesus Christ,
> Son of the Living God,
> Have mercy on me, a sinner.

By repeatedly invoking the proper name of Our Lord, God and Saviour, Jesus Christ we are able to penetrate more deeply into a growing awareness of the presence of God who saves and sanctifies.

Sometimes the whole invocation is said slowly as we dwell on what the words mean to us. We fix our minds directly and deeply on the words of the prayer itself without trying to conjure up any mental picture or intellectual concepts. There should be no straining in our prayer as we allow the Spirit to lead us into the mystery of God himself revealed in Jesus Christ. The frequency with which we say the prayer will gradually accustom us to a more relaxed use of the Divine Name until it becomes the very substance of our prayer life. It is usual to use the Holy Name insistently and quietly before and after other forms of prayer. In this way all our forms of prayer will take their strength from, as well as lead into, the powerful name of the Saviour, through whom we are all saved. 'God gave him the name which is above all other names so that all beings in the heavens, on earth and in the underworld, should bend the knee at the name of Jesus and that every tongue should acclaim Jesus Christ as Lord, to the glory of God the Father.' Philippians 2:9-11.

The Jesus Prayer is an act of deep faith and self-surrender to the indwelling of the Spirit who teaches us to pray without ceasing to Abba, our heavenly Father. 'Everyone moved by the Spirit is a son of God. The spirit you received . . . is the spirit of sons and it makes us cry out, "Abba, Father!" The Spirit himself and our spirit bear

JESUS PRAYER

united witness that we are children of God'. Romans 8:14-16. Great saints down the centuries testify that the Jesus Prayer can so permeate our lives that it becomes second nature to us as we use it throughout our waking hours. In this way we pray without ceasing.

Litanies

LITANY OF THE SACRED HEART

The Sacred Heart of Jesus has long been for us the sign of his great love for us. Jesus said: 'Come to me, all you who labour and are overburdened, and I will give you rest. Shoulder my yoke and learn from me, for I am gentle and humble in heart, and you will find rest for your souls'. Matthew 11:28-29.

Lord, have mercy on us.	**Lord, have mercy on us.**
Christ, have mercy on us	**Christ, have mercy on us.**
Lord, have mercy on us.	**Lord, have mercy on us.**
Christ, hear us.	**Christ, graciously hear us.**
God the Father of heaven,	**have mercy on us.**
God the Son, Redeemer of the world,	**have mercy on us.**
God the Holy Spirit,	**have mercy on us.**
Holy Trinity one God,	**have mercy on us.**
Heart of Jesus, Son of the Eternal Father,	**have mercy on us.**
Heart of Jesus, formed by the Holy Ghost in the womb of the Virgin Mother,	**have mercy on us.**
Heart of Jesus, hypostatically united to the Eternal Word	**have mercy on us.**
Heart of Jesus, of infinite majesty,	**have mercy on us.**
Heart of Jesus, holy temple of God,	**have mercy on us.**
Heart of Jesus, tabernacle of the Most High,	**have mercy on us.**
Heart of Jesus, house of God and gate of heaven,	**have mercy on us.**
Heart of Jesus, burning furnace of charity,	**have mercy on us.**
Heart of Jesus, vessel of justice and love,	**have mercy on us.**
Heart of Jesus, full of goodness and love,	**have mercy on us.**

LITANIES

Heart of Jesus, abyss of all virtues,	**have mercy on us.**
Heart of Jesus, worthy of all praise,	**have mercy on us.**
Heart of Jesus, king and centre of all hearts,	**have mercy on us.**
Heart of Jesus, in which are all the treasures of wisdom and knowledge,	**have mercy on us.**
Heart of Jesus, in which dwells all the fulness of the divinity,	**have mercy on us.**
Heart of Jesus, in which the Father is well pleased,	**have mercy on us.**
Heart of Jesus, of whose fulness we have all received,	**have mercy on us.**
Heart of Jesus, desire of eternal hills,	**have mercy on us.**
Heart of Jesus, patient and abounding in mercy,	**have mercy on us.**
Heart of Jesus, rich unto all that call upon you,	**have mercy on us.**
Heart of Jesus, fountain of life and holiness,	**have mercy on us.**
Heart of Jesus, the propitiation for our sins,	**have mercy on us.**
Heart of Jesus, filled with reproaches,	**have mercy on us.**
Heart of Jesus, bruised for our sins,	**have mercy on us.**
Heart of Jesus, made obedient unto death,	**have mercy on us.**
Heart of Jesus, pierced with a lance,	**have mercy on us.**
Heart of Jesus, source of all consolation,	**have mercy on us.**
Heart of Jesus, our life and resurrection,	**have mercy on us.**
Heart of Jesus, our peace and reconciliation,	**have mercy on us.**
Heart of Jesus, victim for our sins,	**have mercy on us.**
Heart of Jesus, salvation of them that hope in you,	**have mercy on us.**
Heart of Jesus, hope of them that die in you,	**have mercy on us.**

LITANIES

Heart of Jesus, delight of all the Saints,	**have mercy on us.**
Lamb of God, you take away the sins of the world,	**spare us, O Lord.**
Lamb of God, you take away the sins of the world,	**graciously hear us, O Lord.**
Lamb of God, you take away the sins of the world,	**have mercy on us.**
Jesus, meek and humble of heart,	**make our hearts like unto yours.**

Let us pray. Almighty and eternal God, consider the Heart of your well-beloved Son and the praises and satisfaction He offers you in the name of sinners; appeased by worthy homage, pardon those who implore your mercy, in the name of the same Jesus Christ your Son who lives and reigns with you in the unity of the Holy Spirit, one God for ever and ever. Amen.

LITANY OF THE MOST HOLY NAME OF JESUS

The name of Jesus has always been held in special veneration by christians. The angel Gabriel told Our Lady, 'You are to conceive and bear a son, and you must name him Jesus'. Luke 1:32.
Jesus died for us to take away our sins 'but God raised him high and gave him the name which is above all other names so that all beings in the heavens, on earth and in the underworld, should bend the knee at the name of Jesus and that every tongue should acclaim Jesus Christ as Lord, to the glory of God the Father.' Philippians 2:9-11.

Lord, have mercy on us.	**Lord, have mercy on us.**
Christ, have mercy on us.	**Christ, have mercy on us.**
Lord, have mercy on us.	**Lord, have mercy on us.**
Jesus, hear us.	**Jesus, graciously hear us.**
God the Father of heaven,	**have mercy on us.**
God the Son, Redeemer of the world,	**have mercy on us.**
God the Holy Spirit,	**have mercy on us.**
Holy Trinity, one God,	**have mercy on us.**
Jesus, Son of the living God,	**have mercy on us.**

LITANIES

Jesus, splendour of the Father,	**have mercy on us.**
Jesus, brightness of eternal light,	**have mercy on us.**
Jesus, king of glory,	**have mercy on us.**
Jesus, sun of Justice,	**have mercy on us.**
Jesus, Son of the Virgin Mary,	**have mercy on us.**
Jesus most amiable,	**have mercy on us.**
Jesus most admirable,	**have mercy on us.**
Jesus, mighty God,	**have mercy on us.**
Jesus, father of the world to come,	**have mercy on us.**
Jesus, angel of great counsel,	**have mercy on us.**
Jesus most powerful,	**have mercy on us.**
Jesus most patient,	**have mercy on us.**
Jesus most obedient,	**have mercy on us.**
Jesus, meek and humble of heart,	**have mercy on us.**
Jesus, lover of chastity,	**have mercy on us.**
Jesus, lover of us,	**have mercy on us.**
Jesus, God of peace,	**have mercy on us.**
Jesus, author of life,	**have mercy on us.**
Jesus, example of virtues,	**have mercy on us.**
Jesus, zealous lover of souls,	**have mercy on us.**
Jesus, our God,	**have mercy on us.**
Jesus, our refuge,	**have mercy on us.**
Jesus, father of the poor,	**have mercy on us.**
Jesus, treasure of the faithful,	**have mercy on us.**
Jesus, good shepherd,	**have mercy on us.**
Jesus, true light,	**have mercy on us.**
Jesus, eternal wisdom,	**have mercy on us.**
Jesus, infinite goodness,	**have mercy on us.**
Jesus, our way and our life,	**have mercy on us.**
Jesus, joy of angels,	**have mercy on us.**
Jesus, king of patriarchs,	**have mercy on us.**
Jesus, master of the apostles,	**have mercy on us.**
Jesus, teacher of the evangelists,	**have mercy on us.**
Jesus, strength of martyrs,	**have mercy on us.**
Jesus, light of confessors,	**have mercy on us.**
Jesus, purity of virgins,	**have mercy on us.**
Jesus, crown of all sants,	**have mercy on us.**
Be merciful unto us,	**Jesus, spare us.**
Be merciful unto us,	**Jesus, spare us.**
From all evil,	**Jesus, deliver us.**
From all sin,	**Jesus, deliver us.**

LITANIES

From your wrath,	**Jesus, deliver us.**
From the snares of the devil,	**Jesus, deliver us.**
From the spirit of uncleanness,	**Jesus, deliver us.**
From everlasting death,	**Jesus, deliver us.**
From the neglect of your inspirations,	**Jesus, deliver us.**
Through the mystery of your holy Incarnation,	**Jesus, deliver us.**
Through your nativity,	**Jesus, deliver us.**
Through your infancy,	**Jesus, deliver us.**
Through your most divine life,	**Jesus, deliver us.**
Through your labours,	**Jesus, deliver us.**
Through your agony and passion,	**Jesus, deliver us.**
Through your cross and dereliction,	**Jesus, deliver us.**
Through your faintness and weariness,	**Jesus, deliver us.**
Through your death and burial,	**Jesus, deliver us.**
Through your resurrection,	**Jesus, deliver us.**
Through your ascension,	**Jesus, deliver us.**
Through your institution of the most Holy Eucharist,	**Jesus, deliver us.**
Through your joys,	**Jesus, deliver us.**
Through your glory,	**Jesus, deliver us.**
Lamb of God, you take away the sins of the world,	**Spare us, O Jesus.**
Lamb of God, you take away the sins of the world,	**Graciously hear us, O Jesus.**
Lamb of God, you take away the sins of the world,	**Have mercy on us, O Jesus.**
Jesus hear us.	**Jesus, graciously hear us.**

Let us pray. O Lord Jesus Christ, who said: 'Ask and you shall receive, seek and you shall find, knock and it shall be opened unto you'; grant, we beseech you, to us your supplicants, the gifts of your most divine love, that we may love you with our whole heart, and in all our words and works, and never cease from praising you.

O Lord, give us a perpetual fear as well as love of your holy Name, for you never cease to govern those you founded upon the strength of your love. You who live and reign world without end. Amen.

LITANIES

LITANY OF OUR LADY

After the Litany of the Saints which dates from 595, the most ancient is that of Our Lady or the Litany of Loreto which was approved for use in the Church by Pope Sixtus V in 1587. It formed part of the usual Sunday evening service for many years and was preceded by the Rosary.

Lord, have mercy.	**Lord, have mercy.**
Christ, have mercy.	**Christ, have mercy.**
Lord, have mercy.	**Lord, have mercy.**
Christ, hear us.	**Christ, graciously hear us.**
God the Father of heaven,	**have mercy on us.**
God the Son, Redeemer of the world, have mercy on us.	**have mercy on us.**
God the Holy Spirit, Holy Trinity, one God,	**have mercy on us.**
Holy Mary,	**pray for us.**
Holy Mother of God,	**pray for us.**
Holy Virgin of virgins,	**pray for us.**
Mother of Christ,	**pray for us.**
Mother of divine grace,	**pray for us.**
Mother most pure,	**pray for us.**
Mother most chaste,	**pray for us.**
Mother inviolate,	**pray for us.**
Mother undefiled,	**pray for us.**
Mother most lovable,	**pray for us.**
Mother most admirable,	**pray for us.**
Mother of good counsel,	**pray for us.**
Mother of our Creator,	**pray for us.**
Mother of our Saviour,	**pray for us.**
Virgin most prudent,	**pray for us.**
Virgin most venerable,	**pray for us.**
Virgin most renowned,	**pray for us.**
Virgin most powerful,	**pray for us.**
Virgin most merciful,	**pray for us.**
Virgin most faithful,	**pray for us.**
Mirror of justice,	**pray for us.**
Seat of wisdom,	**pray for us.**
Cause of our joy,	**pray for us.**
Spiritual vessel,	**pray for us.**

LITANIES

Vessel of honour,	**pray for us.**
Singular vessel of devotion,	**pray for us.**
Mystical rose,	**pray for us.**
Tower of David,	**pray for us.**
Tower of ivory,	**pray for us.**
House of gold,	**pray for us.**
Ark of the covenant,	**pray for us.**
Gate of heaven,	**pray for us.**
Morning star,	**pray for us.**
Health of the sick,	**pray for us.**
Refuge of sinners,	**pray for us.**
Comfort of the afflicted,	**pray for us.**
Help of Christians,	**pray for us.**
Queen of angels,	**pray for us.**
Queen of patriarchs,	**pray for us.**
Queen of prophets,	**pray for us.**
Queen of apostles,	**pray for us.**
Queen of martyrs,	**pray for us.**
Queen of confessors,	**pray for us.**
Queen of virgins,	**pray for us.**
Queen of all saints,	**pray for us.**
Queen conceived without original sin,	**pray for us.**
Queen assumed into heaven,	**pray for us.**
Queen of the most holy rosary,	**pray for us.**
Queen of peace,	**pray for us,**
Lamb of God, you take away the sins of the world,	**Spare us, O Lord**
Lamb of God, you take away the sins of the world,	**Graciously hear us, O Lord**
Lamb of God, you take away the sins of the world,	**Have mercy on us**

Pray for us, O holy Mother of God
That we may be made worthy of the promises of Christ.

Let us pray. Grant that we your servants, Lord, may enjoy unfailing health of mind and body, and through the prayers of the ever blessed Virgin Mary in her glory, free us from our sorrows in this world and give us eternal happiness in the next. Through Christ our Lord. Amen.

LITANIES

LITANY OF SAINTS

Lord, have mercy	**Lord, have mercy**
Christ, have mercy	**Christ, have mercy**
Lord, have mercy	**Lord, have mercy**
Holy Mary, Mother of God	**pray for us**
Saint Michael	**pray for us**
Holy angels of God	**pray for us**
Saint John the Baptist	**pray for us**
Saint Joseph	**pray for us**
Saint Peter and Saint Paul	**pray for us**
Saint Andrew	**pray for us**
Saint John	**pray for us**
Saint Mary Magdalene	**pray for us**
Saint Stephen	**pray for us**
Saint Ignatius	**pray for us**
Saint Lawrence	**pray for us**
Saint Perpetua and Saint Felicity	**pray for us**
Saint Agnes	**pray for us**
Saint Gregory	**pray for us**
Saint Augustine	**pray for us**
Saint Athanasius	**pray for us**
Saint Basil	**pray for us**
Saint Martin	**pray for us**
Saint Benedict	**pray for us**
Saint Francis and Saint Dominic	**pray for us**
Saint Francis Xavier	**pray for us**
Saint John Vianney	**pray for us**
Saint Catherine	**pray for us**
Saint Teresa	**pray for us**
All holy men and women	**pray for us**
Lord, be merciful	**Lord, save your people**
From all evil	**Lord, save your people**
From every sin	**Lord, save your people**
From everlasting death	**Lord, save your people**
By your coming as man	**Lord, save your people**
By your death and rising to new life	**Lord, save your people**
By your gift of the Holy Spirit	**Lord, save your people**
Be merciful to us sinners	**Lord, hear our prayer**

LITANIES

Jesus, Son of the living God — Lord, hear our prayer
Christ, hear us — Christ, hear us
Lord Jesus, hear our prayer — Lord Jesus, hear our prayer

The Rosary

THE rosary is a vocal and meditative form of prayer which has been very much part of Catholic devotional practice since before the thirteenth century. The Rosary uses words like a mantra so that we can meditate deeply and in peace. It is a simple and effective way of leading us step by step through the essential mysteries of our faith. God reveals his on-going love for us in Christ and the fifteen mysteries are arranged in groups of five decades (chaplets) and follow the historical sequence of the life of Our Lord and his Blessed Mother. Each decade of the rosary is composed of one Our Father, ten Hail Marys and one Glory be to the Father. The rhythm of the prayers helps us to grow in contemplation and brings a stillness so essential to our growth in prayer-life. Each group of the five decades is preceded by the recitation of the Creed and three Hail Marys for faith, hope and charity and concludes with the recitation or singing of one of the anthems to Our Lady.

The scriptural readings are so arranged as to help our thoughts and prayers. They enable us to lift up our minds and hearts to God in gratitude for all he has done for us. Prayer is not so much a matter of talking a great deal but of loving a great deal. Our words in the rosary are the background music of our loving dialogue with God.

THE JOYFUL MYSTERIES

The Annunciation

In the sixth month the angel Gabriel was sent by God to a town in Galilee called Nazareth, to a virgin betrothed to a man named Joseph, of the House of David; and the virgin's name was Mary. He went in and said to her, 'Rejoice, so highly favoured! The Lord is with you.' She was deeply disturbed by these words and asked herself what this greeting could mean, but the angel said to her, 'Mary, do not be afraid; you have won God's favour. Listen! You are to conceive and bear a son, and you must name him Jesus. He will be great and will be called Son of the Most High. The Lord God will give him the throne of his ancestor David; he will rule over the House of Jacob for ever and his reign will have no end.' Mary said to the angel, 'But how can this come about, since I am a virgin?'

THE ROSARY

'The Holy Spirit will come upon you,' the angel answered, 'and the power of the Most High will cover you with its shadow. And so the child will be holy and will be called Son of God. Know this too: your kinswoman Elizabeth has, in her old age, herself conceived a son, and she whom people called barren is now in her sixth month, for nothing is impossible to God.' 'I am the handmaid of the Lord,' said Mary 'let what you have said be done to me.' And the angel left her. Luke 1:26-38.

The Visitation

Mary set out at that time and went as quickly as she could to a town in the hill country of Judah. She went into Zechariah's house and greeted Elizabeth. Now as soon as Elizabeth heard Mary's greeting, the child leapt in her womb and Elizabeth was filled with the Holy Spirit. She gave a loud cry and said, 'Of all women you are the most blessed, and blessed is the fruit of your womb. Why should I be honoured with a visit from the mother of my Lord? For the moment your greeting reached my ears, the child in my womb leapt for joy. Yes, blessed is she who believed that the promise made by the Lord would be fulfilled.' And Mary said:

'My soul proclaims the greatness of the Lord
and my spirit exults in God my saviour;
because he has looked upon his lowly handmaid.
Yes, from this day forward all generations will call me blessed,
for the Almighty has done great things for me.
Holy is his name,
and his mercy reaches from age to age for those who fear him.
He has shown the power of his arm,
he has routed the proud of heart.
He has pulled down princes from their thrones and exalted the lowly.
The hungry he has filled with good things, the rich sent empty away.
He has come to the help of Israel his servant, mindful of his mercy
— according to the promise he made to our ancestors —
of his mercy to Abraham and to his descendants for ever.

Mary stayed with Elizabeth about three months and then went back home. Luke 1:39-56.

THE ROSARY

The Nativity

Now at this time Caesar Augustus issued a decree for a census of the whole world to be taken. This census — the first — took place while Quirinius was governor of Syria, and everyone went to his own town to be registered. So Joseph set out from the town of Nazareth in Galilee and travelled up to Judaea, to the town of David called Bethlehem, since he was of David's House and line, in order to be registered together with Mary, his betrothed, who was with child. While they were there the time came for her to have her child, and she gave birth to a son, her first-born. She wrapped him in swaddling clothes, and laid him in a manger because there was no room for them at the inn. In the countryside close by there were shepherds who lived in the fields and took it in turns to watch their flocks during the night. The angel of the Lord appeared to them and the glory of the Lord shone round them. They were terrified, but the angel said, 'Do not be afraid. Listen, I bring you news of great joy, a joy to be shared by the whole people. Today in the town of David a saviour has been born to you; he is Christ the Lord. And here is a sign for you: you will find a baby wrapped in swaddling clothes and lying in a manger.' And suddenly with the angel there was a great throng of the heavenly host, praising God and singing:

'Glory to God in the highest heaven,
and peace to men who enjoy his favour.' Luke 2:1-14.

The Presentation in the Temple

And when the day came for them to be purified as laid down by the Law of Moses, they took him up to Jerusalem to present him to the Lord — observing what stands written in the Law of the Lord: Every first-born male must be consecrated to the Lord — and also to offer in sacrifice, in accordance with what is said in the Law of the Lord, a pair of turtledoves or two young pigeons. Now in Jerusalem there was a man named Simeon. He was an upright and devout man; he looked forward to Israel's comforting and the Holy Spirit rested on him. It had been revealed to him by the Holy Spirit that he would not see death until he had set eyes on the Christ of the Lord. Prompted by the Spirit he came to the Temple; and when the parents brought in the child Jesus to do for him what the Law required, he took him into his arms and blessed God; and he said:

'Now, Master, you can let your servant go in peace,
just as you promised;
because my eyes have seen the salvation
which you have prepared for all the nations to see,
a light to enlighten the pagans
and the glory of your people Israel'.

As the child's father and mother stood there wondering at the things that were being said about him, Simeon blessed them and said to Mary his mother, 'You see this child: he is destined for the fall and for the rising of many in Israel, destined to be a sign that is rejected — and a sword will pierce your own soul too — so that the secret thoughts of many will be laid bare'. Luke 2:22-35.

The Finding in the Temple

Every year his parents used to go to Jerusalem for the feast of the Passover. When he was twelve years old, they went up for the feast as usual. When they were on their way home after the feast, the boy Jesus stayed behind in Jerusalem without his parents knowing it. They assumed he was with the caravan, and it was only after a day's journey that they went to look for him among their relations and acquaintances. When they failed to find him they went back to Jerusalem looking for him everywhere. Three days later, they found him in the Temple, sitting among the doctors, listening to them, and asking them questions; and all those who heard him were astounded at his intelligence and his replies. They were overcome when they saw him, and his mother said to him, 'My child, why have you done this to us? See how worried your father and I have been, looking for you.'

'Why were you looking for me?' he replied, 'Did you not know that I must be busy with my Father's affairs?' But they did not understand what he meant. Luke 2:41-50.

THE SORROWFUL MYSTERIES

The Agony in the Garden

Then Jesus came with them to a small estate called Gethsemane; and he said to his disciples, 'Stay here while I go over there to pray'. He took Peter and the two sons of Zebedee with him. And sadness came over him, and great distress. Then he said to them, 'My soul is sorrowful to the point of death. Wait here and keep

THE ROSARY

awake with me.' And going on a little further he fell on his face and prayed. 'My Father,' he said 'if it is possible, let this cup pass me by. Nevertheless, let it be as you, not I, would have it.' He came back to his disciples and found them sleeping, and he said to Peter, 'So you had not the strength to keep awake with me one hour? You should be awake, and praying not to be put to the test. The spirit is willing, but the flesh is weak.' Again, a second time, he went away and prayed: 'My Father,' he said 'if this cup cannot pass by without my drinking it, your will be done!' And he came again back and found them sleeping, their eyes were so heavy. Leaving them there, he went away again and prayed for the third time, repeating the same words. Then he came back to the disciples and said to them, 'You can sleep on now and take your rest. Now the hour has come when the Son of Man is to be betrayed into the hands of sinners. Get up! Let us go! My betrayer is already close at hand'. Matthew 26:36-44.

The Scourging at the Pillar

At festival time Pilate used to release a prisoner for them, anyone they asked for. Now a man called Barabbas was then in prison with the rioters who had committed murder during the uprising. When the crowd went up and began to ask Pilate the customary favour, Pilate answered them, 'Do you want me to release for you the king of the Jews?' For he realised that it was out of jealousy that the chief priests had handed Jesus over. The chief priests, however, had incited the crowd to demand that he should release Barabbas for them instead. Then Pilate spoke again. 'But in that case,' he said to them 'what am I to do with the man you call king of the Jews?' They shouted back, 'Crucify him!'

'Why?' Pilate asked them. 'What harm has he done?' But they shouted all the louder, 'Crucify him!' So Pilate, anxious to placate the crowd, released Barabbas for them and, having ordered Jesus to be scourged, handed him over to be crucified. Mark 15:6-15.

The Crowning with Thorns

Pilate then had Jesus taken away and scourged; and after this, the soldiers twisted some thorns into a crown and put it on his head, and dressed him in a purple robe. They kept coming up to him and saying, 'Hail, king of the Jews!'; and they slapped him in the face. Pilate came outside again and said to them, 'Look, I am going to bring him out to you to let you see that I find no case'. Jesus then came out wearing the crown of thorns and the purple robe. Pilate said, 'Here is the man'. When they saw him the chief priests and the guards shouted, 'Crucify him! Crucify him!' Pilate said, 'Take him yourselves and crucify him: I can find no case against him'.

'We have a Law,' the Jews replied, 'and according to that Law he ought to die, because he has claimed to be the Son of God'. John 19:1-7.

Jesus carries his Cross

As they were leading him away they seized on a man, Simon from Cyrene, who was coming in from the country, and made him shoulder the cross and carry it behind Jesus. Large numbers of people followed him, and of women too, who mourned and lamented for him. But Jesus turned to them and said 'Daughters of Jerusalem, do not weep for me; weep rather for yourselves and for your children. For the days will surely come when people will say, 'Happy are those who are barren, the wombs that have never borne, the breasts that have never suckled!' Then they will begin to say to the mountains, 'Fall on us!'; to the hills, 'Cover us!' For if men use the green wood like this, what will happen when it is dry?' Now with him they were also leading out two other criminals to be executed. Luke 23:26-32.

Jesus dies on the Cross

When they reached the place called The Skull, they crucified him there and the two criminals also, one on the right, the other on the left. Jesus said, 'Father forgive them; they do not know what they are doing'. Then they cast lots to share out his clothing. The people stayed there watching him. As for the leaders, they jeered at him. 'He saved others,' they said 'let him save himself if he is the Christ of God, the Chosen One.' The soldiers mocked him too, and when they approached to offer him vinegar they said, 'If you are the King of the Jews, save yourself'. Above him there was an inscription: 'This is the king of the Jews'. One of the criminals hanging there abused him. 'Are you not the Christ?' he said. 'Save yourself and us as well.' But the

THE ROSARY

other spoke up and rebuked him. 'Have you no fear of God at all?' he said. 'You got the same sentence as he did, but in our case we deserved it: we are paying for what we did. But this man has done nothing wrong. Jesus,' he said 'remember me when you come into your kingdom.'

'Indeed, I promise you,' he replied 'today you will be with me in paradise.' It was now about the sixth hour and, with the sun eclipsed, a darkness came over the whole land until the ninth hour. The veil of the Temple was torn right down the middle; and when Jesus had cried out in a loud voice, he said, 'Father, into your hands I commit my spirit'. With these words he breathed his last. Luke 23:33-46.

THE GLORIOUS MYSTERIES

The Resurrection

When the sabbath was over, Mary of Magdala, Mary the mother of James, and Salome bought spices with which to go and anoint him. And very early in the morning on the first day of the week they went to the tomb, just as the sun was rising. They had been saying to one another, 'Who will roll away the stone for us at the entrance to the tomb?' But when they looked they could see that the stone — which was very big — had already been rolled back. On entering the tomb they saw a young man in a white robe seated on the right-hand side, and they were struck with amazement. But he said to them, 'There is no need for alarm. You are looking for Jesus of Nazareth, who was crucified: he has risen, he is not here. See, here is the place where they laid him. But you must go and tell his disciples and Peter, 'He is going before you to Galilee; it is there you will see him, just as he told you' '. Mark 16:1-7.

The Ascension

Meanwhile the eleven disciples set out for Galilee, to the mountain where Jesus had arranged to meet them. When they saw him they fell down before him, though some hesitated. Jesus came up and spoke to them. He said, 'All authority in heaven and on earth has been given to me. Go, therefore, make disciples of all the nations; baptise them in the name of the Father and of the Son and of the Holy Spirit, and teach them to observe all the

THE ROSARY

commandments I gave you. And know that I am with you always; yes, to the end of time'. Matthew 28:16-20.

As he said this he was lifted up while they looked on, and a cloud took him from their sight. They were still staring into the sky when suddenly two men in white were standing near them and they said, 'Why are you men from Galilee standing here looking into the sky? Jesus who has been taken up from you into heaven, this same Jesus will come back in the same way as you have seen him go there'. Acts 1:9-11.

The Coming of the Holy Spirit

When Pentecost day came round, they had all met in one room, where suddenly they heard what sounded like a powerful wind from heaven, the noise of which filled the entire house in which they were sitting; and something appeared to them that seemed like tongues of fire; these separated and came to rest on the head of each of them. They were all filled with the Holy Spirit, and began to speak foreign languages as the Spirit gave them the gift of speech. Now there were devout men living in Jerusalem from every nation under heaven, and at this sound they all assembled, each one bewildered to hear these men speaking his own language. They were amazed and astonished. 'Surely they said 'all these men speaking are Galileans? How does it happen that each of us hears them in his own native language? Parthians, Medes and Elamites; people from Mesopotamia, Judaea and Cappadocia, Pontus and Asia, Phrygia and Pamphylia, Egypt and the parts of Libya round Cyrene; as well as visitors from Rome — Jews and proselytes alike — Cretans and Arabs; we hear them preaching in our own language about the marvels of God.' Everyone was amazed and unable to explain it; they asked one another what it all meant. Some, however, laughed it off. 'They have been drinking too much new wine' they said. Acts 2:1-13.

The Assumption of Our Lady into Heaven

I will tell you something that has been secret: that we are not all going to die, but we shall all be changed. This will be instantaneous, in the twinkling of an eye, when the last trumpet sounds. It will sound, and the dead will be raised, imperishable, and we shall be changed as well, because our present perishable nature must put on imperishability and this mortal nature must

THE ROSARY

put on immortality. When this perishable nature has put on imperishability, and when this mortal nature has put on immortality, then the words of scripture will come true: Death is swallowed up in victory. Death, where is your victory? Death, where is your sting? Now the sting of death is sin, and sin gets its power from the Law. So let us thank God for giving us the victory through our Lord Jesus Christ. I Corinthians 15:51-57.

The Coronation of Our Lady and the Glory of All the Saints

After that I saw a huge number, impossible to count, of people from every nation, race, tribe and language; they were standing in front of the throne and in front of the Lamb, dressed in white robes and holding palms in their hands. They shouted aloud, 'Victory to our God, who sits on the throne, and to the Lamb!' And all the angels who were standing in a circle round the throne, surrounding the elders and the four animals, prostrated themselves before the throne, and touched the ground with their foreheads, worshipping God with these words, 'Amen. Praise and glory and wisdom and thanksgiving and honour and power and strength to our God for ever and ever. Amen'.

Revelation 7:9-12.

Stations of the Cross

The Stations of the Cross

FROM the earliest times christians have traced the footsteps of the Lord as he carried his cross from Pilate's house to Golgotha, the place of the crucifixion. The crusaders are said to have spread this devotion throughout Europe and so for those unable to make the journey to Jerusalem the 'Way of the Cross' was set up in cathedrals and parish churches until now it has become a feature of christian devotion everywhere.

The actual number of stations has varied and at one period there were as many as thirty-six stations recalling the various highlights along the Via Dolorosa [Sorrowful Road] of Our Lord's last journey. In the sixteenth century fourteen stations were chosen and approved by the Church but especially since the Second Vatican Council an additional one has been added, 'the Resurrection of Jesus from the Dead'. This is in keeping with the resurrection piety which permeates our whole approach to suffering and death.

The Stations may be made alone or with others. We may follow the suggested text, meditate on the selection of readings from the Gospel story or just let the Spirit speak to us as we pause before each station remembering what the Lord has done for us. 'All you who pass this way look and see: is any sorrow like the sorrow that afflicts me?' Lamentations 1:12.

The Stations of the Cross: Traditional Form

FIRST STATION
JESUS IS CONDEMNED TO DEATH

THIS response is said before each Station:

We adore you, O Christ, and we bless you.
Because by your holy Cross you have redeemed the world.

Consider how Jesus, after having been scourged and crowned with thorns, was unjustly condemned by Pilate to die on the Cross.

This prayer is said after each station:

I love you Jesus, my Love, above all things;
I repent with my whole heart for having offended you.
Never permit me to separate myself from you again.
Grant that I may love you always, then do with me what you will.

SECOND STATION
JESUS RECEIVES THE CROSS

WE adore ...

Consider how Jesus, in making this journey with the Cross on his shoulders, thought of us, and offered for us to his Father the death he was about to undergo.

I love you Jesus ...

STATIONS OF THE CROSS

THIRD STATION
JESUS FALLS THE FIRST TIME UNDER HIS CROSS

WE adore ...

Consider the first fall of Jesus under his Cross. His flesh was torn by the scourges, his head was crowned with thorns; he had lost a great quantity of blood. So weakened he could scarcely walk, he yet had to carry this great load upon his shoulders. The soldiers struck him rudely, and he fell several times.

I love you Jesus ...

FOURTH STATION
JESUS IS MET BY HIS BLESSED MOTHER

WE adore ...

Consider this meeting of the Son and the Mother, which took place on this journey. Their looks became like so many arrows to wound those hearts which loved each other so tenderly.

I love you Jesus ...

STATIONS OF THE CROSS

FIFTH STATION
THE CROSS IS LAID UPON SIMON OF CYRENE

WE adore ...

Consider how his cruel tormentors, seeing Jesus was on the point of expiring, and fearing he would die on the way, whereas they wished him to die the shameful death of the Cross, constrained Simon of Cyrene to carry the Cross behind our Lord.

I love you Jesus ...

SIXTH STATION
VERONICA WIPES THE FACE OF JESUS

WE adore ...

Consider how the holy woman named Veronica, seeing Jesus so ill-used, and bathed in sweat and blood, wiped his face with a towel, on which was left the impression of his holy countenance.

I love you Jesus ...

STATIONS OF THE CROSS

SEVENTH STATION
JESUS FALLS THE SECOND TIME

WE adore . . .

Consider the second fall of Jesus under the Cross; a fall which renews the pain of all the wounds in his head and members.

I love you Jesus . . .

EIGHTH STATION
THE WOMEN OF JERUSALEM MOURN FOR OUR LORD

WE adore . . .

Consider how these women wept with compassion at seeing Jesus in such a pitiable state, streaming with blood, as he walked along. 'Daughters of Jerusalem,' said he, 'weep not for me, but for yourselves and for your children.'

I love you Jesus . . .

NINTH STATION
JESUS FALLS FOR THE THIRD TIME

WE adore . . .

Consider the third fall of Jesus Christ. His weakness was extreme, and the cruelty of his executioners excessive who tried to hasten his steps when he could scarcely move.

I love you Jesus . . .

TENTH STATION
JESUS IS STRIPPED OF HIS GARMENTS

WE adore . . .

Consider the violence with which Jesus was stripped by the executioners. His inner garments adhered to his torn flesh, and they dragged them off so roughly that the skin came with them. Take pity on your Saviour thus cruelly treated.

I love you Jesus . . .

STATIONS OF THE CROSS

ELEVENTH STATION
JESUS IS NAILED TO THE CROSS

WE adore ...

Consider how Jesus, having been placed upon the Cross, extended his hands, and offered to his Eternal Father the sacrifice of his life for our salvation. Those barbarians fastened him with nails, and then, securing the Cross, allowed him to die with anguish on this infamous gibbet.

I love you Jesus ...

TWELFTH STATION
JESUS DIES ON THE CROSS

WE adore ...

Consider how Jesus, being consumed with anguish after three hours' agony on the Cross, abandoned himself to the weight of his body, bowed his head and died.

I love you Jesus ...

STATIONS OF THE CROSS

THIRTEENTH STATION
JESUS IS TAKEN DOWN FROM THE CROSS

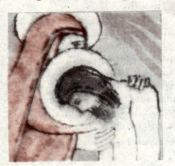

WE adore ...

Consider how, after our Lord has expired, two of his disciples, Joseph and Nicodemus, took him down from the Cross and placed him in the arms of his afflicted Mother, who received him with unutterable tenderness, and pressed him to her bosom.

I love you Jesus ...

FOURTEENTH STATION
JESUS IS PLACED IN THE SEPULCHRE

WE adore ...

Consider how the disciples, accompanied by his holy Mother, carried the body of Jesus to bury it. They closed the tomb, and all came sorrowfully away.

I love you Jesus ...

STATIONS OF THE CROSS

FIFTEENTH STATION
JESUS IS RISEN

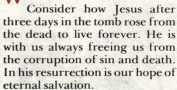

WE adore . . .

Consider how Jesus after three days in the tomb rose from the dead to live forever. He is with us always freeing us from the corruption of sin and death. In his resurrection is our hope of eternal salvation.

I love you Jesus . . .

The Stations of the Cross: A Biblical Form

FIRST STATION
JESUS IS CONDEMNED TO DEATH

PILATE came outside again and said to them, 'Look, I am going to bring him out to you to let you see that I find no case'. Jesus then came out wearing the crown of thorns and the purple robe. Pilate said, 'Here is the man'. When they saw him the chief priests and the guards shouted, 'Crucify him! Crucify him!' Pilate said, 'Take him yourselves and crucify him: I can find no case against him'.

'We have a law,' the Jews replied 'and according to that Law he ought to die, because he has claimed to be the Son of God.' When Pilate heard them say this his fears increased. Re-entering the Praetorium, he said to Jesus, 'Where do you come from? But Jesus made no answer. Pilate then said to him, 'Are you refusing to speak to me? Surely you know I have power to release you and I have power to crucify you?' 'You would have no power over me' replied Jesus 'if it had not been given you from above; that is why the one who handed me over to you has the greater guilt.'. So in the end Pilate handed him over to them to be crucified. John 19:4-11;16.

STATIONS OF THE CROSS

SECOND STATION
JESUS RECEIVES HIS CROSS

'SHOULDER my yoke and learn from me, for I am gentle and humble in heart, and you will find rest for your souls. Yes, my yoke is easy and my burden light'. Matthew 11:29-30.

Ours were the sufferings he bore, ours the sorrows he carried. But we, we thought of him as someone punished, struck by God, and brought low. Yet he was pierced through for our faults, crushed for our sins. On him lies a punishment that brings us peace, and through his wounds we were healed. Isaiah 53:4-5.

THIRD STATION
JESUS FALLS THE FIRST TIME UNDER HIS CROSS

WE had all gone astray like sheep, each taking his own way, and Yahweh burdened him with the sins of all of us. Harshly dealt with, he bore it humbly, he never opened his mouth, like a lamb that is led to the slaughterhouse, like a sheep that is dumb before its shearers never opening its mouth. By force and by law he was taken; would anyone plead his cause? Isaiah 53:6-8.

Yahweh my God, I call for help all day, I weep to you all night; may my prayer reach you, hear my cries for help; for my soul is troubled, my life is on the brink of Sheol; I am numbered among those who go down to the Pit, a man bereft of strength.

Psalm 88:1-4

FOURTH STATION
JESUS IS MET BY HIS BLESSED MOTHER

WHEN they failed to find him they went back to Jerusalem looking for him everywhere. Three days later, they found him in the Temple, sitting among the doctors, listening to them, and asking them questions; and all those who heard him were astounded at his intelligence and his replies. They were overcome when they saw him, and his mother said to him, 'My child, why have you done this to us? See how worried your father and I have been, looking for you'. 'Why were you looking for me?' he replied 'Did you not know that I must be busy with my Father's affairs?'. **Luke 2:45-49.**

I sought him whom my heart loves. I sought but did not find him. So I will rise and go through the City; in the streets and the squares I will seek him whom my heart loves ... I sought but did not find him. The watchmen came upon me on their roads in the City: 'Have you seen him whom my heart loves?' Scarcely had I passed them than I found him whom my heart loves.' **Song of Songs 3:1-4.**

STATIONS OF THE CROSS

FIFTH STATION
THE CROSS IS LAID UPON SIMON OF CYRENE

THEY led him out to crucify him. They enlisted a passer-by Simon of Cyrene, father of Alexander and Rufus, who was in from the country, to carry his cross. **Mark 15:16.**

All I want is to know Christ and the power of his resurrection and to share his sufferings by reproducing the pattern of his death. That is the way I can hope to take my place in the resurrection of the dead. Not that I have become perfect yet: I have not yet won, but I am still running, trying to capture the prize for which Christ Jesus captured me.
Philippians 3:10-13

SIXTH STATION
VERONICA WIPES THE FACE OF JESUS

WITHOUT beauty, without majesty [we saw him], no looks to attract our eyes; a thing despised and rejected by men, a man of sorrows and familiar with suffering, a man to make people screen their faces; he was despised and we took no account of him. **Isaiah 53:2-3.**

As the crowds were appalled on seeing him — so disfigured did he look that he seemed no longer human — so will the crowds be astonished at him, and kings stand speechless before him; for they shall see something never

STATIONS OF THE CROSS

told and witness something never heard before. Isaiah 52:14-15.

My soul thirsts for God, the God of life; when shall I go to see the face of God? I have no food but tears, day and night; and all day long men say to me, 'Where is your God?' Why so downcast, my soul, why do you sigh within me? Put your hope in God: I shall praise him yet, my saviour, my God. Psalm 42:2-3.5.

SEVENTH STATION
JESUS FALLS THE SECOND TIME

HIS state was divine, yet he did not cling to his equality with God but emptied himself to assume the condition of a slave, and became as men are; and being as all men are, he was humbler yet, even to accepting death, death on a cross.

Philippians 2:6-7

During his life on earth, he offered up prayer and entreaty, aloud and in silent tears, to the one who had the power to save him out of death, and he submitted so humbly that his prayer was heard. Although he was Son, he learnt to obey through suffering; but having been made perfect, he became for all who obey him the source of eternal salvation and was acclaimed by God with the title of high priest by the order of Melchizedek.

Hebrews 5:7-10

EIGHTH STATION
THE WOMEN OF JERUSALEM MOURN FOR OUR LORD

LARGE numbers of people followed him, and of women too, who mourned and lamented him. But Jesus turned to them and said, 'Daughters of Jerusalem, do not weep for me; weep rather for yourselves and for your children. For the days will surely come when people will say, 'Happy are those who are barren, the wombs that have never borne, the breasts that have never suckled!' For if men use the green wood like this, what will happen when it is dry?'

Luke 23:27-32.

Acclaim God, all the earth, play music to the glory of his name, glorify him with your praises, say to God, 'What dread you inspire!'

Psalm 66:1-3

You nations, bless our God and make his praise resound, who brings our soul to life and keeps our feet from faltering.

Psalm 66:8-9

God not only heard me, he listened to my prayer. Blessed be God, who neither ignored my prayer nor deprived me of his love.**Psalm 66:19-20.**

NINTH STATION
JESUS FALLS FOR THE THIRD TIME

I CANNOT understand my own behaviour. I fail to carry out the things I want to do, and I find myself doing the very things I hate. Romans 7:15.

The fact is, I know of nothing good living in me — living, that is, in my unspiritual self — for though the will to do what is good is in me, the performance is not, with the result that instead of doing the good things I want to do, I carry out the sinful things I do not want. When I act against my will, then it is not my true self doing it, but sin which lives in me. In fact, this seems to be the rule, that every single time I want to do good it is something evil that comes to hand. In my inmost self I dearly love God's Law, but I can see that my body follows a different law that battles against the law which my reason dictates. This is what makes me a prisoner of that law of sin which lives inside my body. What a wretched man I am! Who will rescue me from this body doomed to death? Romans 7:18-24.

You have given me an inch or two of life, my life-span is nothing to you; each man that stands on earth is only a puff of wind, every man that walks, only a shadow, and the wealth he amasses is only a puff of wind — he does not know who will take it next. So tell me Lord, what can I expect? My hope is in you. **Psalm 39:5-7.**

Yahweh, hear my prayer, listen to my cry for help, do not stay deaf to my crying. I am your guest, and only for a time, a nomad like all my ancestors. Look away, let me draw breath, before I go away and am no more!

Psalm 39:12-13

TENTH STATION
JESUS IS STRIPPED OF HIS GARMENTS

WHEN the soldiers had crucified Jesus they took his clothing and divided it into four shares, one for each soldier. His undergarment was seamless, woven in one piece from neck to hem; so they said to one another, 'Instead of tearing it, let's throw dice to decide who is to have it.' In this way the words of scripture were fulfilled:

They shared out my clothing among them.

They cast lots for my clothes.

This is exactly what the soldiers did. **John 19:23-24.**

While they were there the time came for her to have her child, and she gave birth to a son, her first-born. She wrapped him in swaddling clothes, and laid him in a manger because there was no room for them at the inn.

Luke 2:6-7

STATIONS OF THE CROSS

You are God's chosen race, his saints; he loves you, and you should be clothed in sincere compassion, in kindness and humility, gentleness and patience. Bear with one another; forgive each other as soon as a quarrel begins. The Lord has forgiven you; now you must do the same. Over all these clothes, to keep them together and complete them, put on love. And may the peace of Christ reign in your hearts, because it is for this that you were called together as parts of one body. Always be thankful.

Colossians 3:12-15

ELEVENTH STATION
JESUS IS NAILED TO THE CROSS

WHEN they reached the place called The Skull, they crucified him there and the two criminals also, one on the right, the other on the left. Jesus said, 'Father forgive them; they do not know what they are doing'. Then they cast lots to share out his clothing. The people stayed there watching him. As for the leaders, they jeered at him. 'He saved others,' they said, 'let him save himself if he is the Christ of God, the Chosen One.' The soldiers mocked him too, and when they approached to offer him vinegar they said, 'If you are the King of the Jews, save yourself'. Above him there was an inscription:

STATIONS OF THE CROSS

'This is the king of the Jews'. One of the criminals hanging there abused him. 'Are you not the Christ?' he said. 'Save yourself and us as well.' But the other spoke up and rebuked him. 'Have you no fear of God at all?' he said. 'You got the same sentence as he did, but in our case we deserved it: we are paying for what we did. But this man has done nothing wrong. Jesus,' he said, 'remember me when you come into your kingdom.' 'Indeed, I promise you,' he replied 'today you will be with me in paradise'.

Luke 23:33-43

My breath grows weak, and the gravediggers are gathering for me. I am the butt of mockers, and all my waking hours I brood on their spitefulness. **Job 17:1-2.**

I have become a byword among the people, and a creature on whose face to spit. My eyes grow dim with grief, and my limbs wear away like a shadow.

Job 17:6-7

Pity me, pity me, you, my friends, for the hand of God has struck me. **Job 19:21.**

STATIONS OF THE CROSS

TWELFTH STATION
JESUS DIES ON THE CROSS

FROM the sixth hour there was darkness over all the land until the ninth hour. And about the ninth hour, Jesus cried out in a loud voice, 'Eli, Eli, lama sabachthani?' that is, 'My God, my God, why have you deserted me?' When some of those who stood there heard this, they said, 'This man is calling on Elijah', and one of them quickly ran to get a sponge which he dipped in vinegar, and putting it on a reed, gave it him to drink. 'Wait!' said the rest of them and see if Elijah will come to save him.' But Jesus, again crying out in a loud voice, yielded up his spirit. At that, the veil of the Temple was torn in two from top to bottom; the earth quaked; the rocks were split; the tombs opened and the bodies of many holy men rose from the dead, and these, after his resurrection, came out of the tombs, entered the Holy City and appeared to a number of people. Meanwhile the centurion, together with the other guarding Jesus, had seen the earthquake and all that was taking place, and they were terrified and said, 'In truth this was a son of God.

Matthew 27:45-54

We are only the earthenware jars that hold this treasure, to make it clear that such an overwhelming power comes from God and not

STATIONS OF THE CROSS

from us. We are in difficulties on all sides, but never cornered; we see no answer to our problems, but never despair; we have been persecuted; knocked down, but never killed; always, wherever we may be, we carry with us in our body the death of Jesus, so that the life of Jesus, too, may always be seen in our body. Indeed, while we are still alive, we are consigned to our death every day, for the sake of Jesus, so that in our mortal flesh the life of Jesus, too, may be openly shown. So death is at work in us, but life in you. **2 Corinthians 4:7-12.**

THIRTEENTH STATION
JESUS IS TAKEN DOWN FROM THE CROSS

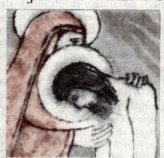

AND many women were there, watching from a distance, the same women who had followed Jesus from Galilee and looked after him. Among them were Mary of Magdala, Mary the mother of James and Joseph, and the mother of Zebedee's sons. When it was evening, there came a rich man of Arimathaea, called Joseph, who had himself become a disciple of Jesus. This man went to Pilate and asked for the body of Jesus. Pilate thereupon ordered it to be handed over.

Matthew 27:55-58

God's love for us was revealed when God sent into the world his only Son so that we could have life through him; this is the love I

STATIONS OF THE CROSS

mean: not our love for God, but God's love for us when he sent his Son to be the sacrifice that takes our sins away. My dear people, since God has loved us so much, we too should love one another.
1 John 4:9-11

FOURTEENTH STATION
JESUS IS PLACED IN THE SEPULCHRE

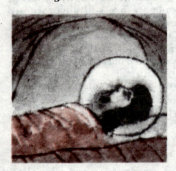

IT was now evening, and since it was Preparation Day [that is, vigil of the sabbath], there came Joseph of Arimathaea, a prominent member of the Council, who himself lived in the hope of seeing the kingdom of God, and he boldly went to Pilate and asked for the body of Jesus. Pilate, astonished that he should have died so soon, summoned the centurion and enquired if he was already dead. Having been assured of this by the centurion, he granted the corpse to Joseph who bought a shroud, took Jesus down from the cross, wrapped him in the shroud and laid him in a tomb which had been hewn out of the rock. He then rolled a stone against the entrance to the tomb. Mary of Magdala and Mary the mother of Joset were watching and took note of where he was laid. **Mark 15:42-47.**

And for anyone who is in Christ, there is a new creation; the old creation has gone, and now the new one is here. It is all God's work. It was God who reconciled

STATIONS OF THE CROSS

us to himself through Christ and gave us the work of handing on this reconciliation. In other words, God in Christ was reconciling the world to himself, not holding men's faults against them, and he has entrusted to us the news that they are reconciled. So we are ambassadors for Christ; it is as though God were appealing through us, and the appeal that we make in Christ's name is: to be reconciled to God.

2 Corinthians 5:17-20

FIFTEENTH STATION
JESUS IS RISEN

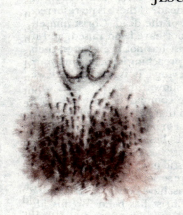

MEANWHILE Mary stayed outside near the tomb, weeping. Then still weeping, she stooped to look inside, and saw two angels in white sitting where the body of Jesus had been, one at the head, the other at the feet. They said, 'Woman, why are you weeping?' 'They have taken my Lord away' she replied 'and I don't know where they have put him.' As she said this she turned round and saw Jesus standing there, though she did not recognise him. Jesus said, 'Woman, why are you weeping? Who are you looking for?' Supposing him to be the gardener, she said, 'Sir, if you have taken him away, tell

STATIONS OF THE CROSS

me where you have put him, and I will go and remove him.' Jesus said, 'Mary!' She knew him then and said to him in Hebrew, 'Rabbuni!' which means Master. Jesus said to her, 'Do not cling to me, because I have not yet ascended to the Father. But go and find the brothers, and tell them: I am ascending to my Father and your Father, to my God and your God.' So Mary of Magdala went and told the disciples that she had seen the Lord and that he had said these things to her. John 20:11-18.

Now if Christ raised from the dead is what has been preached, how can some of you be saying that there is no resurrection of the dead? If there is no resurrection of the dead, Christ himself cannot have been raised, and if Christ has not been raised then our preaching is useless and your believing it is useless; indeed, we are shown up as witnesses who have committed perjury before God that he had raised Christ to life. For if the dead are not raised, Christ has not been raised, and if Christ has not been raised, you are still in your sins. And what is more serious, all who have died in Christ have perished. If our hope in Christ has been for this life only, we are the most unfortunate of all people. But Christ has in fact been raised from the dead,

STATIONS OF THE CROSS

the first-fruits of all who have fallen asleep. Death came through one man and in the same way the resurrection of the dead has come through one man. Just as all men die in Adam, so all men will be brought to life in Christ.
1 Corinthians 15:12-22

The Blessed Sacrament

Prayers Before the Blessed Sacrament

From the earliest times christians have worshipped the Lord Jesus in the Blessed Sacrament. The Blessed Sacrament Chapel is a special feature of our churches and we pray there in peace and quiet to the one who listens. We go out to the world refreshed and with a deeper sense of mission.

Since in Jesus, the Son of God, we have the supreme high priest who has gone through to the highest heaven, we must never let go of the faith we have professed. For it is not as if we had a high priest who was incapable of feeling our weaknesses with us; but we have one who has been tempted in every way that we are, though he is without sin. Let us be confident, then, in approaching the throne of grace, that we shall have mercy from him and find grace when we are in need of help.

Hebrews 4:14-16

He is the image of the unseen God
and the first-born of all creation,
for in him were created
all things in heaven and on earth:
everything visible and everything invisible,
Thrones, Dominations, Sovereignties, Powers —
all things were created through him and for him.
Before anything was created, he existed,
and he holds all things in unity.
Now the Church is his body,
he is its head.

As he is the Beginning,
he was first to be born from the dead,
so that he should be first in every way;
because God wanted all perfection
to be found in him
and all things to be reconciled through him and for him,
everything in heaven and everything on earth,
when he made peace
by his death on the cross.

Colossians 1:15-20

PRAYERS BEFORE THE BLESSED SACRAMENT

Not only that, but I believe nothing can happen that will outweigh the supreme advantage of knowing Christ Jesus my Lord. For him I have accepted the loss of everything, and I look on everything as so much rubbish if only I can have Christ and be given a place in him. I am no longer trying for perfection by my own efforts, the perfection that comes from the Law, but I want only the perfection that comes through faith in Christ, and is from God and based on faith. All I want is to know Christ and the power of his resurrection and to share his sufferings by reproducing the pattern of his death. That is the way I can hope to take my place in the resurrection of the dead. Not that I have become perfect yet: I have not yet won, but I am still running, trying to capture the prize for which Christ Jesus captured me. I can assure you my brothers, I am far from thinking that I have already won. All I can say is that I forget the past and I strain ahead for what is still to come; I am racing for the finish, for the prize to which God calls us upwards to receive in Christ Jesus. We who are called perfect must all think in this way. If there is some point on which you see things differently, God will make it clear to you; meanwhile, let us go forward on the road that has brought us to where we are.

Philippians 3:8-16

Then I saw a new heaven and a new earth, the first heaven and the first earth had disappeared now, and there was no longer any sea. I saw the holy city, and the new Jerusalem, coming down from God out of heaven, as beautiful as a bride all dressed for her husband. Then I heard a loud voice call from the throne, 'You see this city? Here God lives among men. He will make his home among them; they shall be his people, and he will be their God; his name is God-with-them. He will wipe away all the tears from their eyes; there will be no more death, and no more mourning and sadness. The world of the past has gone.'

Revelation 21:1-4

PRAYERS BEFORE THE BLESSED SACRAMENT

You know better than I how much I love you, Lord. You know it and I know it not, for nothing is more hidden from me than the depths of my own heart. I desire to love you; I fear that I do not love you enough. I beseech you to grant me the fulness of pure love. Behold my desire; you have given it to me. Behold in your creature what you have placed there. O God, who love me enough to inspire me to love you for ever, behold not my sins. Behold your mercy and my love.

Francois Fenelon

Lord, I believe in thee; help thou mine unbelief. I love thee, yet not with a perfect heart as I would; I trust in thee, yet not with my whole mind. Accept my faith, my love, my longing to know and serve thee, my trust in thy power to keep me. What is cold, do thou kindle, what is lacking, do thou make up.

Malcolm Spencer

Set our hearts on fire with love to thee, O Christ Our God, that in that flame we may love thee with all our hearts, with all our mind, with all our soul, and with all our strength, and our neighbours as ourselves; so that, keeping thy commandments, we may glorify thee, the giver of all good gifts.

Eastern Orthodox Prayer

Use me, my Saviour, for whatever purpose and in whatever way thou mayest require. Here is my poor heart, an empty vessel; fill it with thy grace. Here is my sinful, troubled soul; quicken it and refresh it with thy love. Take my heart for thine abode; my mouth to spread abroad the glory of thy name; my love and all my powers for the advancement of thy believing people, and never suffer the steadfastness and confidence of my faith to abate.

Dwight Moody

My Lord and my God —
thank you for drawing me to yourself.
Make me desire more deeply
that knowledge of you which is eternal life.
Lord,
you have told us that the pure in heart shall see God
— the single-minded
who do not try to serve two masters,

PRAYERS BEFORE THE BLESSED SACRAMENT

Yahweh is my light and my salvation,
   whom need I fear?
Yahweh is the fortress of my life,
   of whom should I be afraid?

When evil men advance against me
   to devour my flesh,
They, my opponents, my enemies,
   are the ones who stumble and fall.

Though an army pitched camp against me,
   my heart would not fear;
   though war were waged against me,
   my trust would still be firm.

One thing I ask of Yahweh,
   one thing I seek:
   to live in the house of Yahweh
   all the days of my life,
   to enjoy the sweetness of Yahweh
   and to consult him in his Temple.

For he shelters me under his awning
   in times of trouble;
   he hides me deep in his tent,
   sets me high on a rock.

And now my head is held high
   over the enemies who surround me,
   in his tent I will offer
   exultant sacrifice.

I will sing, I will play for Yahweh!
Yahweh, hear my voice as I cry!
   Pity me! Answer me!

My heart has said of you,
   'Seek his face'.
Yahweh, I do seek your face;
   do not hide your face from me.

Do not repulse your servant in anger;
   you are my help.
Never leave me, never desert me,
   God, my saviour!

PRAYERS BEFORE THE BLESSED SACRAMENT

If my father and mother desert me,
  Yahweh will care for me still.

Yahweh, teach me your way,
  lead me in the path of integrity
  because of my enemies;
  do not abandon me to the will of my foes —
  false witnesses have risen against me,
  and breathe out violence.

This I believe: I shall see the goodness of Yahweh,
  in the land of the living.
Put your hope in Yahweh, be strong, let your heart be bold,
  put your hope in Yahweh.

Psalm 27

Eucharistic Exposition and Benediction

Eucharistic Exposition and Benediction

THE structure of the Rite is as follows:

Exposition
Adoration
Benediction
Reposition

Exposition

After the people have assembled, a song may be sung while the minister comes to the altar. If the Holy Eucharist is not reserved at the altar where the exposition is to take place, the minister puts on a humeral veil and brings the sacrament from the place of reservation; he is accompanied by servers or by the faithful with lighted candles. A song such as the following will be suitable:

O salutaris hostia,
Quae caeli pandis ostium;
Bella premunt hostilia,
Da robur, fer auxilium.

Uni Trinoque Domino
Sit sempiterna gloria,
Qui vitam sine termino
Nobis donet in patria.
Amen.

or

O saving victim, opening wide
the gate of heaven to man below;
our foes press on from every side;
your aid supply, your strength bestow.

To your great name be endless praise,
immortal Godhead, one in three;
O grant us endless length of days
in our true native land with thee. Amen.

Latin Texts for the Mass

Latin Texts for the Mass

We give below the Latin Texts for the People's parts of the Ordinary of the Mass.

Response to the Greeting

Amen.
or
Et cum spiritu tuo.

Confiteor

Confiteor Deo omnipotenti et vobis, fratres,
quia peccavi nimis
cogitatione, verbo, opere et omissione:
mea culpa, mea culpa, mea maxima culpa.
Ideo precor beatam Mariam semper Virginem,
omnes Angelos et Sanctos,
et vos, fratres, orare pro me
ad Dominum Deum nostrum.

Kyrie

Kyrie, eleison
   Kyrie, eleison.
Christe, eleison.
   Christe, eleison.
Kyrie, eleison.
   Kyrie, eleison.

Gloria

Gloria in excelsis Deo
   et in terra pax hominibus bonæ voluntatis.
Laudamus te,
   benedicimus te,
   adoramus te,
   glorificamus te,
   gratias agimus tibi propter magnam gloriam tuam,
Domine Deus, Rex cælestis,
   Deus Pater omnipotens.

LATIN TEXTS

Domine Fili unigenite, Jesu Christe,
Domine Deus, Agnus Dei, Filius Patris,
qui tollis peccata mundi, miserere nobis;
qui tollis peccata mundi,
suscipe deprecationem nostram.
Qui sedes ad dexteram Patris, miserere nobis.
Quoniam tu solus Sanctus, tu solus Dominus,
　tu solus Altissimus,
Jesu Christe, cum Sancto Spiritu: in gloria Dei Patris.
Amen.

After the readings

Deo gratias.

Before the Gospel

Dominus vobiscum.
　Et cum spiritu tuo.
Lectio sancti Evangelii secundum N.
　Gloria tibi, Domine.

At the end of the Gospel

Verbum Domini.
　Laus tibi, Christe.

Credo

Credo in unum Deum,
Patrem Omnipotentem, factorem cæli et terræ,
　visibilium omnium et invisibilium.
Et in unum Dominum Jesum Christum,
Filium Dei unigenitum,
　et ex Patre natum ante omnia sæcula.
Deum de Deo, lumen de lumine,
　Deum verum de Deo vero,
　genitum, non factum, consubstantialem Patri:
　per quem omnia facta sunt.
Qui propter nos homines
　et propter nostram salutem
　descendit de cælis.
Et incarnatus est de Spiritu Sancto
　ex Maria Virgine, et homo factus est.

Crucifixus etiam pro nobis sub Pontio Pilato;
  passus et sepultus est,
  et resurrexit tertia die, secundum Scripturas,
  et ascendit in cælum, sedet ad dexteram Patris.
Et iterum venturus est cum gloria,
  iudicare vivos et mortuos,
  cuius regni non erit finis.
  Et in Spiritum Sanctum, Dominum et vivificantem:
  qui ex Patre Filioque procedit.
Qui cum Patre et Filio simul adoratur
  et conglorificatur:
  qui locutus est per prophetas.
Et unam, sanctam,
  catholicam et apostolicam Ecclesiam.
Confiteor unum baptisma in remissionem peccatorum.
Et exspecto resurrectionem mortuorum,
  et vitam venturi sæculi. Amen.

Response to the offertory prayers

Benedictus Deus in sæcula.

Response to the Orate Fratres

Suscipiat Dominus sacrificum de manibus tuis
ad laudem et gloriam nominis sui,
ad utilitatem quoque nostram
totiusque Ecclesiæ sanctæ.

Dialogue before the Preface

Dominus vobiscum.
  Et cum spiritu tuo.
Sursum corda.
  Habemus ad Dominum.
Gratias agamus Domino Deo nostro.
  Dignum et iustum est.

Sanctus

Sanctus, Sanctus, Sanctus Dominus Deus Sabaoth.
  Pleni sunt cæli et terra gloria tua.
  Hosanna in excelsis.
Benedictus qui venit in nomine Domini.
  Hosanna in excelsis.

LATIN TEXTS

Acclamation after the Consecration

1
Mortem tuam annuntiamus, Domine,
et tuam resurrectionem confitemur, donec venias.

2
Quotiescumque manducamus panem hunc
et calicem bibimus,
mortem tuam annuntiamus, Domine, donec venias.

3
Salvator mundi, salva nos,
qui per crucem et resurrectionem tuam liberasti nos.

Pater noster

Præceptis salutaribus moniti,
  et divina insitutione formati,
audemus dicere:

> **Pater noster, qui es in cælis:**
> **sanctificetur nomen tuum;**
>   **adveniat regnum tuum;**
> **fiat voluntas tua, sicut in cælo, et in terra.**
>
> **Panem nostrum cotidianum da nobis hodie;**
> **et dimitte nobis debita nostra,**
>   **sicut et nos dimittimus debitoribus nostris;**
> **et ne nos inducas in tentationem;**
>   **sed libera nos a malo.**

Acclamation after the Pater noster

Quia tuum est regnum,
et potestas, et gloria
in sæcula.

At the Pax

Pax Domini sit semper vobiscum.
  Et cum spiritu tuo.

Agnus Dei

Agnus Dei, qui tollis peccata mundi:
  miserere nobis.
Agnus Dei, qui tollis peccata mundi:
  miserere nobis.
Agnus Dei, qui tollis peccata mundi:
  dona nobis pacem.

Domine, non sum dignus

Domine, non sum dignus ut intres sub tectum meum; sed tantum dic verbo, et sanabitur anima mea.

At the Conclusion

Dominus vobiscum.
  Et cum spiritu tuo.
Benedicat vos omnipotens Deus, Pater, et Filius, ✠ et Spiritus
  Sanctus.
  Amen.
Ite, missa est.
  Deo gratias.